# The Anatomy of United States' Oil Pollution Act of 1990

# The Anatomy of United States' Oil Pollution Act of 1990

Olubunmi Olanrewaju Awoyemi, Ph.D

ISBN: 0996011609
ISBN 13: 9780996011600

# TABLE OF CONTENTS

# ABOUT THE AUTHOR

This legal treatise was a doctoral dissertation submitted in December of 2002 as part of the requirements for the award of the doctoral degree in law, S.J.D/Ph.D, by Tulane University Law School to the author in May 2003. The author, Bunmi Awoyemi, Ph.D is the Managing Partner of the prestigious full service law firm, M.O. Awoyemi & Co. (www.moawoyemi-law.com,bunmi.awoyemi@moawoyemi-law.com) and has been privileged to lead the firm in areas including Oil Pollution law, Maritime law, Environmental law, Aviation law, Corporate Finance law, Project Finance law, Oil, Gas, and Energy Law. He has worked with some of the most prestigious law firms in the world, such as Baker & McKenzie, LLP, Holland & Knight, LL.P. He holds a Ph.D./S.J.D from Tulane University Law School, New Orleans, Louisiana, where he was in the top 5% of his LLM class. He is a New York licensed Attorney, a Solicitor of the Supreme Court of England & Wales, the United States Supreme Court, and the United States Court of International Trade. He also holds an LL.B and B.L from Ogun State University and the Nigerian Law School, respectively. He was Awarded Tulane Law School's Merit Based Scholarship; a recipient of two CALI Excellence for the Future Awards - for obtaining the highest grade in two courses in his LL.M class and is an honored member of 'Strathmore's Who's Who Registry of outstanding professionals.

In the year 2012, he was one of the three finalists invited to Addis Ababa for the final selection interview by the MO IBRAHIM FOUNDATION'S LEADERSHIP FELLOWSHIP for the position of Advisor to the Executive Secretary of the United Nations Economic Commission for Africa out of the over 1,000 applicants worldwide.

The author is highly indebted to the legendary Niels F. Johnsen Professor of Maritime Law and Director Emeritus, Maritime Law

Center, Tulane University Law School, Professor Robert Force for his invaluable contribution to the quality of the treatise through his painstaking and inspiring supervision of the dissertation over a 4 year period.

# INTRODUCTION

## 1. Objectives of this legal treatise

One of the key goals of this legal treatise is to undertake a painstaking textual anatomy of the Oil Pollution Act of 1990 to help academics, lawyers, judges, and students navigate its recondite provisions with relative ease. This treatise consists of eighteen chapters. Chapters eight and nine of this treatise will focus on the effect of the Oil Pollution Act of 1990 on the insurance structure for oil pollution in US and international waters. The two chapters will briefly discuss the financial responsibility requirements and the international oil pollution regimes as they relate to marine insurance. The overall analysis undertaken in this treatise would be helpful to governments at all levels (domestic & foreign), and also to the maritime & transportation, environmental, oil & gas, energy, insurance, banking & financial services, real estate, import & export, and hospitality industries.

This treatise will attempt an extensive textual analysis of the compensation and liability sub-chapter of the Oil Pollution Act of 1990 (OPA).[1] This treatise will also include extensive analysis of OPA jurisprudence and non-OPA jurisprudence construing pre-OPA statutes regulating oil and hazardous substance pollution. My comprehensive analysis of non-OPA jurisprudence would provide guidance to academics, lawyers, judges, students and several business industries in their bid to construe the intricate provisions of the Oil Pollution Act of 1990.

Chapter fifteen undertakes a brief discussion of Pre-OPA statutes and the OPA's effect on them. That chapter has been deliberately included

1 33 USC §§2701-2720, §2751 (The focus of the legal treatise is on sub-chapter one of the OPA).

towards the end of the treatise because by then, almost all the provisions of the compensation and liability sub-chapter of the OPA would have been discussed, thereby facilitating understanding. However, for historical perspective a quick glance of that chapter should be helpful.

The author of this treatise has reproduced the relevant sections of OPA, at the beginning of each discussion of the most important sections of the OPA.

## 2. The Problem with Oil

Crude oil and all the products derived from it are indispensable to our daily life. But, the problem is man's inability to balance the need for a pollution free environment with the necessity of crude oil consumption that has grown exponentially over the years.

Crude oil is a naturally-occurring substance found trapped in certain rocks below the earth's crust.[2] It is a dark, sticky liquid which, scientifically speaking, is classed as a hydrocarbon. This means, it is a compound containing only hydrogen and carbon.[3] Crude oil is highly flammable and can be burned to create energy. Along with its sister hydrocarbon, natural gas, crude oil makes an excellent fuel.[4] Crude oil is measured in barrels. When crude oil first came into large-scale commercial use in the United States in the 19th century, it was stored in wooden barrels. One barrel equals 42 US gallons, or 159 liters.[5] Crude oil serves various purposes in our daily lives. Burning crude oil itself is of limited use. To extract the maximum value from crude, it first needs to be refined into other products.[6] The best-known of these is gasoline, or petrol. However, there are many other products that can be obtained

---

2 See Organization of Petroleum Exporting Countries, FAQ, Crude Oil and its Uses, <http://www.opec.org/> (Last updated May 19, 2001).

3 Id.

4 Id.

5 Id.

6 Id.

when a barrel of crude oil is refined. These include liquefied petroleum gas (LPG), naphtha, kerosene, gas oil and fuel oil.[7] All of these are fuels. Other useful products which are not fuels can also be manufactured by refining crude oil, such as lubricants and asphalt (used in paving roads).[8] A range of sub-items like perfumes and insecticides are also ultimately derived from crude oil.[9]

Furthermore, several of the products listed above which are derived from crude oil, such as naphtha, gas oil, LPG and ethane, can themselves be used as inputs or feed stocks in the production of petrochemicals.[10] There are more than 4,000 different petrochemical products, but those which are considered as basic products include ethylene, propylene, butadiene, benzene, ammonia and methanol.[11] The main groups of petrochemical end-products are plastics, synthetic fibers, synthetic rubbers, detergents and chemical fertilizers.[12] Considering the vast number of products that are derived from it, crude oil is a very versatile substance. Life as we know it today would be extremely difficult without crude oil and its by-products.[13]

Oil continues to remain the world's most important source of energy. According to the reference case of Organization of Petroleum Exporting Countries' (OPEC's) World Energy Model (OWEM), total world oil demand in 2000 was put at 76 million barrels per day (b/d). As world economic growth continues, crude oil demand will also rise to 90.6m b/d in 2010 and 103.2m b/d by 2020, according to the OWEM reference case figures.[14] The OWEM reference case sees oil's share of the world fuel mix falling slightly from over 41 per cent today to just over 39 per cent in 2020.

---

7 Id.

8 Id.

9 Id.

10 Id.

11 Id.

12 Id.

13 Id.

14 See Organization of Petroleum Exporting Countries, FAQ, How much Oil Does the World Consume Each Day? <http://www.opec.org/> (Last updated, May 19, 2001).

However, oil will still be the world's single largest source of energy.[15] The reduction in oil's market share is largely due to the stronger growth enjoyed by other forms of energy, particularly natural gas (see the table below).

| World energy fuel shares (*percent*) | | | | |
|---|---|---|---|---|
| | **1998** | **2000** | **2010** | **2020** |
| Oil | 41.3 | 41.3 | 40.3 | 39.2 |
| Gas | 22.2 | 22.4 | 24.1 | 26.6 |
| Solids | 26.2 | 26.1 | 26.3 | 25.8 |
| Hydro/Nuclear | 10.4 | 10.3 | 9.3 | 8.5 |
| **Total** | **100.0** | **100.0** | **100.0** | **100.0** |
| Source: OWEM Scenarios Report, March 2000 | | | | |

The above statistics underline the fact that crude oil exploration, production, marketing and transportation will continue to be an important part of our daily life for a long time to come, whether we like it or not. There is no doubt that these activities would continue to cause pollution of the waters and the air thereby threatening human and marine life forms. That is why the question of the environmental effect of these activities cannot be ignored. This also explains the United States Congress swift enactment of the Oil Pollution Act of 1990 after the Exxon Valdez oil pollution incident of 1989. It also explains the provision of section 2737 of the Oil Pollution Act of 1990, that bars (notwithstanding any other law), tank vessels that have spilled more than 23, 809.5 barrels (1,000,000 gallons) of oil into the marine environment after March 22, 1989, from operating on the navigable waters of Prince William Sound, Alaska[16] where the exxon valdez oil spill occurred in 1989.

15 See Organization of Petroleum Exporting Countries, FAQ, Will Oil Remain the Most Important Source of Energy? <http://www.opec.org/> (Last updated, May 19, 2001).
16 See 33 USCA §2737.

A statement that captures the mood of the US Congress when it passed the OPA into law is none other than that of President Nixon made over twenty years ago when he said:

*"The basic causes of our environmental troubles are complex and deeply imbedded. They include: our past tendency to emphasize quantitative growth at the expense of qualitative growth, the failure of our economy to provide full accounting for the social costs of environmental pollution; the failure to take environmental factors into account as normal and necessary part of our planning and decision making, the inadequacy of our institutions for dealing with problems that cut across traditional political boundaries; our dependence on conveniences, without regard for their impact on the environment; and more fundamentally, our failure to perceive the environment as a totality and to understand and to recognize the fundamental interdependence of all parts, including man himself."*[17]

President Nixon's statement shows that the cornerstone of the decision of the United States Congress to pass the OPA into law is the effect of oil on water and aquatic life.

*Effects of oil on water:* A review of the available literature on the impact of oil on water reveals that there is a consensus that water can be adversely affected by the presence of oil, its derivatives, or waste. In other words, it is generally agreed that petroleum in water is harmful, even though the extent of the harm might not be agreed upon.[18]*The greatest concerns are for the health and safety of life forms and the long-term ecological and environmental well-being of the planet.*[19]

*Effect of oil on aquatic Life*: Oil, as many other pollutants in water, consumes dissolved oxygen during degradation, and a shortage of oxygen

17 Ex- President Nixon in a message to the U.S Congress. The First Annual Report of the Council on Environmental Quality at 7.

18 S. E. MANAHAM, ENVIRONMENTAL CHEMISTRY 29 (5th ed., 1991).

19 R.O. ANDERSON, FUNDAMENTALS OF THE PETROLEUM INDUSTRY 246 (1984).

could be fatal to the living organisms in water. Many fish kills are caused not by the direct toxicity of pollutants like oil, but by the biodegradation of pollutants, which consumes and causes a deficiency of life sustaining oxygen.[20] On the 4th of February 1999, a 639-foot Japanese-owned bulk carrier called the M/V New Carissa got stuck in the surf after it dropped anchor to wait out a storm before entering Coos Bay in Oregon for a load of wood chips. At least 1, 666.6 barrels of oil leaked into the sea and washed up the beaches. State biologists in Oregon estimate that 115 sea birds died in the area due to exposure to oil.[21] As of April 2001, the United States Coast Guard National Pollution Funds Center had billed this vessel a total of $8, 477, 284.90 for removal costs.[22] The vessel may still incur additional costs depending on the situation of things.

The other known effects of oil on aquatic life include disruption of physiological or behavioral activities that may reduce many species' resistance to infection or stress and interference with reproductive capabilities. Additional effects are disturbance of the food chain, and "direct coating" which impedes the vital processes of respiration and feeding in animals, prevents sunlight penetration to plants, and increases temperature by absorbing solar radiation.[23]Any one, or a combination of these effects, results in massive kills of fish, fish eggs and larvae, birds, otters, crabs, and other animals inhabiting water.[24]These effects could ultimately dislocate the social and economic life of the communities who rely on the contaminated waters for fishing, particularly subsistence fishing.

---

20 S. E. MANAHAM, ENVIRONMENTAL CHEMISTRY at 29.

21 Jeff Barnard, Not quite Free yet, ABC News-Science, February 27, 1999, http://abcnews.go.com/sections/science/DailyNews/coosbay990227.html (last updated, February 24, 2001)

22 See National Pollution Funds Center Oil Spill data, M /V New Carissa, Federal Project Number (FPN) S99018, p 56 (2001) (This information was provided by the National Pollution Funds Center (NPFC) in April of 2001 and the data is on file with the NPFC and is available upon request from the NPFC).

23 The Rio Declaration on Environment and Development, 31 I.L.M. 874 (1992), Principles 6, 7.

24 A government report on the Exxon Valdez spill stated that by 1991 the spill had killed half of Prince William Sound's sea otter population, 580,000 sea birds, and had caused a 70 percent higher death rate in salmon eggs in the region. 21 Envtl. L. Rep. 2234 (1991).

The passing into law of the Oil Pollution Act[25] by the United States Congress ushered in the dawn of a new era in the United States Government's approach to the problem of oil pollution in particular and marine pollution in general. The next part of the introduction will discuss the "Reasons for and events leading to the passing of OPA."

## 3. The Reasons For, And Events Leading To the Passing of OPA

On March 24, 1989, the Exxon Valdez, a supertanker, ran aground on Bligh Reef in Prince William Sound, Alaska. This accident resulted in more than 261, 904.76 (11 million gallons) barrels of crude oil being spilled in Prince William Sound, making it the largest oil spill from a vessel in the history of the United States.[26] The spill had a significant impact on the pristine area in and around Prince William Sound, which is highly dependent on commercial and recreational fisheries and its tourism for its economic well-being.[27] Despite attempts by the oil companies and government to control the spill and contain the damage, hundreds of miles of Alaskan coastline were covered with crude oil, and the habitats of many wildlife and fishery resources were disrupted.[28] Known wildlife losses attributed to the spill as of June 28, 1989, were 81 bald eagles, and 827 sea otters.[29] A number of harbor seals also perished, but the exact number was unknown. A government report released two years after the incident revealed that the spill had a more devastating impact than was first thought. The report revealed that by 1991 the spill had killed half of Prince William Sound's sea otter population, 580,000 sea birds, and had

25 Oil Pollution Act of 1990 (Hereinafter OPA), 33 U.S.C.A. §§ 2701-2761 (West Supp. 1992).

26 S. Rep. No. 99, (101st Cong., 1st Sess. 1989), 1990 United States Code Congressional & Administrative News (U.S.C.C.A.N.) at 750, 1989 WL 225018 (Leg.Hist.), see also, James Barron, Oil Spills Leave Trail of Disturbing Questions, N.Y. TIMES, June 27, 1989, at A1.

27 S. Rep. No. 99, (101st Cong., 1st Sess. 1989), 1990 U.S.C.C.A.N. at 750.

28 Id.

29 1990 U.S.C.C.A.N. at 750.

caused a 70 percent higher death rate in salmon eggs in the region.[30] In addition, there was a disruption to the population of humpback and killer whales in the Prince William Sound area.[31]

The causes of the Exxon Valdez oil spill were thoroughly investigated by the National Transportation Safety Board, the U.S. Coast Guard and other agencies. Several factors were identified as either causes of or possible factors in the accident and the subsequent failure to control the extent of the damage.[32] These factors included the history of alcohol-related problems of the captain of the Exxon Valdez; Coast Guard monitoring of merchant marine personnel; the navigation system and vessel tracking coverage in Prince William Sound; the lack of effective oil spill response capabilities; and the lack of coordination between State and Federal agencies and the private companies involved in the spill and cleanup operations.[33]

In addition, during the weekend of June 23-24, 1989, three incidents involving oil tankers occurred which resulted in the spilling of more than 33, 333.3 barrels (1,400,000 gallons) of oil in U.S. waters.[34] In Rhode Island Sound, a Greek- registered tanker grounded and spilled approximately 10, 000 barrels (420,000 gallons) of No. 2 heating oil. A barge collided with an oil tanker in the Houston Ship Channel in Texas, and released 4000 barrels (168,000 gallons) of crude oil. In the Delaware River, a Uruguayan tanker grounded and spilled 20, 000 barrels (840,000 gallons) of heavy oil.[35]

Investigation of the possible causes of these incidents revealed that there appeared to be similarities between these incidents and the Exxon Valdez spill in Alaska. In addition, the series of accidents between May and July of 1989, demonstrated that the system of regulation and control in place at the time could be improved to prevent future spills and to enhance the capability of oil tanker operators, the oil industry, and others

30 21 Envtl. L. Rep. 2234 (1991).

31 1990 U.S.C.C.A.N. at 750.

32 Id.

33 Id.

34 Id.

35 Id.

to respond effectively to those spills that do occur despite preventative measures.[36]

The US Congress noted in its pre-OPA deliberations that between 1976 & 1989, there were ten major production or transportation accidents that released almost 1,190,476.19 barrels (50 million gallons) of oil in the United States.[37] The Congress said that it could be assumed, therefore, that oil spills can and will occur in the future.[38] The Congress felt that recent experience (1976-1989) had shown that there was a need to improve the ability to prevent future spills and minimize the damage caused by such spills when they occur.[39]

In stressing the need for the passing of the OPA, the Congress observed that the increasing dependence of the United States on foreign oil is another factor which increases the risk of oil tanker groundings or collisions and oil spills.[40] In its statistical analysis of the inescapable nature of the threat of oil spills in the US, the Congress noted that in 1988, the United States imported more than 6 million barrels of oil per day.[41] This translated into approximately 3,800 port calls by oil tankers.[42] The US Congress further noted that while relatively few accidents had occurred in relation to the total amount of oil moving by ship into the United States, with each supertanker carrying more than 1,190,476.19 barrels (50 million gallons) of oil, and making almost 4,000 trips into U.S. ports, the risk posed by oil transportation operations is undeniable.[43] The Congress was convinced based on the outcome of some of the investigations into the various oil spills discussed earlier, that the industry and government were ill-prepared to respond to major oil spill accidents.[44]

---

36 Id.

37 Id. at 751.

38 Id.

39 Id.

40 Id. at 751.

41 Id.

42 Id.

43 Id. at 751.

44 Id.

The OPA legislative history reveals that on June 14, 1989 the American Petroleum Institute (API) released a task force report on oil spills. That report recommended many of the elements contained in the OPA bill. The report had stated that if a 216,000 barrel (9,072,000 gallon) spill was contemplated, "the industry was not prepared anywhere along the coastal U.S. to deal with a spill of this size."[45] Motivated by this API report, the Congress also said "experience at Prince William Sound demonstrated that governments at all levels are similarly ill-prepared to cope effectively with spills of that magnitude."[46]

Under Pre-OPA Federal law, at least five statutes dealt with the issue of oil spill liability and compensation.[47] Each was different, and each was inadequate.[48] The Federal Water Pollution Control Act (or Clean Water Act), which has jurisdiction over most large tanker and inland barge incidents, has historically provided only partial protection. The Act set inappropriately low limits of liability for owners and operators of vessels with respect to Federal oil spill removal costs and natural resources damages, and provided little or no coverage or compensation for other damages.[49]

The US Congress noted that, as documented in a report prepared by the U.S. General Accounting Office (GAO) in 1983, gross inadequacies exist in the FWPA's provisions dealing with spiller responsibility for cleanup costs.[50] Between 1971 and 1982 the United States Government obligated $124 million from the FWPCA's section 311(k) revolving fund, but recovered only $49 million from spillers, for a total expenditure of $75 million in national funds.[51] In individual cases the percentage of clean-up costs expended by the government that was recovered in courts was even lower.[52] Funds also were expended in the costly, time-consuming

45 Id.

46 Id.

47 1990 U.S.C.C.A.N. 722, 724, S. Rep. No. 94, 101ST Cong., (1st Sess. 1989), 1989 WL 225005 (Leg.Hist.)

48 Id. at 724. See the discussion of these statutes in Chapter fifteen.

49 Id. at 724.

50 Id.

51 Id.

52 Id. at 724-25.

litigation required to recoup cleanup expenditures.[53] Relying heavily on the GAO report, the US Congress noted that this report had indicated that, as of 1982 there were 77 cases in litigation involving United States Government efforts to recover $36.5 million.[54]

The Congress also felt that another problem with the FWPCA was that its section 311(k) revolving fund was inadequate to cover large oil spills such as the Exxon Valdez.[55] This fund the Congress noted, had never been funded at the authorized level of $35 million, leaving aside the fact that this amount was far too low.[56] The Congress also pointed out that since the fund was appropriated from the Treasury, it undercut budget reduction goals and ran counter to cost internalization policies.[57] The Congress believed that these policies were exacerbated by the fact that courts had found the FWPCA to provide the only national remedy for recovering oil spill cleanup costs.[58] The Congress was not happy that the courts had held that the government could not use common law nuisance or maritime tort theories to recover its excess costs.[59]

Each of these inadequacies of the FWPCA were adequately addressed in the OPA. For instance a non-preemption clause was included in the OPA to ensure that state governments and private claimants can use common law and state statutory remedies to recover excess costs. It also preserved the right of state governments and the federal government to impose additional civil and criminal penalties on a person who is found to be responsible for an oil spill. Apart from this, Congress created the Oil Spill Liability Trust Fund (the Fund) and pumped up the amount in the Fund to 1 billion US dollars.

The US Congress in its pre-OPA deliberations also noted that in addition to the FWPCA, title III of the Outer Continental Shelf Lands Act

53 Id. at 725.

54 Id.

55 Id.

56 Id.

57 Id.

58 Id.

59 Id.

Amendments, the Deepwater Ports Act, and the Trans-Alaska Pipeline Authorization Act (TAPAA), all played a role in oil spill liability and compensation.[60] But unfortunately, they provided varying and uneven liability standards and scope of coverage for cleanup costs and damages associated with activities covered by each individual law.[61] Moreover, this array of narrowly defined programs could create administrative problems as well. The Congress felt that as a result, the goal of compensating those injured may be complicated by questions of jurisdiction of the various Federal agencies.[62] To buttress this point the Congress cited as example, the fact that when an oil spill occurs it may be necessary to track down the source of the spill before the applicable statute is applied and compensation claims presented.[63] The OPA remedies this type of anomaly by allowing a claimant to present his claim to the Oil spill Liability Trust Fund (the Fund) even where the source of the spill is unknown.

In its Pre-OPA deliberations, the Congress was emphatic and unequivocal about its burning desire to eviscerate the Limitation of Liability Act of 1851 for oil pollution purposes. The Congress was of the view that the 1851 Limitation of Liability Act represented a potentially devastating bar to effective recovery of either cleanup costs or damages.[64] The Congress believed that the Act probably had merit 150 years ago, since its purpose was to further the interests of the United States' budding merchant marine by encouraging shipbuilding and employment of ships.[65] To that end, vessel owner liability was limited to "the amount or value of the interest of such owner in such vessel, and her freight pending" [66] provided that the owner did not have any knowledge of the negligent acts that caused the loss.[67] Congress noted with frustration that

60 Id.

61 Id.

62 Id.

63 Id. at 725.

64 Id.

65 Id.

66 Id.

67 46 App. USC 183(a)

the current application of that law has resulted in situations where the owner pays next to nothing because the vessel and cargo are a total loss following a catastrophic incident.[68] This can be likened to the owner of a vessel walking away from a major oil spill irrespective of the overwhelming evidence showing that the vessel was culpable. Congress noted with dismay that in two Federal cases where the owner of a vessel had invoked the provisions of this Act, courts have held that this law, where applicable, has the effect of limiting recoveries under State law, including provisions allowing unlimited liability.[69] Congress relied on the case of *Esta Later Charters, Inc. v. Ignacio*,[70] where the Ninth Circuit Court of Appeals (on an issue of timing for petitions under the 1851 statute), wrote in dicta on the 1851 statute:

> "Shortly after the close of the middle ages, many European seafaring nationals developed a rule of maritime law that limited a shipowner's liability to the value of the vessel and its cargo. The rule was first adopted in the United States in the Limitation of Liability Act of 1851 ...... and has remained part of U.S. law today, a vestige of a time gone by.[71] No one who has had occasion to study the .... Act has been struck by its lucidity.[72] Misshapen from the start, the subject of later incrustations, arthritic with age, the Limitation Act has "provided the setting for judicial lawmaking seldom equaled."[73] This is an area that could profit from modern legislative attention. Congress might be well advised to examine other approaches or to consider whether the rationale underlying the Liability Act continues to have vitality as we enter the last decade of the twentieth century."[74]

Congressional indignation at the unjust effect of the Limitation of Liability Act may have been further exacerbated by the view of many

---

68 1990 U.S.C.C.A.N. 725..

69 Id. at. 725.

70 1989 A.M.C. 1480, 875 F.2d. 234 (9th Cir. 1989).

71 *Esta Later Charters*, 875 F.2d. at 239.

72 Id. at 235-36.

73 1990 U.S.C.C.A.N. 725-26, (quoting, Esta Later Charters, Inc. v. Ignacio, 875 F.2d. at 239).

74 Id.

legal critics and some courts of law that with the availability of incorporation, insurance and other devices to protect shipowners against major disasters, the Limitation of Liability Act seems oddly out of place in the modern economy.[75] Its application could also lead to wholly unexpected and harsh results.[76] Some commentators had pointed out long before the OPA was passed, for example, that the Limitation of Liability Act could be used to shield shipowners from damages arising from "pollution of navigable waters by oil and other harmful substances."[77] To buttress this critical point, this commentator noted the example of the sinking of the Torrey Canyon, which spilled 120,000 tons of crude oil into the English Channel in 1967. The subsequent clean-up of the beaches and shorelines on both sides of the Channel cost over $16 million; a fund of $50--the value of one salvaged lifeboat--was available to the claimants.[78] That was the reason for the OPA-90 reform, which was a death blow to the continued application of the Limitation of Liability Act to oil pollution incidents. However, it is important to point out that the Limitation of Liability Act only applied in cases where liability was not based on the FWPCA which applied to oil spills before OPA was enacted, and had its own limitation provisions, which was grossly inadequate.

In the hearings before the Senate, witnesses from the Coast Guard, maritime labor, pilots' associations, offshore oil ports, the tanker industry, and the State of Alaska discussed possible modifications in the current system of oil transportation.[79] Those comments were considered in the development of the OPA legislation. Also, in the period following the March 24th Exxon Valdez grounding, six bills were introduced and referred to the Senate Committee on Commerce, Science, and Transportation. The bills related to aspects of the Prince William Sound spill specifically and oil tanker operations in general.[80] The legislative proposals included:

75 *Esta Later Charters*, 875 F.2d. at 239.

76 875 F.2d. at 239.

77 G. Gilmore & C. Black, The Law of Admiralty § 10-4(a), at 824 (2d ed. 1975)

78 See. id. at 823 n. 13e; Benedict on Admiralty, at 236, § 111, at 9-3 (7th ed. 1988).

79 1990 U.S.C.C.A.N. 751.

80 Id. at 751.

requiring double bottoms or double hulls for all newly constructed oil tankers; Federal approval of oil spill contingency plans; an enhancement of Federal licensing regulation for merchant marine personnel; and an increase in Federal authority for oil spill cleanup efforts.[81] The OPA contained some of the provisions of those bills as well as other provisions developed after review of the hearing record and other information made available to this Senate Committee.

Just sixteen months after the Exxon Valdez struck a reef in Alaska's pristine William Sound on March 24, 1989,[82] the Oil Pollution Act of 1990 (the OPA), United States' first comprehensive oil pollution statute swept through Congress. The OPA was a product of the hullabaloos and extensive deliberations that accompanied the Exxon Valdez oil spill earlier extrapolated above. By enacting the OPA into law Congress managed to break nearly two decades of legislative gridlock. The OPA's objectives were to: (1) reduce the possibility of future spills by imposing additional safety, construction and operational requirements on oil tankers; (2) minimize the impact of future spills by establishing a national response plan; (3) ensure that those damaged by spills receive proper compensation for losses suffered.[83] The Act consolidated federal regulatory, liability, and claim procedures applicable to oil spills which were previously governed by a number of different federal statutes. National legislation in effect at that time had been described as a "patchwork of federal and state laws that were unwieldy, inconsistent, inefficient and unnecessarily expensive."[84]

At the time of the accident, the Federal Water Pollution Control Act (FWPCA)[85] stood as the major federal statute that prescribed damages collectible after oil spills. The FWPCA defined a national oil spill policy—allowing recovery by the federal government for expenses incurred

---

81 Id.

82 16 Months After Valdez Spill, Oil Bill Nears Final Passage, N.Y. TIMES, Aug. 3, 1990, at A12.

83 P.L. 101-380, Oil Pollution Act of 1990, Statement By President of The United States, George Bush Upon Signing H.R. 1465, 1990 U.S.C.C.A.N. 861-1, August 18, 1990.

84 David Ashley Bagwell, Hazardous and Noxious Substances, 62 TUL.L.REV. 433 (1988).

85 33 U.S.C.A. §§ 1251-1387 (West 1986 & Supp. 1992).

in the cleanup of oil spills. Although the FWPCA provided for natural resources damages, it failed to address cleanup costs incurred by state governments or private interests, and did not provide compensation for other damages suffered.[86] Instead, these issues remained under the control of state regulation or other federal laws applicable only in specific locations. Maritime scholars had long criticized the FWPCA as a woefully inadequate attempt to address the grave problems caused by oil spills in the United States.[87]

On August 18, 1990, President George Bush signed the OPA into law. The President described the new law as providing "the prevention, response, liability, and compensation components (which) fit together into a compatible and workable system that strengthens the protection of our environment."[88] In other words, Congress sewed up into the OPA, all the scattered compensation and liability provisions that were in a number of federal statutes, and at the same time increased liability limits.[89]

The OPA sets greater monetary liability limits for spills and assesses liability for a broader area of damages. At the same time it allows states to enact or maintain more stringent liability laws.[90] The OPA greatly improved the previously existing scheme, but it still fails to properly define its relationship with international and state law. By maintaining the state's rights to set different and higher liability limits, it fails to set a uniform

---

86 Philip Peterson & Daniel Kopec, Crude Legislation: Liability and Compensation Under The Oil Pollution Act of 1990, 23 RUTGERS L.J. 597 (1992).

87 Soon after the FWPCA was passed, authorities on admiralty law asserted that "the act is as soft and spineless in its drafting as it is muddle-headed in its policy. If it is destined to remain on the books, the courts will have their work cut out for them in making some sense out of its vague, ambiguous and contradictory provisions." GRANT GILMORE & CHARLES L. BLACK, THE LAW OF ADMIRALTY 828 (2d ed. 1975).

88 President's Statement on signing the Oil Pollution Act of 1990, 26 WEEKLY COMP. PRES. DOC. 1265 (Aug. 18, 1990), 1990 U.S.C.C.A.N. 861-1.

89 These legislations are discussed in Chapter Fifteen. See also, 33 USC §§2702 & 2704.

90 33 U.S.C. § 2718(a)(1): "Nothing in this Act or the Act of March 3, 1851 shall – (1) affect or be construed or interpreted as preempting, the authority of any state or political subdivision thereof from imposing any additional liability or requirements with respect to—(A) the discharge of oil or other pollution by law within such state, or (B) any removal activities in connection with such a discharge."

standard on which oil carriers and producers can depend.[91] Additionally, by failing to conform to international agreements, it isolates American Law from the international legal community.[92] This was done deliberately by Congress because its adoption of the 1984 Protocols to the 1969 Civil Liability Convention (CLC) and the 1971 Fund Convention (Fund) would have provided compensation for foreign tanker oil spills and access to up to only $260 million per spill from an international fund.[93] This would have conflicted with the desire of Congress to create a more robust oil spill fund and higher limits of liability. It has been noted that by failing to ratify the 1984 Protocols to the 1969 Civil Liability Convention and the 1971 Fund Convention, a situation may be created in which larger oil shippers seeking to avoid risk are replaced by smaller companies with limited assets and a reduced ability to pay for the clean-up of oil spills.[94]

Although the United States signed the 1969 International Convention and actively participated in the development of its failed 1984 Protocol, it later refused to adhere to this same protocol.[95] Congress realized that the chief stumbling block to ratifying the 1984 Protocols revolved around the issue of preemption of states' rights.[96] The Senate believed that ratifying the 1984 Protocols would leave the states powerless to recover from massive oil spills. (The international conventions are discussed in chapter nine). More specifically, the Senate wanted some assurance that states would be compensated for oil spills that exceeded the limits set forth under the amended CLC and Fund.[97] However, the House of Representatives pushed for a comprehensive oil spill bill that would provide a uniform

91 Philip Peterson & Daniel Kopec, Crude Legislation: Liability and Compensation Under The Oil Pollution Act of 1990, 23 RUTGERS L.J. at 599.

92 Id

93 See 1990 U.S.C.C.A.N. 861-2.

94 See 1990 U.S.C.C.A.N. 861-2.

95 See Susan Bloodworth, Death On The High Seas: The Demise Of Tovalop And Cristal, 13 J. Land Use & Envtl. L. 443, 453 (Spring 1998), (citing Paul S. Edelman, International Convention for Oil Spills, 216 N.Y.L.J. 3, 3 (1996)).

96 See Stephen C. Smith, Comment, An Analysis Of The Oil Pollution Act Of 1990 And The 1984 Protocols On Civil Liability For Oil Pollution Damage, 14 Houston Journal of International Law, 115, 135 (Fall 1991).

97 Id. at 135.

system of liability and compensation, preempting state laws which already addressed the issue.[98] Senate Majority Leader at the time, George Mitchell explicitly stated that federal legislation would not preempt state oil pollution laws.[99] In his opening statement before the Subcommittee on Environmental Protection of the Senate Committee on Environment and Public Works, he said:

*"The only way the citizens of Alaska have any hope of being fully compensated for their losses is under the Alaska State statute, which provides for unlimited, strict, joint and several liability. Had the protocols, or pre-emptive Federal Legislation been in place, Alaskans would have been unable to seek full recovery of their losses. It is inconceivable to me that in the wake of the Alaskan oil spill anyone would want to pre-empt all state oil spill laws."*[100]

Specifically at issue were the laws of approximately thirty-three states that addressed oil spill pollution.[101] The Secretary of Transportation at the time, Samuel Skinner advocated preemption of states rights and the adoption of the 1984 Protocols, saying that "current laws do not offer sufficient protection against foreign tankers that 'want to walk away' from oil spills."[102]

The House continued to push for preemption and the adoption of the 1984 Protocols. In a final attempt, the House proposed two choices regarding preemption: "first, a preemption of only those state laws in conflict with the international protocols when adopted; or second,... the preemption

98 Id.

99 Id.

100 See Pending Oil Spill Legislation: Hearings on S.686, S.687, S. 1066, and S.1223 before the Subcommittee on Environmental Protection of the Senate Committee on Environment and Public Works, 101st Congress, 1st Session 3 (1989) (opening statement of Senator George Mitchell).

101 See Stephen C. Smith, Comment, An Analysis Of The Oil Pollution Act Of 1990 And The 1984 Protocols On Civil Liability For Oil Pollution Damage, 14 Houston Journal of International Law, at 135.

102 Id. at 135-36.

of state liability laws in tandem with a prohibition on state assessing taxes on oil to pay damage claims covered by the federal fund."[103] However, the Senate remained true to the words of Majority Leader Mitchell by refusing to pass any legislation that would preempt state oil pollution laws. Thus, the House conceded, and the Oil Pollution Act of 1990 passed, ending any real chance for future adoption of the 1984 Protocols by the United States.[104]

The non-adoption of the Protocols was a rejection of Samuel Skinner's argument that the benefits achievable under the Protocols clearly outweighed those available under state law. The benefits he identified, included: (a) mechanisms, such as the recognition and enforcement of US judgments abroad, to insure that the assets of the ship-owner or its insurer would be available to meet compensable pollution damage claims; (b) worldwide sharing of the costs of major US oil pollution incidents, and (c) enhancement of the ability of the US to influence the structure of international maritime and environmental regimes and institutions.[105] A number of other reasons for the United States to adopt the 1984 Protocols were also rejected. The Director of the International Oil Pollution Compensation Fund identified at least three additional reasons why the United States should adopt the 1984 Protocols.[106] First, participation by the United States would ensure that insurance certificates are internationally recognized; second international participation in the 1984 Protocols would encourage and provide a means for protecting the marine environment of developing countries; third, victims of oil spill pollution would be ensured compensation for damages suffered without having to resort to costly and time consuming litigation.[107]

---

103 Id. at 136.

104 Id.

105 Colin De La Rue, and Charles B. Anderson, Shipping and The Environment, 59 (Lloyds Shipping Law Library 1998).

106 See Stephen C. Smith, Comment, An Analysis Of The Oil Pollution Act Of 1990 And The 1984 Protocols On Civil Liability For Oil Pollution Damage, Houston Journal of International Law, at 144 (citing, Director of the International Oil Pollution Compensation Fund, A Note Promoting United States' Ratification of the 1984 Protocols 3 (Feb. 22, 1989) (on file with the Houston Journal of International Law)).

107 Id.

During the drafting stages of OPA, the testimony of a group of witnesses, representing environmental organizations, reflected a general mistrust of the Protocol's ability to provide full compensation to pollution victims, but focused on a number of specific issues, such as (a) failure to establish a comprehensive scheme covering all major oil spills by excluding spills of non-persistent oils; (b) failure to implement a system of strict, joint, and several liability by channeling all liability to the vessel owner to the exclusion of operators, pilots, charterers, and crewmembers; (c) failure to impose unlimited liability for pollution damage absent evidence of intentional or reckless conduct on the part of the owner; (d) time bar provisions which would preclude claims for damage, including environmental damage, after six years from the date of the spill incident, and (e) restrictions on the circumstances under which the cost of restoring natural resources could be recovered.[108] These environmental groups continued to see significant advantages of domestic law over the Protocols.[109] They argued that strict liability would not only ensure full recovery of cost, but also induce a higher standard of care.[110] They also expressed concerns about the Protocol's absolute limit on liability, arguing that under federal and state law, compensation funds could be replenished to provide the funds needed to complete a clean up.[111]

108 See. Colin De La Rue, and Charles B. Anderson, Shipping and The Environment, 60 (Lloyds Shipping Law Library 1998).

109 Id. at 60.

110 Id.

111 Id. at 60.

# Chapter One

# SCOPE OF THE OIL POLLUTION ACT OF 1990

## A. SUBSTANCES COVERED-OIL

Statutory provisions:
"§ 2702. Elements of liability

(a) In general

Notwithstanding any other provision or rule of law, and subject to the provisions of this Act, each responsible party for a vessel or a facility from which **oil** is discharged, or which poses the substantial threat of a discharge of oil, into or upon the navigable waters or adjoining shorelines or the exclusive economic zone is liable for the removal costs and damages specified in subsection (b) of this section that result from such incident."[112]

The Act defines oil as follows:

**"oil"** means oil of any kind or in any form, including petroleum, fuel oil, sludge, oil refuse, and oil mixed with wastes other than dredged spoil, but does not include any substance which is specifically listed or designated as a hazardous substance under subparagraphs (A) through (F) of section 101(14) of the Comprehensive Environmental Response, Compensation, and Liability Act [42 U.S.C. 9601] and which is subject to the provisions of that Act [42 U.S.C. 9601et seq.] "[113]

In the OPA, "oil" was originally defined as:

112 33 USC §2702.

113 33 USC §2701(23).

"oil of any kind or in any form, including, but not limited to, petroleum, fuel oil, sludge, oil refuse, and oil mixed with wastes other than dredged spoil, but does not include petroleum, including crude oil or any fraction thereof, which is specifically listed or designated as a hazardous substance under subparagraphs (A) through (F) of section 101(14) of the Comprehensive Environmental Response, Compensation, and Liability Act (42 U.S.C. 9601) and which is subject to the provisions of that Act (42 U.S.C. 9601 et seq.)."[114]

In 1998 the United States Congress amended the original definition of oil in the OPA. This amendment replaced the phrase "but does not include petroleum, including crude oil or any fraction thereof" with the words "any substance."[115] This amendment makes the definition of oil more understandable, because the old phrase appeared to be too restrictive. Now it is clear that any substance specifically listed as hazardous substance under the relevant sections of CERCLA is not oil for the purposes of OPA liability. Section 9607(14) of CERCLA provides:

> "the term hazardous substance does not include petroleum, including crude oil or any fraction thereof which is not otherwise specifically listed or designated as a hazardous substance under subparagraphs (A) through (F) of this paragraph...."

This provision is popularly called the "petroleum exclusion."

First, and most importantly, the Environmental Protection Agency (EPA) has distinguished between oil that naturally contains low levels of hazardous substances and oil to which hazardous substances have been added through use. Although EPA has extended the petroleum exclusion to the former category of oily substances, it has specifically declined to extend such protection to the latter category. In EPA's words: "EPA does not consider materials such as waste oil to which listed CERCLA

114 The Oil Pollution Act 1990, 33 USC §2701(23).

115 33 USCA §2701(23)

substances have been added to be within the petroleum exclusion."[116] EPA's interpretation of the petroleum exclusion comports with the relevant legislative history which indicates that the exclusion was intended for oil spills, not for releases of oil which has become infused with hazardous substances through use.[117] If the oil involved is a product of a hot-rolling process adding hazardous substances to oil, it does not fall within the scope of the petroleum exclusion as construed by the EPA.[118]

## B. PARTIES LIABLE

Statutory provisions:
"§ 2702. Elements of liability

(a) In general

Notwithstanding any other provision or rule of law, and subject to the provisions of this Act, **each responsible party for a vessel or a facility** from which oil is discharged, or which poses the substantial threat of a discharge of oil, into or upon the navigable waters or adjoining shorelines or the exclusive economic zone is liable for the removal costs and damages specified in subsection (b) of this section that result from such incident."[119]

Thus, the Act imposes liability on those who qualify as "**responsible parties**." The "Definitions of the Act defines **responsible parties** as follows:

"§ 2701. Definitions:
For the purposes of this Act, the term--

116 50 Fed.Reg. 13,460 (1985).

117 See S.Rep. No. 848, 96th Cong., 2d Sess. 30-31 (1980), reprinted in A Legislative History, Vol. I, at 405.

118 United States v. Alcan Aluminum Corp., 964 F2d. 252, 266-67 (3rd Cir. 1992).

119 33 USC §2702.

(32) "**responsible party**" means the following:

(A) Vessels

In the case of a vessel, any person owning, operating, or demise chartering the vessel.

(B) Onshore facilities

In the case of an onshore facility (other than a pipeline), any person owning or operating the facility, except a Federal agency, State, municipality, commission, or political subdivision of a State, or any interstate body, that as the owner transfers possession and right to use the property to another person by lease, assignment, or permit.

(C) Offshore facilities

In the case of an offshore facility (other than a pipeline or a deepwater port licensed under the Deepwater Port Act of 1974 (33 U.S.C. 1501 et. seq.), the lessee or permittee of the area in which the facility is located or the holder of a right of use and easement granted under applicable State law or the Outer Continental Shelf Lands Act (43 U.S.C. 1301 – 1356) for the area in which the facility is located (if the holder is a different person than the lessee or permittee), except a Federal agency, State, municipality, commission, or political subdivision of a State, or any interstate body, that as owner transfers possession and right to use the property to another person by lease, assignment, or permit.

(D) Deepwater ports

In the case of a deepwater port licensed under the Deepwater Port Act of 1974 (33 U.S.C. 1501-1524), the licensee.

(E) Pipelines

In the case of a pipeline, any person owning or operating the pipeline.

(F) Abandonment

In the case of an abandoned vessel, onshore facility, deepwater port, pipeline, or offshore facility, the persons who would have been responsible parties immediately prior to the abandonment of the vessel or facility.

The Act provides further guidance by defining the persons who qualify in each of the responsible party categories. Thus, under the Act:
"owner or operator" means (A) in the case of a **vessel**, any person owning, operating, or chartering by demise, the vessel, and (B) in the case of an **onshore facility**, and an **offshore facility**, any person owning or operating such onshore facility or offshore facility, and (C) in the case of any **abandoned offshore facility**, the person who owned or operated such facility immediately prior to such abandonment."[120]

Under the Act: **"vessel"** means every description of watercraft or other artificial contrivance used, or capable of being used, as a means of transportation on water, other than a public vessel.[121]

Likewise, the Act defines facilities as follows:
"facility" means any structure, group of structures, equipment, or device (other than a vessel) which is used for one or more of the following purposes: exploring for, drilling for, producing, storing, handling, transferring, processing, or transporting oil. This term includes any motor vehicle, rolling stock, or pipeline used for one or more of these purposes.[122]
The Act applies to two kinds of facilities, offshore and onshore facilities which are defined as follows:
""offshore facility" means any facility of any kind located in, on, or under any of the navigable waters of the United States, and any facility of any kind which is subject to the jurisdiction of the United States and is located in, on, or under any other waters, **other than a vessel or a public vessel**."[123]

---

120 See 33 USC §2701(26).

121 Oil Pollution Act, 33 USC § 2701(32).

122 33 USC § 2701(9).

123 Id. at §2701(22).

"onshore facility" means any facility (including, but not limited to, motor vehicles and rolling stock) of any kind located in, on, or under, any land within the United States other than submerged land.[124]

Throughout this treatise references will be made to the U.S. Coast Guard's National Pollution Fund Center and the Oil Spill Liability Trust Fund. The National Pollution Fund Center (NPFC) is the fiduciary agent for the Oil Spill Liability Trust Fund (the Fund or OSLTF) that was set up by the U.S. government to ensure that the government can provide enough funding for the removal costs and damages associated with oil spills in the US. The fund consists of the proceeds of per-barrel taxation on oil transported into the US. The NPFC and the Fund is discussed in Chapter Eleven.

The Oil Pollution Act provides that "notwithstanding any other provision or rule of law, and subject to the provisions of the Act, each responsible party for a vessel or a facility from which oil is discharged, or which poses the substantial threat of a discharge of oil, into or upon the navigable waters or adjoining shorelines or the exclusive economic zone is liable for the removal costs and damages that result from such incident."[125]

**Strict Liability**: The basis of liability applicable to oil polluters in OPA cases is not negligence, but rather strict, no-fault liability. The Oil Pollution Act imposes strict liability for oil spills in the navigable waters, exclusive economic zone, or shoreline of the United States on the owner, operator, or demise charterer of a vessel (responsible party).[126] This means that owners, operators, or demise charterers of vessels are jointly and severally liable under the OPA. This has been interpreted as deviating from the well-entrenched rule of general maritime law that allows an owner of a vessel to insulate itself from liability for the acts of a vessel or its crew by bareboat or demise chartering the vessel to another party, as it imposes joint and several liability on each person owning, operating or

---

124 Id. at §2701(24).

125 Oil Pollution Act, 33 USC § 2702(a).

126 33 USC § 2702(a).

demise chartering the vessel.[127] The legislative history of the OPA reveals that the term "liable" or "liability" was taken from the Senate amendment to the House of Representatives OPA bill, and is to be construed to be the standard of liability that obtains under section 311 of the FWPCA for liability for removal costs and damages from discharges of oil.[128] That standard of liability has been determined repeatedly to be strict, joint and several liability.[129]

**Vessel**: Under the OPA, vessel means every description of watercraft or other artificial contrivance used, or capable of being used, as a means of transportation on water, other than a public vessel.[130] This definition of a vessel is an expansive and flexible one, such that in most oil spill incidents it will be easy for an OPA claimant to prove that what caused the oil spill is a vessel because there is an open-ended list of artificial contrivances that are capable of being used as a means of transportation on water. Therefore, this part of the OPA claimants' case will be easy to prove in most cases. If the OPA claimant alleges that the source of the oil spill is a vessel, but fails to show in evidence that the source of the spill is actually a vessel as defined in the OPA, he cannot recover damages and removal costs.

A person whose vessel discharged oil is designated the **responsible party (RP)** under OPA. With respect to vessels, because only *owners, operators, or demise charterers* of vessels are held liable under the OPA, it is certain that *voyage charterers*, as well as *cargo interests* are not subject to any liability under the provisions of the OPA. The fact that cargo owners are not subject to OPA liability is very clear from the legislative history of the statute. The legislative history shows that in the original OPA bill, for oil spills involving tank vessels, liability was to be divided between the vessel owner or operator and the cargo owner with the vessel owner or operator liable for the first 50 percent of the liability limit and the cargo

127 See 3 Benedict on Admiralty, § 112, p. 9-18 (1997). See also, 33 USC § 2701(32)(A).

128 1990 U.S.C.C.A.N. 780, H.R. Conf. Rep. No. 653, 101st Cong., (2nd Sess. 1990), 1990 WL 132747 (Leg.Hist.)

129 1990 U.S.C.C.A.N. 780.

130 33 USCA §2701(37).

owner liable for the second 50 percent.[131] The original intent of Congress was also that if the vessel owner or operator has unlimited liability, the cargo owner was to be liable for up to 50 percent of the applicable limit for the amount of liability which the vessel owner does not compensate.[132] This provision which would have made the owner of the spilled cargo of oil secondarily or partly liable in unlimited liability situations was however expunged by the Congress from the final OPA statute. Some have criticized the non-inclusion of cargo interests in the liability scheme. They believe that OPA's non-inclusion of cargo interests can only help defeat the declared object of Congress, which is to ensure that the claims of future oil- spill victims can be met.[133] "For it excludes from liability the very players in the oil-import game -- American oil companies -- who are rich enough to pay its swinging penalties."[134] But one can make a competing argument that the oil companies' payment of 5 cents per barrel of crude oil into the 1 billion US dollars Oil Spill Liability Trust Fund (Fund) is a type of contribution to the meeting of the liabilities that emanate from oil spills, even though they are not being held directly liable for oil spills. Some other critics suggest that "the escape of cargo owners" from strict liability "could encourage the use of one-ship companies for transportation purposes due to the absence of potential liability of cargo interests."[135] One can make a counter argument that the elaborate scheme for piercing the corporate veil will make it very difficult for a cargo interest that is a parent corporation of a one ship company (transporting the oil) to escape liability. The parent corporation who is also the owner of the cargo of oil could be held directly liable under modern environmental law theories and also under traditional common law theories of environmental corporate liability. This will be discussed more fully in the latter part of this

---

131 1990 U.S.C.C.A.N. 784, H.R. Conf. Rep. No. 653, 101ST Cong., (2nd Sess. 1990), 1990 WL 132747 (Leg.Hist.).

132 1990 U.S.C.C.A.N. 784.

133 See Russell Lewis, U.S. Trade Policy Adrift, 46 Nat'l Rev. No. 7, at 42-43 (Apr. 18, 1994).

134 Id. at 43.

135 Antonio J. Rodriguez & Paul A. C. Jaffe, The Oil Pollution Act of 1990, 15 Tul. Mar. L.J. 1, 27-28 (1990).

chapter. Apart from this, the argument fails to recognize the fact that not all oil cargo interests have subsidiary shipping companies involved in the transportation of their own cargo of oil. Some oil companies would rather use vessel owning or operating companies in which they have no vested interests whatsoever. In those kind of cases, it would not matter if the vessel is a one-ship company, because you cannot hold the cargo owner liable anyway.

Although the OPA's definition of **responsible party** does not expressly include *time charterers* of vessels, it is still not clear whether the courts at their first opportunity to interpret this provision will regard time charterers as operators of vessels.[136] This issue will be discussed later in this chapter.

*Judicial Interpretation of OPA's definition of Facility*[137]*:*

*In United.States. v. Southern Pacific Transportation Co.*,[138] the Federal government sought civil penalties, injunctive relief, and cost recovery for claims arising out of a discharge of diesel fuel into navigable waters of the United States and adjoining shorelines following a freight train derailment on January 27, 1993. The diesel spill in this case came from fuel tanks used to power the train locomotives, not from tanks being used for the commercial production or transportation of diesel fuel.[139] The first claim by the US for relief sought injunctive relief under the Federal Water Pollution Control Act. The second claim sought to recover penalties under

136 See Slaven v. BP America, Inc., 786 F. Supp. 853, 865 (C.D. Cal. 1992). (Holding that a time charterer was an operator of a vessel under the Trans Alaska Pipelines Authorization Act).

137 Please refer to chapter seven which discusses the OPA limitation amount with respect to **facilities** for the explanation of the definition of facility. The discussion below is more appropriate for the current chapter because if it is discussed under the other chapter, it will shift the focus of the reader away from the discussion of the OPA limitation amount in that chapter.

138 CIV. No. 94-6176-HO, 1995 WL 84193 (D. Oregon 1995).

139 Id. at *2.

section 311 of the FWPCA as amended by the Oil Pollution Act of 1990. The US third claim sought recovery under both the FWPCA and the OPA for removal costs incurred by the United States including "administrative and adjudicative costs" it incurred in connection with clean up efforts following the derailment, and reimbursement to the "Spill Fund" (Oil Spill Liability Trust Fund) for any disbursements made in connection with or as a result of the discharge.[140] The US government's right to recovery in this case hinged on its ability to convince the court that OPA's definition of facility included spills from fuel tanks used merely to power train locomotives. The defendant argued that OPA covered spills that occurred in the production and transportation of oil, but not those that occurred in the course of its use by the ultimate consumer.[141] The United States District Court for the District of Oregon agreed with the defendant. The court relied on the plain meaning of section 2701(9) of the OPA, earlier explained above. According to the district court, the definition in section 2701(9) of the OPA confirms Congressional intent that OPA cover only those oil spills occurring in the commercial production or transportation of oil.[142] The Court further held:

*"Where a statute designates certain persons, things, or manners of operation, there is a presumption that omissions are exclusions. ("Expressio unius est exclusio alterius"). See, Boudette v. Barnette, 923 F.2d 754, 756-7 (9th Cir.1991). The OPA definition of facility includes several examples of commercial activity. Therefore, the absence of any language in 33 U.S.C. § 2701(9) relating to the use of oil for consumer purposes creates a presumption that such uses are not within the intended scope of the OPA. This interpretation is consistent with the legislative history of the OPA which reveals that Congress considered the much broader definition of "facility" found in the CWA See S. 1066, 101st Cong., 1st Sess. § 101(8) (1989) (" 'facility' means an onshore facility or an offshore facility other than a public facility") H.R. 1465, 101st Cong., 1st Sess. § 101(7)*

140 Id. at *1.

141 Id. at *2.

142 Id.

*(1989) (" 'facility' means an onshore facility and an offshore facility"). The definition in the final version of the OPA is considerably narrower and specifically focuses on the commercial oil industry."*

Based on the foregoing, the court held that locomotive fuel tanks do not constitute a "facility" under 2701(9) of the OPA. It appears that this decision was well reasoned. Although it involved a freight train derailment in this case, in future cases it might involve any other mode of transportation, for example, bunkers on a non-tank vessel, a vehicular fuel tanker, airplanes etc. If other courts follow the reasoning in this case which appears to be valid, then the principle in this case will apply to all modes of transportation with equal force unless the US Congress amends section 2701(9) and adds the phrase "including discharges of oil being used by consumers for the powering of their several modes of transportation." The possibility of that happening is very remote because of the small volume of oil that can be discharged from the fuel tanks of several modes of transportation, unlike the high volume of oil that can be discharged from facilities and vessels used for the transportation, production and exploration of oil.

But, this decision does not prevent recovery for oil discharges from any mode of transportation or facility involved in the commercial production or transportation of oil. So, even if an oil tanker vehicle spills oil on land that flows or poses a threat of flowing into the navigable waters of the US, the owner or operator of that tanker vehicle will be liable as a responsible party under the Oil Pollution Act of 1990. For instance in the case of *United States v. Mizhir*,[143] the US government brought a successful clean up reimbursement law suit against the owner of an oil delivery truck that crashed his oil delivery truck into a house in Marlborough, New Hampshire, causing a spill of 71.42 barrels (3,000 gallons) of No. 2 fuel oil into a private house and surrounding area that includes the Minnewawa Brook, which flows into the Ashuelot River.

143 *Mizhir*, 106 F.Supp.2d 124 (D. Mass. 2000).

## B.I. RESPONSIBLE PARTY: SHIP OWNER AND OPERATOR LIABILITY IN OPA

The OPA defines the "owner or operator" of a vessel as any "person" owning, operating, or chartering a vessel by demise.[144] Person is defined as an individual, corporation, partnership, association, State, municipality, commission, or political subdivision of a State, or any interstate body.[145] The **demise or bareboat charterer** is basically the lessee of a vessel, usually on a long term contract, often associated with a special finance or purchase agreement.[146] An essential feature of the demise is that the entire command and possession of the vessel is turned over to the charterer.[147] Although the owner retains legal title, the demise charterer is considered the temporary owner, or commonly termed the owner pro hac vice.[148]

The principal provision imposing liability for oil discharges in the US waters prior to the enactment of the OPA was section 311 of the Federal Water Pollution Control Act (FWPCA). Section 311(b) of the FWPCA prohibited the discharge of any oil or hazardous substances in or on the navigable waters of the United States, its shorelines and with certain exceptions, its contiguous zone.[149] The FWPCA provides that the owner or operator of any vessel from which oil or hazardous substance is discharged in violation of section 311(b)(3) of the FWPCA is liable to the US government for actual costs incurred in an amount not to exceed certain limits.[150] The OPA definition of responsible party as an owner and operator of vessel is exactly the same as the definition of a responsible party or polluter in the Federal Water Pollution Control Act (FWPCA). Thus, to the extent a question of interpretation arises with respect to OPA's provisions,

144 33 USCA §2701(26)

145 33 USCA §2701(27).

146 Thomas J. Schoenbaum, Admiralty And Maritime Law, Hornbook Series, WestGroup, §9-3, 635 (2d ed.1994).

147 Id at 635.

148 Id. at 635.

149 33 USC §1321(b)(3)

150 33 USC §1321(f)

judicial and administrative decisions involving section 311 of the FWPCA may be apposite in providing needed guidance on the interpretation of the identical OPA provision. Section 311 remains in effect with respect to oil pollution in US waters, except for the imposition of liability, which is governed by section 2702 of the OPA. Since the OPA imposes liability for removal costs and damages on the person owning or operating a vessel from which oil is discharged, one may look to prior uses of the term "operator" or "operating" in the context of the FWPCA, CERCLA and TAPAA to determine how a court might interpret these terms in OPA cases.

The FWPCA required vessels which trade to the United States to carry certificates of financial responsibility indicating that the vessel would be able to meet the financial liability imposed under the Act.[151] In the regulations implementing this provision, the US Coast Guard defined an "owner" to include the title or equitable owner, including the person whose name appears on the certificate of registry.[152] Based on this provision of the regulation, there is no doubt that the registered owner of a vessel would be primarily liable for removal costs and damages in the unfortunate event of a spill or discharge.

The term "operator" was defined to include any party, including but not limited to an owner, demise charterer, or other contractor who conducts or is responsible for the operation of a vessel.[153] This definition include persons responsible for the vessels in the capacity of a builder, scrapper, repairer, or seller.[154]

The United States Coast Guard had an opportunity to address the question of who may be the operator of a vessel when it first considered what parties were subject to a civil penalty under section 311(b)(6) of the FWPCA. In a 1973 legal opinion of the Coast Guard, the Chief Counsel of the Coast Guard took the position that the term "owner or operator" should be narrowly defined.[155] In this opinion made pursuant to section

151 33 USC §1321(p).

152 33 CFR §130.2(r).

153 33 CFR § 130.2(q).

154 Id.

155 405 Coast Guard Bulletin 1 (1973).

311(b)(6) of the FWPCA, the Chief Counsel opined that the placement of "operating" between" "owning" and "chartering by demise" is intended to make an operator a person in the same class as owner or charterer by demise, thus implying a formalized charter-type situation. This interpretation would foreclose any argument that a facility which is loading a barge or a tug which is towing a barge from point to point is "operating the barge."[156] The Coast Guard's Chief Counsel recognized that the construction given the term "owner or operator" for purposes of the penalty provision in section 311(b)(6) would also have to apply to the cost provision found in section 311(f).[157] This interpretation was upheld a few years later, when the Coast Guard determined that the operator of a tug engaged in towing an unmanned barge, although considered to be a "person in charge" for purposes of reporting a spill from the barge, since the tow boat operator is operationally responsible for the barge, is nevertheless not considered the operator of the barge for purposes of the imposition of a civil penalty under section 311(b)(6).[158]

The courts have however gone beyond this Coast Guard administrative ruling. In the decision in the case of *Tug Ocean Prince Inc. v. US*,[159]which was a decision based on section 311(b)(6) of the FWPCA, the court held that a tenable construction of the statutory language demonstrates that "operator" should be construed to include a tug operating a "dumb" barge. In this case, a tank barge discharged some of its oil cargo in a river after it ran aground on a submerged rock formation while being towed by the tug.

Interpreting the FWPCA, the United States Court of Appeals for the Fifth Circuit has stated that the owner or operator of a vessel or facility is the entity in a position to timely discover discharges, direct the persons who are causing the discharges, and prevent or mitigate any resulting

156 Laurie Frost, Charting Stormy Waters: The Definition of an "Operator" Under The Oil Pollution Act of 1990, 1, 7, 12th New Orleans Maritime Seminar (Jan. 1993).

157 Id at 7.

158 Id, *see also*, 416 Coast Guard Bulletin 2 (1976).

159 Tug Ocean Prince Inc. v. US, 436 F.Supp. 907, 926 (SDNY 1977), *aff'd in part and rev'd in part on other grounds*, 584 F.2d 1151 (2d Cir.1978 ), *cert. denied*, 440 U.S. 959, 99 S.Ct. 1499 (1978).

damages.[160] The United States Court of Appeals for the Eighth Circuit has similarly stated: The owner-operator of a vessel or a facility is the person that: (a) has the capacity to make timely discovery of oil discharges; (b) has power to direct the activities of persons who control the mechanisms causing the pollution; and (c) has the capacity to prevent and abate damage.[161]

The Trans Alaska Pipeline Authorization Act (TAPAA)[162] provides some guidance as well. The Trans Alaska Pipeline Authorization Act is still a binding statute with respect to pipeline oil pollution incidents that took place before the date that the OPA took effect. All post-OPA pipeline oil spill incidents are now dealt with primarily under the OPA. TAPAA imposed strict, joint and several liability on the owner or operator of any vessel discharging oil which has been transported through the Trans Alaska Pipeline, until the oil reaches a port or place where it is offloaded in the United States.[163] In the only reported decision found which addresses the term "operator" under the TAPAA, a court in its decision upon preliminary motions made during trial in a case involving an oil spill in Huntington Beach, held that the owner of the oil, BP Oil Supply Company, and the time charterer, BP Oil Shipping Co., USA, possibly could be an "operator" under the TAPAA.

The court rejected the defendants motion to dismiss in which they argued that as the owner of the oil and the time charterer of the discharging vessel, they were neither the "owner nor the "operator" of the vessel.[164] The court decided that it was possible for the plaintiffs to establish that the charter entered into by BP could make it an "operator" of the vessel under TAPAA.[165] This ruling indicates that courts may look at contractual responsibilities of a time charterer to determine if it could be considered an "operator." Generally, a time charter party is contract

160 See United States v. Mobil Oil Corp., 464 F.2d 1124, 1127, 1973 AMC 427 (5th Cir. 1972).

161 See Apex Oil Co. v. United States, 530 F.2d 1291, 1293 (8th Cir. 1976).

162 43 USC §§1651 *et seq.*

163 43 USC §1653 (c)(1).

164 Slaven v. BP America, Inc., 786 F. Supp. 853, 865 (C.D. Cal. 1992).

165 786 F. Supp. at 865.

to use a ship in order to ship goods (including oil and hazardous substances) for a specific period of time.[166] The time charterer bears the expenses connected to each voyage and pays hire to the carrier based upon the time the ship is under charter.[167] As a basis for their contract, the parties to a time charter party generally use one of the available forms, some of which include; the New York Produce Exchange Form, the "Transtime" form or the "Baltime form- and amend it to suit their needs.[168] Some of the distinctive clauses in time charters could arguably qualify a time charterer as an operator. For instance there is a clause that allows the parties to the time charter to divide responsibilities between themselves. In contrast to voyage charters (which are often contracts of affreightment) where the carrier typically manages the carriage of cargo and cares for the cargo, there is more of a division of responsibility in a time charter.[169] In general, the carrier is to keep the ship properly equipped so that the orders of the time charterer can be properly carried out. The costs are divided so that while the carrier pays fixed costs, the charterer pays variable costs such as bunkering.[170] The charterer is usually responsible for loading and discharge of the cargo. In a time charter party there is also a clause that defines the modus operandi for the individual voyage. The master is under the orders of the charterer. The charterer therefore decides what cargo is to be loaded, where it is to be loaded, and when the loading begins.[171] However, the nautical aspects of the voyage are not under the charterer's control. There is also a clause relating to employment and agency. This clause normally provides that the charterer has the full use of the vessel and the master will comply with the charterer's orders and instructions. The charterer in return normally agrees to indemnify the owner for all liability.[172]

---

166 Thomas J. Schoenbaum, Admiralty And Maritime Law, Hornbook Series, WestGroup, §9-5, 639 (2d. ed. 1994).

167 Id at 639.

168 Id.

169 Id.

170 Id. at 640

171 Id

172 Id

The nature of authority that some of these clauses confer on the time charterer could make him liable as an operator. There is usually freedom of contract in time charter parties which gives the contracting parties the latitude to alter in any way some of the form time charter party clauses. The more responsibility and authority the time charter party clauses confer on the time charterer the more likely the courts would hold a time charterer to be an operator. Based on the three part test formulated by the *Apex Oil Co* court; that the owner-operator of a vessel or a facility is the person that: (a) has the capacity to make timely discovery of oil discharges; (b) has power to direct the activities of persons who control the mechanisms causing the pollution; and (c) has the capacity to prevent and abate damage;[173] one could argue that a time charterer with a lot of authority and responsibility can easily meet the three part test. From the clauses discussed earlier, the time charterer (1) has the capacity to make timely discovery of oil discharges, (2) has the power to direct the activities of persons who control the mechanism causing the oil spill, and (3) has the capacity to prevent and abate damage. Despite the tempting and alluring nature of the preceding argument, a strict constructionist court might decide a case of this nature solely on the fact that the phrase "time charterer" is not mentioned expressly in the definition of responsible party, but the phrase "demise charterer" is expressly mentioned.[174]

The OPA statute does not include the term "ship manager" as a responsible party; however, it is likely that ship managers who exercise day-to-day operational responsibility for the maintenance, safety and seaworthiness of a vessel will be considered "operators" for purposes of liability under both OPA and CERCLA.[175] It is common in the shipping industry for owners to enter into contracts with independent management companies to perform technical and commercial functions relating to the operation of their vessels.[176] It is generally thought that a so called

173 See Apex Oil Co. v. United States, 530 F.2d 1291, 1293 (8th Cir. 1976).

174 33 USCA §2701(32).

175 Colin De La Rue, and Charles B. Anderson, Shipping and The Environment, 659 (Lloyds Shipping Law Library 1998).

176 Id. at 659.

"technical" manager who assumes responsibility for manning, victualling, and equipping a vessel and who is vested with substantial operational control over the vessel will be subject to liability under both the OPA and CERCLA as an "operator," whereas a "commercial" manager who performs such functions as chartering and scheduling of vessel movements, supplying bunkers, or arranging for supervision of cargo loading and unloading activities does not exercise sufficient control over the daily operation of the vessel to be considered an "operator".[177] It appears that commercial managers do not have the type of operational responsibilities that could be connected directly to the cause of a spill. Historically, they have been held not to be liable for maritime torts.[178] Neither OPA nor the case law provides helpful guidance regarding the liability of these various types of ship managers. The legislative history of CERCLA, however, does provide some insight into the nature of the activities required to confer "operator" status on ship managers:

> *"Operator" is the second major class subject to liability under the Act. Operators of vessels do not include those individuals who are not totally responsible for the operation of a vessel. To fall within the definition, the individual must have assumed the full range of operational responsibility. For example, a pilot might be in charge of navigation of a vessel for a short duration, yet he does not meet the definition "operator," since he neither mans nor supplies the vessel. In the case of a facility, an "operator" is defined as a person who is carrying out operational functions for the owner of the facility pursuant to an appropriate agreement.*[179]

In the absence of any interpretative ruling by the courts, the most that can be said at present is that an operator under CERCLA, and by implication under OPA must be one who exercises day to day control over

177 Id. at 659.

178 Benedict on Admiralty, §112a (7th ed. 1991).

179 Colin De La Rue, and Charles B. Anderson, Shipping and The Environment, at 659, *quoting*, H.R. Rep. No. 172, Pt. 1, 96th Cong., 2d Sess. 36-37 (1980), *reprinted in* 1980 USCCAN 6160, 6182-82.

the full range of ship operations.[180] This is likely to encompass any ship manager who assumes contractual responsibility for the vessel's seaworthiness, crewing, maintenance, and general safety so as to be in a position to minimize the risk of pollution.[181]

The Supreme Court recently addressed the issue of what it means to be an operator for CERCLA purposes in *United States v. Bestfoods*.[182] The Court defined an operator as "someone who directs the workings of, manages, or conducts the affairs of a facility."[183] As earlier explained the cases defining "responsible party" under both the FWPCA and CERCLA indicate that a court will look to the degree of control exercised by that party. Despite the potential danger that a court might be influenced by the seriousness of an incident and public outcry, the Supreme Court's decision in *Bestfoods* has made it clear that liability could not be predicated on facts showing less than actual control.

In addition to the *Bestfood* factors discussed above, in order to qualify as operator of a vessel or facility under OPA, the three part test formulated by the *Apex Oil Co* court, discussed earlier in relation to time charter parties is applicable. Thus, an operator of a vessel or a facility is the person that: (a) has the capacity to make timely discovery of oil discharges; (b) has power to direct the activities of persons who control the mechanisms causing the pollution; and (c) has the capacity to prevent and abate damage.[184]

In oil spill incidents in which the owner of the culpable vessel is identifiable and the same vessel is under the control of an operator, a claimant may be able to sue both the owner and operator of the vessel for removal costs and damages. However, the *Bestfoods* "actual control" requirement may be required in order to successfully claim against the operator.

Although application of the FWPCA did not result in expansive interpretation of "owner" or "operator," the greatly expanded OPA liability for costs may motivate governmental and private claimants to seek

180 Colin De La Rue, and Charles B. Anderson, Shipping and The Environment, at 660.

181 Id. at 660.

182 524 U.S. 51, 118 S.Ct. 1876, 141 L.Ed.2d 43 (1998).

183 Bestfoods, 524 U.S. at 66.

184 See Apex Oil Co. v. United States, 530 F.2d 1291, 1293 (8th Cir. 1976).

to expand the scope of these definitions, to add more defendants and to make more assets available to satisfy claims.[185] Courts generally interpret environmental statutes broadly in order to achieve their remedial goals. The owner and operator definition in OPA is sufficiently imprecise that expansive interpretations may be employed by courts so as to reach affiliated companies and to enhance recoveries by claimants.[186]

No other case illustrates this fact better than the case of *Puerto Rico v. M/V EMILY S.*[187] Adopting the theory that a tug and barge acted as a single flotilla, the United States District Court for the District of Puerto Rico in Puerto Rico v. M/V EMILY S. found that both a tug and barge "must be considered a 'discharging vessel" ', thereby making the owner of a non-discharging tug a responsible party. In *Stevens v. The White City*,[188]the United States Supreme Court defined towage as a service rendered by one vessel to aid the propulsion or to expedite the movement of another vessel. The vessel that supplies the power in such an arrangement is typically called a tug, a term, which encompasses many different types of vessels ranging from large, ocean-going ships, to coastal and harbor tugs, and river vessels that push or pull a barge or a fleet of barges. A tug that pushes a barge is properly called a towboat, while the one that pulls a barge is called a tug boat.[189] Generally, a tug cannot be considered a "third party" in order to allow the owner of a barge to avoid liability for an oil spill which occurred while the barge was in the tow of the tug.[190]

In the *M/V EMILY S* case, Metlife Capital Corporation ("MCC") owned the tug EMILY S., although the tug was under bareboat charter at the time of the oil spill in San Juan.[191] MCC filed a motion for partial summary

---

185 Laurie Frost, Charting Stormy Waters: The Definition of an "Operator" Under The Oil Pollution Act of 1990, at 9, 12th New Orleans Maritime Seminar (Jan. 1993).

186 Id at 9.

187 13 F. Supp. 2d 147, 150, 1998 AMC 2020 (D.P.R. 1998); *see also,* Olympic Tug and Barge Co. Inc., v. United States, 1990 AMC 1671, 1674 (W.D. Wash. 1990); The "CIVILTA" and The "RESTLESS", 103 U.S. 699, 701-02 (1880) (holding tug and ship being towed were one vessel).

188 285 U.S. 195, 200, 52 S.Ct. 347, 349, 76 L.Ed. 699, 702 (1932)

189 THOMAS J. SCHOENBAUM, ADMIRALTY AND MARITIME LAW, § 10-1, at 675, Hornbook Series (2d ed. 1994).

190 See United States v. Hollywood Marine Inc., 625 F.2d. 524 (5th Cir. 1980).

191 See M/V EMILY S., 13 F. Supp. 2d at 149.

judgment on grounds that it could not be considered a "responsible party" under OPA because it did not own the barge MORRIS J. BERMAN and because the tug did not discharge oil.[192] The court in M/V EMILY S. noted, however, that OPA changed the "well-entrenched rule of general maritime law" that allows a vessel owner to escape liability by bareboat chartering the vessel to a third party.[193] The court relied on the facts that the barge was (1) a "dumb barge" with no means of self-propulsion and (2) under the tug's complete control.[194] The barge's owner in this case did not have the financial resources to pay for the response costs and natural resource damages associated with a spill of this size, whereas the tug interests was better placed financially.[195] The exposure to the towing company and its underwriters created by this holding is overwhelming; they are now at risk for $100 million in removal costs and third party claims paid by the Fund, plus untold natural resource damage claims and assessment costs.[196] In fact, as of April 2001, the Coast Guard's National Pollution Funds Center had presented bills to MCC and Morris J. Berman (the flotilla) totaling $65, 667, 228.[197] Even though they have incurred such a colossal amount in removal costs and possibly damages, it is still possible that they will be presented with additional bills in the nearest future. As of April 30, 2001, it is so far the highest amount paid by an OPA RP for OPA removal costs and damages. Some have criticized this decision as incorrect,[198] but if one looks at the decision closely there are some merits to the decision.

192 Id. at 150

193 Id.

194 See id.

195 Id.

196 See Larry Kiern and Charlie Papavizas, Coast Guard and Court Rulings Interpreting OPA Raise Serious Questions (visited March 31, 2000) <http://winston.com/newslib.nsf> (choose "Newsletters & Client Memoranda," then choose "Maritime").

197 "See National Pollution Funds Center Oil Spill data, p 13, T /B Morris J . B erman, Federal Project Number 074028 (2001) (This information was provided by the National Pollution Funds Center (NPFC) in April of 2001 and the data is on file with the NPFC and is available upon request from the NPFC).

198 See. Keith B. Letourneau and Wesley T. Welmaker, The Oil Pollution Act Of 1990: Federal Judicial Interpretation Through The End Of The Millennium 12 U.S.F. Mar. L.J. 147, 213 (2000).

The part of the decision relating to the definition of responsible party as including the demise charterer of a vessel and a vessel owner was properly decided. The definition section of the OPA was properly interpreted as deviating from the well-entrenched rule of general maritime law that allows an owner of a vessel to insulate itself from liability for the acts of a vessel or her crew by bareboat or demise chartering the vessel to another party.[199] Apart from this, the OPA's legislative history shows that the US Congress rejected language that would have exempted record owners of vessels from liability.

House Bill 3394 originally proposed the following exception from liability for vessel owners:

> "In those instances, when the owner has transferred possession and right to use the property to another person by means of a lease, assignment, permit, or other similar agreement, the responsible party is that person or persons to whom such property has been transferred by agreement."[200]

However, this language was dropped when House Bill 3394 was consolidated with House Bill 1465.[201] The new OPA regime imposes joint and several liability on each person owning, operating or demise chartering the vessel. This is a congressional repeal of the old maritime rule. No reasonable argument can be made against this aspect of the court's decision.

The rationale articulated above will also apply with equal force in a case involving a vessel in which the owner of the vessel has been identified as a defendant and the same vessel has an operator in charge of its operations. Just like an owner of a vessel cannot insulate itself from liability for the acts of a vessel or its crew by bareboat or demise chartering the vessel to another party under OPA, it also cannot insulate itself from liability by turning over total or partial control of the vessel to a vessel operator. So,

---

199 See 3 Benedict on Admiralty, § 112, p. 9-18 (1997).

200 H.R. 3394, 101st Cong., 135 Cong. Rec. H7899 (daily ed. Nov. 1, 1989).

201 See 135 Cong. Rec. H7965-67 (daily ed. Nov. 2, 1989) (statement of Rep. Stangeland); *see also* Benjamin H. Grumbles & Joan M. Manley, The Oil Pollution Act of 1990: Legislation in the Wake of a Crisis, 10 A.B.A. Sec. Nat. Resources & Env't 35, 168 (Fall 1995).

if the *Apex Oil* factors are satisfied in a lawsuit against the operator of a vessel, the owner of that vessel will be jointly liable under the OPA.

In the *M/V EMILY S* case, the barge involved was a dumb barge that was unmanned and was held strictly liable under the OPA. Even if the barge was not negligent it would still be liable as a responsible party because the OPA imposes strict liability on a vessel that is responsible for the discharge of oil in the navigable waters of the United States of America. Because the owner of the tug was a responsible party under the definition section of the OPA (despite the demise charter) this part of the decision is correct.

The second part of the court's decision dealing with the flotilla rule is a little bit controversial. One can reasonably take positions for or against this aspect of the court's decision. The undisputed facts in the case showed that the barge MORRIS J. BERMAN was a 'dumb' barge loaded with bunker number 6 oil on the date of the spill. The barge was unmanned and had no means of self-propulsion. The barge was, in fact, under the complete control of the tugboat M/V EMILY S and all navigational decisions concerning the barge were made by the crew of the M/V EMILY S. The court observed that under this set of facts, it has been held before that "a tug is thus a necessary adjunct to a barge, and it seems natural to consider the two as a single entity."[202] Some critics of this court's decision referred to the comment of a notable maritime commentator and said that the maritime commentator noted that in pure tort situations "at minimum,..., vessels in the flotilla must be subject to common ownership (including a demise charter)...." [203] The sentence following the quoted text from the commentator referred to is as follows:

202 M/V EMILY S., 13 F. Supp. 2d at 150, *quoting*, In the Matter of Olympic Tug, 1990 WL 166368, 1990 A.M.C. 1671 (W.D.Wash.1990). See also The 'Civilta' and the 'Restless', 103 U.S. 699, 701-02, 26 L.Ed. 599 (1880) (finding that a tug and the ship she was towing were one vessel); see analogous reasoning on factor of control as basis of liability of tug in Sturgis v. Boyer, 65 U.S. 110, 122, 24 How. 110, 16 L.Ed. 591 (1860).

203 See Keith B. Letourneau and Wesley T. Welmaker, The Oil Pollution Act Of 1990: Federal Judicial Interpretation Through The End Of The Millennium 12 U.S.F. Mar. L.J. 147, 213 (2000), quoting, Thomas J. Schoenbaum, Admiralty and Maritime Law § 12-8, at 231 (2d ed. 1994).

"They should also be engaged in a common enterprise and subject to a single command."[204]

Quoting this sentence enables us to get a better understanding of what the commentator was trying to say or what the position of the law is. Looking at this sentence, one of the requirements for applying the flotilla rule is that the tug and the tow should be engaged in a common enterprise and subject to a single command. In the case of *M/V EMILY S,* it seems that these two requirements were satisfied.

For guidance we look to the case of *In The Matter Of Greenhill Petroleum Corp.,*[205] where the court stated as follows:

"The word "command" used in this context is necessarily nautical, referring to the person or captain with the right to control the vessel or vessels at issue. Here, the MISS DORIS (the tow) (emphasis mine) was under the "single command" of Boyd at the time of the accident. Greenhill has failed to show that any other vessel owned by Greenhill in Timbalier Bay was under this "single command" or being navigated in conjunction with the MISS DORIS's venture. In addition, the Court finds that "common venture" should be limited to the particular task at hand, not all work contemplated by the contract."[206]

Both the tug and the tow in the M/V EMILY S case had a common goal in mind, and that was to ensure that tow and its cargo reached its point of destination safely. They were both subject to the tug's command as to nautical matters and other safety related matters at the time of the accident. The only thing that appears to be absent is the common ownership requirement.

One could argue that the commentator's view was made in the context of the interaction between the flotilla rule and the limitation of liability Act of 1851,[207] which has been superseded and repealed by the OPA for

---

204 Thomas J. Schoenbaum, Admiralty and Maritime Law § 12-8, at 231 (2d ed. 1994).

205 1998 AMC 868,1997 WL 567956, *2 (E.D.La. 1997).

206 1998 AMC at 868, 1997 WL 567956, *2 (E.D.La. 1997).

207 46 U.S.C.A. §§ 181-89.

the purposes of oil spill cases.[208] In the context of a limitation proceeding, whether to apply the rule in a particular case depends on the legal relationship of the limiting owner to the injured claimant. If the vessel owner and the injured claimant were parties to a contract (e.g employment contract) at the time of the loss leading to the limitation action, then the owner must include in the limitation fund the value of all the vessels covered by the contract with the injured claimant.[209] All of the limiting owner's vessels necessary for the performance of the contract will make up the "flotilla" whose aggregate value will constitute the fund.[210]

On the other hand, if no privity of contract exists between the vessel owner and the injured claimant, then only the value of the actual offending vessel need be included in the computation of the limitation fund.[211] This concept is often referred to as the "pure tort" limitation to the flotilla rule.[212] Only claimants actually in privity of contract with the owner will have available to them the value of the flotilla in the limitation fund.[213] Claimants not in privity are subject to the pure tort exception to the flotilla rule.[214] In the *M/V EMILY S* case there was no contractual relationship between the tug owner and third party claimants, so one could argue that the tug ought not to have been included as a flotilla by the court. Since the *M/V EMILY S* case was not a limitation action, but rather a motion for summary judgment on the issue of the li-

208 See 33 USCA §2718 (a)-(c).

209 See Sacramento Nav. Co. v. Salz, 273 U.S. 326, 332, 1927 AMC 397, 402 (1927).

210 United States Dredging Corp. v. Krohmer, 264 F.2d 339, 341, 1959 AMC 1110, 1113 (2d Cir. 1959).

211 See Liverpool, Brazil & River Plate Steam Nav. Co. v. Brooklyn E. Dist. Terminal, 251 U.S. 48, 53-54 (1919); *see also*, In re Waterman S.S., 1992 AMC at 2661, 794 F. Supp. at 603-04 (E.D. La. 1992).

212 See, e.g., In re Waterman S.S., 1992 AMC at 2661, 794 F. Supp. at 603-04 (E.D. La.1992) (stating that courts construing the shipowners Limited Liability Act, 46 U.S.C.A. §§ 181-89, have held that when vessels are engaged in a common transportation enterprise they should often be considered one vessel for limitation purposes).

213 See In re North Am. Trailing Co., 763 F. Supp. 152, 163, 1993 AMC 2108 (E.D. Va. 1991).

214 See Kristie Leigh Enters. v. American Commercial Lines, Inc., 168 F.3d 206, 209 n.3, 1999 AMC 1366, 1369 n.3 (5th Cir. 1999); In re North Am. Trailing Co., 763 F. Supp. at 163.

ability of the tug under the OPA, the argument immediately preceding this sentence may not be entirely valid. The limitation Act specifically applies to a particular vessel found liable for a tortuous act like a collision or personal injury. Unlike the Limitation of Liability Act which limits the liability of a vessel to the post casualty value of the vessel, the OPA has its own limitation provision which is applicable to all oil spill cases provided certain exceptions that allow the breaking of limitation do not apply. The limitation provisions of the OPA would hold a vessel liable beyond its post casualty value.

The tort or contract distinction for the purposes of flotilla liability is also unreasonable. Why should a vessel be held liable under the flotilla rule if there is a contractual relationship with a third party and not be held liable where such a contractual relationship does not exist? Although the *M/V EMILY S* court did not criticize the longstanding tort – contract distinction it is something that should be raised by future courts confronted with the issue of the applicability of the flotilla rule in OPA cases where the injured claimant is not in any type of contractual relationship with the responsible party. This is particularly important because until this issue is resolved, the Oil Spill Liability Trust Fund would have to shoulder the responsibility of paying for colossal clean up costs and damages claims. The flexible or relaxed application of the Flotilla rule in OPA, CERCLA and FWPCA cases will ensure that the vessels directly or indirectly connected to oil spill incidents are held liable for clean up costs and damages to the fullest extent possible.

Generally, in a pure tort situation, only the offending vessel causing the injury, will be surrendered unto the court.[215] *Liverpool, Brazil & River Plate Steam Nav. Co. v. Brooklyn E. Dist. Terminal* [216] is the landmark decision holding only the offending vessel liable. There, a tug with a carfloat loaded with railroad cars lashed to its portside and a disabled tug

215 Liverpool, Brazil & River Plate Steam Nav. Co. v. Brooklyn E. Dist. Terminal, 251 U.S. 48, 40 S.Ct. 66, 64 L.Ed. 130 (1919); Murray v. New York Cent. R.R. Co., 287 F.2d 152 (2d Cir. 1961); Harbor Towing Corp. v. Atlantic Mut. Ins. Co., 189 F.2d 409 (4th Cir. 1951).

216 251 U.S. 48, 40 S.Ct. 66, 64 L.Ed. 130 (1919).

on its starboard side was proceeding up the East River. A steamship was damaged while it was moored at a pier in Brooklyn when the carfloat collided with it. All three vessels were under common ownership. The sole question before the Supreme Court was whether the value of the whole flotilla should not have been included in the (limitation) decree. The Court held that only the value of the tug was required by law to be included, because the carfloat, although it was the vessel which collided with the steamship, was a passive instrument in the hands of' the tug, and for the purposes of liability the passive instrument of the harm does not become one with the actively responsible vessel by being attached to it. The Court ruled that the words 'any vessel' in the Act involved in this case meant the offending vessel and not others attached to it, even though all were in common ownership and engaged in a common venture. This doctrine was restated in *Deep Sea Tankers, Ltd. v. The Long Branch,*[217] there two tugs, each with a flotilla, caused the grounding of a tanker owned by the plaintiff by crowding and interfering with its navigation. The court held that only the two tugs could be held liable for their tows were merely 'passive instruments of navigation. They had no motive power of their own.'[218] Both the *Liverpool* and *Deep Sea Tankers* cases limited liability to the tugs as the offending vessel, and exonerated the barges because they were passive instruments. The direct cause of damage and liability in each instance was the action of the tugs. They were the moving components responsible for the injury.

The above argument, though weak in some degree or measure, can be made against the decision of the *M/V EMILY S* court. The tug was a passive instrument in the discharge of the oil that violated OPA. It was not passive in the sense of navigation, but it was passive as to OPA liability because the oil was not discharged from it but rather from the tow. This argument may have been plausible if the tug was not negligent.

A competing and more powerful argument could be made that the tug was not a passive instrument for OPA purposes. The facts of the case revealed that parted towing wire between tug and barge caused the

217 258 F.2d 757 (2d. Cir. 1958).

218 Id. at 773.

grounding of the barge which resulted in the oil spill.[219] Alex L. Parks in his book, The Law Of Tug, Tow, & Pilotage[220] provides a virtual compendium of case law setting forth various duties of the tug, the breach of which may lead to a finding that the tug and its owner were negligent. One of such duties of the tower is that he must furnish a tug of sufficient power, properly equipped for the voyage, manned by a competent master and crew.[221] The tug has a duty to properly make up to her tow, furnishing lines of sufficient length and strength, reasonably inspected for good condition.[222] Although ordinary negligence is not usually an issue in OPA liability cases (because it imposes strict liability) it is very important when it comes to determining whether an oil spill incident was caused solely by a responsible party or by a responsible party in conjunction with a third party. If that third party is in a contractual relationship with the responsible party, the responsible party will not be able to invoke the third party defense in section 2703(a)(3) of the OPA. However, no provision of the OPA stops the US government (through either the Coast Guard, the Environmental Protection Agency or any other agency), or any third party claimant from recovering removal costs and damages directly against the responsible party who has not succeeded in invoking the third party defense as well as against the jointly responsible third party himself. This is particularly important in towage cases where the third party defense will never apply because of the towage contract between the tug and the tow. In such instances, the third party will be jointly and severally liable to any claimant.

Based on the facts of the *M/V EMILY S.* case, one could argue that the tug was a co- responsible party and contributed to the oil spill incident. Why? **Incident** is defined as any occurrence or series of occurrences having the same origin, involving one or more vessels, facilities, or any combination thereof, resulting in the discharge or substantial threat

219 See Puerto Rico v. M/V EMILY S, 132 F.3d 818 (1st Cir. 1997).

220 Alex L. Parks & Edward V. Cattell, The Law of Tug, Tow, & Pilotage 42 (3d ed. 1994).

221 See PARKS & CATTELL, id at 127.

222 Id. at 136-37.

of discharge of oil.[223] **"Incident"** is defined to mean an occurrence or series of related occurrences because, as under other Federal law it was the intent of the Congress that the entire series of events resulting in the spill of oil comprises one "incident".[224] For OPA purposes one can argue that the oil spill that was discharged from the barge was due to an occurrence or series of occurrences having the same origin, involving both the tug (MV Emily S) and the barge (Morris J. Berman), resulting in not just a substantial threat of a discharge, but in an actual discharge from the barge.

Going back to the possible contributory negligence of the tug (M/V Emily S), it is very clear that under towage law, M/V Emily S failed woefully in its duty to properly make up to her tow, and to furnish lines of sufficient length and strength.[225] It was this negligence of the tug that proximately caused the discharge of the oil from the barge. Although the M/V EMILY S court did not pursue this line of reasoning, future courts should not overlook this line of reasoning. Had the towing wire between tug and barge not parted, there would not have been a grounding of the barge which resulted in the oil spill. Because, as under other Federal law it was the intent of the US Congress that the entire series of events resulting in the spill of oil comprise one "incident", the tug MV Emily S., cannot avoid liability. This argument appears to be potent and very persuasive. Although the M/V Emily S. case relates to tow line related negligence, this same line of reasoning should apply to any other case where the negligence of the tug plays a part no matter how infinitesimal in the discharge of oil or hazardous substances.

Many arguments can be made for and against the *M/V EMILY S* court's decision as to combined liability of vessels in OPA cases. The dust raised by the decision is yet to settle and other courts around the country would have the opportunity to address the same issue in the nearest future. But in the mean time it is quite clear that the *M/V EMILY S* court's correct or incorrect interpretation of who constitutes a responsible party under OPA, is a warning signal that tug owners engaged in the transportation of oil

---

223 See. 33 USCA §2701(14).

224 See 1990 USCCAN 780, H.R. Conf. Rep. No. 653, 101ST Cong., (2nd Sess. 1990).

225 See Alex L. Parks & Edward V. Cattell, The Law of Tug, Tow, & Pilotage, at 136-137.

products would need to address with all seriousness pollution insurance coverage issues in their insurance policies.[226] If an oil spill the magnitude of the *M/V EMILY S* case occurs, the lack of adequate insurance coverage could trigger the insolvency of an inadequately capitalized towing company.[227]

The definition section of the United State Coast Guard's regulations on "Financial Responsibility For Water Pollution from vessels" defines an operator as a person who is an owner, a demise charterer, or other contractor, who conducts the operation of, or who is responsible for the operation of, a vessel.[228] It also defines an operator as a builder, repairer, scrapper, lessor, or seller who is responsible, or who agrees by contract to become responsible for a vessel.[229] This same regulation makes the owner, operator, and demise charterer of a vessel strictly, jointly, and severally liable for the costs and damages resulting from an incident or a release or threatened release of oil from a vessel.[230] Builders, repairers, and scrappers, should avoid contractual relationships with owners and bareboat charterers of vessels, that may make them vulnerable to this regulation.

*OPA's definitions of "responsible parties" are not "mutually exclusive*: One other issue that could arise in an OPA case is who ought to be held liable for a discharge from an abandoned vessel or facility. The OPA provides that in the case of an abandoned vessel, onshore facility, deepwater port, pipeline, or offshore facility, the persons who would have been responsible parties immediately prior to the abandonment of the vessel or facility is the responsible party.[231] It appears that this and other expansive definitions of who may constitute responsible parties in section 2701(32)(A)-(F) of OPA are not mutually exclusive, and the Coast

---

226 See Keith B. Letourneau and Wesley T. Welmaker, The Oil Pollution Act Of 1990: Federal Judicial Interpretation Through The End Of The Millennium 12 U.S.F. Mar. L.J. 147, 213 (2000).

227 Id at 213.

228 33 CFR 138.20(b).

229 Id.

230 33 CFR 138.30.

231 33 USCA §2701(32)(F).

Guard, the EPA, and the Department of Justice would want to interpret the definitions broadly to increase the likelihood of recovering removal costs and damages. A quintessential illustration is a recent law-suit concerning an oil well that could be characterized as either an "offshore facility" or an "abandoned facility," where the United States District Court for the Eastern District of Louisiana agreed with the Coast Guard and held that Congress clearly intended that more than one entity could be a responsible party.[232] The court interpreted OPA expansively to extend liability to multiple responsible parties, including some who did not own or even operate the discharging facility.[233] In this case the Coast Guard had responded to a discharge of oil from an abandoned tank battery platform along coastal Louisiana and later sought recovery of its removal costs from Bois D'Arc (BDA), a "lessee or permittee of the area in which the discharging facility is located."[234] The United States District Court for the Eastern District of Louisiana brushed aside BDA's argument that the facility was abandoned, and, therefore, the proper responsible party was the "owner/operator immediately prior to the abandonment."[235] Instead, the court observed that OPA's definitions of "responsible parties" are not "mutually exclusive," that "OPA does not limit the number of responsible parties," and "by defining responsible party broadly, Congress made certain that more than one entity could be held accountable for the costs of pollution."[236] The court also observed that the legislative history demonstrated that OPA's liability provisions should be read "as broadly as the plain language allows."[237] Therefore, the court concluded that an abandoned facility could also be characterized as an offshore facility, that both definitions applied, and that both parties involved could be "responsible parties."[238]

---

232 See United States v. Bois D'Arc Operating Corp., No. 98-157, 1999 WL 130635, at *1-*4 (E.D. La. Mar. 10, 1999).

233 Id. at *3.

234 *See* United States v. Bois D'Arc Operating Corp., No. 98-157, 1999 WL 130635, at *3 (E.D. La. Mar. 10, 1999) (citing 33 USCA s2701(32)(C)).

235 Id. at *3.

236 Id.

237 Id. *at 4.

238 Id. at 3-5.

This court's legal reasoning accords with the articulation of this issue in the context of the FWPCA by the Fifth Circuit Court of Appeals in *United States v. M/V Big Sam,*[239] where the court said:

> "As statutorily defined, the term "owner or operator" refers both to the owner and to the bareboat charterer, and thus in our opinion... affords the government a remedy against either or both. Having in mind the intent of the Act to provide an effective remedy through strict liability for recovering cleanup costs from oil spills on navigable waters, it would seem that this construction is more consistent with the legislative purpose than one that would permit an offending vessel or its owners to insulate themselves from liability through a bareboat charter to, as here, an impecunious and uninsured charterer."

Apart from this, the blanket imposition of strict joint and several liability on responsible parties as explained earlier in this treatise evinces the fact that Congress intended that all potentially liable parties each be held liable for the entire damages and removal costs that emanate from a discharge of oil in the navigable waters of the United States. So, it is safe to conclude that the Congress envisaged the possibility of an oil spill with multiple claimants. In order not to circumvent the ability of this multitude of claimants to recover damages and removal costs, Congress also allowed for the possibility of multiple responsible parties (RPs) who can each be held liable for damages and removal costs that flow from the oil discharge. So, it is possible to have multiple defendants consisting of deep and shallow pockets. A claimant only needs to sue the deep pocket responsible party in order to satisfy its claim.

## B.I.A. Banks Could Pay OPA damages and removal costs claims

Banks have an indirect stake in the Financial Responsibility issue because of their possible exposure to the OPA liabilities of their vessel

239 681 F.2d 432, 438-39, 1983 AMC 2730, 2739 (5th Cir. 1982)

owning and operating borrowers. A claim against a bank that financed the building of an OPA RP vessel and that is still involved in the operations of such vessels because of outstanding loan obligations of the borrower has some prospects. Banks' worst fears about being held liable for oil pollution in the U.S. under the OPA 90 may be exaggerated, but lenders have been warned that they should nevertheless be extremely careful about their relationship with ship owners.[240] A lender can monitor the borrower in the normal way without liability being imposed. However, the line between simple monitoring and participating in the management of the ship could be difficult to define, especially at the beginning of a workout process. Where the monitoring is excessive, it could amount to management. By virtue of this banks providing finance for vessels that are vulnerable to OPA provisions would be doing themselves a lot of good if they include express clauses in the loan agreement disclaiming any liability that the shipowner is subject to under OPA, and requiring that the shipowner indemnify the bank for any costs and liabilities it incurs by virtue of the tortuous acts of the shipowner. Such clauses should provide as follows:

Indemnification Against Liabilities: Mortgagors will protect, indemnify, save harmless and defend Mortgagee from and against any and all liabilities, obligations, claims, damages, penalties, causes of action, costs and expenses (including, without limitation, reasonable attorneys' fees and expenses) imposed upon or incurred by or asserted against Mortgagee by reason of ownership of a mortgagee's interest in the Mortgaged Vessel.[241]

Repossession and foreclosure would very likely leave banks exposed, while obtaining a court sale of the asset is relatively safe. However, lenders should be cautious about more hazy areas such as discussing char-

---

240 Nigel Lowry, Banks' OPA fears may be exaggerated: Lenders warned to take care with shipowners, Lloyd's List Int'l, June 15, 1993, at 8.

241 Steven M. Alden, Real Estate Development and Construction Financing: THE PERMANENT LENDER'S DOCUMENTS, Practicing Law Institute, Real Estate Law and Practice Course Handbook Series, PLI Order No. N4-4506, 325 PLI/Real 409, 469-470 (February 1, 1989).

ters, spending income, equity participation and share pledges.[242] Finance lessors could be liable except a specific exemption was written in. OPA 90's failure to create a qualified exemption for vessel creditors therefore creates a disincentive for lenders to finance fleet modernization and replacement especially for oil tanker fleets. Some commentators have pointed out that lenders must be allowed to exercise financial prudence to protect the quality of their investments without the threat of liability, or lenders will cease to lend to clients who face some degree of environmental risk.[243] Furthermore, when the lack of predictable liability standards renders creditors unsure as to whether their advice to management encouraging environmental diligence will be perceived as management participation, that lender will prefer to remain ignorant as to the nature of a debtor's activities.[244] So, the actual or perceived hazard of incurring liability effectively prevents lenders from acting independently to realize OPA's long term goals by reducing the capacity of lenders to prudently monitor their investments and by decreasing their incentive to encourage environmental diligence.[245]

## B.II. LIABILITY OF PARENT CORPORATIONS AS RESPONSIBLE PARTIES UNDER THE OPA

From the inception of a business entity, three factors influence the form under which the organizers choose to operate: (1) the extent to which the participants are personally liable to business creditors under the applicable commercial law covering the business entity; (2) the tax and regulatory treatment of the business form, including whether the business participants will be taxed at the corporate or individual level; and (3) the

242 Nigel Lowry, Banks' OPA fears may be exaggerated: Lenders warned to take care with shipowners, Lloyd's List Int'l, June 15, 1993, at 8.

243 David C. Read, Note: The Comprehensive Environmental Response, Compensation And Liability Act After United States v. Fleet Factors: New Guidelines Concerning Lender Liability 26 VAL. U. L. Rev. 871, 890 (Summer, 1992).

244 Id. at 890-891.

245 Id. at 891.

current business participants' investment preferences as well as the possibility of attracting additional investment capital in the future.[246] Despite certain federal income tax disadvantages[247] and the increased administrative costs associated with doing business as a corporation or a limited partnership, limited liability traditionally provided the greatest incentive for business organizers to choose one of these two business forms. Today, two or more individuals operating a business have another option, the limited liability company ("LLC").[248] All fifty states and the District of Columbia have enacted LLC legislation.[249] Each state's commercial laws provide company participants with limited liability benefits, the opportunity to manage company affairs, and fewer restrictions on running the company.[250]

One of the most fundamental features of the corporate form is limited liability.[251] Recognizing that a corporation is a "distinct legal entity," separate from the persons comprising it,[252] limited liability provides that shareholder liability shall be limited to the shareholder's investment in the

---

246 See Philip F. Postlewaite & John H. Birkeland, Problems and Materials on the Taxation of Small Business Enterprise: Individual, Partnership, and Corporation 102 (1997).

247 See generally, Stephen Lind et al., Fundamentals of Corporate Taxation 30-31 (4th ed. 1997).

248 Many states define a limited liability company as an unincorporated organization of one or more persons that has limited liability for the business's contractual obligations and other liabilities. See, e.g., Del. Code Ann. tit. 6, § 18-101 (Supp. 1996). *See also* Unif. Ltd. Liab. Corp. Act (ULLCA) § 202(a), 6A U.L.A. 443 (1995) (permitting the formation of single- member LLCs). Most states' LLC acts provide that there must be two or more members to form an LLC. *See* J. William Callison & Maureen A. Sullivan, Limited Liability Companies: A State-By-State Guide to Law and Practice § 3.1, at 30 (1994). See also, N.Y. Ltd. Liab. Co. Law § 102(m) (McKinney Supp. 1997-1998).

249 See for example, Ala. Code §§ 10-12-1 to -61 (1994 & Supp. 1996); Alaska Stat. §§ 10.50.010-.995 (Michie 1996), Ariz. Rev. Stat. Ann. §§ 29-601 to -857 (West Supp. 1997).

250 For a state-by-state review of LLC statutes, *see generally,* J. William Callison & Maureen A. Sullivan, Limited Liability Companies, State Statutes and Federal Materials (1997).

251 See HARRY G. HENN & JOHN R. ALEXANDER, LAWS OF CORPORATIONS AND OTHER BUSINESS ENTERPRISES 130 (3d ed. 1983).

252 See Huard v. Shreveport Pirates, Inc., 147 F.3d 406, 409 (5th Cir.1998) (noting, further, that piercing is a radical remedy warranted only in exceptional circumstances such as fraud or deceit).

corporation.[253] Thus, limited liability effectively encourages investment in high-risk ventures which otherwise might endanger the personal wealth of those providing capital.[254] Limited liability, by its very operation, restricts the assets from which creditors may seek repayment when the corporation is in bankruptcy, default, or must subsequently satisfy legal judgment.[255] When the available assets are inadequate to satisfy the claims of creditors, those creditors often seek to pierce the corporate veil--asserting the theory of inappropriate use of the corporate form to recover directly from shareholders or officers.[256] Unsurprisingly, veil piercing claims have become the most litigated area in corporate law.[257] Nevertheless, the legal standard for determining when to set aside "the corporate veil is notably imprecise and fact-intensive."[258] Veil piercing claims might become one of the most litigated areas in environmental law, especially for environmental statutes like the OPA and CERCLA, because a lot of vessel and facility owners and operators have begun to take advantage of the liability-evading advantages of incorporating subsidiary companies to take over the operation of their vessels and facilities. As earlier explained there are some advantages to doing this.

The face-off between the U.S. Coast Guard and the Protection & Indemnity Clubs (P& I Clubs) on the requirement of the Certificate of Financial Responsibility (this will be discussed in chapter eight) has

---

253 See LEWIS D. SOLOMON ET AL., CORPORATIONS: LAW AND POLICY 241 (2d ed. 1988).

254 See Huard, 147 F.3d at 409 (5th Cir. 1998); *see also* LEWIS D. SOLOMON & ALAN R. PALMITER, CORPORATIONS 70 (2d ed. 1994) (stating that limited liability exists because it facilitates (1) capital formation, (2) desirable management risk- taking, (3) broad based investment diversification, and (4) public stock trading markets).

255 See Robert B. Thompson, Piercing the Corporate Veil: An Empirical Study, 76 CORNELL L. REV. 1036, 1039-40 (1991).

256 See generally 1 WILLIAM MEADE FLETCHER, FLETCHER CYCLOPEDIA OF THE LAW OF PRIVATE CORPORATIONS § 41 (perm. ed. rev. vol. 1990) (explaining that practically all authorities agree that under certain circumstances the corporate form should be disregarded "in the interest of justice in such cases as fraud, contravention of law or contract, public wrong, or to work out the equities among members of the corporation internally and involving no rights of the public or third persons").

257 See Susan Kraemer, Corporate Law, Denv. Law. Rev. 729, 730 (1999)

258 Id. at 730.

led (and may continue to lead) to "restructuring and changes in vessel ownership"(emphasis mine). As industry experts had predicted, many tanker operators have reorganized their corporate structures in an effort to protect their parent companies from the reaches of OPA and its potential for unlimited liability.[259] For instance in a very subtle move, Exxon Corporation has reorganized its shipping subsidiary, Exxon Shipping Company. The subsidiary received a new name, as did each of its U.S.-flagged tankers. Additionally, the subsidiary's board of directors was reshuffled and, for the first time, includes directors from outside the parent corporation. While Exxon Corporation conceded that the move was due, in part, to the impact of OPA 90, it expressly denied that it was a legal maneuver designed to shield itself from the future liabilities of its subsidiary.[260] However it cannot be denied that the reorganization could place further distance between the two companies and their respective assets. One can safely say that if the present trend continues and nothing is done to pierce the corporate veil, it may pave the way for undercapitalized, and substandard operators who will simply walk away from spills, to enter into the market place.

As courts struggle with liability and compensation issues under the OPA, the societal, environmental and economic values that must be balanced are many and varied. The economic and environmental burdens imposed by an oil spill will be decided, in part, by judicially constructed corporate-piercing theory. Imposing the heavy burden of paying for cleanup only on corporate polluters and related companies may help us realize the laudable objective of protecting taxpayers, but could also exacerbate the onerous burden on consumers and on corporations and their employees. It is not a secret that companies do not waste any time in passing on the cost of conforming to additional regulations to sometimes unsuspecting customers. Corporations do not waste any time in reducing their workforce to weather the storm generated by new liability regulations. Limiting corporate responsibility to any particular corporation may

259 Jeffery D. Morgan, The Oil Pollution Act of 1990: A Look at its Impact on the oil industry, 6 Fordham Env. L. J. 1, 9 (1994).

260 Joel Glass, Exxon Plans U.S. Shipping shake-up, Lloyd's List, Mar. 3, 1993 at 1.

preserve the integrity of existing business structures, thereby protecting employees, and sometimes consumers, but it could leave the states governments and the federal government (and taxpayers), with an unacceptable financial burden. This means that in a bid to ensure proper clean up of spills, and payment of claims, human and material resources would be overstretched. How courts resolve these issues will be determined, again at least in part, by how courts address the issues of piercing the corporate veil.

Two choices stare them in the face: they can adopt traditional common law doctrines of piercing the corporate veil, or they can adopt developing theories under federal environmental statutes. They can adopt a mixture of traditional common-law principles and theories under Federal Environmental statutes like the CERCLA and the FWPCA. Traditional piercing doctrine is based mostly upon state court decisions. Federal environmental statutes have prompted federal courts to develop piercing doctrine that facilitates corporate piercing. As evident from the liability-evading strategies of a lot of ship owners and operators explained above, the typical situation in which the veil needs to be pierced is one in which a very large, well- capitalized corporation, A, utilizes a wholly-owned undercapitalized subsidiary, B, to handle and control its shipping needs. The subsidiary actually owns the vessel. If a spill occurs, B, as the record owner, is a "responsible party," but what about the well capitalized A? One common law theory through which A may be held liable is the doctrine of piercing the corporate veil.[261] This doctrine is also applicable in the context of an OPA 90 facility, where a parent company incorporates a subsidiary corporation to handle and control everything relating to its OPA facility, and the subsidiary actually owns the facility.

CERCLA jurisprudence on veil piercing, which will be explored later is apposite in the OPA context, because of oil spills from facilities like pipelines, oil wells, oil storage facilities and so forth. Oil spills from facilities may not be as sudden as oil spills from vessels. Nevertheless, a substantial part of the veil piercing jurisprudence applicable to OPA &

261 See Harry G. Henn & John R. Alexander, Laws of Corporations 70, 344 (3rd ed. 1983).

CERCLA facilities would also apply to OPA vessels. In most cases, it will apply to an OPA vessel that is owned by company B, which is a subsidiary of Company A, or an OPA vessel that is owned by Company C which is subsidiary of Company B. Company B is responsible for managing the day to day operations of Company C's vessel. Company B is a subsidiary of company A. In other words, the vessel involved might be owned by a direct subsidiary of Company A or owned by the subsidiary of a subsidiary. If the veil is successfully pierced in the above example, Company A, the parent company of Company B, and the grand-parent of Company C could be held liable for the oil spill, even though it is not the registered owner of the vessel.

Successor liability could be imposed where a facility from which an oil spill is later found to have taken place has been acquired by another company or corporation. The predecessor corporation may also be held liable. Successor liability could be imposed on the subsequent owner of a vessel, if there was a mystery oil spill with no immediately identifiable Responsible Party, and long-term investigations subsequently identifies the acquired vessel as the source of the oil spill. In that case, both the owner of the vessel at the time of the oil spill, and the subsequent owner of the vessel could arguably be held liable if the corporate veil is successfully pierced.

## B. II(a) Indirect Liability of Parent Corporations - Piercing the Corporate Veil.

The law of piercing the corporate veil is based mostly on state common-law principles, although there is now an established body of Federal Common law on the subject.[262] Even if the parent corporation is organized or located outside of the state in which the casualty occurred, it is likely that a court will, as a practical matter, apply the law of the state of the casualty, or of the state where the court is situated to determine whether to

262 See United States v. Jon-T Chemicals, Inc. 768 F.2d 686 ($5^{th}$ Cir. 1985), *cert. denied*, 475 US 1014 (1986).

pierce the corporate veil.[263] On the other hand, some courts have decided that the law of the state of incorporation is the proper substantive law to apply to a corporate veil issue.[264]

The corporate piercing doctrine is a product of the conflict between society's need to maintain the benefits of the corporate structure and the need to curb abusive uses of that structure. The corporate form is used to limit investor liability to the value of the corporation's assets. Investors are thereby encouraged to pool their collective resources in an economically efficient manner. Such efforts facilitate specialized management and the division of labor. Incorporating for the purpose of limiting liability is accepted as one of the principal purposes of using the corporate form. The doctrine of piercing the corporate veil, under federal common law, regards a corporation as separate from its shareholder corporation so long as: (a) corporate formalities are followed regarding corporate transactions and the proceeds thereof; (b) the procedural formalities of the corporations are observed; (c) the corporations are adequately financed; and (d) the two (or more) corporate entities are held out to the public as separate businesses.[265] In a 1905 decision a Federal Court articulated the approach of the courts to veil piercing and corporate liability, when it said:

> "If any general rule can be laid down, in the present state of authority, it is that a corporation will be looked upon as a legal entity as a general rule, and until sufficient reason to the contrary appears; but, when the notion of legal entity is used to defeat public convenience, justify wrong, protect fraud, or defend crime, the law will regard the corporation as an association of persons. This much may be expressed without approving the theory that the legal entity is a fiction, or a mere mental creation; or that the idea of invisibility or intangibility is a sophism.

---

263 See Verrerieis de L'Hermitage, S.A v. Hickory Furniture Co., 704 F2d. 140 (4th Cir. 1983).

264 See Mikropul Corp. v. DeSimone & Chaplin-Airtech, Inc., 599 F Supp. 940, 942 (S.D.N.Y. 1984).

265 See Harry G. Henn & John R. Alexander, Laws of Corporations at 344 (3rd ed. 1983).

A corporation, as expressive of legal rights and powers, is no more fictitious or intangible than a man's right to his own home or his own liberty."[266]

Courts historically looked through, or "pierced", the parent-subsidiary or corporation-shareholder relationship to find the parent or the shareholder liable for the acts of the corporation. The piercing doctrine was understood as a way to redress the damages caused by the fraudulent acts of a company, when in fact those acts were committed by the parent or owner, hiding behind the corporate structure. The analysis generally was that the subsidiary is no more than the "instrument" of the parent, or that the corporation is only the "alter-ego" of the shareholder. This instrumentality rule requires, for instance, that the parent totally dominate the subsidiary to the extent that the subsidiary manifests no separate interests.[267] In *Anderson v. Abbot*,[268] a bank stock holding company was formed by shareholders of a bank to shift their investment interests from the bank for legitimate business purposes. The court recognized that although limited liability is the rule and not an exception in American law, the exception would be made "when the sacrifice is so essential to the end that some accepted public policy may be defended or upheld."[269] The court in *Anderson* discarded the general rule of shareholder limited liability and held the shareholders of the stock holding company liable in the interest of defending the public against corporate fraud. The *Anderson* court also held that interposition of a corporation will not be allowed to defeat a legislative policy, whether that was the aim or only the result of the liability-evading corporate arrangement. Another 1960 Federal case applying New York law of corporation prescribed a three-part test:

(1) Control, not mere majority or complete stock control, but complete domination, not only of finances, but of policy and business practice in respect to

---

266 See United States v. Milwaukee Refrig. Transit Co., 142 F. 247, 255 (E.D. Wis. 1905).

267 *See* Anderson v. Abbot, 64 S.Ct. 531 (1944).

268 Id.

269 Id. at 538 (quoting Berkey v. Third Ave. Ry. Co., 244 N.Y. 84, 95, 155 N.E. 58, 61).

the transaction attacked so that the corporate entity as to this transaction had at the time no separate mind, will or existence of its own; and

(2) Such control must have been used by the defendant to commit fraud or worse, to perpetrate the violation of a statutory or other positive legal duty, or a dishonest and unjust act in contravention of plaintiff's legal rights; and

(3) The aforesaid control and breach of duty must proximately cause the injury or unjust loss complained of."[270]

Later, courts abandoned the need for a showing of fraud in certain cases.[271] In *United States v. Jon-T Chemicals*, a wholly-owned subsidiary used fraud to collect upland cotton program payments from the United States Department of Agriculture.[272] The *Jon-T* court held that the parent exercised pervasive control over the subsidiary, and was thereby liable for the actions of that subsidiary, even though there was no fraudulent purpose associated with the formation of the subsidiary and all of the corporate formalities had been observed.[273] The court reasoned that, although fraud is an essential element of an alter ego finding in contract veil piercing cases, fraud is not essential in tort cases.[274] This distinction was justified by the court as the difference between a contractual relationship in which both parties bargained and entered freely and the situation in which one party, the tortfeasor, imposed a harm upon the other party without consent.[275] Using the tort and contracts comparison, the court appears to be suggesting that the corporate form represents a bargain with society in which the benefits of enhanced investment and its consequent economic growth are sufficiently beneficial to allow the corporate form to shield investors who otherwise would be held financially responsible

270 See Fisser v. Int'l Bank, 282 F.2d 231, 238 (2d. Cir. 1960) (quoting, in Lowendahl v. Baltimore & Ohio R.R. Co., 247 App.Div. 144, 287 N.Y.S. 62, *affirmed,* 272 N.Y. 360, 6 N.E.2d 56. (1936)).

271 See United States v. Jon-T Chem., 768 F.2d 686, 692 (5th Cir.1985) *cert. denied*, 475 U.S. 1014.

272 768 F.2d 686 (1985).

273 Id. at 686.

274 Id.

275 Id.

for the consequences of their business activities. Traditional state piercing law disregards the corporate form when the investors ignore it, thereby deceiving the public about the true nature of the business and imposing a relationship for which the public did not bargain. In environmental cases, the liability of defendant corporations normally sound in tort than in contract. So, proof of fraud might not be essential to piercing the corporate veil in environmental cases brought under statutes like the OPA and CERCLA.

Traditional state piercing law also disregards the corporate form when the corporation becomes the mere alter ego of the investor. This rationale suggests that the corporate form, when used for committing misdeeds such as fraud, will be ignored just as though the investor shareholder had committed a tort against the public. Perhaps current environmental statutes and concurrently developing piercing law has reached the point at which environmental degradation is analogous to a tort against the public. If such is the case, then traditional state piercing law can be understood as a basis from which the now-emerging federal common law of environmental piercing has developed. Society may be ready to regard pollution as a tort against the public good that was not a part of any bargain, even though the activities which produced the pollution were the consequences of activities undertaken to meet a public need or want.

One commonly repeated refrain is that the alter ego doctrine should apply and make a shareholder personally liable when there is "such unity of interest and ownership that the separate personalities of the corporation and the individual no longer exist and that, if the acts are treated as those of the corporation alone, an inequitable result will follow."[276] Fredrick J. Powell, a leading author on corporate veil piercing in his book, "Parent

276 E.g., Riddle v. Leuschner, 335 P.2d 107, 110-11 (Cal. 1959). This heavily quoted language can be traced to a landmark California case: First, that the corporation is not only influenced and governed by that person, but that there is such a unity of interest and ownership that the individuality, or separateness, of the said person and corporation has ceased; second, that the facts are such that an adherence to the fiction of the separate existence of the corporation would, under the particular circumstances, sanction a fraud or promote injustice. Minifie v. Rowley, 202 P. 673, 676 (Cal. 1921). *See also* John F. Dobbyn, A Practical Approach to Consistency in Veil-Piercing Cases, 19 U. KAN. L. REV. 185, 186 (1971).

And Subsidiary Corporations", formulated a checklist list of factors the courts should take into consideration in deciding whether a subsidiary corporation is a mere instrumentality of its parent corporation.[277] The factors are as follows:

(a) The parent corporation owns all or most of the capital stock of the subsidiary.
(b) The parent and subsidiary corporations have common directors or officers.
(c) The parent corporation finances the subsidiary.
(d) The parent corporation subscribes to all the capital stock of the subsidiary or otherwise causes its incorporation.
(e) The subsidiary has grossly inadequate capital.
(f) The parent corporation pays the salaries and other expenses or losses of the subsidiary.
(g) The subsidiary has substantially no business except with the parent corporation or no assets except those conveyed to it by the parent corporation.
(h) In the papers of the parent corporation or in the statements of its officers, the subsidiary is described as a department or division of the parent corporation, or its business or financial responsibility is referred to as the parent corporation's own.
(i) The parent corporation uses the property of the subsidiary as its own.
(j) The directors or executives of the subsidiary do not act independently in the interest of the subsidiary but take their orders from the parent corporation in the latter's interest.
(k) The formal legal requirements of the subsidiary are not observed.[278]

Veil-piercing cases containing this laundry-list of relevant factors are so numerous that they are virtually innumerable.[279] Usually, the cases

---

277 FREDERICK J. POWELL, PARENT AND SUBSIDIARY CORPORATIONS, at 9 (1931).

278 Id at 9.

279 See William J Rands, Domination Of A Subsidiary By A Parent, 32 Ind. L.Rev. 421, 434 (1999), (hereinafter Rands, Domination) (citing as example, Lowell Staats Mining Co., Inc. v. Pioneer Uravan, Inc., 878 F.2d 1259, 1262-63 (10th Cir. 1989); United States v.

replicate (without attribution) the Powell factors.[280] The cases sometimes add or delete factors.[281] Some decisions say that they are testing for domination.[282] Others say they are testing for alter ego or instrumentality.[283]

Although sometimes decried, laundry-lists of relevant factors can be useful. They are useful for establishing guidelines in the veil-piercing context. Courts pierce the corporate veil when the shareholders fail to abide by a loose set of standards for responsible shareholder conduct, and it is possible to list incidents of bad shareholder conduct that courts do not, or at least should not, tolerate. Asset-stripping comes quickly to mind.[284]

Cathy S. Krendl & James R. Krendl, in their article titled, Piercing the Corporate Veil: Focusing the Inquiry,[285] formulated a shopping list of 31 factors used by courts to justify not piercing the corporate veil. They are:

1. The shareholder is not a party to the contractual or other obligation of the corporation.
2. The subsidiary is not undercapitalized.
3. The subsidiary does not operate at a deficit while the parent is showing a profit.
4. The creditors of the companies are not misled as to which company they are dealing with.

---

Jon-T Chems., Inc., 768 F.2d 686, 691-92 (5th Cir. 1985); Nelson v. International Paint Co. Inc., 734 F.2d 1084, 1093 (5th Cir. 1984); Miles v. American Tel. & Tel. Co., 703 F.2d 193, 195-96 (5th Cir. 1983); DeWitt Truck Brokers, Inc. v. W. Ray Flemming Fruit Co., 540 F.2d 681, 685-87 (4th Cir. 1976); Steven v. Roscoe Turner Aeronautical Corp., 324 F.2d 157, 161 (7th Cir. 1963); Jacobson v. Buffalo Rock Shooters Supply, Inc., 664 N.E.2d 328, 331 (Ill. App. Ct. 1996); St. Peter v. Ampak-Division of Gatewood Prods., Inc., 484 S.E.2d 481, 488-89 (W. Va. 1997); Panamerica Mineral Servs., Inc. v. KLS Enviro Resources, Inc., 916 P.2d 986, 990 (Wyo. 1996).

280 See William J Rands, Domination Of A Subsidiary By A Parent, 32 Ind. L.Rev at 434.

281 Id. at 434

282 Id. at 435

283 Id.

284 See William J Rands, Domination Of A Subsidiary By A Parent, 32 Ind. L Rev. at 436 (hereinafter Rands, Domination).

285 Cathy S. Krendl & James R. Krendl, Piercing The Corporate Veil: Focusing The Inquiry, 55 DENV. L.J. 1, 2 (1978).

5. Creditors are not misled as to the financial strength of the subsidiary.
6. The employees of the parent and subsidiary are separate and the parent does not hire employees of the subsidiary.
7. The payroll of the subsidiary is paid by the subsidiary and the salary levels are set by the subsidiary.
8. The labor relations of the two companies are handled separately and independently.
9. The parent and subsidiary maintain separate offices and telephone numbers.
10. Separate directors' meetings are conducted.
11. The subsidiary maintains financial books and records which contain entries related only to its own operations.
12. The subsidiary has its own bank account.
13. The earnings of the subsidiary are not reflected on the financial reports of the parent in determining the parent's income.
14. The companies do not file joint tax returns.
15. The subsidiary negotiates its own loans or other financing.
16. The subsidiary does not borrow money from the parent.
17. Loans and other financial transactions between the parent and subsidiary are properly documented and conducted on an arm's-length basis.
18. The parent does not guarantee the loans of the subsidiary or secure any loan with assets of the parent.
19. The subsidiary's income represents a small percentage of the total income of the parent.
20. The insurance of the two companies is maintained separately and each pays its own premiums.
21. The purchasing activities of the two corporations are handled separately.
22. The two companies avoid advertising as a joint activity or other public relations which indicate that they are the same organization.
23. The parent and subsidiary avoid referring to each other as one family, organization, or as divisions of one another.

24. The equipment and other goods of the parent and subsidiary are separate.
25. The two companies do not exchange assets or liabilities.
26. There are no contracts between the parent and subsidiary with respect to purchasing goods and services from each other.
27. The subsidiary and the parent do not deal exclusively with each other.
28. The parent does not review the subsidiary's contracts, bids, or other financial activities in greater detail than would be normal for a shareholder who is merely interested in the profitability of the business.
29. The parent does not supervise the manner in which the subsidiary's jobs are carried out.
30. The parent does not have a substantial veto power over important business decisions of the subsidiary and does not itself make such crucial decisions.
31. The parent and subsidiary are engaged in different lines of business.[286]

The presence of one or more of these 31 factors may make a court of law conclude that the veil should not be pierced. The presence of one or more of the Powell factors may make a court of law decide in favor of piercing the corporate veil. So, each case will be decided on its merit.

*Intrusive Daily Control*

Excessive "control" by the parent over the subsidiary is sometimes said to be a sina qua non for piercing the corporate veil of the subsidiary to hold the parent liable. The parent's ability to control the subsidiary is not enough.[287] The parent always has that, and if that were enough, parents

286 Id. at 52-55

287 See, e.g., Craig v. Lake Asbestos of Quebec, Ltd., 843 F.2d 145, 152 (3d Cir. 1988); Jemez Agency, Inc. v. CIGNA Corp., 866 F. Supp. 1340, 1345 (D.N.M. 1994); Scalise v. Beech Aircraft Corp., 276 F. Supp. 58, 62 (E.D. Pa. 1967); Scott v. AZL Resources, Inc., 753 P.2d 897, 901 (N.M. 1988).

would never have limited liability for the debts of their subsidiaries.[288] The parent does not excessively control the subsidiary merely by determining its general policies, exercising supervision[289] or controlling its finances and expenses.[290] The control required is "domination." This usually means intrusive, hands-on, day-to-day control with the parent often leaving no discretion whatsoever to the subsidiary.[291] Moreover, courts frequently say that they require domination with respect to the transaction attacked.[292]

In one case, the parent exclusively controlled the subsidiary's bank account, allowed the subsidiary no discretion in buying and merchandising, and arranged insurance and advertising for the subsidiary without consulting the subsidiary.[293] The two companies had common officers and directors, which, by itself, is almost never considered to constitute excessive control.[294] The court concluded that this micromanaging was "domination" and satisfied the control requirement for piercing the corporate veil. In another case, the majority shareholder of the parent so dominated the operations of the entities that he even dictated to the subsidiary's bookkeeper which bills to pay, when to pay them, and to what extent they

288 See, e.g., Johnson v. Flowers Indus., Inc., 814 F.2d 978, 980 (4th Cir. 1987); United States v. Jon-T Chemicals, Inc., 768 F.2d 686, 691 (5th Cir. 1985).

289 See Carsten Alting, Piercing the Corporate Veil in American and German Law--Liability of Individuals and Entities: A Comparative View, 2 TULSA J. COMP. & INT'L L. 187, 228-29 (1995).

290 See. *id.*

291 See Krivo Indus. Supply Co. v. National Distillers and Chem. Corp., 483 F.2d 1098, 1106 (5th Cir. 1973); In re Catfish Antitrust Litig., 908 F. Supp. 400, 416 (N.D. Miss. 1995); Japan Petroleum Co. (Nigeria) Ltd. v. Ashland Oil, Inc., 456 F. Supp. 831, 841 (D. Del. 1978).

292 See, e.g., Radaszewski v. Telecom Corp., 981 F.2d 305, 306 (8th Cir. 1992); American Protein Corp. v. AB Volvo, 844 F.2d 56, 60 (2d Cir. 1988); Land v. Midwest Office Tech., Inc., 979 F. Supp. 1344, 1349 (D. Kan. 1997); Fleming Cos., Inc. v. Rich, 978 F. Supp. 1281, 1303 (E.D. Mo. 1997); Lane v. Maryhaven Ctr. of Hope, 944 F. Supp. 158, 163 (E.D.N.Y. 1996); National Bond Fin. Co. v. General Motors Corp., 238 F. Supp. 248, 255 (W.D. Mo. 1964); Lowendahl v. Baltimore & O.R. Co., 287 N.Y.S. 62, 76 (N.Y. App. Div. 1 1936); B-W Acceptance Corp. v. Spencer, 149 S.E.2d 570, 576 (N.C. 1966).

293 Consolidated Sun Ray, Inc. v. Oppenstein, 335 F.2d 801 (8th Cir. 1964).

294 See Hystro Prods., Inc. v. MNP Corp., 18 F.3d 1384, 1390 (7th Cir. 1994); see also, Steven v. Roscoe Turner Aeronautical Corp., 324 F.2d 157, 161 (7th Cir. 1963).

should be paid.[295] The majority shareholder of the parent had complete and exclusive control of the subsidiary's fiscal policy. These circumstances constituted domination and satisfied the control requirement for piercing the corporate veil.[296]

One case involved claims asserted by asbestos victims against the parent of a subsidiary engaged in the mining and distribution of asbestos.[297] The parent owned 67.3% of the subsidiary's stock, which is an unusually low percentage for a veil-piercing case, but obviously is high enough to give the parent control over the subsidiary.[298] Nevertheless, the parent placed only three directors on the subsidiary's board, including the parent's chairman. Despite the presence of a mere minority on the subsidiary's board, the Federal District Court for the Eastern District of Pennsylvania found that the parent's control over the subsidiary was "actual, participatory, and pervasive" and thereby satisfied New Jersey's alter ego requirement of dominating control.[299] The parent's chairman wielded complete power over the subsidiary's board, because there was a tacit understanding with the other subsidiary directors never to intervene in the decision-making process.[300] The membership of the parent's chairman on the subsidiary's board resulted in the parent's "omnipresence" in the minds of the subsidiary board members.[301] Moreover, the parent told its shareholders that it would take direct management responsibility for the subsidiary's mining operations and would closely scrutinize its capital expenditures. The chairman promised to report back regularly to the parent's shareholders. The subsidiary, the district court concluded, was nothing more than an "operating division" of the parent.[302] The Third Circuit Court of Appeals reversed, determining that the parent's involvement in the subsidiary's financial and

---

295 See Atlantic Tobacco Co. v. Honeycutt, 398 S.E.2d 641, 645 (N.C. Ct. App. 1990).

296 See id. at 645.

297 Craig v. Johns-Manville Corp., No. 82-0321, 1987 U.S. Dist. LEXIS 4075 (E.D. Pa. June 3, 1987), *rev'd*, Craig v. Lake Asbestos of Quebec, Ltd., 843 F.2d 145 (3d Cir. 1988).

298 1987 U.S. Dist. LEXIS at *8.

299 Id. at 52.

300 *See. id.*

301 Id. at 50.

302 Id.

managerial affairs was neither constant nor day-to-day.[303] It noted that both parent and subsidiary maintained separate books, records, bank accounts, offices and staff, and that each consulted its own financial advisors, accountants and stockbrokers.[304] It determined that the district court's notion of the parent's "omnipresence" on the subsidiary's board was insufficient to meet the control requirement for piercing the corporate veil.[305] "Potential control," it said, "is not enough."[306]

In *In re Accushnet River & New Bedford Harbor Proceedings Re Alleged PCB Pollution*,[307] the United States and the Commonwealth of Massachusetts sought to hold a parent liable for the cost of cleaning the contamination caused by a subsidiary of the New Bedford Harbor and the Accushnet River. The court looked closely for suggestions of pervasive control by the parent company over the subsidiary's hazardous waste disposal policies for an indication that the parent company treated the subsidiary as a mere instrumentality; however, it rejected the plaintiff's pleas that the special problems of cleaning up hazardous waste should be addressed by lowering the standards that make affiliated corporations responsible for the obligations of each member of the group.[308] The parent, the court noted, used a system where all subsidiaries and operating units deposited cash receipts into individual locked box accounts.[309] The parent provided a loan guarantee for the subsidiary, which enabled the subsidiary to obtain lower interest rates on its loans. Loans by the parent to the subsidiary were repaid through inter-company billing instead of formal loan agreements.[310] The parent required the subsidiary to seek prior parental approval for large capital expenditures. It caused the subsidiary to change several accounting procedures, and the subsidiary had to submit financial

303 Craig v. Lake Asbestos of Quebec, Ltd., 843 F.2d 145, 155 (3d Cir. 1988).

304 Id. at 152

305 Id.

306 Id.

307 675 F. Supp. 22 (D. Mass. 1987).

308 In re Accushnet River & New Bedford Harbor Proceedings, 675 F. Supp. at 32.

309 Id at 34.

310 See. id.

reports to the parent during the year.[311] The subsidiary's logo was changed to include the parent's initials. The parent and subsidiary used the same law firm in much of their litigation. The parent purchased an umbrella insurance policy that covered the subsidiary.[312]

The court concluded that the parent's activities did not show an inordinate level of integration and control as to justify piercing the subsidiary's corporate veil.[313] The centralized cash management system was not the equivalent of the intermingling of funds. The court said that if it were "keeping score," the centralized cash management probably would want to check on the "piercing" side of the ledger.[314] The quarterly and annual reports to the parent did not represent an intrusion into the subsidiary's business, as the right of shareholders to be informed is recognized in many public and closely held corporations.[315] Likewise, shareholder control over significant expenditures is not a disregard of corporate separateness.[316] The court also concluded that the parent had respected the separateness of the subsidiary in important ways. It noted that the subsidiary actually was not a "shell" corporation, as evidenced by the subsidiary's $17 million dollar net worth, which was five times more than what it was when the subsidiary had been purchased several years previously. Under the ownership of the parent, the subsidiary had remained profitable. The subsidiary negotiated its own contracts, developed its own customers, arranged its own loans, developed its own budgets, created its own marketing and sales program, hired and fired its own employees, maintained its own financial records and accounts, and regularly conducted board of directors meetings.[317] Although the parent influenced the philosophy and management of the subsidiary, the court found that this was true of all

311 Id.

312 Id.

313 Id.

314 Id.

315 See id at 34

316 See id.

317 See id at 35.

majority shareholders.[318] The court ruled that the circumstances did not justify piercing the corporate veil.[319]

In a Second Circuit Court of Appeals case, a corporation with a claim against a New York corporation sought a judgment against the New York corporation's Swedish parents.[320] The district court imposed legal liability on one of the foreign parents without hesitation and the subsidiary's veil was pierced at least in part because two of the parents' officers and directors, who were also directors of the subsidiary, came to New York and voted at the subsidiary's board meeting to wind down the subsidiary's affairs, resulting in the subsidiary's default on a contract.[321] The Second Circuit reversed.[322] Citing the famous *Lowendahl* case, the Second Circuit said, "control is the key."[323] The parent must exercise complete domination with respect to the transaction attacked. The Second Circuit found that "the strongest piece of evidence to support control was the existence of the interlocking directorates. This commonplace circumstance of modern business did not furnish such proof of control as will permit a court to pierce the corporate veil."[324] Not only did the parent not exert control with respect to the particular contract in question, the subsidiary maintained its own corporate and financial records, held independent board meetings, and maintained separate corporate offices.[325] Though the parent supplied the subsidiary with working capital from time to time, there was not evidence that the subsidiary received financing specifically for the contract in question. There was no evidence of shareholder misbehavior such as asset-stripping.[326]

In the Fourth Circuit case of *Johnson v. Flowers Indus., Inc.*,[327] employees brought suit against their employer (a subsidiary), its parent, and

---

318 Id.

319 Id.

320 American Protein Corp. v. AB Volvo, 844 F.2d 56 (2d Cir. 1988).

321 See id at 62-63.

322 Id. at 62.

323 Id. at 60.

324 Id.

325 Id.

326 Id.

327 814 F.2d 978, 978 (4th Cir. 1987)

another subsidiary, claiming that the parent replaced the plaintiffs with younger employees from the other subsidiary, in violation of the Age Discrimination in Employment Act. The parent, the Fourth Circuit concluded, retained the benefits of limited liability, even though it exercised some control over its subsidiary.[328] The court reasoned that if shareholders were liable whenever they exercised their rightful control, limited liability would become a meaningless fiction.[329] The majority shareholder is entitled to exercise the normal incidents of stock ownership, such as the right to choose directors and set general policies, without forfeiting the protection of limited liability.[330]

The court found a parent company can become the employer of a subsidiary's workers by exercising excessive control in one of two ways. First, it could control the employment practices and decisions of the subsidiary.[331] If it hired and fired the subsidiary employees, routinely shifted them between the two companies, and supervised their daily operations, the parent would then be found to be their employer.[332] Second, the parent might dominate the subsidiary's operations by treating it as its alter ego.[333] The subsidiary might be highly integrated with the parent's business operations, as evidenced by the commingling of funds and assets, the use of the same workforce and business offices for both corporations, the severe undercapitalization of the subsidiary, and the failure to observe basic corporate formalities such as keeping separate books and holding separate shareholder and board meetings.[334]

The plaintiff produced no evidence that the parent excessively interfered with the subsidiary's business operations.[335] The subsidiary's management was responsible for the daily decisions in vital areas of pro-

---

328 Id. at 980

329 Id.

330 See. id at 980-981

331 Id. at 981

332 See. id.

333 Id.

334 Id.

335 Id.

duction, distribution, marketing, and advertising. The subsidiary had a separate board of directors and corporate officers, kept its own business records, and maintained separate bank accounts.[336] Three of the subsidiary's four directors were officers of the parent, and the parent exercised oversight of the subsidiary's activities. However, the court considered those facts to be characteristic of a parent-subsidiary relationship not amounting to domination of the business practices of the subsidiary.[337] In particular, the court found no evidence that the parent controlled the employment practices and decisions of the subsidiary because the parent never hired, fired, promoted, paid, transferred, or supervised any subsidiary employee.[338]

In an effort to bring some cohesion to the judicial discussions of control, Phillip I. Blumberg, in his book, The Law Of Corporate Groups, summarizes by noting that the courts' evaluation of intergroup tort liability have emphasized four factors: (1) parental participation in daily operations; (2) parental determination of important subsidiary policy decisions; (3) parental determination of subsidiary business decisions while bypassing subsidiary managers; and (4) parental issuance of instructions to the subsidiary personnel or the use of parental personnel in the conduct of the subsidiary affairs.[339] The courts in most cases, however, usually acquiesce in the reality of the exercise of control by the parent and determine the parent's liability on the basis of other factors.[340] Essentially, the courts discuss the exercise of control, but control is not usually the critical question.[341]

It would be more accurate to say that piercing the corporate veil is such a confused area of the law that the requirement of control, as with all the other requirements, is treated erratically by the courts. A determination

---

336 See. id. at 982

337 Id.

338 Id.

339 See. Phillip I. Blumberg, The Law Of Corporate Groups: Substantive Law § 10.02 (1987) [Hereinafter Law Of Corporate Groups].

340 Id.

341 Id.

of what constitutes excessive control is a difficult job for a judge because the "separateness" of a parent and subsidiary corporation is formalistic. It is unrealistic to think that a parent and a subsidiary are truly separate, making it hard for a judge to determine when they are not separate. If the subsidiary is treated as an economically viable entity, a higher degree of control by the parent over the subsidiary is tolerated.[342] If something appears amiss, however, such as the manipulation of corporation assets or extensive economic integration, the judge will strictly scrutinize the extensiveness of control. If control is extensive, it will be a factor favoring piercing the corporate veil. If control is not extensive, it will be a factor weighing against piercing the corporate veil.[343]

### *Common Law Theory of Agency*

A parent corporation may also be held liable for the acts of its subsidiary through a common law theory of agency.[344] This is separate from an instrumentality analysis as it follows a contractual or reliance analysis rather than a fraud or misrepresentation analysis. An agency relationship may be established through either express consent, contract, or through actions creating an agency by estoppel argument.[345] An agency theory implies that the parent instructed the subsidiary corporation on its actions-the parent was the principal upon which the burden of liability actually rests. Common law agency theory, however, does not

342 See William J Rands, Domination Of A Subsidiary By A Parent, 32 Ind. L.Rev. at 442.

343 Id. at 443

344 See H.J. Inc., v. International Tel. & Tel. Corp., 867 F.2d 1531 (8th Cir. 1989), *reh'g denied*, 876 F.2d 59, *appeal after remand* 925 F.2d 257 (1991); Mobil Oil Corp. v. Lincar Films, Inc., 718 F. Supp. 260 (D. Del. 1989); Berkey v. Third Ave. Ry., 155 N.E. 58 (N.Y. 1925).

345 Thomas J. Heiden, The New Limits of Limited Liability: Differing Standards and Theories for Measuring a Parent/Shareholder's Responsibility for the Operations of Its Subsidiary, in Protecting the Corporate Parent 1992: Avoiding Liability for the Acts of the Subsidiary 23-25 (Practicing Law Institute ed., 1992).

engender a great deal of scholarly support.[346] This may be because the courts engage in piercing the veil analysis and then apply agency law language.[347] Furthermore, employing a theory of agency could result in the imposition of liability on the parent corporation more frequently than is optimal because the plaintiff need not prove that maintaining the corporate veil is inequitable or unfair, whereas this has to be shown in a piercing the veil inquiry.[348] Instrumentality analysis to pierce the corporate veil is used with greater frequency than common law agency theory.[349]

### B. II(b) Piercing The Corporate Veil Under Federal Environmental Statutes.

There is very little legislative history on CERCLA.[350] This sparsity may be due to the rapidity with which the statute was enacted.[351] Yet, two broad policies of CERCLA have been identified. First, Congress wanted to deal effectively with hazardous waste disposal problems not previously addressed by earlier environmental regulatory statutes,[352] and second, Congress wanted to create an exhaustive system of liability reaching all parties responsible for the improper disposal of hazardous materials. When the OPA was passed into law by the US Congress, they had similar goals in mind for oil pollution.

346 Erika Clarke Birg, Comment: Redefining "Owner Or Operator" Under CERCLA To Preserve Traditional Notions Of Corporate Law, Emory Law Journal, 771, 788 (Spring 1994).

347 Id at 788.

348 Id.

349 Id.

350 Frank A. Grad, A Legislative History of the Comprehensive Environmental Response, Compensation, and Liability ("Superfund") Act of 1980, 8 Colum. J. Envtl. L. 1 (1982).

351 Id. Representative Stockman expressed concern over the statute: "I do not want to see this body stampeded into enactment of a major piece of regulatory legislation." 126 Cong. Rec. 26,759 (1980). However, Representative Moffett stated, "I cannot remember an issue where we have done more work." Id. at 26,763.

352 Id. at 4.

*Plain Language of the Statute*

The CERCLA statute imposes a four-part test in order to assess liability.[353] First, the party charged with liability in the statute must be a "person"[354] according to the statute and fall within one of the four categories of **potentially responsible parties (PRPs)**.[355] Second, the site contaminated must be a "facility"[356] within the meaning of the statute. Third, a hazardous waste release must occur, and fourth, costs must have been incurred in cleaning up the hazardous waste material.[357]

There are four categories of **PRPs** under CERCLA: (1) current owner and operator of a site, (2) owner or operator at time when disposal occurred, (3) generators of hazardous waste, and (4) transporters of hazardous waste.[358] Assuming that a hazardous waste release has occurred and that resources have been expended in cleanup, this part focuses upon the inclusion of parent corporations in the definition of "owner or operator," thus being classified as a current owner and operator or a former owner or operator under CERCLA and apply it to OPA by analogy. This is reasonable because of the similarity in the language of both statutes on this issue.

CERCLA uses alternatively "owner-operator" language in the conjunctive, "owner and operator,"[359] and in the disjunctive, "a person who... owned or operated" a site.[360] Congressional intent with respect to the issue

353 Lynda J. Oswald, Corporate Parent Responsibility for Environmental Liability of the Subsidiary, in Protecting the Corporate Parent 1992: Avoiding Liability for Acts of the Subsidiary 107, 111 (Practising Law Institute ed., 1992).

354 42 U.S.C. § 9601(21) (1982). CERCLA relies upon a definition of "person" to create the categories of PRPs. See H.R. Rep. No. 1016.

355 42 U.S.C. §§ 9601(20)(A), 9607(a) (1982).

356 42 US.C. § 9601(17), (18) (1982).

357 Id.

358 B. Shane Clanton, Comment, Fleeting Security: CERCLA Liability for Secured Creditors, 41 Emory L.J. 167, 171 (1992).

359 42 U.S.C. § 9607(a)(1) (1982).

360 Id. § 9607(a)(2).

of whether the current owner must also be an operator is not apparent. However, courts have not made a distinction on that basis.[361]

In its definition of terms, Congress defines only the disjunctive form, "owner or operator," and does so as follows: The term "owner or operator" means... (ii) in the case of an onshore facility or an offshore facility, any person owning or operating such facility.... Such term does not include a person, who, without participating in the management of a vessel or facility, holds indicia of ownership primarily to protect his security interest in the vessel or facility.[362] This definition is positively circular, yielding no answers as to when a parent corporation may be liable under CERCLA.

If common definitions of the terms owning and operating were accepted, as intended by Congress, the statute could be more precise. Under the lay definition, "owning" would likely mean possessing title or some other similar indicia of ownership to a property or facility. "Operating," in its most probable common definition, would mean "to manage and put or keep in operation...."[363] However, there is an alternative definition. This definition, if accepted, could account for parent corporations being included in the definition of operator. This alternative meaning, "to exert power or influence over"[364] something, connotes greater control and hands-on participation than does the first.

The ready inclusion of a parent corporation within the category of operator could in fact depend upon which definition was intended by Congress. If it is the first, then the inquiry would focus upon whether the parent corporation or the subsidiary corporation managed the facility. If the parent corporation did, then certainly it would be liable as an operator. If it is the second definition, then the inquiry would be whether the

361 Kenneth Berlin, The Environmental Liabilities of Parent Corporations and Minority Shareholders, in Responsibility of the Corporate Parent for the Activities of a Subsidiary 1990 143, 147 (Practising Law Institute ed., 1990) (citing United States v. Moore, 698 F. Supp. 622 (E.D. Va. 1988)).

362 42 U.S.C.A. § 9601(20)(A).

363 Webster's Third New International Dictionary 1580-81 (1986) [hereinafter Webster's International ].

364 Webster's International, id at 1581.

parent corporation exerted power or influence over the facility. As the major shareholder, a parent corporation might readily be found to be an operator because it influences the subsidiary. The question increases in difficulty as we move away from the facility itself and move through the layer of the subsidiary corporation. To be consistent with direct liability, however, there must be power or influence over the hazardous waste activities, not merely the subsidiary in general. There is no direct indication from Congress which definition is appropriate; therefore, there is no certainty regarding the definition.[365] An analysis of other federal environmental statutes may be helpful in discovering the meaning of "owner or operator."

*Definition of "Owner or Operator" in other Environmental Statutes*

CERCLA provides the missing link in a regulatory scheme composed of several statutes: the Clean Air Act (CAA), the Federal Water Pollution Control Act (FWPCA), and the Resource Conservation and Recovery Act (RCRA). Each of these statutes also utilize owner-operator language. Each of these statutes are discussed briefly below.

The CAA defines an "owner or operator" as "any person who owns, leases, operates, controls or supervises...."[366] This definition is seemingly broader than the definition under CERCLA because it embraces those who control or supervise rather than just own or operate. Moreover, it also separates out the concepts of operating as distinct from controlling or supervising. The liability decisions under the CAA also indicate that the courts primarily look at evidence of control or supervision before

---

365 See generally, Edward Hines Lumber Co. v. Vulcan Materials Co., 861 F.2d 155 (7th Cir. 1988).

366 40 C.F.R. § 61.02 (1993). Control is commonly defined as "power or authority to guide or manage" or to "have power over." Webster's International, at 496. Supervise is commonly defined as "to coordinate, direct, and inspect continuously and at first hand the accomplishment of or oversee with the powers of direction and decision the implementation of one's own or another's intentions." Id. at 2296.

imposing liability.[367] For example, in *United States v. Walsh*,[368] the Ninth Circuit Court of Appeals held that the district court correctly required "significant or substantial or real control and supervision over a project" before the officer could be held liable as an operator. Significantly, though, the CERCLA definition does not include either the term "control" or the term "supervise" in its definition of owner or operator. As a logical matter, it is clear that Congress knew how to include these terms if that is indeed what it meant. Alternatively, "controlling" could be considered synonymous with exerting power and influence over something and in fact does encompass the concept of management. Therefore, there may be little substantive difference between operating and controlling. Nevertheless, if Congress in fact meant "control," it could have easily included it in its definition of "owner or operator."

The FWPCA defines "owner or operator" similarly to CERCLA.[369] The statute states that an " 'owner or operator' means... (B) in the case of an onshore facility, and an offshore facility, any person owning or operating such onshore facility or offshore facility."[370] This is no more illuminating than the CERCLA or OPA definition. The case law under the FWPCA does, however, indicate that the corporate veil of a subsidiary may be pierced and a parent corporation may be held derivatively liable under the FWPCA due to the public policy of protecting the environment.[371] There is no evidence that a parent corporation may be held directly liable under the FWPCA.

---

367 United States v. Walsh, 783 F. Supp. 546 (W.D. Wash. 1991), aff'd, 8 F.3d 659 (9th Cir. 1993) (holding defendant liable under CAA as one who "supervised or controlled the work"); United States v. Hugo Key & Son, Inc., 731 F. Supp. 1135, 1141 (D.R.I. 1989) (noting that "Hugo Key was the contractor... and supervised the job"); United States v. Tzavah Urban Renewal Corp., 696 F. Supp. 1013, 1021 (D.N.J. 1988) (defendants "engaged in the supervision" of the project and "hence are 'owners or operators' within the meaning of the Act").

368 8 F.3d at 659.

369 33 U.S.C. § 1321 (1988).

370 Id.

371 United States v. Ira S. Bushey & Sons, Inc., 363 F. Supp. 110, 119 (D. Vt. 1973), *aff'd,* 487 F.2d 1393 (2d Cir. 1973), *cert. denied*, 417 U.S. 976 (1974) (stating that " [t]he public interest in preserving the environmental integrity of Lake Champlain,... a jewel of nature, is sufficiently paramount that the parent corporation... should be accountable").

While RCRA does not define "owner or operator," the statute does regulate some activities of persons who are "owners or operators."[372] However, most of RCRA's liability provisions are concentrated on those who are generators or transporters of hazardous materials.[373] As a result of these differing definitions and the paucity of case law, these other environmental statutes provide little guidance as to whether a parent corporation may be an owner or operator under CERCLA or OPA.

### *The Liability of Parent Corporations Under CERCLA & FWPCA Case Law*

There is a dearth of cases on the issue of piercing the corporate veil under OPA. The U.S. Federal Water Pollution Control Act (FWPCA), as amended by OPA, also has not been used to develop piercing law. Neither OPA, FWPCA nor CERCLA imposes liability on parent corporations by their terms. However, FWPCA's companion legislation directed at land-based releases of hazardous non-petroleum chemicals, CERCLA, has been the substantive basis for the theoretical development of federal corporate piercing doctrine.

#### *A Pre-OPA 90 Case Law*

The most prominent pre-OPA example of piercing the corporate veil occurred in the case of *Amoco Cadiz*[374] where the court found that the parent corporation exercised such day-to-day control over its subsidiaries that the subsidiaries were considered the "mere instrumentalities" of the parent. The court found that Standard Oil Company (Indiana) (parent company) was an alter ego of its ship owning and ship management

---

372 42 U.S.C. §§ 6924, 6925 (1988).

373 Id. § 6928.

374 In re Oil Spill by the Amoco Cadiz, 1984 AMC 2123, 2194 (N.D. Ill. 1984), *aff'd*, 954 F.2d 1279 (7th Cir.1992).

subsidiaries for the disastrous oil spill in March 16, 1978 off the coast of Britany, France.

The Amoco Cadiz, the vessel responsible for the oil spill was a large tank vessel of approximately 230,000 deadweight tons of a class commonly referred to as VLCC.[375] The *Amoco Cadiz* was 1,095 feet long with a beam of 167 feet and a draft, fully loaded, of approximately 65 feet.[376] The registered owner of the Amoco Cadiz was Amoco Transport Company ("Transport"), a Liberian corporation with its principal place of business in Hamilton, Bermuda.[377] From the time of its formation in August 1970, and at all times thereafter material to this court action, Amoco Tankers Company ("Tankers") was a Liberian corporation all of whose stock was indirectly owned by Standard through a chain of wholly owned subsidiaries.[378] At all times material to this action, Standard and consolidated subsidiaries, including Amoco International Oil Company (AIOC), Transport and Tankers (collectively "the Amoco parties"), formed a large integrated petroleum and chemical company conducting operations on a worldwide basis. Standard, as the parent company, concerned itself with overall policy guidance, financing, coordination of operations, staff services, performance evaluation and planning.[379]

The court relied on some factors in reaching this decision. They are as follows:

A. Standard's Control of its subsidiaries:

1. Standard was the controlling parent corporation of a large and intricate corporate structure, the companies of which, including International and Transport, exist and complement one another for the financial benefit of and to carry out the corporate will of Standard.[380]

375 In re Oil Spill by the Amoco Cadiz, 1984 AMC 2135.

376 Id. at 2135.

377 Id. at 2124.

378 Id. at 2125.

379 Id. at 2126

380 Id. at 2181.

2. Standard had a consolidated balance sheet so that the reporting to the Securities and Exchange Commission ("SEC") for Standard included the profit and losses of Amoco International Oil Company (AIOC) and Transport.
3. In its Form 10K filed with the SEC for 1978, Standard described its relationship with its subsidiaries as follows: "Standard and its consolidated subsidiaries (herein sometimes collectively also called 'Standard') form a large integrated petroleum and chemical company that conducts operation on a world-wide basis."
4. Standard described itself as "a parent company concerned with overall policy guidance, financing, coordination of operations, staff services, performance evaluation, and planning for its subsidiaries."
5. None of the stock of AIOC was publicly held. Standard owned 100% of the voting stock of AIOC.
6. As a wholly owned subsidiary of Standard, AIOC was charged with the responsibility of carrying out all of the day-to-day business of Standard in all areas outside of North America. That business included exploration for, sale, and transportation of, crude oil and it refined products.
7. AIOC provided no services outside of Standard's Organization.
8. The Marine Transportation Department of AIOC was responsible for developing, planning and implementing transportation requirements for Standard's consolidated subsidiaries.
9. Within AIOC's Marine Transportation Department, the Marine Operations Department was responsible for the operation of all of Standard's vessels as well as day-to-day planning concerning the vessels.
10. None of the stock of Transport was publicly held. Transport was owned by two subsidiaries of Amoco International Finance Company ("AIFC"), which was itself an 80%-owned subsidiary of Standard. Ownership of the remaining 20% of AIFC was shared by AIOC and Amoco Chemicals Corporation, wholly owned subsidiaries of Standard.
11. In 1978, Transport was the registered owner of all of Standard's foreign, non-U.S. flag vessels, including the *Amoco Cadiz*. All

of Standard's U.S. flag vessels were owned by Amoco Shipping Company, another subsidiary of AIOC.[381]

12. Standard, AIOC, Transport and other Standard subsidiaries were managed by a network of interlocking directors and officers.
13. Clair, who figures prominently at every level of this case, was first employed as an attorney by AIOC in July of 1970. Clair and other AIOC attorneys were reassigned to Standard's legal department in 1973.
14. Clair, an employee of AIOC, became assistant secretary of Tankers when it was formed. Clair never received any compensation from Tankers.
15. Clair also served as assistant secretary of Transport and Amoco Maritime Company.
16. Leslie C. Adams was president of AIOC and a member of Standard's Board in March 1978. He reported to George Meyers, president of Standard, who in turn reported to John E. Swearingen, chairman of the Board of Standard.
17. All of Tankers' directors were employees of AIOC.
18. In 1974, Wren, head of AIOC's New Construction Department, was an officer and director of Tankers, but he was never on Tankers' payroll. He did not recall whether he ever was director of Tankers or whether he ever attended any meetings of its board.
19. In 1974, Haddow, vice president of AIOC's Marine Transportation Department was president and chairman of the board of both Transport and Tankers. He received compensation only from AIOC.
20. In 1978, when the *Amoco Cadiz* grounded, Rinkema was vice president of Marine Transportation Department of AIOC and chairman of Transport. He received no compensation from Transport.
21. Thomas, president and director of Transport in March 1978 was an employee of AIOC. He received no compensation from Transport. Other positions interlocked as well:

381 Id. at 2182.

(a) J. C. Denton, employee of Standard, was secretary of Transport.
(b) F. S. Addy, treasurer of Standard, was vice president of AIOC.
(c) D. E. Wilson, assistant treasurer and associate general counsel of Standard, was treasurer of AIOC.[382]

22. Within the Standard family of corporations, key personnel continuously moved among corporate offices in the parent and its subsidiaries.[383]
23. Standard treated its subsidiaries' operations as its own; its officers and directors had little or no perception of separateness with respect to the various Standard companies. Thus, for example, John Swearingen, Standard's chairman, when he testified that, in approving the purchase of two new VLCCs, the board relied upon the recommendation of the people who ran "our Marine Department," thought that Transport was the subsidiary which handled AIOC's marine operations; in fact, they were carried out in AIOC's own Marine Transport Department.
24. On May 29, 1974, Tankers "sold" the *Amoco Cadiz* to Transport. Both companies were subsidiaries of Standard, which processed the transaction through its legal department.
25. AIOC and Transport could not make all of their own policy decisions, but had to obtain permission from Standard in certain areas.
26. AIOC's employees consulted Standard employees before making major decisions, and would utilize Standard employees to work on AIOC's behalf.
27. Transport's financial records were never audited by AIOC, but by the "internal auditors of Standard Oil" who came from Chicago to Bermuda to examine the books.
28. In April 1978, the accounting functions of Transport were transferred to one of Standard's accounting departments.[384]

---

382 Id.

383 Id. at 2183

384 Id.

B. Standard's Relationship to the VLCC's and especially Amoco Cadiz:

1. Standard was intimately involved in the development and deployment of its VLCCs.[385]
2. AIOC proposed to the Management Committee of Standard's board of directors the purchase of two VLCCs of 230,000 dwt each.[386]
3. The management committee of Standard approved of the project and the two ships eventually became the *Amoco Milford Haven* and the *Amoco Singapore*.
4. On June 16, 1970, Mr. Osment, acting as the president of AIOC and a member of Standard's management committee, proposed to the committee the purchase of two additional VLCCs. The committee approved.
5. Standard's management committee then presented the proposal to Standard's board of directors, which approved of the purchase of the two additional VLCCs which were eventually named the *Amoco Cadiz* and the *Amoco Europa*.
6. Standard's board made the decision based upon AIOC's analysis that the two vessels would be of economic benefit to Standard, and that Standard would save in excess of $9 million by approving a proposal that the design of the new vessels be the same as that of the prior two VLCCs.
7. Financing for the building of the *Amoco Cadiz* was furnished by two other Standard subsidiaries and instructions were sent to the bank by Standard employees on Tankers' stationery.
8. A memorandum dated May 17, 1974, on Standard stationery, from P. James Perille, director of financial evaluations for Standard, requested that Standard's accounting, tax and law departments develop their recommendations on the subject of ownership of the *Amoco Cadiz* and her sister ship, the *Amoco Europa*. The question of what company should own the vessels was raised by

385 Id. at 2184.

386 Id.

Clair, the Standard attorney. The Standard memorandum refers to Transport as "our marine operating company."[387]

9. Clair and Swiger, both attorney at Standard, drafted the so-called chartering and consulting agreements to be signed by employees of AIOC on behalf of both AIOC and Transport.
10. During the course of operations of the VLCCs, meetings were held three times a week among employees of AIOC and Standard to plot the vessels' courses and to determine whether any delays in reaching port could be expected which would endanger crude oil availability for Standard.[388]
11. The *Amoco Cadiz* and all of Standard's vessels were insured through Dradnats Inc., a wholly owned subsidiary of Standard whose function was to see to the insurance needs of the Standard group. Dradnats invoiced Standard for insurance on the vessels nominally owned by Transport.[389]
12. AIOC consulted regularly with personnel in Standard's insurance department to provide them with information concerning the operation and valuation of Transport's vessels.[390]
13. Employees of Standard's insurance department proposed a summary of "our" marine insurance coverage, dealing with various insurance matters pertaining to Standard's vessels, including the VLCC's nominally owned by Transport. The booklet makes no reference to the various legal owners of the ships, but treats the ships as commonly owned assets. All claims were referred to Standard's insurance department.[391]
14. Standard had an oil spill contingency plan for pollution incidents. The persons to be notified were all within Standard and AIOC;

387 Id.

388 Id. at 2184-2185

389 Id. at 2185.

390 Id.

391 Id.

there was no provision for notification of Transport officials, even in the event of an oil spill by a Transport vessel.[392]

The Amoco Cadiz case is no doubt an extension of the traditional veil piercing doctrines discussed extensively above. Although the Amoco Cadiz court appears to have applied traditional veil piercing concepts, it went far beyond that by finding that Standard was liable for the negligence of its subsidiaries under an "intragroup" or enterprise theory of liability, pursuant to which tort liability may be imposed on a parent when its subsidiaries constitute a single economic entity, despite fragmentation by separate incorporation.[393] The court found that as an integrated multinational corporation which is engaged through a system of subsidiaries in the exploration, production, refining, transportation and sale of petroleum products throughout the world, Standard is responsible for the tortuous acts of its wholly owned subsidiaries and instrumentalities, AIOC and Transport.[394] It also concluded that Standard exercised such control over its subsidiaries AIOC and Transport that those entities would be considered to be mere instrumentalities of Standard. Furthermore, Standard itself was initially involved in and controlled the design, construction, operation and management of the *Amoco Cadiz* and treated that vessel as if it were its own.[395]

### *CERCLA Case Law*

Petroleum or Oil is not a CERCLA listed chemical, so CERCLA law cannot be directly applied, but the provisions of CERCLA explicitly support enforcement of the FWPCA and the OPA. A careful review of CERCLA cases and the developing law on piercing under CERCLA may give guidance on what to expect under OPA. Some CERCLA cases have laid a clear road map for piercing to find a responsible party to finance

---

392 Id. at 2185.

393 Colin De La Rue & Charles B. Anderson, Shipping and The Environment, at 666, (Lloyd's Shipping Law Library 1998).

394 In re Oil Spill by the Amoco Cadiz, 1984 AMC at 2194.

395 Id. at 2194.

clean-up costs, stating that the statutory scheme of CERCLA varied traditional corporate principles.[396] Cases decided under state piercing law have not been as expansive in their analysis.

Under CERCLA, the terms "owner" and "operator" have been bifurcated, and liability has been imposed upon parent corporations derivatively as "owners" and directly as "operators."[397] The differing standards for imposing liability are discussed below.

As explained earlier, neither the plain language nor the legislative history of CERCLA addresses whether parent corporations may be held liable for the clean-up costs of their subsidiary's hazardous waste violations. Nevertheless, some courts have found parent corporations liable based on one of two theories. Some courts have found parent corporations liable under the "direct liability" theory, which holds parent corporations directly liable under CERCLA based on their level of involvement in the subsidiary corporation or in operations at the subsidiary's facility.[398] However, courts are in conflict about the level of involvement the parent corporation must exercise over the subsidiary. Some courts hold that a parent's capacity to control the subsidiary's activities is enough while others hold that the parent must exercise actual control over the subsidiary.[399]

---

396 Kelly v. Thomas Solvent Co., 727 F.Supp. 1532, 1542 (W.D.Mich.1989). See also, Idaho v. Bunker Hill Co., 635 F.Supp. 665 (D.Idaho 1986); New York v. Shore Realty, 759 F.2d 1032 (2d Cir.1985); Vermont v. Staco, Inc., 684 F.Supp. 822 (S.D.Ut.1988); United States v. Northernaire Plating, 670 F.Supp. 742 (W.D.Mich.1987); United States v. Ward, 618 F.Supp. 884 (E.D.N.C.1985). For a good review of the CERCLA case law on piercing, see, Elizabeth A. Noonan, To Pierce or Not to Pierce? When is the Question, 68 WASH.U.L.Q. 733 (1990).

397 See generally, Lansford-Coaldale Joint Water Auth. v. Tonolli Corp., 4 F.3d 1209, 1220 (3d Cir. 1993); United States v. Kayser-Roth Corp., Inc., 910 F.2d 24 (1st Cir. 1990), *cert. denied*, 111 S. Ct. 957 (1991); CPC Int'l, Inc. v. Aerojet-Gen. Corp., 777 F. Supp. 549 (W.D. Mich. 1991); Jacksonville Elec. Auth. v. Eppinger & Russell Co., 776 F. Supp. 1542 (M.D. Fla. 1991); John Boyd Co. v. Boston Gas Co., 775 F. Supp. 435 (D. Mass. 1991); *see also* Allen Kezsbom et al., "Successor" and "Parent" Liability for Superfund Cleanup Costs: The Evolving State of the Law, 10 Va. Envtl. L.J. 45, 60 (1990).

398 *See* United States v. Kayser-Roth Corp., 910 F.2d 24, 27 (1st Cir. 1990), *cert. denied*, 111 S. Ct. 957 (1991).

399 *Compare* Idaho v. Bunker Hill Company, 635 F. Supp. 665 (D. Idaho 1986) (holding the parent corporation liable under section 107 because the parent had the capacity to control the hazardous waste practices of the subsidiary) *with*, United States v. Kayser-Roth

In contrast to the direct liability theory, other courts have found parent corporations liable using the "indirect liability" theory. Under the indirect liability theory, courts apply the "alter ego" or "mere instrumentality"[400] doctrine to "determine whether the facts warrant piercing the corporate veil of the subsidiary corporation to impose CERCLA liability on parent corporations." The "alter ego" or "mere instrumentality" doctrines have been discussed earlier.

### *A. Direct Liability Under CERCLA*

Direct liability is "the most common type of liability imposed on **PRPs** under CERCLA."[401] Under the direct liability theory, a parent corporation is liable if it was found to be directly involved in the activities giving rise to the claim against the subsidiary.[402] Whether courts should "expose parent corporations to direct liability implicates a variety of competing policy considerations."[403] Policy considerations militating against direct parent liability are threefold. First, Congress, not the courts, should authorize holding parent corporations liable for the hazardous waste violations of their subsidiaries.[404] Second, it is unnecessary to abandon the

Corp., 910 F.2d 24 (1st Cir. 1990) (holding the parent corporation liable under section 107 because the parent had exercised actual control over the hazardous waste practices of the subsidiary).

400 The mere instrumentality doctrine examines: (1) whether the parent exercises excessive control over the subsidiary; (2) whether wrongful or inequitable conduct was present; and (3) whether there is a causal relationship to the plaintiff's loss. Frederick J. Powell, Parent And Subsidiary Corporations s6, at 9 (1931) [hereafter Parent Corporations].

401 Erika Clarke Birg, Comment, Redefining "Owner Or Operator" Under CERCLA To Preserve Traditional Notions of Corporate Law, 43 Emory L.J. 771, 800(1994) [[hereafter Redefining].

402 Lynda J. Oswald, Corporate Parent Responsibility for Environmental Liability of the Subsidiary, 785 PLI/Corp. 107 (1992) [hereafter Corporate Parent Liability].

403 Ronald G. Aronovsky & Lynn D. Fuller, Liability of Parent Corporations for Hazardous Substance Releases Under CERCLA, 24 U.S.F. L. R ev. 421, 436 (1990) [hereafter Liability].

404 Liability, id. at 436, *see also,* Joslyn Mfg. v. T.L. James & Co., 893 F.2d 80, 83 (5th Cir. 1990).

limited liability concept to finance cleanups necessitated by subsidiary corporation's hazardous waste violations because other sources (i.e. - other PRPs, taxpayers and insurance companies) can provide clean-up funds.[405] Finally, imposing liability on parent corporations "presents serious economic policy concerns" such as increased prices to consumers and increased litigation expenses.[406] Policy considerations favoring direct parent liability are also threefold. First, Congress intended that CERCLA be given broad interpretation,[407] and CERCLA does not preclude a parent corporation's liability for the environmental waste violations of their subsidiary.[408]

Second, direct liability allows courts to hold parent corporations liable "without having to disregard the separate legal existence" of the subsidiary.[409] Finally, the entities best suited to prevent the harm should be burdened with the costs of clean-up instead of other sources, such as other PRPs, taxpayers and insurance companies, who can have little or no control over the subsidiary corporation's waste management activities.[410] Direct liability is based on the theory that the parent corporation is the "operator" of the facility where the hazardous waste is located.[411]

Courts have articulated two tests to determine whether a parent corporation is an operator under CERCLA section 9607: (1) the capacity to control test; and (2) the actual exercise of control test. In all further discussions, section 107 of CERCLA may be used interchangeably with 42 USC §9607.

---

405 Id. at 436

406 Id.

407 See Idaho v. Bunker Hill Co., 635 F. Supp. 665 (D. Idaho 1986) (holding the parent corporation liable under section 107 because the parent had the capacity to control the hazardous waste practices of the subsidiary).

408 Ronald G. Aronovsky & Lynn D. Fuller, Liability of Parent Corporations for Hazardous Substance Releases Under CERCLA, 24 U.S.F. L. Rev. at 437.

409 Id. at 437.

410 Id. at 437-38.

411 See United States v. Kayser-Roth Corp., 910 F.2d 24, 27 (1st Cir. 1990), *cert. denied*, 111 S. Ct. 957 (1991) ("[w]e believe that a fair reading of CERCLA allows a parent corporation to be held [directly] liable as an operator of a subsidiary corporation.").

*The capacity to control test*

The capacity to control test is "based upon mere status as opposed to affirmative acts."[412] It is an inquiry as to whether the parent corporation had the capacity to control the hazardous waste practices at its subsidiary corporation.[413] Numerous federal district courts have recognized the capacity to control test as the requisite level of involvement; however, most federal appellate courts have not recognized the capacity to control test in the parent/subsidiary context.[414] The courts that have rejected this test have held that unexercised capacity to control is insufficient to justify direct parent liability for the acts of subsidiaries which violate CERCLA.[415] *Idaho v. Bunker Hill Co.*,[416] was the first federal case to apply the capacity to control test in assessing direct parent corporation liability. The court concluded that Gulf Resources & Chemical Corporation (Gulf), the parent corporation of Bunker Hill Company, was a past "owner or operator" under section 9607(a)(2) of CERCLA because Gulf had the capacity to control the hazardous waste practices of Bunker Hill.[417] The Bunker Hill court interpreted "owner or operator" to mean one who "has the power to direct the

412 Lynda J. Oswald, Bifurcation of the Owner and Operator Analysis Under CERCLA: Finding Order In The Chaos Of Pervasive Control, 72 Wash. U. L.Q. 223, 260 (1994) [hereafter Bifurcation].

413 See Idaho v. Bunker Hill Co., 635 F. Supp. 665 (D. Idaho 1986).

414 One federal circuit has adopted the capacity to control test, but in the context of a lessor/lessee and not a parent/subsidiary. See Nurad, Inc. v. William E. Hooper & Sons, 966 F.2d 837, 842 (4th Cir. 1992) (Fourth Circuit determined that the focus is not whether the party actually controlled the subsidiary, but rather whether the party had the capacity to control the subsidiary's environmental decisions at the site.) It is inferable that the Fourth Circuit would apply the capacity to control test to the parent/subsidiary context as well because it states "[t]his is the definition of the word 'operator' that most courts have adopted." Id.; Another federal circuit court has recognized the capacity to control test in dicta. In Kaiser Aluminum & Chem. Corp. v. Catellus Dev. Corp., 976 F.2d 1338, 1341 (9th Cir. 1992), the Ninth Circuit identified "[capacity] to control the cause of the contamination" as the applicable standard.

415 Certain Underwriters at Lloyd's, London v. St. Joe Minerals Corp., 90 F.3d 671, 674 (2d. Cir. 1996); In re Bergsoe Metal Corp., 910 F.2d 668 (9th Cir. 1990); United States v. Consolidated Rail Corp., 729 F.Supp. 1461 (D. Del. 1990).

416 635 F. Supp. 665 (D. Idaho 1986).

417 Id.

activities of persons who control the mechanisms causing the pollution... thus having the capacity to prevent and abate damage."[418] The court then applied this test to the parent/subsidiary relationship at issue in Bunker Hill. The court was particularly persuaded by the fact that the parent had at times controlled the subsidiary's board of directors; had received weekly reports of the subsidiary's daily operations; that the subsidiary could not spend in excess of $500 on pollution problems without the parent corporation's approval; and that the subsidiary had limited capitalization of only $1,100 while the parent received in excess of $27 million in dividends.[419] The *Bunker Hill* court thus concluded that Gulf was "intimately familiar with hazardous waste disposal and releases at the... [subsidiary's] facility [and] had the capacity to control such disposal and releases." [420]

This same principle could be applied to OPA vessels and facilities where a parent corporation has the power to direct the activities of persons who control the mechanisms causing the oil pollution, thus having the capacity to prevent and abate damage. However, the merits of the *Bunker Hill* decision are debatable for two reasons. First, the facts of the case suggest that besides having the capacity to control the subsidiary, the parent corporation actually retained control in excess of that normally equated with parental oversight. Thus, the court could have adopted the narrower actual exercise of control test, but instead elected to adopt the much broader capacity to control test. Choosing the capacity to control test was questionable because the test reshapes traditional notions of corporate liability. This reshaping takes place because the capacity to control test is easily satisfied, thus rendering limited liability for the parent corporation essentially nonexistent. One commentator has explained the ease of meeting the capacity to control test as:

"Every parent corporation, by virtue of the power it wields over its subsidiary, could control that subsidiary's activities, including those activities relating

418 Id. at 672 (quoting United States v. Northeastern Pharmaceutical and Chem. Co., 579 F. Supp. 823, 848-49 (W.D. Mo. 1984)).

419 Id.

420 Id

to its environmental matters and the operation of a facility. A literal application of the capacity to control test would thus lead to a finding of parent liability in every case involving a CERCLA violation by a subsidiary."[421]

A literal application of the capacity to control test in OPA cases could also lead to a finding of parent liability in every case involving an OPA violation by a subsidiary.

Second, the *Bunker Hill* court failed to distinguish whether it was holding the parent liable under CERCLA section 9607 as an owner or as an operator.[422] Instead, the court merely stated that it was holding the parent liable as an owner or operator, in essence using the terms interchangeably.[423] However, the terms are not interchangeable. Operator liability is direct liability, and owner liability is indirect liability. [424] Thus, because the court applied the direct liability theory, the parent could only be liable as an operator.[425] The Bunker Hill court's failure to articulate whether it was holding the parent liable as an owner or as an operator when it clearly had to be holding the parent liable as an operator illustrates the confusion among the courts regarding parent liability under section 9607.[426] This confusion demonstrates the need for clarification by either the Supreme Court, the EPA, or Congress.

The district court in *Colorado v. Idarado Mining Co.*[427] adopted a modified version of the capacity to control test. Its modified version included several new criteria, including "the percentage of the subsidiary's stock owned by the parent, whether and to what extent the parent controls the subsidiary's marketing and whether the parent has or exercises

421 Lynda J. Oswald, Bifurcation of the Owner and Operator Analysis Under CERCLA: Finding Order In The Chaos Of Pervasive Control, 72 Wash. U. L.Q. at 260.

422 Id. at 262.

423 *Bunker Hill*, 635 F. Supp at 671-72.

424 Lynda J. Oswald, Bifurcation of the Owner and Operator Analysis Under CERCLA: Finding Order In The Chaos Of Pervasive Control, 72 Wash. U. L.Q. 235, 244-46, 257-58.

425 Id. at 263.

426 See id. at 262 n.184.

427 1987 U.S. Dist. LEXIS 14254 (E.D. Colo. 1987), rev'd on other grounds, 916 F.2d 1486 (10th Cir. 1990), cert. denied, 499 U.S. 960 (1991).

authority to execute contracts on behalf of the subsidiary.'"[428] The *Idarado Mining* court decided that the parent corporation had enough knowledge of and control over the subsidiary's environmental matters to "justify categorizing the parent as an owner or operator."[429]

The merits of the *Idarado Mining* decision are also questionable. First, the court acknowledged that the parent exercised "hands-on control" over the subsidiary's actions.[430] This acknowledgment indicates that the court was really applying the actual control test rather than the capacity to control test.[431] Second, the court's analysis seems to indicate it "was actually engaged in a piercing the veil inquiry under the guise of direct liability... but... failed to make its purpose clear."[432] Finally, as one commentator has argued, the criteria identified by the *Idarado Mining* court focuses on the parent corporation's involvement in the subsidiary itself, not in the facility operated by the subsidiary, as CERCLA requires.[433] According to this commentator, not requiring the focus to be on the facility leaves open the door "for future courts to find [direct] parent liability in inappropriate circumstances."[434] Thus, the *Idarado Mining* decision failed to provide reasonable support for finding parent corporations directly liable as operators under CERCLA section 9607.

### *The Actual Exercise of Control Test*

A majority of the cases examining a parent corporation's liability under the direct liability theory have adopted the narrower actual exercise

428 Id. at *3 (citing United States v. Conservation Chem. Co., 628 F. Supp. 391, 416-20 (W.D. Mo. 1985)).

429 Id. at *5

430 Erika Clarke Birg, Comment, Redefining "Owner Or Operator" Under CERCLA To Preserve Traditional Notions of Corporate Law, 43 Emory L.J. at 808 (citing Idarado Mining, 1987 U.S. Dist. LEXIS 14254, at *8).

431 Id.

432 Id.

433 Lynda J. Oswald, Bifurcation of the Owner and Operator Analysis Under CERCLA: Finding Order In The Chaos Of Pervasive Control, 72 Wash. U. L.Q. at 264.

434 Id. at 265.

of control test.[435] The actual exercise of control test involves examining the relationship between the parent and the subsidiary in order to determine the level of the parent corporation's involvement in the subsidiary's environmental affairs.[436] The actual exercise of control test was originally formulated in *United States v. Kayser-Roth Corporation.*[437] In *Kayser-Roth*, the First Circuit found Kayser-Roth Corporation directly liable for the clean-up costs of its wholly-owned subsidiary, holding Kayser-Roth Corporation to be an operator under CERCLA section 9607.[438] The court determined that to be an operator under CERCLA section 9607 the parent corporation must "at a minimum be actively involved in the activities of the subsidiary."[439] The court concluded that Kayser-Roth exercised actual control over the activities of its subsidiary and thus should be held directly liable as an operator.[440] The court's decision was supported by evidence showing that: (1) Kayser-Roth totally controlled its subsidiary's budget, capital and real estate transactions; (2) Kayser-Roth required that its subsidiary direct all environmental matters to Kayser-Roth; (3) Kayser-Roth controlled its subsidiary's officers and directors; and (4) Kayser-Roth required that any expenditure over $5,000 must be approved by Kayser-Roth. [441]

---

435 Lynda J. Oswald, Corporate Parent Responsibility for Environmental Liability of the Subsidiary, 785 PLI/Corp. 107 (1992) [hereafter Corporate Parent Liability].

436 John S. Boyd Co. v. Boston Gas Co., 992 F.2d 401, 408 (1st Cir. 1993). The court in City of New York v. Exxon Corp., 112 B.R. 540, 548 n.9 (Bankr. S.D.N.Y. 1990) couched it in the following terms: [T]he mere capacity to control the affairs of a subsidiary is not a sufficient basis on which to predicate direct liability under Section 107(a) of CERCLA. We believe that some degree of active participation in and actual control over the affairs of the subsidiary is necessary.... [T]he corporation must [[actually] exercise... control [over] its subsidiary in order to be held liable under section 107(a).

437 910 F.2d 24 (1st Cir. 1990), cert. denied, 498 U.S. 1084 (1991). In John S. Boyd Co. v. Boston Gas Co., 992 F.2d 401 (1st Cir. 1993), the First Circuit concurred with its *Kayser-Roth* holding.

438 *Kayser-Roth,* 910 F.2d at 25-26.

439 Id. at 27.

440 Id. at 27-28

441 Id.

Other courts have also adopted the actual exercise of control test.[442] In *Rockwell Int'l Corp. v. IU Int'l Corp.*,[443] the United States District Court for the Northern District of Illinois determined that mere capacity to control is not enough to impose liability on a parent corporation for its subsidiary's hazardous waste violations.[444] Rather, the parent must actually exercise control over the subsidiary's facility to be held liable.[445] The district court then listed the following factors supporting such liability: (1) the parent hired or approved hiring some of the subsidiary's officers; (2) certain officers of the parent were also officers of the subsidiary; (3) the parent's auditors recommended to the subsidiary how to handle hazardous waste disposal; (4) the parent reviewed the subsidiary's environmental purchases; (5) the parent controlled and monitored the subsidiary's operational plans and procedures; and (6) the parent publicly announced that it operated the subsidiary's facility.[446]

Also in the case of *City of New York v. Exxon*,[447] the Second Circuit Court of Appeals issued a summary judgment ruling that the parent holding company was liable for illegal dumping by its wholly- owned subsidiary. The *Exxon* court pierced the corporate veil both because the parent corporation expected to profit from the activities of its subsidiary and because the parent contributed cash to the same subsidiary when it lost money.[448] The court reached its decision based on CERCLA section

---

442 See Lansford-Coaldale Joint Water Auth. v. Tonolli Corp., 4 F.3d 1209, 1222 n.13 (3d Cir. 1993) (Third Circuit followed the *Kayser-Roth* standard, stating that "operator liability may be established even without evidence that a [parent] corporation controlled the environmental decisions of an affiliated corporation so long as there exist other factors which sufficiently demonstrate pervasive control."); Jacksonville Elec. Auth. v. Bernuth Corp., 996 F.2d 1107, 1110 (11th Cir. 1993) (Eleventh Circuit concluded that the test for direct parent corporation liability as an operator was whether the parent "exercises actual and pervasive control of the subsidiary to the extent of actually involving itself in the daily operations of the subsidiary.").

443 702 F. Supp. 1384 (N.D. Ill. 1988).

444 Id. at 1390

445 Id.

446 Id. at 1390-91

447 1990 Dist. Lexis 3555, at 29-31 (S.D.N.Y.), *aff'd*, 932 F.2d 1020 (2d Cir.1991).

448 Id.

9607.[449] This decision followed earlier CERCLA piercing decisions also based on CERCLA section 9607, which makes liable persons who generate or arrange for the transport and disposal of hazardous materials.[450] In adopting this approach, the court found direct liability under CERCLA's "owner or operator" and "individuals who have control or authority" language rather than relying on traditional corporate piercing doctrine.[451] By using a more expansive approach under CERCLA, the court reached the assets of those who have profited from the environmentally damaging activity, albeit as a result of the activity of a subsidiary. The *Exxon* case may not be applicable to OPA cases because OPA does not impose liability on the shipper of oil. As explained earlier, the legislative history of OPA shows that the US Congress did not intend to impose liability on cargo owners like Exxon. Only an amendment to OPA that mirrors the CERCLA provision that makes shippers of cargo liable, would make the *Exxon* case germane.

### *No Direct Liability*

In contrast to those cases imposing direct liability on parent corporations as operators, the Fifth Circuit in *Joslyn Manufacturing Co. v. T.L. James & Co.*[452] refused to expand the definition of "owner and operator" to include direct liability of parent corporations.[453] The *Joslyn* court

449 42 U.S.C. § 9607(a)(3)-(4) (1988).

450 Exxon, 1990 Dist. Lexis 3555 at 27-28.

451 Id. at 39-40.

452 893 F.2d 80 (5th Cir. 1990), *cert. denied*, 111 S. Ct. 1017 (1991). *Kayser-Roth* rejected the *Joslyn* decision by asserting that the *Joslyn* court declined to hold the parent corporation directly liable as an owner and not as an operator. The *Kayser-Roth* court maintained that operator liability is a direct liability action and owner liability is an indirect liability action. *Kayser-Roth*, 910 F.2d at 27. Thus, the *Kayser-Roth* court felt that *Joslyn* was only addressing owner liability, which is indirect liability, and not operator liability, which is direct liability. Id.

453 *Joslyn*, 893 F.2d at 82. It has been argued that the Fifth Circuit, in *Riverside Market Dev. Corp v. Int'l Bldg. Products, Inc.*, 931 F.2d 327 (5th Cir. 1991), retracted from its *Joslyn* holding. See Jacksonville Elec. Auth. v. Eppinger & Russell Co., 776 F. Supp. 1542,

reasoned as follows. First, the definitional section in CERCLA failed to include the parent corporation of the subsidiary.[454] "CERCLA does not define 'owners' or 'operators' as including the parent company of offending wholly-owned subsidiaries." Thus, if Congress intended parent corporations to be liable as owners or operators under CERCLA section 9607, Congress would have included parent corporations in the section defining owner or operator.[455]

Second, the *Joslyn* court determined that the legislative history of CERCLA failed to show "Congress' intent to alter so substantially the basic tenet of corporate law" that there is limited liability for shareholders, including parent corporations.[456] Imposing direct liability on parent corporations would alter the limited liability protection parent corporations receive.[457]

Just like in CERCLA, the OPA's legislative history does not show Congress' intent to alter substantially the basic tenet of corporate law. The *Joslyn* court further reasoned that imposing direct liability on parent corporations would make parent corporations liable for their subsidiary's hazardous waste violations beyond the amount the parent invested in the subsidiary. Finally, the *Joslyn* court concluded that Congress is capable of passing a statute holding parent corporations liable.[458] As an example the court pointed to 42 U.S.C. s 9601 (20)(A)(iii),[459] which includes a control

1546-48 (M.D. Fla. 1991); However, the Fifth Circuit does not expressly overrule *Joslyn* and never even cites Joslyn in its *Riverside Market* decision. Erika Clarke Birg, Comment, Redefining «Owner Or Operator» Under CERCLA To Preserve Traditional Notions of Corporate Law, 43 Emory L.J. at 804. One commentator stated the best way to reconcile *Riverside Market* with *Joslyn* is to treat the language in *Riverside Market* as mere dicta, and then to assume that the language is not controlling because *Riverside Market*, unlike *Joslyn*, was not considering the liability of a parent corporation. Redefining, id at 804.

454 *Joslyn*, 893 F.2d at 82.

455 Id. at 82-83

456 Id.

457 Id. at 83

458 Id.

459 42 U.S.C. s 9601(20)(A)(iii) (1988). Section 9601(20)(A)(iii) reads as follows: "in the case of any facility, title or control of which was conveyed due to bankruptcy, foreclosure, tax delinquency, abandonment, or similar means to a unit of State or local govern-

test.[460] The court determined that if Congress intended that parent corporations be held liable under section 9607, then Congress would have adopted a control test in section 9607 like Congress did in section 9601 (20)(A)(iii).[461] Thus, because Congress never adopted a control test in section 9607, CERCLA does not impose direct liability on parent corporations for their subsidiary's environmental violations.[462] According to *Joslyn*, the imposition of liability on parent corporations for their subsidiary's hazardous waste violations must be done indirectly through piercing the corporate veil. This is a very strict construction of CERCLA's provisions by the *Joslyn* court.

In all likelihood, this is how the Fifth Circuit Court of Appeals will dispose of OPA cases with similar issues as the *Joslyn* case. The Fifth Circuit Court of Appeals will use the traditional veil piercing doctrines earlier discussed to hold a parent corporation either liable or not liable for the oil spill discharges caused by its subsidiary corporation. If the Fifth Circuit Court of Appeals decides to construct the OPA strictly it will be impossible to hold a parent corporation directly liable for OPA violations of its subsidiary corporation. Because of these conflicting standards from circuit to circuit and from court to court, liability of parent corporations in the nearest future will depend on which circuit of the Courts of Appeal or which District Court is adjudicating the issue. Unless the US Supreme Court intervenes in the future and sets a uniform standard for holding parent corporations directly liable for the environmental law violations of their subsidiaries companies, what we will have is a situation where these three incompatible principles will be applied by different courts. The same parent company could be held liable through the capacity to control test in some courts. In others it could end up being held liable based on the actual control test, while in some others like the Fifth Circuit Court of Appeals, it would escape liability because the courts could decide that

ment, any person who owned, operated, or otherwise controlled activities at such facility immediately beforehand [shall be liable]."

460 *Joslyn*, 893 F.2d at 83.

461 Id.

462 Id. at 82

that parent corporation cannot be held liable except under the traditional common law veil piercing principles.

OPA defendants would definitely attempt to distinguish the CERCLA cases discussed above on the premise that the two statutes are different. However, any company involved in the vessel transportation of oil in the United States or in the exploration, production, distribution and storage of oil through facilities, should understand that itself and its affiliates may be exposed in line with the CERCLA line of cases as well as the Traditional Common Law line of cases discussed above. The CERCLA line of cases will be used by courts of law as well as by the US Coast Guard or the Environmental Protection Agency in deciding who to hold liable as a responsible party for oils spills. These government agencies do not have to wait for a court decision to designate a parent company as a jointly and severally liable responsible party with its subsidiary company.

Based on the above discussions, the following persons could be held liable as responsible parties:

(a) Parent Company of a vessel owning subsidiary company e.g. Standard Oil Company in the Amoco Cadiz case discussed above.

(b) Non- vessel owning sister-subsidiary companies who were deeply involved in the management of the polluting vessel: For instance in the case of *Amoco Cadiz* discussed earlier above, the court held AIOC personally liable even though it was not registered as the actual owner of the vessel Amoco Cadiz. The court held that:

1. As the party which exercised complete control over the operation, maintenance and repair of the *Amoco Cadiz* and the selection and training of its crew, AIOC had a duty to ensure that the vessel was seaworthy and adequately maintained and repaired, and that the crew was properly trained.[463]
2. AIOC negligently performed its duty to ensure that the *Amoco Cadiz* in general and its steering gear in particular were seaworthy, adequately maintained and in proper repair.

---

463 In re Oil Spill by the Amoco Cadiz, 1984 AMC at 2191.

3. AIOC was privy to and had knowledge of the scored rams, slipping belts, maintenance practices and steering gear problems on the *Amoco Cadiz* which made the vessel unseaworthy.[464]
4. The failure of *Amoco Cadiz's* steering gear is directly attributable to an improperly designed, constructed and maintained steering gear system and AIOC knew or should have known of the unseaworthy condition.[465]
5. The negligence of AIOC in failing reasonably to perform its obligations of maintenance and repair of the steering gear system was a proximate cause of the breakdown of the system on March 16, 1978, the grounding of the vessel and the resulting pollution damage.[466]
6. AIOC negligently performed its duty to ensure that the crew of the *Amoco Cadiz* was properly trained.
7. The crew's improper training with respect to the maintenance, operation, inspection and repair of the steering gear system was a proximate cause of the grounding of the *Amoco Cadiz*.467
8. AIOC, as the party which supervised and approved the design and construction of the *Amoco Cadiz*, had a duty to ensure that the design and construction were properly carried out so as to result in a seaworthy vessel. It failed in the duty.[468]
9. AIOC was negligent in operating the *Amoco Cadiz* without a redundant steering system or any other means of controlling the rudder in the event of complete failure of the hydraulic steering system.[469]

(c) The actual vessel owning company.

---

464 Id at 2192.

465 Id.

466 Id.

467 Id.

468 Id. at 2192.

469 Id.

(d) The vessel itself in rem because of the maritime lien that attaches to the vessel because of the maritime tort of marine pollution (this will be discussed below in greater detail in Chapter Thirteen)
(e) The operators of the vessel.
(f) Banks or other financial institutions who hold extensive security interest in the vessel. (This was discussed briefly in Chapter One).
(g) Guarantors who provide the guarantee for the required Certificate of Financial Responsibility (COFR) can be held personally liable up to the amount of the guarantee that they provide. The traditional veil piercing doctrines will be available to pierce the veil of their parent companies as well, should in case the guarantors become insolvent (COFR will be discussed in Chapter Eight).

Even though the traditional veil piercing doctrines and the modern environmental statutes' veil piercing doctrines can be used offensively by claimants against a parent company, parent companies cannot use this doctrines defensively to limit or restrict their own personal liability or the liability of their non-vessel owning subsidiary companies deeply involved in the management or operation of the polluting vessel. In the case of *Amoco Cadiz*, the court held that corporate parents and subsidiaries were not entitled to rely on the Limitation of Liability Act to limit their liability for oil spills occurring when the tanker owned by another subsidiary ran aground, because they were legally separate corporate entities from owner subsidiary and they failed to show that they had requisite possessory, managerial and operational control of the vessel to justify finding they were "owners."[470] This shows that the courts will be very liberal in piercing the corporate veil in order to hold all potential defendants liable to the fullest extent possible for pollution, but they will be very quick to invoke the principle of corporate separateness in order to prevent a corporate parent from invoking limitation of liability as a shield.

Even though the Limitation of Liability Act is of limited application to oil spill incidents because of specific OPA provision to that effect, nevertheless the OPA's limitation provision in section 2704 applies to OPA

470 Matter of Oil Spill by Amoco Cadiz Off Coast of France on March 16, 1978, 1992 A.M.C. 913, 954 F.2d 1279 (7th Cir. 1992).

claims. To the extent that a claimant is bringing suit under the OPA, each responsible party can limit its own liability, but a parent company and its subsidiary companies cannot limit their liability as one entity. Each of them will be jointly and severally liable because they are separate persons under the law. This means that each subsidiary company and the parent company standing alone can be held liable for the entire claim. This means that the combined assets of all the companies will be available to satisfy any eventual judgment that is delivered by the courts.

### B.II(c) Recommendations for Avoiding Parent Corporation Liability

It will be wise for parent companies to restructure their businesses and contractual arrangements to minimize exposure to OPA liability. In his monumental study in 1991, Professor Robert B. Thompson found 637 cases involving corporate groups and piercing the corporate veil. Courts pierced the veil in 237, or 37.21% of those cases.[471] In the light of the result of these types of empirical studies that shows a growing readiness of the courts to pierce the corporate veil, some commentators have suggested different methods for parent corporations to avoid being subjected to liability through the various veil piercing theories under CERCLA and the common law.[472] Because the courts will apply the CERCLA veil piercing theories as well as the common law or traditional veil piercing theories to OPA cases, it is important to discuss some of these suggestions.

Drawing some lessons from some of the cases discussed above addressing this burning issue, there are certain steps that parent corporations may take to avoid, or at the least, minimize their liability under CERCLA

471 Robert B. Thompson, Piercing the Corporate Veil: An Empirical Study, 76 CORNELL L. REV. 1036, 1055 (1991).

472 See generally, John S. G. Worden, CERCLA Liability Of Parent Corporations For The Acts Of Their Subsidiaries, 30 Idaho L. Rev. 73, 87 (1993-94) [Hereinafter Worden CERCLA Liability], John M. Brown, Note & Comment, Parent Corporation's Liability Under Cercla Section 107 For The Environmental Violations Of Their Subsidiaries, 31 Tulsa. L.J. 819, 849 (Summer 1996) [Hereinafter Brown Note].

or OPA for the environmental violations of their subsidiaries. With regard to direct liability as operators, the parent corporation must minimize or avoid controlling those aspects of its subsidiary that invite CERCLA or OPA scrutiny.[473] For example, the subsidiary's board of directors or officers, not the parent corporations, should make decisions regarding environmental matters of the subsidiary.[474] Also, when clean-up becomes necessary, the parent corporation should allow the subsidiary to determine what action to take, and to coordinate that action with government officials.[475] Thus, the parent corporation must not exercise actual control, or demonstrate the capacity to control the subsidiary's environmental affairs. With regard to indirect liability as owners, the subsidiary corporation should make sure that it does not fall within the veil piercing factors.[476] Thus, the subsidiary corporation should have adequate capitalization; there should not be any intermingling of the subsidiary corporation's properties with those held by the parent corporation; the subsidiary must observe the corporate formalities and separateness; the parent must not siphon funds from the subsidiary corporation; the subsidiary should keep its own corporate records; the subsidiary should have its own officers and board of directors; and the parent should not own all the capital stock of the subsidiary.[477] To the extent that there are overlaps in personnel or inter-locking directorships, those individuals should not be given decision-making powers in both entities.[478] Further, officers and directors of the subsidiary must act independently in the interest of the subsidiary and not in the interest of the parent company.[479]

473 John M. Brown, Note & Comment, Parent Corporation's Liability Under Cercla Section 107 For The Environmental Violations Of Their Subsidiaries, 31 Tulsa. L.J at 849 (*quoting*, Worden CERCLA Liability, id. at 87).

474 Id. at 849.

475 Id.

476 Id.

477 Id.

478 Nancy Young, Internationalization: Avoiding Foreign Parent Company Liability For US Subsidiaries, 9 NO 1 Insights 17, 18 ( January 1995).

479 Id. at 18.

When entering into transactions with third parties, each entity should represent itself as a separate entity and not as part of a larger entity of which it is an affiliate.[480] Each entity should have separate letterhead.[481] Transactional documents for each entity should name only the entity entering into the transaction and be signed exclusively by such entity.[482] Similarly, when entering into a transaction requiring financial statement disclosure, only the financial statement of the relevant entity should be disclosed.[483] And when borrowing money from third parties, each entity should cause the lender to rely solely upon the creditworthiness of such entity and not that of its parent or affiliates.[484] Generally, it is not a good idea for a parent company or affiliates to provide guarantees or cross-collateral for a subsidiary.[485]

Finally, any appearance of involvement by the parent company in the day-to-day operations of the subsidiary such as written reports or faxes on such day-to- day operations or policies requiring parental approval for day-to-day business matters should be avoided.[486] Each entity should pay salaries to its own employees (i.e., provide separate checks) and pay its own expenses. If office space and equipment are to be shared between the parent and subsidiary, leases or other contracts should be executed and should be on an arms-length basis.[487]

Further, there should be intercompany administrative service agreements on an arms-length basis for various services (e.g., accounting, legal, Securities and Exchange Commission filing, etc.) to be shared among the entities.[488] If at all possible, each entity should engage in business transactions which are not provided or created by its parent or affiliates (i.e., transactions in which neither its parent nor any of

---

480 Id.

481 Id.

482 Id.

483 Id.

484 Id.

485 Id.

486 Id. at 18.

487 Id.

488 Id.

its affiliates are also parties).[489] The subsidiary's financial statements should be kept separate and not consolidated with the parent company's financial statements. However, if the financial statements are prepared on a consolidated basis, the parent company also should prepare separate financial statements for each subsidiary. In all likelihood, this will require maintaining separate accounting records for each entity.[490] Inter-company transactions should be kept to a minimum. To the extent that they exist, they should be fully documented (i.e., contracts, board resolutions, notes, etc.) and their terms should be on an arms-length basis. For example, inter-company loans should be evidenced by a note (bearing interest at market rates), collateralized (if appropriate), and authorized by proper corporate action and resolutions.[491] Each entity should be capitalized adequately to the extent required by applicable laws and to the extent necessary to carry on its business. Each entity should maintain distinct and separate employment policies. The parent company should avoid exercising control over the subsidiary's employees. For example, the parent company should not hire or fire the subsidiary's employees and should not regulate the terms of employment for such employees (including expatriate employees).[492] In short, the parent and subsidiary corporations must make every effort to make sure that the subsidiary does not look like a mere sham corporation set up by the parent merely to avoid CERCLA or OPA liability.[493]

Some commentators have recommended that control should not be a factor in the tests for stripping the parent of its limited liability.[494] These critics believe that though this may be contrary to the tort principle of making an actor responsible for its own conduct, the emphasis on control

---

489 Id.

490 Id.

491 Id.

492 Id.

493 John M. Brown, Note & Comment, Parent Corporation's Liability Under Cercla Section 107 For The Environmental Violations Of Their Subsidiaries, 31 Tulsa. L.J at 849 (quoting, Worden CERCLA Liability, at 87).

494 See William J Rands, Domination Of A Subsidiary By A Parent, 32 Ind. L.Rev. at 455.

induces parent corporations to steer clear of health and safety issues affecting its affiliates.[495] These critics believe that this type of undesirable behavior is the opposite of what the law should encourage.[496]

## B. II(d) Liability of Successor Corporations under OPA

Because many ship and facility owning and operating corporations have strengthened and continue to strengthen their viability through mergers, acquisitions, as well as take-overs, a legitimate question normally arises as to the potential environmental liability of the acquiring corporation for the environmental liability of the predecessor corporation. To understand how this issue should be handled by the courts in the OPA context, it is important to discuss how the courts have dealt with it in the CERCLA context. I will recommend that this same approach be used by the courts and environmental law enforcement agencies in OPA cases in the future, however, bearing in mind that CERCLA's section 9607 has a wider liability scope than OPA's more limited liability scope.

By enacting the CERCLA, the US Congress sought to achieve a number of goals. Two of the most prominent goals were the identification and cleanup of inactive hazardous waste disposal sites and the imposition of liability for the costs of remedying hazardous conditions on the parties responsible for creating or contributing to such conditions. As extrapolated earlier, section 9607(a) of CERCLA specifically identifies four categories of persons responsible for the costs associated with remedying a hazardous waste site: (1) current owners and operators of the site; (2) persons owning or operating the site at the time of waste disposal; (3) generators of hazardous wastes that were disposed of at the site; and (4) transporters who selected the area as a disposal site.[497] CERCLA, however, does not expressly impose liability on the corporate successors of these responsible parties for costs associated with their predecessors' hazardous waste operations.

---

495 Id. at 455.

496 Id.

497 42 U.S.C. A. § 9607(a)(1988)

The OPA also does not do so expressly. Consequently, an important issue concerning CERCLA's or OPA's reach is to what extent courts will hold corporate successors jointly and severally liable for the removal costs at a waste site or oil spill site (spill from an OPA facility) where the successor's only connection is through their predecessors. Under OPA, successor corporation have to worry about being held jointly and severally liable for damages for oil pollution as provided in section 2702(b)(2)(A)-(F). The one that they have to worry most about is the damages for injury to, destruction of, loss of, or loss of use of, natural resources, including the reasonable costs of assessing the damage, which is exclusively recoverable by a United States trustee, a State trustee, an Indian tribe trustee, or a foreign trustee.[498] For this particular item of damages a responsible party could end up paying damages for several years after the spill. Payment of removal costs of oil spills can go on for several years depending on the magnitude of the spill and the sensitive or pristine nature of the geographical location of the spill, e.g coral reefs, and high population of endangered species. Within this period of time, another company may have acquired the responsible party if he is a corporation. In this kind of situation, the question then is, should the courts just pretend that no one is liable any more for the payment of the balance of the damages and removal costs, or should the successor corporation pay for the environmental "sins" of its predecessor. It is also possible to have situations where there are multiple chains of successor corporations to the originally liable corporation. In this kind of cases, there will be attempts by different successor corporations within a single chain of liability to sue the immediate predecessor corporation for contribution or indemnity. They would need to do this because of the possibility of being held liable as successor corporations.

Although the majority of circuit courts of appeal increasingly agree that Congress intended CERCLA to create liability for successor corporations for the actions of their predecessor,[499] the courts disagree as to the

498 33 USCA §2702(b)(2)(A).

499 See generally, B.F. Goodrich v. Betkoski, 99 F.3d 505 (2d Cir. 1996); Smith Land & Improvement Corp. v. Celotex Corp., 851 F.2d 86, 92 (3d Cir. 1988), *cert. denied*, 488 U.S. 1029 (1989); United States v. Carolina Transformer Co., 978 F.2d 832, 837-38 (4th

proper source and standard for the application of successor liability. While some courts have chosen to follow the traditional corporate rules of successor liability,[500] other courts have chosen to apply the modern expanded doctrines of successor liability.[501] Immediately below, I will discuss the various theories used to determine when a party to a transaction is a successor corporation and the application of these theories in the CERCLA and OPA context.

### *1. Traditional Rule*

The majority of circuits have used the traditional common law principles as a basis for developing a federal common law rule of successor liability to apply in CERCLA cases. Under the traditional common law rule, the liability of a successor corporation invariably depends upon the type of transaction contemplated by the corporation and its successors.[502]

---

Cir. 1992); Mozingo v. Correct Mfg. Corp., 752 F.2d 168, 175 (5th Cir. 1985); Anspec Co. v. Johnson Controls, Inc. 922 F.2d 1240, 1242 (6th Cir. 1991); City Mgmt. Corp. v. U.S. Chem. Co., Inc. 43 F.3d 244 (6th Cir. 1994); United States v. Mexico Feed & Seed Co., 980 F.2d 478, 487 (8th Cir. 1992); Louisana-Pacific Corp. v. Asarco, Inc., 909 F.2d 1260, 1263 (9th Cir. 1990).

500 See Carolina Transformer Co., 978 F.2d, 832, 837-38 (5th Cir. 1991); Louisiana-Pacific Corp., 909 F.2d, 1260,1263 (9th Cir. 1990); Smith Land & Improvement Corp., 851 F.2d 86, 92 (3d Cir. 1988); Anspec Co., 922 F.2d 1240, 1242 (6th Cir. 1990); City Mgmt. Corp., 43 F.3d 244 (6th Cir. 1994).

501 See Mozingo, 752 F.2d at 175; B.F. Goodrich, 99 F.3d at 505; Mexico Feed & Seed Co., 980 F.2d at 487.

502 See, e.g., Carolina Transformer Co., 978 F.2d at 837-38 (adopting a rule for successor liability which relies on federal common law); Louisiana-Pacific Corp., 909 F.2d at 1263 (explaining that because Congress did not address successor liability, the court must look to other decisions for guidance); Mexico Feed & Seed Co., 980 F.2d at 486 (identifying the doctrine of corporate successor liability as being well-settled since before Blackstone); Smith Land & Improvement Corp., 851 F.2d at 92 (stating that Congress must have expected courts to develop a federal common law under the statute). The courts can develop federal common law when the courts find either: (1) that Congress painted with a broad brush and left it to the courts to "flush out" the statute by fashioning a body of substantive law, or (2) that a federal rule of decision is necessary to protect uniquely federal interests. Texas Indus. v. Radcliff Materials, Inc., 451 U.S. 630, 640 (1981) (stating that "there is, of course, no federal general common law" under Erie R. Co. v. Tompkins,

Generally, four types of transactions give rise to the question of successor liability: (1) statutory consolidation,[503] (2) statutory merger,[504] (3) mere purchase of assets,[505] and (4) mere continuation of the old corporation under a new name.[506] In cases of statutory consolidation and statutory merger, the law of corporate successor liability is well established.[507] The corporation resulting from a statutory consolidation assumes the liability of the constituent corporations.[508] Under statutory merger, the remaining corporation assumes the liability for the corporation that was absorbed, at least to the extent of the assets acquired from that corporation.[509] Similarly, if the corporation merely changes its name, the liabilities of the corporation attach to the corporation under its new name.[510] By con-

304 U.S. 64, 78 (1938), but that the majority of courts may formulate "federal common law" in limited areas). Because CERCLA is silent on the issue of successor liability, the majority of circuits concluded that development of federal common law in this area was necessary to fill the legislative gaps in the statute and to protect the uniquely federal interests of developing a uniform system of enforcement for environmental statutes. See, e.g., Carolina Transformer, 739 F. Supp. at 1038; United States v. Distler, 741 F. Supp. 637, 640 (W.D. Ky. 1990) (finding it unlikely that Congress intended to abrogate the common law doctrine of successor liability); Anspec Co., 922 F.2d at 1242 (finding that reliance on federal common law was unnecessary because the CERCLA statute could be construed to favor successor liability). The Sixth Circuit has, however, rejected the notion that it is permissible for courts to create a federal common law of CERCLA successor liability and, instead, relied on the state successor liability doctrine as the proper source of law in CERCLA actions. City Mgmt. Corp., 43 F.3d at 250 (stating that the liability of a successor corporation for CERCLA obligations is determined by reference to state corporation law, rather than federal common law).

503 Statutory consolidation results when constituent companies are wholly and practically dissolved and a new corporation is created. The transaction must satisfy the requirements of the chartering state's corporate law to be a statutory consolidation. 15 William M. Fletcher, Fletcher Cyclopedia of the Law of Private Corporations § 7117 (perm. ed. rev. vol. 1990 & Supp. 1994) (hereinafter Private Corporations).

504 Statutory merger occurs when one corporation absorbs another, the former remaining in existence and the latter ceasing to exist. Id. §7121.

505 Id. §7103.

506 Id. §7102.

507 Id. §7117

508 Id.§7127.

509 Id. §7121

510 Id. §7103.

trast, the application of successor liability to an asset purchase transaction continues to evolve. An OPA facility might be purchased by another corporation, which may be involved in the same business of exploration, transportation, and refining of crude oil.

The general common law rule for asset purchases was that the purchasing corporation was liable only to the extent expressly assumed in the acquisition agreement.[511] This general rule is based upon the premise that when one corporation sells its assets, it transfers an interest distinct from that of the corporate entity itself.[512] The rule protected a bona fide purchaser from liabilities caused by a predecessor corporation of which the bona fide purchaser was unaware at the time of acquisition.[513] This rule of non- liability for asset purchasers has traditionally been subject to four exceptions: (1) an expressed or implied assumption of liability; (2) a transaction amounting to a consolidation or de facto merger; (3) a transaction that was fraudulent or lacking in good faith; or (4) a mere continuation of the transferor by the transferee.[514]

Although the other exceptions are straightforward, the courts have developed tests for the application of the "de facto merger" exception and the "mere continuation" exception. To determine that an asset purchase is actually a de facto merger, the courts consider the following factors: (1) continuity in management, personnel, location of assets, and shareholders; (2) the seller ceases operations, liquidates, and dissolves as legally and practically as possible; and, (3) the purchasing corporation assumes the obligation of the seller necessary for uninterrupted continuation of business operations.[515]

---

511 Id.

512 Id.

513 See Susan M. Girard, An Expansion of Corporate Successor Liability Under CERCLA: United States v. Distler, 3 Vill. Envtl. L.J. 205, 208 (1992).

514 See United States v. Mexico Feed & Seed Co., 980 F.2d 478, 487 (8th Cir. 1992); United States v. Carolina Transformer Co., 978 F.2d 832, 838 (4th Cir. 1992); Louisiana-Pacific Corp. v. Asarco, Inc., 909 F.2d 1260, 1263 (9th Cir. 1990).

515 See Louisiana- Pacific, 909 F.2d at 1264-65. In applying the "de facto merger" exception in a CERCLA context, the Ninth Circuit in Louisiana-Pacific failed to find that the asset purchase was a de facto merger. Id. at 1265. The Ninth Circuit indicated that the most important factor in the de facto merger exception is continuity of shareholders. Id.

Courts of law consider the following factors in applying the "mere continuation" exception: (1) only one corporation remains after the transaction, and (2) an identity of stock, stock holders, and directors exists between the two corporations.[516] Because the application of the traditional exceptions to successor liability has, in some cases, allowed responsible parties to escape liability, some courts have broadened the general rule. For example, some courts have either modified or recast the "mere continuation" exemption to include an element of public policy.[517]

### *2. Expansion of the "Mere Continuation" Exception*

In the past decade, a number of cases have deviated from the traditional continuation rule. These cases can roughly be divided into two groups.[518] In the first group, the courts have applied the "continuity of enterprise," also referred to as the "substantial continuity" theory, which is an expansion of the traditional "mere continuation" rule of non-liability.[519] The substantial continuation theory evolved in contexts where the public policy goal of providing recovery from tainted assets was paramount to the traditional policy goal of limiting successor liability.[520] The test originated

---

at 1264-65. In Louisiana-Pacific, no continuity of shareholders existed where no shares were exchanged (the entire consideration for the transaction was cash, promissory notes, and debt payment). Id. at 1265.

516 Louisiana-Pacific, 909 F.2d at 1265, Mozingo v. Correct Mfg., 752 F.2d 168, 175 (5th Cir. 1985).

517 EPA Memorandum from Courtney Price, Assistant Administrator for Enforcement and Compliance Monitoring, Liability of Corporate Shareholders and Successor Corporations for Abandoned Sites Under the Comprehensive Environmental Response, Compensation, and Liability Act (CERCLA) (June 13, 1984) (hereinafter EPA Memorandum), (citing N.J. Transp. Dep't v. PSC Resources, Inc., 419 A.2d 1151 (Super. Ct. Law Div. 1980); Knapp v. North Am. Rockwell Corp., 506 F.2d 361 (3d Cir. 1974), cert. denied, 421 U.S. 965 (1975)).

518 See, *e.g.*, Mozingo, 752 F.2d at 175 (listing the two groups of cases that have deviated from the traditional continuation rule).

519 Id. at 175.

520 See United States v. Mexico Feed & Seed Co., 980 F.2d 478, 487- 88 (8th Cir. 1992).

in the 1973 labor case of *Golden State Bottling Co. v. NLRB,*[521] in which the Supreme Court held that where a bona fide purchaser acquires a corporation's assets with knowledge that labor wrongs remain unremedied, it is proper to expand the liability net of those responsible for the wrongs to include the purchaser. Under the "substantial continuity" approach, the courts weigh a number of factors. The factors considered are: (1) retention of the same employees, (2) retention of the same supervisory personnel, (3) retention of the same production facilities and location, (4) production of the same products, (5) retention of the same name, (6) continuity of assets, (7) continuity of general business operations, and (8) whether the successor holds itself out to be a continuation of the previous enterprise.[522] In order to avoid liability under the substantial continuity approach, it is important for successor corporations to avoid any of the eight factors listed above. If they can do that, they will be able to avoid liability for the environmental violations of their predecessor corporation. In other words successor corporations should do the following: (1) retain only their own workers, (2) retain no supervisors of the predecessor except as consultants, (3) retained most of their own production facilities, (4) bring in their own managers,(5) produce their own products and sell to their own clients, (6) ensure that the manufacturing process does not materially change and that their equipment largely remains the same, (7) ensure that corporate name of predecessor is not retained and, (8) avoid taking over predecessor's obligations.[523]

This test differs from the "mere continuation" theory in that it does not require a continuity of shareholders or directors between the predecessor and successor corporations. In 1996, the Second Circuit adopted the substantial continuity test in *B.F. Goodrich v. Betkoski.*[524] In the United

521 414 U.S. 168, 180 (1973).

522 See generally, Atlantic Richfield Co. v. Blosenski, 847 F. Supp. 1261, 1289-91 (E.D. Pa. 1994) (listing the Fourth Circuit's tests for substantial continuity); United States v. Carolina Transformer Co., 978 F.2d 832, 838 (4th Cir. 1992); *see also*, United States v. Distler, 741 F. Supp. 637, 642-43 (W.D. Ky. 1990); Mozingo, 752 F.2d at 175.

523 See Witco Corporation v. Elf Atochem North America, 908 F. Supp. 275 (E.D. Pa. 1995).

524 99 F.3d 505 (2d Cir. 1996).

States District Court case of *State of Washington, et al v. United States of America,*[525] the court held that pursuant to the "substantial continuity" test for successor liability, a corporation was liable under CERCLA as successor of prior operators of shipyard, even absent notice to the corporation of potential liability for contamination. This is because the corporation operated the shipyard doing the same kind of business, using the same name, at the same location, for many of the same customers, and using many of the same assets, managers, executives and employees previously used by the prior operators.

The second group of cases deviating from the traditional continuation doctrine applies the "product line" theory of corporate successor liability created by the California Supreme Court in *Ray v. Alad Corporation.*[526] Under the product line theory, successor liability is appropriate where the successor continues to manufacture the same product line under the same name with no outward indication of any change in ownership of the business.[527] Application of the traditional exemptions depends upon the continuity of corporate structure or ownership. Under this modern theory, liability is imposed if the successor corporation continues essentially the same manufacturing or business operation as its predecessor corporation, even if no continuity of ownership exists between them. This could happen if one company sells one of its refineries to another company, and the successor company carries on the same function of oil refining. It could also apply where a company sells some of its pipelines to another company, and the successor company carries on the same function of pipeline transportation of fuel oil.

The California Supreme Court used the product line test in *Ray* to impose successor liability in a products liability claim arising from a defective product manufactured by the predecessor corporation.[528] In

525 930 F.Supp. 474 (W.D. Wash. 1996).

526 560 P.2d 3 (Cal. 1977).

527 *See* Alfred R. Light, "Product Line" and "Continuity of Enterprise" Theories of Corporate Successor Liability Under CERCLA, 11 Miss. C. L. Rev. 63, 66 n.19 (1990) (citing Ray, 560 P.2d at 3).

528 Ray, 560 P.2d at 3.

Pennsylvania, the courts have applied the product line rule in the product liability context but have refused to extend it to the environmental context. That is why the product line rule has not been applied to CERCLA cases in Pennsylvania courts even though the courts embrace the jurisprudential underpinnings of its application to product liability cases.

One case that articulates the stance of the courts in Pennsylvania is the United States District Court case of *United States of America v. Atlas Minerals And Chemicals, Inc., et al.,*[529] The court held as follows:

> "Third-party plaintiffs have been reluctant to argue that the product line exception has any relevance to a CERCLA action. The court agrees that application of the product line exception is unwarranted in this instance. The product line exception is designed to advance the well-settled premise of strict products liability that "the cost of an injury... may be an overwhelming misfortune to the person injured, and a needless one, for the risk of injury can be insured by the manufacturer and distributed among the public as a cost of doing business." *Ray*, 560 P.2d at 8 (citations omitted). Courts applying the product line exception have reasoned that a corporation that acquires the benefits of its predecessor's good will also acquires the built-in resources to meet its various responsibilities, and should assume the concomitant responsibility of redressing any harm caused by a product that it continues to manufacture. These courts have taken the view that the inherent unfairness of forcing an injured consumer to bear the cost of injury justifies an exceptional extension of traditional successor liability rules. These unique concerns simply are not present in this setting."[530]

In the OPA and CERCLA context, those who sue the responsible party are not direct consumers of the injury causing substance. And the strict tort of product liability is not the same as statutorily imposed environmental liability, even though statutory environmental liability also imposes strict liability.

---

529 Civ. A. No. 91-5118, 1995 WL 510304,*1,*113(E.D. Pa. 1995)

530 Id. at 113.

Although application of the product line doctrine has almost exclusively been in the products liability context, at least the state of New Jersey has applied this test to environmental liability claims. In the Superior Court of New Jersey case of *New Jersey Transp. Dep't v. PSC Resources, Inc*,[531] the court held that where a defendant corporation purchased all the predecessor corporation's assets for less than $100 cash and continued the same operation and waste disposal process alleged to be the source of pollution of a lake, defendant was subject to liability for any claims against it arising from discharge of pollutants, either by defendant or its predecessor, onto property of Department of Transportation. It has however been expressly rejected by the Minnesota Supreme Court in the case of *Niccum v. Hydra Tool Corp.*[532] In this case, the Minnesota Supreme Court held: "The majority of courts which have examined the product line exception have declined the invitation to adopt it.... We agree with this reasoning and decline to adopt the product line exception."[533]

If other courts follow the lead of the New Jersey courts, OPA and CERCLA responsible parties will be held liable under this theory. If however the courts decide to follow the Minnesota and Pennsylvania courts' lead, then it is unlikely that OPA or CERCLA responsible parties will be held liable under this product line theory. That will be good for successor corporation-owners or operators of vessels and facilities, but very bad for government, private and trustee claimants under the OPA and CERCLA. It may only take another oil spill on the scale of the Santa Barbara oil spill (this will be discussed later in this treatise) or the Exxon Valdez oil spill for the courts to begin to embrace the New Jersey approach. But the US Congress can make this happen by amending both CERCLA and OPA to include the product line rule. If they do this, the product line rule will apply to all successor corporations which will be very bad for responsible parties. In the absence of congressional action or judicial activism, it is not likely that the product line rule will be applied to OPA and CERCLA cases by most courts in the United States.

---

531 419 A.2d 1151 (N.J. Super. Ct. Law Div. 1980).

532 438 N.W.2d 96, 100 (Minn.1989).

533 Id. at 100.

### B. II(e) Liability of Dissolved Corporations under the OPA

This would apply in OPA cases involving a dissolved corporation later found to be or designated a responsible party (RP) that owned and operated a vessel or facility from which oil was discharged. Where there is delay in identifying the RP, and the RP's corporation is dissolved during investigations, the dissolved corporations jurisprudence will apply.

In order to properly prognosticate what the possible approach of the courts will be in OPA cases involving dissolved corporations, it would be necessary to borrow from CERCLA jurisprudence on this issue. This will be done here.

The common law held that all actions by and against corporations were abated at dissolution.[534] State legislatures reacted to the stringency of the common law rule by extending the life of a corporation beyond dissolution.[535] These statutes, commonly called survival statutes, usually

534 See 15 William M. Fletcher, Fletcher Cyclopedia of the Law of Private Corporations § 8143 (perm. ed. rev. vol. 1990 & Supp. 1994).

535 See Troy Stremming, The Future Course of Oil and Gas Jurisprudence, Note, Corporate Reincarnation ----CERCLA Liability After Corporate Dissolution, 33 Washburn L.J. 874, 884 (Summer 1994) [Hereinafter Stremming Reincarnation](stating that an examination of the laws of the 50 states reveals that the period of time in which a defunct corporation retains the capacity to sue or be sued while winding up its affairs varies dramatically among the jurisdictions. Also citing as example, Delaware, Del. Code Ann. tit. 8, s 278 (Supp. 1991). Delaware allows claims commenced within three years after dissolution or for such longer period as the Court of Chancery shall in its discretion direct. Id. Florida, Fla. Stat. Ann. s 607.1405 (West 1985) (stating that dissolution does not abate or suspend a claim against the corporation); Georgia, Ga. Code Ann. s 14-2-1407 (Harrison 1988). Georgia allows claims brought within two years after the date of filing of articles of dissolution or five years after the date of publication of intent to dissolve, whichever is later. Id. New Jersey, N.J. Stat. Ann. s 14A:12-9 (West Supp. 1992) (stating corporation may sue and be sued as if dissolution never occurred); New Mexico, N.M. Stat. Ann. s 53-16-24 (Michie 1990) (stating that dissolution does not impair any remedy available for or against corporation); New York, N.Y. Bus. Corp. Law s 1006 (McKinney Supp. 1993) (stating that corporation may sue or be sued as if dissolution never occurred); Ohio, Ohio Rev. Code Ann. s 1701. 88 (Anderson 1991) (allowing any claim existing or pending at dissolution to proceed); Arkansas, Ark. Code Ann. s 4-26-1104(a) (1987) (preserving the existence of the corporation as a legal entity indefinitely); California, Cal. Corp. Code s 2011 (West 1992). California allows any claim against a dissolved corporation to the extent of its undistributed assets. Id. California also allows

provide a corporation with a specific period of time to wind up its affairs.[536] Within this time frame, a corporation can sue and be sued.[537] State statutes governing the dissolution of corporations vary. Under some state statutes, corporations are subject to suit any time after dissolution.[538] In other states, corporations are subject to suit after dissolution only when the act giving rise to the claim occurred before dissolution.[539] Corporate dissolution law does not hinder CERCLA claims when the state statutes are of the two types mentioned above.[540]

Whether a dissolved corporation is subject to a CERCLA claim in a state which allows a suit to be brought for claims only arising before dissolution depends on the interpretation of when a claim arises under CERCLA.[541] Most states, however, have corporate dissolution statutes

---

for claims against shareholders who have received distributed assets, but no claim can exceed the amount of the assets. Id. Colorado, Colo. Rev. Stat. s 7-8-22 (1993) (allowing claims commenced within two years after dissolution); Louisiana, La. Rev. Stat. Ann. s 145 (West 1993) (stating that dissolution does not prevent commencement of a proceeding against corporation); Maine, Me. Rev. Stat. Ann. tit. 13-A, s 1122 (West 1993) (allowing claims commenced within two years after dissolution); Maryland, Md. Code Ann. Corps. & Ass'ns s 3-408 (1992) (stating that the corporation continues to exist to satisfy any obligations); Massachusetts, Mass. Gen. Laws Ann. ch. 156B, s 102 (West 1993) (continuing corporation for three years after dissolution to defend claims); Michigan, Mich. Comp. Laws Ann. s 450.1834 (West 1993) (allowing corporation to sue and be sued as if dissolution had not occurred)).

536 See Troy Stremming, The Future Course of Oil and Gas Jurisprudence, Note, Corporate Reincarnation -CERCLA Liability After Corporate Dissolution, 33 Washburn L.J. at 884.

537 See 15 William M. Fletcher, Fletcher Cyclopedia of the Law of Private Corporations § 8143.

538 See, e.g., Md. Code Ann. Corps. & Ass'ns s 3-408 (1992) (stating that the corporation continues to exist to satisfy any obligations); Mich. Comp. Laws Ann. s 450.1834 (West 1993) (allowing corporation to sue and be sued as if dissolution had not occurred).

539 See, e.g., Cal. Corp. Code s 2011 (West 1992); N.M. Stat. Ann. s 53-16-24 (Michie 1990); Miss. Code Ann. s 79-4-14.05 (Supp. 1991).

540 The only state statutes that conflict with CERCLA claims are those that limit corporate liability to a specific period of time after dissolution. See, e.g., Okla. Stat. Ann. tit. 18, s 1099 (West 1993) (allowing claims commenced within three years after dissolution); S.D. Codified Laws An. s 47-7-50 (1993) (allowing claims commenced within two years after dissolution).

541 See Troy Stremming, The Future Course of Oil and Gas Jurisprudence, Note, Corporate Reincarnation ----CERCLA Liability After Corporate Dissolution, 33

which sever a corporation's capacity to sue or be sued a certain number of years after dissolution.[542] These statutes are the primary obstacle to CERCLA claims brought after the expiration of the statutory time limit. Unlike most state statutes, CERCLA does not possess a limited time period following dissolution after which corporate offenders are relieved of liability. Corporate dissolution statutes in most states are patterned substantially after section 105 of the Model Business Corporation Act (1979 Model Act),[543] which allows for a two-year period after dissolution in which claims may be brought. Some states, however, allow a longer period of time to bring suit.[544] The drafters of the Revised Model Business Corporation Act of 1985 (1985 Model Act) made substantial changes to this provision.[545] Under the 1985 Model Act, a claim against a corporation, known or unknown, must be brought within five years of the commencement of the winding-up period.[546] This variation in the amount of time allowed for a claim illustrates how drafters have attempted to balance the competing interests of claimants and dissolved corporations.[547]

The Official Comment to the 1985 Model Act acknowledges that the two-year winding-up period of the 1979 Model Act was an unfairly brief

Washburn L.J. at 885.

542 See generally H. Henn, Handbook of the Law of Corporations and Other Business Enterprises s 1 (2d ed. 1970).

543 Model Business Corp. Act s 105 (1979).

544 See, e.g., Ill. Rev. Stat. ch. 32, P 12.80 (1988) (providing a five-year period after dissolution in which to bring suit).

545 Revised Model Business Corp. Act s 14.06 (1985) (1985 Model Act ). The 1985 Model Act also addresses pre-dissolution and post-dissolution claims separately. Id. at ss 14.06-14.07. Section 14.06 provides for claims that are known at the time of dissolution. Id. at s 14.06. Section 14.07 provides for claims that are unknown at the time of dissolution. Id. at s 14.07. Section 14.07 requires a dissolved corporation to give notice by publication of its dissolution. Id. If notice is given, no claims may be brought against the dissolved corporation more than five years after the published notice of dissolution. Id. If no published notice is given, however, the claims are barred only by the applicable statute of limitations. Id.

546 1985 Model Act s 14.07.

547 See Troy Stremming, The Future Course of Oil and Gas Jurisprudence, Note, Corporate Reincarnation ----CERCLA Liability After Corporate Dissolution, 33 Washburn L.J. at 885.

period of time for a claimant to bring a lawsuit.[548] Permitting the corporation to live indefinitely, however, either leaves other creditors and shareholders without their share of the assets, or uncertain about the assets they will receive.[549] The drafters of the 1985 Model Act struck what they believed to be a reasonable balance between the competing interests of claimants and dissolved corporations by assigning a five-year winding-up period.[550] Although all states have recognized the importance of protecting claimants from complete abatement of claims upon dissolution, state legislatures differ widely on where the balance between these countervailing interests should be struck.[551] The diversity of state statutes undercuts the intent of CERCLA and OPA.[552] Congress expressed a strong concern that liability be applied uniformly among the states to discourage corporations from locating in states with more lenient liability laws.[553] The variation between liability under CERCLA and liability pursuant to state corporate dissolution law leads to the application of **Rule 17(b) of the Federal Rules of Civil Procedure**.[554]

Two commentators[555] articulated the fundamental questions involved in this issue by stating:

---

548 1985 Model Act s 14.07, comment.

549 Id.

550 Id.

551 For example, Colorado allows a two-year period in which to bring suit. Colo. Rev. Stat. s 7-8-22 (1993). Delaware allows a period of three years to bring suit. Del. Code Ann. tit 8, s 278 (Supp. 1991). Illinois extends the period to five years. Ill. Ann. Stat. ch. 805, P 5, s 1280 (Smith-Hurd Supp. 1992).

552 A primary goal of CERCLA is to hold those responsible for hazardous waste sites liable for cleanup costs. H.R. Rep. No. 1016, 96th Cong., 2d Sess. 1 (1980), reprinted in 1980 U.S.C.C.A.N. 6119. This goal is denied if corporations are relieved of liability for hazardous waste cleanup solely because the damages caused by that corporation do not become apparent until after a specific period of time has passed. Id.

553 See, e.g., 126 Cong. Rec. H11,787 (1980). Representative Florio stated that "to ensure the development of a uniform rule of law, and to discourage businesses dealing in hazardous substances from locating primarily in states with more lenient laws, the bill will encourage the further development of a Federal common law in this area." Id.

554 The courts have the option of following Rule 17(b) and looking to state law to find capacity to sue or be sued, or to reject Rule 17(b) and impose liability regardless of dissolution by finding that CERCLA preempted state law.

555 Joel R. Burcat & Craig P. Wilson, Post-Dissolution Liability Of Corporations And Their Shareholders Under Cercla, 50 Business Lawyer, 1273 (August, 1995).

"Is there life after death for a corporation? The answer, at least under CERCLA, is "maybe." A number of courts have examined the question of post-dissolution liability of corporations under CERCLA and are divided on the question. Courts have disagreed as to whether CERCLA preempts state laws of corporate capacity under Federal Rule of Civil Procedure 17(b) and, where preemption has been found, whether CERCLA permits recovery from dissolved corporations. A related question, which has not been directly addressed by these courts, relates to the potential liability of shareholders of dissolved corporations. The factual scenario assumed.....involves a company desiring to dissolve a wholly-owned subsidiary corporation that has been threatened with a cost-recovery action under section 107 of CERCLA. A company faced with this situation generally should not rush to dissolve the subsidiary under the belief that its potential liability will disappear along with the corporate entity. Such liability is likely to remain so long as the assets of the company have not been distributed, even if the entity itself is legally dissolved."[556]

One of the major issues that has generated a lot of controversy among the various courts in the United States is whether **Rule 17(b) of the Federal Rules of Civil Procedure** governs the capacity of a dissolved corporation to sue or be sued or whether some Federal statutes like CERCLA preempts the provisions of this rule. A discussion of Rule 17(b) is undertaken below.

## B. II(f) History of Rule 17(b) of the Federal Rules of Civil Procedure:

Congress adopted the Federal Rules of Civil Procedure in 1938.[557] Rule 17(b) governs the capacity of a party to sue or be sued.[558] The rule states, in part, that "the capacity of a corporation to sue or be sued shall be determined by the law under which it was organized."[559] Rule 17(b)

556 Id. at 1273-74.

557 28 U.S.C. ss 1-86 (1988).

558 28 U.S.C. s 17(b) (1982).

559 Id.

also provides that, except in exceptional circumstances, the capacity to sue or be sued shall be determined by the law of the state in which the district court is held. Courts have held that Rule 17(b) applies to existing, as well as dissolved corporations.[560] The legislative history of Rule 17(b) does not consider the potential conflict between a federal statute, such as CERCLA, and a corporation's capacity to be sued. The drafters of Rule 17(b) attempted to resolve only two issues: 1) whether forum states could insulate their citizens from suit;[561] and 2) whether incorporating states could insulate a company incorporated within its boundaries while the corporation continued to do business in other states.[562] Unfortunately, the legislative history provides little or no assistance in determining whether CERCLA justifies an override of Rule 17(b).

In *United States v. Sharon Steel Corp.*,[563] the Utah District Court resolved the conflict between CERCLA and Rule 17(b) by applying the balancing approach established in the case of *United States v. Gustin-Bacon Division, Certain-teed Products Corp.*[564] The *Sharon Steel* court noted CERCLA's broad remedial purpose and Congress's expressed intent that those responsible for hazardous waste sites bear the cost of clean-up, "notwithstanding any other provision or rule of law."[565] The court in *Sharon Steel* held that CERCLA clearly expresses Congress' intent to supersede any rule that would otherwise relieve a responsible party from

560 See, e.g., Chicago Title & Trust Co. v. Forty-One Thirty-Six Wilcox Bldg. Corp., 302 U.S. 120 (1937) (state that brought corporation into being determines capacity of dissolved corporation); Johnson v. Helicopter & Airplane Servs. Corp., 404 F. Supp. 726 (D.C. Md. 1975) (unless a corporation establishes an independent existence in a foreign jurisdiction, its capacity to be sued is governed only by the state of its incorporation). See 6 Cyclopedia of Federal Procedure s 21 40 (3d ed. 1981). See also Charles A. Wright & Arthur R. Miller, Federal Practice and Procedure: Civil 2d s 1563, at 738 (1971).

561 Hearings on the Rules of Civil Procedure for District Courts Before the House Comm. on Judiciary, 75th Cong., 1st Sess. 10 (1938) (statement of Dean Charles Clark, Reporter, Advisory Committee on Rules of Civil Procedure).

562 Id. at 9-13, 40-43. Incorporating states could not limit a corporation's capacity to be sued in its courts while that corporation continued to do business in foreign states. Id.

563 681 F. Supp. 1492 (D. Utah 1987).

564 426 F.2d 539 (10th Cir. 1970), *cert. denied,* 400 U.S. 832 (1970).

565 681 F. Supp. at 1496.

liability.[566] The court held, therefore, that Rule 17(b) does not stand in the way of CERCLA preemption.[567]

The conflict between CERCLA and Rule 17(b) creates significant confusion in environmental law cases. Rule 17(b) specifically directs the federal courts to defer to state law when determining the capacity of a corporation to be sued.[568] The express language of Rule 17(b), coupled with the courts' long history of recognizing exclusive state control over state-created corporations, directly contradicts the holding in *Sharon Steel.*

Although this discussion is not meant to be an explication of the non-preemption clause of OPA (there is a separate chapter dedicated to that topic), it is necessary to delve into it briefly for the purposes of the current discussion on liability of successor corporations.

Some commentators have suggested that under OPA, state law will probably govern the question of the liability of dissolved corporations because of the non-preemption clause in the OPA.[569] CERCLA does not have a non-preemption clause, so some commentators feel that its express inclusion in the OPA is a license to states to reduce or increase OPA liability. But I disagree. I believe that this suggestion is not a proper articulation of the non-preemption provision of the OPA. A proper understanding of the non-preemption clause of the OPA cannot be achieved without reading section 2702 (a) (Elements of Liability provision of the OPA) together with section 2718 (Non-preemption section) of the OPA. Section 2702 (a) provides in pertinent part:

"Notwithstanding any other provision or rule of law, and subject to the provisions of this chapter, each responsible party for a vessel or a facility from which oil is discharged, or which poses the substantial threat of a discharge of oil, into or upon the navigable waters or adjoining shorelines or the exclusive economic

566 Id. at 1496.

567 Id.

568 28 U.S.C. app. 17(b) (1988).

569 See Colin De La Rue & Charles B. Anderson, Shipping and The Environment, at 669 (Lloyd's Shipping Law Library 1998).

zone is liable for the removal costs and damages specified in subsection (b) that result from such incident."

Section 2718 provides in pertinent part:

"(a) Preservation of State authorities; Solid Waste Disposal Act Nothing in this chapter or the Act of March 3, 1851 shall--

(1) affect, or be construed or interpreted as preempting, the authority of any State or political subdivision thereof from imposing any additional liability or requirements with respect to--
    (A) the discharge of oil or other pollution by oil within such State; or
    (B) any removal activities in connection with such a discharge; or
(2) affect, or be construed or interpreted to affect or modify in any way the obligations or liabilities of any person under the Solid Waste Disposal Act (42 U.S.C. 6901 et seq.) or State law, including common law."

A closer scrutiny of these provisions will reveal that these provisions were included to ensure that states can add to the OPA liability of a responsible party. These provisions were not included to allow the states to reduce or restrict the liability of responsible parties under the OPA. The provisions of state law relating to liability for removal costs and damages cannot obliterate or obstruct the enforcement of the liability provisions of the OPA. That was why section 2702(a) was included. So, any state law that tries to obliterate the essential purpose of making the polluter pay for an oil spill will be preempted by the OPA, despite the non-preemption language in section 2718 of the OPA. The essential goal of section 2718 is to afford a person suing a responsible party pursuant to state law the opportunity to pursue a state law remedy against a responsible party. In other words, Congress did not want OPA to circumvent the application of state oil pollution laws. If this were not so, states would have the authority to replace OPA's strict liability standard with state negligence standard, which would make it impossible to hold responsible parties liable for oil spills, if the responsible party is found to be non negligent. Thus, where a claimant is suing pursuant to the provisions of the OPA, rather than state law, the provisions of state law on liability for oil pollution cannot trump the provisions of the OPA.

## B. II(g) RECOMMENDATIONS

Congress should revise the OPA to clearly express Congress' intent to supersede any rule that would otherwise relieve a responsible party of OPA liability. This can be accomplished by replacing the "notwithstanding any other provision of rule or law" language in section 2702(a) of the OPA with the following phrase:

"The provisions of this statute shall supersede any laws and all state laws insofar as they may now or hereinafter reduce or eliminate the specific liability of any potentially responsible party under this Act." In order to enhance clarity, section 2718 (a)(2) (Non-preemption) of the OPA should be amended by the addition of the phrase "subject to section 2702(a)."

So, after the amendment, it should read:

"Nothing in this chapter or the Act of March 3, 1851 shall—(2) "subject to section 2702(a)," affect, or be construed or interpreted to affect or modify in any way the obligations or liabilities of any person under the Solid Waste Disposal Act (42 U.S.C. 6901 et seq.) or State law, including common law."

These changes will further the purpose of the OPA. It would ensure that the polluter pays irrespective of whether it is a subsidiary corporation, parent corporation, predecessor corporation, successor corporation or dissolved corporation. This will be possible because state statutes that obliterate the provisions of the OPA will be preempted by these provisions. But state statutes that add to the liability of responsible parties, will be upheld because of the non-preemption clause in section 2718(a)(1)-(2).

## C. DISCHARGE

Statutory provisions:
"§ 2702. Elements of liability

(a) In general

Notwithstanding any other provision or rule of law, and subject to the provisions of this Act, each responsible party for a vessel or a facility from which oil is **discharged, or which poses the substantial threat of a discharge** of oil, into or upon the navigable waters or adjoining shorelines or the exclusive economic zone is liable for the removal costs and damages specified in subsection (b) of this section that result from such incident."[570]

The Act defines discharge as follows: ""discharge" means any emission (other than natural seepage), intentional or unintentional, and includes, but is not limited to, spilling, leaking, pumping, pouring, emitting, emptying, or dumping."[571]

"Discharge" means any emission (other than natural seepage), intentional or unintentional, and includes, but is not limited to, spilling, leaking, pumping, pouring, emitting, emptying, or dumping.[572] The proper understanding of the scope of the word "discharge" as used in OPA is very critical for civil and criminal penalty purposes. A responsible party could pay heavy civil fines or go to jail if its discharge of oil is deemed to be a discharge in law.

Section 1321(b)(3) of the FWPCA originally stated:

"The discharge of oil or hazardous substances into or upon the navigable waters of the United States, adjoining shorelines, or into or upon the waters of the contiguous zone **in harmful quantities** (emphasis mine) as determined by the President under paragraph (4) of this subsection, is **prohibited** (emphasis mine), except (A) in the case of such discharges of oil into the waters of the contiguous zone, where permitted under Article IV of the International Convention for the Prevention of Pollution of the Sea by Oil, 1954, as amended, and (B) where permitted in quantities and at times and locations or under such circumstances or conditions as the President may, by regulation, determine not to be

570 33 USC §2702.

571 33 USC §2701(7).

572 33 USC §2701(7).

harmful. Any regulations issued under this subsection shall be consistent with maritime safety and with maritime and navigation laws and regulations and applicable water quality standards." 33 U.S.C. § 1321(b)(3) (1976) (emphasis added)."[573]

However, the above provision was amended in 1978, to provide that a violation could be founded on the discharge of "**such quantities** [of oil or hazardous substances] **as may be harmful**." (Emphasis mine).[574]

One legal commentator in his commentary on the possible scope of the discharge provision of the OPA stated as follows:

"Judicial interpretations of the Federal Water Pollution Control Act (FWPCA) suggest that not all discharges are covered because of the de minimis exception. Generally however, any oil discharge that leaves a "film or sheen upon or discoloration of the surface of the water... or causes a sludge or emulsion... beneath the surface" and does not fall within the aforementioned exceptions is deemed harmful by EPA regulations and is subject to FWPCA and OPA."[575]

The latest developments in this area of the law appears to contradict the commentator's assertion.[576] The de minimis exception is no longer applicable and the case which the commentator cited as authority has been superceded by statute as decided in *Chevron USA Inc. v. Yost*.[577] As explained above, the US Congress in 1978 had amended the FWPCA and

573 33 USC §1321(b)(3).

574 33 U.S.C. § 1321(b)(3) (Supp. V 1981), Pub. L. No. 95-576 § 1(b)(4), 92 Stat. 2467, 2468.

575 See Lawrence I Kiern, Liability, Compensation, Financial Responsibility Under The Oil Pollution Act of 1990: A Review of The First Decade, 24 Tul. Mar. L.J 481, 510 (Spring 2000) (citing as authority, United States v. Chevron Oil Co., 583 F. 2d 1357, 1360, 1362-63, 1979 AMC 602, 604-05, 609-10 (5th Cir. 1978) (interpreting the EPA's "harmful quantity" requirement).

576 Someone else might draw a different conclusion from the commentator's assertion, but reasonable people can disagree.

577 See. 919 F.2d 27 (5th Cir. 1990), *rehearing and rehearing enbanc denied* (1991).

the relevant language changed from **"in harmful quantities"** to read **"in such quantities as may be harmful."**[578]

The court in the superceded case held:

"At the administrative hearing to determine whether civil penalties should be assessed against the owner, operator or person responsible for discharge of oil, the defendant must be allowed to offer proof that its oil spill was not harmful despite the presence of a "sheen" on the water; for such purpose, "not harmful" means only that the quantity of oil spilled was de minimis, not that a harmful quantity was spilled but fortunately did not actually cause any harm."[579]

In the case of *Orgulf Transport Co. v. United States*,[580] the court found that the plain meaning of the amended statute, **"may be harmful,"** led to a distinctly different conclusion and gave different impact to the oil sheen test. The court found that, according to the amended statutory language, "to be prohibited, **the discharge need not actually be harmful; it is prohibited if it may be harmful."**[581] The court stated, "by regulation EPA has determined that any discharge of oil which creates a sheen **'may be harmful."**[582] Thus any discharge, even a **de**

578 Section 1321(b)(3) of the FWPCA originally stated:

"The discharge of oil or hazardous substances into or upon the navigable waters of the United States, adjoining shorelines, or into or upon the waters of the contiguous zone in harmful quantities as determined by the President under paragraph (4) of this subsection, is prohibited, except (A) in the case of such discharges of oil into the waters of the contiguous zone, where permitted under Article IV of the International Convention for the Prevention of Pollution of the Sea by Oil, 1954, as amended, and (B) where permitted in quantities and at times and locations or under such circumstances or conditions as the President may, by regulation, determine not to be harmful. Any regulations issued under this subsection shall be consistent with maritime safety and with maritime and navigation laws and regulations and applicable water quality standards." 33 U.S.C. § 1321(b)(3) (1976) (emphasis added). This provision was amended in 1978, Pub. L. No. 95-576 § 1(b)(4), 92 Stat. 2467, 2468, to provide that a violation could be founded on the discharge of "such quantities [of oil or hazardous substances] as may be harmful." 33 U.S.C. § 1321(b)(3) (Supp. V 1981).

579 United States v. Chevron, 583 F. 2d at 1357.

580 711 F.Supp. 344, 347 (W.D.Ky.1989)).

581 *Orgulf Transport Co.*, 711 F.Supp. at 347.

582 Id. at 347.

**minimis one, will be held to be in violation of the statute if it causes an oil sheen.**[583]

According to this court, the statute no longer requires harmfulness. The court pointed out that the amended language of section 311 was "intended to broaden the reach of the section,"[584] and cited cases to the effect that "there appears to be nothing in the statute or the legislative history of the 1978 amendment indicating that Congress intended the operation of the new standard to be conditioned on the promulgation of new regulations."[585] Thus, for this district court, even de minimis oil spills that cause a sheen upon the water are forbidden by the FWPCA and no longer creates a *Chevron* rebuttable presumption of harmfulness.[586] The *Orgulf* court stated further:

> "Under this broadened statute, the Coast Guard was well within its delegated authority in concluding that a spill presumed to be harmful under the old statute was also a spill which may be harmful under the new. Under these circumstances the court is not required to give the old regulatory language the same interpretation required by the original statute.... The Coast Guard was well within the scope of authority delegated in Congress' amendment in finding *Orgulf* in violation of Section 311."[587]

---

583 Id.

584 Id. at 348.

585 Id. (citing with approval, Healy Tibbitts, 713 F.2d 1469, 1477 (9th Cir. 1983)). Note that the amendment to § 311 of the FWPCA was requested by the EPA because of an injunction that threatened to paralyze EPA's hazardous spill program. 124 CONG. REC. 37,680 (1978). Senator Stafford, a member of the Senate Committee on Environmental and Public Works, stated as follows:

"The proposal clarifies the authority of the administrator in designating hazardous pollutants and determining harmful quantities of such pollutants. The amendment makes it clear that the determination of harmful quantities does not require an assessment of actual harm in the variety of circumstances in which such substances might be discharged. Rather, the determination is based on the administrator's judgment of what quantity may be harmful as a result of its chemical properties, not the circumstances of its release." 124 CONG. REC. 37,683 (1978).

586 *Orgulf Transport Co.*, 711 F.Supp. at 349.

587 711 F.Supp. at 348.

The oil sheen test now stands as a dispositive indicator of pollution. As stated by the Orgulf court:

"EPA has carefully reviewed effects of the recent scientific literature on environmental oil pollution... EPA believes that the literature clearly demonstrates that discharges of small quantities of oil cause environmental harm.... Many types of adverse effects from oil have been extensively documented, proving harmful effects from oil spills and chronic pollution.... Evidence from reviews of laboratory studies further demonstrates that very small amounts of oil, e.g., less than 1 mg/L (1 ppm), can have lethal and sublethal effects on a wide variety of organisms."[588]

The *Orgulf* court's broadening of the oil sheen test's application seems congruent with the federal policies and public sentiment that seek to prohibit oil spills completely. The *Orgulf* decision received a warm endorsement in the case of *Chevron v. Yost.*[589] The court in the *Chevron v. Yost* case, in its rejection of its twelve year old decision in *United States v. Chevron*, held:

"That Congress could have prohibited all discharges through a specific declaration and chose not to do so does not negate the effect of the amendment, a common sense reading of which illustrates that Congress chose to prohibit discharges which might not be harmful. Whether a spill resulted in actual harm to the environment is irrelevant to the determination of whether Section 311's prohibition of discharges of oil in quantities which may be harmful has been violated. The only pertinent inquiry is whether the spill was in a quantity which may be harmful as determined by the EPA. Because EPA has determined that a spill of oil which creates a sheen is a quantity which 'may be harmful,' such a spill is subject to the penalty provisions of 33 U.S.C. § 1321 and 40 CFR Part 110.3. This statement accords with our view that the 1978 amendments gave the EPA broader authority to regulate small spills. With these changed circumstances, we conclude that *Chevron I* does not control this case."[590]

---

588 Id. at 350 (citing 52 Fed. Reg. 10712, 10716 (1985))

589 See 919 F.2d 27 (5th Cir. 1990), *rehearing and rehearing enbanc denied* (1991).

590 919 F.2d at 30-31 (citing with approval, Orgulf Transport Co. v. United States, 711 F.Supp. 344, 347 (W.D.Ky.1989)).

This court clearly rejected the validity and continued application of its earlier decision in *Chevron 1* which the commentator relied on.

## D. EXCLUDED DISCHARGES – 33 USC §2702(c).

The OPA specifically provides that its provisions do not apply to any discharge - (1)permitted by a permit issued under Federal, State, or local law; (2) from a public vessel; or (3) from an onshore facility which is subject to the Trans-Alaska Pipeline Authorization Act (43 U.S.C. 1651 et seq.).[591] The OPA defines public vessel as a vessel owned or bareboat chartered and operated by the United States, or by a State or political subdivision thereof, or by a foreign nation, except when the vessel is engaged in commerce. This means that naval vessels engaged in naval activities and non-commercial activities are totally exempt from liability. This means that if there are two vessels jointly and severally responsible for an oil spill and one is government owned and the other is not government owned, that non-government owned vessel would have to bear the entire liability alone and cannot seek contribution from the government unless the government waives sovereign immunity. If a government owned vessel is bareboat chartered to a private party for commercial purposes both the government and the bareboat charterer are jointly and severally liable because the vessel would not qualify as public vessel as defined by the statute.

Generally, private vessels chartered to the United States government have been characterized as public vessels under the Public Vessels Act ("PVA").[592] Government owned vessels operated by private parties for public purposes also are considered public vessels under the PVA.[593] In

591 33 USC §2702(c)

592 46 U.S.C.App. §§ 781, et seq., see also, Blanco v. United States, 775 F.2d 53, 59-60 (2d. Cir.1985).

593 See Nelsen v. Research Corp. of University of Hawaii, 752 F.Supp. 350, 353 (D.Hawaii 1990) (considering a U.S. research vessel chartered to a university as a PVA public vessel where the university did not acquire any ownership interest and performed research under contract with the United States).

*Santos v. RCA Service Co* [594] it was held that U.S. Navy vessel operated by a private contractor for public purpose is PVA public vessel.

The court in the case of International Maritime Carriers v. The Oil Spill Liability Trust Fund,[595] refused to adjudicate the issue of whether USNS SEALIFT ATLANTIC, a government owned vessel from which oil was spilled is a public vessel. The USNS SEALIFT ATLANTIC was operated by IMC, a private contractor, under a contract with the Navy.[596] IMC brought this action against the Oil Spill Liability Trust Fund (Fund or OSLTF), challenging the Fund's denial of its claim for reimbursement of removal costs incurred under OPA. In its final argument for dismissal for failure to state a claim, the Oil Spill Liability Trust Fund (Fund) characterized the USNS SEALIFT ATLANTIC as a "public vessel."[597] Because discharges from public vessels are expressly excluded from the OPA cost recovery scheme in 33 U.S.C. § 2702(c)(2), the Fund argued that the OPA cannot apply to IMC's claims. Because the court denied IMC's summary judgment motion, the court refused to decide whether the Fund's public vessel argument warranted dismissal.[598]

*Examining what OPA means by "Substantial Threat of A Discharge of Oil."*

The OSLTF or the Fund may be used to respond to a substantial threat of a discharge to prevent, minimize, or mitigate oil pollution from such an. Federal On-Scene Coordinators (FOSC) are the US Coast Guard officers who have been delegated the authority to ensure effective and immediate removal of a discharge, and mitigate or prevent a substantial threat

594 603 F.Supp. 943, 946 (E.D.La.1985).

595 See *IMC*, 903 F.Supp. 1097 (S.D. Tex. 1994).

596 903 F. Supp. at 1104.

597 Id. at 1104.

598 "The Navy, through Military Sealift Command (MSC), contends that the SEALIFT Class tankers, including the SEALIFT ATLANTIC, are public [vessels]. The [United States Coast Guard] USCG's position is that these ships are not public [vessels] under Titles 33 and 46.... I intend to remain silent on the public [vessel] issue, by default taking the USCG position, and reject the claim on reconsideration." IMC, id. at 1104.

of a discharge of oil or hazardous substance release into U.S. surface water.[599] Each Federal-On-Scene Coordinator (FOSC) has the authority to determine whether particular situations present substantial threats of discharge.

1. In making a determination to respond to a substantial threat of discharge, the FOSC should consider the following factors in the context of the overall situation:
   a. The likelihood of a discharge under the circumstances; that the situation presents an unacceptable probability that a discharge will occur without FOSC intervention.[600]
   b. The proximity to navigable waters, the quantity of oil which may be discharged, and the lack of barriers to stop the oil from flowing to the water indicate that a spill will impact navigable waters.[601]
   c. The flow path to surface waters (for land based discharges) as indicated by slope, soil permeability, water table, storm drains, curtain drains, natural or manufactured conduits, or the like.[602]
   d. The condition of or damage to the source, and the environmental factors or weather which may change the conditions, indicate that a spill will occur.
   e. The potential impact of a discharge on the particular environment, including proximity to environmentally sensitive areas, populous areas, etc.
   f. That action must be taken quickly to prevent a spill.[603]

---

599 See U.S. Coast Guard Federal On Scene Coordinator (FOSC), Finance and Resource Management Field Guide, at 17. <http://www.uscg.mil/d1/units/msobos/resources/FFARMGuide.pdf>

600 The US Coast Guard National Pollution Fund Center, Technical Operating Procedures for Determining Removal Costs Under The Oil Pollution Act of 1990, 118 (January 16, 1996).

601 Id. at 118.

602 Id.

603 Id.

2. The FOSC must also document the factors considered and the basis for the decision that a specific situation presented a substantial threat of discharge[604]

## E. GEOGRAPHIC

Statutory provisions:
"§ 2702. Elements of liability

(a) In general

Notwithstanding any other provision or rule of law, and subject to the provisions of this Act, each responsible party for a vessel or a facility from which oil is discharged, or which poses the substantial threat of a discharge of oil, into or upon the **navigable waters or adjoining shorelines or the exclusive economic zone** is liable for the removal costs and damages specified in subsection (b) of this section that result from such incident."[605]
Under the Act, "**"navigable waters"** means the waters of the United States, including the territorial sea."[606]

Likewise, the Act defines the exclusive economic zone as follows:
"**"exclusive economic zone"** means the zone established by Presidential Proclamation Numbered 5030, dated March 10, 1983, including the ocean waters of the areas referred to as "eastern special areas" in Article 3(1) of the Agreement between the United States of America and the Union of Soviet Socialist Republics on the Maritime Boundary, signed June 1, 1990."[607]

604 Id. at 118.
605 33 USC §2702.
606 33 USC §2701(21).
607 33 USC §2701(8).

*Meaning of Navigable Waters Under The OPA*

The Supreme Court has held that the test for whether a body of water is navigable is whether the body of water "in its natural state, is used, or capable of being used, as a highway for commerce, over which trade and travel are or may be conducted in the customary modes of trade and travel in the water."[608] The U.S. Environmental Protection Agency interprets "navigable waters" under the OPA to mean the same as "navigable waters" under the Clean Water Act. According to the EPA:

"What are navigable waters?
"Navigable waters" are broadly defined under the Clean Water Act and Oil Pollution Act to include all waters that are used in interstate or foreign commerce, all interstate waters including wetlands, and all intrastate waters, such as lakes, rivers, streams, wetlands, sloughs, prairie potholes, wet meadows, playa lakes, or natural ponds. Essentially, the term navigable waters refers to any natural surface water in the U.S."[609]

Based on the EPA statement above, the utility and importance of FWPCA or CWA jurisprudence to this issue cannot be overemphasized.

Section 2701 of the OPA provides:

"Notwithstanding any other provision or rule of law, and subject to the provisions of this chapter, each responsible party for a vessel or a facility from which oil is discharged, or which poses the substantial threat of a discharge of oil, into or upon the navigable waters or adjoining shorelines or the exclusive economic zone is liable for the removal costs and damages specified in subsection (b) that result from such incident."

608 Economy Light & Power Co. v. United States, 256 U.S. 113, 121-22, 41 S.Ct. 409, 65 L.Ed. 847 (1921).

609 EPA Emergency Response Program: Oil Spill Prevention, Preparedness & Response (http://www.epa.gov/oilspill/faqs/termfaqs.htm).

This provision of OPA is very important because it can make a world of difference between OPA liability and freedom or exculpation from OPA liability for a Responsible Party (RP). Each phrase in this provision is very important for OPA liability purposes. If the discharge occurs in any one of these three locations, OPA liability will be imposed: (1) Navigable waters, (2) adjoining shorelines, and (3) exclusive economic zone. This subpart will focus on the navigable waters aspect of the above provision.

Section 2701(21) of the OPA defines navigable waters as the "waters of the United States," including the territorial sea. Although the term waters of the United States is not defined by OPA we can get some guidance from the EPA regulations defining the term for FWPCA enforcement purposes. Since the CWA or FWPCA's treatment of the term navigable waters is applicable to OPA it will provide some guidance for us. The EPA regulations[610] provide as follows:

"(s) The term "waters of the United States" means:
(1) All waters which are currently used, or were used in the past, or may be susceptible to use in interstate or foreign commerce, including all waters which are subject to the ebb and flow of the tide; (2) All interstate waters including interstate wetlands; (3) All other waters such as intrastate lakes, rivers, streams (including intermittent streams), mudflats, sandflats, wetlands, sloughs, prairie potholes, wet meadows, playa lakes, or natural ponds, the use, degradation or destruction of which could affect interstate or foreign commerce including any such waters:
(i) Which are or could be used by interstate or foreign travelers for recreational or other purposes; or (ii) From which fish or shellfish are or could be taken and sold in interstate or foreign commerce; or (iii) Which are used or could be used for industrial purposes by industries in interstate commerce; (4) All impoundments of waters otherwise defined as waters of the United States under this definition; (5) Tributaries of waters identified in paragraphs (1) through (4) of this section; (6) The territorial sea; (7) Wetlands adjacent to waters (other than waters that are themselves wetlands) identified in paragraphs (s)(1)-(6) of this section; waste treatment systems, including treatment ponds or lagoons

610 40 CFR §230.3(s).

designed to meet the requirements of CWA (other than cooling ponds as defined in 40 CFR 423.11(m) which also meet the criteria of this definition) are not waters of the United States. Waters of the United States do not include prior converted cropland. Notwithstanding the determination of an area's status as prior converted cropland by any other federal agency, for the purposes of the Clean Water Act, the final authority regarding Clean Water Act jurisdiction remains with EPA."[611]

A United States District Court in Massachusetts in its interpretation of the term navigable waters took note of the provisions of the EPA regulations reproduced above and held that "waters of the United States" describes, in addition to what is obviously navigable, all waters and wetlands that are not navigable or even directly connected to navigable water.[612] It agreed with two cases cited by the plaintiff, the United States Government in the case. The two cases, *United States v. Riverside Bayview Homes, Inc.*,[613] and *Village of Oconomowoc Lake v. Dayton Hudson Corp.*,[614] both describe the term "waters of the United States" as used in the CWA or FWPCA, under very broad terms. The court concluded that because the same language has been interpreted under the Clean Water Act and the EPA considers that term encompasses all waters, "waters of the United States" as used in the OPA properly means all waters and wetlands, not necessarily navigable waters.[615]

The EPA regulations defines "wetlands" as "those areas that are inundated or saturated by surface or ground water at a frequency and duration sufficient to support, and that under normal circumstances do support, a prevalence of vegetation typically adapted for life in saturated soil conditions. Wetlands generally include swamps, marshes, bogs and similar areas."[616]

611 40 CFR §230.3(s).

612 See United States v. George Mizhir, 106 F.Supp.2d 124, 125 (D. Mass. 2000).

613 474 U.S. 121, 132-39, 106 S.Ct. 455, 88 L.Ed.2d 419 (1985).

614 24 F.3d 962, 964-65 (7th Cir.1994).

615 United States v. George Mizhir, 106 F.Supp.2d at 125.

616 40 CFR §230.3(t).

One important distinction between navigable waters jurisprudence for OPA liability and navigable waters jurisprudence for admiralty jurisdiction is that for OPA suits, a more liberal definition of navigable waters is used. For OPA suits, OPA confers subject matter jurisdiction on all Federal District courts. And also allows for concurrent state court jurisdiction. So the requirement of "navigable waters" in the maritime context which is a sine qua non for Federal District Court admiralty jurisdiction is not a requirement for Federal District court jurisdiction in OPA suits, because in OPA suits federal district courts and state courts have been conferred with subject matter jurisdiction.[617] Thus, in the OPA context, the question of "navigable waters" only goes to the issue of the liability of the RP, while in the maritime context, it goes to the issue of the jurisdiction of the Federal District courts.

Relatively few cases have addressed the issue of what navigable waters are for OPA liability. But the cases that have been decided so far point towards a very liberal and landward trend for the finding of navigable waters. One notable case in which this trend of going inland was exhibited is *Avitts v. Amoco Production Co.*[618] The *Avitts* plaintiffs brought claims against Amoco Production under theories of nuisance, trespass, negligence, and breach of contract, in connection with the operation of an active inland oil field.[619] The plaintiffs contended that the defendant's operations contaminated the surface of their properties, allowing oil, saltwater, and waste products to spill onto the surface and seep into the aquifer serving as a freshwater supply.[620] The court reviewed the OPA and found that it did extend to the inland oilfield.[621] Thus OPA applied to oil spills into non-navigable waters that flow into navigable waters. In the view of the court, any other result would undercut Congress's purpose in OPA

617 33 USCA §2717(b)-(c).

618 840 F. Supp. 1116 (S.D. Tex 1994), *vacated on other grounds*, 53 F.3d 690 (5th Cir. 1995). Avitts was vacated as a result of jurisdictional problems, not in relation to the OPA '90 issues presented; however, the Fifth Circuit did question the applicability of OPA '90 to the facts of the case.

619 *Avitts*, 840 F. Supp. at 1117-18.

620 Id. at 1118.

621 Id. at 1122.

of addressing the national danger created by oil spills. According to the *Avitts* court, the facility need not be directly adjacent to navigable waters; the fact that the discharging facility was in the drainage basin for a lake that was part of navigable waters was enough. The court relied on the evidence that showed that the oilfield in question was crossed by two creeks, flowing directly into Clear Lake, a navigable bay ultimately connected to the Gulf of Mexico.[622] The plaintiffs had not shown that oil had flowed into the navigable waters of the United States, but based on section 2702(a) of OPA the court had previously found that the operation posed a substantial threat of discharging oil into the waterways, both through surface and subsurface leakage. In addition to extending OPA in the facts presented in *Avitts*, the court conceded that as one moved further inland, utilization of the substantial threat standard would become "too remote a threat to bring the action within the strictures of the OPA."[623] What this case shows is that the "substantial threat" language in section 2702(a) will in many OPA cases make it very easy for the court to find that the oil was discharged into navigable waters. The decision of the *Avitts* court is in agreement with FWPCA or CWA jurisprudence. For instance in the FWPCA case of *United States v. Earth Sciences, Inc.*,[624] the 10th Circuit Court of Appeals stated:

"It is argued that the creek is not a navigable water subject to regulation under the Clean Water Act. At first blush that argument appears to be plausible. It was stipulated by the parties that the creek is not navigable in fact nor is

622 Id.

623 Avitts, 840 F. Supp. at 1122. See also, Solid Waste Agency of Northern Cook County v. United States Army Corps of Engineers, 121 S.Ct. 675, 682 (2001) (holding: "[a]lthough respondents cite some legislative history showing Congress' recognition of the Corps' assertion of jurisdiction over "isolated waters," as we explained in Riverside Bayview Homes, "[i]n both Chambers, debate on the proposals to narrow the definition of navigable waters centered largely on the issue of wetlands preservation.". Beyond Congress' desire to regulate wetlands adjacent to "navigable waters," respondents point us to no persuasive evidence that the House bill was proposed in response to the Corps' claim of jurisdiction over nonnavigable, isolated, intrastate waters or that its failure indicated congressional acquiescence to such jurisdiction.")

624 599 F.2d 368 (10th Cir.1979).

it used to transport any goods or materials. It is located entirely in Costillo County, Colorado, and below this operation are two reservoirs which collect all of the stream flow to be used for recreation and agricultural irrigation. The defendant would have us review the Clean Water Act in terms of the traditional meaning of "navigable waters," as construed in the line of cases beginning with *The Daniel Ball*, 77 U.S.(10 Wall.) 557, 19 L.Ed. 999 (1870). But the conference committee resolving differences between the Senate and House versions of the Clean Water Act... eliminated the word "navigable" from in front of "waters" in the House bill; thus "navigable waters" was defined as "the waters of the United States, including the territorial seas." The conference report noted the change and declared the term should "be given the broadest possible constitutional interpretation unencumbered by agency determinations which have been made or may be made for administrative purposes." Sen. Conf.Rep. No. 92--1236, 92nd Cong., 2d Sess., reprinted in [1972] U.S.Code Cong. & Admin.News pp. 3668, 3776, 3822. It is stipulated by the parties that the stream supports trout and some beaver, the water collected in the reservoir is used for agricultural irrigation, and the resulting products are sold in interstate commerce. It seems clear Congress intended to regulate discharges made into every creek; stream, river or body of water that in any way may affect interstate commerce. Every court to discuss the issue has used a commerce power approach and agreed upon that interpretation.

... [The defendant] argues the [creek] does not provide a very significant link in the chain of interstate commerce. The stipulation of facts indicates at least some interstate impact from this stream and that is all that is necessary under the [Clean Water Act]. We hold the [creek] is covered by the [Clean Water Act's] definition of navigable waters."[625]

Another case illustrating this landward trend is *Sun Pipeline v. Conewago Contractors, Inc.*,[626] involving the leakage of oil from a six inch petroleum pipeline belonging to the plaintiff. The spill occurred when the defendant struck a pipeline while digging a golf course

625 599 F.2d at 374-75.

626 No. 93-1995, 1994 U.S. Dist. LEXIS 14070 (M.D. Pa. Aug. 22, 1994).

drainage ditch.[627] This allowed 285.71 barrels (12,000 gallons) of petroleum to spout out onto the surrounding land.[628] The plaintiff made allegations under OPA as a basis for recovery, in addition to common law trespass.[629] The defendant contended that OPA's section 2701(8) & (21) shows that OPA was meant to address spills which occurred on the navigable waters of the United States, adjoining shorelines, or the Exclusive Economic Zone. The court took notice of the fact that the site was not adjacent to any shore or shoreline, or within the Exclusive Economic Zone.[630] The only remaining basis of liability was the allegation that this spill would impact the navigable waters of the United States.[631] The court, citing the *Avitts* decision, reasoned that if a spill on an inland area has the proximity to pose the substantial threat of eventually flowing into navigable waters from an adjacent shoreline, through groundwater or some other hydrologic process, OPA would arguably apply.[632] The court reviewed case law under the FWPCA for additional guidance.[633] The definition of "navigable waters of the United States" according to the FWPCA is the same as in OPA.[634]

The *Sun Pipeline* court examined cases under the FWPCA in which wetlands were found to be areas subject to application of that statute, under the notion that contaminants introduced into wetlands will transmigrate or percolate into aquifers, and eventually lead to the navigable waters of the United States.[635] The court observed that several courts have given similarly expansive interpretations to the term "navigable waters," including non-navigable creeks, dry arroyos,[636] tributary

627 Sun Pipeline Co., 1994 U.S. Dist. LEXIS 14070, at *1.

628 Id. at *1.

629 Id. at *2.

630 Id at *5.

631 Id.

632 Id. at *6.

633 Id. at *9.

634 33 U.S.C. § 2701(21).

635 United States v. Riverside Bayview Homes, 474 U.S. 1 (1985).

636 Quivira Mining Co. v. United States, 765 F.2d 126, 130 (10th Cir. 1985); United States v. Phelps Dodge Corp., 391 F. Supp. 1181, 1187 (D. Ariz. 1975).

creeks,[637] and ground water with a hydrological connection to the surface waters.[638]

The *Sun Pipeline* court noted that the key distinction between the Clean Water Act and OPA '90 was one of policy and intent.[639] The Clean Water Act was passed with the goal of remedying pollution within all the nation's waterways,[640] however the Oil Pollution Act of 1990 was directed to the marine environment.[641] The court examined the legislative history of OPA and found that Congress had emphasized the marine area, whereas inland waters definitely took a secondary position.[642] The legislative history of OPA includes statements such as:

> *"This new law, the Oil Pollution Act, is the latest in what I believe is an impressive record of significant marine environmental protection laws which have been developed in the Merchant Marine and Fisheries Committee and approved by this Congress."* [643] *The Oil Pollution Act will provide the assurance we need for the future that we can keep our bays and harbors clean, our wildlife safe, and our beaches free of oil."*[644] *The primary goal of this legislation is to prevent oil spills from occurring in the future. We must make every effort to ensure that accidents like the Exxon Valdez and the Mega Borg do not happen again and that our waterways are free from the ravages of oil."* [645]

OPA was enacted to complement and augment its predecessor federal legislation like the FWPCA.[646] This suggested broad application in

637 *Sun Pipeline Co.*, 1994 U.S. Dist. LEXIS 14070, at *14.

638 McClellan Ecological Seepage v. Weinberger, 707 F. Supp. 1182, 1193-94 (E.D. Cal. 1988).

639 *Sun Pipeline Co.*, 1994 U.S. Dist. LEXIS 14070, at * 17-18.

640 Id. at *17.

641 Id.

642 Id. at 18-32.

643 7136 Cong.Rec. E3021-03 (Jones, W.).

644 8136 Cong.Rec. H6942, (Schneider, H.).

645 9136 Cong.Rec. H6933-02, H6940 (Fields, J.).

646 Sun Pipeline Co., 1994 U.S. Dist. LEXIS 14070, at *32.

coastal shorelines and waterways for OPA.[647] The *Sun Pipeline* court compared OPA's broad application with other statutes directed toward more site-specific problems, such as the Outercontinental Shelf Lands Act and amendments, the Trans-Alaska Pipeline Authorization Act, and the Deepwater Port Act. The court concluded that on the basis of the legislative history of OPA and the wording of the statute, some link, indirect or direct, to U.S. coastal or inland waterways must be demonstrated to invoke the protections of OPA.[648] While the discharge, or threat of discharge, may take place neither in nor over a body of water, there must be some threat that the oil will thereafter make its way into the statutory delineated waterways.[649] The court held that the plaintiffs had not made a specific enough allegation that this migratory pollution would indeed occur.[650] The court granted leave to the plaintiffs to amend the complaint in order to more clearly prove the existence of a proper OPA cause of action.[651]

Based on the *Sun Pipeline* and *Avitts* decisions, it appears that the courts may impose OPA liability to facilities located a little more than a few miles inland, but not those located hundreds of miles inland. For instance in the case of *Rice v. Harken Exploration*[652] the District Court for the Northern District of Texas held that because the Panhandle of Texas is hundreds of miles from costal waters or ocean beaches, discharges of oil and salt water onto land in the Panhandle of Texas are not the type of oil and waste-water spills targeted by the OPA. The court further held that while pollution into Big Creek and the tributaries of Big Creek, into groundwater under Plaintiffs' land, and perhaps eventually into the Canadian River may affect interstate commerce, plaintiffs had no Oil Pollution Act cause of action under the facts of the case.[653] In its

647 Id.

648 Id. at *6.

649 Id. at *37.

650 Id.

651 Id. at *40-41.

652 89 F. Supp.2d 820, 827 (N.D. Tex. 1999).

653 Id. at 827.

affirmation of the decision of the District court, the Fifth Circuit Court of Appeals pointed out that the discharges for which the OPA imposes liability are those into or upon the navigable waters.[654] It pointed out that "navigable waters" do not include groundwater. The court reasoned that "[i]t would be an unwarranted expansion of the OPA to conclude that a discharge onto dry land, some of which eventually reaches groundwater and some of the latter of which still later may reach navigable waters, all by gradual, natural seepage, is the equivalent of a "discharge" "into or upon the navigable waters."[655]

This limitation on the scope of 'navigable waters' under the FWPCA was recently reaffirmed by the Supreme Court in *Solid Waste Agency of Northern Cook County v. United States Army Corps of Engineers.*[656] In this case, a consortium of municipalities sued the United States Army Corps of Engineers, challenging the Corps' exercise of jurisdiction over abandoned sand and gravel pit on which the consortium planned to develop disposal site for non-hazardous solid waste and denial of a Clean Water Act (CWA) or FWPCA permit for that purpose.[657] The Supreme Court held that the Army Corps of Engineers regulation defining "waters of the United States" to include "waters such as intrastate lakes, rivers, streams (including intermittent streams), mudflats, sandflats, wetlands, sloughs, prairie potholes, wet meadows, playa lakes, or natural ponds, the use, degradation, or destruction of which could affect interstate or foreign commerce" exceeded the scope of the Corps' regulatory power under the CWA or FWPCA as applied to the petitioner's land under a regulation known as the "Migratory Bird Rule."[658] This was an attempt by the Army Corps of Engineers to expand the meaning of 'navigable waters' under the "Migratory Bird Rule," encapsulated in 33 CFR § 328.3(a)(3).[659] So, the decision must be restricted to its facts. It is not a new restriction on the landward trend, but rather a nullification of

---

654 See 250 F.3d 264, 271 (5th Cir. 2001).

655 250 F.3d at 271.

656 121 S.Ct. 675 (2001) (Hereinafter SWANCC).

657 Id. at 675.

658 See id. at 678 (quoting 33 C.F.R. § 328.3(a)(3)).

659 U.S. v. Interstate General Co., 152 F.Supp.2d 843, 847 (D. Maryland 2001).

a government agency's regulatory attempt to further expand the landward trend.[660] The overly broad "Migratory Bird Rule" states that the CWA or the FWPCA covers any intrastate waters which could be used by migrating birds that cross state lines or which could be used to irrigate crops sold in interstate commerce.[661]

The case involved several ponds that had formed in pits that were originally part of the sand and gravel mining operation.[662] The Court refused to interpret the FWPCA as extending a government agency's regulatory power to the limits of the Commerce Clause, and held that the application of the FWPCA to the petitioner's land exceeded the authority granted to the Corps under the FWPCA.[663] The Supreme Court distinguished *Riverside Bayview Homes* on the ground that in that case the wetlands in question were adjacent to a body of open water that was actually navigable.[664] The court said:

"We said in Riverside Bayview Homes that the word 'navigable' in the statute was of 'limited effect' and went on to hold that § 404(a) extended to nonnavigable wetlands adjacent to open waters. But it is one thing to give a word a limited meaning and quite another to give it no effect whatever."

According to the Fifth Circuit in *Rice v. Harken Exploration Co.*,[665] under *Solid Waste Agency*, it appears that a body of water is subject to

660 See id at 849 (holding that the SWANCC case was a narrow holding dealing with the Migratory Bird Rule and 33 CFR § 328.3(a)(3)). See also, Headwaters Inc. v. Talent Irrigation District, 243 F.3d 526, 533 (9th Cir. 2001) (holding that unlike in SWANCC, "the irrigation canals in this case are not "isolated waters" such as those that the Court concluded were outside the jurisdiction of the Clean Water Act. Because the canals receive water from natural streams and lakes, and divert water to streams and creeks, they are connected as tributaries to other "waters of the United States.")

661 See 51 Fed.Reg. 41217.

662 *Solid Waste Agency*, 121 S.Ct. at 678.

663 Solid Waste Agency, 121 S.Ct. at 684.

664 Id. at 682-83.

665 *Rice*, 250 F.3d 264, 269.

regulation under the FWPCA if the body of water is actually navigable or is adjacent to an open body of navigable water.[666]

Also, in *Harris v. Oil Reclaiming Co.*,[667] it was held that alleged discharge of relatively limited amount of oil on grounds of oil processing plant in Kansas did not fall within scope of OPA, because the spills occurred miles from any stream, and there was no evidence that oil migrated off the property, entered any stream, river, arroyo, or other tributary of navigable water, or threatened underground aquifer. The court concluded by saying:

> "There is no evidence here, unlike some of the CWA cases, that any underground aquifer is endangered. Instead, during their cross examination of an expert geologist, plaintiffs have simply raised the possibility that--given a flood of virtually biblical proportions, it was conceivable that (to use the geologist's term) a "molecule" of the oil might reach the Arkansas River. While the OPA's definition of "navigable waters" should not be too narrowly construed, to apply the statute under these circumstances would be to render the requirement of an actual or threatened discharge into "navigable waters" to be a meaningless surplusage."[668]

However, by virtue of the expansive approach of the *Avitts* court, one would not even have to demonstrate that the oil actually flowed into a system that leads to a navigable waterway, but simply that there was a "substantial threat" that such a movement could occur. If other courts decide to follow the line of reasoning in *Sun Pipeline* and *Avitts*, oil spill incidents on highways or railroads emanating specifically from onshore-facilities as defined by OPA, with the potential of flowing into watersheds, remotely connected to the navigable waters of the United States, could trigger OPA removal costs and damages liability.[669] Notwithstanding these broad interpretations by the courts so far, OPA's broad applicability is not without re-

---

666 See id. at 680 ("In order to rule for respondents here, we would have to hold that the jurisdiction of the Corps extends to ponds that are not adjacent to open water. But we conclude that the text of the statute will not allow this.")

667 94 F.Supp.2d 1210 (D. Kansas 2000).

668 Harris v. Oil Reclaiming Co., 94 F.Supp.2d 1210, 1214.

669 See 33 USCA 2701(9).

striction, and it may not apply to oil pollution of subsurface waters that do not affect surface waters. [670] This principle was recently reaffirmed by the Fifth Circuit Court of Appeals in *Rice v. Harken Exploration Co.*,[671] when it held that landowners' (appellant's) generalized assertion that covered surface waters would eventually be affected by remote, gradual, natural seepage from contaminated groundwater was insufficient to establish liability under OPA, absent evidence of close, direct and proximate link between discharges of oil and any resulting actual, identifiable oil contamination of particular body of natural surface water.

One important question that must be answered is whether the navigable waters requirement in OPA has been met where the damage suffered by a private third party claimant occurred before the oil entered navigable waters. This question came up in a National Pollution Funds Center (NPFC) Claim adjudication hearing in 1997.[672] In that case a tanker belonging to M & M Fuel Co. ruptured or leaked onto the claimant's property on the 17th of January 1996.[673] A clean up company, Activities Baltimore, was informed of the incident 3 days after the incident.[674] According to an official of the clean-up company, the claimant's yard was in the path of the oil to the water. A hand drawn map of the area of the spill showed that the claimant's property goes to the second fence which is directly adjacent to the property of the Responsible party.[675] The oil entered navigable waters via a storm sewer, via the drainage ditch in front 2407 Ruth Avenue, after following the fence line between 2405 & 2407 Ruth Avenue.

670 See generally, Exxon Corp. v. Train, 554 F.2d 1310, 1312 (5th Cir. 1977); Williams Pipe Line Co. v. Bayer Corp., 964 F. Supp. 1300, 1319- 20, 1326-27 (S.D. Iowa 1997) (discussing judicial interpretations of the FWPCA's application to groundwater); Washington Wilderness Coalition v. Hecla Mining Co., 870 F. Supp. 983, 987-991 (E.D. Wash. 1994); Sierra Club v. Colorado Ref. Co., 838 F. Supp. 1428, 1433-35 (D. Colo. 1993); Kelly v. United States, 618 F. Supp. 1103, 1104-07 (W.D. Mich. 1985).

671 See *Rice*, 250 F.3d 264 (5th Cir. 2001).

672 See John A. Baker, NPFC Claim Summary/Recommendation Form, Claim No 056509-001, pl (John A. Baker, the claimant, filed a claim for damages to Real or Personal property)(on file with the NPFC and available upon request from the NPFC).

673 Id. at 1.

674 Id.

675 Id.

The NPFC claims manager denied the claim saying:

"This claim is denied because the damage suffered occurred before the oil entered a navigable water, and therefore not the result of an "incident." I have discussed this claim with ENS Merriman and have reviewed the case file, I have made a determination that this damage is upstream of an OPA incident."[676]

When one looks at the navigable waters jurisprudence and the earlier analysis of the navigable waters issue, one could argue that the conclusion of the claims manager in this case is somewhat erroneous. First of all, the assertion of the claims manager that the incident in the instant case does not qualify as an OPA incident is flawed. OPA defines "incident" as "any occurrence or series of occurrences having the same origin, involving one or more vessels, facilities, or any combination thereof, resulting in the discharge or substantial threat of discharge of oil."[677] Based on this definition, it is quite clear that the NPFC claims manager had failed to take into consideration the "substantial threat of discharge" aspect of the definition of incident. This definition makes it clear that there need not be an actual discharge of oil but a mere substantial threat of discharge is enough to trigger the application of OPA. Second, the earlier navigable waters analysis makes it clear that the navigable waters requirement is met where there is only a substantial threat of discharge into navigable waters. Therefore if the oil impacts and causes damage to the real or personal property of a claimant before it actually enters into navigable waters, but there was a substantial threat of a discharge into navigable waters when the oil impacted the claimant's property, that claimant's claim should be allowed to the extent that it meets the other statutory and regulatory requirements for claims of that type. It should not fail simply because of the absence of an actual discharge before the oil impacts the property. If a court of law has the opportunity to adjudicate similar cases in the future, the analysis in this chapter should provide some guidance to the courts.

---

676 Id. at 1.

677 33 USCA 2701(14).

The Exclusive economic zone (EEZ) is a zone beyond and adjacent to the territorial sea, in which a coastal state possesses sovereign rights to explore, exploit, conserve, and manage its natural resources, whether living or non-living, of the seabed, subsoil, and superadjacent waters.[678] A coastal state also has powers related to artificial installations, marine scientific research, and marine environment protection.[679] The breadth of the exclusive economic zone could extend beyond 200 nautical miles from the baselines from which the breadth of the territorial sea is measured.[680] The U.S. EEZ (Exclusive Economic Zone) was declared by Presidential Order.[681] On March 10, 1983, U.S. President Ronald Reagan signed proclamation 5030, which established the U.S. Exclusive Economic Zone (EEZ).[682] The area included is equal to two-thirds of all U.S. lands prior to the declaration.[683] The EEZ consists of those areas adjoining the territorial sea of the U.S., the Commonwealth of Puerto Rico, the commonwealth of the Northern Mariana Islands, and U.S. overseas territories and possessions.[684] The EEZ extends up to 200 nautical miles (370 km) from the U.S. coastline. About 15 percent of this area lies on the geologic continental shelf and is shal-

678 See United Nations Convention on the Law of the Sea, Dec. 10, 1982, arts. 56, U.N.Doc. A/CONF. 62/122 (1982), reprinted in 21 I.L.M. 1261, 1280 (1982) [hereinafter UNCLOS III]. The territorial sea is the ocean area extending from the shore of a coastal nation to a maximum of 12 nautical miles under international law. Id. art. 3, 21 I.L.M. at 1280. The coastal nation has complete sovereignty over this area including the air space over the sea as well as its bed and subsoil. Id. art. 2, 21 I.L.M. at 1280.

679 Id.

680 See United Nations Convention on the Law of the Sea, Dec. 10, 1982, arts. 57, U.N.Doc. A/CONF. 62/122 (1982), reprinted in 21 I.L.M. 1261, 1280 (1982) [hereinafter UNCLOS III].

681 See Gloria and the EEZ Scan Program (Last modified Aug. 20, 2001) <http://walrus.wr.usgs.gov/gloria/>

682 NOAA Coastal Services Center - Ocean Planning Information Systems (OPIS) South East: Legislative Summaries (last update March 27, 2002) <http://www.csc.noaa.gov/opis/html/summary/eez.htm>

683 See Gloria and the EEZ Scan Program (Last modified Aug. 20, 2001) <http://walrus.wr.usgs.gov/gloria/>

684 NOAA Coastal Services Center - Ocean Planning Information Systems (OPIS) South East: Legislative Summaries (last update March 27, 2002) <http://www.csc.noaa.gov/opis/html/summary/eez.htm>

lower than 200 meters.[685] Within its EEZ, the U.S. has sovereign rights over all living and non-living resources.[686] Other nations may exercise freedom of vessel navigation and over-flight within the U.S. EEZ.[687]

This means that a discharge from a vessel transporting oil to a foreign adjoining nation could impact US EEZ, if the oil is carried by waves of the sea into the US EEZ. The owners of such vessels would be subject to the provisions of the OPA.

In 1988, President Reagan, acting under his constitutional authority as Commander-in-Chief of the Armed Forces of the United States of America and in accordance with international law, extended the territorial sea to twelve nautical miles under Proclamation No. 5928.[688] President Reagan claimed that the expansion of the territorial sea was necessary to advance national security and other interests of the United States. It also allowed the United States to join the overwhelming number of other nations claiming the twelve-mile limit, and to comply with the suggestion of United Nations Convention on the Law of the Sea (UNCLOS III) that all nations conform to the twelve-mile limit.[689]

685 Id.

686 Id.

687 Id.

688 Proclamation No. 5928, 3 C.F.R. 547, 43 U.S.C. § 1331 (1988) [hereinafter Proclamation or 1988 Proclamation].

689 Id. 1988 Proclamation.

# Chapter Two

# DEFENSES TO LIABILITY
# -33 USC §2703(A)

Statutory provisions:
"§ 2703. Defenses to liability

(a) Complete defenses

**A responsible party is not liable for removal costs or damages** under section 2702 of this title if the responsible party establishes, by a preponderance of the evidence, that the discharge or substantial threat of a discharge of oil and the resulting damages or removal costs were caused solely by--

**(1)** an act of God;

**(2)** an act of war;

**(3)** an act or omission of a third party, other than an employee or agent of the responsible party or a third party whose act or omission occurs in connection with any contractual relationship with the responsible party (except where the sole contractual arrangement arises in connection with carriage by a common carrier by rail), if the responsible party establishes, by a preponderance of the evidence, that the responsible party--

(A) exercised due care with respect to the oil concerned, taking into consideration the characteristics of the oil and in light of all relevant facts and circumstances; and

(B) took precautions against foreseeable acts or omissions of any such third party and the foreseeable consequences of those acts or omissions; or

(4) any combination of paragraphs (1), (2), and (3).

(b) Defenses as to particular claimants

A responsible party is not liable under section 2702 of this title to a claimant, to the extent that the incident is caused by the gross negligence or willful misconduct of the claimant.

(c) Limitation on complete defense

Subsection (a) of this section does not apply with respect to a responsible party who fails or refuses--

**(1)** to report the incident as required by law if the responsible party knows or has reason to know of the incident;
**(2)** to provide all reasonable cooperation and assistance requested by a responsible official in connection with removal activities; or
**(3)** without sufficient cause, to comply with an order issued under subsection (c) or (e) of section 1321 of this title or the Intervention on the High Seas Act (33 U.S.C. 1471 et seq.)"[690]

This chapter analyzes the defenses that are available for use during negotiations with government enforcement agencies, adjudication of claims with the National Pollution Funds Center (NPFC) and private plaintiffs, as well as during enforcement litigation. The three defenses explicitly provided for in OPA are discussed extensively.

The limited defenses provided for by section 2703 of OPA are lost where the responsible party does not report the discharge, or fails to cooperate with or abide by the orders of officials concerned with removal activities.[691] The original OPA bill contained a section which would have made the defenses unavailable to a tanker involved in an incident when operating without a tug escort in Puget Sound waters between Port

690 33 USC § 2703

691 33 USC § 2703(c).

Angeles, Washington, and Vancouver, British Columbia, Canada.[692] This provision was however deleted from the final OPA statute.

Finally, as to a given claimant, the responsible party is not liable to that claimant to the extent that the gross negligence or willful misconduct of that claimant caused the discharge.[693] It is important to note that OPA eliminated the FWPCA defense of government negligence, but the government may still be held directly liable to third parties as a sole cause third party, or indirectly through a contribution action by an RP against the government, subject to the doctrine of sovereign immunity.

The fact that these limited defenses are waived where the responsible party does not report the discharge, or fails to cooperate with or abide by the orders of officials concerned with removal activity gives the regulatory body charged with removal of oil spills, a blank check to take away from the responsible party the rights that the Act has conferred on such a party. The provision appears to be very harsh on the responsible party because it gives the regulatory body an unreasonably wide discretion to wipe out the defenses that may have exculpated a responsible party. However, it is not all bad news for the responsible party (RP) because the Act allows the responsible party to be subrogated to the rights of the U.S. government to bring a claim against a third party whose acts was the sole cause of the spill from the vessel or facility.

The limited defenses were deliberately included by the U.S Congress to circumvent any attempt by the responsible party to raise a plethora of defenses against any claim that might be brought against it by an injured third party claimant. The effect that this provision has on the responsible party is that the traditional defenses on which it used to rely have been taken away from it. It can only rely on the defenses in this Act notwithstanding the provisions of any other law. This is meant to make the polluter pay for any excess oil spill cost just in case its COFR guaranty or P & I Club insurance is inadequate to cover all the clean up cost and damage claims. The intent of Congress was to allow the responsible party to rely

692 1990 U.S.C.C.A.N. 782, H.R. Conf. Rep. No. 653, 101ST Cong., (2nd Sess. 1990), 1990 WL 132747 (Leg.Hist).

693 33 USC §2703(c).

on only OPA defenses in OPA cases. Where the responsible party is being sued under state oil pollution statutes, it can invoke the defenses provided under those state statutes, which means that the responsible party might have no defenses at all; or more defenses than under the OPA; or fewer defenses than under the OPA.[694] This is due to the fact that Congress wanted states to have the liberty to reduce, enlarge or eliminate all OPA defenses in actions commenced exclusively under their respective state statutes.[695]

## A.I. OPA THIRD PARTY DEFENSE -33 USC §2703(a)(3).

The legislative history of the OPA reveals that the requirement that the third party must not be in a contractual relationship with the ship owner (to invoke the third party defense) was included to preclude defendants from avoiding liability by claiming a third party was responsible, when that third party had a contractual relationship with the defendant and was acting, in essence, as an extension of the defendant.[696] "By making owners and operators pay the costs resulting from the acts of irresponsible parties with whom they are in privity, the statute creates incentives for vessel owners to ensure that contractors and subcontractors are competent and reliable."[697]

There has been some interesting jurisprudence on section 2703(a)(3) of the OPA, which prevents the responsible party from utilizing the defense of third party liability where there is a contract between the responsible party and the potentially liable third party. In *International Marine Carriers v. The Oil Spill Liability Trust Fund*,[698] the operator of a

694 See 1990 U.S.C.C.A.N. 728-29, S. Rep. No. 94, 101st Cong. (1ST Sess. 1989), 1989 WL 225005 (Leg.Hist).

695 Id.

696 1990 U.S.C.C.A.N. 734, S. Rep. No. 94, 101st Cong. (1ST Sess. 1989), 1989 WL 225005 (Leg.Hist)

697 Matthew P. Harrington, Necessary and proper, but still unconstitutional: The Oil Pollution Act's Delegation of Admiralty Power to the states, 48 Case W. Res. 1, 18 (Fall 1997), [Hereinafter, Harrington-Necessary].

698 1995 A.M.C. 2072, 903 F.Supp. 1097 (S.D. Tex. 1994).

naval vessel brought an action against the Oil Spill Liability Trust Fund, challenging inter alia, denial of its claim for reimbursement of removal costs incurred under OPA. *International Marine Carriers (*IMC) and the Department of the Navy entered into a contract under which IMC agreed to operate naval vessels on behalf of the United States Military Command.[699] On April 13, 1991, IMC moored one of these vessels, the USNS SEALIFT ATLANTIC, at the Amerada Hess Terminal on the Houston Ship Channel to load jet and bunker fuels.[700] During transfer of the bunker fuel, approximately twelve barrels of bunker fuel spilled from the starboard fuel tank of the USNS SEALIFT ATLANTIC into the Houston Ship Channel. IMC, in accordance with the OPA oil spill response requirements, remediated the spilled bunker fuel, and paid clean-up costs totaling $49,048.19.[701]

On December 26, 1991, IMC filed a claim with the Coast Guard, National Pollution Funds Center, pursuant to section 2713 of the OPA. The claim sought reimbursement of IMC's removal costs from the Oil Spill Liability Trust Fund. On March 3, 1992, the Fund denied IMC's claim on the ground that IMC could not assert a third-party defense to liability under section 2703 of the OPA.

IMC appealed the denial of its claim. The Fund denied IMC's appeal finding that IMC failed to establish a section 2703 defense, in part because there was a contractual relationship between IMC and the Amerada Hess Terminal.

This suit followed the Fund's denial of IMC's appeal, which was a final agency action. IMC's complaint asserted jurisdiction under section 2717(b) of the OPA and section 10(c) of the Administrative Procedure Act ("APA").[702] One of the reasons its claim was denied is that the Fund had concluded that a contractual relationship existed between the operator and the fuel terminal at which fuel spill occurred, thus precluding the operator's assertion of third-party defense to liability under OPA.

699 903 F.Supp. 1097.

700 Id. at 1099

701 Id.

702 5 U.S.C. § 702.

IMC moved a cross-motion for summary judgment on its claim for reimbursement from the Fund on the grounds that the Fund abused its discretion, or acted arbitrarily and capriciously, in denying IMC's OPA claim because no contractual relationship existed between IMC and the fuel terminal (Amerada Hess Terminal) at the time of the fuel transfer. The United States argued that the resolution of this same issue warranted summary judgment in the government's favor, but the court rejected this argument. The court noted that a successful assertion of the section 2703(a)(3) third party defense would require IMC to show that: (1) the Amerada Hess Terminal was the sole cause of the discharge; (2) no contractual relationship existed between the USNS SEALIFT ATLANTIC and the Amerada Hess Terminal at the time of the discharge; and (3) IMC exercised due care and took precautions against foreseeable consequences.[703]

The court noted that the National Pollution Fund Center denied IMC's appeal, on behalf of the Fund, because it determined that IMC's arrangement with the Amerada Hess Terminal was contractual. The court quoted from the fund's final opinion, which states that:

"A contractual relationship... refers to any contractual arrangement, not just direct or indirect contracts. There is a contractual relationship between an oil terminal and a vessel operator to which it is transferring oil. This contractual relationship is even stronger when the oil being transferred is to be used by the vessel for its own bunkers.... The Declaration of Inspection, signed by the Chief Engineer for the ATLANTIC and the dockman for [the] Terminal, further evidences a contractual relationship."[704]

The Fund claimed that: (1) the commercial contacts between IMC and the Terminal are sufficient to imply a contractual arrangement; (2) the Declaration of Inspection evidences this contractual relationship; (3) IMC is an intended third-party beneficiary to the contract between the Navy and the Terminal; and (4) a maritime contract lien arose under 46 U.S.C. § 971,[705]

---

703 903 F.Supp. at 1105

704 Id.

705 The Federal Maritime Lien Act ("FMLA"), 46 U.S.C.A. § 971 (West 1975), provides that: any person furnishing repairs, supplies, towage, use of drydock or marine railway,

when the Terminal transferred fuel to IMC.[706] IMC counter-argued that the Declaration of Inspection is merely a pre-bunkering checklist under 33 C.F.R. Part 156.120, not a contract. IMC did not address the Fund's determination that the commercial contacts constitute an OPA contractual relationship.

The court observed that section 2703(a)(3) of OPA does not explicitly define the phrase "any contractual relationship." The court pointed out that whether the Fund abused its discretion in denying IMC's appeal turns on the reasonableness of the Fund's determination that there was a contract between IMC and the Amerada Hess Terminal.[707]

The court juxtaposed OPA section 2703(a)(3) defense with the analogous CERCLA section 9607(b)(3) third-party defense. Under CERCLA, a contractual relationship "includes, but is not limited to, land contracts, deeds or other instruments transferring title or possession..."[708] The court found that some district courts have limited availability of the CERCLA third-party defense "to situations where the responsible party had no connection to the third party."[709] The court also observed that other courts allow the defense unless the third-party conduct occurs in connection with a contract between the defendant and the third party.[710] The court found

---

or other necessaries, to any vessel, whether foreign or domestic, upon the order of the owner of such vessel, or of a person authorized by the owner, shall have a maritime lien on the vessel, which may be enforced by a suit in rem, and it shall not be necessary to allege or prove that credit was given to the vessel. (Repealed and replaced by 46 U.S.C.A. § 31342 (West 1994)).

706 903 F.Supp. 1097, 1105.

707 Id. at 1105 (the court citing with approval U.S.A., Inc. v. Natural Resources Defense Council, Inc., 467 U.S. 837, 843-46, 104 S.Ct. 2778, 2782-83, 81 L.Ed.2d 694 (1984)).

708 42 U.S.C. § 9601(35).

709 See International Marine Carriers, 903 F.Supp. 1097, 1106 (the court cited with approval, Philadelphia v. Stepan Chemical Co., 18 Envtl.L.Rep. 20133, 20134, 1987 WL 15214 (E.D.Pa.1987); United States v. Stringfellow, 661 F.Supp. 1053, 1061 (C.D.Cal.1987) (holding that the CERCLA third-party defense only applies where "a totally unrelated third party is the sole cause of the release"); O'Neil v. Picillo, 682 F.Supp. 706, 728 (D.R.I.1988), *aff'd*, 883 F.2d 176 (1st Cir.1989), *cert. denied*, 493 U.S. 1071, 110 S.Ct. 1115, 107, L.Ed.2d 1022 (1990)).

710 Id. at 1106 (citing, States v. Monsanto Co., 858 F.2d 160, 169 (4th Cir.1988), cert. denied, 490 U.S. 1106, 109 S.Ct. 3156, 104 L.Ed.2d 1019 (1989); Shapiro v. Alex Anderson, 743 F.Supp. 268, 270-71 (S.D.N.Y.1990); United States v. Hooker Chemicals & Plastics Corp., 680 F.Supp. 546, 558 (W.D.N.Y.1988).

that it has also been held that even an indirect contractual relationship may preclude the defense.[711] While noting that the contractual relationship element to the OPA section 2703 third-party defense is intended to prevent otherwise responsible parties from avoiding liability by pointing to the conduct of foreseeable third parties,[712] the court found that the Fund was reasonable in concluding that section 2703 third-party defense did not extend to the type of arrangement between IMC and the Amerada Hess Terminal at the time of the fuel spill.[713] The court found it reasonable for the Fund to determine that the commercial contacts between IMC and the Terminal, including the Declaration of Inspection, constitute an OPA contractual relationship within the meaning of section 2703(a)(3).[714]

Also in the case of *United States v. JR Nelson Vessel Ltd,*[715] another case that considered the third party defense, the court held that the fact that the RP owner of the discharging party was in a bailment relationship with a third party in whose custody the vessel resided at the time of the discharge, does not entitle the RP to the third party defense.

The United States through a summary judgment motion sought to recover the costs of cleaning up the oil spill that emanated from the defendant's vessel, pursuant to the OPA.[716] The defendant-RP, however, asserted that material issues of fact as to OPA liability existed because any damage sustained by the Nelson (the vessel) that caused it to discharge oil was the result of third-party negligence. The defendant-RP had argued and asserted that, beginning in 1988, and throughout the time relevant to the action, "the Nelson was left in the custody and control of Stephen Clarke, owner and operator of the Greenport Yacht & Shipbuilding Company, for repairs and storage."[717] Having accepted payment for these services, the

711 Id. (citing, *CPC International, Inc. v. Aerojet-General Corp.*, 777 F.Supp. 549 (W.D.Mich.1991) (denying the CERCLA third-party defense where a party acquired a contaminated site from the bankruptcy trustee for the prior owner).

712 Id. (citing, 1990 U.S.CODE CONG. & ADMIN.NEWS 722, 734).

713 Id.

714 Id. at 1106.

715 1998 AMC 2249, 1 F.Supp.2d 172 (E.D.N.Y 1998).

716 1 F.Supp.2d 174.

717 1 F.Supp.2d 174-75.

defendants asserted, Clarke (the third party) made himself a bailee who thereby accepted a duty of care with respect to the condition of the Nelson (polluting vessel).[718] The defendants further argued that a breach of this duty of care would make Clarke at least partially liable for any damages caused by the oil spill. The court rejected this argument as a matter of law because a bailment is a contractual arrangement.[719] The court held that while OPA, allowed third-party negligence to serve as a complete defense, it nevertheless explicitly excludes from that allowance the case of "a third party whose act or omission occurs in connection with any contractual relationship with the responsible party."[720] Thus, the defendant-RP could not avoid summary judgment by claiming that an issue of fact existed as to the purported negligence of Clarke and his company. By virtue of the foregoing, the United States was granted summary judgment.

What the cases discussed above demonstrate is that a slight proof of a contractual relationship between the RP and the negligent third party will not allow the invocation of the third-party defense. In other words, the RP's evidence of the absence of a contractual relationship between itself and the negligent third-party must be very strong. The contract need not be direct and the presence of a contract need not be crystal clear. It also does not seem to matter if the RP is in a contractual relationship with an independent contractor.[721] Where it is not very clear that there is

---

718 Id. at 175.

719 See id. at 175 (*citing*, U.S. v. $79,000 in Acct. No. 2168050/6749900 at the Bank of New York, 1996 WL 648934 at *5 (S.D.N.Y. Nov.7, 1996); 9 N.Y.Jur.2d, Bailments and Chattel Leases, § 1 at 9 (1980).

720 *See. Id.* at 175 (emphasis supplied); (citing, Marine Carriers v. Oil Spill Liability Trust, 903 F.Supp. 1097, 1106 (S.D.Tex.1994) ("OPA section 2703 third-party defense is intended to prevent otherwise responsible parties from avoiding liability by pointing to the conduct of foreseeable third parties"), *see also*, 33 U.S.C. § 2703(a)(3).

721 "For purpose of the Federal Water Pollution Control Act Provision excepting circumstances involving the "Act of a Third Party" from rule imposing liability without fault for government's cleanup costs on a vessel discharging oil in violation of the Act, an example of such "act of a third party" would be a vandal's opening a ship's valve; however, if ship's valve failed because of an act of the installer, ship's owners should not be permitted to avoid liability by claiming that the installer was a third party because he was an independent contractor rather than an employee." Burgess v. M/V Tamano, 564 F.2d 964 (1st. Cir. 1977).

a contractual relationship between an RP and a negligent third party, the courts have been, and may be favorably disposed in the future to holding that there is a contractual relationship in order to ensure that the RP does not hide behind a third party in order to circumvent its responsibility to pay clean-up costs and damages under OPA. This approach of the courts is consistent with the legislative intent of the US Congress earlier discussed.

Generally, the third party defense cannot be successfully invoked by an RP if the alleged sole cause third party is a tug-boat pulling or pushing a barge or a vessel. This is because the tug-boat normally does this pursuant to a contract between itself and the RP.

It is not entirely clear if the third-party defense is available in cases of oil spills caused by the negligence of pilots. Pilotage is a unique service based upon local knowledge and the pilot's expertise in tackling the special conditions prevailing in a given pilotage area.[722] It may be performed in coastal waters, estuaries, rivers, ports, harbors, lakes, enclosed dock waters or any combination of these areas which may come within the jurisdiction of a port or other competent authority.[723]A pilot's function is to combine technical knowledge concerning the operation and handling of different vessel types, and the applicable safety and environmental requirements, with his local knowledge.[724] The latter is manifested in his overall appreciation of the special regulatory requirements and unique conditions which exist in his pilotage area, and with which the master of the vessel cannot be expected to be fully conversant.[725] The prime goal of pilotage is to ensure the safe and efficient passage of ships, regardless of sudden changes in the physical environment or unexpected adversities.[726] In rendering this service, pilots not only contribute to the safety and efficiency of overall maritime traffic in the area concerned (thus aiding also the orderly conduct of other human activities in the area, such as fishing,

722 See International Maritime Pilots Association (IMPA), A message from the IMPA President (last modified April 17, 2002) < http://www.impahq.org/ >

723 Id.

724 Id.

725 Id.

726 Id.

offshore activities, leisure boating, and so on).[727] They also provide an important public service with respect to the protection of the marine environment.[728] "As we live in an increasingly environmentally conscious world, issues of pollution liability and compensation have become highly politically sensitive and often give rise to expensive litigation."[729] Recent maritime accidents have amply demonstrated that pilots can no longer safely assume that they will be spared from direct exposure to environmentalist expectations.[730] The owner and operator of a vessel shares this same concern about exposure to oil pollution liability, due to the negligent navigation of a vessel by a pilot.

There are two types of pilots that vessel owners deal with from day to day: voluntary pilots and compulsory pilots.

*When oil spill is caused by voluntary pilots*: The relation between the vessel owner and the pilot voluntarily employed for the vessel is that of master and servant.[731] The services of the pilot are as much for the benefit of the vessel and cargo as are those of the captain and crew, and his compensation, employment, and liabilities are similar to theirs.[732] The principle of respondeat superior therefore applies, and imposes on both the vessel and the owner, liability for collision or other damage like oil pollution, caused by the pilot's negligence.[733] The relation between owner or master and pilot as that of master and agent or employee is not changed by the fact that the selection of the pilot is limited to those who have been found by examination to possess the requisite knowledge and skill, and have been licensed by the government inspectors.[734] "The liability of vessel and owner for the pilot's negligence remains the same, as long as

---

727 Id.

728 Id.

729 Id.

730 Id.

731 Jody L. Mikasen, Shipping - VIII. Rights, Duties, and Liabilities of Vessels and Owners, § 442- Negligence or Wrongful Acts of Pilot--Voluntary Employment, American Jurisprudence, (Second Edition, Current through the May 2001 Cumulative Supplement).

732 Id. at §442 (citing, The China, 74 US 53, 19 L Ed 67 (1868)).

733 See id. at §442.

734 Id.

the master is at liberty to take a pilot, or not, at his pleasure, for in such a case the master acts voluntarily, though he is necessarily required to select from a particular class."[735] The employment contract between a voluntary pilot and a vessel owner whose vessel is identified as the source of an oil spill creates a contractual relationship between the vessel owner and the voluntary pilot, which vitiates the vessel owner or operator's entitlement to the third party defense in section 2703(a)(3) of the OPA.

*When oil spill is caused by compulsory pilots:* In compulsory pilotage, the vessel owner is required by state law to utilize the services of a local pilot registered with the state, to assist it in the navigation of difficult terrain in intra-state waters. Refusal of a shipowner to use a pilot could subject it to civil fines under state law.

The general maritime rule is that when pilotage is compulsory, a shipowner is not liable in personam for the pilot's negligence,[736] but the vessel is liable in rem.[737] Accordingly, where a compulsory pilot is involved, it is important to sue the vessel in rem to ensure a recovery for pilot negligence. In *Homer Ramsdell Transportation Co. v. La Compagnie Generale Transatlantique*,[738] the Supreme Court articulated the compulsory pilot defense, emphasizing that a shipowner is not liable in personam for damages caused by a compulsory pilot who is solely at fault and exclusively in charge of the vessel at the time of an accident.[739] In *Homer*, a vessel struck and damaged a pier while the crew was acting on the orders of the pilot.[740]

---

735 Id.

736 Homer Ramsdell Transp. Co. v. Compagnie Generale Transatlantique, 182 U.S. 406 (1901).

737 The China, 74 U.S. (7 Wall.) 53, 61 (1868).

738 Dana M. Shelton, Note: The Fifth Circuit Contracts The Compulsory Pilot Defense And Expands the Vessel Master's Duty To Monitor Compulsory Pilots: Avondale Industries v..International Marine Carriers, 9 Tul. Mar. L.J. 485, 488, (summer 1995) (citing, Homer Ramsdell Transportation Co. v. La Compagnie Generale Transatlantique U.S. 406 (1901)).

739 Dana M. Shelton, Note: The Fifth Circuit Contracts The Compulsory Pilot Defense And Expands the Vessel Master's Duty To Monitor Compulsory Pilots: Avondale Industries v. International Marine Carriers, 9 Tul. Mar. L.J. at 488.

740 Id. at 488.

Although on board at the time of the allision, the vessel's officers took no part in the navigation of the ship.[741] The Court held that the shipowner was "not liable for injuries inflicted exclusively by negligence of a pilot accepted by a vessel compulsorily."[742]

Some courts have refused to extend the above jurisprudence to the oil spill context, by holding that compulsory pilots who bring vessels through channels and direct the navigation of vessels at the time of grounding are not third parties within section 311 of the FWPCA.[743] For instance, in the case of *Burgess v. M/V Tamano,*[744] the First Circuit Court of Appeals held that even though a compulsory pilot might be regarded as an independent contractor, he is at all times subject to the ultimate control of the ship's master.[745] The Supreme court case to which the *Burgess* court cited had stated:

"The services of the pilot are as much for the benefit of the vessel and cargo as those of the captain and crew. His compensation comes from the same source as theirs. Like them he serves the owner and is paid by the owner. If there be any default on his part, the owner has the same remedies against him as against other delinquents on board. The difference between his relations and those of the master is one rather of form than substance. It is the duty of the master to interfere in cases of the pilot's intoxication or manifest incapacity, in cases of danger which he does not foresee, and in all cases of great necessity.[746] The master has the same power to displace the pilot that he has to remove any subordinate officer of the vessel. He may exercise it or not, according to his discretion."[747]

This approach of holding a shipowner liable in personam for the acts of compulsory pilots in the oil pollution context is inconsistent with the

741 Id.

742 Homer Ramsdell Transportation Co. v. La Compagnie Generale Transatlantique 182 U.S. 406 (1901)).

743 See. In re Oriental Republic of Uruguay, 821 F.Supp. 928, 1993 AMC 502 (D. Del. 1992).

744 564 F.2d 964, 981-82, 1977 AMC 1892 (1st Cir. 1977).

745 564 F.2d at 982, (*citing*, China, 74 U.S. at 67-68, 19 L.Ed. 67 (1868)).

746 China, 74 U.S. at 67.

747 Id. at 67-68.

approach of the courts under general maritime law. One could argue that since compulsory pilots are not usually in any contractual relationship with the shipowner, the third party defense should apply to oil spill incidents caused solely by the negligence of compulsory pilots. It is however important to emphasize that if the shipowner is found to have contributed slightly to an oil spill incident, the third party defense should be unavailable in the compulsory pilot context. Vessel owner contribution might be found if the master of the vessel failed to observe and monitor the activities of a compulsory pilot, and that failure causes an oil spill.[748] The effect of slight contribution to an oil spill by a ship owner is discussed later.

The first hurdle that an RP must surmount in order to successfully invoke the third party defense as explained above is to prove that there is no contractual relationship between himself and the sole cause-third party. The second hurdle which is a more difficult one to surmount is provided for in section 2703(a)(3)(A)&(B) of the OPA. This section provides that the RP can only invoke the third party defense if it exercised due care with respect to the oil concerned, taking into consideration the characteristics of the oil and in light of all relevant facts and circumstances and took precautions against foreseeable acts or omissions of any such third party and the foreseeable consequences of those acts or omissions.

For instance in *United States Of America v. George MIZHIR,* [749] the United States brought an action for reimbursement of funds expended by the Oil Spill Liability Trust Fund for the cleanup of an oil spill allegedly caused by the defendant, George Mizhir ("Mizhir").[750] The court noted that Mizhir, the person designated as the responsible party for the oil spill could not, as a matter of law, avail himself of the responsible third party defense, because he was negligent or failed to exercise due care. The absence of negligent behavior under the circumstances is a sine qua non to the successful invocation of the responsible third party defense. The court

748 Avondale Industries Inc. v. International Marine Carriers Inc., 15 F.3d 489, 493, 1994 AMC 1555, 1560 (5th Cir. 1994).

749 106 F.Supp.2d 124, 2000 WL 914108 (D.Mass. 2000).

750 106 F.Supp.2d at 124.

found that the service records from Bergevins (the company that serviced Mizhir's truck) indicated that its mechanic inspected the truck and told Mizhir the brakes were "unsafe" and "not to drive truck." The court found that, Mizhir was clearly aware of the dangerous condition of his brakes and that it was foreseeable that they might fail, but nevertheless drove the truck, which made him culpably negligent under the circumstances, and this made it impossible for him to take advantage of this OPA defense.[751]

FWPCA jurisprudence on the third party defense is also relevant and applicable to the OPA. FWPCA cases dealing with the third party defense also require a proof of the exercise of due diligence by the invoking RP. They also require adequate proof that the RP took precautions against foreseeable acts of third parties. A FWPCA case that illustrates the approach of the courts on this issue is the case of *Cities Service Pipeline Co. v. The United States.*[752] The Plaintiff-RP in this case owned an underground pipeline through which it transported oil under pressure. Where the pipeline crossed a waterway it was covered by mud. On the evening of March 20, 1980, the pipeline burst, spewing approximately 8800 barrels of oil into Carpenter's Bayou, a shallow, slow-running creek.[753] The Plaintiff cleaned up the mess at a cost of some $880,000. It then brought this action under the Federal Water Pollution Control Act (FWPCA), 33 U.S.C. § 1321(i)(1) (1976), to recover its cleanup costs from the United States.[754] The Plaintiff alleged that the spill was caused solely by the act of a third party. The court noted that even if arguendo, the third party defense were applicable to the discharge from the plaintiff's pipeline, the plaintiff must nevertheless establish that it could not have prevented the spill through the exercise of due care.[755] The court found that the plaintiff had failed to establish that it was unable to prevent the spill through the exercise of due care.[756]

751 Id. at 128.

752 20 ERC 1350, 4 Cl. Ct. 207 (1983).

753 Id. at 207.

754 Id.

755 Id. at 209 (*citing as example*, Travelers Indemnity Co. v. United States, 230 Ct.Cl. 867, *cert. denied*, 459 U.S. 1015, 103 S.Ct. 374, 74 L.Ed.2d 508 (1982)).

756 Id. at 209.

The court based its conclusion of lack of proof of due care on the plaintiff's metallurgy expert testimony that the pipeline had been damaged by heavy equipment.[757] The metallurgy expert had explained that when a pipeline is damaged and remains unrepaired, forces are set in motion that inevitably lead to a rupture.[758] The expert pointed out that first, the impact itself causes the pipe metal to become brittle, diminishing its resistance to fracture.[759] Second, the injury may cause surface cracks that grow in length and depth with the passage of time.[760] Finally, the injury leaves dents and gouges that focus internal stresses onto the damaged area.[761] The increased pressure in the area of a dent or gouge is created because the pipeline loses its circular shape. The internal pressure is then unevenly distributed around the pipeline's perimeter. The oil flowing through the pipe pushes outward on the dent in order to restore the pipeline's circular shape, subjecting the damaged area to high bending stresses.[762] The *Pipeline* court believed that this means that a pipeline that is operating at some 950 pounds per square inch (psi), as this pipeline did on the night of the rupture, was experiencing a much greater pressure in the area of the dent or gouge.[763] It reasoned that this intense pressure caused further deterioration of the damaged metal, increasing its brittleness and enlarging surface cracks until the pipeline bursts, as this one did.[764]

It found that the plaintiff was aware that the pipeline might sustain damage from heavy equipment. It was also aware that, upon sustaining a dent or gouge, the pipeline would be subjected to continuous stresses

757 Id.

758 Id.

759 Id.

760 Id.

761 Id.

762 Id. at 209, n1.

763 Id at 209, n2 (The court noted that pursuant to regulations of the Department of Transportation, a pipeline may be operated at 80% of the pressure for which it has been hydrostatically tested. 49 C.F.R. § 195.406(a)(3) (1982). Ten years prior to the rupture the pipeline had been tested at 1260 psi, which meant it could be operated up to 1000 psi. Under the metallurgist's analysis, it would appear that after the damage some portions of the pipeline were subjected to pressures exceeding those permitted by the regulations).

764 Id.

and deterioration that would inevitably lead to a rupture.[765] The court also believed that the plaintiff should also have been aware that rupture of a pipeline transporting oil under pressure poses risks that far exceed those from other types of leaks.[766] The court noted that the explosive force of this rupture sent oil hurtling over a 10 acre area, blackening the tops of pine trees 400 yards away. The court noted that according to the plaintiff, such a rupture would normally discharge a minimum of 3000 barrels (125,000 gallons) of oil before the flow could be stopped. The court noted that because of a mechanical failure, this rupture in fact resulted in a discharge of almost three times that quantity of oil.[767]

The court pointed out that these are facts the plaintiff could not responsibly ignore.[768] The court held that damage to the pipeline and the consequent rupture were foreseeable, particularly where the pipe was not covered by solid ground but only by the soft and shifting mud of the bayou.[769] Therefore the risk of damage from equipment used near the pipeline or from objects floating in the bayou should have been apparent.[770] The court also observed that where the pipeline traversed a flowing body of water, an additional danger existed because any oil spilled would be carried downstream and dispersed, endangering a large area and rendering cleanup efforts difficult and expensive.[771] The court observed that while the bayou was normally not very deep or fast running, its water level was known to rise sharply during heavy rainfalls. Damage from floating objects was therefore foreseeable.[772]

The court noted the plaintiff regularly inspected the pipeline right-of-way, principally by aerial overflights.[773] The purpose of those inspections was to detect hazardous activities near the pipeline. The court lamented

---

765 Id.

766 Id.

767 Id. at 209, n3.

768 Id.

769 Id. at 209-10

770 Id. at 210.

771 Id.

772 Id.

773 Id.

the fact that such inspections could not assure detection of all potential damage to the pipeline.[774] The court observed that the plaintiff had no program for visually inspecting the pipeline itself, even at those points where it was most vulnerable or where a rupture would cause particularly grievous harm. Nor did plaintiff run periodic hydrostatic tests of the pipeline for the purpose of locating and repairing weak spots.[775] The court pointed out that it is inevitable that a pipeline will suffer damage from time to time. The court relied on plaintiff's expert witness explanation that "mechanical damage is a common cause of in- service pipeline failures.[776] The court rejected the plaintiff's argument that it had no responsibility to discover and repair such damage.[777] The court observed that although in plaintiff's view, it was entitled to stand by and let the injury work its way into a rupture which spewed massive quantities of oil into the nation's waterways, the court would not accept this proposition. Based on the foregoing, the court concluded that the plaintiff shared culpability for the rupture because of its protracted failure to detect and repair the damage.[778] This sharing of culpability by the plaintiff therefore disqualifies the plaintiff from invoking the third-party defense.

*THIRD PARTY MUST BE SOLE CAUSE OF THE SPILL*

The court also held that even if the plaintiff were entirely without fault for the rupture, the court would grant defendant's motion because plaintiff had failed to establish that the oil spill was caused solely by the act of a third party within the meaning of the FWPCA. The court noted that while the plaintiff showed that a third party may have damaged the pipeline, it also established that this damage alone was insufficient to cause a rupture. The court held that the plaintiff's use of the pipeline,

774 Id.

775 Id.

776 Id.

777 Id.

778 Id.

over a period of what may have been ten years, was as much a cause of the oil spill as the initial damage.[779] While acknowledging that no culpability attached to the plaintiff's actions that amounted to normal use of the pipeline, the court noted however, that it is not merely culpable acts that will preclude a plaintiff's recovery for oil cleanup costs.[780] **"Any conduct, however slight, on the part of an owner or operator contributing to a spill... negates relief."**[781] The court reasoned that it is clear from the language of the FWPCA: To recover, a plaintiff must establish not merely that the oil spill was the result of one or more of the causes listed in section 1321, but also that no other cause contributed to the spill.[782] The court held that the plaintiff's own contributing actions-- even those that are entirely innocent--will preclude recovery because they are not among the causes listed in section 1321(i)(1); causation therefore could not be confined as required by that section.[783]

The court held that even though ten years may have passed since the third party action that caused the initial damage, that damage would never have matured into a rupture without plaintiff's continuing use of the pipeline and the resultant wear and tear. The court decided that under these circumstances, it would offend common sense to hold that the third party was the sole cause of the oil spill.[784]

All OPA responsible parties would be unable to invoke any of the defenses in the Act if they are found to have contributed in any way to the discharge. Such contribution need not be negligent for the courts to find the RP culpable. The express provision in section 2703(a) of OPA dictates this outcome even though it seems harsh. This section specifically provides:

---

779 Id. at 210.

780 Id.

781 Id., (*citing*, Reliance Insurance Co. v. United States, 230 Ct. Cl. 390, 677 F.2d at 849 (Ct. Cl. 1982)).

782 Id.

783 Id. at 210-11.

784 Cities Service Pipeline v. United States, 4 Cl. Ct. 207, 211 (Cl. Ct. 1983).

"A responsible party is not liable for removal costs or damages under section 2702 of this title if the responsible party establishes, by a preponderance of the evidence, that the discharge or substantial threat of a discharge of oil and the resulting damages or removal costs were caused "solely by ....." (emphasis mine).

The key phrase that dictates this outcome is "solely by."

This requirement that the invoked defense be the sole cause of the discharge will be almost impossible to sustain in most cases because of the foreseeability and due care requirements inherent in all the defenses. Because of the foreseeability and due care requirement an RP could be charged with constructive knowledge of something it never actually knew. The imputation of constructive knowledge will in most cases defeat the invocation of the three OPA defenses.

The third party defense might be applicable in cases involving criminal acts of third parties, but the courts are not likely to relax the due care and foreseeability requirement simply because of the criminal nature of the acts of a third party. The application of the due care and foreseeability requirement is particularly important for OPA and CERCLA third party defense cases because of the specific express provision to that effect in both statutes. One case that underlines the importance of these two requirements is the FWPCA case of *Union Petroleum Corp. v. United States*.[785] Here, the United States Court of Claims held that the plaintiff Petroleum company was entitled to recover expenses it incurred in cleaning up oil that was spilled when unknown vandals, during a labor strike at company's oil terminal, opened valves on two railroad tank cars. The court found that the discharge was established to have been caused solely by the act of the unknown vandal third parties, that is, the discharge occurred despite the oil company's reasonable precautions against vandalism.[786] This case shows that the courts would and should still require the proof of due diligence and foreseeability in OPA, CERCLA and FWPCA

785 651 F.2d 734 (Ct. Cl. 1981).

786 651 F.2d at 734.

third party defense cases involving the acts of vandals. One of the things that dictated the outcome of the *Union Petroleum* case was the security measures put in place by the plaintiff, Union Petroleum Corporation.

Security Measures Taken by Union Petroleum in Response to the Labor Strike.

On April 3, 1975, a labor union steward notified plaintiff's operations manager, Mr. Forest, that the union would go on strike at 4:00 p.m. that day.[787] He immediately put Union Petroleum's pre-established contingency plans into effect. Mr. Forest first called the Revere Police Department and requested two officers on a 24-hour basis. At least two Revere police officers were continually on duty at the Union yard beginning at approximately 8:00 p.m. on April 3, 1975.[788] The court noted in footnote one of its decision, that the plaintiff's efforts to secure extra protection from police and from its private security company were sufficient to meet the "reasonableness" standard required, especially since the plaintiff had no reason to anticipate the sort of senseless vandalism which subsequently occurred.[789]

On the morning of April 4, 1975, Mr. Forest telephoned Hallmark Security, the private security agency employed by Union for 3 to 4 years prior to the strike.[790] He testified that in his conversation with Mr. Prew, President of Hallmark Security, he requested that a security guard be stationed in the gasoline yard.[791] The guard was expected to watch the gasoline loading rack, walk the perimeter of the yard, past Gates 4 and 5 along the west side of the premises, and check in back of the Airborne Freight warehouse and in the area of the railroad tank cars at the extreme northern end of the yard.[792]

Also on April 3, 1975, Mr. Forest informed a Mr. Mark Hoyt at Airborne Freight of the strike, and asked him to leave all the lights on in back of the warehouse. Mr. Forest testified that he observed that these

787 Id. at 738.

788 Id.

789 Id. at 738, n1.

790 Id.

791 Id.

792 Id.

lights were in fact on for the duration of the strike.[793] Mr. Forest testified that these lights "were on day and night" throughout the strike, beginning at 4:00 p. m. on the first day. Mr. Forest's testimony was corroborated by that of Mr. Johnson, a Union salesman on special duty the night of the spill. He testified that on the night of the spill "the racks and the complete area was lighted."[794] Finally, at least two Union employees were stationed in the control shack in the yard during the strike. Although some parts of the yard, including Gate 1, could not be seen from the control shack, the tank car loading racks were visible.[795] The court was convinced that Union Oil exercised due care because of the security measures that it put in place to forestall vandalism.

The outcome in the *Union Oil* case may have been different if that area was a vandalism and theft prone area. In that case a more extensive and elaborate security scheme would have been required because of the labor strike. If this kind of security measure was not put in place then the court would have held that the plaintiff-RP had failed to exercise due care against a foreseeable act of a third party. For instance in the another FWPCA case of *Proctor Whole Sale Co. v. United States,*[796] where the court relied heavily on another United States Court of Claims decision in *City of Pawtucket v. United States,*[797] the court made it clear that a claimant cannot recover, even if a vandal or third party immediately caused the spillage, if the claimant does not prove that it acted reasonably to prevent or forestall such intervention by the third party.[798] The burden of proof lies on the claimant.[799] The court found that Proctor Wholesale, the RP, did not exercise the required level of reasonable care.[800] The court noted that the spill occurred about forty days after the plaintiff acquired the property,

793 Id.

794 Id.

795 Id.

796 215 Ct. Cl. 1049, No. 398-76, 1978 WL 23785, *1 (1978).

797 211 Ct. Cl. 324 (1976).

798 1978 WL 23785, at *1.

799 Id.

800 1978 WL 23785, at *2.

with two oil tanks on it, from the City of Hickory.[801] The court lamented the fact that plaintiff apparently did not even trouble to ascertain for sure what the tanks contained, although it was quite aware of their existence.[802] The court also found that although Proctor was aware that third persons could gain access to the property and the tanks, it took no action prior to the spill to restrict or prevent such access to the area on which the tanks were located.[803] It noted particularly that: (1) there was no fence around the tanks or the property, (2) there was no external lighting on the property to help prevent vandalism, and (3) the area was not patrolled by police or other security personnel.[804] The court also noted that there was no single dike or beam around the tanks to retain oil accidentally or intentionally discharged from the tanks.[805] The court also lamented the fact that the company was clearly on notice from the type of the tanks that they might well contain oil or a comparable substance,[806] but yet nothing whatsoever was done in the forty days after the property on which the tanks stood was transferred from the City of Hickory to Proctor.[807] The court held that Forty days is not too short a period within which a property owner should take preventive action against spillage of oil (or a comparable substance) located on its property.[808]

The court concluded by saying:

"The result is that, here as in City of Pawtucket, supra, 'it was the omissions of plaintiff which gave the third party easy access to the tank area and created a situation conducive to vandalism,' and 'it cannot be said that a vandal was the sole cause of the spill within the meaning' of the statute. Because of its total and negligent inaction for a period of more than a month, plaintiff has failed to

---

801 Id.

802 Id.

803 Id.

804 Id at *2.

805 Id.

806 Id.

807 Id.

808 Id.

establish that the discharge was caused 'solely' by an act or omission of a third party. "IT IS THEREFORE ORDERED AND CONCLUDED that defendant's motion for summary judgment is granted, plaintiff's cross-motion for summary judgment is denied, and the petition is dismissed."[809]

In the *City of Pawtucket v. United States*,[810] a case on which the above *Proctor Wholesale Co.* case relied, the City of Pawtucket (City) sought reimbursement from the United States Government for clean-up expenses it incurred combating an oil spill from two city-owned storage tanks. The United States Court of Claims in its findings of fact noted that the City acquired the storage tanks in January 1974, when it purchased the land on which they were located.[811] No plans were made for the use of the oil in the tanks; even though plans were discussed concerning destruction of the tanks themselves.[812] Attempts to sell the oil failed when it proved to be 'stale' and unmerchantable.[813] The Court noted that at the time the City took possession, security facilities were in a state of disrepair.[814] Surrounding fences were incomplete and featured gaping holes through which even City employees gained access to the tanks.[815] Floodlights illuminating the tank area had burned out.[816] The lock on the gate did not have a key. The tanks' spigots were unlocked. Drainage facilities to protect against accidental spillage were in disrepair.[817] No action was taken with regard to the security facilities during the eight months of City ownership which preceded the oil spill.[818]

Based on these facts, the court found that it was the omissions of the plaintiff which gave the third party easy access to the tank area and creat-

809 Id.

810 211 Ct. Cl. 324, 1976 WL 23902, at *1.

811 1976 WL 23902, at *1.

812 Id. at *1.

813 Id.

814 Id.

815 Id.

816 Id.

817 Id.

818 Id.

ed a situation conducive to vandalism.[819] The court relied on the evidence that showed gaping holes in the protective fence, lack of lighting in the tank area, lack of a working lock on the gate (City personnel desiring access were forced to crawl under the fence), unprotected oil tank spigots, improper drainage spouts for possible overflow oil, and a variety of what the court called "almost 'Keystone Kop' antics of local guards and officials."[820] All of the above led the court to conclude that the City was definitely a major contributing cause to the oil spill. The court also held that in view of the above, it could not be said that a vandal was the sole cause of the spill within the meaning of 33 U.S.C. § 1321 (i)(1).[821]

A case that illustrates adequate care against foreseeable criminal acts of third parties is *General Motors Corp. v. United States*.[822] General Motors Corporation sought reimbursement for clean-up expenses it incurred in combating an oil spill from tanks it owned in Bristol, Connecticut.[823] The facts of the case which the government admitted, revealed that on or about April 18, 1973, oil in harmful quantities was discharged into the Pequabuck River, navigable waters of the United States from an onshore facility (known as the Northside Plant) owned and maintained by General Motors' New Departure-Hyatt Division in Bristol.[824] General Motors had ceased using the plant for manufacturing operations in 1971, and prepared to offer it for sale. At the time of the discharge, the facility was maintained in a closed condition, and the oil tanks had been drained, except for a reserve needed to provide boiler fuel for heating the facility to protect against equipment freezing in the

819 Id. at *2.

820 Id.

821 Id at *2, (*citing*, Tanker Hygrade No. 18, Inc. v. United States, 208 Ct.Cl. 488, 492-3, 526 F.2d 805, 807 (1975), *cert denied*, 426 U.S. 920 (1976) (holding that plaintiff is required to prove that the discharge was caused solely by an act or omission of a third party)).

822 213 Ct. Cl. 703 (1977).

823 213 Ct. Cl. at 703.

824 Id. at 703.

event of extremely cold weather.[825] The oil storage tanks were protected by a 10-foot high fence topped with barbed wire, with the fence chained and locked.[826] A second fence 12 feet high and topped with barbed wire surrounded the perimeter of the plant.[827] This fence was also chained and locked. In addition, the plant was regularly patrolled by the Bristol Police Department and by General Motors personnel on weekends.[828] In spite of these security precautions, vandals gained access to the tanks on April 18, 1973, and opened at least two of the valves on the tanks, and the oil spill resulted.[829] The court rejected the government's attempt to invoke the case of *City of Pawtucket v. United States,*[830] discussed above. The *General Motors Corp* court pointed out that the facts in that case are quite different from those in the instant controversy.[831] The court noted that the city, plaintiff in that case, was guilty of numerous omissions, and those omissions constituted a cause of the oil spill there.[832] The court pointed out that in the *City of Pawtucket* case a third party was not the sole cause, and thus the city was not entitled to recover.[833] Based on the facts of the case outlined above, which the government admitted, the *General Motors* court concluded that the situation in the instant case is different from the situation in the *City of Pawtucket* case. Based on the foregoing reasoning the court distinguished the *City of Pawtucket* case and refused to follow its reasoning as requested by the government defendant in the case.

In other cases, however, the security of valve mechanisms has played a key role in determining whether reasonable care was exercised to prevent vandalism. For instance in *Chicago, Milwaukee, St. Paul Pacific Railroad*

---

825 Id.

826 Id.

827 Id.

828 Id.

829 Id.

830 211 Ct. Cl.324(1976).

831 213 Ct. Cl. at 704.

832 Id. at 704.

833 Id.

*Corp. v. United States,*[834] the United States Court of Claims allowed an RP to recover removal cost because the valve handle was protectively removed. Whereas in *Anglo Fabrics Co. v. United States,*[835] an RP was not allowed to recover removal costs because the protection of the valve against vandalism was inadequate. Also in *M/V Anna-Maria & Elena, Inc. v. United States,*[836] the RP was not allowed to recover removal costs from the government because the "minimal step" of chaining or removing valve handles was not taken by the RP. In the *City of Pawtuckett v. United States,*[837] discussed earlier, recovery was disallowed because the spigots were left unlocked. In *Travelers Insurance Co. v. United States,*[838] the Court of Claims denied recovery because the handle was left on the valve. In *Minneapolis Park & Recreation Board v. United States,*[839] recovery was denied because valve handle was not removed and vandals had previously broken the padlock on the door.

It follows, therefore, that the failure to properly tighten the cap and plug would breach the duty of reasonable care.[840] If, therefore, the RP fails to tighten the plug and valve, it could not be considered blameless if a vandalism- related spill resulted.

A renowned legal commentator articulated the nature of the due care that an RP must take against foreseeable acts of vandalism when he said:

---

834 *Chicago, Milwaukee, St. Paul Pacific Railroad Corp. v. United States,* 216 Ct.Cl. at 160, 575 F.2d 839, 842 (1978) (holding that owners exercised reasonable care to forestall third-party intervention in abandoned meat-packing plant in which burglars opened valves causing oil to seep into navigable waters of United States, where owners had acquired plant only ten days before burglary, valves had been closed and each valve handle protectively removed, entire assemblage was protected against accidental overflow by capped vent pipe, there was perimeter fence around facility and there was outside lighting; thus owners were entitled to be reimbursed by United States for costs incurred in cleanup and removal of the oil).

835 227 Ct.Cl. 604, 605 (1981).

836 14 Env't Rep.Cas. (BNA) 1314, 1316 (Ct.Cl.), *opinion adopted,* 225 Ct.Cl. 535 (1980).

837 211 Ct.Cl. 324, 326, 546 F.2d 430 (1976).

838 2 Cl.Ct. 758, 762 (1983).

839 18 Env't Rep.Cas. (BNA), 1015, 1016 (Ct.Cl.), *opinion adopted,* 231 Ct.Cl. 738 (1982).

840 See Total Petroleum Co. v. United States, 12 Cl.Ct. 178, 183 (1987) (failure to reasonably adhere to established safety procedures precludes recovery of clean-up costs for oil spill).

"What is required is merely the conduct of the reasonable person of ordinary prudence under the circumstances, and the greater danger, or the greater responsibility, is merely one of the circumstances, demanding only an increased amount of care."[841] "If the risk is an appreciable one, and the possible consequences are serious, the question is not one of mathematical probability alone. It may be highly improbable that lightning will strike at any given place or time; but the possibility is there, and it may require precautions for the protection of inflammables. As the gravity of the possible harm increases, the apparent likelihood of its occurrence need be correspondingly less to generate a duty of precaution."[842]

The above cases also demonstrate clearly that the exercise of adequate precaution and due care against foreseeable criminal acts of third parties cannot be overemphasized and is a sine qua non to the successful invocation of the third party defense in OPA, FWPCA and CERCLA cases.

The NPFC Claims Division in its adjudication of claims by Responsible Parties invoking the third party defense and filing claims for reimbursement of removal costs and damages, has followed the approach of the courts in the CERCLA and FWPCA cases discussed above. For instance in an NPFC claim filed in 1997 by a corporate RP-Claimant, and administratively closed the same year, the claimant's third party defense was rejected initially by the NPFC Claim Management Division because of the emphasis placed on the requirement that the RP be absolutely free from contributory fault.[843] The third party defense also failed because the RP initially failed to prove that he exercised due care or took precautions against foreseeable acts or omissions of third parties or the foreseeable consequences of those acts or omissions.[844] This case involved an oil spill caused by a third party's accidental striking of a pipeline belonging to

841 See. W. Prosser & W. Keeton, Prosser & Keeton on Torts, § 34 at 209 (1984) (hereafter cited as Prosser).

842 Id. at § 31, p 171.

843 See NORCO Pipeline Inc., NPFC Claim Summary/Recommendation Form, Claim No 9C6408-001, p1 (10/09/1997) (on file with the NPFC and available upon request from the NPFC).

844 Id. at 1.

the RP.[845] The third party was a contractor hired by the Marshall County Conservation District and was not in any form of contractual relationship with the RP.[846] The third party was repairing a levee with a dragline when the accident occurred.[847] The ruptured pipeline discharged approximately 13.071 barrels (549 gallons) of unleaded gasoline into the surface water and drainage ditch.[848] The RP's pipeline was located on the east bank of the Illinois River and threatened the waters of the River and nearby wetlands.[849] The initial claim and the third party defense invoked by the RP-Claimant failed for four reasons: (1) The RP-Claimant failed to properly mark the pipeline in accordance with Federal Regulations; (2) The pipeline markers were not of the proper character; (3) The right of way was not properly maintained by the RP-Claimant; (4) The RP-Claimant failed to maintain a written program to notify regular excavators as required under Federal Law.[850] After the RP's claim and defense was denied by the NPFC, it filed a new claim for reconsideration of the initial claim.[851] Because the RP proved by a preponderance of the evidence in the reconsideration claim that he exercised due care and took adequate precautions against foreseeable acts or omissions of third parties his third party defense was allowed.[852]

The NPFC Claim Management Division reversed itself on all the four grounds on which it based its initial decision to deny the RP's claim and defense. The main contention in the initial claim, which remained the same in the reconsideration claim was whether the RP complied with the provisions of 49 CFR 195.410. This provision prescribes minimum requirements for operating and maintaining pipeline systems constructed with steel pipe.[853] 49 CFR 195.410 provides in pertinent part:

---

845 Id.

846 Id.

847 Id.

848 Id.

849 Id. at 1.

850 Id.

851 Id.

852 Id. at 3.

853 49 CFR §195.400.

"(a) Except as provided in paragraph (b) of this section, each operator shall place and maintain line markers over each buried pipeline in accordance with the following:

(1) Markers must be located at each public road crossing, at each railroad crossing, and in sufficient number along the remainder of each buried line so that its location is accurately known.

(2) The marker must state at least the following on a background of sharply contrasting color:

  (i) The word "Warning," "Caution," or "Danger" followed by the words "Petroleum (or the name of the hazardous liquid transported) Pipeline", or "Carbon Dioxide Pipeline," all of which, except for markers in heavily developed urban areas, must be in letters at least 1 inch (25 millimeters) high with an approximate stroke of 1/4 -inch (6.4 millimeters).

  (ii) The name of the operator and a telephone number (including area code) where the operator can be reached at all times."[854]

This regulation in part provides that pipelines be marked in such a manner that the location of the pipeline is accurately known.[855] The RP provided evidence to support its contention that there were no Department of Transportation (DOT) interpretations of this section which sets forth the number of markers required per foot of pipeline.[856] The evidence was a letter from the Department of Transportation Office of Pipeline Safety, dated July 2, 1997.[857] Statements from this letter indicated that the criteria for line markers vary depending on the circumstances such as general accessibility to the pipeline, operator control of the area and land use.[858] The Claims Manager pointed out that the RP's pipeline was located in a conservation District, to which access was very limited.[859] The Claims

854 49 CFR §195.410.

855 See NORCO Pipeline Inc., NPFC Claim Summary/Recommendation Form, Claim No 9C6408-001, at 1.

856 Id. at 1.

857 Id.

858 Id. at 1.

859 Id. at 1.

Manager relied on evidence provided by the RP which showed that there was a locked gate entrance to the District. The Claims Manager pointed out that although the NPFC was aware of the use of the land initially (when the first claim was adjudicated), it was unaware of how remote and secure the area was.[860] The Claims Manager relied on evidence submitted by the RP which indicated that access to the District was limited by a locked gate which could only be opened with the authorization of the State.[861]

In this reconsideration claim, the RP-Claimant provided additional and more compelling evidence regarding the remoteness of the pipeline location which the Claims Manager found persuasive in accepting the claimant's contention that the markers which were in place were in fact adequate to mark the pipeline and comply with the regulations.[862] Evidence presented by the claimant in support of this reconsideration indicated that there were six pipeline markers, including an aerial marker (aerial markers are conspicuous signs that warns people that a pipeline is present in a particular place) which included the claimant's name and phone number (as required by the regulations) at the entrance to the Conservation District.[863] Additionally, from the entrance to the spill site, there were seven more pipeline markers. These markers were all placed within two feet of the pipeline.[864] Because of the remoteness of location and security which surrounded the RP's pipeline, the NPFC was of the opinion that the markers used were sufficient to adequately mark the pipeline in accordance with the Federal Regulations.[865]

On the second ground upon which it denied the initial claim, the NPFC also reversed itself. The contention was whether the pipeline markers were not the proper character.[866] As pointed out earlier in the regulations reproduced above, certain wordings are required to appear on the pipeline

860 Id. at 2.
861 Id.
862 Id. at 2.
863 Id.
864 Id.
865 Id.
866 Id. at 2.

markers. The evidence (photographs) presented in the initial unsuccessful claim showed that not all the markers had such language.[867] Upon reconsideration however, the RP provided sufficient evidence that these markers were old markers from the prior owner of the pipeline, and simply had not been removed.[868] The evidence presented by the RP showed that all of the markers that the RP installed were in compliance with the Federal Regulations.[869] The Claims Manager concluded by saying:

"Based on the analysis above, which concluded that the number of NORCO pipeline markers are adequate to mark the pipeline, the "old" markers are not relevant to this decision."[870]

The NPFC also reversed itself on the third ground upon which it denied the initial claim. The contention was whether the right of way was not properly maintained by the RP-Claimant. One of the reasons the NPFC's Claims Manager granted the RP's claim upon reconsideration, was the location of the RP's pipeline within a Conservation District.[871] The Claims Manager noted that the very nature of such a District is to preserve the land in a relatively "natural" state.[872] It was therefore not reasonable to have a real "clearing" near the pipeline. The Claims Manager also accepted the claimant's contention that the clearing around the right of way was obvious, but not so barren as to defeat the purpose of the District.[873] The RP also presented evidence that it had requested permission to clear the vegetation, but the request was denied.[874] The RP-Claimant was only allowed to clear an 8" diameter, which it did. The Claims Manager concluded that given the use of the land, this was probably reasonable. The Claims Manager also relied on additional evidence presented by the RP

867 Id.

868 Id.

869 Id.

870 Id.

871 Id. at 2.

872 Id.

873 Id.

874 Id.

which showed that the closest line was approximately two (2) feet from the spill site.[875]

The NPFC also reversed itself on the fourth ground upon which it denied the initial claim. The contention here was whether the RP failed to maintain a written program to prevent damage to pipelines as required by Federal Regulations. This Federal Regulation is codified in 49 CFR §195.442. This regulation provides in pertinent part:

"(a) Except as provided in paragraph (d) of this section, each operator of a buried pipeline must carry out, in accordance with this section, a written program to prevent damage to that pipeline from excavation activities. For the purpose of this section, the term "excavation activities" includes excavation, blasting, boring, tunneling, backfilling, the removal of aboveground structures by either explosive or mechanical means, and other earthmoving operations."[876]

The Claims Manager found that although the claimant failed to comply with this provision, compliance was impossible because the regulation was not in effect at the time the oil discharge incident took place, therefore the third party defense could not be denied on this ground.[877]

Based on the foregoing the NPFC granted the claim of the RP and upheld its third party defense. This NPFC claim is a prototypical example of how the NPFC and the courts of law will approach claims dealing with the third party defense. Every conceivable regulation that goes to the issue of exercise of due care as well as adequate precaution against foreseeable acts or omissions of third parties will be invoked by the NPFC or sole-cause third parties to defeat an RP's claim for reimbursement against the Fund or indemnity against alleged sole-cause third parties. This will invariably place an RP under the onerous burden of proving that it did not violate the regulations invoked to defeat his third party defense. The claimant in the above illustration obviously failed woefully to carry that burden in its initial claim, but succeeded in meeting its burden when the claim

875 Id.

876 49 CFR §195.442.

877 See NORCO Pipeline Inc., NPFC Claim Summary/Recommendation Form, Claim No 9C6408-001, at 2.

was reconsidered. Not every claimant would be as fortunate as NORCO Pipeline Inc. (the RP) was.

Another NPFC claim that illustrates the approach of the NPFC Claims Division to third party defenses under OPA and the likely approach of the courts of law is the Bergerson Enterprises claim against the Oil Spill Liability Trust Fund, which was administratively closed in 1995.[878] This claim was submitted by Bergerson Enterprises, the owner of the T/B Maddie M (vessel) for reimbursement of uncompensated removal costs.[879] The claimant as the owner of the vessel was designated as the Responsible Party (RP). He asserted the third party defense in the OPA.[880] The oil pollution incident in this case occurred when "someone" (vandals) went onto the barge, hooked up a generator (battery) to the fuel tank, and pumped fuel oil out of the tank.[881] After pumping an unknown quantity of oil, the vandals left the scene, leaving the battery hooked up to the fuel tank.[882] As a result of leaving the battery hooked up, fuel oil spilled into the waters of Tillamook Bay.[883] The NPFC's Claims Division's Case Team III upheld the claimant's third party defense.[884] The decision to uphold this defense was based on the fact specific analysis of the incident.[885] The Claims Division pointed out that it has been established in the courts in CERCLA cases, that a valid third party defense requires that one be able to prove by a preponderance of the evidence how the incident started, how it progressed, and that the third party was not associated contractually with the RP.[886] The Claims Division also emphasized that one must be able to show by

878 Bergerson Enterprises, NPFC Generic Document-FPN: 133038, Final Decision on Third Party Defense, Claim No 133038-001, pl (07/26/1995), (on file with the NPFC and available upon request from the NPFC).

879 Bergerson Enterprises, NPFC Generic Document-FPN: 133038, E-mail: Third Party Defense, Claim No 133038-001, pl (07/25/1995).

880 Id.

881 Id.

882 Id.

883 Id.

884 Bergerson Enterprises, NPFC Generic Document-FPN: 133038, Final Decision on Third Party Defense, Claim No 133038-001, pl (07/26/1995).

885 Id. at 1.

886 Id. at 1.

a preponderance of the evidence that the RP exercised due care in safe-guarding against the incident.[887]

On the first requirement of proof that a third party caused the oil spill, the Claims Managers noted that the local police were able to determine how the perpetrators caused the incident; how they got on board the vessel, and how the actual act of vandalism was accomplished.[888] The Claims Managers observed that the police were able to describe the perpetrators as individuals who must have had a rather sophisticated knowledge of this type of vessels and fuel tanks in order to accomplish this act.[889] The Claims Managers found that although investigations did not point to one person or group of persons, this was not fatal to granting the defense.[890] The Claims Managers noted that in the area where the incident occurred - namely a port – there would be a significant number of persons who could accomplish this act.[891]

On the second requirement of proof that the RP must exercise due care in safe-guarding the incident, the Claims Managers were convinced that the security arrangements made for the Dock and the vessel were adequate enough to satisfy this requirement.[892]

*Security at the Dock*: The Claims Managers found that the RP moored the vessel at the most secure marina/port in the region.[893] There were prominent "No Trespassing" signs at the port; frequent patrols by the local

---

887 Id.

888 Id.

889 Id. see also, Bergerson Enterprises, NPFC Generic Document-FPN: 133038, E-mail: Third Party Defense, Claim No 133038-001, p1 (07/25/1995)(The claimant indicated that the type of vandalism involved in this case requires a certain sophistication with this type of vessel, fuel tanks, and "hot wiring," in general).

890 Id., see also Bergerson Enterprises, NPFC Generic Document-FPN: 133038, E-mail: Third Party Defense, Claim No 133038-001, p1 (07/25/1995)(The Police report of the vandalism indicated that there were no leads or suspects. The claimant also indicated that there were no "disgruntled" employees that would have had access and/or motive to do this act. Subsequent conversations with the Claimant's Attorney and the Port Manager, did not shed any more light on the "who" aspect of the third party defense test).

891 Id.

892 Id. at 1.

893 Id.

police; located approximately fifty yards from the Coast Guard Station, which is manned on a 24 hour basis.[894] No similar acts of vandalism had been reported in this port.[895]

*Security on the Vessel*: The vessel involved is an open barge – flat pile driving barge with crane driver.[896] All machinery located on the vessel were welded down; fuel tank, and "dry shack" storage areas were both secured with padlocks.[897] Based on the foregoing reasoning and findings of fact by the Claims Managers, they concluded that the claimant had done all he could possibly do to prevent this type of pollution incident. The approach of the claims managers in the instant claim under discussion is similar to the approach of the courts in the CERCLA and FWPCA cases analyzed above.

Another NPFC Claims Division case illustrates the difficulty of successfully proving the third party defense by a preponderance of the evidence. In an NPFC claim filed by Plantation Pipeline Company (Plantation) on December 5, 1994 for uncompensated removal cost and for payments made for damages to real or personal property, the RP-Claimant's claim was denied because (1) the claimant failed to prove that the oil spill was an OPA incident; (2) the claimant failed to prove that the damage to its pipeline that caused the oil spill was a result of the act or omission of a third party; (3) the claimant failed to prove that it exercised due care under the circumstances.[898] In this case, Plantation, the claimant-RP discovered a leak in a pipeline owned by it of approximately 165 barrels

---

894 Id.

895 Id., see also Bergerson Enterprises, NPFC Generic Document-FPN: 133038, E-mail: Third Party Defense, Claim No 133038-001, p 2 (07/25/1995)(The General "criminal" offenses reported in this port before the instant incident included stealing of gas cans from the deck of vessels).

896 Id.

897 Id., see also, Bergerson Enterprises, NPFC Generic Document-FPN: 133038, E-mail: Third Party Defense, Claim No 133038-001, p 2 (07/25/1995)(The claimant indicated that all padlocks were in place at the time the incident occurred).

898 See Plantation Pipeline Company, NPFC Generic Document, Claim Recommendation, Claim No 9C4041-001, p 1-3 (4/17/1996) (on file with the NPFC and available upon request from the NPFC).

of gasoline.[899] The leak occurred in a residential neighborhood in Cobb County, Georgia.[900]

*Plantation's failure to prove that this was an OPA incident:* The NPFC Claims Managers observed that the EPA's report on the incident evinced the fact that the pipeline leak posed no potential for surface water contamination.[901] According to the EPA report, the closest waterway, Sweetwater Creek, was approximately five miles away.[902] Apart from that the EPA's primary concern in the instant case was air pollution and soil contamination rather than water pollution.[903] The EPA's report also failed to document or record any mention that the company's clean up activities were in any way coordinated or directed by the Federal-On-Scene Coordinator (FOSC).[904]

On May 4, 1992 at 10:31 AM gasoline was discovered in a culvert or transverse drain behind a home, which Plantation believed leaked from its leaking pipeline.[905] Although it was not clear whether the EPA knew of the oil in the culvert, Plantation did advise the State of Georgia's Environmental Protection Division (EPD) of the discharge in the culvert.[906] According to the EPD's report on the incident, Plantation conducted extensive soil and groundwater sampling due to the alleged discharge in the culvert.[907] However the result of the test or sampling showed low concentrations levels of gasoline contamination in the surrounding soil.[908] The Oil spill Liability Trust Fund can only be used for the payment of cleanup costs for oil spills that impact navigable waters or pose a substantial threat of impacting same. That was why Plantation argued that the gasoline from its pipeline discharged into US navigable waters, and therefore

899 Id. at 1.
900 Id.
901 Id. at 2.
902 Id.
903 Id.
904 Id.
905 Id.
906 Id.
907 Id.
908 Id. at 2.

the incident fell under OPA jurisdiction.[909] According to Plantation, a natural spring fed this culvert. The culvert emptied into a beaver pond that emptied into a wetland, an unnamed tributary, the Sweetwater Creek and into the Chattahoochee River, a US navigable water.[910] Plantation therefore concluded that the culvert was a US navigable water. The Claims Managers however noted that the owner of the wetland had since developed it for commercial use.[911] The NPFC Claims Division observed that based upon its review of all the documentation obtained up to the date of the closing of the claim, Plantation had failed to provide any evidence that it notified the EPA of the alleged discharge from the culvert.[912] The EPA's report on the incident which stated categorically that the discharge posed no threat to surface waters, contradicted Plantation's assertion that an OPA incident had occurred.[913]

*Plantation's failure to prove that the damage to its pipeline that caused the oil spill was a result of the act or omission of a third party:* The dents on Plantation's pipeline were found to be the immediate cause of the oil spill.[914] Plantation tried to prove that the dent to its pipeline was not caused during the installation of the pipeline in 1968.[915] It pointed accusing fingers at Gemcraft Homes, Inc. (Gemcraft) as the sole cause third party of the incident.[916] According to Plantation, Gemcraft's construction equipment dented its pipeline while building the homes at 7047 and 7049 Ivy Pointe Drive in the late 1980's.[917] These two homes were built on opposite sides of the pipeline where the leak occurred.[918] According to Plantation, the dents caused by Gemcraft's equipment weakened the metal pipeline

909 Id.

910 Id.

911 Id.

912 Id.

913 Id.

914 Id. at 3.

915 Id.

916 Id.

917 Id.

918 Id. at 3.

that eventually caused the 1992 leak.[919] Plantation argued that Gemcraft was the only company conducting extensive construction activity at this site at the time. The Claim Management Division rejected this assertion because information supplied by Plantation itself showed that other companies were digging in the same general area to install utilities to the homes Gemcraft built.[920] Although Plantation argued that the debris found between the cracked pipeline and the top soil pointed to the culpability of Gemcraft, the Claims Managers rejected the argument because Plantation did not provide additional information that proved the debris belonged to Gemcraft.[921] Furthermore, Plantation failed to show that the debris in question was not in any way associated with its activities or that it did not bury the debris.[922]

Plantation provided three reasons why the dents in the pipeline were not caused during its installation in 1968.[923] First, the Pipeline was visually inspected in an open trench before being buried with soil.[924] Second there was no building debris within the soil cover in 1968 because the land was not occupied at the time.[925] And thirdly, the damage combined with normal operating pressure cycles, would not have allowed the fatigue life of the pipeline to maintain its integrity without leaking earlier.[926] To prove its assertion, Plantation hired Stress Engineering Services, Inc. (SES) to conduct a failure analysis of the damaged pipeline. SES concluded that the damage did reduce the life span of the pipeline to no more than six years, and that the dent did occur around after 1985.[927] The NPFC also hired its own expert, GAB Business Services Inc. (GAB) to determine the cause of the leak. GAB hired a subcontractor, H & A Corporation (H & A), and the subcontractor participated in SES's metallurgical testing on the damaged

919 Id.
920 Id.
921 Id.
922 Id.
923 Id.
924 Id. at 3.
925 Id.
926 Id.
927 Id. at 3.

pipeline.[928] The NPFC's expert could not establish the time period when the pipeline incurred the dents.[929]

All the above arguments of the claimant were rejected by the NPFC Claims Division. On the first argument, the Claims Managers found that Plantation had failed to support or document the assertion.[930] On the second argument, it was also found that Plantation did not provide supporting evidence that documents the assertion. Plantation also failed to explain how some of the debris such as wooden poles and railroad ties, are used at a home construction site.[931] On the third assertion, the Claims Division noted the fact that its own expert's opinion on the possible date of the dent contradicts the assertion of Plantation's expert that it happened in the late 1980s. The Claims Division refused to rule out the possibility that Plantation exposed the damaged section of the pipeline.[932] For instance the facts revealed that Plantation owned a smaller, 14-inch pipeline that ran parallel with the damaged pipeline. Plantation failed to indicate the exact time it installed the smaller pipeline, or whether it had exposed this pipeline near the area of the damaged pipeline.[933] Based on a meticulous review of all the information provided by Plantation, the NPFC's expert, and the office of pipeline Safety (OPS), the Claims Division concluded that Plantation had failed to meet its burden that the cause of the purported OPA incident is the sole fault of a third party.[934] The Claims Division also found that the information with which Plantation attempted to implicate Gemcraft was speculative and insufficient to link Gemcraft, the home builder, to the oil pollution incident.

This NPFC case was correctly decided. A contrary opinion would have created an atmosphere where almost any one could be held liable as a sole cause third party for an OPA incident. It also shows that evidence

928 Id. at 3-4.

929 Id. at 4.

930 Id.

931 Id.

932 Id.

933 Id.

934 Id. at 4.

that is speculative in nature would not satisfy the threshold requirement for proving sole fault of third parties. The instant case also underlines the difficulty of proving sole fault of third parties in oil spills from dented and cracked pipelines. It will be very difficult for RP-Claimants to prove: (1) the exact time of the dent (2) that a particular third party actually caused the dent (3) that it did not cause the dent itself either at the time of installation or at the time it was installing sister- pipelines close to the damaged pipeline.

*Lessons learned from Plantation's failure to prove third party culpability*: This case shows that documentation of activities or a paper trail is very important for the avoidance of future OPA pipeline oil spill related liability. Documenting every activity that occurs during the installation of a pipeline could make a world of difference between OPA liability running into millions or billions of dollars or total exculpation from OPA liability. For instance all oil or petrochemical companies who own or operate pipelines should make sure that they document the fact that their newly installed or newly renovated pipelines were visually inspected in an open trench before being buried in the soil. It is also important for them to document whether the land on which the pipelines are located was occupied at the time of their installation and whether there was no building debris within the soil cover at that time. This is very critical because it is reasonable to argue that a third party involved in some construction work on the land above or around the pipeline caused the dent leading to the spill. This will require a regular inspection of the vicinity of the pipeline and documentation of third party activity that could cause pipeline rupture. Thorough inspection should be carried out by geologists, seismologists and other experts to see if any damage has been or could be caused by such third party activities. Copies of such documentations should be filed with appropriate government agencies or departments like the Office of Pipelines Safety, US Coast Guard, The Environmental Protection Agency, and others. This documentation could serve as a line of defense against possible future OPA liability and could help to guarantee a successful invocation of the OPA or CERCLA third party defense.

*Plantation's failure to prove that it exercised due care*: The NPFC's Claims Division concluded that Plantation failed to exercise due care in this incident. The Office of Pipeline Safety (OPS) within the US department of Transportation regulates the pipeline industry. This agency sets minimum standards for installation and maintenance of pipelines as well as minimum guidelines for spill prevention and cleanup. Regulations for pipeline installation maintenance and leak prevention codified in 49 CFR §195 became effective on April 1, 1970. The regulation for spill response plans became effective on May 5, 1993. Plantation installed its pipeline in 1968, before the effective date of 49 CFR 195. Therefore design regulations for steel pipes were not mandatory for Plantation in this case.[935] The NPFC's expert after mechanical testing and chemical analysis concluded that Plantation's damaged pipe did meet or exceed standards established by the American Petroleum Institute. (Some of the design requirements set forth in the regulations refer to standards established by the American Petroleum Institute).[936]

However the Claims Division observed that current regulations require the industry to install all buried pipes in a manner that minimizes the introduction of secondary stresses and possibility of damage to the pipe.[937] The regulations also require the industry to bury the pipe at a depth to allow for soil cultivation. It was also noted that the regulations require the industry to perform soil backfilling in a manner that protects the pipe's protective outer coating and provides firm support for the pipe.[938] The Claims Division observed that Plantation had failed to provide any evidence that it exercised due care in this regard. The Claims Division pointed out that Plantation had failed to prove that it inspected the pipeline in the open trench. Plantation had also failed to prove its assertion that it was industry practice in 1968 to inspect the pipeline in an open trench.[939]

935 Id. at 4.

936 Id.

937 Id.

938 Id.

939 Id.

The Claims Manager pointed out that although the claimant had a number of leak prevention measures in place as is required under 49 CFR § 194 (rules for spill response plans), it had failed to explain why those measures did not prevent the May 1992 leak.[940] For instance the regulations require pipeline operators to test for external and internal corrosion. According to plantation, it uses a magnet flux instrument (smart pig) and an electronic kaliper to detect the presence of an anomaly in its pipeline. Both tests failed to detect the dents or the leak in the pipeline.[941] Although Plantation's expert stated in his report that neither the smart pig nor the electronic kaliper could have detected the dents, this was contradicted by an official of the Office of Oil Pipeline Safety (OPS).[942] This official concluded that smart pigs can identify dents, although the device is used primarily to detect corrosion.[943] The OPS official noted that the test results must be examined carefully to find pipeline dents.[944] So it logically follows that if this test was carefully examined the dent would have been detected before it worsened into a rupture of the pipe.

Apart from this Plantation usually monitored the amount of gasoline that enters and leaves the pipeline. The Claims Manager noted that by reconciling two amounts, the pipeline company could determine if a leak had occurred.[945] Plantation also routinely measured by computer the pressure through out the pipeline. At least one Plantation employee reviewed the pressure readings at all times, and was capable of immediately shutting down operations if a potential problem was detected.[946] The OPS regulations require pipeline companies to monitor pipeline pressure. The Claims Manager pointed out that Plantation had failed to explain why these two spill detection systems failed to alert the company of the gasoline leak.[947]

---

940 Id.

941 Id. at 4.

942 Id.

943 Id.

944 Id.

945 Id. at 5.

946 Id.

947 Id.

Plantation also failed to explain why its bi-weekly aerial patrols failed to alert it of Gemcraft's purported activities. The Claims Manager also pointed out that Plantation was not a first time or second time offender in relation to oil leaks. Between 1987 and 1996, Plantation had reported 45 accidents from its pipelines to OPS.[948] Outside force damage to the pipelines caused eleven of the accidents. However, during this period of time, OPS had cited Plantation three times for violations of pipeline regulations.[949] This unfavorable reputation of Plantation made it even harder for it to extricate itself from liability in this case. This shows that environmental integrity is always important in oil spill cases. A pipeline company that has operated responsibly will find it easier to prove due care compared to a company that is a regular violator of pipeline safety regulations. Based on the foregoing, the NPFC Claims Division concluded that Plantation could not successfully invoke the OPA third party defense.

Another NPFC Claims Division case that illustrates the possible approach of the courts is the case of *Reliance Insurance Company (Reliance)*.[950] *Reliance* was the insurer of the owners of the vessel, DRAGON LADY, and was by virtue of that a subrogor of the rights of the owners of the vessel. The facts of this case were quite straight forward and the third party defense was relatively easy for the subrogor to prove. On December 8, 1997, the pleasure yacht DRAGON LADY was docked at the Sundance Marina in the North Portland Harbor on the Columbia River in Oregon.[951] The Coast Guard's Marine Safety Office (MSO) Portland was notified by Portland Emergency 911 Dispatch that three boats were on fire in the marina. The MSO field officers arrived on scene while the vessels were ablaze.[952] According to the Federal On-Scene Coordinator (FOSC), fire department reports, and witnesses, the fire originated on the vessel

948 Id. at 5.

949 Id.

950 Reliance Insurance Company, NPFC Generic Document, Claim No 138009-001, p 1 (10/16/2000) (on file with the NPFC and available upon request from the NPFC).

951 Id. at 1.

952 Id.

TENDER VITTLES, which was docked between the other damaged vessel and the DRAGON LADY.[953] The insurers of the TENDER VITTLES confirmed that the fire originated on the TENDER VITTLES. The fire spread to the DRAGON LADY which sustained extensive hull damage and sank after the fire was extinguished.[954] Upon sinking, the DRAGON LADY discharged diesel oil into the water. Because the DRAGON LADY discharged the oil, its owners were deemed the Responsible Party (RP) as defined in the OPA.[955] The Claims Manager noted that there was no contractual relationship between the vessel that was the source of the fire and the designated RP.[956] The only relationship the RP had with the TENDER VITTLES was that it docked its boat next to the TENDER VITTLES.[957] The Claims Manager relied on the testimony of witnesses that saw the fire spread from the TENDER VITTLES to the DRAGON LADY.[958] The Claims Manager also relied on investigative reports of the Portland Bureau and the Oregon State Fire Marshall to conclude that TENDER VITTLES, the third party, was the sole cause of the spill.

The Claims Manager also found that the owner of the DRAGON LADY had exercised sufficient due care against foreseeable acts of third parties. The Claims Manager relied on a telephone interview with the Federal-On-Scene Coordinator (FOSC), in which he stated that the owners of the DRAGON LADY had violated no rules or regulations.[959] The FOSC had stated specifically that the Dragon Lady was properly moored in the slip at the marina.[960] In addition, the claims manager relied on the assertion of the claimant that the DRAGON LADY was in good operating condition and was securely moored at its regular mooring place in a commercial marina.[961] The Claims Manager pointed out that

953 Id.

954 Id.

955 Id.

956 Id. at 2.

957 Id.

958 Id.

959 Id. at 2-3.

960 Id. at 3.

961 Id.

there was no evidence to indicate that the TENDER VITTLES was a potential fire hazard and therefore, no evidence that the DRAGON LADY owners were negligent in mooring next to it.[962] The Claims Manager noted that the diesel oil leaked from the DRAGON LADY's internal fuel tanks which, according to the FOSC, melted because the fire was very hot.[963] The Claims Manager noted that the manufacturer properly installed the tanks on board. The Claims Manager also pointed out that the owner's proper docking of the vessel in good condition in a marina and storing of the diesel oil in the factory-installed internal fuel tanks showed that the RP exercised due care.[964]

The claims manager further observed that the owners of DRAGON LADY could not have reasonably foreseen that the boat next to theirs would catch fire, that the fire would spread to their boat, that the fire would so severely damage their boat and that the fire department would use water to cool the boat down after the flames were already extinguished which all in combination would cause their boat to sink and spill diesel fuel.[965] The Claims Manager further found that the precautions that the owners took to prevent an oil spill were: (1) owning a seaworthy yacht, (2) keeping the diesel in the internal fuel tanks, and (3) docking in a commercial marina.[966] The Claims Manager concluded that there was no evidence that the owners of DRAGON LADY could have taken any additional reasonable precautions to prevent this incident since it was not reasonably foreseeable.[967] Based on the foregoing analysis and reasoning, the Claims Manager decided that the claimant as subrogor to the rights of the RP had proven by a preponderance of evidence that the discharge was caused solely by the acts of a third party, and had therefore met its burden under 33 USC 2703(a)(3).[968]

962 Id. at 3.

963 Id.

964 Id.

965 Id.

966 Id.

967 Id. at 3.

968 Id. at 3.

## A.II. OPA ACT OF GOD DEFENSE - 33 USC §2703(a)(1).

There have been relatively few OPA cases addressing the scope of the Act of God defense specifically guaranteed in section 2703(a)(1) of the Act. These cases will be discussed in the latter part of this chapter. However there are a number of FWPCA and CERCLA cases that have addressed the scope of the Act of God defense. In most of these cases, the RP is usually suing as plaintiff to recover removal cost from a government Fund by virtue of freedom from liability because of the possible application of the "act of God" defense. In others the RP is the defendant being sued by the government for recovery of removal costs. These cases will be discussed succinctly in this part of chapter two. These cases are applicable to the OPA because of the very similar provisions of "act of God" in the statutes.

OPA defines "act of God" as "an unanticipated grave natural disaster or other natural phenomenon of an exceptional, inevitable, and irresistible character the effects of which could not have been prevented or avoided by the exercise of due care or foresight."[969] The FWPCA on its part defines "act of God" as "an act occasioned by an unanticipated grave natural disaster."[970] The first part of the OPA definition of Act of God mirrors the FWPCA provision. OPA then goes on too add more words and phrases to its definition of "act of God" to make it more cumbersome for an RP to successfully plead or invoke this defense. OPA's addition of words and phrases like "inevitable," "irresistible character," "exceptional," and "natural phenomenon" will make it harder under the OPA to invoke this defense than under the FWPCA.

969 33 USCA §2701(1).

970 Federal Water Pollution Control Act Amendments of 1972 (Clean Water Act), § 311(a)(12), (i)(1)(A), 33 U.S.C.A. § 1321(a)(12), (i)(1)(A).

## FWPCA ACT OF GOD DEFENSE CASES

### Sabine Towing & Transp. Co. v. United States.[971]

On the 29th of March, 1975, plaintiff's vessel, the T/S Colorado, struck an unknown underwater object in the Hudson River channel.[972] The Colorado was bound for Rensselaer, New York, with a cargo of petroleum products, and was opposite Roger's Island at the time of the incident. Although the crew did not realize that the ship's hull had been ruptured, the No. 2 port wing tank had suffered a tear that was some 20 feet long and 3-4 inches wide.[973] During the time the Colorado was moving up the Hudson, there was a freshet condition in the river, an increased rate of flow due in this instance to rain and the spring runoff of melted snow.[974] Freshets raise the level of the river, but they also wash down sediment, gravel, logs, rocks and other debris. Although there is no way to determine what may be rolled down the river and embedded during a freshet, it is "normal practice" (emphasis mine) not to interrupt regular navigation on this account.[975] It was assumed through all of the litigation in this case that the object that the Colorado struck was something that had been deposited in the river bed during the freshet that then existed.

There was no significant oil spillage from the ship until the ruptured tank was opened for discharging at Rensselaer. The opening released a partial vacuum in the tank that had been created as the oil inside had cooled from its high loading temperature and allowed 714.28 -1, 190.47 barrels (30,000 to 50,000 gallons) to escape out of the tear and into the Hudson. The Plaintiff contracted to have the oil cleaned up, and the cost had been stipulated at $113,943.41.[976] The plaintiff, the owner of the dis-

971 666 F.2d 561 (Ct. Cl. 1981).

972 666 F.2d. at 562.

973 Id. at 562-63.

974 Id. at 563.

975 Id. at 563.

976 Id.

charging vessel, T/S Colorado, brought this suit to recover his cost of cleaning up the oil spill that emanated from his vessel. He wanted to accomplish this by invoking the "act of God" defense in the FWPCA.

The *Sabine* court traced the strict liability encapsulated in the FWPCA to the Water Quality Improvement Act of 1970,[977] which repealed the Oil Pollution Act, 1924 and its amendments,[978] and established more stringent liability.[979] It is this liability section, as incorporated into the Federal Water Pollution Control Act Amendments of 1972,[980] that the *Sabine* court utilized in its construction of the "act of God" defense invoked by the plaintiff in this case.

*Sabine* (plaintiff) sought from the court the application of the defense that its spill was caused "solely by an act of God."[981] The questions relevant to our current discussion that was presented are whether the unknown debris that the Colorado (Sabine's vessel) struck, or the freshet condition that deposited it, falls within the meaning of "an act of God" as used in the statute.[982]

The *Sabine* court noted the FWPCA's definition of the phrase "an act of God" as "an act occasioned by an unanticipated grave natural disaster."[983] Because the legislative history of this definition is sparse, the court noted that there was a temptation to resort to the common-law meaning of "act of God" to help in determining how the phrase should be applied in FWPCA's section 1321 cases.[984] However the *Sabine* court decided not to yield to such interpretative temptation, due to the Supreme Court case of *Milwaukee v. Illinois*[985] where the Supreme Court in the

977 Pub.L.No. 91-224, 84 Stat. 91 (1970).

978 Pub.L.No. 91-224 at title I, s 108, 84 Stat. 113.

979 Pub.L.No. 91-224 at title I, s 102, 84 Stat. 91.

980 Pub.L.No. 92-500, title III, s 311, 86 Stat. 862 (1972) and codified at 33 U.S.C. s 1321 (1976).

981 *Sabine*, 666 F.2d. at 564.

982 Id. at 564.

983 33 U.S.C. s 1321(a)(12).

984 *Sabine*, 666 F.2d. at 564

985 451 U.S. 304 101 S.Ct. 1784, 68 L.Ed.2d 114 (1981) (federal common law supplanted by any federal statute addressing the question).

United States cautioned on the inappropriateness of using judicially created rules of decision in areas where Congress has legislated. This United States Supreme Court case was decided the same year as the *Sabine* case, but shortly before it. Were it not for this Supreme court decision, maybe the Sabine court would have borrowed from common law jurisprudence on "act of God." Following the binding United States Supreme Court decision in *Milwaukee v. Illinois,* the *Sabine* court concluded that common-law cases on acts of God, to the extent that they embody judicial decisions on allocating the burden of mishap, should not be used in determining the allocation that Congress intended in section 1321 of the FWPCA.[986]

Having resolved to look solely within the four walls of the FWPCA instead of common law jurisprudence, the *Sabine* court dug intensively into the legislative history of the FWPCA for answers. The court found that the definition of "act of God" as it appears at section 1321(a)(12) emerged from the conference committee for the final version of the Water Quality Improvement Act of 1970.[987] The House version of the Act had left the phrase undefined, and the definition in the Senate version was one that the conference committee was concerned did not require a lack of foreseeability.[988] The Senate provision read: "an act occasioned exclusively by violence of nature without the interference of any human action." The conference committee's substitution, as the conference report explained, was intended to be very restrictive.[989] The term "act of God" is defined to mean an act occasioned by an unanticipated grave natural disaster. The *Sabine* court pointed out that this definition varies from that of the Senate definition and, under this definition, only those acts about which the owner could have had no foreknowledge, could have made no plans to avoid, or could not predict would be included.[990] Thus, grave natural disasters which could not be anticipated in the design, location, or opera-

986 *Sabine*, 666 F.2d. at 564.

987 Id. at 564.

988 Id.

989 Id. at 564, (*citing*, Conf.Rep.No. 940, 91st Cong., 2d Sess., reprinted in (1970) U.S. Code Cong. & Ad.News 2712, 2719).

990 *Sabine*, 666 F.2d. at 564.

tion of the facility or vessel by reason of historic, geographic, or climatic circumstances or phenomena would be outside the scope of the owner's or operator's responsibility.[991]

The Sabine court reasoned that the definition, as enacted, should be strictly construed.[992] The court observed that the conference committee made it clear that an occurrence shall be an "act of God" if it results solely from a grave natural disaster and if that grave natural disaster is wholly unanticipated.[993]

On the first question of whether there was a "grave natural disaster," the *Sabine* court held that based on the facts of the case before it, there was none. The court found that neither the spring runoff of melted snow nor the object struck by the Colorado was a disaster as the word is commonly used.[994] For the common usage of the word "disaster" the court turned to the Webster's New Collegiate Dictionary, which defines disaster in the following ways:

> "( A) sudden calamitous event bringing great damage, loss, or destruction; broadly : a sudden or great misfortune "syn DISASTER, CALAMITY, CATASTROPHE, CATACLYSM shared meaning element: an event or situation that is regarded as a terrible misfortune"[995]

The *Sabine* court relied heavily on uncontradicted statistical testimony at the trial that the flow rate on the Hudson on the day of the incident was equaled or exceeded on 25 percent of all the days in that water year and that those days were evenly distributed over that year.[996] Based on this uncontradicted testimony, the *Sabine* court pointed out that to contend that the freshet on March 29, 1975, was a disaster is to contend that the

---

991 Id. at 564, (*citing*, Conf.Rep.No. 940, 91st Cong., 2d Sess., reprinted in (1970) U.S. Code Cong. & Ad. News 2712, 2722).

992 *Sabine*, 666 F.2d. at 564.

993 Id.

994 Id. at 564-565.

995 See. Webster's New Collegiate Dictionary (1973).

996 *Sabine*, 666 F.2d. at 565.

Hudson is in a disaster condition one-quarter of the time.[997] Furthermore, it noted that Congress restricted its definition to "grave" disasters, making clear that the occurrence must be of great magnitude before it falls within the liability exception of section 1321.[998]

On the second point, whether the circumstances of the hull rupture were "unanticipated" within the meaning of section 1321, the court held that they were not.[999] The *Sabine* court noted the frequency of freshet conditions on the Hudson and the fact that the danger that they cause are well known to those who navigate the river. The *Sabine* court read the tight language of the conference committee report as clearly indicating that Congress did not mean to allow recovery for spills resulting from events as regular and predictable as freshets.[1000]

The court rejected Sabine's argument that anticipatable or not, it still could not have avoided the accident without suspending its operations, and that Congress could not have intended that shippers stop using the Hudson whenever there is danger from freshets.[1001] The court was convinced that the plaintiff's argument overstated the burden that section 1321 imposes.[1002] The *Sabine* court in its reasoning pointed out that if shippers have established a general practice not to interrupt normal navigation during freshets and, presumably, to absorb in their operating costs any damage to their ships from freshet-related incidents, then it does not seem harsh for Congress to require shippers also to absorb the costs of cleaning up any oil that is spilled when those accidents occur.[1003] The court pointed out further that it would be inconsistent with the strictness with which the conference committee recommended that "unanticipated" for the purposes of section 1321 be read, to allow the section to cover regular and frequent

---

997 Id.

998 Id. at 565.

999 Id. at 565.

1000 Id.

1001 Id.

1002 Id.

1003 Id. at 565.

conditions, like freshets, where the dangers are expected and where the losses are normally worked into the cost of doing business.[1004]

The plaintiff's final argument was that it is wrong to construe the "act of God" defense narrowly.[1005] The contentions basically were: (1) that a strict reading would discourage spillers from making cleanups themselves and (2) that the defenses are remedial and thus should be broadly construed.[1006] The court held that a holistic reading of section 1321 warrants a rejection of those arguments.[1007] The court pointed out that this section places the primary responsibility for oil spill cleanup on the President. The court observed that even though spillers may clean up their own spills, the section specifically does not rely on their doing so.[1008] The court noted that the general conception of the section is that the Government will perform the cleanup operations and recoup its costs from the spillers, subject to certain liability defenses.[1009] The inclusion of those defenses in section 1321(i) is not encouragement to spillers to clean up their spills themselves but only a way to keep constant the allocation of the cost.[1010] Spillers who clean up may recover costs from the Government in just those situations in which the Government would have had to have borne the costs itself.[1011] The court held that since the liability of the spiller does remain constant, irrespective of who actually makes the cleanup, there can be no special inducement in section 1321(i) for the spiller to do so.[1012]

Noting that the entire history of section 1321 shows Congress's desire for a comprehensive solution to the oil spill problem, the court held that it is section 1321 that is remedial and not any of the defenses to it.[1013] It is section 1321 as a whole that should be construed liberally. Based on the

1004 Id.
1005 Id.
1006 Id.
1007 Id.
1008 Id.
1009 Id.
1010 Id.
1011 Id.
1012 Id.
1013 Id. at 565-566.

foregoing, the *Sabine* court held that the circumstances found to surround the plaintiff's oil spill were not "an act of God" within the meaning of 33 U.S.C. s 1321(i)(1) (A) and that the plaintiff is not eligible under that section to recover its cleanup costs from the Government.[1014]

As earlier explained the additional phrases and words added to the definition of "act of God under the OPA would make it even harder for RP's to successfully invoke the this defense. The word "inevitable" used in the OPA definition of "act of God" means, incapable of being avoided and evaded.[1015] The synonyms for this word includes, certain, ineluctable, ineludible, inescapable, inevasible, necessary, returnless, unavoidable, unescapable, and unevadable.[1016] Related words includes, ineliminable, sure, unpreventable; decided, settled; destined, foreordained; inexorable, and inflexible.[1017] All these synonyms and related words for the word "inevitable" points to the fact that it must not have been anticipated or avoidable in any way. Any disaster or other natural phenomenon of whatever shape or form would not qualify as "act of God," unless they fit into this definitional structure. Therefore, if the disaster is eluctable, eludible, escapable, evasible, avoidable, eliminable, preventable, and evadable the "act of God" defense cannot be invoked successfully.

*RP MUST EXERCISE DUE CARE*

One important phrase in the OPA definition of "act of God" is the part that says "the effects of which could not have been prevented or avoided by the exercise of due care or foresight."[1018] This means that even if the disaster or natural phenomenon is subjectively unanticipated, that alone would not satisfy the "act of God" defense. By "subjectively unanticipated," I mean that there are some natural disasters that some areas are prone to occasionally (once in three or four years) but which the RP may not

1014 Id. at 566.

1015 See. Merriam-Webster's Collegiate Dictionary (2001).

1016 Merriam-Webster's Collegiate Thesaurus (2001).

1017 Id.

1018 33 USC §2701(1).

subjectively anticipate, but could have objectively anticipated. So, there is a difference between subjective and objective anticipation. The defense can only be invoked if the unanticipated disaster produces effects which could not have been prevented. Even if the RP is anticipating an earthquake (in an area like San Francisco where earthquakes often happen) in the abstract, it must put measures in place in order to eliminate or at least minimize the potential for an oil spill or the potential subsequent damage or harm. The kind of measures that a person puts in place in an earthquake prone area should be more stringent than what a person puts in place in a non-earthquake prone area. Also, the nature of measures put in place in an earthquake prone area should differ from what is put in place in a typhoon prone area, in that the former produces effects that the latter does not.

Although it is difficult to exercise due care with respect to something you cannot subjectively anticipate, there are general measures that the RP can exercise, having due regard to the industry's basic traditions, nature of the activity and the particular geographic location. If the effects produced by the disaster are avoidable by the exercise of due care and due care was not actually exercised, the RP cannot invoke the defense.[1019] Since the RP is the one invoking the defense, he carries the burden of proving that an "act of God" caused the discharge of the oil. Therefore, the RP must introduce sufficient evidence that proves that it was not culpable in any way. This should also be specifically pled in the answer as an affirmative defense, if it is invoking the act of God defense as a defendant or in the complaint if it is invoking the act of God defense as a plaintiff. The OPA non-RP claimant does not bear the burden of proof on this issue, because it is an affirmative defense by the OPA RP.

The inclusion of the due care requirement in the definition of "act of God" also means that the RP must be free from fault and must not have contributed in any way to the discharge. If the discharge is caused by a combination of an "act of God" and the fault of the RP whether

1019 See, e.g., Travelers Indemnity Co. v. United States, 230 Ct.Cl. 867, *cert. denied*, 459 U.S. 1015, 103 S.Ct. 374, 74 L.Ed.2d 508 (1982).

negligent or non-negligent, the RP will be absolutely liable.[1020] This issue of combination of an RP's fault and an "act of God" will be discussed further below.

### Kyoei Kaiun Kaisha, Ltd., V. M/V Bering Trader.[1021]

The defendant vessel, the M/V AOYAGI MARU, was moored to the M/V BERING TRADER while it was anchored in Lost Harbor, Alaska. An approaching storm and the dragging of the M/V BERING TRADER's anchor required the separation of the vessels. During separation, a mooring line became tangled around the propeller of the M/V AOYAGI MARU, and the ship grounded on the rocky shore.

The plaintiff, United States moved for summary judgment on defendants' liability under the Federal Water Pollution Control Act (FWPCA), 33 U.S.C. § 1321(f), for the cost of the Coast Guard's activities in preventing a threatened oil spill from defendants' grounded vessel.

The *M/V Bering Trader* court noted that the defendants tried to make a half-hearted attempt to show that "an act of God" was the sole cause of the grounding.[1022] In support of their defense, defendants had cited a remark by the captain of the Bering Trader, "I believe the wind in excess of 100 knots (reported at Dutch Harbor) should be considered the cause of the accident."[1023] The court pointed out however that the defendants had failed to put forth any evidence that the weather on the night of the grounding could not have been foreseen or guarded against, as required by this "act of God" defense.[1024] Instead of that, the court found that the Coast Guard's navigation guide for Alaska in effect at the time of the grounding warned that the "weather of the Aleutians is characterized by persistently overcast

1020 See, e.g, Reliance Insurance Co. v. United States, 230 Ct.Cl. 390, 394, 677 F.2d 844, 848 (1982).

1021 795 F.Supp. 1054 (W.D. Wa. 1991).

1022 795 F.Supp. at 1056, n2.

1023 Id. at 1056, n2.

1024 Id.

skies, strong winds, and violent storms... winds are variable, local, and often strong... a maximum wind of 104 knots has occurred at Adak."[1025]

The *M/V Bering Trader* court held that the defenses to liability, must be narrowly construed because the unambiguous intent of Congress was to impose liability on the polluting vessel except in very rare circumstances.[1026] Congress intended its strict liability system to make owners or operators liable if their actions contributed in any way to an accident, without regard to whether or not their actions were negligent.[1027] Only in situations where the accident was completely beyond the control of the polluting vessel would they be excused from liability.[1028] Based on this, the court held that regardless of whether actions aboard of the BERING TRADER contributed to the grounding, if the AOYAGI MARU is in any way responsible defendants are liable for clean-up costs.[1029]

On the issue of AOYAGI MARU's contribution to the discharge, the United States alleged that lack of communication aboard the AOYAGI MARU during unmooring contributed to the ship's grounding. The government contended that there was no communication between the stern of the AOYAGI MARU, where lines mooring the two ships together were secured, and the bridge, where the captain gave orders to the deck crew over loudspeakers during unmooring.[1030] The United States concluded that this lack of communication caused the captain of the AOYAGI MARU to engage her engines without knowing whcther the mooring lines were clear of the ship, which led to the ship's propeller becoming entangled in a

1025 Id. (*citing*, National Oceanic and Atmospheric Administration, United States Coast Pilot, v. 9, 198 (13th ed. 1987)).

1026 Id. at 1056 (*citing*, United States v. West of England Ship Owner's Mut. Protection & Indem. Ass'n, 872 F.2d 1192, 1200 (5th Cir.1989) (Congress endorsed an absolute liability system with very limited exceptions).

1027 West of England Ship Owner's Mut. Protection & Indem. Ass'n, 872 F.2d 1192, 1196- 1199 (5th Cir. 1989).

1028 Reliance Ins. Co. v. United States, 677 F.2d 844, 849, 230 Ct.Cl. 390 (Ct. Cl. 1982) (any conduct, however slight, on the part of an owner or operator contributing to a spill negates relief, even though such conduct might have operated in concert with greater third-party conduct to produce the spill).

1029 795 F.Supp. at 1056.

1030 Id. at 1056.

mooring line that was still in the water.[1031] The court agreed with the government's argument because the exhaustive depositions of the AOYAGI MARU's captain and crew contained uncontroverted statements describing events aboard the vessel which supported the government's argument. Because of evidence of fault or contributory fault by the RP the court held that the defendant was liable to the United States government for the clean up costs incurred because of the oil discharge. In all OPA cases, freedom from fault no matter how slight is a sine qua non to the successful invocation of the "act of God" defense or any other defense provided for in section 2703(a) of the Act.

### Liberian Poplar Transports Inc v. United States.[1032]

Owner of vessel brought action to recover costs of clean up of oil spill into river. On government's motion for summary judgment, the Claims Court, Futey, J., held that discharge of oil into the river that occurred when thunder storms arrived during transfer of oil to vessel did not come within the FWPCA's exception for "act of God" so as to enable the vessel owner to recover clean up costs from the United States,[1033] because had the ship's crew monitored their radio for weather conditions they could have anticipated and taken precautions against the storm.[1034]

The Plaintiff -RP argued unsuccessfully that because the storm was not well forecasted, and was not visually foreseeable by the ship's watch, that the storm was not anticipated.[1035] In its rejection of this argument, the court pointed out that the statute and the legislative history do not subscribe to a subjective test for anticipation.[1036] The court held that whether the crew did or did not actually anticipate the storm was beside

1031 Id.

1032 1992 AMC 2253, 26 Cl. Ct. 223 (U.S. Cl. Ct. 1992).

1033 26 Cl. Ct. 223.

1034 Id. at 223.

1035 Id. at 226.

1036 Id.

the point.[1037] The court reasoned that if the crew had monitored the radio for weather conditions, they clearly could have anticipated and taken precautions against the storm.[1038] The court found that even though the storm was not well forecasted, it was in fact forecasted at least a half-hour before it hit and there was an indication of bad weather in a storm watch issued approximately an hour before the storm struck.[1039] The court concluded that the storm could have been anticipated and the plaintiff had failed to establish the act of God defense.[1040] Based on the foregoing, the United States Government's motion for summary judgment was granted.

### St. Paul Fire & Marine Insurance Co., v. The United States.[1041]

The oil spill here in question occurred in 1976 when one of Wellen Oil Co.'s (subrogor of the plaintiff-insurer) storage tanks ruptured; the oil broke through a retaining wall into a river. In its original as well as its amended complaint, the plaintiff alleged that the rupture of the oil tank "was caused solely by an act of God or an act or omission of a third party or a combination of the foregoing."[1042] In its rejection of the plaintiff's allegation, the court noted that during discovery, the plaintiff produced an engineering report prepared in connection with prior litigation involving the same incident, which contradicted the allegation of the plaintiff.[1043] The court relied on the conclusion of the report that "the tank failure was due to severe differential settlement of the sub-structure below the tank floor plates" and that such settlement was entirely foreseeable when the

1037 Id.

1038 Id.

1039 Id.

1040 Id.

1041 4 Cl. Ct. 762, 20 ERC 1788 (1984).

1042 4 Cl. Ct. 768.

1043 Id. at 768.

tank was erected.[1044] By virtue of this report and the precedent in *Sabine Towing & Transportation Co. v. United States,*[1045] the *St. Paul Fire & Marine Insurance Co.,* the court held that such soil settlement was not an act of God within the meaning of section 1321(i)(1)(a) of the FWPCA.[1046]

## CERCLA ACT OF GOD DEFENSE CASES

Section 9607(b) of the CERCLA provides for three defenses for a person who discharges hazardous substances.[1047] CERCLA provides in pertinent part:

> "There shall be no liability under subsection (a) of this section for a person otherwise liable who can establish by a preponderance of the evidence that the release or threat of release of a hazardous substance and the damages resulting therefrom were caused solely by--
>
> (1) an act of God;
>
> (4) any combination of the foregoing paragraphs."

Section 701(1) of CERCLA defines the term, "act of God" to mean "an unanticipated grave natural disaster or other natural phenomenon of an exceptional, inevitable, and irresistible character, the effects of which could not have been prevented or avoided by the exercise of due care or foresight.

These CERCLA provisions are identical to that of OPA, thus CERCLA act of God Defense cases would provide useful guidance for OPA cases.

---

1044 Id.

1045 666 F.2d 561, 229 Ct.Cl. 265, 269-70 (1981).

1046 St. Paul Fire & Marine Insurance Co., 4 Cl. Ct. at 768.

1047 Comprehensive Environmental Response, Compensation, and Liability Act of 1980, §107(b), as amended, 42 U.S.C.A. §9607(b).

## United States v. Allen.[1048]

This was an action filed by the government under § 9607(a)(1) and (2) of the CERCLA for the recovery of response costs incurred by the government in connection with the cleanup of a hazardous waste site.[1049] This location was occupied by a transformer repair facility owned and operated by Allen Transformer Company. The individual defendant, was the president of the Allen Transformer Company. Allen Transformer Company was initially formed in 1968 by a group of individuals to manufacture transformers. Subsequently, the operation changed and the primary focus of operations was the repair of transformers.[1050] Hazardous substance was spilled when fire caused the capacitors in the transformers to burst. The hazardous substance at issue was polychlorinated biphenyls (PCBs). This substance or fluids contaminated with this substance were contained in transformers and capacitors handled by Allen Transformer Company (hereinafter Company).[1051]

The defendant argued that the fire that caused the capacitors to burst was an "act of God" within the meaning of the statute.[1052] It argued that the largest discharge of PCBs on the site was the result of this act of God.[1053] In its rejection of the defendant's act of God defense, the court observed that it has been noted that the act of God defense is narrow and is limited to exceptional natural phenomena.[1054] The court held that it does not believe a fire of unknown origin is the type of natural disaster contemplated by the act of God defense.[1055] The court also held that assuming arguendo that the fire could constitute an act of God, the fire was not the sole cause of the

1048 See United States v. Allen, Civil No. 90-2093, 1990 U.S. Dist. LEXIS 19955 (W.D. Ark. 1990).

1049 *Allen*, 1990 U.S. Dist. LEXIS 19955, at *1.

1050 Id. at *1.

1051 Id.

1052 Id. at 19.

1053 Id.

1054 Id. at 19 (*citing*, United States v. Stringfellow, 661 F.Supp. 1053, 1061 (C.D. Cal. 1987)).

1055 Id.

releases at issue.[1056] The court found that there were multiple causes of the releases at issue.[1057] Specifically, the court relied on information provided the court which established that on several other occasions PCB contaminated material was released or disposed of at the site.[1058] Based on this, the court granted the government's motion for summary judgment on the issue of CERCLA liability, and rejected the act of God defense. So an OPA RP should not count on the act of God defense simply because the oil spill was caused by a fire whose origin is unknown. It should be traceable to a natural phenomenon. For instance the strike of lightning is known to cause wild bush or brush fire in dry weather. An OPA RP who invokes the act of God defense would need to trace the origin of the fire to a natural phenomenon.

## United States v. Amtreco Inc.[1059]

In this case, the United States sued the defendant corporation and its sole owner/shareholder under the CERCLA, seeking to recover costs connected to cleanup of site used by defendants to treat wooden fence posts.[1060] Parties cross-moved for summary judgment. The defendants claimed inter alia that an act of God or a flood caused the contamination. The court rejected this defense as having no merit because the flood referred to did not occur until after the cleanup was already in progress. Hence the United States was granted its summary judgment.[1061]

This shows that even if a subsequent flood spreads the oil to areas hundreds of miles away from where the discharge occurred, the RP will still be liable to claimants for OPA oil spills. Only an antecedent flood that solely causes an oil spill will be analyzed under the act of God defense. If the court finds that it occurred subsequent to the spill the court will

1056 Id.

1057 Id.

1058 Id.

1059 809 F.Supp. 959 (M.D. Ga 1992).

1060 809 F.Supp. at 969.

1061 Id. at 969.

not proceed further to consider if the flood qualifies as act of God. This means that even if antecedent flooding caused the oil spill, that alone will not entitle the RP to the act of God defense. The RP has to prove by a preponderance of the evidence that the flood possessed the kind of characteristics that qualifies it as an act of God.

## United States v. Stringfellow.[1062]

In this case the United States and California sought to recover costs of remediation from owners and operators of toxic waste disposal site, generators of waste, and transporters of waste from generators to facilities.[1063] United States and California moved for partial summary judgment. In its partial grant of the motion for summary judgment the court held inter alia, that heavy rainfall was not exceptional natural phenomenon and was not "act of God" within meaning CERCLA.[1064]

The defendants had argued that the heavy rainfall in 1969 and 1979 which played a role in the pollution was a natural disaster which constituted an act of God. However, the Court found that the rains were not the kind of "exceptional" natural phenomena to which the narrow act of God defense of section 9607(b)(1) applies.[1065] The court held that the rains were foreseeable based on normal climatic conditions and any harm caused by the rain could have been prevented through design of proper drainage channels.[1066] Furthermore, the court found that the rains were not the sole cause of the release.[1067] Therefore, the Court concluded that the rains were not sufficient to establish an act of God defense pursuant to CERCLA section 9607(b)(1).[1068]

1062 661 F. Supp 1053 (C.D. Cal. 1987).

1063 661 F.Supp. at 1053.

1064 Id. at 1053.

1065 Id. at 1061.

1066 Id.

1067 Id.

1068 Id.

### United States v. Barrier Industries Inc.[1069]

In October, 1995, the United States commenced this action under the CERCLA, seeking (i) recovery of response costs expended by the Environmental Protection Agency ("EPA") in cleaning up a former site of (bankrupt) defendant Barrier Industries, Inc. ("Barrier"), operated by Barrier's principal, defendant Kurt Wasserman ("Wasserman").[1070] From 1978 through December, 1993, defendant Barrier used hazardous substances in the manufacture of janitorial chemicals at its facility in Port Jervis, New York.[1071] Numerous spills of these hazardous substances occurred in the plant prior to December, 1993. In December, 1993, the Port Jervis Building Department condemned the building, but in early January, 1994, further spills were detected.[1072] On January 25, 1994, a representative of the EPA inspected the site and ordered corrective action, which commenced on February 15, 1994, resulting in the clean-up costs here claimed.[1073]

Wasserman, who operated the Barrier site, did not contest that the Government has established a prima facie case of his liability under CERCLA, but contended that a genuine issue existed as to whether it was entitled to the "act of God" defense allowed by CERCLA § 9607(b).[1074] Specifically, Wasserman argued that spills occurring in January, 1994 were caused by a bursting of pipes occasioned by "an unprecedented cold spell."[1075] The court in its rejection of this defense found that nothing documented on the evidentiary record before the Court remotely suggested that this "cold spell" falls within the CERCLA definition of an "act of God," i.e., "an unanticipated natural disaster or other natural phenomenon of an exceptional, inevitable, and irresistible character, the effects

1069 991 F.Supp. 678 (S.D.N.Y. 1998).

1070 991 F.Supp. at 679.

1071 Id.

1072 Id.

1073 Id.

1074 Id. at 679.

1075 Id.

of which could not have been prevented or avoided by the exercise of due care or foresight."[1076] The court also held as other courts before it have, that § 9607(b), by its terms, permits such a defense only if the release or threatened release of hazardous substances was caused "solely" by the act of God.[1077] The court found that the Government had adduced substantial undisputed evidence that numerous other factors antedating the cold weather of January, 1994 causally contributed to the problems at the Barrier site.[1078] Based on the foregoing, Wasserman's "act of God" defense was out rightly rejected by the court.[1079]

### United States v. Alcan Aluminum Corp.[1080]

The United States government brought action under CERCLA against, inter alia, aluminum manufacturer to recover response costs.[1081] In September of 1985, in the wake of a Hurricane called "Hurricane Gloria", approximately 2, 380.95 barrels (100,000 gallons) of oily waste contaminated with hazardous substances were discharged from the Butler Tunnel into the Susquehanna River.[1082] EPA's response costs in addressing this release totaled $1,302,290.18. Response actions included " 'containing an oily material on the river through the use of absorbent booms; immediately removing and disposing of 161,000 pounds (over 80 tons) of oil and chemical-soaked debris and soil, monitoring, sampling and analysis of air and water, and conducting hydrogeologic studies.' "[1083] Alcan's used emulsion was commingled in the waste materials discharged into the Susquehanna River in September of 1985.[1084] The waste oils removed

1076 42 U.S.C. § 9601(1).

1077 991 F.Supp. at 679.

1078 Id. at 679-80.

1079 Id.

1080 892 F.Supp. 648 (M.D. Pa. 1995).

1081 892 F.Supp at 648.

1082 Id. at 651.

1083 Id. at 651-52.

1084 Id. at 652.

from the Susquehanna River contained cadmium, chromium, copper, lead and zinc.[1085] The United States District Court, Middle District of Pennsylvania, Edwin M. Kosik, J., entered judgment against the manufacturer, and the manufacturer appealed. The Court of Appeals, vacated and remanded the case to the District Court. On cross-motions for summary judgment, the District Court, Vanaskie, J., held among other things that the manufacturer could not prevail on the act of God defense.[1086]

In its Motion for Summary Judgment, Alcan, the discharger argued that any release of hazardous substances was caused solely by an act of God, specifically, Hurricane Gloria.[1087] Alcan contended that the release occurred in connection with the torrential downpour of rain associated with the hurricane.[1088] The court noted that under the act of God defense, no liability attaches to a person who would otherwise be liable if that person can establish that the release of the hazardous substance and the damages which result were caused solely by an act of God. The court referred to the case of *United States v. Stringfellow*,[1089] where the defendants had contended that "heavy rainfall" was a natural disaster which constituted an act of God.[1090] The court noted and agreed with the conclusion of the court in that case that heavy rainfall was "not the kind of 'exceptional' natural phenomenon" to which the "act of God exception applies."[1091]

Alcan, had argued that the release at the site was caused not simply by heavy rainfall but by a hurricane which is "a grave natural disaster or phenomenon."[1092] It had also asserted that the hurricane was "unanticipated" as far north and inland as Pennsylvania.[1093] The court however rejected this "act of God" defense of Alcan for three reasons. First, no reasonable factfinder could conclude that Hurricane Gloria was the sole

1085 Id.

1086 Id. at 648.

1087 Id. at 658.

1088 Id.

1089 661 F.Supp. 1053 (C.D.Cal.1987).

1090 *Alcan*, 892 F.Supp at 658.

1091 Id. at 658.

1092 Id.

1093 Id.

cause of the release and resulting response costs. Two million gallons of hazardous wastes were not dumped into the borehole by an act of God, and were it not for the unlawful disposal of this hazardous waste, Hurricane Gloria would not have flushed 100,000 gallons of this chemical soup into the Susquehanna River.[1094]

Second, the effects of Hurricane Gloria could "have been prevented or avoided by the exercise of due care or foresight."[1095] The court reasoned that exercise of due care or foresight would have militated against dumping hazardous wastes into mine workings that inevitably lead to such a significant natural resource as the Susquehanna River.[1096]

Finally, the *Alcan* court recognized as the Court in *Stringfellow* recognized; heavy rainfall is "not the kind of 'exceptional' natural phenomenon to which the act of God exception applies."[1097] Accordingly, the court found it appropriate to enter judgment in favor of the Government on Alcan's act of God defense. This case illustrates that natural disasters do not automatically qualify for the act of God Defense. So, the owner of a facility in a typhoon, hurricane or earthquake prone area should not count on this defense simply because there is a typhoon or hurricane or an earthquake in the area. It is very strictly construed and in most cases the act of God defense will be denied.

## United States v. M/V Santa Clara I[1098]

On the evening of January 3, at approximately 5:50 p.m., the M/V SANTA CLARA I departed Port Elizabeth for what was intended to be a short overnight transit to its next port of call, Baltimore, Maryland. During the course of that overnight transit, the vessel encountered a storm

1094 Id.

1095 See id., see also, 42 U.S.C. § 9601(1).

1096 *Alcan*, 892 F.Supp at 658.

1097 Id. at 658, see also *Stringfellow*, 661 F.Supp. at 1061.

1098 887 F.Supp. 825 (D.SC. 1995).

approximately thirty miles off the coast.[1099] According to the affidavits of the crew, the storm caused the vessel to pitch and roll violently for several hours and resulted in damage to the ship and to much of its cargo.[1100] Reconstruction of weather data from buoys in the area indicated that the sea heights reached eighteen feet and the winds gusted to fifty knots.[1101] When the storm subsided, the crew noticed that twenty-one shipping containers had been lost overboard and much of the cargo had broken loose below decks. Four of the twenty-one containers lost overboard were loaded with the barrels of arsenic trioxide.[1102] A fifth container of arsenic trioxide remaining on board was damaged such that some of its barrels fell overboard.[1103] The crew determined that approximately 441 barrels of arsenic trioxide had been lost overboard. The vessel also suffered stowage collapse of sundry cargo including the magnesium phosphide.[1104]

In the action arising from this loss overboard of containers of arsenic trioxide, as well as a spill on board the vessel of magnesium phosphide, the vessel owner and operator asserted third-party claims against the shippers and consignees of those chemicals, seeking contribution and indemnification pursuant to bills of lading and under the CERCLA.[1105] On owner's and operator's motion for summary judgment, as well as summary judgment motions by shipper of arsenic trioxide and consignee of magnesium phosphide, the District Court, Norton, J., held inter alia that the act of God defense provided by CERCLA was inapplicable to the plaintiff's case.[1106]

The court believed that there was ample evidence in the record about the events surrounding the offshore storm on the night of January 3, 1992 to conclude that the act of God defense is not available to any of the

---

1099 887 F.Supp. at 829.

1100 Id. at 829-30.

1101 Id. at 830.

1102 Id.

1103 Id.

1104 Id.

1105 Id. at 825.

1106 Id.

parties.[1107] The court found that even a poorly forecasted storm has been held under the FWPCA not to constitute an act of God because it was predicted and was avoidable.[1108] The court found that the evidence in the record showed clearly that inclement weather offshore was predicted by the National Weather Service and known by the captain and crew prior to their departure from Port Elizabeth.[1109] The court pointed to the fact that several crew members stated that they were told to expect bad weather and were directed to take extra precautions to insure that the vessel and its cargo were secure for rough seas.[1110] The court held that even if the evidence demonstrated that the storm was worse than predicted, the storm the M/V SANTA CLARA I encountered was not the type of "unanticipated grave natural disaster" or "other natural phenomenon of an exceptional, inevitable, and irresistible character, the effects of which could not have been prevented or avoided by the exercise of due care or foresight."[1111] Based on the above reasoning the court denied the act of God defense.

Even though some courts in circumstances other than environmental pollution have held that a "rogue" or "freak" wave affecting a vessel was an act of God, the relevance and applicability of these decisions to OPA and CERCLA cases is quite questionable. Why? (1) Because of the public policy behind environmental legislations like OPA and CERCLA; and (2) because of the elaborate and expansive definition of "act of God" in OPA and CERCLA.[1112] Just like the *Sabine* court resisted the temptation of borrowing the common law's construction of the "act of God defense", courts construing the act of God defense of OPA should resist any temptation to look outside statutes like CERCLA, FWPCA and OPA itself for answers. These three statutes have similar or identical provisions on the act of God defense and by virtue of this, complement each other. They all further the

1107 Id. at 843.

1108 Id. (*citing*, Liberian Poplar Transp., Inc. v. United States, 26 Cl.Ct. 223, 226 (1992)).

1109 Id. at 843.

1110 Id.

1111 See id, see also, 42 U.S.C. § 9601(1).

1112 See Ferromontan v. Geroge Town Steel Corp. 535 F.Supp. 1198, 1210 (D.S.C. 1982) (Interpreting the Harter Act "act of God" defense).

goal of protecting the environment and making polluters imbibe a culture of environmental responsibility and sensitivity. Most of the statutes that enshrine the act of God defense have diametrically opposite objectives to the environmental statutes like OPA, CERCLA and FWPCA. For instance the Harter Act[1113] and the Carriage of Goods by Sea Act (COGSA),[1114] both provide for the act of God defense, but these two statutes are aimed at allocating liability between a ship owner and a shipper for damage to cargo belonging to the shipper during the marine transportation of the cargo. Whereas OPA, CERCLA and FWPCA are aimed at ensuring that a polluter is held strictly liable for polluting the environment. The courts would in all likelihood construe OPA's act of God defense more strictly than courts would under COGSA and the Harter Act, because the objectives of OPA differ sharply from the objectives of these statutes.

### OPA- United States v. JR Nelson Vessel Ltd[1115]

This action was brought by the United States for recovery of costs for cleaning up an oil spill and for a declaratory judgment that the defendants were responsible for the removal from a harbor of their vessel that had been determined to be a hazard to navigation.[1116] The United States moved for summary judgment and the motion was granted by the court. A Coast Guard investigatory report, determined the Nelson's (defendant's vessel) sinking had been the result of holes in the vessel's starboard side that had been caused by the pounding of the unattended vessel against its mooring during a storm.[1117] The defendants argued that the vessel was damaged by the severity of the storm and that was what caused the oil spill. Rejecting this defense the court stated:

1113 46 USCA app. § 190-195.

1114 46 U.S.C. app. §§ 1300-1315 (1988).

1115 1 F.Supp.2d. 172.

1116 Id. at 173.

1117 Id. at 174.

"The defendants also make much of the severity of the storm that damaged the Nelson. While OPA does allow that "an act of God," is a complete defense to liability, 33 U.S.C. § 2703(a)(1), the Act defines the term as "an unanticipated grave natural disaster or other natural phenomenon of an exceptional, inevitable, and irresistible character...." 33 U.S.C. § 2701(1). The defendants make no effort to establish that the storm was of such a magnitude."[1118]

Due to the defendants non-presentation of evidence that showed that the storm was unanticipated or a natural phenomenon of an exceptional, inevitable, and irresistible character; the court granted the governments motion for summary judgment.

An NPFC Claims Division case decided in 2000 illustrates the approach of the NPFC and the possible approach of the courts of law to the OPA act of God defense. This case and the second one which will be discussed after this one shows that the CERCLA and FWPCA act of God defense cases would continue to provide guidance to the courts and to the Fund. The approach of the NPFC is consistent with the earlier extensive analysis of the approach in CERCLA and FWPCA cases.

In the NPFC Claims Division case of *Apex Towing Company* administratively closed in 2000, a corporate claimant, Apex Towing Company, submitted a claim to the NPFC for reimbursement of its removal costs and salvage activities in the amount of $2.7 million dollars.[1119] On June 16, 1995, the tug M/V SONDRA B (SONDRA B or the tug), a 3800 Horse Power push boat, was up bound on the Mississippi River with seven barges in tow.[1120] Four barges were loaded and grouped on the port side of the tow; the three empty barges were positioned on the starboard side. The tow was arranged so that six barges were attached to the front of the tow; a

1118 Id. at 176, n2.

1119 Apex Towing Company, NPFC Claim Summary/Recommendation Form, Claim No 085114-001, p 1-2 (03/03/2000) (on file with the NPFC and available upon request from the NPFC).

1120 Id. at 1.

single port side barge was faced up to the SONDRA B.[1121] At this time, the Mississippi River was experiencing the effects of extremely heavy spring rains in the Midwest area of the United States.[1122] The run off from the rains resulted in high water levels and rapid and unpredictable rises and falls on the Upper Mississippi River.[1123] The June 7, 1995 and June 14, 1995, editions of the US Coast Guard's Notice to Mariners (Notices to Mariners) advised mariners that these rises and falls could result in damages to the Aids to Navigation System, and that the system could be unreliable and mariners should transit all areas with due caution.[1124] At approximately 2130 hours on 16 June 1995, the tug approached the bridge span of the Highway 80 Bridge in the Vicksburg, Mississippi area.[1125] The bridge span is located at Mississippi River, Mile 435.7 LMR. The Flotilla's two forward barges, Apex 3506 and 3603, were loaded with slurry oil.[1126] They cleared the bridge span; however, at this point the river overwhelmed the tug's forward momentum and pushed the entire tow into the bridge's concrete spans.[1127] The aft two barges struck the spans on their port sides, causing the wire holding the forward four barges to part.[1128] The forward barges began to turn around, striking the spans. The 3603, the second barge, port side became caught between the starboard side of the tow and the span.[1129] It turned in on itself and inverted. The tow then broke at this time. Five of the seven barges broke free and floated down river.[1130]

The 3506 received extensive hull damage on its port side. The 3506 and 3603 began discharging slurry oil into the water.[1131] Approximately 20, 000 barrels (840,000 gallons) of slurry oil was discharged along with

1121 Id.
1122 Id.
1123 Id.
1124 Id.
1125 Id.
1126 Id.
1127 Id. at 1.
1128 Id.
1129 Id.
1130 Id.
1131 Id. at 2.

202.38 barrels (8,500 gallons) of diesel fuel and 2.38 barrels (100 gallons) of thermal fluid heater oil. The tug and barges were owned and operated by Apex Towing Company, who took responsibility for the discharge and initiated removal activities. In a supplement to its claim, Apex asserted an entitlement to an act of God defense, citing the flood of 1995 and exceptionally strong and unpredictable currents in the Vicksburg area of the lower Mississippi River.[1132] Apex argued that the flood and currents were an unanticipated grave natural disaster, which could not have been prevented or avoided by the exercise of due care or foresight. To substantiate its act of God Defense assertion, Apex relied on the investigative report of the Coast Guard, called the Marine Casualty Investigative Reports (MCIR).[1133] Apex argued that MCIR concluded that there was no negligence on the part of the captain of the SONDRA B and that expecting him to foresee the situation would have been beyond the scope of a prudent mariner.[1134] On July, 18, 1998, the NPFC Claims Division issued a letter to Apex denying the act of God Defense, stating that Apex had not met its statutory burden of establishing entitlement to the defense.[1135] The NPFC based its denial on the grounds that the flooding and associated currents were not solely an act of God. The NPFC' s denial letter explained that for an incident to be solely an act of God, it has to be abnormal or unusual, strictly natural in origin, and inevitable.[1136] The NPFC letter defined "abnormal" to mean "so unusual that it cannot be anticipated or expected."[1137]

The NPFC also based its denial on the failure of Apex to show that the incident could not have been avoided by due care and prudent seamanship.[1138] The denial letter explained that the event must be entirely absent of human agency and that a Coast Guard determination of non-negligence does not mean there was an absence of human agency.[1139] In other words,

1132 Id.

1133 Id.

1134 Id.

1135 Id.

1136 Id.

1137 Id.

1138 Id. at 2.

1139 Id.

an RP's lack of fault is not relevant in determining entitlement to the act of God defense. Apex was allowed extension of time to resubmit its request for reconsideration. The NPFC granted the request and Apex submitted its request for reconsideration on October 26, 1998 making almost the same arguments it had made in its unsuccessful first claim.[1140] In addition to that it also argued that the NPFC's decision to deny the claim was directly contrary to the Coast Guard's conclusion that the captain of the SONDRA B was not negligent. It also argued that the NPFC abused its discretion because it created a new standard, "lack of human agency," which is not supported by OPA or the regulations.[1141]

In its decision, the Claims Division relied heavily on some of the FWPCA cases analyzed earlier. The NPFC Claims Division found that floods and periodic storm events are not acts of God under the FWPCA and CERCLA.[1142] The NPFC rejected the claimant's argument that the Flood of 1995 and the strong unpredictable currents constitute an act of God because the flood was an extreme flood and the river current velocity was exceedingly strong and the current patterns were inconsistent and unpredictable at River Mile A.H.P. 435.7.[1143] The NPFC rejected this argument for several reasons. Most importantly, the NPFC noted that Apex personnel stated that they were aware of the flood, therefore, the flood conditions were not unanticipated.[1144] The NPFC pointed out further that because strong and unpredictable currents are often associated with flood conditions, Apex could not argue that these currents would be unanticipated.[1145]

The NPFC found further that floods and periodic storm events are not acts of God.[1146] They pointed out further that springtime floods in the

1140 Id.

1141 Id. at 2.

1142 Id.

1143 Id.

1144 Id. at 3.

1145 Id.

1146 Id. at 4, (relying on United States v. Stringfellow, et al., 661 F.Supp. 1053, 1061 (C.D. Cal. 1987)(holding that heavy rainfall is not a natural disaster constituting an act of God because it is foreseeable based on normal climatic conditions and harm caused by rain could have been prevented).

Midwest area of the United States are not unusual. Nor is it unusual for rains from Midwest floods to affect water levels in the Mississippi River. They believed that these were normal climatic conditions. In other words, they could predict the unpredictability of the currents and water levels. If an owner is aware of this unpredictability, but nevertheless sails in such conditions, it should know that it not only risks damage to the vessel, it also risks damage to the marine environment. The NPFC Claims Division noted specifically that even extreme floods on the Mississippi River at the Vicksburg Bridge are not unusual. They pointed to a report prepared and submitted by Lamy Chopin, Jr., a civil engineer and surveyor for the Claimant. The NPFC noted that the report states that "during the 50-year period prior to the casualty, five years had flood stages greater than 47.0 feet.[1147] They noted that the report categorized the flood of 1995 as an extreme flood, the seventh highest stage recorded since the gauge was installed at the Vicksburg Bridge in 1934.[1148] They further observed that as recently as 1983, the river reached a stage of 49.3 feet. Based on this reasoning, the Claims Division of the NPFC concluded that Apex could have anticipated that spring floods in the Midwest could subsequently result in high river stages on the Mississippi River in the Vicksburg area.

The Claims Division noted further that strong currents associated with flood waters are not unusual and can be anticipated.[1149] The NPFC pointed to the part of the Chopin report which states that during extreme floods "the current velocities in a river may increase significantly along the inside of a bend in a river and may tend to cross parts of the convex bank or bar.[1150] As a result this change in flow can cause inconsistent and unpredictable current patterns in the area below the bend." The NPFC noted that the tug's captain in anticipation of strong current velocities, specifically chose to transit the bridge spans on the outer bend of the river, where the current velocities could be slower.[1151]

---

1147 Id. at 4.

1148 Id.

1149 Id.

1150 Id.

1151 Id.

The NPFC Claims Division noted further that even if extreme flooding on the Mississippi River had not occurred in prior years, the flood conditions and associated strong currents in this case could have been anticipated.[1152] The Claims Manager noted that in the spring of 1995, weeks prior to the incident, the Midwest area of the United States experienced heavy rains.[1153] The rain waters drained into creeks; the run off eventually progressed into tributaries of the Mississippi River and ultimately into the Upper Mississippi River. The high waters moved downstream toward the lower Mississippi River. The Claims Manager noted that these events were widely covered in the media and a general advisory was stated in the Notices to Mariners.[1154]

Apex had emphasized the gravity of the flood and currents. It admitted that it was aware of the flood conditions, but maintained that the gravity of these circumstances, i.e., the extremely high river stage and strong, fast, unpredictable currents, could not be anticipated, and thus was an act of God. To substantiate the gravity of the event, Apex cited historical data reflecting that the river stage in June 1995 was the fifth highest in the last 50 years and the highest in the preceding 12 years. Apex argued that since the previous high flood stage was 12 years prior, in 1983, that it could not have anticipated that the river stage would be so high on June 16, 1995.[1155] This argument was rejected by the NPFC Claims Division. The NPFC noted that the data in the Chopin report evinces the fact that this same Mississippi River at the Vicksburg bridges had been at flood stages of 47.0 or higher in 1973, 1975, 1979, 1983 and June 1995, the year of this incident.[1156] The NPFC observed that of the five highest river stages in the past 22 years, the 1995 flood stage was the lowest, at 47.0 feet.[1157]

The Claims Division also noted that Apex had not established that the effects of the floodwaters and strong currents could not have been

1152 Id.

1153 Id. at 4.

1154 Id.

1155 Id. at 4-5.

1156 Id.

1157 Id. at 5.

prevented or avoided by the exercise of due care or foresight.[1158] Apex provided affidavits from top company officials which inter alia stated that Apex could not have foreseen navigational problems to their tug and tow because they were not aware of any navigational problems in the vicinity of the river at the bridges at Vicksburg.[1159] Nor were they aware of other similar tugs and tows that had experienced such problems. In its rejection of this argument, the NPFC found that the argument does not establish that the effects of the flood and the currents could not have been prevented or avoided by the exercise of due care or foresight.[1160] The NPFC found that the argument only revealed that the affiants were relying on other incidents on the Mississippi River in order to foresee the effects on their tug and tow.[1161] The NPFC observed that the scope of unanticipated circumstances and foreseeability cannot be interpreted narrowly. The NPFC referred to the Chopin report which stated that the river current velocity was exceedingly strong, probably six to eight knots or 10 to 34.4 feet per second.[1162] The report also stated that this velocity would exert a significant force on the up bound barge tow. In fact, the tug was overwhelmed by the strong current just north of the Vicksburg bridge.[1163] The NPFC found that it was foreseeable that the tug and barges, transiting up river into increasingly higher and faster waters, could encounter unpredictable currents and suffer navigational problems.[1164] The NPFC found that Apex towing could have prevented or avoided the effects of the floodwaters and associated currents by using a higher-powered tug that could have safely maneuvered through the currents.

Apex also cited to the Marine Casualty Investigative Reports (MCIR) to substantiate that the flood and associated currents could not be anticipated. The MCIR stated that "expecting [the captain of the tug] to

---

1158 Id.

1159 Id.

1160 Id.

1161 Id.

1162 Id.

1163 Id.

1164 Id.

foresee the situation would have been beyond the scope of the prudent mariner."[1165] The NPFC pointed out that this statement is vague in that it does not clarify what the "situation" is. The NPFC pointed out further that even if it exonerates the captain of the tug, it does not relieve Apex Towing of its responsibility to prevent or avoid the effects of the flood waters and strong currents by exercising due care and foresight.

The NPFC also pointed out that assuming arguendo that the flood and strong associated currents were an act of God under the FWPCA, the incident was not solely caused by the floods and strong currents.[1166] The NPFC's Claim Division pointed out that "caused solely by" means an owner or operator will be exonerated from liability in those situations which are completely beyond his control and are entirely caused by the act of God.[1167] The Claims Manager noted that Apex chose not to interrupt its normal navigation in the face of the floods, which they admitted they were aware of. The NPFC noted further that Apex chose to transit the flotilla into this riskier environment with an under powered tug to tow the barges.[1168] The Claims Manager pointed out that this under powered tug was the proximate cause of the discharge of oil.[1169] The Claims Manager noted that at the Vicksburg Bridge, the current became overwhelming for the SONDRA B and began to negate forward momentum. The current pushed the entire tow toward the right descending bank onto the concrete bridge spans. The Claims Manager inferred from the facts of the case that the manner in which the oil spill occurred reflects that the decision to navigate into higher and faster waters with an under powered tug contributed to the discharge.[1170]

The NPFC Claims Division also found that a lack of negligence on the part of the owner of the tug does not mitigate strict liability under

1165 Id.

1166 Id at 6.

1167 Id. (citing, Travelers Indemnity Co. and The Liberal Market Inc. v. United States, 230 Cl.Ct. 867, 868-69 (1982)).

1168 Id.

1169 Id.

1170 Id.

the FWPCA and OPA so as to entitle an RP to an act of God Defense.[1171] The NPFC cited to the case of *United States v. Tex-Tow, Inc.*,[1172] where the Seventh Circuit Court of Appeal held that neither clean-up liability nor liquidated damages liability is premised on a finding of fault and the defense of act of God leaves open the possibility that a faultless owner or operator will nevertheless be liable because of the inapplicability of the narrow defense. The NPFC further found that Congress intended, and the courts agree, that the strict liability scheme makes owners or operators liable if their actions in any way contributed to the incident, without regard as to whether their actions were negligent or culpable.[1173] The Claims Division found that notwithstanding that Apex's decision to navigate into an increasingly riskier environment with an inadequately powered tug may not have been negligent, that does not mitigate Apex's strict liability for removal costs and damages because Apex's decision contributed to the incident.[1174]

Finally, the NPFC found that the NPFC had not abused its discretion in determining that Apex was not entitled to an act of God defense because it had not created a standard inconsistent with OPA or associated regulations.[1175] The NPFC found that when it said in its denial letter in response to the initial claim that an act of God event must be "entirely absent of human agency," it merely meant that the act of God event must be the sole cause of the discharge and that a claimant must not contribute to the cause of the discharge by any human act or human omission.[1176] Apex argued that this standard was an onerous one, because the only way it could have avoided the incident and avoided any human agency would have been not to travel upriver at all.[1177] In its rejection of this argument, the Claims Division found that Apex certainly took some risks in operating in these

---

1171 Id.

1172 589 F.2d 1310, 1315 (7th Cir. 1978).

1173 Apex Towing Company, NPFC Claim Summary/Recommendation Form, Claim No 085114-001, at 6 (03/03/2000).

1174 Id. at 6.

1175 Id.

1176 Id.

1177 Id.

known conditions; however, Apex could have prevented or avoided the effects of the high river water and associated currents by utilizing an adequately powered tug.[1178]

Based on the foregoing reasoning and findings, the reconsidered Apex claim was once again denied and its act of God defense failed. This case underlines the difficulty of proving the OPA act of God defense.

Another NPFC's Claim Division case that illustrates the approach of the US Coast Guard National Pollution Funds Center and possible approach of courts to the OPA act of God defense is the case of *Cummins Investment Corporation*.[1179] In 1999, Cummins Investment Corp., the owner of the Frontier Terminal, filed a claim with the Fund for $400,431.49 for removal costs, asserting an act of God defense.[1180]

On or about June 9 1998 there was a discharge from the Frontier Terminal of approximately 23.80 barrels (1,000 gallons) of blending product of AC20 (asphalt oil, kerosene, etc) into the Navigation Channel and eventually into the Arkansas River, a navigable waterway of the United States.[1181] Specifically the claimant asserted that a violent storm with multiple lightning strikes in the vicinity of the Terminal produced naturally generated electricity which built to an extent that it caused a direct interference with the electrical system of the Terminal. It was this interference that caused damage to the blending unit, which in turn caused the escape of material into the area in excess of the retention capacity available.[1182]

The NPFC Claims Division denied the claim for a number of reasons. First, the NPFC relied heavily on a report submitted by a forensic engineer it hired to investigate and provide information regarding whether lightning could have caused such an incident and whether the

---

1178 Id.

1179 Cummins Investment Corp., NPFC Claim Summary/Recommendation Form, Claim No 088176-002, p 1 (12/08/1999) (on file with the NPFC and available upon request from the NPFC).

1180 Id. at 1.

1181 Id.

1182 Id.

claimant could have done anything to prevent the incident.[1183] Based on the report the NPFC rejected the claimant's characterization of the storm as being violent in nature and also found that thunderstorms are foreseeable events in Oklahoma.[1184] The NPFC found that there was no evidence provided to support the position of the claimant that the storm was so unusual in nature as to not be prevented against.[1185] The NPFC noted the finding in the report that storms of that nature are not a rare or unusual occurrence in Oklahoma at this time of the year.[1186] The report indicated that Oklahoma is second only to Florida in the number of thunderstorms per year.[1187] In addition, there was evidence that indicated that Oklahoma has approximately 50 to 60 days of thunderstorms per year. There was further evidence that indicated that the month of June has on average 10 thunderstorm days in Oklahoma, and are not unusual occurrences.[1188] The NPFC found that the claimant presented no evidence that this thunderstorm, although severe, was unusual in either its intensity or frequency for the month of June in Oklahoma.[1189]

The NPFC found that there was no physical evidence of a lightning strike to the Terminal which would cause a malfunction of the controller to activate the flow control valve and the blender/mixer pumps.[1190] The NPFC noted that a lightning strike has therefore been eliminated as the cause of the discharge of oil from the Terminal. The NPFC pointed to the findings of the investigation that the discharge occurred when the computerized control-led flow control valves of the blender/mixer malfunctioned and the hand operated gate valves upstream of the flow control valves were in an open position.[1191] The NPFC noted that while the pumps and the flow control valves can be activated only from the processor in the Waugh

---

1183 Id.

1184 Id. at 2.

1185 Id.

1186 Id.

1187 Id.

1188 Id. at 2.

1189 Id.

1190 Id.

1191 Id.

computerized controller, the hand operated gate valves were manually operated by the terminal operator.[1192]

The NPFC Claims Division also found that the claimant knew of the risk and failed to act reasonably to prevent such an incident.[1193] The NPFC also found that although the malfunction which occurred at the Waugh controller arguably could not have been prevented, the discharge of material from the Terminal could have been prevented if Frontier was in compliance with industry standards which directs that hand gate valves should not be left in an open position with no terminal operator present.[1194] The NPFC also found that the discharge would not have occurred if the hand gate valves were not open. The NPFC noted particularly that in the period from 1992-1994 the computer controlled blending/mixing system containing the Waugh controller was purchased from and installed by Fluid Specialties, Inc. (Fluid).[1195] Fluid provided on-site training to the Frontier Terminal employees. The NPFC noted that there was no evidence that this training addressed how the system would operate in an electrical storm, or what actions should be taken in the event of such a storm.[1196] The NPFC pointed out that it is reasonable to expect that a lightning strike or a lightning storm could cause some type of damage to the electrical system of a facility such as Frontier Terminal.[1197] It was therefore critical that there be some other safety mechanisms in place to ensure that an incident such as this one did not occur.[1198] The NPFC noted that the report indicated that the Terminal had suffered electrical damage from a storm at least once in the past. In that electrical damage, a flow control valve was damaged and was subsequently replaced prior to this incident.[1199] The NPFC noted that no other changes were made to the procedures despite this earlier inci-

---

1192 Id.

1193 Id. at 3.

1194 Id.

1195 Id.

1196 Id.

1197 Id. at 4.

1198 Id.

1199 Id.

dent. It also pointed out that the malfunction in the way the processor was supposed to operate could only produce a discharge if the three manual hand valves were left in an open position.[1200] The NPFC noted further that although the Waugh controller malfunctioned and turned on as a result of lightning in the vicinity, no product would have made its way out of the loading arm if they were left in a closed position.[1201] The NPFC observed that subsequent to the incident, changes were made to prevent the activation of the three pumps by the Waugh controller without manually turning on the switch to complete the control circuit from the Waugh controller to the pump starters.[1202] These changes was an indication that a better operating procedure could have been put in place to prevent the incident from happening. The Claims Manager said:

"In fact, the fact that they changed this procedure after the incident, lends credibility to the argument that this was a failure to take reasonable precautions."[1203]

On the standard operating procedures in place at the time of the incident, the NPFC found them to be inadequate. According to the investigative report, the standard operating procedures which were in place on June 9, 1998, directed the terminal operator to open all hand gate valves at the beginning of his shift and to leave them open for the duration of that shift.[1204] The NPFC pointed out that this direction resulted in there being no intermediate means to prevent an accidental spill from occurring in the event of the malfunction of the automatic controls. The NPFC concluded that this procedure is not recommended and is not in line with industry standards.[1205] Based on the foregoing, the NPFC denied the claim of Cummins Investment Inc.

1200 Id.

1201 Id.

1202 Id.

1203 Id. at 5.

1204 Id. at 4.

1205 Id.

## A.III. ACT OF WAR - 33 USC §2703(a)(2).

The OPA in section 2703 (a)(2) provides that an RP is not liable for removal costs or damages if the RP establishes by a preponderance of the evidence, that the discharge or substantial threat of a discharge of oil and the resulting damages or removal costs were caused solely by an act of war. At the time this treatise was written, there was no case on record that construed the OPA act of war defense. But there is at least one CERCLA case that has construed the act of war defense. This case will provide some guidance for OPA cases and would be discussed in the latter part of this subpart.

The word 'war' has been defined as a 'hostile contention by means of armed forces against a foreign power or against an opposing power in a state.[1206] ' Figuratively 'war' is used poetically or rhetorically to indicate any kind of active hostility or contention between living beings, or a conflict between opposing forces or principles.[1207] The Supreme Court of South Carolina in the case of *West v. Palmetto State Life Insurance Co.*,[1208] defined war as follows:

"The definition of war in Corpus Juris, 67 C.J. 336, is as follows: "War in the legal sense is the state of nations among whom there is an interruption of all pacific relations and a general contestation of arms by authority of the several sovereigns; it is not a mere contest of force, but must be an armed struggle carried on between two political bodies each of which exercises de facto authority over persons within a determinate territory, and its existence is determined by the authorized political department of the government. So, lawful war can never exist without the actual concurrence of the war-making power, but may exist prior to any contest of the armed forces. The courts are bound by a declaration or determination by the proper department of government that a war exists, while until there has been such a declaration or determination the courts cannot take judicial notice of the existence of a war by their government." Very pointed is

1206 See Gitlow v. Kiely, 44 F.2d 227, 233 (S.D.N.Y. 1930).

1207 44 F.2d at 233.

1208 25 S.E 2d 475, 477 (S.C. April 27, 1943).

the following from the same Volume, Page 338: "A court cannot, however, take judicial notice of a war by its government until there has been some act or declaration creating or recognizing the existence of war by the department of the government clothed with the war-making power."[1209]

The court in the case of *Savage v. Sun Life Assurance Co. of Canada*,[1210] also articulated the scope of the term "act of war" when it said:

"There can be no doubt that the attack by the Japanese Navy and its air force was intended as an act of war on its part, which eventuated inevitably in a declaration of war by both countries. However, the word or term as used in this policy must be interpreted in a manner that can be applied and understood in a more definite sense, rather than depend upon the violence or inconsequential nature of the acts of the attacker. If a state of war is to be judged by the latter circumstances, it would exist or not according to the opinion of the particular court construing it. On the other hand, if it is held to mean a condition accepted or recognized by the political authority of the government which is attacked, whether through an actual declaration of war or other acts clearly demonstrating such position, then we would have a criterion which could be readily understood and applied to cases, no matter what the circumstances might be. The attack by the Japanese armed forces upon the Panay in China has been alluded to in the above decisions as illustrating a case that might have led to war, but did not, with different views by the state and federal courts as to its weight. To this might be added the many attacks by German submarines upon American vessels, which led up to the first World War; but it could hardly be said that in any of these a provision such as the one in the policy involved here would have justified the conclusion that the death of an American officer or seaman, killed thereby, resulted 'from war or any act incident thereto."

"Granting that many wars have been fought without formal declaration by the governments involved, nevertheless, they were prosecuted by the mutual participation and attacks of the armed forces of each against the other. In other words, the war-making authority on each side accepted the actual conditions

1209 Id. at 477.

1210 57 F.Supp. 620, 621 (W.D. La 1944).

and brought into play the power of their armed forces in definite, hostile contest. Yet, when the bombs of the Japanese naval air force began falling upon our warships and installations at Pearl Harbor we were at peace with that nation, in fact, actually negotiating (certainly in good faith on our part, although fraudulently and deceitfully by the Japanese) for settlement of our differences by peaceful means. That condition certainly continued and there was no war until the first bomb landed against us. Must it be said that from that moment we were at war or would it be more reasonable, in the construction of the language of this policy, to say that it contemplated a condition where both we and the nation attacking us would first have to know and understand that we were engaged in a conflict of arms?"[1211]

Some other courts have articulated an opposite view of war. They have held that in private matters, unaffected by a public interest, the courts are free to take judicial notice of the existence of a war although no formal declaration of war has been made by the Federal government. For instance in the case of *Western Reserve Life Insurance Co. v. Meadows*,[1212] the court held that there may be war or a state of war without a declaration of war by the department of government clothed with the war-making power. The court in *Pang v. Sun Assurance Co. of Canada*,[1213] after referring to several decisions by United States courts, said:

"Those cases are authority for the admitted proposition that no 'formal' declaration is necessary to the creation of a 'state of war', and that by making payment to the officers and men engaged on a war basis and other informal acts the Congress recognizes the existence of a 'condition' of war."[1214]

---

1211 57 F.Supp. at 620-21.

1212 261 S.W. 2d. 554 (S.C. Tex Nov. 11 1953).

1213 37 Hawaii 208, 218 (S.C. Hawai Oct. 24 1945).

1214 Id. at 218, see also, Hamilton v. McClaughry, C.C., 136 F. 445, 451 (C.C.D Kansas, April 12 1905); Bas v. Tingy, 4 Dall. 37, 1 L.Ed. 731, 733-734 (1800); State of Virginia v. West Virginia, 11 Wall. 39, 20 L.Ed. 67, 72-73 (1870); Wharton v. Wise, 153 U.S. 155, 38 L.Ed. 669, 676 (1894).

Edwin Borchard, discussing under the title 'When Did the War Begin,' the decision of the United States Circuit Court of Appeals in New York Life Insurance Company v. Bennion,[1215] and other decisions, said:

"It is common knowledge that war may exist without a declaration thereof.' And on the authorities reviewed he expressed this conclusion: 'It thus appears that war may be deduced from the circumstances as a fact and may exist independently of a declaration by Congress."[1216]

Many definitions of war and many decisions reflect the common understanding of war as war in fact. The opinion in *the Prize cases (The Amy Warwick),*[1217] quotes with approval a definition of war as 'That state in which a nation prosecutes its right by force.' In *Stankus v. New York Life Insurance Co.,*[1218] the court said, citing authorities: 'A conflict between the armed forces of two nations under authority of their respective governments would be commonly regarded as war.' In the same opinion the court said that: 'The existence of a war is not dependent upon a formal declaration of war.'[1219] The Supreme Court of Maine in an 1860 opinion stated as follows:

"But every forcible contest between two governments, de facto, or de jure, is war. War is an existing fact, and not a legislative decree. Congress alone may have power to 'declare' it beforehand, and thus cause or commence it. But it may be initiated by other nations, or by traitors; and then it exists, whether there is any declaration of it or not. It may be prosecuted without any declaration; or Congress may, as in the Mexican war, declare its previous existence. In either case it is the fact that makes 'enemies', and not any legislative Act."[1220]

1215 158 F.2d 260 (10th Cir. 1946).

1216 Edwin Borchard, 'When Did the War Begin,' the decision of the United States Circuit Court of Appeals in New York Life Insurance Company v. Bennion, and other decisions, 47 Columbia L. Rev., 742, 745, 748 (1947).

1217 2 Black. 635, 17 L.Ed. 459, 476 (1862).

1218 312 Mass. 366, 44 N.E.2d 687, 688, 689 (S.C. Mass. Oct. 29 1942).

1219 Id. at 689.

1220 Dole v. Merchants' Mutual Marine Ins. Co., 51 Me. 465, 470 (1863).

Since we are faced with two conflicting and contending opinions on the issue of when war has actually begun in law, one would have to actually wait to see what position a court of law would take. But what this dilemmatic situation does tell us is that even where we have open hostilities between the US and another country that alone may not guarantee the successful invocation of the act of war defense if a court of law decides to follow the cases that hold that only an official declaration of war would suffice as war. On the other hand if a court of law follows the competing precedents that hold that an official declaration need not be made for there to be war, then the RP invoking an act of war defense has a better chance of successfully invoking the defense. But even in that kind of situation it would still be very difficult to successfully invoke the defense as epitomized in the case of *United States v. Shell Oil Co.*[1221] *Shell* will be discussed in the latter part of this chapter.

One thing that is clear from the first contending view as articulated in the *West v. Palmetto State Life Insurance Co.,*[1222] case is that there must be an official declaration and even if hostilities have not begun, but a declaration has been made, that alone will satisfy the act of war requirement. A hypothetical situation that could help to better explain this situation is as follows:

A foreign flagged supertanker carrying oil was sailing to a seaport in the US and during the voyage, a war declaration was made against the country whose flag the vessel carries, and by virtue of that, sanctions are imposed on that country which include a ban on direct sea transportation to the US by vessels carrying that country's flag. The declaration punishes the owner and operator of a violating vessel with forfeiture of the vessel and its cargo. That declaration was made just as the supertanker was about to enter US navigable and territorial waters and the vessel on learning of the declaration of war and the sanctions tries to get out of US waters, but is pursued by US naval ships resulting in the grounding of the supertanker and in the discharge of thousands of barrels of oil into US waters.

1221 841 F.Supp. 962, 966 (C.D. Cal. 1993).

1222 25 S.E 2d 475, 477.

In the above situation, the owner of the foreign flagged supertanker can successfully invoke the act of war defense even though hostilities like bombings and shootings have not broken out between both countries yet. It is clearly an act of war despite the absence of usual violence associated with war. So, the key factor to look at in the first school of thought is whether there has been a cloak of officialdom putting no one in doubt that both nations are at war.

On the other hand if the second school of thought that says there need not be an official declaration of war for there to be war, as long as there is conflict or forcible contest between the armed forces of two nations under authority of their respective governments prevails, then despite the declaration of war in the hypothetical, the supertanker may not be able to invoke the "act of war" defense.[1223] This is due to the absence of conflict or forcible contest between the armed forces of the US and that foreign nation under authority of the government of the US and the government of that foreign country. Therefore, the first school of thought looks at the cloak of officialdom, while the second school of thought focuses on the presence of officially sanctioned hostilities between both countries with all the trappings of war.

If a court of law were to follow the first school of thought, even the bombing of a supertanker carrying oil within US waters by international terrorists or the armed forces of a foreign nation leading to the discharge of oil into the navigable waters of the US may not be sufficient to invoke the act of war defense because of the absence of an official declaration of war by the governments of the US and/or the government of the foreign country. On the other hand if a court of law were to follow the second school of thought, the "act of war" defense could be invoked successfully in that kind of situation, except for one involving international terrorists not having the official backing or sponsorship of any nation. But, for both schools of thought, the bombing of a supertanker by a domestic terrorist may not be sufficient to invoke the act of war defense, because it is devoid of the requirement that the hostilities be between two nations. If

1223 Pang v. Sun Assurance Co. of Canada, 37 Hawaii 208, 218 (S.C. Hawai Oct. 24 1945).

the domestic terrorist did the act because it was sponsored by a foreign government and was thus acting as a traitor, then it might still qualify as an "act of war."

Even in this kind of situation the courts would still require that the RP prove that the discharge was caused solely by the "act of war." Even where a vessel has been attacked within US territory, the owner and operator of that vessel is not supposed to walk away from the vessel. He has to take adequate precaution against an oil spill by contacting the necessary government agencies like the US Coast Guard's National Response Center, the Environmental Protection Agency and all other government agencies charged with the responsibility of protecting US waters from pollution. By so doing the threat of a substantial discharge of oil from the vessel into US waters could be eliminated or minimized substantially. If the owner of the vessel decides to walk away simply because it believes that it is entitled to the act of war defense, that owner may either lose the "act of war defense" or may be deemed to have contributed to the spill by his actions. Section 2703(c) of OPA provides that the defenses enumerated in section 2703(a) does not apply with respect to an RP who fails or refuses to report the incident as required by law, if the RP knows or has reason to know of the incident. "Incident" is not limited to the discharge itself but includes any occurrences or series of occurrences having the same origin, involving one or more vessels, facilities, or any combination thereof, resulting in the discharge or substantial threat of discharge of oil.[1224] This shows that a state sponsored attack on an oil carrying supertanker or facility would qualify as an incident if it could cause a discharge of oil into US navigable waters. So, it must be reported as quickly as possible.

The FWPCA has an act of war defense that would apply to oil spills caused by wars fought between 1972 and August 18, 1990 when OPA was enacted. The OPA specifically provides in section 2717(e) that:

"Nothing in this title shall apply to any cause of action or right of recovery arising from any incident which occurred prior to August 18, 1990. Such claims shall be adjudicated pursuant to the law applicable on the date of the incident."

---

1224 33 USCA §2701(14).

Obviously, the OPA act of war defense cannot be invoked for war induced oil spills that occurred prior to August 18, 1990. Whereas, CERCLA applies retroactively and its act of war defense can be invoked for spills of hazardous substances that occurred prior to its enactment, even stretching as far back as World War II. It has been held that retroactive application of CERCLA does not violate due process; because CERCLA's language and legislative history reveal Congress' conscious intent to compel correction of careless disposal of hazardous waste in the past by the nation's industries.[1225] Unlike CERCLA cases that usually involve wars fought decades ago, OPA's "act of war" defense is limited to wars fought after August 17, 1990. I will now undertake a brief analysis of the only CERCLA "act of war" case that could provide needed guidance for future OPA act of war cases.

## United States v. Shell Oil Co.[1226]

The governments of United States and California brought this action under CERCLA against some oil companies and the landowner for response costs incurred in cleaning up hazardous waste site.[1227] This Superfund site known as the McColl Superfund Site comprised roughly twenty-two acres in Fullerton, California.[1228] It was bordered by housing developments, a country club golf course, a regional park, and an oil field. The Site was divided into two distinct areas: the Ramparts area and the Los Coyotes area. The Ramparts area occupied vacant land. It contained six large pits, or sumps. The Los Coyotes area was land that once was part of the Los Coyotes Country Club golf course. It contained six sumps which underlie what were portions of the golf course. The hazardous waste located at the McColl Site consisted of acid sludge byproducts of alkylation processes used by the oil companies during World War II to produce high octane aviation fuel. During the war, the oil companies

1225 United States v. Shell Oil Co., 841 F.Supp. 962 (C.D. Cal. 1993).

1226 841 F.Supp. 962, 966 (C.D. Cal. 1993), *affirmed in,* 281 F.3d. 812 (9th Cir. 2002).

1227 Id. at 962.

1228 Id. at 966.

produced this aviation fuel in extraordinary quantities at the demand of, and in fulfillment of supply contracts with, the federal government.[1229]

Under the government's regulatory scheme, the contracting companies were subject to considerable oversight by government agencies, and any oil company that refused to comply with regulations could be taken over by the government and individuals who interfered with the government's regulation of industry and acquisition of supplies would have been subject to criminal prosecution.[1230] The government's demand at the Fullerton, California site of the aviation fuel production became so great that the oil companies were unable to dispose of the waste sludge on their premises.[1231] The government urged the companies not to allow the storage problem to interfere with the oil production, and 'with at least tacit approval from the government,' the companies arranged for the sludge to be transported from the facilities to the McColl site, where the waste was stored in unlined pits.[1232] The dumping stopped after the War, but by the 1990's, the sludge was oozing up from the ground, a portion of which had been developed into a golf course.

The McColl property became a Superfund site, and the federal government and the State of California incurred response costs for which they sought reimbursement from the oil companies and the present site owner under section 9607(a) of CERCLA. The district court found that the necessary elements set forth in section 9607(a) were satisfied and that the federal government and the State of California were entitled to reimbursement from the defendants.[1233] The district court concluded that the sludge-filled pits, or sumps, were 'facilities' as defined by CERCLA, and that the seepage of the sludge constituted a release of 'hazardous substances' under CERCLA.[1234]Due to the fact that the oil companies produced the oil and contracted for the transportation of the sludge for dumping, they were

1229 Id.

1230 Id.

1231 Id. at 967.

1232 Id.

1233 Id. at 969-70.

1234 Id. at 969.

found to be generators and arrangers liable under section 9607(a)(3).[1235] Likewise, the present owner of the McColl site was found to be an owner and operator and was liable under section 9607(a)(1).[1236]

The oil companies raised section 9607(b)(2)'s act of war defense, which was rejected by the court.[1237] The defendants claimed that the dumping of the sludge occurred only because vast amounts of fuel had to be produced for the government during the War; thus, an act of war had caused the contamination.[1238] Emphasizing that the liability provisions of CERCLA are broad in scope and that section 9607(b)'s defenses have repeatedly been held to be extremely narrow, the court disallowed the defense.[1239] The court noted that 'act of war' is neither defined in CERCLA, nor addressed by the statute's legislative history.[1240] The court noted that on the basis of the legislative history, and with CERCLA's overall slant in favor of imposing liability, one leading commentator has opined that the act of war defense presumes "governmental sponsorship" and "formalization of hostilities," and contemplates "a confrontation of organized forces, acts of state, massive violence, and overwhelming influence that are unlikely to be found in the domestic Superfund context."[1241] Although it is unlikely in a domestic Super Fund context, it is highly possible in an OPA liability context because the OPA allows foreign countries to recover removal costs and damages from RPs for oil spills originating in US navigable waters, Outer Continental Shelf facility, deepwater port, and from vessels transporting Trans Alaska Pipeline oil that impacts the territorial sea, internal waters, and adjacent shoreline of foreign nations.[1242] So,

1235 Id. at 970.

1236 Id.

1237 Id. at 970-72.

1238 Id. at 970.

1239 Id. at 970-72.

1240 Id. at 970-71.

1241 Id. at 971 (*citing*, 4 William H. Rodgers, Jr., Environmental Law: Hazardous Wastes and Substances § 8.13(C)(3)(c) (1992) (pointing to "the environmental terrorism inflicted on the air and water of the Persian Gulf by the troops of Saddam Hussein" as a prototypical example)).

1242 See 33 USCA §2707(a)-(b).

nations like Canada and Mexico adjacent to US territory would be able to invoke OPA liability and compensation provisions and an RP could invoke the "act of war" defense in those types of cases. While CERCLA does not extend beyond US territory, OPA extends far beyond US territories and covers oil pollution impacting foreign countries, as long as the requirement of section 2707(a)-(c) of OPA is satisfied by foreign claimants.

Looking to precedent not involving environmental issues, the court noted that although the seizure of property from those who support an enemy has been held to be an act of war, courts have repeatedly distinguished such situations from those where the government agrees to compensate owners for the use of their property during hostilities.[1243] Similarly, Civil War cases indicate that only acts of the government in appropriating property in order to destroy or weaken the enemy, as opposed to action taken to supply the military, constitute acts of war.[1244] The Court found that none of these act of war' interpretations supported the oil companies' position.[1245] Critical to the court's determination was the contractual relationship between the oil companies and the government and the voluntary nature of the oil companies' entry into the war contracts.[1246] Also vital was the oil companies' readiness to have the excess sludge transported for dumping.[1247] The district court held that it was inconsequential whether the oil companies' voluntary entry into the war production effort was motivated by profit or a sense of civic duty.[1248] Although the court recognized the far reaching nature of the government regulation during the War, it discounted that element because of the companies' voluntary entry into the contracts.[1249] The court was not impressed by the fact that uncooperative companies were subject to government seizure.[1250] The non-coercive

---

1243 Shell Oil Co., 841 F.Supp. at 971-72.

1244 Id. at 971-72.

1245 Id.

1246 Id.

1247 Id. at 967.

1248 Id.

1249 Id.

1250 Id. at 966-67.

nature of the defendants' acts was the most important factor in the court's refusal to accept the defendant's invocation of the act of war defense.

This case buttresses the fact that the "act of war" defense will be strictly construed against an RP. So, even where it is established that there is a war situation in existence, for the RP to successfully invoke the act of war defense, it must prove that the oil spill was caused by circumstances that fall within the normal trappings of war between nations, like excessive force, violence, hostility and conflict. So, if an enemy bomb or weapon of war hits a vessel or facility and it causes an oil spill that impacts the navigable waters of the US, that will clearly qualify as "act of war." But the events in the *Shell* case does not come close to this type of situation because the oil companies were in contractual relationship with the government and were in control of the circumstances of the spill, by knowingly arranging for the disposal of the hazardous substances involved. One cannot reasonably argue that the spill was caused by an act of war because the oil companies anticipated the manner of disposal of the substances and executed it themselves.

One interesting thing about this case was that the defendants had filed counter-claims against the government as well as cross-claims against each other for the pollution. The court allowed a bifurcation of the defendant's cross claims and counter claims holding that the Federal Rule of Civil Procedure 42(b) authorizes the Court to order a separate trial of any claim including counterclaims, cross-claims, or any other issue for purposes of convenience, avoiding prejudice, expedition, or judicial economy.[1251] The court noted that the principal goal of Rule 42(b) is to promote efficient judicial administration, and only one of the conditions set forth in the rule need be served to justify a separate trial.[1252] The court specifically held that the possibility of a future finding of partial liability on the part of the governments ought not stand as a bar to expeditious recovery of response costs, since the defendants will be reimbursed in the event

1251 *Shell Oil Co.*, 841 F.Supp. at 974.

1252 Id. at 974-75.

the governments are found liable.[1253] The Court found that allowing the governments to recover their response costs before resolving Defendants' counterclaims and cross-claims could not unduly prejudice Defendants as they will be reimbursed in the future for any costs paid to the Superfund that are properly attributable to other parties.[1254] In contrast, the Court took the view that litigating the cost recovery together with the cross and counterclaim aspects of the action would inappropriately prejudice the public welfare by slowing replenishment of the Superfund.[1255]

Therefore, the Court concluded that bifurcation of Defendants' counterclaims and cross-claims from the remaining portion of the cost recovery phase of the litigation will best serve the Court's and litigants' economy of time and effort.[1256] The court bifurcated Defendants' counterclaims and cross-claims from the remainder of the cost recovery phase.[1257] The court also stayed litigation of Defendants' counterclaims and cross-claims for contribution pending completion of the governments' cost recovery phase of this action.[1258] Because of the decision of the court to stay further proceedings in the issue of contribution among the contending parties, this aspect of the *Shell* case did not come up again until 1998.

The importance of this aspect of the case is that it shows that if the RP cannot invoke the 'act of war' defense successfully, it might be able to force a substantial contribution from the United States to the costs of cleanup and remediation of the pollution. In *United States v. Shell*,[1259] (Shell II) after reviewing the evidence and applying such equitable factors as appeared appropriate, the court found that the Government bore total responsibility for any waste at the CERCLA hazardous waste site attributable to the World War II aviation gas program for three reasons: (1) such a result simply places the cost of the war on the United States

1253 Id. at 975, (citing, United States v. Western Processing Company, 734 F.Supp. 930, 939-40 (W.D.Wash.1990)).

1254 Id. at 975.

1255 Id.

1256 Id.

1257 Id. at 975-76.

1258 Id. at 976.

1259 *Shell II*, 13 F.Supp.2d 1018 (C.D. Cal. 1998)

and thus on society as a whole, (2) the Oil Companies were unable to transport aviation gasoline (avgas) waste to Richmond for recycling due to the unavailability of tank cars, and (3) the Oil Companies were unable to construct treatment plants due to the War Production Board's (WPB's) refusal to issue priorities. Each of these reasons appeared to the Court to be a compellingly appropriate equitable factor to support the Court's conclusion.[1260]

In *Shell II* most of the facts and evidence that were not sufficient to prove "act of war," were enough to prove that government contributed to the spill. Shortly after the December 7, 1941, bombing of Pearl Harbor by the Japanese, Congress enacted the First War Powers Act "to expedite the prosecution of the war effort."[1261] This Act gave broad power to the President to issue Executive Orders concerning the war effort. In January 1942, President Roosevelt issued Executive Order 9024, which established the War Production Board (WPD).[1262] Pursuant to Executive Order 9024, the Chairman of the WPB was empowered to issue directives to industry in connection with war procurement and production, including directives with respect to purchasing, contracting, specification, construction, requisitioning, plant expansion, conversion and financing.[1263]

The court pointed out that even if the Court were of the view that, during the pendency of the war, the Oil Companies were responsible for facilitating the proper disposal of avgas waste, the Court is convinced that the Oil Companies had no reasonable recourse to on-land dumping of the sludge due to the conduct of the WPB.[1264] The court found that the Oil Companies had made a strong showing that this was indeed the case. The defendants proved that in the years prior to the war effort, acid sludge was routinely transported in special lead-lined tank cars to the Shell Point facility in Richmond, California, for reprocessing into

1260 Id. at 1026-27.

1261 See *Shell II*, 13 F.Supp.2d 1021, see also, 55 Stat. 838, 839 (1941) (codified at 50 U.S.C.App. § 611 (repealed 1966)).

1262 Id. at 1021.

1263 Id.

1264 *Shell II*, 13 F.Supp.2d at 1027.

fertilizer.[1265] Between 1936 and 1939, when tank cars were available, the Oil Companies transported more than 86,000 tons of sludge to the Shell Point facility.[1266]

During the war, the lead-lined tank cars were needed by the Government for war purposes.[1267] Thus, the cars were rarely available for the transportation of sludge to Shell Point. Indeed, in his testimony before the Los Angeles Planning Commission in May 1942, Eli McColl stated that the reason he was applying for permit to dump waste at the McColl Site was that the Government would not allow his or the companies he represented to use tank cars to ship acid to northern California for use as fertilizer.[1268] Between 1941 and 1943, the total amount of sludge transported to Shell Point dropped to less than 2,000 tons. As soon as tank cars again became readily available near the end of the war, the large-scale transportation of sludge to Shell Point via tank cars resumed.[1269] The court found that given the pattern of transport both before and after the war, one can be sure that had lead-lined tank cars been available throughout the war years, the Oil Companies would have made use of them.[1270]

The facts also revealed that from the beginning of the avgas program, the Government was aware that spent alkylation acid and acid sludge were produced in the manufacture of avgas and that increasing production of avgas would increase the amount of spent alkylation acid and acid sludge produced.[1271] The construction of new facilities to reprocess these avgas byproducts required WPB approval because without WPB approval the materials needed for construction could not be obtained. Decisions on the construction of such plants were made pursuant to the WPB's powers to allocate resources for the war effort.[1272]

---

1265 Id. at 1027.

1266 Id. 1027-28.

1267 Id. at 1028.

1268 Id.

1269 Id.

1270 Id.

1271 Id.

1272 Id.

During the war, Shell sought to build a spent alkylation acid decomposition plant in Houston. It sought to spend more than $1 million of its own funds to this end. On October 13, 1944, the Inorganic Acids Committee of the WPB rejected this request on the ground that when considering the need for fresh acid, an original sulfuric acid plant could be built with fewer resources than a spent acid decomposition plant.[1273] Similarly, the stipulated facts established that Texaco sought to build an acid re-concentrator to treat both spent acid and acid sludge as part of a larger proposal. The WPB eliminated this portion of the proposal on the ground that the acid requirements of Texaco could be provided from other sources.[1274]

After review of evidence of the denial of these two attempts to obtain priorities for the construction of treatment plants, as well the evidence submitted concerning the denial of the Tidewater request and the grant of the Stauffer request, the court found that it was clear that the Government's policy with respect to spent acid or acid sludge was not to grant priorities unless the plant was needed to provide fresh acid for use in the manufacture of avgas.[1275]

The court acknowledged that it was likely that this policy was that which best furthered the war effort. The court noted however, that it came at the expense of the environment as, in combination with the unavailability of tank cars, it left the Oil Companies with no reasonable choice but to dump acid sludge.[1276] The *Shell II* court noted further:

> "Simply put, the Government's war requirements created the waste and Government acts or omissions foreclosed the reasonable alternative methods of disposal (transportation via tank cars for recycling or construction of regeneration plants) of the waste. Having created the problem and foreclosed the possible solutions, the Government will receive a 100 percent allocation of waste attributable to the avgas program."[1277]

---

1273 Id.

1274 Id.

1275 Id.

1276 Id.

1277 Id. at 1028.

In its finding that holding the government liable places the cost of the war on the United States and thus on society as a whole, the court relied on the case of *FMC Corp. v. U.S. Department of Commerce*,[1278] where the Third Circuit Court of Appeals wrote:

> "Furthermore, we point out that at bottom our result simply places a cost of the war on the United States, and thus on society as a whole, a result which is neither untoward nor inconsistent with the policy underlying CERCLA."[1279]

The *Shell II* court found this statement of equal force in the context of this allocation proceeding.[1280] The court pointed out that the avgas program is one in which the degree of Government oversight was extraordinarily high.[1281] The court observed that if the Oil Companies' performance in the supply of avgas had fallen short of requirements, the Government could have gone so far as to seize the plants.[1282] The *Shell II* court pointed out further that an allocation to the Government of liability for waste that is attributable to a war-time program is wholly consistent with the policy underlying CERCLA and indeed simply places a cost of the war on the United States and thus on society as a whole.[1283] The court found further that so long as responsibility being allocated is responsibility only for waste attributable to avgas production, it stands to reason that just as the American public stood to benefit from the successful prosecution of the war effort, so too must the American public bear the burden of a cost directly and inescapably created by the war effort, the production of avgas waste.[1284] Based on the foregoing reasoning, on the manner of allocating the clean up costs, the court found that the oil companies were liable for

1278 Id. at 1027 (*citing*, 786 F.Supp. 471 (E.D.Pa.1992), affirmed at 29 F.3d 833 (3rd Cir.1994)).

1279 29 F.3d at 846.

1280 *Shell II*, 13 F.Supp.2d at 1027.

1281 Id. at 1027.

1282 Id.

1283 Id.

1284 Id. at 1027.

zero percent of the clean-up costs while the US government was liable for 100 percent of the clean-up costs.

There could have been a different outcome in this case if the Oil Companies were not inhibited from transporting avgas waste to Richmond for recycling due to the availability of tank cars, and if the Oil Companies were able to construct treatment plants due to the War Production Board's (WPB's) readiness or willingness to issue priorities. In that situation the Oil Companies would not have had any excuse for the pollution or the dumping of the waste on land that consequently became a CERCLA Super Fund site. The *Shell II* case shows that if an RP fails in its attempt to invoke the "act of war" defense, because of a court's reliance on either the first or second school of thought for determining "act of war," it could alternatively sue the government for contribution provided the requirements of a contribution action against the government, discussed later in chapter ten are satisfied.

## Other issues related to the OPA Defenses

If the responsible party refuses to pay removal costs and damages as required by section 2702(d)(B), it could lose its third party defense because section 2703(c)(2) provides specifically that the complete defenses in section 2703(a) do not apply with respect to a responsible party who fails or refuses to provide all reasonable cooperation and assistance requested by a responsible official in connection with removal activities. Failure to make removal costs and damages payments as requested by a responsible government official could qualify as "failure to provide all reasonable cooperation and assistance."[1285] The consequences of the RP losing its defenses is that it would not be able to recover 100% of its removal costs and damages from the NPFC. Although that should not circumvent its ability to sue the sole cause third party for contribution or indemnity or its ability to limit its liability to the OPA limit of liability.

---

1285 See 33 USCA §2703(c)(2)

2702(D)(1)(B)(I)[1286] is restricted to the third party defense and does not in any way affect the complete defenses of Act of war or Act of God,[1287] that a responsible party might be entitled to. Unlike in cases involving the third party defense, if either the act of war or act of God defense is successfully invoked, the responsible party is not required to pay removal costs and damages to any claimant. In situations like these, the Fund shoulders the responsibility of paying the removal costs as well as damages of claimants.[1288] This type of outcome is logical because if the oil spill is caused by the act of God, or act of war, there will be no one to hold responsible for the oil spill. If the responsible party decides to voluntarily shoulder the responsibility of paying for removal costs and damages, it might not succeed in obtaining reimbursement from the Fund. The RP entitled to an act of war or act of God defense will not be able to sue any third party for indemnification or contribution, in that the spill was not caused by any third party. But, the decision of an RP to refuse to pay removal costs and damages when requested by the US Coast Guard or the EPA because it is sure that it is entitled to either the act of God or act of War defense could turn out to be a very costly one. This is because the RP may have to litigate the issue of its entitlement to these defenses which it must prove by a preponderance of the evidence. As discussed earlier in this treatise, these defenses are very difficult to invoke successfully. So, the RP cannot predict a favorable outcome in the litigation. Apart from the difficulty of predicting a favorable outcome, section 2704(c)(3) of OPA specifically provides:

"(c) Limitation on complete defense
Subsection (a) of this section does not apply with respect to a responsible party who fails or refuses--

---

1286 "(B) Subrogation of responsible party

If the responsible party alleges that the discharge or threat of a discharge was caused solely by an act or omission of a third party, the responsible party--

(i) in accordance with section 2713 of this title, shall pay removal costs and damages to any claimant."

1287 33 USCA §2703(a)

1288 See 33 USCA §2712(a).

(3) without sufficient cause, to comply with an order issued under subsection (c) or (e) of section 1321 of this title, as amended by this Act, or the Intervention on the High Seas Act (33 U.S.C. 1471 et seq.)."

Section 1321(e) of the FWPCA to which the above OPA section refers provides:

"(e) Civil enforcement

(1) Orders protecting public health

In addition to any action taken by a State or local government, when the President determines that there may be an imminent and substantial threat to the public health or welfare of the United States, including fish, shellfish, and wildlife, public and private property, shorelines, beaches, habitat, and other living and non-living natural resources under the jurisdiction or control of the United States, because of an actual or threatened discharge of oil or a hazardous substance from a vessel or facility in violation of subsection (b) of this section, the President may--

(A) require the Attorney General to secure any relief from any person, including the owner or operator of the vessel or facility, as may be necessary to abate such endangerment; or

(B) after notice to the affected State, take any other action under this section, including issuing administrative orders, that may be necessary to protect the public health and welfare."

This provision of Section 1321(e) of the FWPCA empowers the President to issue administrative orders. Most of these powers have been delegated to the US Coast Guard, the Environmental Protection Agency (EPA) and other government agencies. If they issue this order and the RP fails to obey them the RP could be faced with a loss of a the defenses to which it is entitled. But there is a limiting phrase in section 2703(c )(3) of the OPA that minimizes the harshness and draconian nature of the provision. That phrase is the phrase "who fails or refuses without sufficient cause to comply with an order issued." If the RP has sufficient cause for not complying, it would not lose its right to invoke the OPA defenses.

Section 1321(c) of the FWPCA provides in pertinent part:

"(c) Federal removal authority

(1) General removal requirement

(A) The President shall, in accordance with the National Contingency Plan and any appropriate Area Contingency Plan, ensure effective and immediate removal of a discharge, and mitigation or prevention of a substantial threat of a discharge, of oil or a hazardous substance--
  (i) into or on the navigable waters;
  (ii) on the adjoining shorelines to the navigable waters;
  (iii) into or on the waters of the exclusive economic zone; or
  (iv) that may affect natural resources belonging to, appertaining to, or under the exclusive management authority of the United States.

(B) In carrying out this paragraph, the President may--
  (i) remove or arrange for the removal of a discharge, and mitigate or prevent a substantial threat of a discharge, at any time;
  (ii) direct or monitor all Federal, State, and private actions to remove a discharge; and
  (iii) remove and, if necessary, destroy a vessel discharging, or threatening to discharge, by whatever means are available.

(2) Discharge posing substantial threat to public health or welfare

(A) If a discharge, or a substantial threat of a discharge, of oil or a hazardous substance from a vessel, offshore facility, or onshore facility is of such a size or character as to be a substantial threat to the public health or welfare of the United States (including but not limited to fish, shellfish, wildlife, other natural resources, and the public and private beaches and shorelines of the United States), the President shall direct all Federal, State, and private actions to remove the discharge or to mitigate or prevent the threat of the discharge.

(B) In carrying out this paragraph, the President may, without regard to any other provision of law governing contracting procedures or employment of personnel by the Federal Government--
  (i) remove or arrange for the removal of the discharge, or mitigate or prevent the substantial threat of the discharge; and
  (ii) remove and, if necessary, destroy a vessel discharging, or threatening to discharge, by whatever means are available."

Subsection (c) gives sweeping powers to the President (or the delegatee of his power) to ensure adequate containment and removal of oil spills.

The President or the government agency to which these powers have been delegated will issue administrative orders to ensure the enforcement of these provisions. One of such orders might be an order ordering the RP to destroy its own multi-million dollar vessel or facility with self-destructive explosives in order to minimize the effects of an actual or threatened oil spill. Thus, this order could be issued if there is no actual oil spill but only a determination by the EPA or the US Coast Guard that the vessel or facility poses a substantial threat of a discharge into navigable waters. It is only logical that an RP or its insurer may resist the order to destroy the vessel or facility because of the value of the vessel or facility and because of the belief of the RP that it is possible to prevent an oil spill under the circumstances without destroying the vessel or facility. Such disobedience by the owner or operator of the vessel or facility could strip it of its OPA defenses. The EPA or the US Coast Guard in its administrative hearings might determine it to be a disobedience of administrative orders. Once this happens, the RP may need to challenge the administrative order in a competent court of law. The only way a court of law that decides to step in can overturn the administrative decision is presentation of convincing evidence by the RP that it had sufficient cause for refusing to comply with the administrative order.

If an RP decides not to pay for any portion of the removal costs when requested by the Federal On Scene Coordinator or any other statutorily competent federal official because it is convinced of its entitlement to the defenses of Act of God or Act of War, that could also pose a danger to the RP. This is because of the difficulty of successfully invoking these defenses which the court construe very narrowly and grant in only exceptional or extreme situations. This has been explained extensively in the earlier part of this treatise.

Because of the difficulty of successful invocation of these defenses and the onerous burden of proof that the RP has to discharge in cases involving these two OPA defenses, the RP could pay dearly for not complying with payment requests. Until the issue is litigated before a court of law successfully, the RP could be gambling with OPA liability. This is because the court of law could decide that the oil spill was caused by both the RP in combination with one of the defenses. If a court of law finds that it was not caused solely by any of the defenses in section 2703(a) of the OPA, the RP would be held liable. But the RP would have lost the opportunity of controlling the cost of clean up and the size of damages. The US government would have dictated the cost of clean up because it was given the leeway to handle clean up efforts at standard government contract rates which is usually higher than the contract rates the RP would have paid those oil spill response organizations it might have privately retained under the Oil Spill Response Program of the National Contingency Plan. The NPFC would have played a primary and exclusive role in the settlement or litigation of removal costs and damage claims against the Fund due to the RP's denial of responsibility for the oil spill. The Fund would then have been subrogated to all the rights of those third parties and definitely sue to recover the exact amount it paid the private third parties plus interest. It is possible that if the RP had accepted to participate in the clean-up effort it could have minimized the private claimant's clean-up costs. It may also have litigated some damages claims successfully against certain third parties. These exact same cases that an RP may have litigated and defeated successfully in court could be settled for millions of dollars by the Fund, since it knows that it could sue the RP successfully and recover the amount. There are however some advantages that the RP could derive from the subrogation action. Since it is a subrogation action, the RP is entitled to all the defenses it could have invoked against the third party claimant. The NPFC is also limited to only the rights, claims, and causes of action that the third party claimant has under any other law.[1289] This means that if the NPFC pays any bogus claim of a third party, it might not be able to recover the amount successfully from the RP. Since the Fund is merely standing in the shoes of the third party claimant it cannot have more rights than the original third party claimant would have, except for that which OPA itself has conferred on it. For instance section 2715(c) of OPA provides that in subrogation actions against the RP or its guarantor, the Fund can recover interest (including prejudgment interest), administrative and adjudicative costs, and attorney's fees. This gives the government additional rights. If the size of the oil spill is moderate, in-

1289 See 33 USCA §2715(a).

terest (including prejudgment interest), administrative and adjudicative costs, and attorney's fees could be larger than the costs of removal and amount of damages combined. This is where the RP will feel the pain of a subrogation action the most.

The danger involved in refusing to obey an administrative order is further exacerbated by the usual difficulty of pre-enforcement review of administrative orders. Prior to 1986, CERCLA was silent as to whether review of administrative orders was available, but the majority of the courts considering the issue found that the statute implicitly barred review.[1290] In 1986, Congress codified the judicially created bar to judicial review in the Superfund Amendments and Reauthorization Act (SARA).[1291]

Unfortunately, Congress has left other federal environmental statutes like the FWPCA silent as to whether pre-enforcement review is precluded,[1292] leaving the recipients of administrative orders in doubt as to whether to challenge the validity of the order in court. Because of Congress' silence, courts are left to guess Congress' intent, searching for hints in the statutes' language, legislative histories, and purposes.[1293] When administrative orders are issued to address emergency hazards to human health or the environment, the policies supporting a bar to pre-enforcement review are overriding.[1294] However, when environmental statutes are silent as to

1290 See e.g., Wagner Elec. Corp. v. Thomas, 612 F.Supp. 736 (D.Kan.1985) (holding that actions seeking to review the merits of an order prior to an attempt by the EPA to enforce it are not ripe for review under the Administrative Procedure Act).

1291 Pub.L. No. 99-499, 100 Stat. 1613 (1986). The SARA amendments added § 113(h) which expressly bars review of § 104 and § 106(a) orders. 42 U.S.C. § 9613(h) (1988).

1292 Neither the Resource Conservation and Recovery Act of 1976 (RCRA), 42 U.S.C. §§ 6901-6922(k) (1988) nor the Federal Water Pollution Control Act (FWPCA), 33 U.S.C. §§ 1251-1387 (1988) expressly provide for, or preclude, pre- enforcement review.

1293 See, e.g, Block v. Community Nutrition Inst., 467 U.S. 340 (1984). The standards for whether Congress intended to preclude judicial review of statutory claims and constitutional claims should not be confused. The Supreme Court has repeatedly held that "where Congress intends to preclude judicial review of constitutional claims its intent to do so must be clear." Webster v. Doe, 486 U.S. 592 (1988). *See also* Weinberger v. Salfi, 422 U.S. 749 (1975); Johnson v. Robison, 415 U.S. 361 (1974).

1294 Hodel v. Virginia Surface Mining & Reclamation Ass'n, 452 U.S. 264, 299-300 (1981) (citing Calero-Toledo v. Pearson Yacht Leasing Co., 416 U.S. 663, 677-80 (1974);

pre-enforcement review, a challenge to an administrative order may force EPA to litigate the validity of the order. As a result, little or no response actions take place to abate the environmental hazard, litigation expenses mount, and the resources of the EPA and the judiciary are wasted. The sensitive nature of environmental hazards and the costs of litigation are such that Congress must clearly establish whether administrative orders under the federal environmental statutes are reviewable. When pollution to the environment poses a hazard of impending significant damage, immediate action by either the EPA, the Coast Guard or the recipient of the order is required under the FWPCA. Immediate remedial action prevents further contamination that could require more complex and expensive remediation efforts. The longer environmental hazards remain, the greater the possibility of migration of pollutants into surface or groundwater, air, or soil. Greater migration of pollutants into environmental media complicates cleanup because it requires that remedial efforts be taken upon a greater volume of the environmental media, involving additional time and resources. The implication of this is that the EPA or the US Coast guard and responsible parties will waste their time, efforts, and resources in litigation rather than using those resources to abate the environmental hazard.

As explained earlier, the FWPCA is silent as to whether pre-enforcement review of administrative orders is available even though judicial review of orders is explicitly provided for by section 309(b) of the Act when EPA brings an enforcement action or seeks to enforce a compliance order.[1295] Under the FWPCA, emergency abatement of water pollution is handled through the district courts rather than via administrative orders.[1296] The issue of pre-enforcement review arises most often when

---

Boddie v. Connecticut, 401 U.S. 371, 378-79 (1971); Ewing v. Mytinger & Casselberry, Inc., 339 U.S. 594, 599-600 (1950); Fahey v. Mallonee, 332 U.S. 245, 253-54 (1947); Yakus v. United States, 321 U.S. 414, 442-43 (1944); Bowles v. Willingham, 321 U.S. 503, 519-20 (1944); Phillips v. Commissioner, 283 U.S. 589, 595-99 (1931); North Am. Cold Storage Co. v. Chicago, 211 U.S. 306, 315-21 (1908).

1295 See David Montgomery Moore, Comment, PRE-Enforcement Review Of Administrative Orders To Abate Environmental Hazards, 9 Pace Env. L. Rev 675, 701 (Spring 1992).

1296 See FWPCA §§ 311(e), 504, 33 U.S.C. §§ 1321(e), 1364 (1988).

EPA issues an administrative compliance order under section 309(a)(3) of the Act[1297] and prior to any agency attempt to enforce the order.[1298] Civil penalties may be assessed administratively,[1299] but are explicitly subject to pre-enforcement review pursuant to section 309(g)(8) of the Act.[1300]

In determining whether pre-enforcement review of compliance orders is available under the FWPCA, courts have focused on the language of the statute, its structure, objectives, legislative history and the nature of the administrative action involved.[1301] Under this analysis, it has been held that the statutory scheme of the FWPCA provides "clear and convincing evidence" that Congress intended to preclude pre-enforcement review of administrative compliance orders issued under the FWPCA.[1302] The courts have recognized that by providing a detailed mechanism for judicial review of compliance orders once EPA seeks to enforce them, Congress impliedly precluded judicial review of orders prior to their enforcement.[1303] EPA cannot force recipients of orders to comply with the Act unless an enforcement action is brought in the district court.[1304] Thus, the recipient of an administrative compliance order is afforded a full opportunity to oppose an order and is entitled to review once EPA chooses to enforce the order.[1305] Furthermore, because EPA has the option of issuing a compliance order or directly bringing an action in district court,

1297 33 U.S.C. § 1319(a)(3) (1988).

1298 See, e.g., Hoffman Group, Inc. v. EPA, 902 F.2d 567 (7th Cir.1990). Jurisdiction may be sought pursuant to the Federal Declaratory Judgment Act, 28 U.S.C. §§ 2201, 2202 (1988), and federal question jurisdiction pursuant to 28 U.S.C. § 1331 (1988).

1299 FWPCA § 309(g), 33 U.S.C. § 1319(g) (1988).

1300 CWA § 309(g)(8), 33 U.S.C. § 1319(g)(8) (1988). Notices of appeal of an administrative penalty assessment must be filed in the appropriate court within 30 days from the date an administrative penalty order is issued. Id. Administrative penalty assessments will be upheld unless they are not supported by substantial evidence or they constitute an abuse of discretion. Id.

1301 Southern Pine Assoc. v. United States, 912 F.2d 713, 715 (4th Cir.1990) (quoting Block v. Community Nutrition Inst., 467 U.S. 340, 345 (1984)).

1302 *Southern Pines Assoc.*, 912 F.2d at 715-16.

1303 Hoffman Group, Inc. v. EPA, 902 F.2d 567, 569 (7th Cir.1990).

1304 CWA § 309(b), 33 U.S.C. § 1319(b) (1988).

1305 *Hoffman*, 902 F.2d at 569-570.

the recipient of a compliance order is in no worse position for EPA's having issued a compliance order rather than immediately bringing an enforcement action.[1306] For OPA defenses purposes the power of the EPA to choose either the option of issuing a compliance order or directly bringing an action in district court is very critical because, if the order is issued and the RP disobeys the order, it could be deemed by the EPA or the US Coast Guard to have disobeyed an administrative order and consequently lose its OPA defenses to which it might be otherwise entitled. That will make him it equally liable for the cost of clean up and damages as any ordinary responsible party would be.

The policy rationale for precluding review of FWPCA compliance orders is similar to that for administrative orders under the other environmental statutes. Congress provided the EPA with flexibility to address environmental problems quickly, without becoming entangled in litigation.[1307] In barring pre-enforcement review, due process is not denied because no property rights are implicated until EPA seeks an injunction or penalties in an enforcement proceeding in the district court.[1308] Agency action amounting to mere assertion of jurisdiction over an environmental issue is not final agency action and will not be subject to pre- enforcement review under the exhaustion and ripeness doctrines.[1309] In *Deltona Corp.*

---

1306 *Southern Pines Assoc.*, 912 F.2d at 715, n. 3.

1307 Id. at 716.

1308 Id. at 717.

1309 See FTC v. Standard Oil Co., 449 U.S. 232, 239-243 (1980), see also, Solar Turbines, Inc. v. Seif, 879 F.2d 1073, 1080 (3d Cir.1989) (applying finality and exhaustion to EPA action under the Clean Air Act). *Compare to* Abbott Labs. v. Gardner, 387 U.S. 136, 149 (1967). In *Ciba-Geigy Corp. v. EPA*, 801 F.2d 430 (D.C.Cir.1986), the Circuit Court for the District of Columbia held that a letter issued by EPA constituted final agency action and imposed sufficient hardship on the recipient to warrant review. Id. at 437. In that case, compliance with the terms of the letter would have resulted in a 50% loss in sales of the pesticide at issue. Id. at 432. The court found that judicial review would not disrupt the orderly process of administrative decision-making, or threaten health or safety. Id. at 437-438. The court quoted *Independent Bankers Assoc. v. Smith*, 534 F.2d 921, 929 (D.C.Cir.), *cert. denied*, 429 U.S. 862 (1976), for the proposition that "an agency's interpretation of its governing statute, with the expectation that regulated parties will conform to and rely on this interpretation, is final agency action fit for judicial review." Id. at 438.

*v. Alexander*,[1310] the Court of Appeals for the Eleventh Circuit held that judicial review of a landowner's challenge to an Army Corps of Engineers' denial of a dredge-and-fill permit was precluded.[1311] The court found that since the Corps had not yet assessed the property to determine jurisdiction, agency action was not final.[1312] The court determined that allowing the Corps to make a wetland determination prior to judicial review of the action promoted the policies supporting the exhaustion requirement.[1313] Similarly, the issuance of a cease-and-desist order is a mere assertion of jurisdiction, not a final agency action subject to review.[1314]

All that the above goes to show is the difficulty of making a decision on whether to obey or disobey administrative orders. The question of which is the proper decision to make is a catch 22 question and it would depend on the circumstances in each case. An attorney should advise clients on which course of action to take only when he or she has a comprehensive

---

1310 682 F.2d 888 (11th Cir.1982).

1311 682 F.2d at 888.

1312 Id. at 893.

1313 Id.

1314 See generally, Route 26 Land Development Ass'n v. United States, 753 F.Supp. 532, 539 (D.Del.1990) (holding that the CWA impliedly precluded this type of review. The court held that assertion of jurisdiction alone did not constitute final agency action, relying upon the Third Circuit Court of Appeals holding in Solar Turbines Inc. v. Seif, 879 F.2d 1073 (3d Cir.1989) (holding that a Clean Air Act compliance order was not a final agency action). Further, the court found that the issue could not be ripe until the ultimate effect of the Corps assertion of jurisdiction is known. 753 F.Supp. at 540. See also Leslie Salt Co. v. United States, 22 Envtl.L.Rep. (Envtl.L.Inst.) 20,359 (N.D.Cal. Dec. 31, 1991); Mulberry Hills Dev. Co. v. United States, 772 F.Supp. 1553, 1557 (D.Md.1991) (holding that the CWA does not provide for pre-enforcement review); Banks v. Page, 768 F.Supp. 809 (S.D.Fla.1991); Hampton Venture No. One v. United States, 768 F.Supp. 174 (E.D.Va.1991) (Corps jurisdictional determination not final agency action) McGown v. United States, 747 F.Supp. 539 (E.D.Mo.1990); United States v. Hobbs, 21 Envtl.L.Rep. (Envtl.L.Inst.) 20,830 (E.D.Va. Aug. 22, 1990); Fiscella & Fiscella v. United States, 717 F.Supp. 1143 (E.D.Va.1989).

In contrast, the Court of Appeals for the Ninth Circuit has allowed review of CWA compliance orders or cease-and-desist orders. In Swanson v. United States, 600 F.Supp. 802 (D.Idaho 1985), aff'd 789 F.2d 1368 (9th Cir.1986), the plaintiff sought declaratory and injunctive relief in the form of a decree that the land in question was not a navigable water of the United States. Id. at 1370. See also Bailey v. United States, 647 F.Supp. 44 (D.Idaho 1986).

grasp of the provisions of the OPA, its implementing regulations, FWPCA and CERCLA case law and the facts of the particular case. An attorney who fails to do this might be subjected to negligent representation liability for being negligent in his offering of advice to his client. Before advising a client to disobey an administrative order, an attorney must make sure that the provisions of the OPA, its implementing regulations, FWPCA and CERCLA case law and the facts of the particular case are overwhelmingly in his client's favor. Considering the amount of liability an RP client of an attorney might be subjected to, a judicial finding that the attorney is liable for negligent representation could cause a law practice to fail, because he might have to pay in damages to his client, the amount the client had to pay as an OPA RP.

## PROOF OF CAUSATION FOR LIABILITY OF RP

*OPA DAMAGES*: It is important to point out that an OPA plaintiff suing for damages would have to discharge its burden of proof and burden of production by proving that the RP is liable for OPA damages because the oil spill from the responsible party's (RP) vessel or facility caused the damages for which it is suing. If the OPA claimant can meet that burden, then the burden of production will shift to the RP. Depending on the specific OPA damage claim filed by the plaintiff, the RP must then produce evidence that shows that even though there was an oil spill from its vessel or facility, that spill did not cause an damage to the claimant."[1315] Because the burden of persuasion on the issue of liability and the original burden of production on the issue of causation rests on the OPA plaintiff's shoulders, it must discharge this burden or risk summary judgment or judgment as a matter of law before or after the verdict. If the OPA claimant meets its burden of production on the issue of causation, then the RP must produce evidence that shows that the oil spill from its vessel or facility did not cause an OPA damage to the claimant, or otherwise risk the entry of summary judgment or judgment as a matter of law before or after

1315 See 33 USC §2702(b)(2)(A)-(F).

the verdict against it. If the OPA claimant is unable to meet the burden of production on the issue of causation by the RP, then the RP does not have to come forward with any evidence of lack of causation, because the burden of production has not shifted. And in all likelihood, that will be the end of court proceedings.

In the alternative, the RP could frame lack of causation as an affirmative defense. But, this could then mean that it bears the original burden of production on the issue of lack of causation. So, it is wiser not to raise causation as an affirmative defense.

*OPA REMOVAL COSTS*: For removal costs claims however, proof of causation is not needed as part of the elements of the plaintiff's case against an RP. If tests carried out by the US Coast Guard show that the oil in the water is the RP's oil, then the RP has the obligation to undertake the removal of the spilt oil or reimburse private and government claimants for their clean up expenses up to the RP's limit of liability under OPA. If the US Coast Guard finds that oil from another known or unknown source is in close proximity to or commingled with the oil from the RP, the Coast Guard need not prove causation. This means that the US Coast Guard can sue the RP for the entire removal costs of the RP's oil and the removal costs of the oil belonging to the other known or unknown source. In most cases an RP would like to raise causation as an affirmative defense in removal costs claims. However, unlike in damage claims, an RP can only raise the three OPA defenses in section 2703(a) in removal cost claims. The OPA defenses provision in section 2703(a) are identical to the defenses provision in section 9607(b) of CERCLA. It would be proper to look to CERCLA case law for guidance on the question of whether proof of causation is required in removal cost claims. All the cases discussed involve removal cost claims, not claims for natural resources damage assessment and restoration.

The case that discussed this issue extensively is *United States v. Shell Oil Co.*,[1316] where the defendant invoked a plethora of defenses to its potential CERCLA liability. For the purposes of this analysis only the defense of

1316 1992 WL144296, No. CV. 91-0589-RJK (C.D. Cal. 1992).

proximate cause and causation that Shell invoked will be discussed. In the courts rejection of the defense of causation by Shell, the court agreed with the Second Circuit decision in *N.Y. v. Shore Realty Corp,*[1317] where it was held that CERCLA's section 9607(a)(1) unequivocally imposes strict liability without regard to causation and to interpret section 9607(a)(1) as including a causation requirement makes superfluous the affirmative defenses provided in 9607(b), each of which carves out from liability an exception based on causation."[1318] The *Shell* court also agreed with the Fourth Circuit case of *United States v. Monsanto,*[1319] where the Circuit Court found that the legislature had eliminated the element of causation from the plaintiff's liability case. As such a defense of lack of causation is irrelevant in determining the scope of liability, whether joint and several or apportioned."[1320]

The *Shell* court in its rejection of the causation defense relied also on the case of *United States v. Stringfellow,*[1321] a district court decision in the Ninth Circuit where the court held that § 9607(a) (Liability provision) does not contain a causation requirement and that plaintiffs do not have to prove traditional causation. The court also agreed with the Ninth Circuit case of *Levin Metals Corp. v. Parr-Richmond Terminal Co.*,[1322] where it was decided that in order for a plaintiff to claim declaratory judgment in a § 9607 case, it or must base the claim of non-liability on one or more of the three CERCLA statutory defenses. Based on its application of and agreement with the foregoing cases, the *Shell* court concluded that causation and other similar or associated defenses have no part in a § 9607 claim and are stricken. These CERCLA jurisprudence are applicable to OPA cases because of the identical language of OPA and CERCLA defenses provisions.

The Third Circuit case of *United States v. Alcan Aluminum Corp.*,[1323] also considered this issue. The *Alcan* court observed that the legislative

---

1317 759 F.2d 1032, 1044 (2d. Cir.1985).

1318 See Shell Oil Co., 1992 WL144296, at * 5, see also, 42 U.S.C. § 9607(a)(1), §9607(b).

1319 858 F.2d 160, 167 (4th Cir. 1988).

1320 Shell Oil Co., 1992 WL144296, at * 5 (citing, United States v. Fairchild Industries, 766 F.Supp. 405, 410 (D. M.D 1991)).

1321 661 F.Supp. 1053, 1060-1 (C.D.Cal.1987).

1322 799 F.2d 1312, 1317 (9th Cir.1986).

1323 964 F.2d. 252, 264 (3 rd Cir. 1992).

history supported the Government's argument that CERCLA does not require the plaintiff to establish a specific causal relationship between a generator's waste and the release or the plaintiff's incurrence of response costs, especially in cases where the hazardous waste is from multiple sources. The court also pointed out that that the early House of Representatives' version of CERCLA imposed liability upon those persons who "caused or contributed to the release or threatened release."[1324] However, the version ultimately passed by Congress deleted the causation requirement and instead imposed liability upon a class of responsible persons without regard to whether the person specifically caused or contributed to the release and the resultant response costs.[1325] The court emphasized the fact that Congress added three limited defenses to liability based on causation which are contained in 42 U.S.C. § 9607(b): acts of God, acts of war, and acts or omissions of a contractually unrelated third party when the defendant exercised due care and took appropriate responses. The court held that imputing a specific causation requirement would render these defenses superfluous. The court concluded in sum, that the legislative history indicates that Congress considered and rejected a requirement that the plaintiff establish that the defendant's waste caused or contributed to the release or the incurrence of response costs.[1326] The *Alcan* court also pointed out that decisions rejecting a causation requirement between the defendant's waste and the release or the incurrence of response costs are well-reasoned, consistent with the plain language of the statute and consistent with the legislative history of CERCLA.[1327]

No provision of the OPA dictates a different outcome for OPA cases. These cases should provide enough guidance for OPA cases. Only an amendment to the OPA that inserts a causation requirement for removal costs liability would warrant a different outcome for OPA cases. That amendment is highly unlikely because of the polluter pay principle and

1324 See. 964 F2d. at 264-65, see also, H.R. 7020, 96th Cong., 2d Sess. § 3071(a)(D), 126 Cong.Rec. 26,779.

1325 See id. at 265, see also, 126 Cong.Rec. 31,981-82.

1326 Id. at 265.

1327 Id. at 266.

the heavy burden that the Oil Spill Liability Trust Fund would have to shoulder in oil spill cases where the RP is able to avoid OPA liability simply because of a government or private claimant's inability to establish causation in removal cost claims.

# Chapter Three

# ASSERTING CLAIMS AGAINST A RESPONSIBLE PARTY: PRELIMINARY PROCEDURES –A 33 USC § 2714

Generally, responsible parties (RPs) for a vessel or a facility are liable for removal costs and damages, including interest thereon, resulting from their OPA incident (i.e., oil discharged into, or posing a substantial threat to U.S. surface waters (including the EEZ) on or after 19 August 1990). If possible, the source of the oil spill must be designated by a government official. Once the source is designated, the official notifies the "responsible party" (i.e., the owner or operator of the source) of the designation by means of a written "Notice of Designation."[1328] The responsible party then advertises (in newspapers, on radio, etc.) that designation and the procedures by which claims may be presented to the responsible party or that party's guarantor. If the responsible party denies the designation,[1329] the source of the discharge is a public vessel, or the source of the discharge is unknown, the National Pollution Funds Center (NPFC) advertises the procedures by which claims may be presented to the Fund.[1330] This process is explained further below.

RPs are also responsible for handling claims for such removal costs or damages; if they do not, then they are also liable for the costs incurred by the Fund in handling claims. To begin the claims process, section 2714 of OPA, provides that once an incident becomes known, the source or sources of a discharge or threat shall be designated where possible and appropriate. And, if the designated source is a vessel or a facility, the RP and the guarantor, if known, shall be immediately notified of the designation. "Designation"

1328 33 CFR § 136.305

1329 33 CFR § 136.307

1330 33 CFR 136.309(d)-(e).

is an OPA term of art used in connection with the initiation of the claims process. It frequently overlaps with the On Scene Coordinators' (OSCs' or FOSC's) need to identify the potential RPs to ascertain their present intentions with respect to removing the oil or its threat.[1331] However, formal notification of designation, with its five day period after receipt in which to deny the designation, will likely not assist OSCs in determining what immediate action needs to be taken to remove the oil.[1332]

*Authorities and Responsibilities:*

1. Secretary of Department in which the Coast Guard is Operating: Executive Order 12777 delegated the functions vested in the President by section 2714 of OPA to the Secretary of Department in which the Coast Guard is operating (Department of Homeland Security).[1333]
2. Commandant of the Coast Guard: The Secretary of Transportation delegated those functions to the Commandant of the Coast Guard in 49 CFR Part 1.[1334]
3. Chief of the Office of Marine Safety, Security, and Environmental Protection: The Commandant of the Coast Guard redelegated those functions pertaining to designation of source and notification of responsible parties to the Chief of the Office of Marine Safety, Security, and Environmental Protection, and Coast Guard predesignated On-Scene Coordinators.[1335]
4. Director, National Pollution Funds Center: The Commandant of the Coast Guard redelegated those functions pertaining to advertising for claims under 2714 (b) to the Director, National Pollution

1331 The National Pollution Fund Center's Technical Operating Procedures (TOPs) for the Designation of Source under the Oil Pollution Act of 1990, 418 (May 20, 1996).

1332 Id. at 418.

1333 Id.

1334 Id.

1335 Id.

Funds Center. The Chief of the Office of Marine Safety, Security, and Environmental Protection redelegated the functions pertaining to designation of source and notification of responsible parties and guarantors to the Director, National Pollution Funds Center jointly with Coast Guard predesignated On-Scene Coordinators.[1336]

5. Coast Guard On-Scene Coordinators. The Chief of the Office of Marine Safety, Security, and Environmental Protection redelegated the functions pertaining to designation of source and notification of responsible parties and guarantors to Coast Guard predesignated on-scene Coordinators jointly with the Director, National Pollution Funds Center.[1337]
6. Federal On-Scene Coordinators. The National Contingency Plan requires, "The OSC/RPM shall, to the extent practicable, collect pertinent facts about the identification of potentially responsible parties; the nature, amount, and location of the discharged or released materials; the probable direction of travel of discharged or released materials; whether the discharge is a worst case discharge as discussed in section 300.324 of the NCP; the pathways to human and environmental exposure; the potential impact on human health, welfare, and safety and the environment; whether the discharge or release poses a substantial threat to the public health or welfare of the United States as discussed in section 300.322 of the NCP; the potential impact on natural resources and property which may be affected; priorities for protecting human health and welfare and the environment; and appropriate cost documentation."[1338]

*Investigative Considerations:*

A. Objectives of the FOSC's Investigation/Fact Gathering: The FOSC is supposed to - (1). Identify the source of the discharge or substantial threat

1336 Id.

1337 Id.

1338 Id.

of discharge. (2) Confirm whether the substance discharged or threatened to be discharged is oil. (3) Identify the navigable water into which the oil was discharged or which is threatened by a discharge. (4). Establish the pathway from the source to the navigable water. (5) Determine the occurrence or series of occurrences which resulted in the discharge or substantial threat of discharge. (6) Fully identify the responsible party(ies): the owners and operators of the vessel or facility that was the source of the discharge, as defined in OPA section 2701. Strive to get as much timely information as possible including names, addresses, telephone/telex/fax numbers, resident for service of process, those authorized to speak and act for the RP in this situation (particularly where the RP is an organization), how they can be contacted, their tax ID numbers, and the pertinent structure (i.e. whether the RP is a dissolved, successor, parent, subsidiary corporation or a partnership), etc of the organization.[1339]. This has been discussed earlier in this dissertation.(7) Establish facts to support a determination as to whether the responsible party may have a defense to liability under OPA section 2703 (a). If an RP raises a potential defense or it appears to the FOSC that the OPA incident may involve a defense, the FOSC is supposed to contact the NPFC for further guidance. In no case is the FOSC (or other government personnel) authorized to make any statements about whether the defense is valid or not; because that is a legal conclusion to be made at the appropriate time during the cost recovery/claims/civil penalty process by someone authorized to do so.[1340] (8) Determine whether exceptions to limits of liability may apply in accordance with OPA section 2704 (c).[1341]

In cases where an oil spill was not discovered on time and the source of the discharge is a vessel whose owner deliberately failed to report the oil spill and changed the name of the vessel in order to avoid OPA liability, the FOSC or state OSC should utilize the Lloyd's Register of Ships to trace the new name of the vessel. This will be useful even if the vessel has changed its name more than once or twice. In addition to this, the FOSC or state OSC can engage the services of some consultants who specialize

1339 Id. at 420.

1340 Id.

1341 Id.

in tracking the movement of vessels to help track the movement of the discharging vessel trying to evade OPA liability. Once the vessel with the new name or possibly new color or flag sails again into US waters it can be arrested.

*Actual Designation of Source And Notification of RP:*

A. General Procedures.

1. Federal On-Scene Coordinators (and State On-Scene Coordinators using the Oil Spill Liability Trust Fund (OSLTF) under OPA State Access) are supposed to:
   a. Conduct investigations, "to the extent practicable", to identify the source of the discharge or substantial threat of discharge. FOSCs is required to promptly determine the source of the oil pollution, and where it involves a vessel or a facility, identify any potential RPs to ascertain their present intentions with respect to removing the oil or the threat of its discharge.[1342] In doing so, they are supposed to attempt to fully identify the potential RPs: names, addresses, telephone/telex/fax numbers, resident agents or agents for service of process, those authorized to speak and act for the RP in this situation (particularly where the RP is an organization) and how they can be contacted, their tax ID number, and information concerning RP organizational structures which could assist in this endeavor.[1343]
   b. Assess possibility for OPA claims: The OSC must determine whether third party claims for removal costs or damages due to the incident are possible. Criteria for determining the possibility of claims are listed in paragraph below. When the possibility of claims is unknown, the OSC is supposed to re-

1342 Id at 423.

1343 Id. at 423.

quest that the NPFC issue a Notice of Designation. The NPFC should be advised of the potential for claims and provided with all identification information in every case.[1344]

c. Advise/work with NPFC: If claims are reasonably possible due to the incident, the OSC must notify the NPFC either by phone or message of the identity of the source vessel or facility and the responsible parties. The notification must include the address and contact information for the responsible parties. The OSC must work with the NPFC case officer to select the appropriate means of advertising or direct notifications to reach potentially injured parties.[1345]

2. National Pollution Fund Center (NPFC) Case Officer/Case Team.
   a. Assess: The NPFC Case officer/Case Team will also assess the possibility of claims based on their experience with similar incidents. If they determine that designation is appropriate, they may contact the OSC and request that the OSC provide source and responsible party information.[1346] Again, the OSC is required to advise the NPFC of the potential for claims and provide it with all identification information in every case.[1347]
   b. Make Designation: The NPFC case officer is required to arrange for the formal designation and notification to the responsible parties and guarantors, if known.[1348] In those rare situations which require immediate or expedited designation, the OSC may make the formal designation and notification to the local representative of the responsible party, but the OSC must coordinate that designation with the NPFC case officer. The FOSC's immediate concerns, however, will normally be

1344 Id.

1345 Id.

1346 Id.

1347 Id.

1348 Id.

better served with the use of administrative orders, thus leaving the formal notice of designation to the NPFC.[1349]

c. Accept denial/advertising: The designation should advise the responsible party that any denial must be made in writing within 5 days of receipt to the NPFC case officer or as indicated in the designation letter. If the OSC elects to receive the RP's denial, the OSC must then establish a process to ensure that any denial is received within the required time and that the NPFC Case Officer is notified[1350] This provision is very critical to the possible or eventual liability of a responsible or non-responsible party. Failure to respond with a denial before the expiration of the five day denial requirement could be fatal to the RP's or non-RP's successful invocation of a complete defense to OPA liability. Therefore, even if he is entitled to any of the defenses specified in section 2703(a) of the OPA, sloppy and uncoordinated response to the Notice of Designation would make an otherwise non-responsible party, a responsible party for OPA purposes. That is why owners and operators of vessels and facilities connected with oil should hire or retain attorneys or legal consultants with marine or oil pollution law expertise. These experts should be contacted immediately after the oil spill occurs, so that they can swing into action immediately to ascertain if any of the OPA defenses are applicable to the specific incident.

d. Monitor/Advertise for Fund or RP: If the RP denies the designation or the RP is unknown, the NPFC generally advertises on behalf of the Fund. If the RP fails to advertise as required, the NPFC may advertise on the RP's behalf.[1351]

*Contents of Notifying Letter*: The notifying letter should contain the following information:

1349 Id. at 423-24.

1350 Id. at 424.

1351 Id.

(1) The name and other unique identifying information of the vessel or facility designated as the source. (2) The location, date, and time of the incident. (3) The specific body(ies) of water affected or threatened. (4) Procedures to deny designation and requirement to deny in writing within 5 days after receipt of notification. (5) The name, address, phone and fax numbers of the federal official to be contacted for additional information or denial of designation.[1352]

(6) Requirements for advertising for claims (or information that the NPFC will establish requirements for advertising through separate correspondence when the Coast Guard OSC issues the notification) including the fact that the NPFC will advertise on behalf the RP if the RP fails to deny the designation and then does not comply with the advertising requirements.[1353] (7) The date of the designation and the date that the notification was issued.[1354]

*Criteria for evaluating possibilities of claims:*

1. Removal costs (consistent with the National Contingency Plan (NCP) and under normal circumstances coordinated with the FOSC) may be the subject of OPA claims when incurred by:
   (a) State or local agencies responding to the spill.[1355] (b) Indian tribe responding to the spill. (c) Federal agencies responding to the spill. (d) Other persons conducting removal actions. (e) The FOSC are required to consider the use of Pollution Removal Funding Authorizations (PRFAs) when other federal, state, or local agencies are conducting removal actions under the direction of the FOSC. Use of PRFAs establishes the scope of work and assures funding, and thus is preferred over the claims process. The NPFC Technical Operating

1352 Id.

1353 Id. at 425.

1354 Id.

1355 Id. at 426.

Procedures (TOPS) on Resource Documentation for PRFA procedures provides more insight into this.[1356] (f) The FOSC should determine the nature, amount, and location of the discharged oil; the probable direction of travel of the oil; and whether or not the spill was contained in determining if other entities may incur removal costs to remove oil from water, shorelines, or property.[1357]

2. Damages may be anticipated as a result of an oil spill depending on:
   (a) Magnitude of the spill.[1358]
   (b) Area of the spill and impact on:
      (1) Environmentally sensitive areas - obtaining preliminary evaluation by Scientific Support Coordinator and/or cognizant federal, state, or Indian tribe trustee is critical.
      (2) Real or personal property - checking impact on boats, docks, nets, beach, shoreline, marinas, etc is very important.
      (3) Areas of potential subsistence use – querying the local Fish and Wildlife Department or any other cognizant state representatives.
      (4) Business or property generating governmental revenues – checking with state or local officials concerning tax, royalty, or fee assessments is very important.
      (5) Business or private enterprise causing change in income or profits –checking if the clean up prevents access to commercial enterprise, closes areas used for transit of watercraft or closes bridges affecting vehicle traffic, affects use of beaches, or damages inventory of waterside businesses such as hatcheries. (Note alternative income or profits available as a result of the incident or reasonable

1356 Id.

1357 Id.

1358 Id. at 427.

under the situation since claimants are required to mitigate damages.)

(6) Activities of state and local representatives in providing increased or additional services in connection with the incident such as security, traffic control, evacuations, arranging access.[1359]

(c) Consider the type of oil spilled, length of time in one area, and the concentration.

(d) Consider the type of natural resource potentially affected. Again, seek advice from the Scientific Support Coordinator, and/or cognizant federal, state, or Indian tribe trustee.

(e) Consider the effectiveness, or anticipated effectiveness, of the removal activities, including how much of the oil was contained, whether all the oil can be removed, etc.[1360]

*ADVERTISING REQUIREMENTS:*

A. General. It is not necessary to require public advertising in every Notice of Designation. Use of the OSLTF by the On Scene Coordinator (OSC) gives rise to a potential claim against the RP for federal removal costs, and the Notice of Designation also serves to make the RPs aware of this liability under OPA. When required, however, the advertising is supposed to be designed to reach as many potential claimants as possible.[1361]

B. Forms of Advertising. The forms of advertisement are specified in 33 CFR 133.311 and include the following: (1) Paid advertisements in newspapers having general circulation which encompasses the spill area. (2) Posting notices at marinas, marine supply stores, bait and tackle shops, and other appropriate business establishments or public facilities in the specific area. (3) Direct mailing of notices to known individual claimants or categories of potential claimants, e.g., towboats which may have been

1359 Id.

1360 Id. at 427.

1361 Id. at 428.

delayed by a waterway closing. (4) News releases or paid announcements on radio or television broadcasts serving the general area. (5) Other advertising methods as specified by the NPFC.[1362]

C. Content of Advertising. The content of advertisements is specified in 33 CFR 136.313. Each advertisement or notification is to contain the following information or to indicate where this information may be contained: (1) Location, date and time of the incident. (2) Geographical area affected. (3) Quantity/type of oil involved (when pertinent). (4) Name or other description of the designated source. (5). Name of the responsible party (the person to whom the Notice of Designation is addressed unless otherwise stipulated). (6) Name, address, telephone number, office hours, and work days of the person or persons to whom claims are to be presented and from whom claim information can be obtained. (7) The procedures by which a claim may be presented.[1363] (8) Notification that if the RP denies or does not resolve a claim within 90 days after the date of submission, the claimant may then submit the claim to the National Pollution Funds Center (cm), 4200 Wilson Boulevard, Suite 1000, Arlington, VA 22203-1804, for consideration for payment from the Oil Spill Liability Trust Fund.[1364] (9) Unless specifically authorized by the NPFC, the advertisement/notification must be in English.[1365]

*Sample NPFC Notice Of Designation With Advertising*

Certified Mail Return Receipt Requested Number:
RP Name
RP Address
RP City, State, Zip Code
Subject: NOTICE OF DESIGNATION
Re: Federal Project Number [FPN]

1362 Id.

1363 Id.

1364 Id. at 429.

1365 Id.

On [Date of incident], your [facility/vessel] the [source name] [discharged oil into the / ran aground and posed a substantial threat of a discharge of oil in] [body of water], a navigable water of the United States. The Oil Pollution Act of 1990, 33 USC 2701, requires that we formally designate the [source name] as the source of the [discharge / substantial threat] and notify you that as its [owner/operator/licensee/lessee/permittee/holder], you incur certain legal responsibilities to the U.S. Government and others damaged by this incident. You are liable for removal costs and damages as specified in 33 USC 2702 and must advertise the procedures by which persons who have claims for removal costs and damages may submit their claims to you, as specified in 33 USC 2714.

You must publicly advertise this designation and the procedures by which claims may be presented to you. The advertisement must begin within 15 days of the date of this letter and must continue for no less than 30 days. Enclosure (1) outlines the required content of this advertisement and enclosure (2) is a sample advertisement. You may choose to follow this sample but are not required to do so as long as your advertisement contains the required information. Your advertisement must be disseminated in such a manner that all potential claimants are notified. To accomplish this, we require that you advertise in the newspapers having general circulation in the area(s) affected. We also require that you post notices in marinas affected and provide direct notification where individuals have been identified as receiving damages from your spill. You may propose other methods of advertisement and notification, but they may be used only when approved in advance by the National Pollution Funds Center.

You are directed to inform us of the specifics of your advertising, including the name of any newspaper or other publication in which the advertisement is run, the geographical area covered by the publication, and how often the advertisement will appear, as appropriate. Send us copies of the advertisement and advise us in writing that you have begun advertising within 20 days of receipt of this letter, otherwise we will assume that you did not comply with these requirements. If you do not comply with these requirements, the National Pollution Funds Center will advertise for claims. If we advertise, you will be charged for our costs, as well as for the costs of any administration, adjudication and payment of claims. You may deny this designation within 5 days of receipt of this Notice of Designation. Your denial must be in writing, identify this Notice of Designation, give the reasons for the denial, include a copy of all supporting documents, and must be submitted to "+ ClaimsManager +", Claims Manager, at the above address. If you deny this designation, the National Pollution Funds Center will advertise for claims. If we advertise and you are later judged to be responsible for the discharge, you will be charged for our costs, as well as for the costs of any administration, adjudication and payment of claims.

You may contact the Claims Manager, [Claims Manager name] at [Telephone #] if you have any questions. The FAX number is [Fax #].

Sincerely,
[signature]
Encl: (1) Content of Advertisements
(2) Sample Advertisement
Copy: FOSC, other RPs, Guarantors

**NPFC's STANDARD CLAIM FORM- -**

**National Pollution Funds Center Standard Claim Form**

4200 Wilson Blvd., Suite 1000
Arlington, VA 22003-1804
(703) 235-4764 or (800) 280-7118

This form may be used for submitting claims to the U.S. Coast Guard, National Pollution Funds Center, for potential compen-sation from the Oil Spill Liability Trust Fund for uncompensated removal costs or damages resulting from an incident under the Oil Pollution Act of 1990.

**1. Claimant Name:** ______________________________

Address: ______________________________

______________________________

Social Security #: __________ Home Tel. #: ( ) __________

Tax I.D.#: __________ Work Tel. #: ( ) __________

**2. Incident Information:**

Date: ______________________ Time: ____________________________

Name of vessel or facility causing damage: ____________________

Geographic location of incident: ____________________________

Brief description of the incident: ___________________________

_______________________________________________________________

_______________________________________________________________

**3. Type(s) of claim(s) and total amount for costs and damage(s) claimed: $**

_______________________________________________________________

_____________ Removal Costs _______________ Subsistence Use

_____________ Profits and Earning Capacity

_____________ Natural Resources _____________ Public Services

_____________ Government Revenue __________ Real or Personal Property

**4. Has claimant communicated with the responsible party?**

☐☐No ☐☐Yes

**5. Has the claim been submitted to the responsible party?**

☐☐No ☐☐Yes Date Submitted ____________________________________

**6. If the claim has been submitted to the responsible party, what action has been taken?**

No Action _____ Denial ______ Paid in Part ______ Other (explain): _____

_______________________________________________________________

_______________________________________________________________

**7. Has claimant commenced any action in court against the responsible party?** ☐☐No ☐☐Yes

If yes, provide the name, address, phone number of your attorney, the court in which action is pending and the civil action number __________________

_______________________________________________________________

**8. Has claimant submitted or planned to submit the loss to an insurer?** ☐☐No ☐☐Yes

If yes, provide the name, address, and phone number of the insurer, and the policy number ______________________________

**National Pollution Funds Center Standard Claim Form**

4200 Wilson Blvd, Suite 1000 Page 2

Arlington, VA 22203-1804

(703) 235-4764 or (800) 280-7118

Submit a separate Page 2 for each type of claim. Attach additional information as necessary.

**9. Claimant Name:** ______________________________

Soc. Sec. #: ____________ Tax I.D. #: ____________

**10. Type of claim submitted and claim amount: $** ____________

________Removal Costs ________ Subsistence Use

________Profits and Earning Capacity

________Natural Resources________ Public Services

________Government Revenue ________ Real or Personal Property

**11. Description of the nature and extent of damages claimed:** ________

______________________________

______________________________

**12. Description of how the incident caused the damage:** ________

______________________________

______________________________

**13. Description of actions taken by claimant/representative to avoid or minimize damages:** ______________________________

______________________________

______________________________

**14. Witnesses:**

Name: ____________ Tel. No: ____________

Address: ________________________________________

________________________________________________

Name: ____________________ Tel. No: ________________

Address: ________________________________________

________________________________________________

Name: ____________________ Tel. No: ________________

Address: ________________________________________

________________________________________________

I, the undersigned, agree that upon acceptance of any compensation from the Fund, I will cooperate fully with the United States in any claim or action by the United States to recover the compensation. The cooperation shall include, but is not limited to, immediately reimbursing to the Fund any compensation received from any other source for the same costs and/or damages and, providing any documentation, evidence, testimony, and other support, as may be necessary for the Fund to recover such compensation.

I, the undersigned, certify that, to the best of my knowledge and belief, the information contained in this claim represents all material facts and is true. I understand that misrepresentation of facts is subject to prosecution under Federal law (including but not limited to 18 U.S.C. 287 and 1001).

**15.** ____________________ **16.** ____________________

Claimant's Signature Date Legal Representative Date

8/93

**Designation of The Source of Oil Spill - Not An Indispensable Requirement For Liability To The Government.**

It has been held that the OPA does not require designation of the source of an oil spill.[1366] The OPA designation of source section provides that the President shall, where possible and appropriate, designate the source or sources of the discharge or threat.[1367] The key phrase in this section is the phrase "where possible and appropriate" (emphasis mine). In the case of *United States v. Murphy Exploration And Production Co.*,[1368] the responsible party's (Murphy) challenge to the lack of formal designation under section 2714 of OPA was held to be unpersuasive. The Court agreed with the government's argument that the government reasonably ascertained that formal designation was inappropriate because there was no possibility of third party claims arising out of the spill, and therefore, advertising was unnecessary.

The Ninth Circuit Court of Appeals, held that the owner of an oil pipeline was not entitled to declaration that a rail authority and its general contractor were "responsible parties," under Oil Pollution Act, for purposes of all future litigation, despite the fact that the owner of the ruptured pipeline established that the rail authority and contractor were sole causes of the oil spill that occurred during construction of a railway station. The court held that the finding that the oil pipeline operator was not liable does not warrant such a declaration; because the statute required only declaration of liability for removal costs or damages, not declaration that would act as prophylactic measure preventing any future suits against the oil pipeline owner for any act relating to the spill.[1369]

1366 See United States of America v. Murphy Exploration And Production Co. 939 F.Supp. 489 (E.D.La 1996), *see also*, 33 USCA §2714.

1367 33 USCA §2714(a)

1368 United States of America v. Murphy Exploration And Production Co. 939 F.Supp. 489 (E.D.La 1996)

1369 Unocal Corp. v. United States, 222 F.3d 528 (9th Cir. 2000), *see also*, 33 U.S.C.A. § 2717(f)(2).

# Chapter Four

# A. REMOVAL COSTS UNDER OPA

"§ 2702. Elements of liability

(a) In general

Notwithstanding any other provision or rule of law, and subject to the provisions of this Act, each responsible party for a vessel or a facility from which oil is discharged, or which poses the substantial threat of a discharge of oil, into or upon the navigable waters or adjoining shorelines or the exclusive economic zone is liable for the **removal costs** and damages specified in subsection (b) of this section that result from such incident.

(b) Covered removal costs and damages

(1) Removal costs

The removal costs referred to in subsection (a) of this section are--

**(A)** all removal costs incurred by the United States, a State, or an Indian tribe under subsection (c), (d), (e), or (l) of section 1321 of this title under the Intervention on the High Seas Act (33 U.S.C. 1471 et seq.), or under State law; and

**(B)** any removal costs incurred by any person for acts taken by the person which are consistent with the National Contingency Plan."[1370]

**

1370 33 USC § 2702.

The Act requires the responsible party to pay all removal costs including the costs to prevent, minimize, or mitigate oil pollution in any case in which there is a substantial threat of, or an actual discharge of oil.[1371] The responsible party must pay removal costs incurred by the United States, a state government, or an Indian tribe pursuant to the Federal Water Pollution Control Act,[1372] or state law as well as removal costs incurred by any person for acts consistent with the National Contingency Plan (NCP).[1373] Section 2701(30) defines "remove" or "removal" as containment and removal of oil or a hazardous substance from water and shorelines or the taking of other actions as may be necessary to minimize or mitigate damage to the public health or welfare, including, but not limited to, fish, shellfish, wildlife, and public and private property, shorelines, and beaches. Removal costs is defined as the costs of removal that are incurred after a discharge of oil has occurred or, in any case in which there is a substantial threat of a discharge of oil, the costs to prevent, minimize, or mitigate oil pollution from such an incident.[1374] The responsible party can recover removal costs that exceed its OPA limits if it acted and is acting in consonance with the requirements in the OPA and the implementing regulations. This would include the amount expended in the cleanup that exceeds the OPA limit, and the cost of putting equipment and labor on standby, which was done to minimize the substantial threat of a discharge of oil into or upon the navigable waters or adjoining shorelines or exclusive economic zone.

The implementing regulations throw more light on the issue of removal costs by providing that "a claim for removal costs may be presented by any claimant."[1375] The utilization of the phrase "any claimant" in § 2702(b)(1) (B) shows that all removal costs incurred by private third parties or oil spill responders in an effort to prevent or minimize oil spills is refundable by the Fund and all those engaged in those activities

1371 33 USC § 2702(a).

1372 33 U.S.C. §§ 1251- 1387 (1988).

1373 33 USC § 2702(b)(1).

1374 33 U.S.C. §2701(31)

1375 See 33 C.F.R. §136.201.

can file claims against the Fund, provided they follow the procedure for doing so.

The utilization of the phrase "any claimant" also is a demonstration of the resolve of the U.S. Congress to broaden the category of those who can recover in cases of oil pollution in order to encourage people to respond to distress calls involving oil pollution. Any third party who is involved in the removal activity is entitled to a private cause of action against the Fund or the responsible party. The OPA procedure for asserting claims against the Fund applies to any claimant irrespective of whether it is the responsible party or just a third party. These third parties would include those who have incurred removal costs as well as those who have suffered some damages as a result of the spill. It would also include Federal, state and Indian Tribe trustees making a claim for natural resources damage and restoration.

*All Claimants Must Prove Removal Costs*: In order for any claimant to prove its case, it must establish—

"(a) That the actions taken were necessary to prevent, minimize, or mitigate the effects of the incident;
(b) That the removal costs were incurred as a result of these actions;
(c) That the actions taken were determined by the Federal-On-Scene-Coordinator (FOSC) to be consistent with the National Contingency Plan (NCP) or were directed by the FOSC."[1376]

Responsible Parties (RPs) are liable for "all removal costs" incurred by the government that result from the RPs oil pollution incident. Although not necessary for RP liability, removal costs must be "consistent with the NCP" to be payable from the OSLTF.[1377] For instance under CERCLA's section 9607(a)(4)(A),

1376 33 C.F.R. § 136.203. (The FOSC is the Federal official pre-designated by the Environmental Protection Agency (EPA) or the U.S Coast Guard to direct and coordinate all efforts for removal of a discharge, or the mitigation or the prevention of a substantial threat of a discharge, of oil).

1377 US Coast Guard National Pollution Funds Center, Technical Operating Procedures For Determining Removal Costs Under The Oil Pollution Act of 1990, at 109 (January 16, 1996).

which is similar to OPA's provision on consistency with the NCP, all costs that the United States may recover from a responsible party in a CERCLA response action must not be inconsistent with the NCP. However despite this provision, no CERCLA defendants can legally contend that the United States must establish that all its incurred costs are not inconsistent with the NCP before it can obtain partial summary judgment on the issue of liability.[1378] This is because it is well established that a showing that costs are not inconsistent with the NCP is not required for CERCLA liability in government actions against CERCLA PRP's.[1379] Generally OPA and CERCLA removal costs liability hinges on whether plaintiffs incurred any response cost. Whether some of those CERCLA or OPA response costs are inconsistent with the NCP is a triable issue of fact which goes to the amount, not the fact, of defendants' liability.[1380] Thus, when the issue of amount is in dispute and there is a contention as to its inconsistency with the NCP, that issue may survive a motion for summary judgment. However, this contrasts with private recovery actions against the Fund and the responsible party in which a private party must show that incurred costs are consistent with the NCP in establishing liability.[1381] In addition, it is well established that defendants bear the burden of showing that the United States government's incurred costs are inconsistent with the NCP.[1382] Thus, the issue of whether the costs recoverable by the United States are not inconsistent with the NCP is not relevant for the purposes of determining a summary judgment motion on removal costs liability. It may however become germane when the issue of amount or quantum of costs is being adjudicated.

---

1378 See United States v. Amtreco Inc. 809 F.Supp 959, 967 (M.D. Ga 1993).

1379 See United States v. Mottolo, 695 F.Supp. 615, 630 (D.N.H.1988) ("Liability hinges on whether plaintiffs incurred any response costs.... Whether some of those response costs are inconsistent with the NCP is a triable issue of fact which goes to the amount, not the fact, of defendants' liability."); *see also* United States v. R.W. Meyer, Inc., 889 F.2d 1497, 1508 (6th Cir.1989), cert. denied, 494 U.S. 1057, 110 S.Ct. 1527, 108 L.Ed.2d 767 (1990); United States v. Northeastern Pharmaceutical & Chemical Co., 810 F.2d 726, 747-48 (8th Cir.1986), *cert. denied*, 484 U.S. 848, 108 S.Ct. 146, 98 L.Ed.2d 102 (1987); United States v. Kramer, 757 F.Supp. 397 (D.N.J.1991); United States v. Western Processing Co., 734 F.Supp. 930, 942-43 (W.D.Wash.1990).

1380 See United States v. Mottolo, 695 F.Supp. at 630

1381 See, *e.g.*, County Line Invest. Co. v. Tinney, 933 F.2d 1508 (10th Cir.1991).

1382 See R.W. Meyer, Inc., 889 F.2d at 1508; Northeastern Pharmaceutical, 810 F.2d at 747-48; Mottolo, 695 F.Supp. at 630.

Federal On-Scene Coordinators ( FOSCs) are responsible for exercising effective financial management and cost controls during the response, including verification of removal costs and certification of consistency with the NCP, as outlined in the Technical Operating Procedures.[1383]

The concept of consistency encompasses carrying out the purposes of the NCP and substantially complying with the NCP process, specifically: (a) The removal activity was deemed necessary for the cleanup or the prevention of an oil spill and not otherwise contrary to the NCP (e.g., the limitations on use of dispersants or in-situ burning).[1384] (b) The removal activity must have been authorized by a federally approved response plan, the FOSC or the RP, or was condoned by the FOSC or RP. If there is no FOSC or RP involvement in the incident, good cause must have been shown for the lack of coordination with the FOSC.[1385] (c) The removal activity must be within the scope of the tasking, either in the federally approved response plan or given by the FOSC or RP. Absent clear tasking, it must be shown that the activity conducted was a customary removal action under the circumstances or there was good cause for the deviation from the norm. The FOSC may terminate authorized activities and may ratify unauthorized ones for good cause if they are otherwise consistent with the NCP.[1386]

*Roles And Responsibilities In Determining Removal:*

A. The Federal On-Scene Coordinator's (FOSC ) Role.

1. Authority: The FOSC has been delegated the authority to ensure effective and immediate removal of a discharge, and mitigation

---

1383 US Coast Guard National Pollution Funds Center, Technical Operating Procedures For Determining Removal Costs Under The Oil Pollution Act of 1990, at 109 (January 16, 1996).

1384 US Coast Guard National Pollution Funds Center, Technical Operating Procedures For Determining Removal Costs Under The Oil Pollution Act of 1990, 109-110 (January 16, 1996).

1385 Id. at 110.

1386 Id.

or prevention of a substantial threat of a discharge oil into U.S. surface waters (including the Exclusive Economic Zone). The FOSC verifies whether a particular cost was incurred for removal and was consistent with the NCP. The FOSC is not allowed to incur costs which are unnecessary for the removal or inconsistent with the NCP. In other words, the FOSC removal activities should be as effective and economical as possible under the circumstances.[1387]

2. Establishing the purpose for which a removal cost was incurred: In making the determination regarding removal actions and resulting costs, the FOSC is guided by the criteria set out above and should, therefore, be prepared to document the following:
   "a. Why a particular action was necessary to contain or remove oil pollution, or necessary to minimize or mitigate oil pollution damage to the public's health and welfare.
   b. That the action falls within phases II-IV," Operational Phases of Response for Oil Removal.[1388]
3. Documenting removal costs: NCP Sections 300.315 and 5.7 of Appendix E to the NCP require the FOSC to collect and maintain documentation "to support full cost recovery". Such documentation should include both reimbursable and non-reimbursable Government costs allocable to the removal effort (non-reimbursable costs are those costs which cannot be reimbursed to the agency because it has already received appropriated funds for that purpose). Routine incidents are responded to in a routine manner, and the response activities are clearly outlined in FOSC Pollution Reports (POLREPs) and other reports. When the purpose of the cost is not clear, however, the FOSC may be required to provide further explanation of the determinations made regarding removal actions.[1389]

---

1387 Id. at 111.

1388 Id.

1389 Id.

B. National Pollution Funds Center Role.

1. Authority. The NPFC has been solely delegated authority to pay removal costs. The NPFC was established as a separate Coast Guard Headquarters Unit to maintain a degree of independence from the operational environmental protection programs. Thus, the NPFC has a responsibility to establish and enforce appropriate limits on the use of the OSLTF, balanced against the operational requirements of the FOSC.[1390]
2. The Case Officer /Case Team. The Case Officer represents the NPFC for all incident specific matters with the exception of particular claims matters. The Case Officer and the Case Team support the operational requirements of the FOSC while also ensuring that the uses of the OSLTF are appropriate. They are tasked with verifying that the resource/cost documentation meets all the guidelines in the Technical Operating Procedures.[1391]

The following are examples of documentation that could be appropriate and necessary to support this type of claim:

"a. dates on which work was performed;

b. daily records of personnel costs for individuals that worked on the removal, including the name of the laborer, the labor category, a description of the task performed and how it relates to the removal actions, the number of hours worked documented on the official time attendance record, and the hourly rate paid to the laborer,

c. daily records of all travel costs, by person, including: travel authorizations; vouchers showing starting point, destination, and transportation method; receipts (hotel, airline, etc.); and proof of payment,

d. daily records of equipment costs incurred for each Removal action including a description of the equipment and how it relates to the removal actions, the time used, and the rates for use;

e. description and cost of purchased supplies and materials consumed during the removal action including receipts for the supplies and materials and a

---

1390 Id.

1391 Id.

description of how the supplies or materials relate to the removal actions; and

f. contractor and consultant costs documented on invoices paid by the claimant including a detailed description of activities performed and how they relate to the removal actions, daily cost records of all personnel, equipment, supplies, and material used by the contractor to perform the removal actions."[1392]

Although claimants are not generally required to fill out standard claim forms in order to successfully recover removal costs or damages from the Fund, it generally advisable to fill out the standard forms. This will make for easy and prompt processing of all claims. Incomplete applications can cause delay in the processing of claims. There are guidelines to follow in the completion of claim forms. These guidelines are discussed below.

## GUIDELINES ON COMPLETING STANDARD CLAIM FORMS FOR REMOVAL COSTS

The Fund guidelines cover OPA removal costs and each item of damages. This part of chapter four will only explain the aspect relating to removal costs. It will discuss recovery of removal costs by State governments, Non- State governments, and all other than state governments from the Fund. This guidance is a manifestation of the fact that the Fund is not going to act like a cash cow for anyone to show up with a claim and just collect their claim, no questions asked. The claim recovery process is a rigorous process that ensures that only valid claims rather than frivolous claims are paid. Since the Fund is limited in amount, these safeguards ensure that the Fund is not easily dissipated.

1392 The US Coast Guard National Pollution Funds Center, Claimant's Information Guide, Chapter 7, at 565-566 (September 1993).

## Removal Cost by state Governments

"**1. EVIDENCE OF INCIDENT**: State governments are supposed to provide one or more of the following:

a. On Scene Commander's (OSC) report or justification why there is no OSC report.
b. Information on when the state notified the Coast Guard or EPA and with whom the state government talked.[1393]
c. Newspaper reports describing the incident (contemporaneous not historical.)
d. Witness statement(s) concerning the spill.[1394]

**2. GENERAL INFORMATION**:

"a. A detailed description of actions taken.
b. A letter, signed by the head of the state government (State Governor, Mayor, etc.), granting the person who signed this claim the authority to bind the government in a settlement; OR,
c. A copy of letter previously filed with NPFC with signature of the head of government or the individual showing authorization to sign such claims.
d. Analysis of substance spilled showing that it was oil, and that it was not contaminated with CERCLA substances.
e. Complete investigation file on identity of responsible party (RP).
f. Map of area impacted and/or sufficient description to clearly describe the threat to navigable waters.
g. Report from the FOSC that actions were necessary, appropriate and consistent with the NCP."[1395]

**3. CONTRACTOR COSTS**:

"a. Delivery tickets, receipts, invoices, or similar records with descriptions of work performed and daily break-down of activities and costs.
b. Paid invoices for subcontractors and materiel suppliers.

---

1393 National Pollution Funds Center's Supplemental Claims Guidance on Completing Standard Claims Forms, 3 (July 18, 1997).

1394 Id. at 3.

1395 Id. at 3.

c. Invoices from and proof of payment to responsible parties, state and local governments, anyone else who might have carried some of the cost of the removal.
d. Basis for Comparison of rates charged.
e. Rates of any negotiated, open contract between the state and the Contractor.
f. Contractor's published rates with proof that they have actually charged these rates in the past.
g. Signed disposal manifests and proof of payment for disposal."[1396]

**4. GOVERNMENT LABOR AND EQUIPMENT RATES:**

"a. Payroll verification of the hourly rate the government paid its personnel at the time of the incident.
b. Verification of the standard government equipment and maintenance rates for the equipment used at the time of the incident; OR,
c. Signed and dated contemporaneous records of the incident which include the hourly rates for labor and equipment. The date on the records should be within the time of the response to the incident. Total cost of the state response set out in contemporaneous records must match the claim amount.
d. Explain whether the rates given are inclusive of benefits, overhead, etc. If the rates do include these amounts, an explanation of the formula used to calculate them must be provided, along with evidence that these overhead rates are charged to other parties. Rates under OMB A-87 should be provided.
e. Certification that the rates used reflect actual costs incurred by the government and do not include any punitive damages or fees."[1397]

**B. Other Governments**

"1. Same as above except that justification that is supported by existing data provided by State Governments is acceptable. (i.e. Local governments and municipalities need not provide data to show that the substance was oil, provided the State Government has already done so.)[1398]

---

1396 Id.

1397 Id.

1398 Id. at 4.

**C. ALL others**

"1. Provide as much of the above data as is possible.

a. Include detailed account of circumstances and reasoning that led to removal efforts.

b. Replace the word "government" as used above with the words: "your company, firm or business."[1399]

c. Disregard item 2.b. above regarding "prior signature authorization."[1400]

1. The National Contingency Plan (40 CFR Part 300), Subpart D, OPERATIONAL

RESPONSE PHASES FOR OIL REMOVAL, outlines the scope of activities which constitute a response to an oil incident to conduct removal. The four phases of response are as follows: I. Discovery or Notification. II. Preliminary Assessment and Initiation of Action. III. Containment, countermeasures, cleanup, and disposal. IV. Documentation and Cost Recovery.

*Phase I – Discovery or Notification:*

Phase I Activities are activities conducted to discover oil spills or to notify appropriate authorities of oil spills- this phase has been discussed in the earlier part of this chapter.

*Phase II Preliminary Assessment And Initiation Of Action – Activities And Removal Costs Including Assessment Phase Costs:*

A. Phase II Activities: These activities are conducted to gather information about the reported incident and plan appropriate actions. These activities are necessary whether or not the Responsible Party (RP) is taking action. The costs incurred in this phase are eligible for funding from the

1399 Id.

1400 Id.

Fund subject to thresholds for access to the Fund defined in subparagraph D.2 below. Phase II also includes the "initiation of action" activities which would immediately follow the determination the FOSC that further action is required.[1401]

B. Assessment Phase: Phase II includes the "assessment phase" between notification of a discharge and the determination by the FOSC : i) that either nothing beyond initial assessment needs to be done; or ii) that further action or presence is required. The nature of pollution response sometimes results in an initial mobilization of more resources than are actually needed to respond to an incident. Because this mobilization of resources may potentially result in costs which appear to exceed those necessary to conduct the actual cleanup, the Coast Guard (CG) has elected not to charge the RP for assessment phase costs depending on such circumstances as whether the RP is responding responsibly to the incident. The discretion to bill an RP for some or all Federal removal costs incurred during the assessment phase rests with the NPFC, and FOSCs are required to avoid advising RPs about whether certain charges will or will not be billed.[1402]

C. Use of the Fund for Phase II Costs:

"The FOSC should obtain a Federal Project Number (an FPN) and corresponding ceiling (and begin documenting all Federal removal costs ) when:

1. The FOSC expects to incur "out-of-pocket" costs to conduct the assessment phase or any part of the response; or
2. The FOSC determines that a continued presence is required to ensure proper removal actions (the initiation of action part of Phase II) and no "out-of-pocket" costs are expected, but internal costs (costs of FOSC personnel and equipment) are expected to exceed $500.[1403]

D. Examples of Phase II – are as follows:

---

1401 US Coast Guard National Pollution Funds Center, Technical Operating Procedures For Determining Removal Costs Under The Oil Pollution Act of 1990, 113 (January 16, 1996).

1402 Id. at 113.

1403 Id.

1. Assessment: (a) Evaluate magnitude/severity, (b) Assess feasibility of removal.
2. Initiation of action: (a) Identify the RP, (b) Notify affected natural resource trustees and other affected agencies. (c) Plan further action, (d) Indicate RP to clean up, (e) Issue administrative orders."[1404]

E. Some Examples of Costs Eligible for Direct Charge to the Fund for Phase II Activities for Assessment though these Costs may be Recovered from the RP as discussed in subparagraph B above :

(1) Temporary Duty per diem, travel and transportation in accordance with Federal travel regulations. (2) Contractor costs, such as drilling test wells, performing hydrological surveys. (3) Consumables or services specifically purchased during the response, such as film purchased to document the incident. (4) Replacement, repair, renovation or cleaning of equipment (whichever is most cost effective) to the extent that the loss or damage is due to the specific response and not the result of improper maintenance, improper use of the equipment, or the actions of others unrelated to the removal. (5) Long distance telephone charges. (6) Costs of transporting and staging of required supplies and equipment.[1405]

F. Some Examples of Costs Eligible for Charge to the Fund for Phase II Activities for Initiation of Action and Subsequent Recovery from the RPs:

(1) Local and Temporary Duty travel, transportation, and any per diem. (2) Contractor costs, such as contract cleanup expertise. (3) Consumables or services specifically purchased during the response, such as sorbent, supplies, incident-specific vehicle and equipment lease/rentals.(4) Replacement, repair, renovation or cleaning of equip ment C to the extent that the loss or damage is due to the specific response and not the result of improper maintenance, improper use of the equipment, or the actions of others unrelated to the removal. (5) Reservist orders. (6) Auxiliarist orders. (7) Government personnel assigned, such as scientific support, FOSC personnel, strike team personnel, legal support for administrative orders, etc., at standard costs. (8) Government facility use, such as office space at standard cost. (9) Government vehicles, boats, aircraft use at standard

1404 Id. at 113.

1405 Id. at 114

costs. (10) Government systems use.(11) Costs of transporting and staging of required supplies and equipment."[1406]

*Phase III – Containment, Countermeasures, Cleanup, And Disposal – Activities And Removal Costs:*

A. Phase III Activities: These activities are the traditional cleanup activities. If the RPs are taking proper action, the FOSC only conducts those activities necessary to ensure that immediate and effective removal takes place. Monitoring activities ought to be restricted to those necessary to ensure proper removal and should not become so onerous as to discourage RPs from conducting their own cleanups. Again, the costs incurred in this phase are eligible for funding from the Fund subject to thresholds for access to the Fund specified in paragraph C of Phase II discussed above.[1407]

B. Examples of Federal Phase III Removal Activities when the RP Performs Cleanup include: (1) Analyzing water samples to determine source, (2) analyzing water samples to determine spread. (3) measuring and sampling, (4) monitoring fate and effect of oil, (5) restricting access to area, controlling traffic, and (6) reviewing and directing actions by the RP.[1408]

C. Examples of Costs Eligible for Charge to the Fund for Phase III Removal Activities when the RP Performs Cleanup:

"(1) Local and Temporary Duty travel, transportation, and any per diem. (2) Contractor costs, such as security contractors, technical assist team contractors. (3) Consumables or services specifically purchased during the response, such as supplies, sorbent, incident specific vehicle and equipment lease/rentals. (4) Replacement, repair, renovation or cleaning of equipment - to the extent that the loss or damage is due to the specific response and not the result of improper maintenance, improper use of the equipment, or the actions of others unrelated

1406 Id.

1407 Id. at 115.

1408 Id.

to the removal. (5) Long distance telephone charges. (6)Reservist orders. (7) Auxiliarist orders. (8) Government personnel assigned, such as scientific support, FOSC personnel, strike team personnel, legal support for administrative orders, etc., at standard costs. (9) Government or leased facility use, such as office space at standard cost, mobile command post lease. (10) Government vehicles, boats, aircraft use at standard costs. (11) Government systems use, such as telecommunications systems, computer systems. (12) Government or contract laboratory sample analysis, such as Coast Guard Marine Safety Lab services at standard costs. (13) Costs of transporting and staging of required supplies and equipment.[1409]

D. Examples of Federal Removal Activities in Addition to those Listed in paragraph B above when the RP is not Known ("Mystery Oil Spills") or Fails to Perform Immediate and Effective Removal :

(1) Controlling the source of discharge. (2) Controlling the spread of oil.[1410] (3) Placement of physical barriers to deter the spread of the oil and to protect the natural resources and sensitive ecosystems.[1411] (4) Controlling of the water discharged from upstream impoundment. (5) Capturing, cleaning, and emergency care for oiled animals. (6) Cleaning oil from beaches, shoreline, piers, boats, private and public property. (7) Excavating contaminated soils. (8) Providing alternative drinking water. (9) Providing for temporary relocation or evacuation where necessary to protect public health. (10) Removing debris from shorelines prior to oiling to facilitate later cleanup. (11) Removing and, if necessary, destroying a vessel to limit discharge when properly authorized. (12) Using chemicals and other materials in accordance with subchapter J of the NCP to restrain the spread of oil and mitigate its effects. (13) Properly disposing of recovered oil and contaminated materials.[1412]

E. Examples of Costs Eligible for Charge to the OSLTF in Addition to those Listed in paragraph C for Phase III removal Activities when the FOSC Determines it

1409 Id.

1410 Id.

1411 Id. at 116.

1412 Id.

Necessary to Arrange for Removal, in Addition to, or instead of, a RP's Removal Efforts:

(1). Purchase of equipment, such as boom, skimmers, transfer systems, pumping systems, dracones, vapor analyzers, gas indicators, protective gear. Purchase of nonexpendable equipment" (generally those items, of value greater than $1000 with useful life greater than 1 year).[1413] In its acquisition of Property Items the FOSCs should only purchase property with OSLTF funds when operational necessity directly related to the removal dictates or when it is clearly more beneficial to the Government than leasing.[1414] When making decisions to buy versus lease property, and operational conditions permit, units should factor in the costs necessary to acquire, maintain, and dispose of the property, not just the purchase price versus the costs of leasing.[1415] Many of these considerations are appropriately addressed through the planning process before a spill occurs.[1416] Documentation of the factors considered in purchasing property during a spill are critical in cost recovery and litigation efforts and shall be documented to the greatest extent possible.[1417] FOSCs should be aware that property purchased for removal activities will be billed to the RP at 100% of the cost.[1418] Accordingly, whenever feasible, the FOSC should provide the responsible party the opportunity to purchase or otherwise directly supply the property needed for removal activities.[1419] Upon case completion, any property purchased and provided by the responsible party shall be returned to the responsible party.[1420]

(2) Government equipment inventory use at standard cost, such as boom, skimmers, transfer systems, pumping systems, dracones, vapor analyzers, gas indicators, protective gear.[1421] (3) Purchase of water as alternative drinking water. (4) Contract for temporary lodging for evacuees. (5)

---

1413 Id.

1414 Id. at 120.

1415 Id.

1416 Id.

1417 Id.

1418 Id. at 120-21.

1419 Id. at 121

1420 Id. at 122.

1421 Id. at 116.

Contract for temporary feeding for evacuees. (6) Contract for cleanup labor. (7) Contract for diving, and when necessary to control the source or spread of oil, salvage operations. (8) Contract for disposal. (9) In special circumstances, contract for temporary docking of salvaged vessel. (10) Rental/purchase of fencing, barricades, and security material. (11) Traffic control. (12) Contract for capturing, cleaning and emergency care for oiled animals, such as costs to capture, clean, temporarily care for, and release birds oiled by spill, or dispose of dead animals. (13) Repair of damages caused by cleanup activities, such as damage to lawns by vehicles. [Note that such costs may also be the subject of a claim for property damage per standard NPFC claims procedures if not handled as part of the removal.] (14) Replacement of oiled equipment and property which cannot be cleaned cost-effectively. (15) Decontamination of oiled equipment. (16) Replacement of excavated soils."[1422]

*Phase IV – Governmental Documentation And Cost Recovery – Activities And Removal Costs:*

A. Phase IV Activities: These activities are the documentation and reporting activities necessary to support cost recovery and record uses of the OSLTF. The costs incurred in this phase are also eligible for funding from the OSLTF to the extent that they can be identified with and attributed to specific incidents.[1423]

B. Examples of Phase IV Activities :

"(1) Collect and safeguard information, samples, and reports. (2) Interview witnesses and investigate causes. (3) Consolidate information and prepare reports. (4) Transmit reports to appropriate officials. (5) Verify report information. (6) Bill RPs. C. Examples of Costs Eligible for Charge to the OSLTF for Phase IV Removal Activities (1) Local and TDY travel and transportation. (2) Reservists orders. (3) Government personnel services. (4) Government and leased facility use, such as

1422 Id.

1423 Id. at 117.

office space. (5) Lease/purchase computer systems. (6) Government systems use at standard cost. (7) Overnight/express delivery services. (8) Warehousing/storage services, such as costs to store records, samples. (9) Contract clerical services. (10) Contract documentation services. (11) Government or leased communications systems, such as paging systems, cellular phones, and facsimile equipment normally charged at standard rates plus any identifiable direct costs."[1424]

### *Other Removal Cost Issues:*

*Spills from Federal Vessels or Facilities*: Title I of OPA excludes discharges from public vessels and Federal facilities. (This was discussed earlier). Consequently, there is no Federal liability under OPA and the remedial aspects of OPA (such as the initiation of natural resource damage assessments, state access, and the OPA claims process) are not available for spills from public vessels and Federal facilities. However, the OSLTF is still available to FOSCs to clean up or prevent oil discharges, even if OPA is otherwise inapplicable.[1425] However, the Federal agency whose vessel or facility spilled the oil is responsible under the NCP for funding and handling its own cleanups.[1426] The CG technical operating procedures (TOPS) require that the OSLTF should only be used in Federal spills (other than incidental FOSC costs) as a last resort, when the responsible agency cannot handle a cleanup.[1427] The TOPS also require that:

1. When the responsible agency is capable of funding the cleanup but lacks the resources to properly conduct the cleanup, the FOSC should attempt to establish a Interdepartmental Purchase Request (MIPR) or similar reimbursable agreement, as time permits, to establish direct upfront funding of the FOSC removal activities.[1428]

---

1424 Id.

1425 US Coast Guard National Pollution Funds Center, Technical Operating Procedures For Determining Removal Costs Under The Oil Pollution Act of 1990, at 124 (January 16, 1996).

1426 Id.

1427 Id.

1428 Id. at 125.

FOSCs are encouraged to contact the cognizant NPFC Regional Manager for assistance in establishing such agreements.

2. Where the OSLTF is used to clean up a Federal spill, the NPFC will normally seek reimbursement from the responsible agency. FOSCs should immediately notify the cognizant NPFC Regional Manager whenever it appears necessary to use the OSLTF for a Federal spill.[1429]

*Spills Involving Both Removal Costs and Potential Claims*: The Coast Guard (CG) TOPS provide some insight on how this type of situation should be handled.

1. When an incident involves removal actions under the direction of the FOSC as well as potential damage claims under OPA, the actions of the FOSC should be coordinated with the NPFC case officer/claims representatives to ensure a cost-effective use of all OSLTF monies.[1430]
2. There are overlaps between removal costs and damages. For example, the cost incurred by the FOSC for cleaning boats oiled due to a spill is a valid removal cost while costs incurred by individuals for cleaning their own boats oiled due to a spill are also valid claims.[1431] Further, a boat owner may have a property damage claim for permanent damage to the boat even after the FOSC has cleaned it.[1432] In most cases, it is more efficient to handle boat cleaning as a removal cost because this ensures control over the disposition of the oil and the costs of the cleaning.[1433] Any property damage can be handled separately as a claim.[1434]
3. Additionally, there are situations where property is cleaned by the FOSC only to be replaced as the result of a claim. An example might be oiled wooden piers which although cleaned by the FOSC

1429 Id.

1430 Id. at 125.

1431 Id.

1432 Id.

1433 Id.

1434 Id.

as removal must still be torn out and replaced due to the residual damage.[1435] Close coordination allows the selection of the most cost-effective approach which in some cases is to simply replace the property as a removal cost in the first place.[1436]

*Oil Wells/Pits/Facilities*: The CG TOPS also provide some insight on how spills from these type of sources should be dealt with.

1. The Fund is available for removal of oil discharged, or substantial threat of discharge, from "abandoned" wells, pits, and related facilities.[1437] The use of the term "abandoned" in this context indicates that such wells are no longer in active production, but does not mean that they were properly abandoned in accordance with applicable state law.[1438] Generally, these facilities are "orphans" presenting special problems in identifying the responsible parties for the discharge or substantial threat.[1439]
2. Types of Facilities.
   "(a) The wells themselves: Wells no longer in production, whether or not they have been plugged and abandoned, properly or improperly.[1440]
   (b) Related facilities: These include abandoned refineries and above ground storage tanks, or production field tank batteries, used to gather, treat, and store crude oil; together with any associated well head assemblies ("Christmas trees") and gathering lines, pumps, compressors, etc.[1441]
   (c) Pits: Holding and containment pits used for storage, treatment, or otherwise to collect oil wastes and effluents associated with oil wells or refineries. Cleanup or remediation of pits contaminated with hazardous substances, whether or not

---

1435 Id.
1436 Id.
1437 Id. at 127.
1438 Id.
1439 Id.
1440 Id.
1441 Id. at 127.

mixed with oil wastes, must be treated with CERCLA monies or the SuperFund.[1442]

3. Identification of Responsible Party: The FOSC is required to begin appropriate research, including title searches, as early as possible to identify the responsible parties."[1443]

*Laundry List of Regulatory Requirements for Reimbursement of Eligible Claimants:* The implementing regulations provide a laundry list of general requirements for filing a claim. Because they are so many, I will highlight only some of them: All claimants including the responsible party, bears the burden of providing all evidence, information, and documentation deemed necessary by the Director, NPFC, to support their claims. In addition:

"(a) Each claim must be in writing for a sum certain for compensation for each category of uncompensated damages or removal costs resulting from an incident. If at any time during the pendency of a claim against the Fund the claimant receives any compensation for the claimed amounts, the claimant shall immediately amend the claims.[1444]"

This provision would apply to a responsible party who has a complete defense of fault of a third party and has made a successful claim against that third party that covers some or all his removal costs. It would also apply to a third party who has fully or partially succeeded in his claim against the responsible party for removal costs and damages. It is imperative that they amend their claims against the fund to reflect the true position of things.

Furthermore:

"(b) Each claim must be signed in ink by the claimant certifying to the best of the claimant's knowledge and belief that the claim accurately reflects all material facts."[1445]

---

1442 Id.

1443 Id.

1444 33 C.F.R. § 136.105(a)-(c).

1445 33 C.F.R. § 136.105(a)-(c).

*Removal costs and multiple items of damages:* "(a) A claimant must specify all of the claimant's known removal costs or damages arising out of a single incident when submitting a claim. (b) Removal costs and each separate category of damages (as described in subpart C of this part) must be separately listed with a sum certain attributed to each type and category listed. (c) At the sole discretion of the Director, NPFC, removal costs and each separate category of damages may be treated separately for settlement purposes."[1446]

In addition each claim must include at least the following as applicable:

"(1) The date, time, and place of the incident giving rise to the claim. (2) The identity of the vessel causing or suspected to have caused the removal costs or damages claimed and the basis for such identity or belief. (3) A general description of the nature and extent of the impact of the incident, the costs associated with the removal actions, and damages claimed by category, including for any property, equipment or similar item damaged. (4) An explanation of how and when the removal costs or damages were caused by, or resulted from, an incident. (5) Evidence to support the claim. (7) A description of the actions taken by the claimant, or other person on his behalf, to avoid or minimize removal costs or damages claimed. (8) A copy of written communications and the substance of verbal communications, if any, between the claimant and the responsible party and a statement indicating that the claim was presented to the responsible party and guarantor, the date it was presented, that it was denied or remains not settled and, if known, the reason why it was denied or remains not settled. (9) A statement by the claimant that no action has been commenced in court against the responsible party or, if an action has been commenced, a statement identifying the claimant's attorney and the attorney's address and phone number, the civil action number, and the court in which the action is pending. (9) In the discretion of the director of the NPFC, any other information deemed relevant and necessary to properly process the claim for payment."[1447]

1446 33 CFR § 136.109.

1447 33 C.F.R. § 136.105(e)(2)(3)(4)(6)(7)(10)(12)(13).

*Other Compensation:* 33 C.F.R. §136.113 mandates all Fund claimants to include an accounting, including the source and value, of all other compensation received, applied for, or potentially available as a consequence of the incident out of which the claim arises including, but not limited to, monetary payments, goods or services, or other benefits.

*Settlement And Notice To Claimant:* 33 C.F.R §136.115 (a) stipulates that payment in full, or acceptance by the Fund claimant of an offer of settlement by the Fund, is final and conclusive for all purposes and, upon payment, constitutes a release of the Fund for the claim. In addition, acceptance of any compensation from the Fund precludes a claimant from filing any subsequent action against the responsible party to recover costs or damages which are the subject of the compensated claim. Acceptance of any compensation also constitutes an agreement by a claimant to assign to the Fund any rights, claims, and causes of action the claimant has against the responsible party for the costs and damages which are the subject of the compensated claims and to cooperate reasonably with the Fund in any claim or action by the Fund against any person to recover the amounts paid by the Fund. The cooperation shall include, but is not limited to, immediately reimbursing the Fund for any compensation received from any other source for the same costs and damages and providing any documentation, evidence, testimony, and other support, as may be necessary for the Fund to recover from any person.

## RECOVERING COSTS OF MONITORING DAMAGES AND CLEAN UP

One very important question that has generated some controversy in the past is the question of whether the damages recoverable in section 2702(b) of the OPA includes monitoring costs. The definition section of the OPA, provides that damages" means damages specified in section 2702(b) of the statute, and includes the cost of assessing these damages.[1448] The National Oceanic and Atmospheric Administration final rule

1448 33 U.S.C.A §2701(5).

concerning liability for oil spills reiterated this definition of damages recoverable under the OPA, by providing in its rules that damages means damages specified in section 2702(b) of OPA, and includes the costs of assessing these damages, as defined in section 2701(5) of the OPA.[1449] These rules shed more light on the ability of the trustees and the government to recover monitoring costs by providing as follows:

> "reasonable assessment costs means assessment costs that are incurred by trustees in accordance with this part. In cases where assessment costs are incurred but trustees do not pursue restoration, trustees may recover their reasonable assessment costs provided that they have determined that assessment actions undertaken were premised on the likelihood of injury and need for restoration. Reasonable assessment costs also include: administrative, legal, and enforcement costs necessary to carry out this part; monitoring and oversight costs; and costs associated with public participation."[1450]

These rules were challenged in the case of *General Electric Co. v. U.S. Dept. of Commerce*,[1451] where General Electric, the petitioner, filed for a review of the rules, but the District of Columbia Circuit Court of Appeal found that the National Oceanic and Atmospheric Administration's (NOAA) final rules concerning liability for oil spills under Oil Pollution Act (OPA) properly held responsible parties accountable for monitoring and oversight costs, i.e., costs associated with trustee monitoring of implementation of restoration plans and their environmental consequences.[1452]

Another case in which the issue of recoverability of monitoring costs came up is the case of *United States v. Conoco, Inc*,[1453] where the United States sued an oil company for recovery of costs of monitoring clean-up for oil pipeline spills. Both parties filed summary judgment motions. The

---

1449 15 CFR § 990.30.

1450 Id.

1451 128 F.3d 767 (D.C. Cir. 1997).

1452 Oil Pollution Act of 1990, § 1002(b)(2)(A), 33 U.S.C.A. § 2702(b)(2)(A); 15 C.F.R. § 990.30.

1453 916 F.Supp. 581 (E.D. La. 1996).

District Court held that monitoring costs were included in removal costs that government could seek to recover from a responsible party under the Oil Pollution Act. The court believed that the United States advanced a straightforward reading of the provisions of the OPA 90, which specifically supports recovery by the government of the cost of monitoring the efforts of the responsible party who undertakes to clean up its own oil spill. The court rejected the oil company's argument that simply because the government is authorized by 33 USCA § 1321 to monitor private cleanup activities does not mean that the cost of the monitoring is chargeable to the private actor.[1454] The court noted that the statute expressly authorizes the government to monitor the cleanup and removal efforts of the responsible party. The court decided to give a broad reading to the OPA's definition of "removal" as including not only the actual containment or removal of oil but also *such other actions as are necessary* (emphasis mine) to minimize or mitigate damage to the public health or welfare.[1455] The court found that monitoring costs falls under the category of "such other actions as are necessary". According to the government, oversight by the Coast Guard in this case was necessary to minimize and mitigate such damages because the Coast Guard had to determine whether the oil company's activities were sufficient to contain the spill(s).[1456] Also in the case of *United States v. Hyundai Merchant Marine Co*,[1457] another recent case that addressed the issue of recoverability of monitoring costs, the main contention was the purport of section 2701(30) of OPA 90. This OPA 90 definition section defines "remove" or "removal" as the containment and removal of oil or a hazardous substance from water and shorelines or the taking of other actions *as may be necessary* to minimize or mitigate damage to the public health or welfare, including, but not limited to, fish, shellfish, wildlife, and public and private property, shorelines, and beaches. The main dispute was the interpretation of the phrase "as may be necessary." Hyundai, the defendant contended that the United States may

1454 Id. at 583.

1455 33 U.S.C. § 2701(30).

1456 916 F.Supp. 581, 583 (E.D. La. 1996)

1457 48 ERC 1385, 1999 A.M.C. 1521, 29 Envtl. L. Rep. 21, 172 F.3d 1187 (9th Cir.1999).

not recover costs unless the district court determines they were "necessary" to mitigate or prevent a discharge of oil.[1458] In its rejection of the defendant's contention, the court noted that, the words "as may be necessary" do not purport to be a limitation on reimbursement, but rather are more naturally read as an acknowledgment of executive discretion in determining the steps a particular situation requires. The court also pointed out that in any event, the relevant term in § 2702(a) is "removal costs," not "removal." The court further found that the former is defined at section 2701(31) as the "costs to prevent, minimize, or mitigate oil pollution," and the word "necessary" was nowhere to be found in this more pertinent definition.

The *Hyundai Merchant* court also noted that, if Congress were to establish a standard for establishing which actions of the Coast Guard were reimbursable, one would expect to find it in the liability portion of the statute, not in the definitions section. The court pointed out that the liability section, § 2702(b), specifies what removal costs are recoverable under § 2702(a). It defines them as "all removal costs incurred by the United States." (Emphasis added.) Nothing in the liability section limits the United States to recovery of "necessary" removal costs.

Hyundai argued that the United States should not have a blank check permitting it to undertake all kinds of unnecessary and unreasonable actions at Hyundai's expense. The court pointed out in passing, however, that many of the actions that Hyundai now regarded as unreasonable or unnecessary appear so, if at all, only by hindsight.[1459] The court noted further that the grounding of the Hyundai No. 12 contained the seeds of a major ecological disaster and in the circumstances, it was only prudent for the government to rush personnel and equipment to the scene and maintain them there until the threat was over. The court also pointed out that be that as it may, the OPA 90 does not restrict the recovery of the United States to costs that were prudent, or necessary, or reasonable.[1460] As of

1458 172 F.3d 1187, 1191.

1459 Id. at 1191

1460 Id.

April 2001, the M/V Hyundai had been billed a total of $2, 219, 926 for oil spill removal related costs.[1461]

*Limitations on Monitoring Costs:* It is important to point out that even though the OPA permits recovery of monitoring costs there are some limitations on this item of recovery. The monitoring costs must not be unreasonable and capricious under the circumstances. The most apposite case on this issue is the case of *United States v. Murphy Exploration and Production Co.*[1462] In this case the defendant/responsible party (RP) challenged the amount the United States Coast Guard claimed they had expended on monitoring the clean up and removal effort of the responsible party. Murphy, the defendant relied on the stipulated fact that the Coast Guard paid $3,767.00 per hour for total overflight cost of $16,951.50 on July 23, 1992, when it (Murphy the responsible party) leased a helicopter the previous day, on July 22, 1992, at a rate of $900.00 plus $378.00 in non-rate charges for a daily total of $1,278.00.[1463] The court pointed out that the facts show that Murphy, who was actively engaged in the cleanup, incurred less charges for its 48 helicopter overflights over a three day period and maintained that those helicopters were available for government use. The Court's analysis was further guided by Judge Holland who, according to the Court's research, was the only court at the time to have passed directly on this issue under the OPA:

"Firstly, one can hardly say that the requisite nexus or causation exists as between a pollution incident and a cost authorized by an FOSC [federal on-scene coordinator] to, for example, replace a piece of equipment which had failed in the course of a prior, unrelated pollution incident. Secondly, to suggest that a cost is recoverable if the requisite causation exists simply because the FOSC authorized it in substance deprives a responsible party of any judicial review, and such a position would pose a serious due process problem. The court's example is of

1461 See Appendix 1, p 40, M/V Hyundai, Federal Project Number (FPN) 172001 (2001).

1462 43 ERC 1701, 1996 A.M.C. 2883, 136 Oil & Gas Rep. 440, 939 F.Supp. 489 (E.D. La. 1996).

1463 939 F.Supp. 489, 493.

course an extreme one. The more likely situation is one where the FOSC has authorized an expenditure and the potentially responsible party views it as significantly disproportionate to the facts of the incident. As to such questions and as already suggested, fairness and proportionality come into consideration as a part of the arbitrariness analysis. It is simply not rational to use a large vessel to go after a spill of a few gallons of oily water from a frozen pipe, which is known to have already been repaired or sealed off. Here again, expert testimony may very well be necessary in a seriously contested response situation."[1464]

The *Murphy Exploration and Production Co.* court noted that the due process ramifications inherent in the government's position were significant, and the government had failed to demonstrate a non-arbitrary rational basis for authorizing the challenged helicopter expenditures and that Murphy had otherwise shown that the Coast Guard acted arbitrarily and capriciously in the causing this expenditure to be made. The Court concluded that it would be remiss in allowing such an arbitrary, capricious and irrational expenditure of fiscal resources, and will permit recovery for the overflight on July 23, 1992, in the amount of $1,278.00, based on the rational July 22, 1992, rate of $900.00 per hour plus $378.00 in non-rate charges.[1465] This case underscores the importance of seizing the clean-up effort initiative from the United States Coast Guard. If Murphy had not seized the initiative in the clean-up/clean-up monitoring effort, they might not have had the opportunity to compare the Coast Guard's monitoring costs figures with theirs, and this would have led to payment of capricious and outrageous amounts as monitoring costs. So, once an oil spill has been verified and the responsible party has accepted its designation as the responsible party, it ought to make costs control its number one priority.

---

1464 Id. at 493 (citing, *United States v. Hyundai Merchant Marine Co., Ltd., Civ.* Act. A94-0391-CV (HRH) (D.Alaska Jan 26, 1996) (Order on Motion for Partial Summary Judgment/Removal Costs), slip op. at pp. 9-10.

1465 939 F.Supp. at 493.

# Chapter Five

# DAMAGES

This chapter will refer to the US Coast Guard's Oil spill Liability Trust Fund as the Fund or OSLTF from time to time. "The Fund" is discussed in a separate chapter later on in this treatise. A quick glance at that discussion might help in the understanding of the current discussion.

Generally, section 2702 (a) of OPA holds an RP for a vessel or a facility from which oil is discharged or which poses the substantial threat of a discharge of oil, into or upon the navigable waters or adjoining shorelines or the exclusive economic zone of the US, liable for the removal costs and damages. The OPA also makes the responsible party liable for damages, for injury to natural resources, injury to real or personal property (including economic losses resulting from that injury), loss of subsistence use of natural resources, loss of revenues (including federal, state or local taxes) on the use of natural resources and real or personal property, loss of profits and impairment of earning capacity resulting from such pollution, and the costs of providing additional public services during or after removal activities.[1466] Each element of liability is discussed below.

## A. NATURAL RESOURCE DAMAGES

Statutory provisions:

"§ 2702. Elements of liability

(a) In general

1466 33 USC §2702(b)(2).

Notwithstanding any other provision or rule of law, and subject to the provisions of this Act, each responsible party for a vessel or a facility from which oil is discharged, or which poses the substantial threat of a discharge of oil, into or upon the navigable waters or adjoining shorelines or the exclusive economic zone is liable for the removal costs and **damages** specified in subsection (b) of this section that result from such incident.

(b) Covered removal costs and damages

**

(2) Damages

The damages referred to in subsection (a) of this section are the following:

**(A) Natural resources**

Damages for injury to, destruction of, loss of, or loss of use of, **natural resources**, including the reasonable costs of assessing the damage, which shall be recoverable by a United States trustee, a State trustee, an Indian tribe trustee, or a foreign trustee."[1467]

**"§ 2706. Natural resources**

(a) Liability

In the case of natural resource damages under section 2702(b)(2)(A) of this title, liability shall be--

**(1)** to the United States Government for natural resources belonging to, managed by, controlled by, or appertaining to the United States;
**(2)** o any State for natural resources belonging to, managed by, controlled by, or appertaining to such State or political subdivision thereof;

---

1467 33 USC § 2702

**(3)** to any Indian tribe for natural resources belonging to, managed by, controlled by, or appertaining to such Indian tribe; and

**(4)** in any case in which section 2707 of this title applies, to the government of a foreign country for natural resources belonging to, managed by, controlled by, or appertaining to such country.

(b) Designation of trustees

(1) In general

The President, or the authorized representative of any State, Indian tribe, or foreign government, shall act on behalf of the public, Indian tribe, or foreign country as trustee of natural resources to present a claim for and to recover damages to the natural resources.

(2) Federal trustees

The President shall designate the Federal officials who shall act on behalf of the public as trustees for natural resources under this Act.

(3) State trustees

The Governor of each State shall designate State and local officials who may act on behalf of the public as trustee for natural resources under this Act and shall notify the President of the designation.

(4) Indian tribe trustees

The governing body of any Indian tribe shall designate tribal officials who may act on behalf of the tribe or its members as trustee for natural resources under this Act and shall notify the President of the designation.

(5) Foreign trustees

The head of any foreign government may designate the trustee who shall act on behalf of that government as trustee for natural resources under this Act.

(c) Functions of trustees

(1) Federal trustees

The Federal officials designated under subsection (b)(2) of this section--

**(A)** shall assess natural resource damages under section 2702(b)(2)(A) of this title for the natural resources under their trusteeship;

**(B)** may, upon request of and reimbursement from a State or Indian tribe and at the Federal officials' discretion, assess damages for the natural resources under the State's or tribe's trusteeship; and

**(C)** shall develop and implement a plan for the restoration, rehabilitation, replacement, or acquisition of the equivalent, of the natural resources under their trusteeship.

(2) State trustees

The State and local officials designated under subsection (b)(3) of this section--

**(A)** shall assess natural resource damages under section 2702(b)(2)(A) of this title for the purposes of this Act for the natural resources under their trusteeship; and

**(B)** shall develop and implement a plan for the restoration, rehabilitation, replacement, or acquisition of the equivalent, of the natural resources under their trusteeship.

(3) Indian tribe trustees

The tribal officials designated under subsection (b)(4) of this section--

**(A)** shall assess natural resource damages under section 2702(b)(2)(A) of this title for the purposes of this Act for the natural resources under their trusteeship; and

**(B)** shall develop and implement a plan for the restoration, rehabilitation, replacement, or acquisition of the equivalent, of the natural resources under their trusteeship.

(4) Foreign trustees

The trustees designated under subsection (b)(5) of this section--

**(A)** shall assess natural resource damages under section 2702(b)(2)(A) of this title for the purposes of this Act for the natural resources under their trusteeship; and

**(B)** shall develop and implement a plan for the restoration, rehabilitation, replacement, or acquisition of the equivalent, of the natural resources under their trusteeship.

(5) Notice and opportunity to be heard

Plans shall be developed and implemented under this section only after adequate public notice, opportunity for a hearing, and consideration of all public comment.

(d) Measure of damages

(1) In general

The measure of natural resource damages under section 2702(b)(2)(A) of this title is--

**(A)** the cost of restoring, rehabilitating, replacing, or acquiring the equivalent of, the damaged natural resources;

**(B)** the diminution in value of those natural resources pending restoration; plus

**(C)** the reasonable cost of assessing those damages.

(2) Determine costs with respect to plans

Costs shall be determined under paragraph (1) with respect to plans adopted under subsection (c) of this section.

(3) No double recovery

There shall be no double recovery under this Act for natural resource damages, including with respect to the costs of damage assessment or restoration, rehabilitation, replacement, or acquisition for the same incident and natural resource.

(e) Damage assessment regulations

(1) Regulations

The President, acting through the Under Secretary of Commerce for Oceans and Atmosphere and in consultation with the Administrator of the Environmental Protection Agency, the Director of the United States Fish and Wildlife Service, and the heads of other affected agencies, not later than 2 years after August 18, 1990, shall promulgate regulations for the assessment of natural resource damages under section 2702(b)(2)(A) of this title resulting from a discharge of oil for the purpose of this Act.

(2) Rebuttable presumption

Any determination or assessment of damages to natural resources for the purposes of this Act made under subsection (d) of this section by a Federal, State, or Indian trustee in accordance with the regulations promulgated under paragraph (1) shall have the force and effect of a rebuttable presumption on behalf of the trustee in any administrative or judicial proceeding under this Act.

(f) Use of recovered sums

Sums recovered under this Act by a Federal, State, Indian, or foreign trustee for natural resource damages under section 2702(b)(2)(A) of this title shall be retained by the trustee in a revolving trust account, without further appropriation, for use only to reimburse or pay costs incurred by the trustee under subsection (c) of this section with respect to the damaged natural resources. Any amounts in excess of those required for these reimbursements and costs shall be deposited in the Fund.

(g) Compliance

Review of actions by any Federal official where there is alleged to be a failure of that official to perform a duty under this section that is not discretionary with that official may be had by any person in the district court in which the person resides or in which the alleged damage to natural resources occurred. The court may award costs of litigation (including reasonable attorney and expert witness fees) to any prevailing or substantially prevailing party. Nothing in this subsection shall restrict any right which any person may have to seek relief under any other provision of law."[1468]

**Natural Resources Damage Assessment and Restoration** – 33 USC §§ 2702(b)(2)(A) & 2706.

The OPA allows a United States trustee, a State trustee, an Indian tribe trustee, or a foreign trustee to recover "damages for injury to, destruction of, loss of, loss of use of, natural resources, including the reasonable costs of assessing the damage."[1469] Natural resources includes land, fish, wildlife, biota, air, water, ground water, drinking water supplies, and other such resources belonging to, managed by, held in trust by, appertaining

---

1468 33 USC §2706

1469 See 33 USCA §2702(b)(2)(A).

to, or otherwise controlled by the United States (including the resources of the exclusive economic zone), any State or local government or Indian tribe, or any foreign government.

Indian tribe means any Indian tribe, band, nation, or other organized group or community, but not including any Alaska Native regional or village corporation, which is recognized as eligible for the special programs and services provided by the United States to Indians because of their status as Indians and has governmental authority over lands belonging to or controlled by the tribe.[1470]

A natural resource trustee is a federal official designated by the President of the United States who acts on behalf of the residents of the nation. A state trustee is a state official designated by the governor of a state who acts on behalf of the residents of the State. An Indian trustee is an Indian official designated by the governing body of any Indian tribe who acts on behalf of the residents of the tribe. A foreign trustee is a foreign official designated by the head of any foreign government, who acts on behalf of the residents of the foreign country.

The primary duties of trustees include, (a) participating in National Response System preparedness and response activities intended to avoid or minimize injury to natural resources;(b) assessing damages for injury to, destruction of, loss of, or loss of natural resources under their trusteeship; (c) obtaining compensation from the responsible party for these damages through negotiation or litigation; and (d) developing and implementing a plan for restoration of injured resources.[1471]

Federal trustees are made up of Secretaries of Interior, Commerce, Agriculture, Defense and Energy as land managing agencies, for natural resources located on, over, or under land administered by each agency. Secretaries of Commerce and Interior are responsible for general categories of natural resources, including their supporting ecosystems.[1472] A state

1470 33 USCA § 2701(15).

1471 See National Contingency Plan (NCP) CFR 300.210(c )(4), 300.615(c)(3)(i), 300.910(a),CERCLA section 107(f)(2) and CWA section 311 (as amended by OPA section 2706).

1472 NCP 40 CFR 300.600.

trustee is the official(s) designated by the Governor of each State to act as trustee for natural resources within the State's boundaries or for resources belonging to, controlled by, or appertaining to the State. The designated official is normally the head of an agency responsible for environmental protection or fish and wildlife management. States may designate more than one trustee agency.[1473] An Indian trustee is a Tribal chairman, head of the tribe's governing body, or an individual selected by the tribe to act as trustee on behalf of a tribe. The Secretary of the Interior may act as trustee if requested by the tribe.[1474]

Federal & State Agencies and Indian Tribes may be co-trustees for the same natural resource. The Department of the Interior and States are co-trustees for migratory birds. Federal land management agencies (other than Interior) are co-trustees with Interior, Commerce, and/or States and possibly Indian tribes for most living natural resources on Federal lands. The Departments of the Interior and Commerce can be co-trustees for certain natural resources: sea turtles are the trust responsibility of Commerce in the water and Interior on land. States are co-trustees with Interior and Commerce for sea turtles both at sea and on land.[1475]

Most natural resource trustees are natural resource and land managers. Carrying out these responsibilities requires expertise in disciplines such as biological sciences, chemistry, hydrology, geology, range/timber/wildlife/fisheries management, and park/recreation management. As resource managers, trustees want to avoid injury to their trust resources.[1476] Staff with scientific expertise and knowledge of trustee resources

---

1473 NCP, 40 CFR 300.605.

1474 NCP, 40 CFR 300.610.

1475 Department of Interior Office of Environmental Policy and Compliance-- Response and Natural Resource Trusteeship Training Module On NRDA For Personnel Involved In Emergency Response To Oil Spills And Hazardous Substance Releases Under The National Oil And Hazardous Substances Pollution Contingency Plan <http://www.doi.gov/oepc/response/a09.htm> (last updated May 4, 2000).

1476 Department of Interior Office of Environmental Policy and Compliance-- Response and Natural Resource Trusteeship Training Module On NRDA For Personnel Involved In Emergency Response To Oil Spills And Hazardous Substance Releases Under The National Oil And Hazardous Substances Pollution Contingency Plan <http://www.doi.gov/oepc/response/a03.htm> (last updated, May 4, 2000).

are good sources of information for assisting On-Scene Coordinators in identifying and deciding on protection priorities of sensitive resources.[1477] By participating in both preparedness and response activities, trustees can help minimize injury to natural resources, which has the additional benefit of reducing the ultimate cost of an incident to the responsible party. Trustees are often on the scene relatively early in response activities, to begin natural resource damage assessment work.[1478] Information that trustees gather for natural resource damage assessment purposes can be useful to the On-Scene Coordinator in making response decisions.[1479]

Natural resource damage assessment under the OPA is the process of (1) collecting and analyzing information to evaluate the nature and extent of injuries resulting from an incident, (2) determine the restoration actions needed to bring injured natural resources and services back to baseline, and (3) making the environment and public whole for interim losses.[1480] The OPA provides that the President of the United States acting through the Under Secretary of Commerce for Oceans and Atmosphere shall promulgate regulations for the assessment of natural resources damages (under section 2702(b)(2)(A) of the statute) resulting from a discharge of oil.[1481] By virtue of this provision of the OPA, the National Oceanic and Atmospheric Administration (NOAA), a government agency under the Department of Commerce was given the power to make the required regulations. The NOAA engaged in a six-year rule-making process, four years longer than the two years required by Congress, and promulgated its final rule in 1996. This rule making process involved many years of information-gathering and analysis of public comment on approaches to developing natural resource damage assessment procedures.[1482]

---

1477 Id.

1478 Id.

1479 Id.

1480 Oil Pollution Act Regulations, Natural Resources Damage Assessments, CFR § 990.30 (July 2000).

1481 33 USCA § 2706 (c) (1).

1482 See Colin De La Rue & Charles B. Anderson, Shipping And The Environment, 542 (Lloyd's Shipping Law Library 1998).

The American Institute of Marine Underwriters (AIMU), and liability insurer, Water Quality Insurance Syndicate (WQIS) lodged an appeal against the final NOAA regulations for evaluating environmental damage under OPA. Interested parties had 90 days in which to register their opposition to the regulations, which were issued by the National Oceanic and Atmospheric Administration in January of 1996. The Institute and the Syndicate filed their petition with the Court of Appeals of the United States for the District of Columbia just prior to the deadline.[1483]

WQIS and AIMU followed this path because review of any regulation promulgated under the OPA may be had upon application by any interested person only in the Court of Appeals of the United States for the District of Columbia.[1484] Any such application is required to be made within 90 days from the date of promulgation of such regulations. The OPA provides that any matter with respect to which review could have been obtained under section 2717(a) of the OPA shall not be subject to judicial review in any civil or criminal proceeding for enforcement or to obtain damages or recovery of response costs. It seems that this requirement of early challenge to the implementing regulations was aimed at preventing any thing that could slow down environmental law enforcement agents in the performance of their duties. It may have also been aimed at preventing violators of the OPA from making baseless challenges to the validity of any OPA implementing regulation in enforcement proceedings.

WQIS and AIMU claimed that the Natural Resources Damage assessment regulations in the form in which they were, posed a serious threat to the ability of marine underwriters to provide pollution liability cover in the US. They claimed that the regulations make it difficult, if not impossible for marine insurers to anticipate liability costs arising from oil pollution incidents, and thus for them to establish proper reserves for the underwritten risks.[1485] They also said that insurance cover for vessels

1483 Liz Shuker: US insurers seeking pollution review. Lloyd's List Int'l April 8, 1996, at 1.

1484 33 USCA §2717(a).

1485 Liz Shuker: US insurers seeking pollution review. Lloyd's List Int'l April 8, 1996, at 1.

trading in US waters would be withdrawn as a result, severely impeding US domestic maritime trade. The P & I Clubs that insure 90 percent of the world's vessels were also opposed to the regulations. According to Walter Kramer, President of the American Institute of Marine Underwriters, the responsible party to an oil spill, or his insurer, could be forced to conduct an expensive restoration program for many years, or, alternately, choose to pay for the costs of the restoration plan in advance with little or no right to challenge the cost.[1486] The OPA provides that the measure of damages payable to a trustee for lost or damaged natural resources shall be the cost of restoring, rehabilitating, replacing, or acquiring the equivalent of the damaged natural resources as well as the diminution in value of those natural resources pending restoration, plus the cost of assessing those damages.[1487]

It is important to point out that the natural resources damage provision of OPA does not allow private parties to bring suit. Only a United States trustee, a state trustee, an Indian tribe trustee, or a foreign trustee can recover damages.[1488] It is also important to point out that this item of damages is subject to the limitation provisions of OPA.[1489] But in most oil spill cases, it would constitute a disproportionate percentage of the limited damages a responsible party might have to pay under the provisions of OPA. The OPA provides that the sums recovered under the OPA by a Federal, State, Indian, or foreign trustee for natural resource damages under section 2702(b)(2)(A) of this Act shall be retained by the trustee in a revolving trust account, without further appropriation, for use only to reimburse or pay costs incurred by the trustee under section 2706(c) of the OPA with respect to the damaged natural resources.[1490] Any amounts in excess of those required for these reimbursements and costs shall be deposited in the Fund.[1491] This provision will ensure that the money recovered

---

1486 Id. at 2.

1487 Oil Pollution Act § 2706(d)(1).

1488 Id. § 2702 (b)(2)(A).

1489 Id. § 2704 (a) (1).

1490 33 USCA § 2706(f).

1491 33 USCA §2706(f).

by the trustees are not used to meet other non-OPA related government expenses. It will ensure that recovery by trustees does not become another source of revenue for the Federal, state or municipal governments. The provision also ensures that the trustees do not have to go cap in hand before congress to beg for reimbursement money for the costs that they have incurred in the course of their legal duties. It will also keep the Fund robust for the payment of future removal costs and damages claims that may be presented to it.

*Citizen Suits Allowed*: In order to ensure that Federal officials are not slack or dragging their feet in the performance of their natural resources damage assessment and restoration duties that are non-discretionary; the OPA provides that review of actions by any Federal official where there is alleged to be a failure of that official to perform a duty under this section that is not discretionary with that official may be initiated by any person in the district court in which the person resides or in which the alleged damage to natural resources occurred.[1492] The court may award costs of litigation, including reasonable attorney and expert witness fees to any prevailing or substantially prevailing party.[1493] The OPA makes it clear that nothing in this provision restricts any right which any person may have to seek relief under any other provision of law.[1494] This means that citizen-suits may be brought under various environmental statutes to compel Federal officials to perform non-discretionary duties imposed on them by the natural resources damage assessment provisions of the OPA. These suits are usually brought solely to compel performance, not to seek damages for civil wrongs by Federal officials. The courts are usually liberal in the award of attorney's fees in these type of cases because they recognize that the citizen bringing the suit may not derive any direct benefit from the suit. Since it is being brought on behalf of all citizens to safeguard the interest of all, it would not be fair not to grant attorney's fees

1492 33 USCA §2706(g).
1493 33 USCA§2706(g).
1494 33 USCA§2706(g).

in these type of cases. That is probably why the OPA recognized the need to allow recovery of attorney's fees and expert witness fees.

*No Double Recovery*: The OPA does not permit double recovery of damage to natural resources. The OPA specifically provides that there shall be no double recovery under this chapter for natural resource damages, including with respect to the costs of damage assessment or restoration, rehabilitation, replacement, or acquisition for the same incident and natural resource.[1495]

**A.I (a) The Relationship of NOAA's OPA-NRDA Regulations with DOI's CERCLA- NRDA Regulations.**

The NOAA final rules on natural resources damage assessment and restoration also explains its relationship to the Comprehensive Environmental Response, Compensation, and Liability Act's (CERCLA), 42 U.S.C. 9601 natural resource damage assessment regulations.[1496] The NOAA rules provides as follows:

(a) *General*: Regulations for assessing natural resource damages resulting from hazardous substance releases under the Comprehensive Environmental Response, Compensation, and Liability Act of 1980, as amended (CERCLA), 42 U.S.C. 9601 et seq., and the Federal Water Pollution Control Act (Clean Water Act), 33 U.S.C. 1321 et seq., are codified at 43 CFR part 11. The regulations were written and are being enforced by the Department of Interior (DOI). The CERCLA regulations originally applied to natural resource damages resulting from oil discharges as well as hazardous substance releases. This part supersedes 43 CFR part 11 with regard to oil discharges covered by OPA.[1497]

1495 33 U.S.C.A. §2706(d)(3).

1496 Natural Resources Damage Assessments, CFR § 990.20 (July 2000).

1497 15 CFR §990.20(a).

(b) *Assessments commenced before February 5, 1996*: "If trustees commenced a natural resource damage assessment for an oil discharge under 43 CFR part 11 prior to February 5, 1996 they may complete the assessment in compliance with 43 CFR part 11, or they may elect to use this part, and obtain a rebuttable presumption."[1498]

(c) *Multiple Causes or Oil and hazardous substance mixtures*: "For natural resource damages resulting from a discharge or release of a mixture of oil and hazardous substances, trustees must use 43 CFR part 11 in order to obtain a rebuttable presumption."[1499]

Except in the situations specifically mentioned above, generally, the provisions of the NOAA's Damage Assessment and Restoration Regulations apply exclusively to oil spill cases and supercedes the provisions of the CERCLA regulations. The NOAA regulation also provides that any determination or assessment of damages to natural resources made by a trustee in accordance with this part shall have the force and effect of a rebuttable presumption on behalf of the trustee in any administrative or judicial proceeding under OPA. The practical effect of this "rebuttable presumption" is not totally clear. As will be explained below, CECRLA also allows this "rebuttable presumption." One commentator has argued that, consistent with Rule 301, Federal Rules of Evidence, the CERCLA presumption should only shift the burden of coming forward with evidence to the defendant, and should leave the burden of persuasion on the trustee plaintiffs.[1500] Since the CERCLA rebuttable presumption is identical to that provided for in the OPA, one could also argue that consistent with Rule 301, Federal Rules of Evidence, the OPA "rebuttable presumption" should only shift the burden of coming forward with evidence to the RP, and should leave the burden of persuasion on the trustee-plaintiffs.

---

1498 Id. at §990.20(b).

1499 Id. §990.20(c).

1500 Menefee, Recovery for Natural Resource Damages Under Superfund: The Role of the Rebuttable Presumption, 12 Envtl. L. Rep, (ELI) 15,057, 15,061-64 (1982).

Once the RP successfully comes forward with sufficient rebuttal evidence the rebuttable presumption dies.[1501]

It is important to undertake a brief analysis of the DOI regulations for several reasons. Firstly, because the NOAA regulations specifically provide that where there is a discharge of mixture of oil and hazardous substances the DOI regulations must be applied by the trustees. Secondly, because the NOAA regulations permit trustees who commenced a natural resource damage assessment for an oil discharge under the DOI regulations (43 CFR part 11) prior to February 5, 1996 to continue using those regulations. Thirdly, because until the passage of the NOAA regulations in 1996 by the NOAA, the DOI regulations applied with full force to all OPA cases. Fourthly, because it is vital to a better understanding and appreciation of the NOAA regulations which will be discussed later in this chapter.

### A.I(a)(i) DOI's NRDA Regulations

Under CERCLA natural resource damages is defined as monetary compensation for injury to, destruction of, or loss of natural resources.[1502] Restoration or rehabilitation means actions undertaken to return an injured resource to its baseline condition, as measured in terms of the injured resource's physical, chemical, or biological properties or the services it previously provided, when such actions are in addition to response actions completed or anticipated, and when such actions exceed the level of response actions determined appropriate to the site pursuant

---

1501 See *General Elec. Co. v. U.S. Dept. of Commerce*, 128 F.3d 767, 772, 327 U.S.App.D.C. 33, 38 (D.C. Cir. 1997), where the court noted: "As agency counsel described it at oral argument, the rebuttable presumption thus functions as nothing more than a "burden shifting exercise." Whatever the rebuttable presumption means and however it will work in practice, issues we need not resolve at this time, one thing is clear--before trustees can take advantage of the presumption, they must prove that their damage assesments are "reliable and valid for the particular incident."

1502 CERCLA §9607(a)(4)(C).

to the National Contingency Plan (NCP).[1503] "Natural resource damage assessment" or "assessment" is the process of collecting, compiling, and analyzing information, statistics, or data through prescribed methodologies to determine damages for injuries to natural resources.[1504]

Pursuant to express statutory authority, the Department of the Interior (Interior) issued regulations to provide a framework and standards for the NRDA process.[1505] The Superfund law (CERCLA) authorizes NRDA when there is a release of a hazardous substance (oil was included in the past until the NOAA regulations were promulgated in 1996). The Clean Water Act (CWA) or the FWPCA authorizes NRDA when there is a discharge of a hazardous substance or oil into navigable waters. Certain categories of parties responsible for a release or discharge, known as "responsible parties" (RPs) are liable for natural resource damages if the release or discharge results in injury to natural resources. Natural resources include land, fish, wildlife, plants, air, and water that the government manages on behalf of the public. Only designated "trustees" may recover natural resource damages. The primary Federal trustees are Interior (including the Fish and Wildlife Service, the National Park Service, and the Bureau of Land Management), NOAA, and the Department of Agriculture's Forest Service. State and Tribal trustees commonly include fish and game, park, and water management authorities.

Trustees must use recovered damages to fund restoration, rehabilitation, replacement, or acquisition of the equivalent of the injured or lost natural resources. As earlier explained, these actions, often referred to collectively as "restoration," are principally designed to return injured resources to baseline (i.e., the condition that would have existed if the release or discharge had not occurred). Restoration may also compensate for the public's interim loss of injured resources from the onset of injury until baseline is restored. In contrast, response actions, normally conducted by the U.S. Environmental Protection Agency (EPA) or State or Tribal response agencies, focus on controlling exposure to a released substance

1503 43 CFR §11.14(ll).

1504 43 CFR s 11.14(aa).

1505 See. 43 CFR §11.10-§11.93.

and removing the substance in order to protect human health and the environment from threats of additional harm. Thus, although response can reduce or even eliminate the need for restoration in some cases, the two types of action are distinct.

The hazardous substance NRDA regulations provide optional procedures that trustees may use to conduct their assessments. Trustees generally use the regulations as a framework for settlement negotiations with RPs. However, if trustees and RPs fail to reach settlement and trustees must file suit, Federal and State trustees who comply with the regulations have an advantage, known as a "rebuttable presumption," in litigation.[1506] This means that the trustees determinations as to damages will be taken as valid unless the RP can show in evidence that it is not valid. The regulations provide an administrative process that involves preparation of various documents and coordination with interested parties. The regulations also include a range of technical procedures for the actual determination of injuries and damages.

Under the regulations, there are four phases of an NRDA: Preassessment, Assessment Plan, Assessment Implementation, and Post-Assessment.[1507] Once trustees discover or are informed about a release or discharge, they may enter the Preassessment phase.[1508] Based on certain requirements, trustees perform a Preassessment Screen to determine whether additional assessment work is warranted.[1509] They document their determination, and if work is warranted, they proceed to the Assessment Plan phase.[1510] During the Assessment Plan phase, trustees prepare an Assessment Plan describing how they intend to determine injuries and damages.[1511] This phase also involves coordination among trustees and between trustees and response agencies, involvement of the RP, and

1506 42 USCA §9607(f)(2)(C).

1507 43 CFR §11.13.

1508 Id.

1509 43 CFR §11.23.

1510 Id.

1511 43 CFR §11.30-38.

opportunity for public comment on the Assessment Plan.[1512] After the Assessment Plan is drafted and made available for public review, trustees enter the Assessment Implementation phase, in which they perform the work described in the Assessment Plan.[1513]

The regulations contain two general types of assessment procedures for determining injury and damages. The procedures are the "Type A" procedures and the "Type B" procedures. "Type A" procedures are standardized procedures for simplified assessments requiring minimal field observation that are available to determine damages for minor spills in certain environments.[1514] "Type B" procedures are more detailed procedures for assessments in other cases.[1515] The regulations provide criteria for using a type A procedure, type B procedures, or both.

The Department of Interior is developing type A procedures in stages. Currently there are appears to be two type A procedures: one for minor spills in coastal or marine areas that incorporates a computer model called the Natural Resource Damages Assessment Model for Coastal and Marine Environments (NRDAM/CME); and one for minor spills in the Great Lakes that incorporates a computer model called the Natural Resource Damages Assessment Model for Great Lakes Environments (NRDAM/GLE).[1516] Trustees must supply a number of data inputs to operate the NRDAM/CME and the NRDAM/GLE. After trustees supply the data inputs, the models themselves perform the remaining calculations necessary to establish if there has been an injury, quantify the extent of injury, estimate the cost of restoration actions, and value economic losses.[1517] Trustees supply limited data, such as the amount and duration of the spill; the name of the substance that entered the coastal or marine environment; mass or volume of the identified substance; year, month, day, and hour when the identified substance first entered a coastal or marine environment; latitude

---

1512 Id.

1513 43 CFR §11.40.

1514 Id.

1515 43 CFR 11.60.

1516 43 CFR §11.40 as amended by FR 60457, 60459 (1997).

1517 62 FR 60457, 60457 (1997).

and longitude, stated in degrees and decimal minutes, where the identified substance entered a coastal or marine environment; at least one set of data on prevailing wind conditions for each day of the 30- day period beginning 24 hours before the identified substance entered a coastal or marine environment, (each set must include: Wind velocity stated in knots or meters per second; and Corresponding wind direction stated in the degree angle of the wind's origin; response actions taken (volume of substance removed, time frame of removal of substances; documentation that a closure was ordered by an appropriate agency as a result of the release (provinces where closure occurred, length of shoreline closed, number of days of closure); quarterly implicit price deflator for the Gross National Product (base year 1992) for the quarter in which the identified substance entered a coastal or marine environment; currents (for a rectangular geographic area encompassing the area affected by the release stated in terms of the northern- and southern-most latitude, and the eastern- and western-most longitude); hour of high tide on the day that the identified substance entered a coastal or marine environment (tidal range at point that the identified substance entered a coastal or marine environment stated in meters; and whether the tide in the area affected by the release is diurnal (i.e., completes one full cycle every day) or semi-diurnal (i.e., completes two full cycles every day)); and modifications to the NRDAM/CME Databases (if any) (documentation of the source of the modification).[1518]

The NRDAM/CME and NRDAM/GLE determine the physical fate of the spilled substance, and estimate acute lethal effects. The models then estimate and sum the cost of restoring baseline and the value of certain lost interim public uses, such as hunting, fishing, bird-watching, and beach visitation. Because type A procedures are intended for minor spills, the regulations place a $100,000 cap on their use if trustees intend to obtain a rebuttable presumption.[1519]

The Type B model is intended for application in large and exceptionally destructive or damaging spills or releases.[1520] When trustees use type

1518 43 CFR §11, App. II, §11.41.

1519 43 CFR §11.44.

1520 42 USCA §9651(c)(3).

B procedures, they determine injury and damages through scientific and economic studies.[1521] The regulations include both specific definitions of injury for each category of natural resource and provisions allowing trustees to establish additional injuries if certain criteria are met.[1522] For example, for ground water resources, an injury to the ground water resource has resulted from the discharge of oil or release of a hazardous substance if the following changes in the physical or chemical quality of the resource is measured: "(i) Concentrations of substances in excess of drinking water standards, established by sections 1411-1416 of the Safe Drinking Water Act, or by other Federal or State laws or regulations that establish such standards for drinking water, in ground water that was potable before the discharge or release."[1523]

The regulations provide guidance on the selection of testing and sampling methodologies to determine whether an injury has occurred and whether a pathway of exposure exists.[1524] A "pathway" is the route or medium through which oil or a hazardous substance is or was transported from the source of the discharge or release to the injured resource.[1525] If an injury has occurred and a pathway exists, trustees then quantify the injury by: (1) identifying the functions, or "services," such as habitat, recreation, erosion control, provided by the resource; (2) determining the baseline level of such services; and (3) quantifying the reduction in service levels as a result of the release or discharge.[1526] "Services" means the physical and biological functions performed by the resource including the human uses of those functions. These services are the result of the physical, chemical, or biological quality of the resource."[1527]

After determining and quantifying injury, trustees identify a reasonable number of possible restoration alternatives, including natu-

---

1521 43 CFR §11.61.

1522 43 CFR §11.62.

1523 Id. at §11.62(c).

1524 43 CFR §11.63, §11.64.

1525 43 CFR § 11.14(dd).

1526 43 CFR §11.70-72.

1527 43 CFR § 11.14(nn).

ral recovery.[1528] Trustees select one of the alternatives based on several factors, including technical feasibility, relationship of costs to benefits, and consistency with response.[1529] Trustees then document their decisions in a Restoration and Compensation Determination Plan, which is subject to public review and comment.[1530] After the public comment period, trustees estimate the cost of implementing the selected restoration alternative.[1531] Trustees may also, but are not required to, determine the value of the associated public interim losses using methodologies authorized by the regulations. The trustees would need to determine the compensable value which is the amount of money required to compensate the public for the loss in services provided by the injured resources between the time of the discharge or release and the time the resources and the services those resources provided are fully returned to their baseline conditions.[1532] The compensable value includes the value of lost public use of the services provided by the injured resources, plus lost nonuse values such as existence and bequest values. "Existence value" is the value of ensuring just the existence of natural resources, knowing that one may never use the resource. The benefit derived from it is the mere knowledge of the existence of the resource. "Bequest value" is the benefit derived from knowing a resource will be passed on to future generations.

Compensable value is measured by changes in consumer surplus, economic rent, and any fees or other payments collectable by a Federal or State agency or an Indian tribe for a private party's use of the natural resources; and any economic rent accruing to a private party because the Federal or State agency or Indian tribe does not charge a fee or price for the use of the resources.[1533] Use value is the value of the resources to the public attributable to the direct use of the services provided by the

1528 43 CFR § 11.73(a)(1), §11. 80(c).

1529 43 CFR §11.82.

1530 43 CFR §11.81.

1531 43 CFR §11.83.

1532 43 CFR §11.83(c)(1).

1533 Id.

natural resources.[1534] Nonuse value is the difference between compensable value and use value, as those terms are used in this section of the DOI regulations.[1535] Estimation of option and existence values shall be used only if the authorized official determines that no use values can be determined. The DOI regulations give the trustees the option of choosing one or more of many alternative methodologies depending on the particular circumstances of each case. They are as follows:

(a) Valuation methodologies: The authorized official may choose among the valuation methodologies listed in this section of the DOI regulations to estimate willingness to pay (WTP) or may choose other methodologies provided that the methodology can satisfy the acceptance criterion in paragraph (c)(3) of this section (which provides that other valuation methodologies that measure compensable value in accordance with the public's WTP, in a cost-effective manner, are acceptable methodologies to determine compensable value under this part).[1536] Nothing in this section of the DOI regulations precludes the use of a combination of valuation methodologies so long as the authorized official does not double count or use techniques that allow any double counting to be estimated in the final damage calculation. This allows for flexibility to trustees when undertaking the valuation of a lost resource. The limit put on them with regard to double count ensures that the principle of "no double recovery" (emphasis mine) imposed on trustees by CERCLA is not rendered nugatory.[1537]

(b) Market price methodology: This methodology may be used if the natural resources are traded in the market. In using this methodology, the authorized official should make a determination as to whether the market for the resources is reasonably competitive. If the authorized official determines that the market for the resources, or the services provided by the resources, is reasonably

1534 Id.

1535 Id.

1536 43 CFR §11.83(C)(2).

1537 Id.

competitive, the diminution in the market price of the injured resources, or the lost services, may be used to determine the compensable value of the injured resources. For instance the amount it costs to buy or replace an endangered specie or other sea creatures which may not be endangered species.[1538]

(c) Appraisal methodology: Where sufficient information exists, the appraisal methodology may be used. In using this methodology, compensable value should be measured, to the extent possible, in accordance with the applicable sections of the "Uniform Appraisal Standards for Federal Land Acquisition" (Uniform Appraisal Standards), Interagency Land Acquisition Conference, Washington, DC, 1973 (incorporated by reference, see 43 CFR § 11.18). The measure of compensable value under this appraisal methodology will be the difference between the with- and without-injury appraisal value determined by the comparable sales approach as described in the Uniform Appraisal Standards.[1539]

(d) Factor income methodology: "If the injured resources are inputs to a production process, which has as an output a product with a well-defined market price, the factor income methodology may be used. This methodology may be used to determine the economic rent associated with the use of resources in the production process. This methodology is sometimes referred to as the "reverse value added" methodology. The factor income methodology may be used to measure the in-place value of the resources."[1540] For example, if a trustee extracts groundwater and uses materials such as chlorine to purify the water for distribution and sale to households, any change in net income caused by contamination would be a measure of the value of the ground-water resource (assuming the price of the water and variable costs of production do not change).[1541]

---

1538 Id.

1539 43 CFR §11.83(c) (2).

1540 Id.

1541 See PTI Environmental Services, Technical Memorandum 2, Assessing Damages to Ground Water Resources From Releases of Hazardous Substances, at 14 (Prepared for

(e) Travel cost methodology: "The travel cost methodology may be used to determine a value for the use of a specific area. An individual's incremental travel costs to an area are used as a proxy for the price of the services of that area. Compensable value of the area to the traveler is the difference between the value of the area with and without a discharge or release. When regional travel cost models exist, they may be used if appropriate."[1542] This method is not relevant to assessing damages to a particular natural resource except in cases where there is a direct connection between the recreational activity and the natural resources injured.[1543] For instance, contamination of hot springs or mineral baths resulting in injury to other resources, such as fisheries, which provide recreational services.[1544]

(f) Hedonic pricing methodology: The hedonic pricing methodology may be used to determine the value of nonmarketed resources by an analysis of private market choices. The demand for nonmarketed natural resources is thereby estimated indirectly by an analysis of commodities that are traded in a market.[1545]

(g) Unit value methodology: Unit values are preassigned dollar values for various types of nonmarketed recreational or other experiences by the public. Where feasible, unit values in the region of the affected resources and unit values that closely resemble the recreational or other experience lost with the affected resources may be used.

(h) Contingent valuation methodology: This is the most controversial of all the valuation methodologies. The contingent valuation methodology includes all techniques that set up hypothetical markets to elicit an individual's economic valuation of a natural

---

Washington Dept. of Ecology, June 1991).

1542 43 CFR §11.83(c) (2)(iv).

1543 See PTI Environmental Services, Technical Memorandum 2, Assessing Damages to Ground Water Resources From Releases of Hazardous Substances, at 15 (Prepared for Washington Dept. of Ecology, June 1991).

1544 Id.

1545 Id.

resource.[1546] This methodology can determine use values and explicitly determine option and existence values. This methodology may be used to determine lost use values of injured natural resources. The DOI regulations emphasize that the use of the contingent valuation methodology to explicitly estimate option and existence values should be used only if the authorized official determines that no use values can be determined. The DOI regulations also permit other valuation methodologies. It provides that other valuation methodologies that measure compensable value in accordance with the public's Willingness To Pay (WTP), in a cost-effective manner, are acceptable methodologies to determine compensable value under the DOI regulations.[1547]

Once the trustees have calculated damages, they enter the Post-Assessment phase. In this phase, the trustees prepare a Report of Assessment detailing the results of the Assessment Implementation phase.[1548] The trustees present the Report to the RPs, along with a demand for damages and reasonable assessment costs.[1549] Trustees have the authority to settle their damages claims at any time. However, if the RPs do not agree to pay within 60 days of receipt of the demand, then the trustees may file suit.[1550] Once damages have been awarded or settlement has been reached, trustees officials establish an account for the recovered damages and prepare a post-assessment Restoration Plan.[1551] All sums (damage claim and assessment costs) recovered pursuant to section 9607(f) of CERCLA or sections 311(f)(4) and (5) of the CWA by the Federal government acting as trustee shall be retained by the trustee, without further appropriation, in a separate account in the U. S. Treasury.[1552] For state trustees such sums shall be placed in a separate

1546 Id.
1547 43 CFR §11.83(c)(3).
1548 43 CFR §11.90.
1549 43 CFR §11.91.
1550 43 CFR §11.91(d).
1551 43 CFR §11.92.
1552 43 CFR §11.92(a)(1).

state treasury account.[1553] Indian tribe trustees must keep such sums in a tribal treasury or it should be placed by the responsible party or parties in an interest bearing account payable in trust to the Indian tribe.[1554]The trustees must provide for public comment on the Plan and then implement the Plan using the natural resource damages recovered.[1555]

### A.I (a)(ii) The Concept Of Natural Resources Damage In OPA

The concept of natural resources damage assessment in the OPA is based on the concept of natural resources damage assessment in CERCLA. The rules take into consideration existing common law rules for developing a theory of natural resource damages.[1556] A fundamental principle of the theory developed in the rule is that natural resource damages are compensatory, not punitive. CERCLA itself calls for compensatory rather than punitive damages,[1557] so also does the OPA. This principle is consistent with the common law, which disfavors punitive damages, and is basic to the theory underlying the common law of damages, which is that money can be used to provide substitutionary relief. The money awarded as compensation using common law principles represents a rough measure that approximately represents the value of the thing that is lost.[1558] Rules have been developed by the courts for the measurement of damages so that cases can be resolved, and perhaps more importantly, settled in accordance with common law principles. Settlements become possible because the range of outcomes given a particular set of facts is predictable. The mandate to establish regulations for the assessment of damages to natural resources included a mandate to develop methodologies that are based upon the best

1553 43 CFR §11.92(a)(2).
1554 43 CFR §11.92(a)(3).
1555 43 CFR §11.93.
1556 51 FR 27674, 27680.
1557 Id. at 27680.
1558 Id.

available procedures.[1559] This directive implies that compensatory damages were intended. The expensive and complex process of studying existing injury measurement and economic compensation techniques would have been unnecessary if punitive damages were intended.[1560] The procedures for determining punitive damages could have involved the simple publication of penalty fee tables.[1561] Finally, it should be noted that a variety of criminal or other punitive statutes may apply to actions for which natural resource damages may be sought. Through those statutes, penalties may be sought where appropriate.[1562] That is why section 2718(a) & (c) of the OPA specifically allows the Federal government, state governments and political subdivision of states to impose additional requirements, liabilities and civil or criminal penalties on responsible parties.[1563]

**A.I(a)(iii)What the Federal On Scene Coordinator is required to do with regard to trustees.**

As explained earlier, Federal On-Scene Coordinators (FOSC) are US Coast Guard officers who have been delegated the authority to ensure effective and immediate removal of a discharge, and mitigate or prevent a substantial threat of a discharge of oil or hazardous substance release into U.S. surface waters.[1564] The FOSC verifies whether a particular cost was incurred for removal and was consistent with the National Contingency Plan (NCP). This shows that the FOSC's ability to carry out his or her functions effectively is pivotal to well-organized oil spill response, assessment, and restoration activities.

---

1559 Id.

1560 Id.

1561 Id.

1562 Id

1563 33 USCA 2718 (a) & (c).

1564 See U.S. Coast Guard Federal On Scene Coordinator (FOSC), Finance and Resource Management

Field Guide, at 17. <http://www.uscg.mil/d1/units/msobos/resources/FFARMGuide.pdf>

During preparedness activities On-Scene Coordinators must:

1. Consult trustees in writing the Fish and Wildlife and Sensitive Environments Plan of the Area Contingency Plan: Section 300.210(c )(4) of the National Contingency Plan (NCP) calls for preparation of a plan that identifies fish and wildlife and sensitive environments in the area covered by the Area Contingency Plan (ACP) and strategies for protecting and treating them, for inclusion in the ACP. The plan is to be prepared in consultation with the U.S. Fish and Wildlife Service in the Department of the Interior and the National Oceanic and Atmospheric Administration in the Department of Commerce, and other interested natural resource management agencies and parties. This list essentially covers the natural resource trustees.

   In developing the fish and wildlife and sensitive environments plan for the ACP, the On-Scene Coordinator should contact all trustees responsible for resources in the area under consideration. This will usually include the Department of the Interior, the Department of Commerce through NOAA, other Federal land managers in the area, State natural resource agencies, and tribal trustees in the area. Subpart G of the NCP calls for trustees to provide information on sensitive environments and assistance in identifying or recommending response techniques in the ACP.[1565]
2. On-Scene Coordinators must request trustee approval of preauthorization plans for dispersants and other chemical countermeasures: Under the NCP, On-Scene Coordinators must obtain the concurrence of the Department of Commerce and Department of the Interior natural resource trustees for plans pre-approving use of chemical countermeasures during emergency response.

During response activities, On-Scene Coordinators must:

1. Notify trustees of incidents:[1566] Trustees must be notified of spills and releases so they can begin taking appropriate actions. The

1565 40 CFR 300.615(c )(3)(i).

1566 40 CFR 300.135(j)(1), 300.305(e), and 300.320(a)(5).

NCP requires the On-Scene Coordinator to notify all trustees, not just the Federal trustees. The Area Contingency Plan should include a notification protocol worked out between the On-Scene Coordinator and the Federal, State, and Indian tribal trustees. In the case of spills that cross an international boundary, the On-Scene Coordinator may be required to notify foreign trustees as well. The trustee notification requirement is different from the Regional Response Team (RRT) notification requirement. Some trustees, usually the Interior and Commerce trustees, are RRT members, so when the RRT is notified, these trustees will be, also. Other trustees will not be covered by RRT notification and must be notified separately and even when the RRT is not notified. The On-Scene Coordinator is not obliged to notify the trustees him or herself, but must ensure that timely notification occurs.

2. Consult trustees about protection priorities and methods: Section 300.135(j)(2) of the NCP requires the On-Scene Coordinator to coordinate all response activities with the affected natural resource trustees, and, for oil spills, to consult with the affected trustees on the appropriate removal action to be taken. During this consultation, the trustees will advise the On-Scene Coordinator as to which resources are considered most sensitive to the spilled material. The requirement to consult trustees on actions to remove oil applies to all trustees, not just the Federal trustees.
3. Share non-monetary response resources with natural resource trustees conducting Natural Resource Damage Assessment activities so long as this does not hinder response activities: Sections 300.305(e) and 615(c )(3)(iii) of the NCP provides for the On-Scene Coordinator to make response resources such as aircraft, vessels, and booms, available to natural resource trustees for use in NRDA activities, so long as these activities and use of these resources do not interfere with response actions. This may also involve advising trustees when space is available on over-flights of the spill area.
4. Provide funding from the On-Scene Coordinator's budgetary ceiling for the incident to pay for natural resource trustees' assistance

to the On-Scene Coordinator on response to oil spills: The Oil Spill Liability Trust Fund is available under certain circumstances to fund removal of oil under section 311 of the Clean Water Act. Section 300.335(b) of the NCP provides that Federal agencies assisting the On-Scene Coordinator in response to an oil spill may be reimbursed. Trustees apply to the On-Scene Coordinator for funding for response activities. The On-Scene Coordinator is responsible for approving the funding level and the work that trustees perform with this money. Because this funding is restricted to removal activities, it may not be used for any Natural Resources Damage Assessment (NRDA) activities. Trustees submit all required documentation and requests for reimbursement to the On-Scene Coordinator.

### A.I (a)(iv) National Oceanic and Atmospheric Administration Oil And Hazardous Substance Spill Cost Reimbursement

As earlier indicated, stewardship of the Nation's natural resources is shared among several Federal agencies, states and tribal trustees. However, NOAA is the principal Federal trustee for natural resources in the coastal and marine environment.[1567] NOAA's trust resources include, sediment and water quality, anadromous species (fish, like salmon, that spawn in freshwater and then migrate to the sea); commercial and recreational fishery resources; endangered and threatened marine species and their habitats (e.g., sea turtles); marine mammals (e.g., whales, dolphins and seals); marshes, mangroves, sea grass beds, coral reefs, and other coastal habitats; and all resources associated with National Marine Sanctuaries and National Estuarine Research Reserves (e.g., coral reefs and sea grasses). NOAA provides an integrated approach to natural resource damage assessment and restoration. Where possible, NOAA nego-

1567 About DARP, NOAA's web site for the Damage Assessment and Restoration Program (DARP) <http://www.darp.noaa.gov/about.htm> (Last Updated September 7, 2000).

tiates cooperative settlements with the parties responsible for the injury, minimizing litigation. By working together with responsible parties and co-trustees to collect data, conduct assessments and carry out restoration actions, NOAA works to restore a clean and healthy environment as quickly and effectively as possible.

In an appropriation statute called the Departments of Commerce, Justice, And State, The Judiciary, And Related Agencies Appropriations Act, 1991, the United States Congress provided, that notwithstanding any other provision of law, in fiscal year 1991 and thereafter, sums provided by any party or governmental entity for natural resource damage assessment, response or restoration activities conducted or to be conducted by the NOAA as a result of any injury to the marine environment and/or resources for which the NOAA "acts as trustee" (emphasis mine) of said marine environment and/or resources, shall be deposited in the Damage Assessment and Restoration Revolving Fund and said funds so deposited shall remain available until expended.[1568] In 1992 the United States Congress passed the National Oceanic And Atmospheric Administration Authorization Act into law.[1569] This statute provided that notwithstanding any other provision of law, amounts received by the United States "as reimbursement of expenses" related to oil or hazardous substance spill response activities, or natural resource damage assessment, restoration, rehabilitation, replacement, or acquisition activities, conducted (or to be conducted) by the NOAA-- (1) shall be deposited into the Fund; (2) shall be available, without fiscal year limitation and without apportionment, for use in accordance with the law under which the activities are conducted; and (3) shall not be considered to be an augmentation of appropriations.[1570] The term 'expenses' is defined to include incremental and base salaries, ships, aircraft, and associated indirect costs. But it does not include base salaries and benefits of National Oceanic and Atmospheric Administration Support Coordinators."[1571]

---

1568 104 Stat 2101, 2105, Pub.L 101-515 (HR 5021), November 5, 1990.

1569 106 Stat 4270, 4282, October 29, 1992, 33 USCA §2706.

1570 106 Stat 4282, Pub.L 102-567 (HR 2130), October 29, 1992.

1571 106 Stat 4282, Pub.L 102-567 (HR 2130), October 29, 1992

## A.I (a)(v) NOAA's Rapid Assessment Program

NOAA's Rapid Assessment Program (RAP) consists of an on-call team of NOAA scientists and contractors responsible for evaluating spills of oil and hazardous substances.[1572] Following the accidental release of such materials, NOAA, as natural resource trustee, has only a brief window of opportunity to begin assessing the impacts. The emergency nature of spills makes it difficult to design and implement effective field studies. Thus, in January 1992, NOAA's Damage Assessment and Restoration staff created the RAP.[1573]

### Goal

The goal of the RAP is to collect perishable data and information, photographs and videotape in a timely manner to determine the need for a natural resource damage assessment. Information collected soon after the spill is critical to designing assessment studies, initiating restoration planning, and may be used later as evidence in support of a damage claim.[1574]

### Why RAP was Created

In the past, the first efforts following a spill focused on clean-up. Damage assessment studies or surveys lagged weeks or months behind the response effort.[1575] Although responders may have collected information and samples useful to the natural resource damage assessment and restoration process, damage assessment was necessarily a secondary

---

1572 National Oceanic Atmospheric Administration Rapid Assessment Program, <http://www.darp.noaa.gov/darporg/rap.htm> (last updated April 14, 1997).

1573 Id.

1574 Id.

1575 Id.

concern.[1576] The RAP team was developed to provide a quick response capability exclusively for damage assessment.[1577]

### How RAP Works

The RAP has established emergency notification procedures with the United States Coast Guard and within NOAA to ensure prompt response to significant spills.[1578] Once alerted to a spill, RAP staff consult with co-trustees at the state and federal levels and evaluate the potential for injury to NOAA trust resources.[1579] If the spill is expected to have significant effects, NOAA staff determine whether to initiate natural resource damage assessment and restoration activities based on the scientific, economic and legal merits of the case, as well as the potential for the successful restoration of injured resources. In many cases, the spiller of the oil works cooperatively with NOAA to develop restoration-based settlements.[1580] To support RAP, NOAA has developed an emergency procedures manual and a comprehensive training program that provide guidance for the collection of environmental and economic data as well as internal consistency among NOAA staff and regional contractors.[1581] Natural resource economists may go to the spill site to evaluate the potential for recreational and other human-use losses. Typical tasks conducted on-site by resource economists include collecting data on recreational and commercial uses affected by the spill, and documenting beach, fishing and waterway closures.[1582]

RAP is coordinated from Seattle, Washington and regional responders are located in Anchorage, Alaska; Sandy Hook, New Jersey; St.

1576 Id.

1577 Id.

1578 Id.

1579 Id.

1580 Id.

1581 Id.

1582 Id.

Petersburg, Florida; Seattle, Washington; Long Beach, California; and Silver Spring, Maryland. These NOAA regional scientists work full-time on damage assessment cases and are also the primary damage assessment responders for spills in their area.[1583] Additionally, NOAA has four rapid assessment contractors located in Seattle, Washington; Boston, Massachusetts; Narragansett, Rode Island; and Columbia, South Carolina. NOAA's quick response mechanism allows the mobilization of contractor personnel or other specialized support to the site of an incident within six hours of notification.[1584] NOAA staff have started regional pre-oil spill planning with Federal, state and tribal co-trustees.[1585] Because measuring the effects of oil spills is difficult and complex, increased emphasis on pre-oil spill planning will expedite assessment and permit cases to move more rapidly toward restoration.[1586]

## A.I(a)(vi) THE NATIONAL OCEANIC ATMOSPHERIC ADMINISTRATION'S FINAL RULES ON NATURAL RESOURCES DAMAGE ASSESSMENT AND RESTORATION

The regulations are codified in 15 CFR §§ 990.10 - 990.66 and are divided into six subparts. The regulation states in subpart A, that "the goal of the Oil Pollution Act of 1990 (OPA), 33 U.S.C. 2701 *et seq*., is to make the environment and public whole for injuries to natural resources and services resulting from an incident involving a discharge or substantial threat of a discharge of oil (incident)." The regulation provides further that:

"this goal is achieved through the return of the injured natural resources and services to baseline and compensation for interim losses of such natural resources and services from the date of the incident until recovery. The purpose

1583 Id.

1584 Id.

1585 Id.

1586 National Oceanic Atmospheric Administration Rapid Assessment Program, <http://www.darp.noaa.gov/darporg/rap.htm> (last updated April 14, 1997).

of this part is to promote expeditious and cost-effective restoration of natural resources and services injured as a result of an incident. To fulfill this purpose, this part provides a natural resource damage assessment process for developing a plan for restoration of the injured natural resources and services and pursuing implementation or funding of the plan by responsible parties. This part also provides an administrative process for involving interested parties in the assessment, a range of assessment procedures for identifying and evaluating injuries to natural resources and services, and a means for selecting restoration actions from a reasonable range of alternatives."[1587]

Assessment of natural resource damage under the final rule is divided into three phases: (1) the pre-assessment phase; (2) the restoration planning phase; and (3) the restoration implementation phase.

**1.** *The pre-assessment phase:* The purpose of this subpart is to provide a process by which trustees determine if they have jurisdiction to pursue restoration under OPA and, if so, whether it is appropriate to do so.[1588] "Upon learning of an incident, trustees must determine whether there is jurisdiction to pursue restoration under OPA." To reach this decision, trustees must decide if:

"(1) An incident has occurred, as defined in the OPA, 33 U.S.C. 2701(14)). (2) The incident is not:

(i) Permitted under a permit issued under federal, state, or local law; or

(ii) From a public vessel; or

(iii) From an onshore facility subject to the Trans-Alaska Pipeline Authority Act, 43 U.S.C. 1651, *et se.*; (3) Natural resources under the trusteeship of the trustee may have been, or may be, injured as a result of the incident.

(b) Proceeding with preassessment: If the conditions listed above are met, trustees may proceed under this part. If one of the conditions is not met, trustees may not take additional action under this part, except action to finalize this determination. Trustees may recover all reasonable assessment costs incurred up to this point provided that conditions

1587 Oil Pollution Act Regulations, Natural Resources Damage Assessments, CFR § 990.10 (July 2000).

1588 Determination of jurisdiction, 15 CFR § 990.41(a).

in paragraphs (a)(1) and (a)(2) of this section were met and actions were taken with the reasonable belief that natural resources or services under their trusteeship might have been injured as a result of the incident."[1589]

*Determination to conduct restoration plan:* "(a) If trustees determine that there is jurisdiction to pursue restoration under OPA, trustees must determine whether:
(1) Injuries have resulted, or are likely to result, from the incident;
(2) Response actions have not adequately addressed, or are not expected to address, the injuries resulting from the incident; and
(3) Feasible primary and/or compensatory restoration actions exist to address the potential injuries.[1590]

Injury is defined as an observable or measurable adverse change in a natural resource or impairment of a natural resource service. Injury may occur directly or indirectly to a natural resource and/or service. Injury incorporates the terms "destruction," "loss," and "loss of use" as provided in OPA.[1591] If these criteria are met, the trustees may issue a Notice of Intent to Conduct Restoration Planning."

*Proceeding with preassessment*: If the conditions listed in paragraph (a) of this section are met, trustees may proceed under § 990.44 of this part. If one of these conditions is not met, trustees may not take additional action under this part, except action to finalize this determination. However, trustees may recover all reasonable assessment costs incurred up to this point. "Trustees may conduct data collection and analyses that are reasonably related to Pre-assessment Phase activities.[1592] Data collection and analysis during the Preassessment Phase must be coordinated with response actions such that collection and analysis does not interfere with response actions." Trustees are allowed to collect and analyze the following types of data during the Preassessment Phase:

---

1589 Id. § 990.41(b).
1590 Id. § 990.42 (a)-(b).
1591 Id. § 990.30.
1592 Id. at §990.43.

"(a) Data reasonably expected to be necessary to make a determination of jurisdiction under § 990.41 of this part, or a determination to conduct restoration planning under § 990.42 of this part; (b) Ephemeral data; and (c) Information needed to design or implement anticipated assessment procedures under subpart E of this part."[1593]

The regulations also require that should the trustees decide to proceed with restoration planning, they have to open a publicly accessible administrative record to document the basis for their decisions pertaining to restoration.[1594] The administrative record should be opened concurrently with the publication of the Notice of Intent to Conduct Restoration Planning. "Depending on the nature and extent of the incident and assessment, the administrative record should include documents relied upon during the Assessment."[1595] It particularly requires Federal trustees to maintain the administrative record in a manner consistent with the Administrative Procedure Act.[1596] The construction of NOAA's final rule created a built-in defense for a responsible party against a trustee's Natural Resources Damage Assessment (NRDA) because the creation of an administrative record means that the NRDA is only subject to an "arbitrary and capricious" standard of review under the Administrative Procedure Act (APA).[1597]

2. *Restoration Planning Phase*: Restoration Planning is the second phase of the damage assessment process. The restoration planning phase is the fulcrum of the natural resource damage process. The purpose of this phase is twofold: the determination and quantification of the injury to natural resources; and the selection of a restoration plan.[1598]

---

1593 Id. § 990.43.

1594 Id. at §990..45(a).

1595 Id. § 990.45(a).

1596 5 U.S.C. §§551-59, §§701-06.

1597 See International Marine Carriers v.The Oil Spill Liability Trust Fund, 903 F. Supp. 1097, 1101, 1995 AMC 2072 (S.D. Tex 1994) (applying administrative record review to decisions made by the NPFC, concerning claims presented to the Fund under OPA); see also 5 U.S.C. § 702 (1994).

1598 15 CFR § 990.50 (July 2000).

Injury evaluation is divided into two proceedings: (1) injury determination and (2) injury quantification. "Injury" is defined quite vaguely as an observable or measurable adverse change in a natural resource or impairment of a natural resource service.[1599] The injury determination process consists of analyzing the exposure of the resource to the discharged oil and whether a pathway exists from the discharge to the resource,[1600] establishing a causal link between the incident and the injury. Once the existence of injury is determined, the trustees proceed to quantifying the injury.[1601] Injury quantification consists of comparing the degree of injury to the baseline condition of the resource. Baseline means the condition of the natural resources and services that would have existed had the incident not occurred. Baseline data may be estimated using historical data, reference data, control data, or data on incremental changes (e.g., number of dead animals), alone or in combination, as appropriate.[1602] The purpose of injury quantification is to clarify the needed scale and design of future restoration actions. To quantify the injury the trustees are free to use a variety of conceptual bases, including the physical extent of damages or services lost. The trustees must also consider the time necessary for natural recovery of the resources.[1603] This part of the regulations has been criticized as being inadequate because the trustees are given very speculative bases for quantifying injury, and the cost of restoration is not relevant in the injury quantification process.[1604] It would be better to put off quantifying the injury until the restoration selection process.[1605]

After determining and quantifying injury, the trustees must develop a plan to restore the injured natural resource. Before selecting their preferred restoration plan, the trustees must develop and consider a range

1599 Id. at §990.30.

1600 Id. at §990.51(b)(2).

1601 Id. § 990.51.

1602 Id. § 990.30.

1603 Id. § 990.53(b)(2).

1604 Thomas J. Schoenbaum, Analysis of The Department of Commerce's Final Rule On Natural Resources Damages, 3 Mar. L. Prac. 1122, 1124 (1996).

1605 Id. at 1124.

of possible alternatives, including natural (no action) restoration.[1606] Each alternative must provide for two different restoration requirements: (1) a primary restoration action, which consists of a plan to return the damaged area to its baseline physical, chemical, and biological condition; and (2) compensatory restoration, which is a monetary damage assessment that represents the interim resource loss between the time of damage to the time of full recovery.[1607]

In selecting between alternatives the trustees must employ a process referred to in the regulations as scaling, which ensures that the restoration action appropriately addresses the injury resulting from the discharge. Scaling appears to be a way for determining the appropriate extent of a restoration action. The scaling process, which is employed both for primary and compensatory restoration, is an analysis of the injury on the basis of resources and/or services lost.[1608] This appears to be another exercise in attempting to quantify the damage caused by the incident; in this respect scaling is a duplication of the injury quantification process. If the trustees determine that neither the resource or service approaches to scaling are appropriate, they may use a valuation approach. In this proceeding natural resources must be explicitly valued in monetary terms. Both use and non-use values can be considered. For the latter, a wide variety of speculative techniques are allowable, including contingent valuation, hedonic price models and models of market supply and demand.[1609]

After the trustees have developed a reasonable range of restoration alternatives under § 990.53, they are required to evaluate the proposed alternatives based on, at a minimum:

> "(1) The cost to carry out the alternative; (2) The extent to which each alternative is expected to meet the trustees' goals and objectives in returning the injured natural resources and services to baseline and/or compensating for interim losses; (3) The likelihood of success of each alternative; (4) The extent to

---

1606 15 CFR § 990.53.

1607 Id. § 990.53 (c).

1608 Id. § 990.53(d)(2).

1609 Id. § 990.53(d)(3).

which each alternative will prevent future injury as a result of the incident, and avoid collateral injury as a result of implementing the alternative; (5) The extent to which each alternative benefits more than one natural resource and/or service; and (6) The effect of each alternative on public health and safety."[1610]

Once the trustees have developed a range of restoration alternatives, they must select a restoration plan after public review and comment.[1611] The trustees must prepare and circulate both a Draft Restoration Plan and a Final Restoration Plan for public comment before making their selection.[1612] The Draft Restoration Plan should include:

"(i) A summary of injury assessment procedures used; (ii) A description of the nature, degree, and spatial and temporal extent of injuries resulting from the incident; (iii) The goals and objectives of restoration; (iv) The range of restoration alternatives considered, and a discussion of how such alternatives were developed under Sec. 990.53 of this part, and evaluated under § 990.54 of this part; (v) Identification of the trustees' tentative preferred alternative(s); (vi) A description of past and proposed involvement of the responsible parties in the assessment; and (vii) A description of monitoring for documenting restoration effectiveness, including performance criteria that will be used to determine the success of restoration or need for interim corrective action."[1613]

3. *Restoration Implementation Phase:* Upon completion of the Restoration Planning Phase, the trustees must implement the decisions concerning restoration. These tasks include: (1) closing the administrative record;[1614] (2) presenting a demand for implementation and/or the payment of damages by the responsible parties;[1615] (3) monitoring and supervising

---

1610 Id. § 990.54(a)(1)-(6).
1611 Id. § 990.55(a).
1612 Id. § 990.55(a).
1613 Id. § 990.55(b)(1)(i)-(vii).
1614 Id. § 990.61(a).
1615 Id. § 990.62(a).

restoration actions;[1616] and (4) determining that final restoration has been achieved.[1617] The trustee can enforce their determinations by bringing a civil suit or by seeking an appropriation from the Oil Spill Liability Trust Fund.[1618]

*Coordination among trustees*: In order to prevent a situation where many trustees (Federal v. State Trustees, Indian Tribe Trustees v. State Trustees) may have to litigate against each other, the NOAA regulations provides a mechanism for coordination among multiple trustees. This may not arise in typical oil pollution incidents, but it could happen occasionally. The regulations provide that if an incident affects the interests of multiple trustees, the trustees should act jointly in order to ensure that full restoration is achieved without double recovery of damages. For joint assessments, trustees must designate one or more Lead Administrative Trustees to act as coordinators.[1619] Lead Administrative Trustees (or LAT) are the trustees who are selected by all participating trustees, whose natural resources or services are injured by an incident, for the purpose of coordinating natural resource damage assessment activities. The LAT(s) should also facilitate communication between the On Scene Coordinator (OSC is the United Coast Guard Official that supervises clean up response) and other natural resource trustees regarding their activities during the response phase.

"If there is a reasonable basis for dividing the natural resource damage assessment, trustees may act independently, so long as there is no double recovery of damages. Trustees may develop pre-incident or incident-specific memoranda of understanding to coordinate their activities."[1620]

*Participation of Responsible Parties :* (1) Invitation : Trustees must invite the responsible parties to get involved in the natural resource damage assessment.[1621] The invitation to participate should be in writing, and a written response by the responsible parties is needed to confirm the

1616 Id. § 990.66(a)(3).
1617 Id. § 990.66(a)(4).
1618 Id. § 990.64.
1619 15 CFR §990.14.
1620 Id. §990.14(a)(2)-(3).
1621 Id. §990.14(c)(1)-(4).

interest in participation. (2) Timing: The invitation to participate ought to be extended to known responsible parties as soon as possible, but not later than the delivery of the "Notice of Intent to Conduct Restoration Planning," to the responsible party.[1622] (3) Agreements. "Trustees and responsible parties should consider entering into binding agreements to facilitate their interactions and resolve any disputes during the assessment. To maximize cost-effectiveness and cooperation, trustees and responsible parties should attempt to develop a set of agreed-upon facts concerning the incident and/or assessment."[1623] (4) Nature and extent of participation:

"If the responsible parties accept the invitation to participate, the scope of that participation must be determined by the trustees, in light of the considerations in paragraph (c)(5) of this section. At a minimum, participation will include notice of trustee determinations required under this part, and notice and opportunity to comment on documents or plans that significantly affect the nature and extent of the assessment. Increased levels of participation by responsible parties may be developed at the mutual agreement of the trustees and the responsible parties. Trustees will objectively consider all written comments provided by the responsible parties, as well as any other recommendations or proposals that the responsible parties submit in writing to the Lead Administrative Trustee. Submissions by the responsible parties will be included in the administrative record. Final authority to make determinations regarding injury and restoration rest solely with the trustees. Trustees may end participation by responsible parties who, during the conduct of the assessment, in the sole judgment of the trustees, cause interference with the trustees' ability to fulfill their responsibilities under OPA and this part."[1624]

*Trustees use formula-based assessments or other non-field procedures*

OPA does not prohibit formula-based methods or specific procedures. However, when using pure formula methods, including methods which

1622 Id.

1623 Id.

1624 Id. §990.14(c)(1)-(4).

assess a fixed dollar amount of natural resource damages on a unit of discharge, or affected area, the Trustee has the burden to prove that any method or procedure used accurately identifies and quantifies injury to the natural resource(s) and that the amounts claimed are in accordance with the acceptable measure of damages outlined at 33 US C § 2706(d).[1625]

An oil incident may occur in an area in which the environment is already degraded by previous pollution or as a result of other factors. Any methods or procedures used that do not take this into account may not satisfy the claimant's burden to prove the injury for which damages are claimed resulted from the incident.[1626]

### *Statute of Limitations*

The Statute of Limitations (SOL) under OPA for the filing of NRD claims with the NPFC is the later of three years from the date the injury and connection with the discharge was reasonably discoverable with due care, or three years from the date the assessment is completed in accordance with the damage assessment regulations published by the National Oceanic and Atmospheric Administration at 15 CFR Part 990.[1627] Following the U.S. Comptroller General's decision that the NPFC could not adjudicate claims for natural resource damages under OPA, any NRD claims previously received were rejected or were held at the NPFC.[1628] If those rejected claims were originally submitted within the statute of limitations (SOL), they can be resubmitted for adjudication.[1629] However, the NPFC will not be able to adjudicate any claims that are not submitted within the SOL.[1630] Any Trustee who has a claim for which the SOL

1625 NPFC Fund Use Reference Guide, Supplement to the Coast Guard Marine Safety Manual, Volume IX, Chapter 6, at 619 (May 2000).

1626 Id. at 619.

1627 Id. at 620.

1628 Id.

1629 Id.

1630 Id. at 620-21.

deadline will expire in the near future should immediately file a claim with the NPFC to ensure that this requirement is met.[1631]

*Trustees utilization of NOAA regulations*

Neither OPA nor the claims regulations require Trustees to assess damages in accordance with the NOAA regulations.[1632] However, the OPA "rebuttable presumption" and the more generous statute of limitations (SOL) period for submitting claims to the NPFC (within 3 years from the date the assessment is completed in accordance with the NOAA damage assessment regulations) are available to a NRD claimant only if the assessment is completed in accordance with the NOAA regulations.[1633] It therefore seems that it will be wiser to use the NOAA regulations. But this also shows that a trustee is free to use the DOI regulations if he is ready to forfeit the advantages of using the NOAA regulations.[1634]

### A.I(a)(vii) Differences Between NOAA's NRDA Regulations and DOI's NRDA Regulations

The two regulations differ in certain respects. The NOAA regulations contains three phases compared to DOI's four phases. The DOI's regulations are more comprehensive than that of NOAA. Both DOI and NOAA differ in their methods of assessing public loss of values, which may have been engendered by the healthy debate among legal commentators on this issue. While the DOI regulation is based primarily on monetary valuation of natural resources and services, NOAA regulations places primary emphasis on the cost of actual restoration as the primary measure of assessment. This seems to be a better approach, since the goal of government

---

1631 Id.

1632 Id. at 621.

1633 Id.

1634 Id.

is to see that the natural resource is returned to the state in which it was before spill damages occur. Both the NOAA and the DOI have adopted the reasonable cost limitation principle on assessment costs. DOI has applied a limitation of assessment costs to not exceed the damages to be recovered, under the standard of not grossly disproportionate expenses. The NOAA on its part does not require early estimate of total damages likely to result, instead it simply requires that a cost effective performance must govern every stage of the procedures. The only requirement is an avoidance of unnecessary and excessive costs. The trustees are required to determine an appropriate relationship between assessment costs, the costs of restoration, and compensation sought because of the incident.

The DOI and NOAA regulations define injury differently. In the DOI regulations, specific delimiting categories of injuries are enumerated. In the NOAA regulations, injury is defined as any observable or measurable adverse change or any impairment of natural resource services.

### A.I(a)(viii) CRITICISMS OF NOAA REGULATIONS

First, although the process is streamlined, it is open-ended and vague, with virtually unlimited discretion in the hands of the trustees.[1635] Because of the enormous number of discretionary decisions, the process will move very slowly, and there will be ample opportunity to challenge the trustees' decisions. Second, although the regulation attempts to focus on restoration, there is ample authority to allow the trustees to levy virtually unlimited monetary damages to compensate for "non-use" values using questionable valuation methodologies. Again, the extent these methods are used is a case-by-case judgment by the trustees.[1636] NOAA regulations clearly give government trustees broad discretion to assess natural resource damages using a wide range of methods, some of which may not withstand scientific scrutiny. The NOAA rule, for example, authorizes

---

1635 Thomas J. Schoenbaum, Analysis Of The Department Of Commerce's Final Rule On Natural Resources Damages, 3 Mar. L. Prac. 1122, 1125 (1996).

1636 Id. at 1125.

trustees to use field studies, laboratory procedures, models, and literature reviews in the assessment process, subject only to the requirements that the procedures be "appropriate" for a particular injury, "reliable," and "valid."[1637] These procedures are not described in the rule itself, but rather in "guidance documents" which are not published in the Federal Register and are available only upon request.[1638] An issue therefore immediately arises as to whether an assessment based upon these guidance documents has been made "in accordance" with the regulations so as to have the benefit of the presumption of correctness. It has been suggested that NOAA's failure to publish the guidance documents in the Federal Register will invalidate any aspect of the rules that the guidance documents purportedly supplement or qualify.[1639] NOAA, however, has failed to address this fundamental administrative law issue and simply suggests that the "guidance documents are truly complementary, and not required to understand how to plan assessments in accordance with this rule."[1640] In NOAA's view, any procedure which complies with the general standards for reliability will be deemed to be in accordance with the regulations and entitled to the rebuttable presumption.[1641]

*Challenge to NOAA's Final Rule:* In *General Electric Co. v. United States Department of Commerce*,[1642] the United States Court of Appeals for the District of Columbia addressed a broad challenge to the substantive and procedural provisions of OPA's final rule, raised by numerous industry and insurance company petitioners. Industry petitioners argued that NOAA acted arbitrarily and capriciously by authorizing trustees to employ "contingent valuation" as an assessment technique.[1643] These

---

1637 Richard B. Stewart et al., Evaluating the Present Natural Resource Damages Regime: The Lawyer's Perspective, in Natural Resource Damages: A Legal, Economic and Policy Analysis 171, 181 (Richard B. Stewart ed., 1995).

1638 Id. at 181, n91

1639 Id.

1640 Natural Resource Damage Assessments, 61 Fed. Reg. 440, 458 (1996).

1641 See id. at 459.

1642 128 F.3d at 769-771 (D.C. Cir. 1997).

1643 Id. at 771.

petitioners also argued that NOAA exceeded its authority by requiring the removal of residual sources of contamination that the Coast Guard and EPA left behind.[1644] Insurance petitioners asserted that the final rule impermissibly applied retroactively, and that it violated OPA by allowing trustees to recover passive-use, or non-use values, by failing to reiterate OPA's damage limitation, by impairing the right of responsible parties to seek contribution, and by granting trustees "uncontrolled discretion."[1645]

The court distinguished rebuttable presumptions created by agencies, from those created by Congress.[1646] The court pointed out that Agency presumptions are only appropriate "when proof of one fact renders the existence of another fact so likely that assuming the existence of the inferred fact is both sensible and time-efficient."[1647] Congress, on the other hand, is free to adopt rebuttable presumptions for policy reasons. [1648] Thus, the court recognized that congressionally created rebuttable presumptions, unlike agency rebuttable presumptions, do not have to operate "sensibly." Noting that Congress created OPA's rebuttable presumption that the trustees' assessment is correct, the court ignored NOAA's role in fashioning the basis of that presumption in its final rule. Because trustees must comply with NOAA's regulatory scheme to earn the rebuttable presumption, the agency rebuttable presumption standard should apply when trustees employ agency regulations to assess natural resource damages. Yet, a troublesome aspect of NOAA's final rule is that it authorizes trustees to use various assessment procedures set forth in guidance documents that are not part of the final rule.[1649] Consequently, if a trustee follows these guidance documents, the question arises as to whether the Natural Resources Damage Assessment (NRDA) was prepared in accordance with NOAA's

1644 See id.

1645 Id.

1646 Id. 771-72.

1647 Id. at 771

1648 See id.

1649 See Charles B. Anderson, Damage to Natural Resources and the Costs of Restoration, 72 Tul. L. Rev. 417, 486-87 (1997).

regulations, thereby entitling the assessment to the benefit of a rebuttable presumption.[1650] NOAA's final rule also authorizes trustees to consider both active losses, that is, loss of actual use of a natural resource, and passive-use or non-use losses, which is defined as the "value individuals place upon the existence of natural resources, even if they never plan to make active use of them."[1651] Most certainly, America's natural treasures have intrinsic value to the public at large, whether an individual American ever visits or uses them. OPA's text does not address recovery for passive-use, or non-use damages.

In Appendix B to the final rule's preamble, NOAA included the technique known as "contingent valuation" as a method trustees could choose to employ to measure passive-use or non-use damages.[1652] This technique consists of surveying a hypothetical market and asking survey participants how much they would pay to protect a given natural resource.[1653] NOAA's Panel on Contingent Valuation concluded that, when conducted under strict guidelines, contingent valuation "can produce estimates reliable enough to be the starting point of a judicial process of damage assessment."[1654] Despite the Panel's view of the preliminary nature of a contingent valuation assessment, however, the rebuttable presumption created by Congress seemingly would treat the contingent valuation damages found by a trustee as evidence against a responsible party, absent evidence to the contrary. Thus, a responsible party is placed in the unenviable position of having to rebut a speculative category of damages that is not specified in OPA. NOAA attempted to sidestep the controversy in its regulations by stating that "NOAA supports the use of all of the procedures discussed in Appendix B of the preamble which includes contingent valuation as reliable and valid within the appropriate context and when performed in accordance with accepted professional

---

1650 See id. at 487.

1651 Id.

1652 *General Electric*, 128 F.3d at 772.

1653 Id.

1654 Natural Resource Damage Assessments under the Oil Pollution Act of 1990, 58 Fed. Reg. 4601, 4610 (1993) (reporting decision of NOAA's panel on contingent valuation).

practices."[1655] It is questionable, therefore, whether contingent valuation is even part of the NOAA regulations since it is only mentioned in an appendix attached to the final rule's preamble.

In addition to procedural objections, industry petitioners in General Electric argued that NOAA acted arbitrarily and capriciously by failing to bar contingent valuation altogether.[1656] The court dismissed this argument, relying upon its earlier decision in United States Department of the *Interior v. Ohio*,[1657] in which the court held that the "Interior Department had not acted arbitrarily or capriciously by authorizing CERCLA trustees to use contingent valuation." The court noted that nothing in NOAA's panel report or the administrative record cast doubt on its *Ohio* decision.[1658] Industry petitioners also argued that NOAA acted arbitrarily in allowing recovery of passive-use damages for temporary losses of natural resources because passive-use losses can only occur when resources are lost forever.[1659] The court found that this issue was not ripe for adjudication until a trustee actually assesses damages for temporary losses in a particular case.

As to removal authority, industry petitioners argued that where the final rule authorized the trustees to "remove conditions that would prevent or limit the effectiveness of any restoration action (e.g., residual sources of contamination)," NOAA exceeded its statutory authority by authorizing trustees to remove residual oil.[1660] The court found that NOAA did not exercise "reasoned decision-making," and vacated this portion of the final rule, remanding it for further agency action.[1661] The controversy over the removal of residual oil involves decisions about the adequacy of restoration, and whether the Coast Guard, EPA, or NOAA makes the determination about whether cleanup efforts are complete. Thus, NOAA's decision

1655 *General Electric,* 128 F.3d at 773.

1656 See id. at 773-74.

1657 Id. at 773. See also Ohio v. United States Dep't of Interior, 880 F.2d 432, 478 (D.C. Cir. 1989).

1658 See *General Electric*, 128 F.3d at 773.

1659 See id. at 773-74.

1660 Id. at 774.

1661 Id. at 769.

in its final rule allowing trustees to remove residual oil failed to account for the role of other federal agencies in the cleanup process.

Like industry petitioners, insurance petitioners argued that OPA does not authorize the recovery of passive-use values.[1662] The court disagreed, noting that nothing in OPA sections 2702 and 2706 "excludes passive-use values."[1663] The court held that "these two sections simply provide for recovery of diminished value without indicating whether the value is of the active or passive variety."[1664] Relying upon OPA's legislative history and its prior decision in *Ohio*, the court found that Congress "clearly intended to authorize trustees to recover passive-use values."[1665] That conclusion, however, is difficult to reconcile with OPA's express language, which details the recovery of loss of use damages but makes no reference to passive-use or non-use damages.[1666] Lastly, insurance petitioners argued that the final rule gives trustees "uncontrolled discretion."[1667] The court summarily dismissed this charge because the final rule requires the NRDA plan to be "reliable and valid for the particular incident," which the court believed adequately constrained trustee discretion.[1668]

In the initial DOI rules, the compensation methodology for NRD faced a judicial bump in the road. A very interesting case deciding the validity of the compensation methodology in the DOI NRDA rules is *Ohio v. United States Department of the Interior.*[1669] In this case several petitioners sought review of the DOI regulations governing the recovery of money from those responsible for spills of oil or hazardous substances that cause damage to natural resources. DOI promulgated the regulations pursuant to CERCLA. The regulations prescribed assessment methods for quantifying damages to natural resources that petitioners complained would cause flawed dam-

1662 General Elec., 128 F.3d at 776, 778.

1663 Id. at 778.

1664 Id.

1665 Id.

1666 See id. See also 33 U.S.C. §§ 2702, 2706 (1994 & Supp. III 1997).

1667 *General Electric*, 128 F.3d at 778.

1668 Id.

1669 880 F.2d 432.

age assessments. The court rejected most of the challenges to the DOI's rules. However, it overturned significant components of the rules.

State and environmental petitioners raised a number of issues concerning DOI's choices of economic values and policies in challenging the regulations. The petitioners complained that resource valuation pursuant to DOI's regulations undervalued the damages recoverable from parties responsible for harm to the environment. Industry petitioners on their part complained that the regulations overstated damage cost estimates. The District of Columbia Circuit Court of Appeals rejected all but three of the challenges to the regulations. The court struck down two parts of the Interior rules and remanded a third for clarification.

The first rule to be struck down by the *Ohio* Court was the "lesser of" rule that limited compensation to the lesser of the cost of restoration of damaged natural resources or the cost of compensation for the loss of their use.[1670] State and Environmental Petitioners challenged the DOI's "lesser of" rule, insisting that CERCLA requires damages to be at least sufficient to pay the cost in every case of restoring, replacing or acquiring the equivalent of the damaged resource.[1671] They further argued that because in some, or probably a majority of cases, lost-use-value will be lower than the cost of restoration, the DOI's rule will result in damages award too small to pay for the costs or restoration.[1672] It appears that the "lesser of" rule will systematically under-compensate the public because use value does not really capture value because value may outrun willingness to pay. Second, the court overruled the DOI's hierarchy of methods for assessing damages to natural resources because of its excessive reliance on market price to determine the value of injured natural resources.[1673] All of the rules that the court struck down tended to reduce the measure of damages. The court found that the lesser of rule was contrary to the "clearly expressed intent of Congress."[1674] The court also held that the regulation

1670 Id. at 438.

1671 Id. at 441.

1672 Id.

1673 Id.

1674 Id.

prescribing a hierarchy of methodologies by which the lost-use value of natural resources may be measured, which focuses exclusively on the market values for such resources when market values are available, is not a reasonable interpretation of the statute.[1675]

There is no record of any filing of a NRDA claim by foreign trustees to date which seems to suggest that they might not be entitled to Fund money. However when it comes to US domestic trustees there is no doubt that they are now entitled to Fund money without the need for direct congressional appropriation. This is due to the NPFC decision to discard the-Comptroller General's opinion, issued in late 1995, that OPA provides for payment of NRD from the Oil Spill Liability Trust Fund (OSLTF) only by appropriation.[1676] It instead decided to adopt the different interpretation of OPA, issued in late 1997 by the Department of Justice (DOJ), Office of Legal Counsel, opining that natural resource damages are payable from the OSLTF without further appropriation, like other damages and removal costs.[1677] However most NRDA claims have been filed directly with an RP.

Due to the new interpretation by the DOJ that the NPFC decided to adopt, there is now one recorded OPA NRDA claim against the Fund. This claim was filed on September 2, 1999 by the National Oceanic & Atmospheric Administration Damage Assessment Center (NOAA DAC) as Lead Administrative Trustee on behalf of the Department of Interior and the Government of America Samoa.[1678] The incident in this claim was named the Pago Pago Longliners Stranding.[1679] This claim was specifically filed for Emergency Restoration/ Damage Assessment. The NOAA DAC sought to recover $6,424,683 as Emergency Restoration Claim,

---

1675 Id.

1676 NPFC Fund Use Reference Guide, Supplement to the Coast Guard Marine Safety Manual, Volume IX, Chapter 6, at 616 (May 2000).

1677 Id. at 616.

1678 See. NOAA DAC, NPFC Natural Resource Damage Claims Division, Former Claim No H99024-DN1, Claim No 142006-OC1, at 1, (09/17/1999) (on file with the NPFC and available upon request from the NPFC).

1679 Id. at 1.

while it sought $347,538.53 for Damage Assessment.[1680] The RP in this case was referred to as "identified but not viable."[1681] On December 10, 1991, Hurricane "Val" struck and caused widespread damage to the South Pacific Islands of America Samoa. During the storm, nine foreign-owned fishing vessels broke their moorings and were driven aground on the reefs within Pago Pago Harbor on the Island of Tutuila.[1682] According to a US Coast Guard assessment conducted on December 11, 1991, about 35.71 barrels (1,500 gallons) of oil was discharged into the surrounding waters during the grounding incident. After the US Coast Guard removed 250 barrels (10,500 gallons) of diesel, lube and hydraulic oil from three of the vessels, rough weather prevented further oil removal, leaving about 428.57 barrels (18,000 gallons) of oil and an undetermined amount of ammonia on the vessels.[1683] Following the grounding, the US Coast Guard received several reports of sheening and/or small discharges of oil from the abandoned vessels.[1684] On or about May 19, 1999, the US Coast Guard determined that the nine vessels "continue to pose a substantial threat to the fragile environment" and that it intended to eliminate the risk of pollutant discharge by removing all ammonia and oil from the vessels.[1685]

Planned US Coast Guard actions were expected to result in injuries to natural resources. The NOAA DAC as Lead Trustees prepared an emergency restoration plan so that restoration was concurrent with US Coast Guard's response efforts.[1686] This approach was intended to prevent additional injury associated with rebuilding causeways for restoration efforts after the US Coast Guard completed its response actions; and takes advantage of the cost savings associated with using the causeways constructed for the response action and employing the US Coast Guard salvage equipment already deployed to the island.[1687] The Natural

1680 Id. at 1.
1681 Id.
1682 Id.
1683 Id.
1684 Id.
1685 Id. at 1.
1686 Id.
1687 Id.

Resources Damage Claims Division of the NPFC meticulously adjudicated this claim and recommended that it be accepted, noting the unique, emergency nature of this environmental assessment and restoration action.[1688]

Many more claims of this nature that were denied because of the Comptroller General's opinion, may now be refiled again if they were not time barred at the time they were initially filed.[1689] So, trustees can dust their files once again and attempt recovery from the Fund for NRD.

## B OTHER DAMAGES RECOVERABLE BY GOVERNMENTAL ENTITIES

### 1. Recovery of Damages for loss of Revenue- 33 USC § 2702(b)(2)(D).

"Statutory provisions:
§ 2702. Elements of liability

(a) In general

Notwithstanding any other provision or rule of law, and subject to the provisions of this Act, each responsible party for a vessel or a facility from which oil is discharged, or which poses the substantial threat of a discharge of oil, into or upon the navigable waters or adjoining shorelines or the exclusive economic zone is liable for the removal costs and **damages** specified in subsection (b) of this section that result from such incident."[1690]

"(b) Covered removal costs and damages

**

1688 Id. at 1.

1689 NPFC Fund Use Reference Guide, Supplement to the Coast Guard Marine Safety Manual, Volume IX, Chapter 6, at 620.

1690 33 USC 2702(a).

(2) Damages

The damages referred to in subsection (a) of this section are the following:

**

**

**(D) Revenues**

Damages equal to the net loss of taxes, royalties, rents, fees, or net profit shares due to the injury, destruction, or loss of real property, personal property, or natural resources, which shall be recoverable by the Government of the United States, a State, or a political subdivision thereof."[1691]

The OPA allows recovery of "[d]amages equal to the net loss of taxes, royalties, rents, fees, or net profit shares due to the injury, destruction, or loss of real property, personal property, or natural resources," but only the Government of the United States, a State, or a political subdivision can pursue such claims.[1692] Similar economic losses for offshore spills had previously been recognized under the 1978 Amendments to the Outer Continental Shelf Lands Act.[1693] The implementing regulations provide that a claim for net loss of revenue due to the injury, destruction, or loss of real property, personal property, or natural resources may be presented only by an appropriate claimant sustaining the loss.[1694] This means that the Government of the United States, a State, or a political subdivision should only assert a claim if it sustained the loss in revenue. It is not inconceivable that there could be an oil spill incident that might trigger different layers of revenue losses to different tiers of government, Federal, State and municipal. The amount of compensation allowable is the total net revenue

1691 33 USC § 2702(b)(2)(D).

1692 33 USCA § 2702(b)(2)(D).

1693 43 U.S.C. § 1813(a)(2)(F) (1988). This provision, which was repealed by OPA, allowed recovery of the loss of tax revenue for one year.

1694 33 CFR §136.225.

actually lost.[1695] If the government bringing an OPA suit is proceeding against the responsible party solely on the OPA liability regime, liability limits set forth in the OPA would be applicable.

Recovery of loss of revenue is not automatic. The government claimant has to overcome some evidentiary and procedural hurdles in order to recover. A claimant must establish--(a) The identification and description of the economic loss for which compensation is claimed, including the applicable authority, property affected, method of assessment, rate, and method and dates of collection; (b) That the loss of revenue was due to the injury to, destruction of, or loss of real or personal property or natural resources; (c) The total assessment or revenue collected for comparable revenue periods; and (d) The net loss of revenue.[1696]

Despite the evidentiary hurdle stipulated in the implementing regulations, recovery of revenue losses still presents several difficult questions of proof. Typically, claims for economic losses raise critical issues of standing, causation, remoteness, and mitigation, presenting major barriers to recovery.[1697] For example, what causal relationship is required between the governmental revenue loss and the damaged property or resource?[1698] As to causation, OPA uses the term "due to," but no Congressional insight is provided regarding the meaning of this term. Must the loss be reasonably foreseeable, or a direct and immediate consequence of the environmental incident? Furthermore, does the victim-government have a duty to mitigate its loss with other revenue-generating measures?[1699] In this vein, the evaluation of the net loss of revenues will require consideration of increases in other revenues, such as increases in income, sales and lodging taxes which are frequently associated with the removal effort.[1700] These and other legal and factual questions will require judicial definition before

1695 33 CFR § 136.229.

1696 33 CFR § 136.227.

1697 Thomas J. Wagner, Recoverable Damages Under The Oil Pollution Act Of 1990, 5 U.S.F. Mar. L.J. 283, 291 (1993) (hereinafter Wagner, Recoverable damages).

1698 Id. at 291.

1699 Id.

1700 Id. at 292.

OPA can provide a reasonable, realistic and predictable measure of recovery for governmental revenue losses.[1701]

But the Fund's guidelines on completing of standard claims forms might provide some insight.

The guidelines provide:

"A State or Local Government should provide:

**1. EVIDENCE OF INCIDENT**: Provide one or more of the following:

a. Report from Federal On Scene Coordinator (federal government official in charge of environmental issues in the region) or justification why there is no FOSC report.[1702]

b. Information regarding any notification of the Coast Guard or Environmental Protection Agency, when the state or local government made the notification, to whom they made the notification.[1703]

c. If applicable, any reports from the State or Federal natural resource trustees.

d. Newspaper reports describing the incident which ran contemporaneously with incident.

e. Witness statement(s) concerning the spill.

f. Pictures of damaged property, if applicable.[1704]

**2. GENERAL INFORMATION**:

a. A letter, signed by the head of the state government (State Governor, Mayor, etc.), granting the person who signed this claim the authority to bind the government in a settlement OR a claim signed by the head of government or by the individual already authorized to sign such claims in a letter previously filed with the NPFC,[1705]

b. A narrative description of what revenues were impacted and how the spill caused a loss of revenues,

---

1701 Id. at 292.

1702 National Pollution Funds Center's Supplemental Claims Guidance on Completing Standard Claims Forms, 3, 12 (July 18, 1997).

1703 Id. at 12.

1704 Id.

1705 Id.

c. A copy of all investigative files into the identity of the party responsible for the spill.
d. Copies of statutes, regulations, ordinances, etc. outlining the applicable authority to raise such revenues, property affected, method of assessment, rate of assessment, and method and dates of collection of assessment,
e. Government financial reports showing total assessment or revenue collected for comparable periods,
f. Details of any expenses not paid out by government during the period being claimed.
g. Details and explanation of net loss of revenue."[1706]

The NPFC and courts of law will demand a government claimant's compliance with the requirements of the statute and implementing regulations with respect to this head or item of damage. For instance in a loss of government revenue claim filed for reconsideration by the state of Alabama in 1996, the NPFC Claim Management Division denied the claim of the state of Alabama because it failed to prove that the alleged loss of rent, fees and taxes were due to injury, destruction, or loss of real property, personal property, or natural resources.[1707] The state of Alabama had also failed to prove that the rent, fees, and taxes lost were due to an oil pollution incident.[1708] This claim had been denied earlier on June 3, 1996, but it was submitted unsuccessfully for reconsideration.

The claim involved a vessel that posed a substantial threat of discharge of oil into navigable waters of the United States. The vessel developed some engine problems while berthing in the Port of Mobile.[1709] The berthing costs were paid for by the vessel operator, from the vessel's entry date until abandonment on March 31, 1994.[1710] The vessel was not allowed

---

1706 Id.

1707 See. State of Alabama, NPFC Claim Summary/ Recommendation Form, Claim No 084026-003, 1, 2 (7/31/1996) (on file with the NPFC and available upon request from the NPFC).

1708 Id. at 2.

1709 Id. at 1.

1710 Id.

to leave the port because it had not resolved some pollution and Safety of Life at Sea Convention issues.[1711]

The situation of the vessel took a turn for the worse on January 31, 1994, by virtue of which the Coast Guard responded to a distress call. The Coast Guard contracted an oil pollution cleanup and removal company to remove the oil from the vessel.[1712] This removal operation lasted until March 14, 1994. At that point the contracted company had removed most of the oil from the vessel and discontinued the major removal operations.[1713] From then on, the Coast Guard checked the vessel once or twice a month, pumping it out as needed.[1714] Between April 27, 1994 and May 18, 1994 the state of Alabama moved the vessel from one berthing dock to another.[1715] On November 29, 1994, the Commandant gave authorization to sink the vessel as a reef.[1716] A contract for the sinking was awarded on June 23, 1995. Between July 10, 1995 and September 27, 1995, the sinking of the vessel as a reef was concluded.[1717]

The problem here was that since the operator had abandoned the vessel on March 31, 1994, there was no one to hold responsible for the payment of the port docking fees and taxes, which was an appreciable source of government revenue. In its rejection of the claim of the State of Alabama, the Claims Manager noted that the vessel's agent made an agreement with the State at the docks.[1718] He also noted that by virtue of this agreement, the owners of the vessel, not the Coast Guard, were obliged to pay for the berthing fees, whether or not there was a pollution incident.[1719] The Claims Manager also reasoned that the mere fact that the Coast Guard monitored and performed certain oil pollution and pumping operations did not itself make the Coast Guard liable for berthing costs, nor should

1711 Id.
1712 Id.
1713 Id.
1714 Id.
1715 Id. at 1.
1716 Id.
1717 Id.
1718 Id. at 2.
1719 Id.

there be an inference that Coast Guard had taken over the vessel.[1720] The Claims Manager also found that there was no contract, agreement, or understanding that the Coast Guard would be responsible or pay for the berthing costs.[1721] In addition the Claims Manager pointed out that it was the State of Alabama that decided to move the vessel from site to site, not the Coast Guard.[1722] The Claims Manager noted further that at no time did the State make their concerns over lack of payment to the Coast Guard, nor did they mention to the Coast Guard that they expected to be paid by the Coast Guard.[1723] In conclusion, the Claims Manager found that the costs incurred by the State of Alabama were due to the vessel owner's breach of a commercial berthing contract, rather than the oil pollution incident.[1724] The Claims Manager also denied the State's other claims for removal costs because they were neither consistent with the National Contingency plan nor directed by the FOSC.[1725]

## 2. Recovery of damages for net costs of providing additional public services – 33 USC § 2702(b)(2)(F).

Statutory provisions:
"§ 2702. Elements of liability

(a) In general

Notwithstanding any other provision or rule of law, and subject to the provisions of this Act, each responsible party for a vessel or a facility from which oil is discharged, or which poses the substantial threat of a discharge of oil, into or upon the navigable waters or adjoining shorelines or the exclusive economic zone is

1720 Id.
1721 Id.
1722 Id. at 2.
1723 Id.
1724 Id. at 2.
1725 Id.

liable for the removal costs and **damages** specified in subsection (b) of this section that result from such incident."[1726]

"(b) Covered removal costs and damages

**

(2) Damages

The damages referred to in subsection (a) of this section are the following:

**(F) Public services**

Damages for net costs of providing increased or additional **public services** during or after removal activities, including protection from fire, safety, or health hazards, caused by a discharge of oil, which shall be recoverable by a State, or a political subdivision of a State."[1727]

The OPA allows the recovery of public services damages for net costs of providing increased or additional public services during or after removal activities, including protection from fire, safety, or health hazards, caused by a discharge of oil, but limits authorized claimants to only a State, or a political subdivision of a State.[1728] Under the OPA, State mean the several States of the United States, the District of Columbia, the Commonwealth of Puerto Rico, Guam, American Samoa, the United States Virgin Islands, the Commonwealth of the Northern Marianas, and any other territory or possession of the United States.[1729] So, private causes of action are not allowed for this item of damage. The Federal government is not an authorized claimant under this section.[1730] A State government

1726 33 USCA §2702(a).

1727 33 USCA §2702(b)(2)(F).

1728 33 USCA §2702(b)(2)(F), see also, 33 CFR §136.237.

1729 33 USCA 2701(36).

1730 33 CFR §136.237.

or the political subdivision of a State can only file a claim if it actually incurred the additional costs.

In order to prevent this from being used by the state or political subdivision as another way of generating revenue, the implementing regulations added some evidentiary burdens on the claimants. In addition to the requirements discussed above, a claimant must establish: (a) The nature of the specific public services provided and the need for those services; (b) That the services occurred during or after removal activities; (c) That the services were provided as a result of a discharge of oil and would not otherwise have been provided; and (d) The net cost for the services and the methods used to compute those costs.[1731]

The recovery of increased public services (other than removal costs) represents a new element not formerly authorized by environmental statutes. Normally, expenditures for public services, even in response to a catastrophe, are paid by the public rather than the tortfeasor.[1732] The jurisprudence disallowing this recovery generally holds that expenditures for general public services funded by public taxation (as distinguished from property damages or specific cleanup costs) are to be borne by the public at large unless the legislative authority, which established the tax-funded general services, expressly imposed these general costs upon particular parties (i.e. tortfeasors).[1733] OPA provides this statutory authorization for recovery of the costs of these increased public services from specific responsible parties (vessel and facility owners and operators). OPA recoveries will be statutorily limited to the net costs of increased public protection services and will not include the underlying fixed costs which would have been incurred in any event.[1734] This means that the state government or its subdivision would need to show in evidence that it has not included underlying fixed costs.[1735]

1731 33 CFR § 136.239.

1732 Koch v. Consol. Edison Co., 468 N.E.2d 1, 7-8 (N.Y.1984).

1733 468 N.E.2d 1, 8.

1734 33 CFR §136.241.

1735 33 CFR §136.241.

The Fund's supplemental guidelines on filling out the standard claim forms also provide more insight into what a state or municipal government ought to provide in order to ensure quick and easy processing of their claims. A State or Municipal Government should provide:

"1. **EVIDENCE OF INCIDENT**: (Provide one or more of the following.)

a. Report from Federal On Scene Coordinator (federal government official in charge of environmental issues in the region) or justification why there is no FOSC report.
b. Information regarding any notification of the Coast Guard or Environmental Protection Agency, when the state or local government made the notification, to whom they made the notification.
c. If applicable, any reports from the State or Federal natural resource trustees.
d. Newspaper reports describing the incident which ran contemporaneously with incident.
e. Witness statement(s) concerning the spill.[1736]

**2. GENERAL INFORMATION**:

a. A letter, signed by the head of your government (State Governor, Mayor, etc.), granting the person who signed this claim the authority to bind the government in a settlement OR a claim signed by the head of government or by the individual already authorized to sign such claims in a letter previously filed with the NPFC.
b. Reports showing that the increased public services were required due to the discharge, specifying if the increased services were due to fire, safety, or health hazards.[1737]
c. Detailed description of what increased services were necessary and why, including a distinction between removal activities, safety acts, and law enforcement acts, and a statement regarding whether the increase was actually incurred or was due to a diversion of resources normally available.[1738]

---

1736 National Pollution Funds Center's Supplemental Claims Guidance on Completing Standard Claims Forms, at 13 (July 18, 1997).

1737 Id. at 13.

1738 Id.

d. Daily reports of the activities of the government personnel and equipment involved.[1739]

**3. GOVERNMENT LABOR AND EQUIPMENT RATES:**

a. Payroll verification of the hourly rate the government paid its personnel at the time of the incident.[1740]

b. Verification of the standard government equipment and maintenance rates for any equipment claimed; OR,

c. Signed and dated contemporaneous records of the incident which include the hourly rates for labor and equipment. (The date on the records should be within the time of the response to the incident.)[1741]

d. An explanation from the state as to whether the rates given are inclusive of benefits, overhead, etc. If the rates do include these amounts, an explanation of the formula used to calculate them must be provided. Rates under OMB A-87 should be provided.

e. A certification that the rates used reflect actual costs incurred by the government and do not include any punitive damages or fees."[1742]

One major problem state governments may experience in the filing of this item of damages is time limitations. This is particularly common in relation to governments because of a system of administration marked by officialism, red tape, and proliferation. The state government or political subdivision of a state government that wants to file a damage claim for the cost of providing increased public services should make sure they observe the time limitation provisions of the OPA discussed in the latter part of this treatise. No matter how valid the claim may be, it would be denied if it is filed after the expiration of the statutory time limitation. For instance in an NPFC claim decided in 1997, a very good claim that should have succeeded was denied because of the failure of a state government to adhere

1739 Id.

1740 Id.

1741 Id.

1742 Id.

to the time limitation provisions.[1743] In January 1991, an oil spill was discovered in Hometown, Pennsylvania.[1744] The Spill source was a gasoline service station's underground storage tanks, which leaked oil into the ground.[1745] The oil then migrated into the sewer system, a pond, and an unnamed tributary of the Little Schuylkill River. The State of Pennsylvania alleged that it incurred increased public service costs when it provided bottled water and eventually converted area residents' water system to public utilities.[1746] From the documentation presented it appeared that the costs were incurred from the period of January 1991 through July 5, 1994. The claim was not received by the NPFC until the 22nd of July 1997. The Claims Manager found that the period of limitations for submitting a claim under section 2712(h)(2) of the OPA had already expired.

One very interesting thing that this claim brought to the fore is the difficulty of determining if some claims should be categorized as damages or removal costs. For instance in this NPFC claim, the state government's claim included over $7,000 cost for laboratory analyses. The claims manager noted that these type of costs are generally considered removal costs, compensable under OPA.[1747] The Claims Manager noted however that the analyses in the instant case was specifically related to periodic monitoring of the pollution levels in the drinking water, which was more of a damage assessment.[1748] More like a property damage appraisal, since they were appraising the quality of the drinking water.[1749] The importance of determining if a claim qualifies as removal costs or rather as damages cannot be overemphasized because of the 6 year time limitation for removal costs which is three years longer than the three years time limitation for damage claims. If the Claims manager had found the laboratory analyses to be re-

---

1743 See Commonwealth of Pennsylvania, NPFC Claim Summary/Recommendation Form, Claim No 056032-003, p1 (7/31/1997) (on file with the NPFC and available upon request from the NPFC).

1744 Id. at 1.

1745 Id.

1746 Id. at 1.

1747 Id.

1748 Id.

1749 Id.

moval costs, the state of Pennsylvania may have recovered it from the Fund because it would have had up to July 5, 2000 to file a removal costs claim.

Another example of claims by state or municipal governments to recover damages for the increased cost of providing public services is an NPFC claim, decided in 1998. In that case an unnamed barge anchored in a harbor was reported to be sinking.[1750] The US Coast Guard and the claimant (a county sheriff's office) responded to the incident.[1751] The claimant asked for overtime, boat fuel and boat cleaning costs. The Claims manager granted the claim because the records of the Coast Guard showed that the claimant worked with the Coast Guard to forestall the sinking of the unmanned barge.[1752] The records did not indicate that their assistance was not needed.[1753] Apart from this, overtime was documented in the Pollution Reports (POLREP) file. The claimant produced a receipt for the boat fuel, and an estimate for the cleaning of the boat from the waterline up, including all topside surfaces ($12/ft X 25' boat = $300).[1754]

Sometimes the NPFC could deem a removal cost claim to be a claim for damages for the net costs of providing increased or additional public services in order to prevent hardship to the claimant. This is particularly important in cases where the NPFC has no rates to compare the specific response items to. For instance, in an NPFC claim decided in 1999, the Norwalk Fire and Police Departments responded to the report of an oil spill.[1755] According to the Norwalk Fire Department, officials from both departments were called in from their homes and required to fill in for other officials required to be involved in the incident.[1756] On an initial re-

---

1750 San Juan County Sheriff's Office, NPFC Claim Summary/Recommendation Form, Claim No 137015-001, p1 (06/03/1998) (on file with the NPFC and available upon request from the NPFC).

1751 Id. at 1.

1752 Id. at 1.

1753 Id.

1754 Id.

1755 City of Norwalk, NPFC Claim Summary/ Recommendation Form, Claim No 999128-002, p1 (01/18/1999) (on file with the NPFC and available upon request from the NPFC).

1756 Id. at 1.

sponse basis, the Norwalk Fire Department deployed containment and sorbent booms in an effort to minimize their potential damages.[1757] During this same period of time, police officials conducted an investigation into the discharge and a fruitless search for an RP. The Claims manager noted that the response conducted by the Norwalk township, was in line with their State pre-approved emergency response.[1758] It was determined to be consistent with the National Contingency Plan (NCP) by the EPA FOSC.[1759] The Claims Manager observed that a review of the costs in the response/ investigation effort was conducted, but unfortunately, the NPFC had no rates for fire or police to compare these line items to.[1760] Based on the dilemmatic circumstance which it faced, the Claims Manager decided that the NPFC could only examine the costs from the perspective of actually being "increased" public services costs.[1761] The Claims Manager found that these charges met the legal definition of "costs of increased public services" and were reimbursable because these were costs for personnel called in to replace others that were required for the oil spill response.[1762] This example illustrates the fact that in certain situations it is possible to categorize a claim as removal costs and as damages for increased costs of providing public services. This will be done where the removal costs claim is in danger of being denied and the claimant is likely to go away empty handed.

## B. DAMAGES RECOVERABLE BY ANY PARTY

In authorizing private remedies for oil spill damages, the OPA directly addresses one of the chief flaws in the former FWPCA and CERCLA. CERCLA authorized only federal remedies for removal costs and natural resource

---

1757 Id.

1758 Id. at 1.

1759 Id.

1760 Id.

1761 Id. at 1.

1762 Id.

damages;[1763] there were no private remedies.[1764] While the FWPCA only preserved private remedies in very limited situations. Although the FWPCA did preserve or save the rights of private claimants for property damage by oil or hazardous substance under state statutory provisions, OPA's treatment of Responsible Parties (RPs) is a sharp departure from the FWPCA, as the FWPCA did not directly make an RP liable to anyone other than the United States, and then only for removal costs and natural resources damages. The OPA explicitly provides for private party recovery of property damages and removal costs, economic losses, and damages for loss of subsistence use of natural resources. These items of damage are discussed further below.

### 1. Recovery of loss of subsistence use of natural resources - 33 U.S.C.A. § 2702(b)(2)(C).

Statutory provisions:
"§ 2702. Elements of liability

(a) In general

Notwithstanding any other provision or rule of law, and subject to the provisions of this Act, each responsible party for a vessel or a facility from which oil is discharged, or which poses the substantial threat of a discharge of oil, into or upon the navigable waters or adjoining shorelines or the exclusive economic zone is liable for the removal costs and damages specified in subsection (b) of this section that result from such incident."[1765]

"(b) Covered removal costs and damages

**

1763 33 U.S.C. § 1321(f)-(h) (1988).

1764 Middlesex City Sewage Auth. v. National Sea Clammers Ass'n, 453 U.S. 1, 15 (1981); OKC Dredging, Inc. v. Amerada Hess Corp., 1981 AMC 1927 (S.D.Ala.1979).

1765 33 USC §2702(a).

(2) Damages

The damages referred to in subsection (a) of this section are the following:

**

**(C) Subsistence use**

Damages for **loss of subsistence use of natural resources**, which shall be recoverable by any claimant who so uses natural resources which have been injured, destroyed, or lost, without regard to the ownership or management of the resources."[1766]

**

OPA specifically provides that damages for loss of subsistence use of natural resources shall be recoverable by any claimant who uses natural resources which have been injured, destroyed or lost, without regard to the ownership or management of the resources.[1767] A claim for loss of subsistence use of natural resources may be presented only by a claimant who actually uses, for subsistence, the natural resources which have been injured, destroyed, or lost, without regard to the ownership or management of the resources.[1768] An example of a claimant in this category is someone who depends on the fish or shrimp in the oil polluted river or ocean for subsistence living or survival.

In the case of *In the Matter of The Petition of CLEVELAND TANKERS, INC., for Exoneration From or Limitation of Liability*,[1769] the court addressed the issue of recovery of loss of subsistence use of natural resources provided for by the OPA.[1770] In this case, the petitioner's vessel,

1766 33 USC §2702(b)(2)(C).

1767 33 U.S.C.A. § 2702(b)(2)(C).

1768 33 CFR s 136.219.

1769 1992 A.M.C. 1727, 791 F.Supp. 669 (S.D. Mich. 1992).

1770 33 U.S.C.A. § 2702(b)(2)(C).

the M/V JUPITER, docked at Total's dock in the Saginaw River at Bay City, Michigan. The JUPITER was carrying a cargo of gasoline. As the JUPITER was unloading the gasoline at the Total dock an explosion and fire occurred. As a result of this accident the JUPITER broke loose from its mooring at the Total dock and drifted into the navigation channel of the river. The explosion and fire damaged the JUPITER to such an extent that the vessel partially sank in the channel. The JUPITER blocked all commercial navigation in the channel causing the Coast Guard to close the channel until October 22, 1990. In the wake of the accident, litigation ensued. In February 1991, Cleveland filed a Petition for Exoneration from or Limitation of Liability. The court entered an Order which provided for notice of Cleveland's Petition, enjoined suits against Cleveland, and directed the filing of claims.[1771] Parties whose business interests were adversely affected by accident between vessel and dock filed economic damages claims against the vessel owner and the dock owner.[1772] The court held that the claimants could not recover damages under § 2702(b)(2)(C) because they did not use the river for "subsistence use." The court noted that the term subsistence use relates to use of a natural resource, such as water, to obtain the minimum necessities for life. The court rejected the claimants attempt to stretch the term subsistence use well beyond its plain meaning to include as "subsistence" any business activity.[1773]

A year later another court in the case of *Sekco Energy, Inc. v. M/V Margaret Chouest*,[1774] arrived at a similar decision as the earlier court. In this case the owner of a drilling platform brought an action against the owner and charterer of the vessel which was towing seismic cable which struck a leg of the platform, causing it to rupture and spill mineral oil into the ocean, with result that the platform operations were halted during pollution investigation. The court held that subsection (C) provides no ground for damages

---

1771 791 F.Supp. at 671.

1772 Id. at 669.

1773 Id. at 678, n7, the court noted that "Subsistence" is defined as: "means of subsisting... the minimum (as of food and shelter) necessary to support life... a source or means of obtaining the necessities of life." Webster's Ninth New Collegiate Dictionary, 1176 (1986).

1774 1994 A.M.C. 1515, 23 Envtl. L. Rep. 21,248, 820 F.Supp. 1008 (E.D. La 1993).

for the plaintiff because his use of natural resources did not "relate to use of a natural resource, such as water, to obtain the minimum necessities for life," but, rather than using natural resources in this manner, the plaintiff had a commercial purpose in drilling for hydrocarbons.[1775] The implementing regulations provides that the amount of compensation allowable is the reasonable replacement cost of the subsistence loss suffered by the claimant if, during the period of time for which the loss of subsistence is claimed, there was no alternative source or means of subsistence available.[1776]

In order to prevent double recovery, the implementing regulations provides further that the reasonable replacement cost must be reduced by: (1) All compensation made available to the claimant to compensate for subsistence loss; (2) All income which was derived by utilizing the time which otherwise would have been used to obtain natural resources for subsistence use; and (3) Overheads or other normal expenses of subsistence use not incurred as a result of the incident.[1777]

To ensure that it is not an all comers affair, the statute also imposes some proof requirements on those claiming loss of subsistence use. A claimant must provide (a) The identification of each specific natural resource for which compensation for loss of subsistence use is claimed; (b) A description of the actual subsistence use made of each specific natural resource by the claimant; (c) A description of how and to what extent the claimant's subsistence use was affected by the injury to or loss of each specific natural resource; (d) A description of each effort made by the claimant to mitigate the claimant's loss of subsistence use; and (e) A description of each alternative source or means of subsistence available to the claimant during the period of time for which loss of subsistence is claimed, and any compensation available to the claimant for loss of subsistence.[1778]

The provisions of the Fund's guidelines for filing out a standard claim form also provide some insight into some of the additional information a claimant under this subpart must provide. Firstly, they need to provide

1775 820 F.Supp. 1008, 1015.

1776 33 CFR s 136.223.

1777 Id.

1778 33 CFR § 136.221.

almost the same information as is required in the "Evidence of Incident" section for government claimants, claiming damages for cost of providing additional public services, plus pictures of damaged property. In addition to this, they must provide the following information:

"GENERAL INFORMATION:

a. A statement identifying each natural resource on which the claimant subsists and a description of how the claimant uses it.[1779]
b. A statement from a federal or state Natural Resource Trustee of how and to what extent subsistence use was affected by injury to or loss or natural resources.[1780]
c. A certification from a Native American tribe that the claimant is a bona fide user of natural resources for subsistence.
d. If applicable, statements from witnesses that the claimant is a bona fide user of natural resources for subsistence.
e. A description of any efforts the claimant made to mitigate his or her losses.
f. A description of any alternate sources or means of subsistence available to the claimant and whether and how he or she utilized these sources.[1781]
g. A breakdown of costs associated with alternative sources or means of subsistence - receipts from stores, purchases of goods, etc."[1782]

## 2. Recovery For Economic Loss or Damage To Real or Personal Property - 33 USCA §2702(b)(2)(B).

Statutory provisions:
"§ 2702. Elements of liability

(a) In general

---

1779 National Pollution Funds Center's Supplemental Claims Guidance on Completing Standard Claims Forms, at 7(July 18, 1997).

1780 Id. at 7.

1781 Id.

1782 Id.

Notwithstanding any other provision or rule of law, and subject to the provisions of this Act, each responsible party for a vessel or a facility from which oil is discharged, or which poses the substantial threat of a discharge of oil, into or upon the navigable waters or adjoining shorelines or the exclusive economic zone is liable for the removal costs and damages specified in subsection (b) of this section that result from such incident."[1783]

"(b) Covered removal costs and damages

**

"(2) Damages

The damages referred to in subsection (a) of this section are the following:

**

**(B) Real or personal property**

Damages for injury to, or economic losses resulting from **destruction of, real or personal property**, which shall be recoverable by a claimant who owns or leases that property."[1784]

The OPA provides that damages for injury to, or economic losses resulting from destruction of, real or personal property, shall be recoverable by a claimant who owns or leases that property.[1785] This item of damage appears to be consistent with prior law. The Robins Dry Dock Rule generally bars economic maritime tort recovery, unless there is a physical damage to a proprietary interest of the claimant.[1786] "Proprietary interest" has

---

1783 33 USC § 2702(a).

1784 33 USCA §2702(b)(2)(B).

1785 33 USCA §2702(b)(2)(B).

1786 Robins Dry Dock & Repair Co. v. Flint, 275 U.S. 303, 48 S.Ct. 134 (1927) (holding that time charterers did not have property interest in vessel authorizing recovery against

been defined by the Fifth Circuit to mean that "a party must have control over the property tantamount to full ownership."[1787] The OPA phrase "who owns or leases the property" brings this OPA provision close to the Robins Dry Dock requirement of physical damage to a proprietary interest.

*Recent OPA Jurisprudence on Economic Loss*: In the case of *Sekco Energy, Inc. v. M/V Margaret Chouest,*[1788] the court held that the Robins Dry Dock rule precluding recovery for purely economic loss in certain negligence actions would not bar recovery under the Oil Pollution Act by the owner of an oil platform for economic loss resulting from shutdown of operations for pollution investigation after the platform was struck by seismic cable being towed by the vessel owned and chartered by defendants. In order to fully appreciate the concept of economic loss under the OPA it is important to point out that section 2702 (b)(2)(B) is not a blank check for recovery of economic loss, because it limits the circumstances under which a claimant can recover economic losses. Section 2702 (b)(2)(B) specifically provides that the responsible party is liable for damages for injury to, or economic losses **resulting from destruction of real or personal property**, (which) shall be recoverable by a claimant who "owns or leases that property."

The *M/V Margaret Chouest* court undertook a thorough analysis of this subsection of the OPA. The *Chouest* court found as a matter of law that the plaintiff could not recover damages under subsection (B). The court noted that even though the plaintiff alleged a loss of personal

---

repairer negligently causing delay).

1787 J. James Cooper, James P. Lam, Recovery of Economic Damages For Delayed Offshore Production, 28 J. Mar. L. & Com. 323, 326 (1997). (Citing, Texas E. Transmission Corp. v. McMoran Offshore Exploration Co., 877 F.2d 1214, 1225 (5th Cir.), *cert. denied*, 493 U.S. 937 (1989) (a proprietary interest requires "actual possession or control, responsibility for repair and responsibility for maintenance"); Testbank, 752 F.2d at 1034 (Williams, J., concurring) ("the legal synonym for 'proprietary interest' is ownership"); Vicksburg Towing Co. v. Mississippi Marine Transp. Co., 609 F.2d 176, 177 (5th Cir. 1980) (the difference between recovery by an owner when its property is damaged and recovery by others is "meaningful, real, and dispositive"); Naviera Maersk Espana, S.A. v. Cho-Me Towing, Inc., 782 F. Supp. 317, 320 (E.D. La. 1992) (describing ownership as "wide ranging control"). Id at 326, n 11.

1788 820 F.Supp. 1008, 1994 A.M.C. 1515, 23 Envtl. L. Rep. 21,248 (E.D La. 1993).

property, i.e. revenue, the plaintiff did not allege injury to personal or real property.[1789] The *Chouest* court read "injury" to mean physical injury; and further pointed out that "injury" does not encompass economic loss because where Congress intended recovery for "loss," it specifically used that word.[1790] The court gave as an example, the clear and unambiguous wording of subsection (B) which, specifically allows recovery for "economic losses" **resulting from the destruction of real or personal property.** The court concluded that, even though the plaintiff claimed a loss of revenue, that loss did not result from the destruction of any real or personal property.[1791] The reasoning of the court is logical, since it will not be equitable to allow the plaintiff to get two bites at the apple, in that the recovery of lost profits and earning capacity allowed in section 2702 (b)(2)(E) is a form economic loss recovery.

Although the Fifth Circuit Court of Appeals in *Reserve Mooring Inc. v. American Commercial Barge Line,*[1792] disapproved of the part of the *M/V Margaret Chouest* decision discussing the Robins Dry Dock Rule requirement of physical damage in a pure maritime negligence situation (not discussed here), the part of the *M/V Margaret Chouest* decision discussed above was left undisturbed by the Fifth Circuit. Therefore, *M/V Margaret Chouest's* analysis of section 2702 (b)(2) (B) & (E) of the OPA is still good law after *Reserve Mooring.*

One legal commentator criticized the typical indifference, with which the US Congress declined to define several key terms and concepts in its enactment. For example, OPA authorizes recovery of "economic loss" resulting from "destruction"--but not "injury"--to real or personal property (but evidently not to natural resources).[1793] Such economic loss may be recovered only by a claimant who owns or "leases" the destroyed

---

1789 Id. at 1015.

1790 Id.

1791 Id. at 1015.

1792 251 F.3d 1069 (5th Cir. 2001).

1793 Thomas Wagner, Recoverable Damages Under The Oil Pollution Act Of 1990, 5 U.S.F. Mar. L.J. 283, 297 (1993).

property. None of the quoted terms are defined either under OPA or under the FWPCA.[1794] While statutory definition of such common terms is ordinarily unnecessary, clarity becomes critical in the context of the other "economic loss" provision, which allows recovery by any claimant of lost profits and earnings' impairment due to injury, loss, or destruction of property or resources.[1795] Thus, only a limited class of claimants may recover "economic losses" caused by property destruction under subsection 2702(b)(2)(B), while anyone may recover lost profits and impairment of earning capacity caused by injury, destruction, or loss of property or natural resources under subsection 2702(b)(2)(E).[1796] This commentator also asked the probing question; "can a more remote claimant, who would be denied recovery of economic losses as a non-owner/lessee under subsection 2702(b)(2)(B), recover lost profits under subsection 2702(b)(2)(E) even though the owner/lessee would be denied recovery because the property was not destroyed?[1797] A counter argument could be made that injury is in itself a partial destruction as opposed to a total loss. However, the OPA implementing regulations responded to some of these criticisms by providing specific guidelines on recovery of this item of damages. Under these regulation that will be discussed further in the latter part of this chapter, economic loss resulting from injury to real or personal property is recoverable.[1798] Therefore, there need not be destruction of real or personal property to recover.

One legal critic pointed out further that since, loss of profit and impairment of earning capacity are commonly considered "economic losses," without some definition of terms or greater precision of expression,

1794 33 U.S.C. § 2701 (Supp. II 1990); 33 U.S.C. § 1321 (1988 & Supp. II 1990). The term "lessee" is defined in OPA in the context of an oil or gas lease under the Submerged Lands Act (43 U.S.C. § 1301 (1988)) or under the Outer Continental Shelf Lands Act (43 U.S.C. § 1331 (1988)). Presumably, the term "leases" referred to in subsection 2702(b)(2)(B) is intended to be a lease in a more general sense.

1795 33 U.S.C. § 2702(b)(2)(E).

1796 Thomas Wagner, Recoverable Damages Under The Oil Pollution Act Of 1990, 5 U.S.F. Mar. L.J. at 297.

1797 Id. at 298

1798 33 CFR § 136.215

these two sections are hopelessly in conflict.[1799] Neither has supremacy, and giving effect to one will frequently violate the tenets of the other.[1800] These two subsections dictate opposite answers. While "sensible" conclusions and limitations may be ultimately reached by the courts, such sensible conclusions cannot be inferred from the statutory language, which is imprecise and contradictory.[1801]

The implementing regulations allow a claim for injury to, or economic losses resulting from the destruction of, real or personal property to be presented only by a claimant either owning or leasing the property.[1802] Also, any claim for loss of profits or impairment of earning capacity due to injury to, destruction of, or loss of real or personal property must be included as subpart of the claim under this section and must include the proof required under § 136.233 (§ 136.233 provides the nature of proof required in order to recover damages for loss of profits and earning capacity). As part of the evidential and standing requirement, a claimant must establish by proof:

(1) An ownership or leasehold interest in the property;
(2) That the property was injured or destroyed;
(3) The cost of repair or replacement; and
(4) The value of the property both before and after injury occurred.

(b) In addition, for each claim for economic loss resulting from destruction of real or personal property, the claimant must establish--

(1) That the property was not available for use and, if it had been, the value of that use; (2) Whether or not substitute property was available and, if used, the costs thereof; and (3) That the economic loss claimed was incurred as the result of the injury to or destruction of the property."[1803]

---

1799 Thomas Wagner, Recoverable Damages Under The Oil Pollution Act Of 1990, 5 U.S.F. Mar. L.J. at 297.

1800 Id. at 297

1801 Id. at 298

1802 33 CFR § 136.213.

1803 33 CFR s 136.215

The United States Coast Guard has promulgated some regulations for determining the compensation allowable for damage to real or personal property.[1804] Section 136.217 of the implementing regulations provides that the amount of compensation allowable for damaged property is the lesser of--(1) Actual or estimated net cost of repairs necessary to restore the property to substantially the same condition which existed immediately before the damage;(2) The difference between value of the property before and after the damage; or (3) The replacement value. The regulations also provide that the compensation for economic loss resulting from the destruction of real or personal property may be allowed in an amount equal to the reasonable costs actually incurred for use of substitute commercial property or, if substitute commercial property was not reasonably available, in an amount equal to the net economic loss which resulted from not having use of the property. When substitute commercial property was reasonably available, but not used, allowable compensation for loss of use is limited to the cost of the substitute commercial property, or the property lost, whichever is less. The implementing regulations prohibit compensation in any shape or form for loss of use of **noncommercial property.**[1805]

One question that should agitate the minds of lawyers, judges and legal scholars is whether damage to real or personal property not caused directly by the oil discharge can be recovered under this item of damage. In other words if the damage to the real or personal property of a private claimant was caused by the removal activities of the United States Coast Guard or the Environmental Protection Agency (EPA) or removal and cleanup contractors hired by them, can the private claimant recover under this item of damages? The answer to this difficult question is yes. The reason the answer to the question is in the affirmative is the plain language of section 2702 of OPA, which provides:

"Notwithstanding any other provision or rule of law, and subject to the provisions of this chapter, each responsible party for a vessel or a facility from which

1804 Compensation Allowable, 33 C.F.R. § 136.217 (2000).
1805 33 CFR §136.217.

oil is discharged, or which poses the substantial threat of a discharge of oil, into or upon the navigable waters or adjoining shorelines or the exclusive economic zone is liable for the removal costs and damages specified in subsection (b) **that result from such incident**."[1806]

The key phrase in this provision is "damages specified in subsection (b) that result from such incident." If the damages to the claimant's property is connected to activities aimed at containing and preventing the exacerbation of the oil spill, those damages should qualify as OPA damages. One illustration of this is an NPFC Claims Division decision involving a claim for damage to real property by a private claimant. In this case, oil leaked from an abandoned well into the Black River, near Chatham Township, Ohio on June 11, 1996.[1807] There was no identifiable Responsible Party for the spill and the EPA Federalized the spill. During the clean up, the Federal On Scene Coordinator (FOSC) hired trucks to remove oil, soil, and the like.[1808] Some trucks also brought in fill dirt and stone. The claimant brought this damage to Real or Personal Property claim and alleged that due to heavy traffic, the foundation of his house was damaged. The claimant provided the NPFC claim management Division with two written estimates to repair the damage – one was for $6,900 and the other was for $7,400.[1809] The Claims Manager recommended that the claimant should be paid the first estimate of $6,900.[1810] This recommendation was approved by the NPFC Claim Supervisor.[1811] The claims managers reached that conclusion because the facts showed that in order to respond to the spill from the abandoned well, the FOSC actually had to construct a gravel road past the claimant's property onto the site

1806 33 USCA §2702(a).

1807 See Charles M. Manik, NPFC Claim Summary/ Recommendation Form, Claim No 096025-001, pl (2/9/2000) (on file with the NPFC and available upon request from the NPFC).

1808 Id. at 1.

1809 Id.

1810 Id.

1811 Id. at 2.

of the spill.[1812] This road, at its closest point, was approximately 20-30 yards from the claimant's home, and could only be used by one truck at a time.[1813] There were times when up to six or eight trucks were lined up on the previously existing road with their engines running, waiting for their turn to transverse the road being built.[1814] The major question was whether it was possible that the vibrations from trucks passing or from their idling engines could have caused the cracks to the claimant's basement. The NPFC contacted James Lewis, a Professional Engineer with the US Coast Guard Facilities Design and Construction Command, Atlantic, who evaluated the information provided by the claimant and the FOSC and provided an analysis of the facts of the case, the types of soil in that area, and the amplitude of the ground vibrations caused by the response activities. He then opined that "my background in geo-technical engineering, through 10 years of experience with the Norfolk District Army Corps of Engineers and graduate studies in the field, leads me to believe that the claim has merit."[1815] Based on this testimony and evaluation of the engineer, the Claims manager reached the decision that favored the claimant.

A court of law would probably follow the same line of reasoning as the case management division of the NPFC did in this case. This goes to show that the damage to real or personal property need not emanate directly from the oil itself. All damages to real or personal property that occur **as a result of removal activities** could qualify as OPA damages. Although this was a mystery oil spill with no identifiable Responsible Party, there is a lesson that can be learned from it. Responsible Parties (RPs) should endeavor to take over response activities as quickly as possible. This is only possible if the RP already has a response program or plan in place that can anticipate removal cost related damages. In such situations the oil spill response and removal companies engaged by RP because of their experience in oil spill response would avoid taking measures that could lead to the RP being subject to additional damages.

---

1812 Id. at 1.

1813 Id.

1814 Id.

1815 Id. at 1.

The Fund's guidelines for completion of standard Claims form for recovery from the Fund requires that claimants under this subpart present some additional information.

They are as follows:
"DAMAGE TO PERSONAL PROPERTY
**A. ALL**
**1. EVIDENCE OF INCIDENT AND DAMAGE**: The claimant must provide one or more of the following:

a. A description of the incident.[1816]
b. Copy of title or license for the property, in their own name.[1817]
c. Pictures or videotape of the damage, if available.
d. Pictures or statements from witnesses that the property was within the area impacted by the oil spill. (May be shown by marina records or other contemporaneous business records showing the location of the property at the time of the spill.) If available, pre-spill and post-spill photos should be provided.[1818]

**2. GENERAL INFORMATION**:

a. Two estimates of the activities / costs required to repair or replace damaged property; OR
b. Copies of paid bills for repair or replacement of damaged property.
c. An accounting of all those expenses the claimant did not incur because he was unable to use the property (i.e. saved expenses).
d. If the property is leased by the claimant, a copy of any rental or charter agreements applicable to the property.
e. A copy of any rental agreement or other agreement the claimant may have entered to obtain substitute property to use while the property was damaged.
f. Copies of receipts or bills for all extra expenses incurred by use of substitute property.[1819]

1816 National Pollution Funds Center's Supplemental Claims Guidance on Completing Standard Claims Forms, at 5 (July 18, 1997).

1817 Id. at 5.

1818 Id.

1819 Id. at 5.

## DAMAGE TO REAL PROPERTY

**A. ALL**

**1. EVIDENCE OF INCIDENT AND DAMAGE**: The claimant must provide one or more of the following:

a. A description of the incident.

b. Copy of the claimant's lease or deed to the property in question showing his interest in the real property.[1820]

c. Pictures or videotape of damage, if available.

d. Maps or legal documents describing the location to show that the property was within the area impacted by the oil spill.

e. Pre-spill and post-spill property appraisals.[1821]

**2. GENERAL INFORMATION**:

a. Two estimates setting out the activities and cost necessary to repair the damage; OR

b. Copies of paid bills for repair of damage.

c. Comparison of the costs to other reasonable and comparable repairs conducted in the general area of the spill.[1822]

d. Any property appraisals MUST meet the following standards--

   (1) Be done to professional standards.[1823]

   (2) Contain sufficient information to show that the decrease in value is attributable to the spill rather than market conditions.[1824]

   (3) Address the general economic trend in relevant real estate markets before and after the spill.

   (4) Address the amount of time before the real estate will regain any loss in valuc attributable to the spill.[1825]

e. If applicable, evidence that the property was "on the market" at time of spill.

---

1820 Id.

1821 Id.

1822 Id.

1823 Id. at 5.

1824 Id.

1825 Id.

f. An accounting of all those expenses the claimant did not incur because he was unable to use the property. (i.e. saved expenses).[1826]
g. A copy of rental agreements and/or leases for any substitute property which had to be utilized while the claimant's property was unavailable.[1827]
h. Copies of receipts or bills for all extra expenses incurred by use of substitute property."[1828]

## 3. **Recovery For Loss of Profits And Earning Capacity -** 33 USC § 2702(b)(2)(E).

Statutory provisions:
"§ 2702. Elements of liability

(a) In general

Notwithstanding any other provision or rule of law, and subject to the provisions of this Act, each responsible party for a vessel or a facility from which oil is discharged, or which poses the substantial threat of a discharge of oil, into or upon the navigable waters or adjoining shorelines or the exclusive economic zone is liable for the removal costs and damages specified in subsection (b) of this section that result from such incident."[1829]

"(b) Covered removal costs and damages

**

(2) Damages

1826 Id. at 5.
1827 Id. at 6.
1828 Id.
1829 33 USC §2702(a).

The damages referred to in subsection (a) of this section are the following:

**

**

**(E) Profits and earning capacity**

Damages equal to the **loss of profits or impairment of earning capacity** due to the injury, destruction, or loss of real property, personal property, or natural resources, which shall be recoverable by any claimant."[1830]

The OPA provides that damages equal to the loss of profits or impairment of earning capacity due to the injury, destruction, or loss of real property, personal property, or natural resources, shall be recoverable by any claimant. [1831] The scope of damages for which the Oil Pollution Act allows recovery is much broader than that previously permitted under maritime tort law. Admiralty has traditionally prevented plaintiffs from asserting a right to recovery for purely economic losses in the absence of any damage to person or a property interest.[1832] This rule, first announced in *Robins Dry Dock & Repair Co. v. Flint*,[1833] functions as a rule of proximate cause, foreclosing recovery for damages remote to the incident giving rise to the tort. The Robins Dry Dock rule has been used to severely limit claims for purely economic loss on a number of occasions. Although the rule is admittedly arbitrary in nature, it is motivated by a desire to prevent unbounded or unlimited exposure, and thus to decrease the likelihood that socially beneficial activity will be impeded by unlimited liability.[1834] The concern is that "liability for pure financial harm, insofar as it

---

1830 33 USC § 2702(b)(2)(E).

1831 "PROFITS AND EARNING CAPACITY.—Damages equal to the loss of profits or impairment of earning capacity due to the injury, destruction or loss of real property, or natural resources, which shall be recoverable by any claimant." 33 USC § 2702(b)(2)(E).

1832 See Robins Dry Dock & Repair Co. v. Flint, 275 U.S. 303, 308-09 (1927).

1833 Id.

1834 Id.

is proved vast, cumulative and inherently unknowable in amount, could create incentives that are perverse."[1835] Thus, prior to the passage of the Act, certain limited classes of claimants were able to recover for damages to their businesses under maritime tort law.

Most federal circuits also hold that maritime tort law permits recovery for only physical loss to a proprietary interest and for economic loss accompanied by such physical loss.[1836] The majority of the circuits do not allow recovery under maritime tort law for economic losses when the party seeking to recover those losses has not suffered physical damage to proprietary interest.[1837] An exception has been carved out of this rule in favor of commercial fishermen who may recover for the revenue forgone as a result of an oil spill.[1838] *Louisiana ex rel. Guste v. M/V Testbank*[1839] contains examples of those parties who might suffer economic losses following an oil spill and cannot assert a claim under maritime tort law:

1. Shipping and/or other shipping type interest unable to traverse the area of the spill. This includes claims with respect to vessels actually in the area at the time or rerouted around the area at the time, marina and boat rental operators, whole sale and retail seafood enterprises not actually engaged in fishing, shrimping, crabbing or oystering in the mandated area, seafood restaurants, tackle and bait shops.
2. Fishermen, oystermen, shrimpers and crabbers who engaged in these activities for recreational purposes only.[1840]

Under the maritime law prevailing in most circuits, none of those claimants could recover.[1841] In sharp contrast to the Robins Dry Dock

1835 See Barber Lines A/S v. M/V Donau Maru, 764 F.2d. 50, 55 (1st Cir. 1985).

1836 Getty Ref. and Mktg. Co. v. M/T Fadi B, 766 F.2d 829, 832, 1985 AMC 2579, 2583-84 (3d Cir. 1985).

1837 See, e.g., Louisiana ex rel. Guste v. M/V Test bank, 752 F.2d 1019, 1021, 1985 AMC 1521, 1524 (5th Cir. 1985) (enbanc), *cert denied,* 477 U.S. 903, 1986 AMC 2704 (1986).

1838 Union Oil Co. v. Oppen, 501 F.2d 558, 1975 AMC 416 (9th Cir. 1974).

1839 524 F.Supp. at 1170, 1982 AMC 2246 (E.D. La. 1981).

1840 *Testbank*, 524 F.Supp. at 1174, 1982 AMC at 2252.

1841 Under Kinsman Transit Co. v. City of Buffalo, 388 F.2d 821, 1968 AMC 293 (2d Cir. 1968), at least the claimants listed in item one could recover.

Rule, this section of OPA does not require ownership or proprietary interest in the damaged property. The classes of claimants able to recover under OPA seem broader than previously allowed, and it appears that the new provision has come to replace the general maritime law rule that prevented some categories of claimants from recovery. This means that the categories of people listed above who could not recover damages under general maritime law may be able to do so now under the new OPA regime.

The implication of this is a monumental increase in liability for the responsible party and its insurer and it also appears to have automatically upset settled general maritime law principles that had hitherto governed this area prior to the promulgation of the OPA. This may now give an avalanche of claimants the leeway to institute legal actions, which would not have had a chance of succeeding under the general maritime law regime that governed those issues, prior to the OPA.

In *the Matter of the Complaint of Ballard Shipping Company*,[1842] the court found that Congress's enactment of the OPA, which allows recovery for certain damages resulting from oil spills, including 'loss of profits or impairment of earning capacity,' may permit application of the economic harm provisions of a Rhode Island statute in actions arising out of incidents occurring after August 18, 1990, the effective date of the statute. The court concluded that OPA, however, does not apply to the instant action, which arose out of an oil spill occurring in 1989.

One legal critic also pointed out that assuming that the Robins-TESTBANK rule has been abrogated by this enactment, OPA provides no guidance regarding the critical questions of standing, foreseeability, and causation.[1843] The implementing regulations may not have addressed the question of causation or foreseeability but it seems that it addresses the issue of standing. The implementing regulations spell out the type of claimants that are authorized to claim loss of profits and earning capacity.[1844] It provides as follows:

1842 810 F.Supp. 359, 1993 A.M.C. 1413, 23 Envtl. L. Rep. 21,241 (D.R.I.1993).

1843 Id. at 298

1844 Authorized claimants, 33 C.F.R. § 136.231.

"(a) A claim for loss of profits or impairment of earning capacity due to the injury to, destruction of, or loss of real or personal property or natural resources may be presented by a claimant sustaining the loss or impairment. The claimant need not be the owner of the damaged property or resources to recover for lost profits or income.

(b) A claim for loss of profits or impairment of earning capacity that also involves a claim for injury to, or economic losses resulting from destruction of, real or personal property must be claimed under § 136.213." (§ 136.213 provides the nature of proof required in order to recover damages for injury to real or personal property).

"(c) A claim for loss of profits or impairment of earning capacity that also involves a claim for loss of subsistence use of natural resources must be claimed under § 136.219."[1845] (The claimant in this kind of case must proceed under the "loss of subsistence use" authorized claimants regulations instead of proceeding under "loss of profits and earning capacity regulations").

A legal commentator has suggested that tying the statutory subsections together, OPA might be liberally read to provide that any claimant can recover as damages resulting from an incident, lost profits or impairment of earning capacity due to property or natural resource injury, destruction or loss.[1846] While this approach allows access to economic recoveries without regard to direct physical impact, there is no reasonable and predictable rule that will allow private parties to resolve all their legitimate differences short of litigation; the courts must define, on a case-by-case basis, the parameters of this new remedy. The attractiveness of the Robins rule was its clarity, predictability and certainty. It was a workable formula used by private interests to adjust their disputes without the undue time, expense and effort required to formally adjudicate claims in the courts.[1847] The failing of the Robins rule was its denial of recovery of

1845 Id. § 136.231

1846 Thomas Wagner, Recoverable Damages Under The Oil Pollution Act Of 1990, 5 U.S.F. Mar. L.J. at 298.

1847 See TESTBANK, 752 F.2d at 1032; William Tetley, Q.C., Damages and Economic Loss in Marine Collision: Controlling the Floodgates, 22 J.MAR.L. & COMM. 539, 569-75 (1991) [hereinafter Tetley, Controlling the Floodgates].

non-remote economic damages directly resulting from the tortuous event or the spread of the spilled oil.

One critic suggested that the legislative abrogation of the Robins rule might return private parties to the doctrinal struggle of applying legal concepts of standing, duty, foreseeability, and causation to putative economic consequences of some physical event.[1848] In its use of the phrase "any claimant," Congress probably eschewed the Robins prerequisite proprietary interest in the impacted property or resource.[1849] This interpretation, however, does not resolve all the issues. I disagree with the suggestions of a legal critic who believes that the challenge to standing may be revived against remote claimants, such as prospective purchasers or users of property, and future, even unborn--claimants seeking recovery of long term "projected" economic consequences.[1850] The reason for my disagreement is the clear wording of the implementing regulations discussed earlier under subsection (B). Since subsection (B) of the regulations require proof of an ownership or leasehold interest in the property, there is no way a prospective buyer can have standing to sue. I also do not see how an unborn child can prove ownership. We do not need to look outside the four walls of the OPA for answers on the issue of standing. The question of whether the holders of future interests can sue is an entirely different issue, which is outside the scope of this research.

A major distinction between recovery for damage to real and personal property and recovery for loss of earning capacity is that in the former you must hold the ownership or lessee/lessor interest in the property, while in the latter, you need not hold the ownership or lessee/lessor interest in the damaged property or natural resources to recover. The legislative history of the OPA reveals that the US Congress by way of example explained that a fisherman may recover lost income due to

---

1848 Thomas Wagner, Recoverable Damages Under The Oil Pollution Act Of 1990, 5 U.S.F. Mar. L.J. at 298.

1849 Id at 298.

1850 Id.

damaged fisheries resources, even though the fisherman does not own those resources.[1851]

To recover for loss of profits and earning capacity, the claimant must prove the following:

"(a) That real or personal property or natural resources have been injured, destroyed, or lost; (b) That the claimant's income was reduced as a consequence of injury to, destruction of, or loss of the property or natural resources, and the amount of that reduction; (c) The amount of the claimant's profits or earnings in comparable periods and during the period when the claimed loss or impairment was suffered, as established by income tax returns, financial statements, and similar documents. In addition, comparative figures for profits or earnings for the same or similar activities outside of the area affected by the incident also must be established. (d) Whether alternative employment or business was available and undertaken and, if so, the amount of income received. All income that a claimant received as a result of the incident must be clearly indicated and any saved overhead and other normal expenses not incurred as a result of the incident must be established."[1852]

The amount of compensation allowable for loss of profits and earning capacity is limited to the actual net reduction or loss of earnings or profits suffered. Calculations for net reductions or losses must clearly reflect adjustments for: (a) All income resulting from the incident; (b) All income from alternative employment or business undertaken;

(c) Potential income from alternative employment or business not undertaken, but reasonably available; (d) Any saved overhead or normal expenses not incurred as a result of the incident; and (e) State, local, and Federal taxes.[1853]

One thing that is worth noting is that section 2702(b)(2)(E) which creates a private cause of action mentions natural resources. It provides that

1851 1990 U.S.C.C.A.N. 781, H.R. Conf. Rep. No. 653, 101ST Cong., (2nd Sess. 1990).

1852 33 CFR s 136.233.

1853 33 CFR § 136.235.

damages equal to the loss of profits or impairment of earning capacity due to the injury, destruction, or loss of .... natural resources shall be recoverable by any claimant. This provision does not in any way create private damages causes of action for injury to, destruction of, loss of, loss of use of, natural resources. Only a United States trustee, a State trustee, an Indian tribe trustee, or a foreign trustee can recover damages for injury to, destruction of, loss of, loss of use of, natural resources. Private claimants can only recover for the loss of profits and earning capacity engendered by injury to, or destruction of...natural resources. This very important distinction must not be overlooked.

One other thing that is evident in all the implementing regulations is the zero tolerance that regulators have for claimants who fail to mitigate their damages. That is why in almost all the implementing regulations the amount of compensation allowable is reduced to the amount it would have been if the claimant had mitigated damages. That is why the implementing regulations for loss of profits and earning capacity requires that calculations for net reductions or losses must clearly reflect adjustments for potential income from alternative employment or business not undertaken, but reasonably available.[1854] The implementing regulations for damages to real or personal property and economic loss resulting from injury or destruction of real or personal property, penalize claimants who fail to mitigate their damages by providing that if substitute commercial property was reasonably available, but not used, allowable compensation for loss of use is limited to the cost of the substitute commercial property, or the property lost, whichever is less.[1855] The implementing regulations for loss of subsistence use of natural resources requires that the claimant present in evidence (a)A description of each effort made by the claimant to mitigate the claimant's loss of subsistence use; and (b) A description of each alternative source or means of subsistence available to the claimant during the period of time for which loss of subsistence is

1854 33 CFR § 136.235.

1855 33 CFR §136.217.

claimed.[1856] All private claimants should make reasonable effort to mitigate their damages to prevent a reduction in their recovery of damages.

The provisions of the guidelines to filing out a standard claim form also provide some insight into some of the additional information a claimant under this subpart must provide. Firstly, they need to provide almost the same information as is required in the "Evidence of Incident" section for government claimants, claiming damages for cost of providing additional public services, plus pictures of damaged property. The information required covers the following category of claimants: (1) Individual salary-earner, (2)Generic Business, (3)Hotels & Motels, (4) Retail Business, (5)Fishing / Marine Charters. The following information should be provided:

"A. Employee Losses

**GENERAL INFORMATION**:

a. A statement from the claimant as to how the oil spill led to the loss of income or earning.[1857]
b. An affidavit from private claimant's employer stating that he did not work during the period claimed or that his income was reduced during the period claimed due to the oil spill and stating whether the business has or will file a claim for lost profits due to the spill.[1858]
c. Copies of his pay stubs, receipts, etc. for his pay before, during, and after the incidents.[1859]
d. Personnel records from the private claimant's employer showing how many employees were employed before and during the spill and which were retained or hired after the spill.[1860]
e. A description of the private claimant's efforts to mitigate loss, including copies of letters, records of State Employment Office, etc. which show that

---

1856 33 CFR §136.221.

1857 National Pollution Funds Center's Supplemental Claims Guidance on Completing Standard Claims Forms, at 8 (July 18, 1997).

1858 Id. at 8.

1859 Id.

1860 Id.

he made a good faith search for employment after losing his job. Should include details of his job hunting experience, including any job offers made during the time period claimed.[1861]

f. Copies of receipts of any expenses incurred in job hunting.[1862]

g. Signed copies of Income Tax Returns and schedules for at least two years prior to the spill.

h. Details of any employment expenses not incurred during the period being claimed (e.g. commuting costs, etc.).

i. Copies of pay stubs from any substitute or alternative employment taken during the time of the spill.

j. Copies of receipts of any expenses incurred in obtaining and maintaining any alternative employment.[1863]

B. Generic Business; Hotels and Motels

**1. EVIDENCE OF INCIDENT**: (Provide one or more of the following.)

Same as paragraph A1. above.

**2. GENERAL INFORMATION**:

a. A description of business lost due to oil spill and documentation supporting any such loss.[1864]

b. Copies of any agreements and copies of letters of cancellation resulting directly from the spill.

c. Maps or other description of the area to show that your business was in the area impacted by the spill.

d. Copies of monthly, interim and annual financial statements for at least two years prior to the spill and the year of the spill.[1865]

e. Signed copies of Income Tax Returns and schedules for at least three years prior to the spill.

f. Details on efforts to mitigate losses or reasons why this was not feasible.

---

1861 Id.

1862 Id.

1863 Id.

1864 Id. at 9.

1865 Id.

g. A statement from you as to how the oil spill led to the loss of income or earning capacity and statements from any witnesses you may have. If applicable, please explain earnings anomalies.[1866]
h. Daily and monthly occupancy information for two years prior to the spill and the year of the spill.[1867]

### C. Retail Business

**1. EVIDENCE OF INCIDENT**: Same as paragraph A.1. above. In addition to this a retail business claimant must provide one or more of the following

**2. GENERAL INFORMATION**:

a. A description of business lost due to oil spill and supporting documentation.
b. A statement from you as to how the oil spill led to the loss of income or earning capacity.
c. Maps or other description of the area to show that your business was in the area impacted by the spill.
d. Copies of monthly, interim and annual financial statements for at least two years prior to the spill and the year of the spill.
e. Signed copies of Income Tax Returns and schedules for at least three years prior to the spill
f. Details of your efforts to mitigate losses or reasons why this was not feasible.
g. If applicable, please explain any earnings anomalies.[1868]

### D. Fishing / Marine Charters

**1. EVIDENCE OF INCIDENT**: (Provide one or more of the following.)
Same as paragraph A.1. above.

**2. GENERAL INFORMATION**:

a. A description of business lost due to oil spill and supporting documentation.[1869]
b. A statement from you as to how the oil spill led to the loss of income or earning capacity.

---

1866 Id. at 9.
1867 Id.
1868 Id. at 10.
1869 Id. at 11.

c. Maps or other descriptions of the area to show that your business was in the area impacted by the spill.
d. Evidence that the vessel(s) which are the subject of the claim were in the area impacted by the spill and were unable to carry on their business because of the spill.[1870]
e. Copies of monthly, interim and annual financial statements for at least two years prior to the spill and the year of the spill.
f. Signed copies of Income Tax Returns and schedules for at least three years prior to the spill.
g. Details of any expenses not paid out by business during the period being claimed.[1871]
h. Booking records for three years prior to the spill and the year of the spill.
i. List of published and/or non-published charter rates, especially rates for any services (such as sport fishing) that the business specializes in.[1872]
j. Copies of any logs relating to boating activities for the year prior to the spill and the year of the spill.[1873]
k. Registration documents for the vessel for which claim is made, copies of business license, vessel license, fishing license or permit, and the captain's license.[1874]
l. Details of efforts to mitigate losses or reasons why this was not feasible."[1875]

A prospective claimant under this head or item of damages ought to avoid bargaining away his or her right to bring this type of claim. Prospective claimants should also endeavor to prove their claims by a preponderance of the evidence. The Fund is not a cash cow for any Tom Dick and Harry to collect money. A 1997 NPFC Claims Division decision aptly illustrates the need to avoid these types of roadblocks to successful claims. In this NPFC Claims Division decision, a corporate claimant filed

1870 Id.
1871 Id.
1872 Id.
1873 Id.
1874 Id. at 11.
1875 Id.

a claim against the Fund for lost profits and earning capacity as a result of an oil spill that occurred on March 8, 1994.[1876] The source/RP of the spill was designated as Conoco Oil Company's Glenrock Refinery.[1877] The oil had seeped over many years from a storage tank, through the ground and into the river. As part of the removal activities the RP set up recovery trenches and wells on the claimant's property.[1878] The RP worked out an access agreement to use the impacted portion of the claimant's property.[1879] Although the RP denied the Coast Guard's designation of source they cleaned the spill and continued to monitor the well as needed.[1880] The claimant was not required to present the claim to the RP, because the RP denied the designation.[1881] The claimant alleged it lost profits and earning capacity from its sod farm.[1882] The claimant alleged that it intended to develop 26 acres of land, which were being occupied by the wells/trenches of the RP at the time the claim was filed with the NPFC.[1883] The Claims Manager denied the corporate claimant's claim in its entirety.[1884]

First, the NPFC Claims Manager pointed out that whatever the intended plans may have been, the claimant signed an access agreement which gave the RP the rights to that portion of the property in question.[1885] The Claims Manager found that there could be no expansion when such an agreement subsists.[1886] The Claims Manager further found that the claimant was receiving compensation for the RP's access rights.[1887] Therefore,

---

1876 Brubaker Ranches, Inc., NPFC Claim Summary/Recommendation Form, Claim No. 024021-003, p1 (05/12/1997) (on file with the NPFC and available upon request from the NPFC).

1877 Id. at 1.

1878 Id.

1879 Id.

1880 Id.

1881 Id.

1882 Id.

1883 Id.

1884 Id. at 1.

1885 Id.

1886 Id.

1887 Id.

there were no uncompensated lost profits from the alleged future development of the property.[1888]

Second, the Claims Manager found that the claimant's assertion that the impacted portion of the property was to be used for expanding its sod farm was not substantiated by any submitted evidence.[1889] It was also decided that the claimant's assertion of expansion with an unsupported guess of how much would have been lost over future years was speculative.[1890] In conclusion, the Claims Manager found that notwithstanding the access agreement, the claimant still had not proven that it could not expand its sod farm anyway.[1891] The Claims Manager found that the claimant's property appraisal indicated that there was a total of 95 acres available for use, but only 28 were in use.[1892] The Claims Manager further observed that if the 26 impacted acres were unavailable, that still left 41 acres to expand.[1893] Because of this reasoning, the Claims Manager held that the corporate claimant still had failed to prove its alleged loss of profits and earning capacity.[1894]

This case may have had a different outcome if: (1) there was no access agreement between the claimant and the designated RP; (2) a substantial percentage of the claimant's land was impacted, thus foreclosing possible expansion; (3) If the claimant had proved by a preponderance of the evidence that it was planning an expansion. Future claimants should avoid the mistakes of the claimant in this case.

Another good example of damage claims for loss of profits and earning capacity is an NPFC Claims Division claim that was decided in 1999. In that case, a corporate claimant inter alia, filed a claim for loss of profits and earning capacity for damages caused by an oil spill that occurred on

---

1888 Id. at 1.

1889 Id.

1890 Id.

1891 Id.

1892 Id.

1893 Id.

1894 Id.

February 5, 1997.[1895] The NPFC settled the loss of profits and earning capacity claim for $21,756 because the claimant proved that (1) it diverted its employees from boat repair activities to repair docks damaged by the oil spill;[1896] (2) in order to maintain normal business operations, it incurred employee overtime costs; (3) it incurred costs in hiring contractors to temporarily replace its employees who were engaged in removal activities; (4) at the time of the spill it operated the Sunset Marina and that it incurred lost profits from its operation of the Sunset Marina; (5) that most of its extra labor and contractor costs arose solely from the oil spill.[1897] The Claims Manager relied on the review of a claim adjuster contracted by the NPFC to investigate and authenticate the documents presented by the claimants. It was the recommendation of the contractor that the claimant should be paid $21, 756 for its loss of profits and earning capacity claim. The contractor's recommendation was accepted by the NPFC Claims Manager.[1898] This claim underlines the importance of proper and well organized documentation of receipts, invoices and other documents that will make the job of the Claims Manager easier. A clumsy or disorganized documentation or lack of documentation could be fatal to a successful claim no matter how valid the claim may look on its face.

Tabular Representation of OPA Removal Costs and Damages Bills above $100,000 charged to the Responsible Parties by the United States Coast Guard's National Pollution Funds Center.[1899]

---

1895 Maine Shipyard & Maine Railway, NPFC Claim Summary & Recommendation Form, Claim No 017404-003, at 1, (03/26/1999) (on file with the NPFC and available upon request from the NPFC).

1896 Id. at 1.

1897 Id.

1898 Id. at 2.

1899 See. National Pollution Funds Center Oil Spill data, p 1-56 (2001) (Contains the amount billed to the OPA Responsible Party as of April 2001, the Case Names, and the Federal Project Number for each case) (This information was provided by the National Pollution Funds Center (NPFC) in April of 2001 and the data is on file with the NPFC and is available upon request from the NPFC).

| Federal Project Number (FPN) | CASE NAME | AMOUNT BILLED |
|---|---|---|
| 011015 | T/B Sarah Frank | $893, 209.22 |
| 011214 | T/B Smithtown | $118,644.33 |
| 012600 | Dade Oil Company | $477, 218.94 |
| 013102 | T/B RTC | $164,946.29 |
| 013213 | M/V (Various Derelict Vessels) | $330, 129.83 |
| 014021 | New York City Metropolitan | $120, 406.61 |
| 014504 | Roosevelt Drive | $1, 813, 290.70 |
| 014600 | Standard Tank Cleaning Corp. | $2, 483, 837.00 |
| 014601 | M/V Tank Master No. 1 | $509, 006.96 |
| 015502 | Mizhir Oil Co. | $252, 871.32 |
| 015504 | Muller Park Realty | $131, 441.18 |
| 016112 | Maj. Gen. WM. H. Hart | $285, 610.84 |
| 016203 | M/V Scandia & T/B North Cape | $1, 921, 369.90 |
| 016401 | M/V Nickpatrick & M/V Mariner | $229, 001.07 |
| 016405 | T/V Julie N | $470, 811.49 |
| 016501 | Superior Products Dist. Inc. | $1, 118, 960.40 |
| 016600 | Green Pond Road | $183, 161.46 |
| 016602 | Clair Pine Service Center | $173, 330.71 |
| 017011 | Sundance Petroleum PCB Oil | $116, 203.02 |
| 017502 | Southington CT | $3, 146, 638.50 |
| 017504 | Green Tannery | $720, 081.90 |
| 018504 | W & S Laundry #2 | $489, 980.26 |
| 018600 | Matt Petroleum Co. | $1, 112, 267.00 |
| 022019 | MacMillan Ring Free Oil Co. | $1, 567, 094.70 |
| 023025 | Continental Steel | $549, 900.93 |
| 024021 | Glenrock | $1, 543, 319.70 |

| Federal Project Number (FPN) | CASE NAME | AMOUNT BILLED |
|---|---|---|
| 025022 | Warden Oil | $113, 552.91 |
| 025033 | Maysville KY Spill | $196, 253.63 |
| 025040 | Clinton County Site | $189, 836.32 |
| 026003 | Wayne County | $313, 388.24 |
| 026008 | Iowa Malleable Iron | $106, 665.16 |
| 51020 | Star Enterprises | $5, 346, 549.80 |
| 051023 | CG & T Refinery Inc. | $1, 705, 573.30 |
| 051035 | Coastal Properties East Inc. | $270, 831.61 |
| 052030 | Sovereign Oil | $250, 199.18 |
| 053001 | Allegro Oil & Gas Inc. | $2, 296, 725.90 |
| 053026 | Island Realty | $1, 426, 948.20 |
| 053520 | Colonial Pipeline Company | $580, 416.59 |
| 054006 | Burlington Asphalt Corp. | $389, 304.58 |
| 054509 | M/V Saudi Diriyah | $430, 335.78 |
| 054528 | M/V Isomeria | $245, 705.93 |
| 055028 | CG & T Drums | $193, 370.12 |
| 055034 | T/B Bunker | $640, 197.76 |
| 056032 | Home Town Gasoline | $2, 367, 015.90 |
| 056034 | T/V Anitra | $288, 802.29 |
| 056509 | M & M Fuel Company | $128, 808.22 |
| 057010 | Clean Habits | $216, 228.07 |
| 057016 | Sunken Deck Barge | $251, 321.36 |
| 071031 | T/B Vistabella | $3, 371, 130.10 |
| 071057 | Dixie Transmission Oil | $213, 060.09 |
| 072007 | Lagoon Marina Restaurant | $233, 276.37 |
| 072026 | St. Eustatious Oil Refinery | $209, 737.23 |

| Federal Project Number (FPN) | CASE NAME | AMOUNT BILLED |
|---|---|---|
| 072055 | S/V Miss Pammy | $121, 622.64 |
| 073041 | F/V Big Mama | $237, 792.82 |
| 073044 | M/V Miss Beholden | $220, 748.37 |
| 073082 | F/V Red Diamond | $101, 762.75 |
| 073088 | T/B (Tampa Bay Collision) | $1, 891, 355.20 |
| 074011 | M/V Joan McCalister | $197, 985.28 |
| 074028 | T/B Morris J. Berman | $65, 667, 228.00 |
| 074041 | F/V Little Wendy D | $104, 732.91 |
| 074051 | Guanica Southwest Sugar | $1, 292, 068.40 |
| 075012 | M/V Firat | $509, 243.90 |
| 075068 | M/V Theresia | $377, 715.85 |
| 075072 | M/V Orfeo – Drums | $334,488.21 |
| 075083 | M/V Defiant | $296, 511.68 |
| 077013 | M/V Igloo Moon | $120, 979.65 |
| 077023 | San Juan Port Authority | $353, 171.35 |
| 077049 | M/V Marlago I | $291, 364.16 |
| 077054 | GC Quality Lubricants | $2, 584, 562.30 |
| 077056 | M/V Fortuna Reefer | $339, 521.53 |
| 078049 | M/V Author | $218, 853.49 |
| 081011 | T/B Coastal 2509 | $743, 592.55 |
| 81022 | Derelict Barges | $548, 222.59 |
| 081054 | Chain Oil & Gas Co. | $123, 728.11 |
| 082056 | Cattle Farms | $1, 029, 822.50 |
| 982090 | Babin Construction Co. | $677, 439.14 |
| O82105 | S. Parish Oil Co. | $663, 607.88 |
| 083058 | T/B IB-2629 | $169, 149.61 |

| Federal Project Number (FPN) | CASE NAME | AMOUNT BILLED |
|---|---|---|
| 083062 | Unocal Corporation | $341, 380.64 |
| 083069 | T/B Hollywood 2303 | $190, 195.35 |
| 083094 | Marco of Iota Inc. | $2, 769, 581.50 |
| 083095 | T/B Ken Adams #3 | $1, 245, 746.20 |
| 084026 | M/V Antares | $647, 076.34 |
| 084080 | Resources Securities Corp | $124, 219.70 |
| 084122 | Sunchase Exploration Pipeline | $111, 543.42 |
| 085013 | San Jacinto Pipelines | $17, 316, 423.00 |
| 085019 | F/V Bayou Princess | $485, 660.09 |
| 085027 | Mongrue Oil Co. | $106, 700.12 |
| 085046 | Needham Resources Inc. | $207, 492.14 |
| 085048 | T/S Berge Banker | $509, 267.41 |
| 085050 | Riverbend Operating | $494, 229.12 |
| 085067 | Mystery Spill | $641, 541.99 |
| 086024 | Intercoastal Oil Company | $3, 045, 440.60 |
| 086075 | T/B Buffalo | $1, 374, 610.00 |
| 086113 | T/B Buffalo | $149, 694.00 |
| 086120 | Voda Petroleum Site | $524, 337.02 |
| 086126 | USS Cabot | $239, 633.82 |
| 086136 | Riverbend Facilities | $682, 877.53 |
| 086149 | Somerset Refining | $671, 542.60 |
| 086205 | M/V Babuyan | $118, 172.67 |
| 087149 | Overholt Trucking Tank Farm | $2, 641, 001.10 |
| 087151 | USS Cabot | $2, 878, 213.90 |
| 087183 | Lake Palourde Barge | $276, 011.61 |
| 087186 | Bayou Sorrel Barge | $286, 683.12 |

| Federal Project Number (FPN) | CASE NAME | AMOUNT BILLED |
|---|---|---|
| 087190 | Indian Refinery | $921, 235.50 |
| 087209 | Lake Maurepas Aban Barge | $169, 786.23 |
| 087248 | Oil Production Facility | $158, 678.00 |
| 087249 | Oil Tank Facility | $469, 571.04 |
| 088040 | Mid America Oil | $1, 126, 416.70 |
| 088049 | Minden Airport | $187, 408.92 |
| 088066 | Custom Blended Oils | $232, 828.30 |
| 088067 | M/V Stone Fueler & T/B S-7 | $138, 190.51 |
| 088078 | T/V Red Seagull | $112, 597.50 |
| 088081 | Hudson oil Refinery | $676, 817.53 |
| 088107 | M/V Florida Sea Horse | $415, 578.51 |
| 088135 | Reclaim Environmental | $101, 678.09 |
| 088153 | Laforte Spill | $185, 669.06 |
| 088182 | M/V Kriti Amethyst | $164, 478.04 |
| 088189 | Vermillion Bay Barges | $409, 374.17 |
| 088233 | Abandoned Well | $161, 219.61 |
| 088242 | Iowa Sanitation Enviro. | $348, 926.71 |
| 088262 | Bonne Terre Tire Fire | $496, 300.03 |
| 088276 | A – 1 Septic SRVC | $960, 437.20 |
| 08T077 | T/B Natchez | $1, 345, 517.90 |
| 093022 | Petroleum Specialties | $2, 632, 247.60 |
| 094016 | T/B Cleveco | $6, 239, 815.40 |
| 094023 | Scott Contracting | $149, 732.48 |
| 095003 | T/B A – 410 | $190, 980.63 |
| 095020 | Lakeside Refinery | $4, 630, 333.10 |
| 096003 | Griffith Oil | $116, 589.47 |

| Federal Project Number (FPN) | CASE NAME | AMOUNT BILLED |
|---|---|---|
| 096008 | Edward A. Kidston | $2, 378, 535.60 |
| 096025 | Frank Madison | $430, 555.52 |
| 096026 | Nacelle Land & Mgmt | $342, 129.56 |
| 096034 | Zephyr Refinery | $3, 118, 493.00 |
| 098003 | Crystal Refinery | $3, 913, 077.60 |
| 09T018 | M/V Jupiter | $766, 801.58 |
| 110004 | T/V American Trader | $553, 275.35 |
| 111013 | M/V Zim Canada | $193, 592.19 |
| 112022 | Unocal Corporation | $262, 117.13 |
| 113017 | Quik Chek Gas | $574, 181.09 |
| 114005 | Bush Oil Company | $120, 282.00 |
| 114006 | Four Corners Pipeline | $217, 149.62 |
| 114009 | Naples Truck Stop | $2, 360, 873.40 |
| 114016 | Taylor & Mcilhenny Inc. | $322, 656.95 |
| 117002 | M/V Cape Mohican | $1, 194, 719.90 |
| 117022 | F/V Three Daughters | $103, 502.70 |
| 117026 | Toro Canyon | $231, 949.66 |
| 118004 | M/V Kure | $431, 181.28 |
| 118005 | M/V Lady Christine | $375, 608.49 |
| 118011 | Derelict Flotilla | $191, 989.27 |
| 118032 | M/V Command | $1, 233, 657.40 |
| 131013 | Texaco Oil Co. | $124, 847.17 |
| 131019 | F/V Tenyo Maru | $6, 058, 313.30 |
| 132013 | Crazy Bob's Trucking Co. | $216, 887.59 |
| 133017 | Southern Pacific Transportation | $252, 316.94 |
| 134024 | M/V An Ping 6 | $145, 581.83 |

| Federal Project Number (FPN) | CASE NAME | AMOUNT BILLED |
|---|---|---|
| 135002 | F/V Bremeva | $107, 345.89 |
| 136015 | City of Newport Pier | $365, 234.51 |
| 136023 | Garfield Road Fire | $252, 327.52 |
| 136045 | V 1 Petroleum | $1, 544, 140.30 |
| 138021 | Payless Gas | $581, 349.55 |
| 138030 | M/V Debbie Wines | $146, 773.84 |
| 141004 | T/S Star Connecticut | $141, 951.58 |
| 141031 | F/V Hui Feng | $109, 947.25 |
| 142005 | F/V Eiju Maru No. 21 | $233, 802.70 |
| 144002 | F/V Jin Shiang Fa | $367, 832.17 |
| 146037 | Chevron Pipeline | $981, 976.41 |
| 146046 | M/V Sea Tiger | $211, 376.03 |
| 148027 | Tesoro Oil Corp | $155, 356.84 |
| 172001 | M/V Hyundai | $2, 219, 926.00 |
| 172035 | M/V La Poncena | $530, 918.56 |
| 173006 | F/V Sotrudnichestvo | $1, 782, 550.20 |
| 173044 | M/V Karen | $273, 833.73 |
| 173048 | C/S Yorktown Clipper | $257, 086.28 |
| 174018 | T/V Eastern Lion | $197, 297.63 |
| 174037 | F/V All Alaskan | $754, 746.17 |
| 176010 | M/V Citrus | $492, 646.04 |
| 177006 | M/V Baneasa | $489, 260.82 |
| 177013 | M/V Pan Dynamic | $134, 609.37 |
| 178010 | M/V Kuroshima | $3, 069, 100.80 |
| 999318 | Vessel Scott Lynd | $158, 685.20 |
| 9C5067 | N E Utilities | $305, 997.34 |

| Federal Project Number (FPN) | CASE NAME | AMOUNT BILLED |
|---|---|---|
| 9C5200 | State of Texas | $209, 236.66 |
| 9C6235 | Washtenaw County, MI | $133, 597.90 |
| 9C6447 | Smith Oil | $102, 430.07 |
| 9C7013 | State of New York | $1, 049, 214.00 |
| 9C7593 | Burgess Tank Farm | $590, 161.97 |
| A99002 | Abandoned Well | $137, 789.79 |
| A99009 | Garden Grove Mainten | $281, 755.00 |
| B00400 | F/V Jessica Ann | $930, 510.09 |
| B00403 | P/C Rose of Sharon | $485, 264.11 |
| B99014 | Jonas Equities | $887, 653.67 |
| G99032 | Lake Underground | $1, 523, 275.80 |
| H99011 | F/V Van Loi | $216, 584.95 |
| J99051 | M/V Wilderness Adv. | $347, 210.20 |
| M00016 | M/V Sergo Zakariadze | $613, 222.90 |
| M99019 | M/V Pacific Mako | $626, 448.89 |
| M99027 | M/V Star Evviva | $439, 488.92 |
| N00018 | Bayou Creek Oil Site | $269, 949.85 |
| N00120 | F/V Troy and Trey | $109, 087.21 |
| N00131 | F/V St. Vincent | $120, 817.68 |
| N00138 | Floyd County Tire Fire | $220, 156.69 |
| N00153 | Northstar Petroleum | $229, 443.90 |
| N99002 | SP45 Chevron | $101, 500.95 |
| N99072 | Abercrombie Well No. 1 | $1, 898, 517.20 |
| N99102 | Fireball Production | $387, 444.50 |
| N99109 | Western Oil & Gas Inc. | $1, 348, 019.60 |
| N99187 | Claremark Oil | $100, 004.66 |

| Federal Project Number (FPN) | CASE NAME | AMOUNT BILLED |
|---|---|---|
| N99209 | Wood Energy Remediation | $556, 396.92 |
| N99248 | M/T Nord Jahre Princess | $326, 803.66 |
| N99255 | 20 House Boats & P/C | $663, 119.46 |
| N99259 | M/V Union Faith | $1, 060, 397.40 |
| N99260 | LaStrada Facility | $210, 059.08 |
| N99269 | Abandoned Oil Refinery | $581, 918.77 |
| N99274 | Kirby Tire Recycling | $1, 015, 956.00 |
| P00056 | Patuxent River Spill | $4, 040, 924.70 |
| P99500 | P/C Pork N Beans | $114, 899.40 |
| S99018 | M/V New Carissa | $8, 477, 284 |

# Chapter Six

# RECOVERY OF INTEREST – 33 USC § 2705(A)

The OPA does not make any specific provision for the recovery of interest by Responsible parties against the Fund, but the statute makes provision for the recovery of interest by every claimant against the responsible party. [1900] The use of the word "claimant" (emphasis mine) in section 2705(a) of OPA indicates that it covers every claimant. The statute defines "claimant as any person or government who presents a claim for compensation under the OPA.[1901] This means that all claimants bringing action against the responsible party to recover removal costs and damages directly or by subrogation will be entitled to recover interest from the responsible party. Such claimants would include trustees of all tiers of government in the United States, tribal trustees, foreign government trustees, the Fund by subrogation action, as well as private citizens. The OPA also does not specifically provide for the recovery of interest by non-responsible party claimants against the Fund.

The United States, as sovereign, is immune from suit except if it consents to be sued, and "a waiver of sovereign immunity cannot be implied but must be unequivocally expressed."[1902] The government expressly waived its immunity from suit by allowing OPA claimants to file claims against the Fund, which is part of the government. The waiver of immunity from suit does not constitute a waiver of immunity to interest recovery. The basic rule of sovereign immunity has led to what is known as the no-interest rule: "In the absence of express congressional consent to the award of interest separate from a general waiver of immunity to

1900 33 U.S.C. §2705(a).

1901 33 U.S.C. §2701(4).

1902 See United States v. $30,006.25 (Thirty Thousand Six Dollars 25/100), 2000 WL 1879124, see also, United States v. Mitchell, 445 U.S. 535, 538, 100 S.Ct. 1349, 63 L.Ed.2d 607 (1980).

suit, the United States is immune from an interest award."[1903] For well over a century, the United States Supreme Court, executive agencies, and Congress itself consistently have recognized that federal statutes cannot be read to permit interest to run on a recovery against the United States unless Congress affirmatively mandates that result."[1904]

In *Gatlin Oil Company v. United States Dept. of Transportation*,[1905] a case in which the respondent sought to recover interest from the Fund, the Fourth Circuit Court of Appeals held that the defendant/respondent, Gatlin Oil, was not entitled to an award of interest against the United States. The court recognized the long-standing principle that the no-interest rule prohibits an award of interest against the government in the absence of an express waiver of sovereign immunity from an award of interest.[1906] The *Gatlin Oil* court noted that traditionally, Congress has manifested intent to make such a waiver expressly, but an express waiver of immunity from interest is not found in the Oil Pollution Act.[1907] The *Gatlin Oil* court pointed out that the Supreme Court has recognized that the no-interest rule is inapplicable in situations where the government has "cast off the cloak of sovereignty and assumed the status of a private commercial enterprise," and that this is consistent with the Court's holding in *Standard Oil Co. v. United States*.[1908] In that case, the government issued insurance policies, which insured a steamship and her freight against war risks.[1909] When loss occurred, the payment of interest was questioned. The policies issued by the government indicated that "claims would be paid within thirty days after complete proofs of interest and loss had been filed....".[1910] Furthermore, the insured were permitted to sue the government under the

1903 See Library of Congress v. Shaw, 478 U.S. 310, 314, 106 S.Ct. 2957, 92 L.Ed.2d 250 (1986).

1904 Id. at 316, 106 S.Ct. 2957; *see* also Edwards v. Lujan, 40 F.3d 1152, 1153-54 (10th Cir.1994); Sandia Oil Co. v. Beckton, 889 F.2d 258, 261 (10th Cir.1989).

1905 48 ERC 1208, 29 Envtl. L. Rep. 20,605, 169 F.3d 207 (4th Cir. 1999).

1906 See *Gatlin Oil*, 169 F.3d 207, 213.

1907 Id.

1908 Id. (*citing*, Oil Co. v. United States, 267 U.S. 76, 45 S.Ct. 211, 69 L.Ed. 519 (1925)).

1909 *Standard Oil Co*, 267 U.S. at 76-77, 45 S.Ct. 211.

1910 Id. at 79, 45 S.Ct. 211.

policy "in case of disagreement."[1911] The Court determined that the government had assumed the status of a private insurance company.

The *Gatlin Oil* court found that with respect to the Oil Pollution Act, the government does not issue any policies, nor does it assume any risk on behalf of claimants, and that the Act provides limited compensation when the party responsible for an oil spill is unavailable, since it does not function as a private insurance company. The court rejected *Gatlin Oil Inc.'s* reliance on the provisions of the Postal Reorganization Act of 1970. The court explained that in the case of *Loeffler v. Frank*,[1912] Congress established that the Postal Service's liability was equivalent to any other business.[1913] Because Congress "launched the Postal Service into the commercial world," it is presumed that Congress "waived any otherwise existing immunity of the Postal Service from interest awards."[1914] The Court in *Loeffler v. Frank* had decided that the Postal Service could be subjected to an interest award in a Title VII suit due to congressional waiver of immunity.

The *Gatlin Oil* court pointed out that in contradistinction to the situation in *Loeffler v. Frank* there is no evidence that Congress intended the Oil Spill Liability Trust Fund (the Fund) to function like a commercial enterprise or to have liability like that of any other business, and an award of interest against the Fund does not appear to have been contemplated by Congress. This is a logical conclusion since the Fund does not engage in any profit making venture, the main reason for its existence is to help in funding cleanup activities and paying valid oil spill damage claims. The court found that the Act contains no provisions that would make such an award possible. The court found that the Act does establish that a responsible party (or the responsible party's guarantor) is "liable to a claimant for interest on the amount paid in satisfaction of a claim...." (section 2705(a) of OPA). The court noted that based on the definition of a "responsible party," in which, an onshore facility like Gatlin Oil, is defined as "any

---

1911 Id.

1912 486 U.S. 549, 108 S.Ct. 1965, 100 L.Ed.2d 549 (1988).

1913 See *Gatlin* Oil, 169 F.3d 207, 214, (*citing*, id. at 556, 108 S.Ct. (1965)).

1914 Id. at 214. (*citing*, v. Frank, 987 F.2d 1072, 1076-77 (4th Cir.1993)).

person owning or operating the facility, except a Federal agency, State...." (section 2701(32)(B) of OPA), the federal government is not included in the definition of responsible party.[1915] The court confirmed that even though the government is not liable for interest under the Act, it can recover interest as a cost incurred by the Fund. The court noted that the Attorney General is authorized under the Act to commence an action on the Fund's behalf to recover compensation paid by the Fund, as well as costs incurred by the Fund.[1916] The court concluded that section 2715(c) of OPA expressly permits the Fund to recover interest on the money that it had expended, but it does not do any more than provide for the reimbursement of the Fund for expenses it should not have to bear. Based on the foregoing, the no-interest rule was applied to the case and the court reversed and vacated the contrary District Court's finding on the issue, and remanded the case for further proceeding consistent with its ruling.[1917]

A responsible party who has exceeded the OPA liability limits and wants to get reimbursement from the Fund for what it has paid as interest (including prejudgment interest) to other claimants, should not be allowed to get a reimbursement for what it paid as interest because the statute provides specifically that the payment of interest is not subject to the limitation provision of the statute. Only those items of damages and costs that are subject to the limitation provision of OPA can arguably be collected by the responsible party from the Fund. This section of the statute is in my opinion one of the most subtle sections of the statute which ship owners have to be aware of, since their guarantors cannot be held liable for the payment of interest above the amount they have provided as financial responsibility, they would have to bear this burden alone. It becomes a nightmare for shipowners where the interest was accumulated over a number of years and the spill is a medium or large oil spill. Apart from that, because the *Gatlin Oil* decision already bars recovery of inter-

1915 Id.

1916 33 U.S.C. See § 2715(c).

1917 See *Gatlin* Oil, 169 F.3d 207, 214, (*citing*, of Congress v. Shaw, 478 U.S. 310, 311, 106 S.Ct. 2957, 92 L.Ed.2d 250 (1986).

est by claimants generally, RPs are most likely caught by the *Gatlin Oil* decision.

*The OPA interest recovery scheme:* Generally, subject to some specific exceptions, the period for which interest shall be paid is the period beginning on the 30$^{th}$ day following the date on which the claim is presented to the responsible party or guarantor and ending on the date that the claim is paid.[1918] 33 U.S.C. §2705(b)(2)& (3) of the OPA excludes this period for which payment of interest is mandated if the guarantor of the responsible party makes an offer to the claimant that in amount is greater than or equal to what is finally paid in satisfaction of the claim, provided that such offer is made within 60 days after the date on which the claim is presented in consonance with §2713 (claims procedure section); and if justice demands that it be excluded (this is where default in conforming to the time requirement is due to uncontrollable circumstances). The interest includes prejudgment interest and it is calculated at the average of the highest rate for commercial and finance company paper of maturities of 180 days or less obtaining on each of the days included within the period for which interest must be paid to the claimant, as published in the Federal Reserve Bulletin.[1919] In general, interest (including prejudgment interest) under this section of the OPA is in addition to damages and removal costs for which claims may be asserted under section 2702 of the statute and shall be paid without regard to any limitation of liability under section 2704 of the Act.[1920] Because of the non-applicability of the limitation provision to the payment of interest, it is advantageous for a responsible party to settle a claim as quickly as possible to prevent unnecessary accumulation of interest that may very well exceed the amount it might be able to get as reimbursement from the Fund. But the statute creates an exception for guarantors of the responsible party, by providing that nothing in the statute (including the interest provisions) shall impose liability with respect to an incident on any guarantor for damages or re-

1918 33 U.S.C. §2705(b)(1).

1919 33 U.S.C. §2705(b)(4)-(5).

1920 33 U.S.C. §2705(b)(5).

moval costs which exceed, in the aggregate, the amount of financial responsibility which that guarantor has provided for a responsible party.[1921] The statute in effect pegs the total liability of the guarantor in direct action claims brought against the guarantor to the amount provided for financial responsibility. This means that guarantors of responsible parties are fully immune to the "interest recovery without regard to limitation"(emphasis added) provision of the statute.

The court in the case of *National Shipping Co. of Saudi Arabia (NSCSA) v. Moran Mid-Atlantic Corp.*,[1922] decided that the prejudgment interest provision contained in the OPA only applies to cases under OPA brought by a claimant against a "responsible party," and does not apply to actions under the OPA's contribution provision brought by a responsible party against a third party. This is a reasonable decision because the interest provision (section 2705) of the OPA specifically mentions the responsible party as the person responsible for the payment of interest. There is no affirmative provision in this section that allows the responsible party to recover interest from a jointly and severally liable third party. The only way a person designated the responsible party can recover interest is by proving that it was not liable at all for the spill. It can do this by proving that the oil spill was caused solely by a third party with whom it had no contractual relationship. If such proof of non-responsibility is accepted either by a court or by the Fund, that sole-cause third party will be regarded as the responsible party for indemnity purposes and the person originally designated the responsible party would be entitled to indemnification for all it has paid as cleanup costs and damages.[1923] It would also be entitled to payment of interest by virtue of the interest recovery provision in section 2705 of the statute, which imposes liability on only responsible parties.

In the case of *Unocal Corp. v. United States*,[1924] the owner of an oil pipeline that ruptured during construction of a railway station by the gov-

1921 33 U.S.C. §2705(b)(5)(B) & 33 U.S.C. §2716(g).

1922 Moran, 924 F.Supp. 1436, see also, Oil Pollution Act of 1990, §§ 1005(a), 1009, 33 U.S.C.A. §§ 2705(a), 2709.

1923 33 USC.§2702(d)(1)(A)-(B).

1924 Unocal Corp, 222 F.3d 528 (9th Cir. 2000).

ernment, brought an action against the rail authority and others, seeking reimbursement of cleanup costs arising from oil spill under theories of negligence, breach of contract, and quasi-contract, among others. The owner of the pipeline was designated the responsible party and it undertook the clean-up effort. The court found that the owner of the oil pipeline was not negligent in responding to the oil spill that occurred during the construction of railway station, and thus was not liable under the OPA. The court's finding was supported by sufficient substantial evidence that showed that the discharge was caused solely by acts or omissions of the rail authority and its general contractor. The court further found that the owner of the ruptured pipeline exercised due care with respect to the pipeline, and that owner took precautions against foreseeable acts or omissions of third parties and their consequences.[1925]

The court held that the owner of the oil pipeline was entitled to prejudgment interest from the rail authority, based upon its finding that the rail authority caused the oil spill during construction of the railway station. The court also held that although the owner of the pipeline was considered a "responsible party" under the Act, it could also be deemed a "claimant," for purposes of the section providing for interest.[1926]

The defendants (second responsible parties) in the *Unocal Corp* case relied on the case of *National Shipping Co. of Saudi Arabia v. Moran Mid-Atlantic Corp*,[1927] but the *Unocal Corp* court rejected the case and regarded the defendant's reliance on it as misplaced. In *Moran*, the plaintiff's boat collided with the defendant's, causing an oil spill. After the cleanup, the plaintiff, a responsible party under the OPA, sued the defendant for contribution. The district court concluded that the defendant was not a "responsible party" under the OPA because it had been acting under a contractual relationship with the plaintiff.[1928] The *Moran* court had buttressed the fact that prejudgment interest is only appropriate under

1925 Unocal Corp, 222 F.3d 528, *see also*, 33 USCA §2703(a)(3)(A)-(B).

1926 *See*. Unocal Corp, 222 F.3d 528, *see also*, Oil Pollution Act of 1990, §§ 1001(4), 1005(a), 1008(a), 33 U.S.C.A. §§ 2701(4), 2705(a), 2708(a).

1927 Moran, 924 F.Supp. 1436 (E.D.Va.1996).

1928 Id. at 1446 n 4.

the OPA in claims against "responsible parties."[1929] Because the defendant was not a "responsible party," the district court in *Moran* denied the plaintiff's request for prejudgment interest. The *Unocal Corp* court held that in the instant case, in contrast, the jury found that the defendants were responsible parties under the OPA. Therefore, *Moran* was inapposite, and an award of prejudgment interest was appropriate in this case.[1930] The *Unocal Corp* analysis shows that where the government is the sole-cause of an oil spill, subject to the sovereign immunity doctrine - it may be required by the courts to reimburse the original RP for its interest payments. This is quite different from situations where the RP is merely filing a claim for reimbursement of interest payments with the Fund because it has exceeded its liability limits under OPA for an oil spill caused solely by it, or because it was jointly and severally liable with a private or governmental third party.

1929 See Unocal Corp, 222 F.3d 540, see also, 33 U.S.C. § 2705(a).

1930 Id. at 540, n5.

# Chapter Seven

# LIMITS ON LIABILITY - 33 U.S.C. § 2704

Statutory provisions:
"§ 2704. **Limits on liability**

(a) General rule

Except as otherwise provided in this section, the total of the liability of a responsible party under section 2702 of this title and any removal costs incurred by, or on behalf of, the responsible party, with respect to each incident shall not exceed--

**(1)** for a tank vessel, the greater of--

**(A)** $1,200 per gross ton; or

**(B)** **(i)** in the case of a vessel greater than 3,000 gross tons, $10,000,000; or

**(ii)** in the case of a vessel of 3,000 gross tons or less, $2,000,000;

**(2)** for any other vessel, $600 per gross ton or $500,000, whichever is greater;

**(3)** for an offshore facility except a deepwater port, the total of all removal costs plus $75,000,000; and

**(4)** for any onshore facility and a deepwater port, $350,000,000.

(b) Division of liability for mobile offshore drilling units

(1) Treated first as tank vessel

For purposes of determining the responsible party and applying this Act and except as provided in paragraph (2), a mobile offshore drilling unit which is being used as an offshore facility is deemed to be a tank vessel with respect to the discharge, or the substantial threat of a discharge, of oil on or above the surface of the water.

(2) Treated as facility for excess liability

To the extent that removal costs and damages from any incident described in paragraph (1) exceed the amount for which a responsible party is liable (as that amount may be limited under subsection (a)(1) of this section), the mobile offshore drilling unit is deemed to be an offshore facility. For purposes of applying subsection (a)(3) of this section, the amount specified in that subsection shall be reduced by the amount for which the responsible party is liable under paragraph (1).

(c) Exceptions

(1) Acts of responsible party

Subsection (a) of this section does not apply if the incident was proximately caused by--

**(A)** gross negligence or willful misconduct of, or

**(B)** the violation of an applicable Federal safety, construction, or operating regulation by, the responsible party, an agent or employee of the responsible party, or a person acting pursuant to a contractual relationship with the responsible party (except where the sole contractual arrangement arises in connection with carriage by a common carrier by rail).

(2) Failure or refusal of responsible party

Subsection (a) of this section does not apply if the responsible party fails or refuses--

**(A)** to report the incident as required by law and the responsible party knows or has reason to know of the incident;

**(B)** to provide all reasonable cooperation and assistance requested by a responsible official in connection with removal activities; or

**(C)** without sufficient cause, to comply with an order issued under subsection (c) or (e) of section 1321 of this title or the Intervention on the High Seas Act (33 U.S.C. 1471 et seq.).

(3) OCS facility or vessel

Notwithstanding the limitations established under subsection (a) of this section and the defenses of section 2703 of this title, all removal costs incurred by the United States Government or any State or local official or agency in connection with a discharge or substantial threat of a discharge of oil from any Outer Continental Shelf facility or a vessel carrying oil as cargo from such a facility shall be borne by the owner or operator of such facility or vessel.

(4) Certain tank vessels

Subsection (a)(1) of this section shall not apply to--

**(A)** a tank vessel on which the only oil carried as cargo is an animal fat or vegetable oil, as those terms are used in section 2720 of this title; and

**(B)** a tank vessel that is designated in its certificate of inspection as an oil spill response vessel (as that term is defined in section 2101 of Title 46) and that is used solely for removal.

(d) Adjusting limits of liability

(1) Onshore facilities

Subject to paragraph (2), the President may establish by regulation, with respect to any class or category of onshore facility, a limit of liability under this section of less than $350,000,000, but not less than $8,000,000, taking into account size, storage capacity, oil throughput, proximity to sensitive areas, type of oil handled, history of discharges, and other factors relevant to risks posed by the class or category of facility.

(2) Deepwater ports and associated vessels

(A) Study

The Secretary shall conduct a study of the relative operational and environmental risks posed by the transportation of oil by vessel to deepwater ports (as defined in section 1502 of this title) versus the transportation of oil by vessel to other ports. The study shall include a review and analysis of offshore lightering practices used in connection with that transportation, an analysis of the volume of oil transported by vessel using those practices, and an analysis of the frequency and volume of oil discharges which occur in connection with the use of those practices.

(B) Report

Not later than 1 year after August 18, 1990, the Secretary shall submit to the Congress a report on the results of the study conducted under subparagraph (A).

(C) Rulemaking proceeding

If the Secretary determines, based on the results of the study conducted under this subparagraph (A), that the use of deepwater ports in connection with the transportation of oil by vessel results in a lower operational or environmental risk than the use of other ports, the Secretary shall initiate, not later than the 180th day following the date of submission of the report to the Congress under subparagraph (B), a rulemaking proceeding to lower the limits of liability under this section for deepwater ports as the Secretary determines appropriate. The

Secretary may establish a limit of liability of less than $350,000,000, but not less than $50,000,000, in accordance with paragraph (1).

(3) Periodic reports

The President shall, within 6 months after August 18, 1990, and from time to time thereafter, report to the Congress on the desirability of adjusting the limits of liability specified in subsection (a) of this section.

(4) Adjustment to reflect Consumer Price Index

The President shall, by regulations issued not less often than every 3 years, adjust the limits of liability specified in subsection (a) of this section to reflect significant increases in the Consumer Price Index."[1931]

The congressional decision to limit a vessel owner's liability under OPA is firmly rooted in economic theory. Under the statute, the owner of a large vessel, is exposed to much greater liability than the owner of small vessel.[1932] This scheme places the greatest exposure upon those who are in a position to obtain the most benefit from maritime commerce. Certainly, the owners of a large cargo vessel receive a greater benefit from the vessel's activity than the owners of the tug boat which assists with the cargo vessel's docking procedure. The owners of large vessels, therefore, are in a better position to insure against an oil spill or to absorb the cost of a spill and pass the cost on to their customers.[1933] By placing the greatest risks of operating a vessel in the navigable waters of the United States upon those who receive the greatest benefits from doing so, the statute's liability scheme allows the costs associated with oil spills to be spread among all those who benefit from maritime commerce, including those who consume products which are shipped

---

1931 33 USC §2704

1932 See National Shipping Co. of Saudi Arabia (NSCSA) v. Moran Mid-Atlantic Corp., 924 F.Supp. 1436, 1447, n7 (E.D. Va. 1996), *see also*, 33 U.S.C. § 2704(a).

1933 See *Moran*, 924 F.Supp. 1436, 1447.

from overseas.[1934] Oil spill from large tank vessels are likely to be more harmful to the marine environment than those from small tank vessels because discharge will probably be greater.

Liability of various shapes and sizes accompany the transportation, exploration, refining, marketing and storage of oil as defined in the OPA no matter the geographical location of the oil spill. But the exact size and shape of the responsible party's liability depends on whether the source of the discharge is a tank vessel, non-tank vessel, onshore facility, offshore facility, deepwater port, mobile offshore drilling unit, outer continental shelf facility, and a vessel carrying oil as cargo from the outer continental shelf facility.[1935]

Even though the OPA is silent on the procedure for utilizing its limitation provisions, it is important to point out that all the items of damages listed in the statute as well as all the removal costs are all subject to the liability limits in the statute. This means that a responsible party sued solely under the OPA could still limit its liability to the OPA limits. Under these circumstances, the liability of the responsible party would be determined by the OPA limitation formula, rather than the Limitation of Liability statute.[1936]

It does not appear that the responsible party can include what it pays as criminal or civil fines and penalties in the limitation figure. In other words it would have to pay the penalty involved without getting any reimbursement from the Oil Spill Liability Trust Fund (the Fund). This is because of the "additional requirement, liabilities and penalties provision" (emphasis mine) of the OPA.[1937] It provides that nothing in the OPA, the Limitation of Liability Act of March 3, 1851 (46 U.S.C. 183 et seq.), or section 9509 of title 26, shall in any way affect, or be construed to affect, the authority of the United States or any State or political subdivision thereof -(1) to impose additional liability or additional requirements; or (2) to impose, or to determine the amount of, any **"fine or penalty"** (emphasis

1934 Id. at 1447.

1935 33 USCA §2704(a)-(b) & (c)(3).

1936 46 App. U.S.C.A. § 183

1937 33 USCA §2718(c )

mine) (whether criminal or civil in nature) for any violation of law; relating to the discharge, or substantial threat of a discharge, of oil.

A responsible party cannot be assured that limitation of liability will hold until investigation and possible litigation are resolved. Because of the unusual length of time investigation normally takes, a responsible party may need to continue to make payments for clean up even after such payments have exceeded its possible limitation. This is imperative because the RP cannot preempt the result of the investigation. The only remedies that will be open to the responsible party are (1) litigating the accuracy of the outcome of the investigation, (2) presenting a claim to the Oil Spill Liability Trust Fund for reimbursement of excess payments made, and (3) if possible sue the National Pollution Funds Center (NPFC) for denying a claim for reimbursement.

The Oil Pollution Act contains liability limits which are significantly higher than the limits contained in the CWA or FWPCA, and other previous legislation. For instance, a tank vessel's liability is now $1,200 per gross ton or $10,000,000 for a vessel over 3,000 tons (or $2,000,000 for a smaller vessel), whichever is the greater. [1938] A tank vessel is a vessel that is constructed or adapted to carry, or that carries, oil or hazardous material in bulk as cargo or cargo residue, and that - (A) is a vessel of the United States; (B) operates on the navigable waters (meaning the waters of the United States, including the territorial sea); or (C) transfers oil or hazardous material in a place subject to the jurisdiction of the United States.[1939]

The new OPA limit for vessels is a 3,900% increase on the old liability limits of the FWPCA. This monumental increase in the limits on liability appears to be too drastic, considering the fact that Congress could have

1938 The new limits contained in 33 USCA section 2704 of the Oil Pollution Act are as follows:

(1) Tank vessel over 3,000 tons--$1,200 per gross ton or $10,000,000, whichever is greater.

(2) Tank vessel of 3,000 gross tons or less--$1,200 per gross ton or $2,000,000, whichever is greater.

(3) Other vessels--$600 per gross ton or $500,000, whichever is greater.

1939 33 USCA §2701(34).

introduced gradual increases in the liability limits, which could be subject to upward or downward review depending on the prevailing circumstances at the time. The Congress decided to do the opposite by allowing only upward adjustment of the liability limits to reflect Consumer Price Index. Section 2704(d)(4) provides that the President shall, by regulations issued not less often than every 3 years, adjust the limits of liability specified in subsection (a) (liability limits) of this section to reflect significant increases in the Consumer Price Index. In 1991, the president by an executive order delegated this duty to the Secretary of Transportation.[1940] The legislative history of the OPA reveals the possible intent of Congress in including the consumer price index requirement. The Congress noted that in several of the existing Federal laws on oil spills, the liability limits have not been increased in 10 years so that, in real dollars, the liability limits have been decreasing over time.[1941] The Congress noted that in order to prevent further diminution of compensation, this consumer price index provision requires the President to adjust the limits on liability by regulation not less often than every three years, to take into account significant increases in the Consumer Price Index.[1942] Under the FWPCA the limit was $150 per gross ton or $250,000, whichever was greater.[1943] Although considerably higher, the new limits are dwarfed by the actual amount spent by Exxon following the spill from the EXXON VALDEZ, which is reported to be in excess of $12,000,000,000.[1944]

The United States Congress amended the OPA on November 20, 1995, via the Edible Oil Regulatory Reform Act.[1945] This amendment resulted in the amendment of sections 2704(a)(1), and 2716(a) of the OPA. In 1998 there

1940 See Ex. Ord. No. 12777, Oct. 18, 1991, 56 F.R. 54757.

1941 1990 U.S.C.C.A.N. 735, S. Rep. No. 94, 101ST Cong., 1ST Sess. 1989, 1989 WL 225005 (Leg.Hist.)

1942 1990 U.S.C.C.A.N. 735.

1943 33 USCA § 1321(f)(1).

1944 See Dr. Dagmar Schmidt Etkin, Financial Costs of Oil Spill in the United States, 224 (1998), Alaska Court Allows More Exxon Valdez Claims, Oil Spill Intelligence Rep. Cutter Info. Group), Nov. 25, 1999, at 3-4.

1945 33 USCA §2720, Pub.L. 104-55, §2(d)(1).

was a further amendment that added subsection (c)(4) to section 2704.[1946] Both amendments were geared towards the same purpose – treating tank vessels carrying vegetable oil differently for the purposes of limitation of liability under the Act. The new subsection added in 1998 specifically provides that subsection (a)(1) (provision on limitation figure for tank vessels) shall not apply to: (A) a tank vessel on which the only oil carried as cargo is an animal fat or vegetable oil, as those terms are used in section 2720 of this Act; and (B) a tank vessel that is designated in its certificate of inspection as an oil spill response vessel (as that term is defined in section 2101 of Title 46), and that is used solely for removal. This means that a tank vessel carrying edible oils is treated as a non-tank vessel and subject to lower liability limits.

The amendment or exception for tank vessels carrying animal fat or vegetable oil was made to reduce unnecessary regulatory burdens on the transportation of less harmful oil. It was a recognition of scientific facts that showed that animal fat or vegetable oil was not as harmful (non-toxic) to the marine environment as crude oil. The legislative history of the amending legislation reveals that Congress was not satisfied with the overly broad definition of "oil," in the OPA which made the statute applicable not only to toxic oils such as petroleum oil, but also to non-toxic agricultural products such as animal fats and vegetable oils.[1947] The Congress was upset that these non-toxic substances, which are used to make foodstuffs and other consumer products, were unfortunately being regulated to the same degree as petroleum and other toxic oils.[1948] That is why section 2720(a) of the OPA as amended provides that:

> "except as provided in subsection (c) of this section, in issuing or enforcing any regulation or establishing any interpretation or guideline relating to the transportation, storage, discharge, release, emission, or disposal of a fat, oil, or

---

1946 33 USCA §2704(c )(4), Pub.L. 105-383, §406(2), added paragraph 4.

1947 1995 USCCAN 476, H.R. Rep. No. 104-262(I), 104TH Cong., 1ST Sess. 1995, 1995 WL 255962 (Leg.Hist.).

1948 1995 USCCAN 481, H.R. Rep. No. 104-262(II), 104TH Cong., 1ST Sess. 1995.

grease under any Federal law, the head of that Federal agency shall: (1) differentiate between and establish separate classes for-
(A) animal fats and oils and greases, and fish and marine mammal oils, within the meaning of paragraph (2) of section 61(a) of Title 13, and oils of vegetable origin, including oils from the seeds, nuts, and kernels referred to in paragraph (1)(A) of that section; and (B) other oils and greases, including petroleum; and (2) apply standards to different classes of fats and oils based on considerations in subsection (b) of this section."

Section 2720 provides further in subsection (b) that:

"in differentiating between the class of fats, oils, and greases described in subsection (a)(1)(A) of this section and the class of oils and greases described in subsection (a)(1)(B) of this section, the head of the Federal agency shall consider differences in the physical, chemical, biological, and other properties, and in the environmental effects, of the classes."[1949]

The amendments further provide that:

"none of the funds made available by this Act or subsequent Acts may be used by the Coast Guard to issue, implement, or enforce a regulation or to establish an interpretation or guideline under the Edible Oil Regulatory Reform Act (Public Law 104-55), or the amendments made by that Act [Pub.L. 104- 55, Nov. 20, 1995, 109 Stat. 546, enacting this section and amending sections 2704 and 2716 of this title], that does not recognize and provide for, with respect to fats, oils, and greases (as described in that Act, or the amendments made by that Act) differences in- (1) physical, chemical, biological and other relevant properties; and (2) environmental effects."[1950]

This amendment was enacted because it proposed only minor changes and it was supported by a broad-based and influential food in-

1949 33 USCA §2720.

1950 33 USCA §2720, see also, Pub.L. 105-277, Div. A, § 101(g) [Title III, § 343], Oct. 21, 1998, 112 Stat. 2681-473.

dustry coalition that included: the American Fats and Oils Association, the Institute of Shortening and Edible Oils, the National Fish Meal and Oil Association, the National Renderers Association and the U.S. Canola Association.[1951] The Animal Fats/Vegetable Oil coalition represented an industry responsible for handling more than 25 billion pounds of animal fats and vegetable oils in the United States each year.[1952] Because of the industry's wide reach, it garnered bipartisan congressional support that included over 80 cosponsors by late September 1995.[1953]

Some critics believe that the proponents of the amendments failed to provide persuasive evidence of the need for changing the liability limit, e.g. by showing that non-petroleum oils as a whole are less expensive to remove or less injurious to claimants than petroleum oils.[1954] Instead, they generally pointed to the non-toxic character of non-petroleum oils and the industry's good safety record. Some critics of these amendments have noted that by carving out special treatment for non-petroleum oil tankers, proponents of the measure have made it more likely that consumers of petroleum oil will subsidize the environmental costs of the non-petroleum oil industry through the Oil Spill Liability Trust Fund (OSLTF) to which the non-petroleum industry and its consumers do not contribute.[1955] The reason for this is that many pollution response costs do not vary with the type of oil cargo involved in the spill.[1956] For example, as the recent case of the T/B ERIE near Tampa Florida, illustrates, the costs to respond to an incident involving a vegetable oil barge can be remarkably similar, if not identical, to a petroleum oil barge.[1957] On December 10, 1995, the barge

1951 See Lawrence Kiern, The First Session of the 104th Congress and Legislation To Amend the Oil Pollution Act of 1990, 6, Fifteenth New Orleans Maritime Seminar (1996).

1952 1995 U.S.C.C.A.N. 481, H.R. Rep. No. 262(II), 104TH Cong., 1ST Sess. 1995, 1995 WL 588679 (Leg.Hist.).

1953 See Lawrence Kiern, The First Session of the 104th Congress and Legislation To Amend the Oil Pollution Act of 1990, at 6, Fifteenth New Orleans Maritime Seminar (1996).

1954 Id at 8.

1955 Id. at 10

1956 Id. at 9.

1957 Id.

carried a cargo of 17,857.14 barrels (750,000 gallons) of vegetable oil on its voyage in the Gulf of Mexico, when it was lost after its own tug was damaged when it struck the tow. The Coast Guard dispatched aircraft and cutters which located the abandoned oil-laden barge, vectored a salvage tug to it, and towed the damaged tug to Tampa. The Coast Guard's response costs to that substantial threat of a discharge would have been the same irrespective of oil carried by the barge.[1958] Therefore, that case serves to illustrate what experience has taught in other oil pollution incidents when the Coast Guard has responded to pollution threats presented by vessels carrying non-petroleum oils. It goes to show that in **"substantial threat of discharge"** situations, the cost of responding by the US Coast Guard to the threat of petroleum or vegetable oil spills is virtually the same.

The US Congress provided some additional reasons for their decision to introduce this edible oil reform to the OPA. For instance they emphasized the fact that animal and vegetable oil are essential components to human and wildlife diets.[1959] They further observed that there are notable differences in the manner in which animal fats and vegetable oils and other non-animal fats and vegetable oils are transported.[1960] Congress relied on a report that showed that vessels carrying petroleum oils can exceed 500,000 deadweight tons.[1961] In contrast, vegetable oils typically are carried on small parcel tankers ranging from 30,000 to 45,000 deadweight tons.[1962] Further, differences exist in the size of the tanks in vessels carrying these two kinds of products. Large tankers carrying petroleum oil may have 10 large center tanks and 15 wing tanks with individual tank capacities reaching approximately 592,000 tons or 4,228,571 barrels (177,600,000 gallons) of oil.[1963] Parcel tankers carrying vegetable oil typically have about 30 to 35 cargo tanks that range from 1,000 to 3,500 tons

1958 Id. at 10.

1959 1995 U.S.C.C.A.N. 481, H.R. Rep. No. 262(II), 104TH Cong., 1ST Sess. 1995, 1995 WL 588679 (Leg.Hist).

1960 1995 U.S.C.C.A.N. 481.

1961 Id.

1962 Id.

1963 Id.

capacity each.[1964] With regard to transfer operations, the typical amount of vegetable oil loaded or offloaded during a transfer ranges from 500 to 5,000 tons. In contrast, a tanker carrying petroleum commonly loads or offloads its entire cargo during one transfer operation.[1965]

The US Congress also pointed out that spills of animal fats or vegetable oils are likely to be smaller and to occur less frequently than spills of non-animal fats and vegetable oils.[1966] Congress referred to data compiled by the Coast Guard which revealed that, from 1986 to 1992, animal fats and vegetable oils together accounted for only about 0.4 percent of the oil spill incidents in and around U.S. waters (both in terms of incidents and their volume).[1967] Less than half of those spills were in water. Further, these spills were generally very small. Only thirteen of those spills were greater than 23.80 barrels (1,000 gallons).[1968] Thus, only about 0.02 percent of all oil spill incidents in and around U.S. waters over the last seven years were spills of animal fats or vegetable oils greater than 23.80 barrels (1,000 gallons).[1969]

The legislative history of the OPA provides further insight into why the US Congress was particularly concerned about the importance of treating these non-petroleum oils differently from petroleum oils. The Congress believed that separate response requirements that recognize the different characteristics of animal fats and vegetable oils within separate classes should be established pursuant to this amendment.[1970] The Congress reasoned that although spills of any type of oil may have some similar environmental impacts under certain conditions, in many significant respects spills of animal fats and vegetable oils are very different than those of toxic oils in the way they affect the environment.[1971] The US Congress

1964 Id.

1965 Id.

1966 Id.

1967 Id. at 481-82.

1968 Id.

1969 Id.

1970 1995 USCCAN 482, H.R. Rep. No. 104-262(II), 104TH Cong., 1ST Sess. 1995, 1995 WL 255962 (Leg.Hist.).

1971 1995 USCCAN 481, H.R. Rep. No. 104-262(II), 104TH Cong., 1ST Sess. 1995.

was convinced that non-toxic animal fats and vegetable oils by their very nature do not have the same overall environmental impact as toxic oil.[1972] Consequently, agencies should provide flexibility for different response strategies for animal fats and vegetable oils recognizing their non-toxic and readily biodegradable nature.[1973]

The US Congress noted that one response strategy appropriate for toxic oils that may not be appropriate for animal fats and vegetable oils is containment and removal.[1974] The Congress warned that amassing non-toxic and readily biodegradable animal fats and vegetable oils, through the use of typical type contain-and-remove strategy commonly used for toxic petroleum oils, may have an unintended detrimental effect given the likelihood of oxygen depletion and increased possibility of immersion of wildlife in created pools of oil resulting from this containment technique.[1975] Congress noted further that considering the non- toxic, biodegradable, and non-persistent properties of animal fats and vegetable oils, use of intrusive methodologies appropriate for toxic oil spills may actually cause more damage to the environment than the spill left undisturbed.[1976] Congress believed that in the case of animal fats and vegetable oils, alternative approaches such as dispersement, dilution, or agitation, as well as no action may be more appropriate and should be permissible response techniques.[1977] The US Congress was convinced beyond any doubt that these alternative approaches are consistent with the National Contingency Plan and would protect the shorelines as well as serve to minimize harm to wildlife and the environment.[1978] Without this reform legislation, several government agencies responsible for environmental protection would have continued to give the same treatment to animal fats and vegetable oils and toxic petroleum oil. The response methods for dealing with

1972 Id. at 481.

1973 Id. at 481-82.

1974 1995 USCCAN 482, H.R. Rep. No. 106, 104TH Cong., 1ST Sess. 1995.

1975 Id. at 481-82.

1976 Id.

1977 Id.

1978 Id.

petroleum oil would have been applied in animal fats and vegetable oil spills.

The US Coast Guard's implementing regulations for the Certificate of Financial Responsibility (COFR) requirement (which will be discussed in chapter eight) began to treat animal fat and vegetable oil differently from toxic petroleum oil for the purposes of a COFR by virtue of the Edible Oil Regulatory Reform Act. The COFR regulations treat the guarantor of a tank vessel on which the only oil carried as cargo or cargo residue is an animal fat or vegetable oil, as "other vessels." By virtue of being treated as "other vessels," its COFR guarantee is limited to the greater of $500,000 or $600 per gross ton.[1979] This means that the responsible party also is subject to the limitation amount applicable to "other vessels" in section 2704(a)(2) of the OPA.

The second part of the amendment[1980] relating to oil spill response tank vessels appears to have been made to motivate those type of tank vessels to respond to oil spill incidents without fearing that they would be subject to the elaborate liability scheme in the OPA. When they engage in salvage and oil spill minimizing and mitigating efforts they can act in the most prudent and non-negligent manner possible without being subject to the strict civil and criminal penalty provisions of the OPA and other federal statutes.

Despite complaints about the huge increase in OPA liability limits, the European Union (EU) considered a proposal to promulgate an EU environmental regulation patterned after the OPA.[1981] The proposed legislation was called EUROPA.[1982] This call for an OPA like regulation was

---

1979 33 CFR §138.80(f)(1)(i) & (ii).

1980 33 USCA §2704(c)(4)(B).

1981 See Keith Wallis, International: Asia: P&I chief warns on **Erika** action, Lloyd's List Int'l, Oct. 4, 2000, at 5 (reporting the warning that was sounded by George Greenwood, who retired as chairman of the international group of P&I clubs in October 2000, at a Hong Kong Shipowners Association lunch, that shipowners will be adversely burdened if individual governments and regional organizations such as the European Commission push through their own maritime regulations in the wake of the **Erika** disaster).

1982 See Julian Bray, Heidenreich proposes radical rules shake-up, Lloyd's List Int'l, March 22, 2000, at 1. (Mr. Heidenreich warned during his keynote address to the Connecticut Maritime Association's conference: "This may be far-fetched, but if the

due to the massive oil that was spilt from the vessel called Erika.[1983] This vessel split in two in stormy seas off the coast of Brittany on December 12, 1999. An estimated 15,000 tons of diesel oil drifted at sea within two weeks of the ship's break up.[1984] After the ballyhoo that the Erika incident generated, the International Maritime Organization (IMO) quickly moved to increase the limits of liability in the CLC of 1992, by pumping up the amount of limitation. This was done to prevent piecemeal legislation by several EU countries that were parties to the 1992 CLC. The provisions of the post-1992 increase in the CLC limitation amount is discussed in Chapter Nine.

Apart from vessels, the OPA allows lessees and permitees of onshore facilities, offshore facilities, deepwater ports, and mobile offshore drilling units to limit their liability under the OPA.[1985]

Under the OPA, a responsible party also includes the lessee of an offshore facility or the permittee of the area in which it is located, as well as any person owning or operating an onshore facility except a government body. Facility means any structure, group of structures, equipment, or device (other than a vessel) which is used for one or more of the following purposes: exploring for, drilling for, producing, storing, handling, transferring, processing, or transporting oil. This term includes any motor vehicle, rolling stock, or pipeline used for one or more of these purposes.[1986] Offshore facility means any facility of any kind located in, on, or under any of the navigable waters of the United States, and any facility of any

---

industry doesn't act now someone else may act for it. This is not a case of 'if it isn't broke, don't fix it' because the present system is completely broke. The Erika disaster had catalysed opinion towards the tanker industry. The Erika incident, which was unfortunately a serious environmental tragedy, has become the wake-up call that the tanker industry needed. Now we are facing EurOPA 2000 which could end up to be similar to OPA 90. Hopefully that will not happen. Our industry does not need a situation where there is an uneven application of regulations where some shipowners can slip by and hurt our industry."

1983 See Oil Hits French Coast, BBC News Online (Dec. 25, 1999) (last modified, April 16, 2002) <http://news.bbc.co.uk/hi/english/world/europe/newsid_578000/578071.stm>

1984 Id.

1985 33 USCA §§2704(a)(3)-(4), 2704(b).

1986 33 USCA §2701(9)

kind which is subject to the jurisdiction of the United States and is located in, on, or under any other waters, other than a vessel or a public vessel.[1987] Onshore facility means any facility (including, but not limited to, motor vehicles and rolling stock) of any kind located in, on, or under, any land within the United States other than submerged land. Lessee means a person holding a leasehold interest in an oil or gas lease on lands beneath navigable waters (as that term is defined in section 1301(a) of title 43) or on submerged lands of the Outer Continental Shelf, granted or maintained under applicable State law or the Outer Continental Shelf Lands Act (43 U.S.C. 1331 et seq.). A permittee means a person holding an authorization, license, or permit for geological exploration issued under section 11 of the Outer Continental Shelf Lands Act (43 U.S.C.1340) or applicable State law.[1988] Section 101 of the US Senate amendment to the House of Representatives version of the OPA bill contained definitions of terms used in the Act. The terms "vessel", "public vessel", "owner or operator", "onshore facility", "offshore facility", "barrel", "person", "navigable waters", "remove" and "removal" and "territorial seas" were defined by reference to existing definitions contained in either section 311 or section 502 of the Federal Water Pollution Control Act (FWPCA).[1989]

Section 2704(a)(3) of the OPA provides that the total liability of a responsible party under section 2702 of the OPA and any removal costs incurred by, or on behalf of, the responsible party, for an **offshore facility** except a deepwater port shall not exceed the total of all removal costs plus $75,000,000. Section 2704(a)(4) provides that for any **onshore facility** and a **deepwater port**, the total liability shall not exceed $350,000,000. An "onshore facility" is defined as "any facility (including, but not limited to, motor vehicles and rolling stock) of any kind located in, on, or under, any land within the United States other than submerged land."[1990]

---

1987 33 USCA §2701(22)

1988 33 CFR 2701(28).

1989 See 1990 U.S.C.C.A.N. 779, H.R. Conf. Rep. No. 653, 101ST Cong., (2nd Sess. 1990), 1990 WL 132747 (Leg.Hist.), Pub.L. 101-380, OIL POLLUTION ACT OF 1990, *see also* 33 U.S.C. A.§§1321, 1362.

1990 33 USC 2701(24).

Section 2701(6) of OPA provides that a "Deepwater Port" is a facility licensed under the Deepwater Port Act of 1974.[1991] Section 1502(10) of the Deepwater Port Act defines "deepwater port" as:

"any fixed or floating manmade structures other than a vessel, or any group of such structures, located beyond the territorial sea and off the coast of the United States and which are used or intended for use as a port or terminal for the loading or unloading and further handling of oil for transportation to any State, except as otherwise provided in section 1522 of this title. The term includes all associated components and equipment, including pipelines, pumping stations, service platforms, mooring buoys, and similar appurtenances to the extent they are located seaward of the high water mark."

The definition of a deepwater port contained in the Deepwater Port Act does not include facilities used exclusively for production, transportation and storage of oil produced from adjacent OCS (Outer Continental Shelf) mineral leases, which constitute an incident of the lease development, and which are not intended to serve as a link in the nation's transportation network.[1992]

For an offshore facility this provision makes it clear that liability is unlimited with respect to removal costs but limited with respect to damages. This means that removal costs would not be counted towards limitation. If there is an oil spill from an offshore facility that results in removal costs of over $200,000,000 dollars and damages of only $500,000, the limitation of liability provision in section 2704(a)(4) will be worthless to the responsible party because it will not be able to apply the limitation provision to the removal costs of over $200,000,000. Because its liability for damages is far below the limitation amount, it will not be able to apply the limitation amount to damages claims. If this section is amended to reflect section 2704(a)(1)-(2) where the limitation figure for tank and non-tank vessels applies to both removal costs and damages, the responsible

1991 33 USCA §1501-1524.

1992 See Get Oil Out! Get Oil Out! Inc. v. Exxon Corp., 586 F.2d 726 (9th Cir. 1978).

party in my hypothetical will be able to apply the limitation amount of $75,000,000 to the $200,000,0000 removal costs. It is reasonable to criticize the possible rationale for treating oil spills from vessels differently from oil spills from offshore facilities.

The limitation amount for onshore facilities and deep water ports is the highest of all the limitation amounts in the OPA. Even though the OPA imposes unlimited liability for removal costs in offshore facility oil spills, this provision does not in any way eliminate or eviscerate the defenses to liability provisions in section 2703(a) of the statute. If the owner or operator of an offshore facility has a legitimate defense to liability that is recognized under section 2703(a) of OPA, that person will be free from any liability whatsoever in relation to the oil spill. The reason for my reasoning is the absence of any express provision in section 2704(a)(3) disallowing the invocation of the defenses to liability provision in section 2703(a). What makes this argument more compelling is the express provision in section 2704(c)(3) eliminating the defenses to liability provision for removal costs emanating from Outer Continental Shelf facilities. The implication of this is that the defenses will be available for all offshore-facility oil spills but unavailable in relation to removal costs claims for Outer Continental Shelf facilities.

OPA defines a mobile offshore drilling unit as a vessel (other than a self- elevating lift vessel) capable of use as an offshore facility.[1993] Section 2704(b) divides the liability for mobile offshore drilling units (MODU) by treating it first as tank vessel and then treating it as facility for the purposes of excess liability. This section makes the treatment in the following ways:

"(1) Treatment First as tank vessel: For purposes of determining the responsible party and applying this chapter and except as provided in paragraph (2), a mobile offshore drilling unit which is being used as an offshore facility is deemed to be a tank vessel with respect to the discharge, or the substantial threat of a discharge, of oil on or above the surface of the water.

1993 33 USCA §2701(18).

(2) Treated as facility for excess liability: To the extent that removal costs and damages from any incident described in paragraph (1) exceed the amount for which a responsible party is liable (as that amount may be limited under subsection (a)(1) of this section), the mobile offshore drilling unit is deemed to be an offshore facility. For purposes of applying subsection (a)(3) of this section, the amount specified in that subsection shall be reduced by the amount for which the responsible party is liable under paragraph (1)."

The implication of this division of liability is that if the actual or eventual liability of a mobile offshore unit is equal to or below the liability amount specified for tank vessels (section 2704(a)(1)), the tank vessel limitation amount would be applied for the purposes of limitation. But on the other hand, if the actual or eventual liability of a mobile offshore drilling unit exceeds the liability limit for tank vessels, the offshore facility liability limitation would be applicable to the mobile offshore drilling unit. The implication of this for the mobile offshore drilling unit is that it will not be able to limit its liability for removal costs.

The earlier hypothetical on the effect that the responsible party's inability to limit removal costs liability would have, applies with equal force to a mobile offshore drilling unit that incurs excess liability. In a typical excess liability situation, the MODU-responsible party will be first of all liable in the amount of either 2 million US dollars or 10 million US dollars depending on its size, afterwards it would be liable for the entire removal costs plus 75 million US dollars (limit for offshore oil spill damages). The MODU-responsible party can deduct what it has paid under the tank vessel liability provision from the 75 million US dollars, but it cannot deduct it for removal costs purposes because removal costs are subject to unlimited liability. This means that if the MODU-responsible party is sued for damages or a claim for damages is presented to it, it can limit its liability for those damages to 75 million US dollars less the amount it has already paid as a tank vessel. This means that if it has paid 10 million US dollars as a tank vessel it would not have to pay more than 65 million US dollars as damages.

It is very important to point out that the mobile offshore drilling unit (MODU) provision on treatment of the MODU-responsible party as a tank vessel for limitation purposes relates only to the discharge, or the substantial threat of a discharge, of oil on or above the surface of the water. It does not in any way cover the discharge, or the substantial threat of a discharge, of oil below the surface of the water. The provision on treatment of the MODU as a facility for excess liability also does not in any way cover the discharge, or the substantial threat of a discharge, of oil below the surface of the water.[1994]

The legislative history of the OPA reveals the intent of the US Congress on the issue of allocation of liability between owners and operators MODUs responsible for oil spills on Outer Continental Shelf land and lessees and permittees of the area in which an outer continental shelf (OCS) facility is located. The US Congress observed that one of its intentions is that a major deficiency of title III of the Outer Continental Shelf Lands Act Amendments of 1978 be corrected by the OPA bill.[1995] Under that title, the owner or operator of an OCS facility as well as vessels transporting OCS oil were held liable for all the cost of clean-up, which included the restoration of natural resources.[1996] Congress noted that often, that owner or operator is an independent drilling contractor and not the actual holder of the rights to produce the oil.[1997] This technical feature of the 1978 Act changed the way in which OCS leaseholders and drilling contractors had historically allocated liability, through contracts and indemnity agreements.[1998] The OPA bill was supposed to restore the balance among leaseholders and drilling contractors on the OCS, leaving the possibility of further adjustment in their internal allocation of liability through indemnity agreements.[1999]

The bill accomplished this by defining "owner or operator" for OCS facilities to mean the lessee or permittee of the area in which the facility

---

1994 See 33 USCA §2704(b)(1)-(2).

1995 1990 U.S.C.C.A.N. 733, S. Rep. No. 94, 101ST Cong., 1ST Sess. 1989, 1989 WL 225005 (Leg.Hist.).

1996 1990 U.S.C.C.A.N. 733.

1997 Id. at 733.

1998 Id.

1999 Id.

is located (or the holder of the OCS rights).[2000] But the Congress jettisoned this proposal and in the final OPA statute expanded the definition of owner or operator of a facility without maintaining the status quo. OPA provides that a responsible party in the case of an offshore facility is the lessee or permittee of the area in which the facility is located or the holder of a right of use and easement granted under applicable State law or the Outer Continental Shelf Lands Act (43 U.S.C. 1301-1356) for the area in which the facility is located (if the holder is a different person than the lessee or permittee).

The original OPA bill's definition of the owner or operator was thus expanded in the final OPA statute by including the holder of a right of use and easement granted under applicable State law or the Outer Continental Shelf Lands Act. The holders of such easements or right of use can be different persons from the lessee or permitee. This purported expansion in the final OPA statute does not seem to cover independent drilling contractors using MODUs. Independent drilling contractors using MODUs are mere contractors and they are not the actual holders of the rights to produce the oil. They are not permitees because a "permittee" means a person holding an authorization, license, or permit for geological exploration issued under section 11 of the Outer Continental Shelf Lands Act (43 U.S.C. 1340) or applicable State law.[2001] They are also not lessees because a "lessee" means a person holding a leasehold interest in an oil or gas lease on lands beneath navigable waters (as that term is defined in section 1301(a) of Title 43) or on submerged lands of the Outer Continental Shelf, granted or maintained under applicable State law or the Outer Continental Shelf Lands Act (43 U.S.C. 1331 et seq.).[2002] Neither are they holders of a right of use and easement. They are mere independent contractors.

The intent of Congress was that, where a mobile offshore drilling unit is being used as an offshore facility, and there is a discharge of oil on or above the surface of the water, the owner or operator of the unit is liable,

---

2000 Id.

2001 33 USCA §2701(28).

2002 33 USCA §2701(16).

up to the limits established by the OPA bill for tank-vessels.[2003] If costs exceeded that limit, the excess costs was supposed to be borne by the lessee or permittee.[2004] This part was deleted from the final OPA statute and instead the excess cost is to be borne by the owner or operator of the MODU. As extrapolated earlier the owner or operator of the MODU is treated as a facility for excess liability purposes. Congress, in its allocation of liability between owners and operators of MODUs and lessees and permitees of the area in which they are located, intended that if a discharge of oil from a MODU occurs below the surface of the water, only the lessee or permittee should be liable.[2005]

This means that in any discharge, or the substantial threat of discharge, of oil below the surface of offshore water, liability must be borne by the lessee or permittee and /or the holder of the easement and right of use, but not by the owner or operator of the MODU.[2006] If Congress had wanted to hold the owner or operator of the MODU liable for offshore oil spills below the surface of the water, it would have stated it expressly in section 2704(b). Instead of providing for this expressly, Congress in order not to place any one in doubt as to what its real intent is, stated expressly in section 2704(b)(1) that the liability of a MODU is limited to the discharge, or the substantial threat of a discharge, of oil on or above the surface of the water. This area will no doubt generate litigation in the future, especially when government and private claimants try to hold the owner and operator of a MODU responsible for OCS oil spills below the surface of the water. The courts should follow my earlier line of reasoning. The legislative history as well as a strict construction of section 2704(b)(1)-(2) would no doubt help to resolve cases of this nature in favor of the owner or operator of a MODU.

Congress has made it clear that nothing stops the responsible party from claiming contribution and indemnity from a third party whose negligence was the actual or contributing cause of the oil spill.[2007] The

2003 1990 U.S.C.C.A.N. 734.

2004 1990 U.S.C.C.A.N. 734.

2005 Id.

2006 1990 USCCAN 734.

2007 See 33 USCA §§2709-2710.

statute also allows the responsible party to enter into indemnification agreements with third parties, and gives him the right to enforce such agreements. But the OPA provides that such agreements cannot reduce or eliminate the liability of the responsible party for oil spills. So, if there is an indemnity agreement between the owner and operator of the MODU and the permitee or lessee of the offshore area in which it is located, that agreement can allow the permitee or lessee to claim indemnity from the owner and operator of the MODU for oil spills below the surface of the water. But, the MODU and the permitee or lessee of an offshore facility will not be jointly and severally liable for oil spills below the surface of the water even where it was caused solely or contributorily by the negligence of the MODU. The government and third parties may only sue the permitee or lessee of the OCS facility. Afterwards the permitee or lessee of the OCS facility can sue for indemnity or contribution depending on the provision of the contract between both parties.

It also must be emphasized that the Oil Pollution Act provides for unlimited liability where a pollution incident is determined to have been proximately caused by (1) gross negligence or willful misconduct, or (2) the violation of an applicable federal safety, construction, or operating regulation. Further, any potential limitation of liability would be waived where the responsible party does not report the discharge or fails to cooperate with or abide by the orders of officials concerned with removal activities.[2008] The legislative history of the OPA reveals the possible intent of the US Congress's in restricting the application of the limitation provision of the OPA. The US Congress observed that a limit on liability is clearly of benefit to an owner or operator subject to the provisions of the OPA.[2009] It believed however that such a benefit should not be conferred in instances where the conduct of the owner or operator indicates that such owner or operator is not, in good faith, attempting to comply with the applicable regulations or statutory requirements.[2010] It

---

2008 33 USCA §2704(c).

2009 1990 U.S.C.C.A.N. 735, S. Rep. No. 94, 101ST Cong., (1st Sess. 1989), 1989 WL 225005 (Leg.Hist).

2010 1990 U.S.C.C.A.N. 735-36.

concluded that in these instances, where compliance perhaps could have prevented or mitigated the effects of an oil spill, no such limits should apply.[2011]

OPA section 2704(c) (1)(A)'s inclusion of the disjunct "or" between the two phrases "gross negligence" and "willful misconduct," seems to suggest that Congress wanted the two phrases to be used interchangeably. But the use of "or" does not necessarily mean that Congress wanted both phrases to have the same meaning. US tort law is dictated by a mixture of state common law and state statutes. So the phrase gross negligence or willful misconduct is susceptible of differing definitions depending on the locus of injury, because the law of the place of injury would govern.[2012] **This will make it difficult for this discussion to settle on a particular definition of these terms**. However, gross negligence generally implies willful or intentional misconduct. It is defined as the thoughtless disregard of consequences which may ensue from an act, and an indifference to the rights of others.[2013] Unlike the failure to use ordinary and reasonable care in simple negligence, gross negligence justifies the imposition of liability and damages, even when the parties have provided in a contract against liability.[2014] Gross negligence has also been defined as the intentional disregard of the consequences of an action which would most likely adversely affect the life and property of another.[2015] Commentators have acknowledged that there is no generally accepted meaning aside from more than ordinary inadvertence or inattention.[2016] The Black's Law Dictionary

---

2011 Id. at 736.

2012 See Black Diamond S. S. Corp. v. Robert Stewart & Sons, 69 S.Ct. 622 (1949) (holding that in the absence of some overriding domestic policy translated into law, the right to recover for a tort depends upon law of place where tort occurred).

2013 See Cauble v. Mabon Nugent & Co., 594 F.Supp. 985, 993 (S.D.N.Y. 1984).

2014 See Hong Kong Export Credit Ins. Corp. v. Dun and Bradstreet, 414 F.Supp. 153, 160 (S.D.N.Y.1975).

2015 BLACK'S LAW DICTIONARY 1033 (6th ed. 1990).

2016 PROSSER AND W. PAGE KEETON, THE LAW OF TORTS §34 (5th ed. 1984). Originally, gross negligence was seen as very great negligence, without even the slightest care. Id. Today, most courts admit that gross negligence differs and is not quite a reckless disregard of consequences, and is different from ordinary negligence in degree, not in kind. Id.

shed some light on the difference between ordinary negligence and gross negligence by providing thus:

> "The element of culpability which characterizes all negligence is in gross negligence magnified to a high degree as compared with that present in ordinary negligence. Gross negligence is a manifestly smaller amount of watchfulness and circumspection than the circumstances require of a person of ordinary prudence."[2017]

Some courts have held that the legal standard for finding "gross negligence" is different from that which is required to find "willful misconduct." First, it is generally recognized that willful or wanton misconduct is separate and distinct from negligence, involving different principles of liability and different defenses.[2018] Some courts have found that unlike negligence, which implies a failure to use ordinary care, and even gross negligence, which connotes such a lack of care as may be presumed to indicate a passive and indifferent attitude toward results, willful misconduct is not marked by a mere absence of care.[2019] Rather, it "involves a more positive intent actually to harm another or to do an act with a positive, active and absolute disregard of its consequences."[2020]

The courts have also held that in order to be held liable for willful and malicious conduct, one must act intentionally, deliberately and purposefully.[2021] A willful act is one done intentionally, or on purpose, and not accidentally, and willfulness implies intentional wrongdoing.[2022] An injury is willful where the act which produced it was intended to have that effect.[2023] A tort having some of the characteristics of both negligence

---

2017 BLACK'S LAW DICTIONARY 1033 (6th ed. 1990).

2018 See Shepardson v. McLellan 59 Cal.2d 83, 89, 27 Cal.Rptr. 884, 378 P.2d 108 (1963) [willful misconduct]; see also Palazzi v. Air Cargo Terminals, Inc. 244 Cal.App.2d 190, 195, 52 Cal.Rptr. 817 (1966) [wanton misconduct].

2019 See Calvillo-Silva v. Home Grocery, 80 Cal. Rptr. 2d. 506, 517 (S.C. Cal. 1998).

2020 Id. at 517.

2021 See Cagle v. U.S., 937 F.2d 1073 (6th Cir. 1991).

2022 Irwin J. Schiffres, 74 American. Jurisprudence. Torts § 21 (2d ed. 1974).

2023 Id.

and willfulness occurs when a person with no intent to cause harm intentionally performs an act so unreasonable and dangerous that he knows, or should know, it is highly probable that harm will result.[2024] In other words, willfulness is regarded as sufficiently established where there is a knowledge that the act will probably result in an injury to another, and an utter disregard of the consequences.[2025] Although no mischief of any kind is intended, if a person commits an act which is dangerous to others, and which evinces a reckless disregard of consequences, he is answerable for the resulting injuries.[2026]

We can look to the FWPCA for some guidance on the interpretation of the limitation breaking provision of OPA. The FWPCA also provided that limitation would not hold if the oil pollution was caused by the willful negligence or willful misconduct within the privity and knowledge of the owner.[2027] The OPA changed the previous FWPCA standard of "willful negligence or willful misconduct" and replaced it with "gross negligence or willful misconduct." Thus, OPA retained one of the phrases in the previous statute but changed one.

It appears that section 2704(c)(1)(B)'s provision that limitation will be lost if the RP or an agent or employee of the responsible party, or a person acting pursuant to a contractual relationship with the responsible violates applicable Federal safety, construction, or operating regulation is a provision that indicates the fact that privity and knowledge of the owner will cause limitation to be lost. Like the FWPCA, OPA does include the requirement that the willful misconduct and gross negligence be within the privity and knowledge of the owner of the offending vessel or facility. The implication of this broad provision that causes the RP to lose its limitation under OPA by holding it vicariously liable is that the RP would

2024 Id., see also, Calvillo-Silva v. Home Grocery, 80 Cal. Rptr. 2d. at 516 (holding that willfulness generally is marked by three characteristics: (1) actual or constructive knowledge of the peril to be apprehended; (2) actual or constructive knowledge that injury is a probable, as opposed to a possible, result of the danger; and (3) conscious failure to act to avoid the peril).

2025 Irwin J. Schiffres, 74 American. Jurisprudence. Torts § 21.

2026 Id.

2027 33 USCA 1321(f)(1).

have to incur great transaction costs in monitoring the activities of employees and other third parties in contractual relationship with it. The RP would also have the incentive to select the most environmentally responsible and sensitive third party contractors, who may charge higher fees for their activities which will probably be carried out with the best available environmental control technology. The type of third parties that owners and operators of vessels and facilities normally have contractual relationship with, which could expose them to vicarious liability under 2704(c)(1) include suppliers of bunkers, ship builders and repairers, vessel masters, pilots, mobile off-shore drilling companies, members of a vessel's navigation crew, operators of pipelines, tug boat owners, manufacturers of vessel parts and drilling equipment, etc. The only limitation to the vicarious liability of the ship owner is that the plaintiff must prove that the oil spill incident was proximately cause by the third party.

Because the provisions of the FWPCA is quite similar to that of OPA, FWPCA case law interpreting "willful misconduct" should provide some guidance in OPA cases. In *Steuart Transportation Co. v. Allied Towing Corp.*,[2028] FWPCA limit of liability was granted to the owner of an oil barge which sank in heavy weather causing a release of oil, despite the courts finding that the flanges securing a cowling on the barge were badly deteriorated and scrapper plugs had not been removed thereby allowing seawater to fill the pump room and accumulate on deck leading to the loss of the barge and subsequent oil discharge. The court found that "willful negligence" within the meaning of the FWPCA refers to reckless disregard for probable consequences of voluntary act or omission.[2029]

The case of *Tug Ocean Prince v. United States*,[2030] decided in 1978 noted that the phrases "willful misconduct" and "willful negligence" had not been defined. The court noted the dearth of cases in which the terms had been explained at the time and the research of the court disclosed

2028 596 F.2d 609, 612, 1979 AMC 1187 (4th Cir. 1979).

2029 Id. at 609, (citing, Billingsley v. Westrac Co., 365 F.2d 619, 621-23 (8th Cir. 1966); F. W. Myers & Co. v. United States, 360 F.Supp. 429, 434-35 (Cust.Ct.1973); cf. In re Tug Ocean Prince, Inc., 584 F.2d 1151, 1162-63 (2d Cir. 1978) (defining "willful misconduct")).

2030 584 F.2d 1151, 1163 (2d. Cir 1978), *cert. denied*, 440 US 959 (1979).

none. The court noted that the phrase "willful misconduct", has been defined with reference to cases arising under the Warsaw Convention,[2031] which excludes any limitation of liability if the damage is caused by the carrier's willful misconduct.[2032] The Court pointed out that in those cases arising under the Warsaw Convention, this same court had established the following criteria for a finding of willful misconduct: an act, intentionally done, with knowledge that the performance will probably result in injury, or done in such a way as to allow an inference of a reckless disregard of the probable consequences.[2033] The court held that if the harm results from an omission, the omission must be intentional, and the actor must either know the omission will result in damage or the circumstances surrounding the failure to act must allow an implication of a reckless disregard of the probable consequences.[2034] The court held that the knowledge required for a finding of willful misconduct is that there must be either actual knowledge that the act, or the failure to act, is necessary in order to avoid danger, or if there is no actual knowledge, then the probability of harm must be so great that failure to take the required action constitutes recklessness.[2035]

The *Tug Ocean* court denied limitation on the ground that the owner failed to inform one of the pilots about a second pilot's unfamiliarity with a section of the river where the spill occurred.[2036] Limitation was also denied because the defendant knew that deckhands were sent below for coffee, thereby eliminating them as a lookout, yet failed to take any steps to halt this practice.[2037] The court held that given the conditions at the time of the accident, the ice along the bank, the possibility of the buoys having been moved by the ice, the darkness, and the ebbing tide, all of which the

2031 49 Stat. 3000, Article 25(1).

2032 584 F.2d. at 1162.

2033 Id. at 1162-63 (*citing*, Pekelis v.Transcontinental & Western Air, 187 F.2d 122 (2d Cir.), *cert. denied*, 341 U.S. 951, 71 S.Ct. 1020, 95 L.Ed. 1374 (1951)).

2034 Pekelis v. Transcontinental & Western Air, 187 F.2d at 122.

2035 *Tug Ocean Prince*, 584 F.2d at 1163 (citing, Berner v. British Commonwealth Pacific Airlines, Ltd., 346 F.2d 532 (2d Cir. 1965)).

2036 Id. at 1163.

2037 Id.

defendant knew or should have known, the defendant's failure to act allows an inference of a reckless disregard of the probable consequences.[2038]

The court emphasized that the determination of willful misconduct does not rest solely because of the second pilot's unfamiliarity with the river, nor does it attach necessarily because of any navigational mistakes, it is, rather, the combination of factors which together indicate a probable consequence of damage resulting from several failures to act, and by continuing to fail to act in the face of that probability, that indicates a reckless disregard of the consequences.[2039] The court further held that while any one of the faults of defendant alone, even within privity, may not constitute "willful misconduct", on the entire record the various inactions and gross disregard of the potential harm amount to willful misconduct within the meaning of the statute.[2040] The court noted that the implications of a contrary decision is that it would be difficult to imagine what would be necessary to make a tug company liable for the costs of cleaning a negligent oil spill save an admission of an actual intent to do so, and this would extend to the tugboat industry an almost absolute exemption from liability for pollution cleanup costs.[2041]

One other issue that needs to be addressed is whether the gross negligence and willful misconduct provision in section 2704(c)(1) of the OPA forecloses the possibility of recovering common law punitive damages in oil spill cases. Such a discussion should also focus on how section 2704(c)(2) would impact the Pennsylvania rule or how the Pennsylvania rule could impact this section. A discussion of the issue of distribution of liability between a vessel owner and the manufacturer of a defective vessel equipment that proximately causes an oil spill, as well as distribution of liability between the vessel owner and the builder of its vessel, where the vessel is found to fall below minimum construction standards under federal regulations is also important. But such discussions are outside the scope of this treatise.

---

2038 Id.

2039 Id. at 1163-64.

2040 Id. at 1164.

2041 Id.

The term "Outer Continental Shelf facility" under OPA means an offshore facility which is located, in whole or in part, on the Outer Continental Shelf and is or was used for one or more of the following purposes: exploring for, drilling for, producing, storing, handling, transferring, processing, or transporting oil produced from the Outer Continental Shelf.[2042] Section 2704(c)(3) of the OPA provides that notwithstanding the limitations established under subsection (a) of this section and the defenses of section 2703 of the OPA, all removal costs incurred by the United States Government or any State or local official or agency in connection with a discharge or substantial threat of a discharge of oil from any Outer Continental Shelf facility or a vessel carrying oil as cargo from such a facility shall be borne by the owner or operator of such facility or vessel. This section makes it abundantly clear that where the spill is from any Outer Continental Shelf facility or a vessel carrying oil as cargo from such a facility, the liability of the owner or operator of such facility or vessel with respect to removal costs shall be unlimited. If the owner or operator of such facility or vessel successfully proves that it is entitled to any of the defenses in section 2703(a), its liability with respect to removal costs would still be unlimited. However, the defenses in section 2703(a) of the OPA and the limitation provisions for vessels (section 2704(a)(1)-(2)) and offshore facilities (section 2704(a)(3)) will still be applicable to the damage claims (section 2702(B)(2)) of all claimants. This important distinction must not be overlooked.

The legislative history reveals that the original OPA bill allowed a total liability limit of $100 million for oil spills from Outer Continental Shelf facilities. This limitation provision was eventually deleted from the final OPA statute.[2043] The US Congress had a lot reasons for not allowing any limitation on recovery of removal costs for Outer Continental Shelf facility oil spills.

One of the reasons Congress deleted the controversial limitation provision is the Santa Barbara Channel oil blow out incident that occurred in California in 1969. On January 28, 1969, Union Oil Company's well on outer continental shelf lands in the Santa Barbara Channel blew out,

2042 33 USCA §2701(25).

2043 See 1990 USCCAN 735.

creating an oil slick of about fifty square miles which caused severe property and environmental damage.[2044] On that day, oil began to escape under and near Union Oil Company of California's Platform 'A' located on the Outer Continental Shelf of the United States in the Santa Barbara Channel.[2045] Certain operations conducted on Platform 'A' resulted in the release of unascertained amounts of crude oil from the ocean floor underneath and near Platform 'A'.[2046] Such crude oil release was carried by natural forces of winds and tides to various areas of the ocean's surface and towards and in some instances to the adjacent coast lines.[2047] An unascertained amount of damage resulted from this occurrence.[2048] There immediately developed a political climate of great concern over any further drilling on continental shelf lands in the Channel.[2049] A further consequence of the Union Oil disaster was the collapse of the insurance market covering damages caused by offshore oil spills.[2050]

The OPA legislative history reveals that the Congress believed it had several good reasons for maintaining one policy with respect to oil tankers and other facilities handling oil, but a different one with respect to Outer Continental Shelf facilities (OCS).[2051] Congress noted that, first, spills from OCS facilities will by definition occur in areas which are environmentally sensitive, while tanker accidents may not.[2052] Congress noted that these oil wells and platforms are by virtue of what they are--that is, facilities located on the continental shelf--located close to shores, bays

---

2044 See Pauley Petroleum Inc., et al v. The United States, 591 F.2d 1308, 1311 (U.S. Ct of Cl. 1979).

2045 See Union Oil Company et al v. James J. Oppen And John J. Masterson et al, 501 F.2d 558, 559 (9th Cir. 1974).

2046 *Union Oil Company*, 501 F.2d at 559.

2047 Id. at 559.

2048 Id.

2049 *Pauley Petroleum*, 591 F.2d at 1311.

2050 Id. at 1311.

2051 1990 U.S.C.C.A.N. 748, S. Rep. No. 94, 101ST Cong., (1st Sess. 1989), 1989 WL 225005 (Leg.Hist).

2052 1990 U.S.C.C.A.N. 748.

and estuaries.[2053] Indeed, many of them are visible from the beaches of Southern California, which is one of the reasons for the widespread public opposition to them in that State.[2054] Congress also noted that a vessel may break up on the high seas. Or, even if it is close to land, the prevailing winds may blow the oil offshore.[2055] But not so with OCS spills: they will almost invariably be within a few miles of a coast line, as in the case of the Santa Barbara blowout.[2056]

Second, Congress noted that like airline tragedies, although spills for OCS facilities may be infrequent, they will likely be catastrophic when they do occur.[2057] Vessels--even extremely large ones such as the Amoco Cadiz and the Exxon Valdez--carry finite supplies of oil, and usually only a portion of the cargo is lost because they are compartmentalized. Such was the case with the Exxon Valdez, which lost only a fraction of the total amount of oils she was carrying.[2058] Congress noted that OCS spills, in contrast, can involve prodigious and seemingly unlimited quantities of crude oil.[2059] The size of such spills can be enough to fill hundreds of even thousands of tankers the size of the Exxon Valdez.[2060]

Finally, Congress observed that OCS spills are often difficult to control.[2061] It pointed out that welding steel plates below the waterlines of a leaking supertanker is extraordinarily difficult.[2062] But it is much more difficult to cap a well which has blown out three miles beneath the oceans surface.[2063]

To buttress these points, Congress cited two OCS spills as illustrations. Congress referred to the Santa Barbara blowout earlier discussed.

---

2053 Id.

2054 Id.

2055 Id.

2056 Id.

2057 1990 U.S.C.C.A.N. at 748.

2058 Id.

2059 Id. at 749.

2060 Id.

2061 Id.

2062 Id.

2063 Id.

Congress noted that it occurred in a well 5.5 miles from shore.[2064] The lease operators had failed to install casing to the full depth of the well, so crude oil under high pressure was able to move through porous work and then through a fault line to the ocean floor.[2065] The oil was dispersed over 800 square miles of ocean and 100 miles of coastline, and while the major flow was halted in about a month, seepage was being observed as late as October 1970, according to a report prepared for the Federal Water Quality Administration.[2066]

Congress further noted that probably the world's most expensive oil spill was another OCS blowout, the IXTOC I, which occurred on June 3, 1979.[2067] According to a report prepared for the Bureau of Land Management, which the Congress relied on, the discharge of oil from this incident was over 5 million barrels (210,000,000 gallons) **within eight months**.[2068] To cap the IXTOP blowout required eight months--until March 1980. When the Exxon Valdez oil spill happened, many people were shocked and horrified. But the ship spilt about 261, 904 barrels (11 million gallons), almost nothing compared with a total of about 10,190,476 barrels (428 million gallons) for the IXTOC I and other less-known spills.[2069]

Congress noted that it was for these reasons that the Department of the Interior (DOI) adopted a policy of requiring those engaged in OCS operations to bear the full and complete cost of cleanup.[2070] The 1969 DOI regulations were then enacted into federal law by the Congress in the 1978 amendments to the Outer Continental Shelf Lands Act (OCSLA),[2071] which is incorporated in Title III of the OCSLA. Finally, in its rejection of the limitation in the original bill Congress stated:

---

2064 Id.

2065 Id.

2066 Id.

2067 Id.

2068 Id.

2069 The Environment - A Global Challenge: Largest Oil Spills (Last updated Jan. 2002) <http://library.thinkquest.org/26026/Statistics/largest_oil_spills.html>

2070 1990 U.S.C.C.A.N. 749.

2071 Id.

"The majority of OCS facilities are outside the 3 mile limit, and therefore are not subject to state laws. Unlimited liability is not a question of accounting. It is a policy decision that the financial burden of a spill can deter negligence. Insulating those responsible for a spill from the full costs of their actions removes this deterrence. The current law for OCS facilities works, and it works well. Twenty years of experience have demonstrated this truth. And the proper action is to leave that law as is."[2072]

It is most likely that in the nearest future this zero tolerance for OCS oil spills will continue to be applied irrespective of its punitive effect on owners and operators of OCS facilities. Considering the fact that no defenses are available to prevent unlimited liability for removal costs in OCS facility oil spills, the responsible party will be doing itself a lot of good if it ensures that it procures adequate insurance as well as adequate certificate of financial responsibility guarantee. Apart from this, the responsible party should have in place proactive response and clean up plans to reduce removal costs to the barest minimum. The responsible party should take the removal action initiative away from the US Coast Guard. If the responsible party has instituted and internalized response programs, it would have entered into discounted retainer services with salvage and oil spill response organizations. In the absence of this, the Coast Guard might engage contractors at contractually fixed rates that are usually many times higher than usual contract rates.[2073]

The Oil Pollution Act appears to remove the anomaly that existed under the Federal Water Pollution Control Act. The owner who voluntarily undertook cleanup operations could not credit those expenses against its overall limit if the government subsequently effected further cleanup.

2072 1990 U.S.C.C.A.N. 749.

2073 See States v. Murphy Exploration and Production Co., 43 ERC 1701, 1996 A.M.C. 2883, 136 Oil & Gas Rep. 440, 939 F.Supp. 489 (E.D. La. 1996) (holding that the due process ramifications inherent in the government's position were significant, and the government had failed to demonstrate a non-arbitrary rational basis for authorizing the challenged helicopter expenditures and that the plaintiff had otherwise shown that the Coast Guard acted arbitrarily and capriciously in the causing this expenditure to be made.)

Under the OPA, when the RP exceeds the statutory limit, it can get a refund from the Oil Pollution Liability Trust Fund (the Fund or OSLTF).[2074]

One National Pollution Fund Center claim decided on August 16, 2000 illustrates the manner in which a Responsible Party can make such claims when it exceeds its statutory limit.[2075] In that case, at 1300 hours, on March 18, 1996, the hull of a 27 year old single-skin inland barge (Buffalo 292) belonging to Buffalo Marine Services Inc., catastrophically failed forward of the number 3 port and star board cargo tanks.[2076] The vessel's midsection buckled in a 30-degree bend.[2077] As a result, approximately 5,000 barrels (210,000 gallons) of intermediate Fuel Oils 380 (IFO-380) discharged into the Galveston Bay entrance, next to the Houston Ship channel, where it crossed the Gulf Intracoastal Waterway.[2078] The spilled oil moved into the Gulf of Mexico, and eventually covered the Texas coast from Brownsville to near Sabine Texas (Louisiana/ Texas border) on the Gulf Coast, or approximately 300 miles of shoreline.[2079] This did not include islands, coves, bays and peninsulas that were also coated by the oil.[2080]

Buffalo assumed responsibility for the cleanup that cost almost $20,000,000. Coast Guard removal costs were $1, 367,170.71 which was billed, but not paid.[2081] The Claims Manager noted that records in the NPFC data base indicated that two billings were made, however since Buffalo Marine greatly exceeded their limits, payments by Buffalo would result in a 100% reimbursement for Coast Guard costs.[2082] The Claims Manager pointed out that the Deputy Chief of the NPFC Claims Division, indicated

2074 33 USCA §2708

2075 See Buffalo Marine Services Inc., NPFC Claim Summary/Recommendation Form, Claim No 086075-001, 1, 2 (08/16/2000) (on file with the NPFC and available upon request from the NPFC).

2076 Id. at 2.

2077 Id.

2078 Id. at 2.

2079 Id.

2080 Id.

2081 Id.

2082 Id.

that no further cost recovery actions were warranted.[2083] Therefore, there was no expectation that the RP would pay the $1, 367, 170.71 Coast Guard bill.[2084] There was no plan to recoup this cost from the RP and there was no expectation that the RP would try to recoup this particular cost since it would not have to pay it.[2085] The Claims Manager noted that that the RP claimant took responsibility right from the beginning and followed the requirements of the National Contingency plan by utilizing an Oil Spill Removal Organization (OSRO) and responding to all reports of oil impact.[2086] Several days into the oil spill, the OSRO contracted by the RP-claimant established itself as the primary contractor and incorporated numerous Oil Spill Removal Organizations (OSROs) as its subcontractors.[2087] The NPFC Claims Manager pointed out that this action helped to standardize costs, and it established an accounting system that continued throughout the spill in the Houston/Galveston area.[2088] The Claims Manager also noted that the insurance underwriters of the RP's barge and the RP himself assumed all financial responsibility for the spill.[2089] They paid all submitted removal costs.[2090] The Claims Manager pointed out that pursuant to section 2704 of the OPA, the limitation applicable to the RP in this case is the greater of $1,200 per gross ton or $2,000,000 unless the incident was caused by the gross negligence or willful misconduct of the RP.[2091]

The Claims Manager did not find any evidence of gross negligence or willful misconduct by the RP. This limitation amount was applied to the RP in this case because the barge was less than 3,000 gross tons. The Claims Manager pointed out that the removal costs incurred by the RP in this case greatly exceeded the vessel's Limits of Liability.[2092] Since the

---

2083 Id.

2084 Id.

2085 Id.

2086 Id. at 2.

2087 Id. at 3.

2088 Id. at 3.

2089 Id.

2090 Id.

2091 Id.

2092 Id. at 3.

RP's underwriters had paid all contractors' removal costs, all amounts in excess of the vessel's Limits of Liability were being claimed for reimbursement from the Oil Spill Liability Trust Fund by the RP.[2093] The RP through its attorneys submitted a claim for $19,028,142.46 with invoices that matched the total figure.[2094] The RP had also provided documents that showed that it was able to renegotiate or reduce/delete some subcontractor costs, and also deleted duplicates or overcharges. The Claims Manager noted that after this renegotiating action the amount of $18,031,215.35 firmly represented the actual final removal costs incurred.[2095] The director of the NPFC determined that Buffalo Marine Services' Limit of Liability would be upheld. Upon adjudication of the claim the Claims Manager determined that only $14,922,026.19 would be paid for the instant claim. This is $4,106,116.27 less than the amount the claimant had planned to recover from the Fund. This happened because of the adjudication methodology that the NPFC applied to the RP's claim as well as deduction of $2,000,000 which was the liability amount the RP was responsible for by virtue of section 2704(a)(1)(B)(ii) of the OPA.

The Claims Manager looked at each invoice and the supporting daily expenditures and costs to ensure that all charges were for services rendered, that were reasonable, and that they were compensable costs under OPA.[2096] This methodology would apply to removal cost claims by any claimant not just the RP. The measurement method devised, reviewed and approved was based in large part on the creation of a new comparative tool to determine the reasonableness of claimed costs. In this case, the NPFC Claim Management Division developed a regional cost calculation for both services (labor) and materials/equipment.[2097] The process also took into account the reasonable fluctuations in the many company costs and considered regional and incident-related influences on costs.[2098]

2093 Id.

2094 Id.

2095 Id.

2096 Id. at 4.

2097 Id.

2098 Id.

This methodology accounted for all personnel costs, all standard vehicles and boats, and the bulk of the disposable cleanup equipment.[2099] Unique items like large skimmers, shrimp vessels, aircraft, separation chemicals and waste reduction products were reviewed where possible and significant overcharges were noted and adjusted.[2100] The Claims Management Division conducted a 100% review of all invoices and created an "exception"-type report for items that stood out as egregious. These were items like multifunction machines, (fax/copier/telephone) at $125 per day which were determined to be either acceptable (dropped off the list of egregious costs), or recorded for deduction on the accompanying spreadsheets.[2101]

Based on the application of this methodology and after interaction with the accountants representing the RP, and several meetings at the NPFC and response to numerous requests for additional information, the Claims Manager concluded that over two million dollars in removal and response costs could not be approved because of three reasons: (1) Limited documentation for and lack of cost breakdown for a claim of $471,852 which the RP paid to a clean up contractor;[2102] this was the Claims Manager's determination despite the fact that the claimant was able to provide two invoices that evinced the payment. The lesson to be learnt from this is that merely producing invoices does not suffice, in order to recover, the RP's invoice must contain a thorough breakdown of every cost paid; (2) No documentation of any type was provided for a maritime response claim of $414,092.46;[2103] (3) The costs for the use of a particular vessel were incurred without the request or approval of the NPFC, an approval which is a sine qua non to the recoverability of removal cost claims by all claimants. The costs involved was $213,900. A total amount of $2,106,116.27 was therefore deducted from the claim.[2104] Also deducted from the claim was the amount of $2,000,000 which was the limitation amount applicable to the RP.

2099 Id.

2100 Id. at 4.

2101 Id.

2102 Id. at 5.

2103 Id.

2104 Id.

# Chapter Eight

# FINANCIAL RESPONSIBILITY

Statutory provisions:

"§ 2716. **Financial responsibility**

(a) Requirement

The responsible party for--

**(1)** any vessel over 300 gross tons (except a non-self-propelled vessel that does not carry oil as cargo or fuel) using any place subject to the jurisdiction of the United States; or

**(2)** any vessel using the waters of the exclusive economic zone to transship or lighter oil destined for a place subject to the jurisdiction of the United States;

shall establish and maintain, in accordance with regulations promulgated by the Secretary, evidence of financial responsibility sufficient to meet the maximum amount of liability to which the responsible party could be subjected under section 2704(a) or (d) of this title, in a case where the responsible party would be entitled to limit liability under that section. If the responsible party owns or operates more than one vessel, evidence of financial responsibility need be established only to meet the amount of the maximum liability applicable to the vessel having the greatest maximum liability.

(b) Sanctions

(1) Withholding clearance

The Secretary of the Treasury shall withhold or revoke the clearance required by section 91 of the Appendix to Title 46 of any vessel subject to this section that does not have the evidence of financial responsibility required for the vessel under this section.

(2) Denying entry to or detaining vessels

The Secretary may--

**(A)** deny entry to any vessel to any place in the United States, or to the navigable waters, or

**(B)** detain at the place,

any vessel that, upon request, does not produce the evidence of financial responsibility required for the vessel under this section.

(3) Seizure of vessel

Any vessel subject to the requirements of this section which is found in the navigable waters without the necessary evidence of financial responsibility for the vessel shall be subject to seizure by and forfeiture to the United States.

(c) Offshore facilities

(1) In general

(A) Evidence of financial responsibility required

Except as provided in paragraph (2), a responsible party with respect to an offshore facility that--

**(i)** **(I)** is located seaward of the line of ordinary low water along that portion of the coast that is in direct contact with the open sea and the line marking the seaward limit of inland waters; or

**(II)** is located in coastal inland waters, such as bays or estuaries, seaward of the line of ordinary low water along that portion of the coast that is not in direct contact with the open sea;

**(ii)** is used for exploring for, drilling for, producing, or transporting oil from facilities engaged in oil exploration, drilling, or production; and

**(iii)** has a worst-case oil spill discharge potential of more than 1,000 barrels of oil (or a lesser amount if the President determines that the risks posed by such facility justify it),

shall establish and maintain evidence of financial responsibility in the amount required under subparagraph (B) or (C), as applicable.

(B) Amount required generally

Except as provided in subparagraph (C), the amount of financial responsibility for offshore facilities that meet the criteria of subparagraph (A) is--

**(i)** $35,000,000 for an offshore facility located seaward of the seaward boundary of a State; or

**(ii)** $10,000,000 for an offshore facility located landward of the seaward boundary of a State.

(C) Greater amount

If the President determines that an amount of financial responsibility for a responsible party greater than the amount required by subparagraph (B) is justified based on the relative operational, environmental, human health, and other risks posed by the quantity or quality of oil that is explored for, drilled for, produced, or transported by the responsible party, the evidence of financial responsibility required shall be for an amount determined by the President not exceeding $150,000,000.

(D) Multiple facilities

In a case in which a person is a responsible party for more than one facility subject to this subsection, evidence of financial responsibility need be established only to meet the amount applicable to the facility having the greatest financial responsibility requirement under this subsection.

(E) Definition

For the purpose of this paragraph, the seaward boundary of a State shall be determined in accordance with section 1301(b) of Title 43.

(2) Deepwater ports

Each responsible party with respect to a deepwater port shall establish and maintain evidence of financial responsibility sufficient to meet the maximum amount of liability to which the responsible party could be subjected under section 2704(a) of this title in a case where the responsible party would be entitled to limit liability under that section. If the Secretary exercises the authority under section 2704(d)(2) of this title to lower the limit of liability for deepwater ports, the responsible party shall establish and maintain evidence of financial responsibility sufficient to meet the maximum amount of liability so established. In a case in which a person is the responsible party for more than one deepwater port, evidence of financial responsibility need be established only to meet the maximum liability applicable to the deepwater port having the greatest maximum liability."[2105]

This chapter and the next chapter of the treatise will discuss the impact that the OPA and its financial responsibility requirements have on Protection & Indemnity (P & I) pollution insurance structure.

This chapter will focus on the following issues: (I) A brief history of the certificate of financial responsibility. (II) Analysis of the criteria for

2105 33 USC §2716

obtaining the Certificate of Financial Responsibility (COFR) as spelt out in the Coast Guard Regulation. (III) The face-off between the Protection & Indemnity Clubs (P & I Clubs) and the United States Coast Guard and its impact on the Maritime Industry. (IV) Mobil Shipping and Transportation Company led the way for several other COFR applicants to follow. (V) Insurance Industry's solution to the stand-off and its impact on P & I Clubs.

The conclusion reached in this chapter is that the train-wreck scenario threatened by the P & I Clubs did not take place after all. Gasoline also appears to be much cheaper than it was seven years ago, contrary to the dooms day predictions of the P & I Clubs. It will also reveal that neither of the disputing parties in the face-off between the P & I Clubs and the Coast Guard emerged the winner. The real winner was the insurance industry, which was able to devise a timely and auspicious solution to the dispute that was threatening U.S. oil trade. The loser, however, was monopoly, which was exemplified by the strangle hold that the P & I Clubs maintained and sustained in their provision of oil pollution insurance cover to 90% of the world's ocean-going vessels. Although the P & I Clubs still provide oil pollution insurance cover to almost all the vessel owners who carry the COFR guaranty from other insurers, the fact that new insurers have entered into the market is nevertheless a step in the right direction.

OPA 90's requirement that all vessel owners and operators in United States waters maintain evidence of financial responsibility of a specified amount affects everyday vessel operations. Evidence of such financial responsibility must be reflected in a document called a **Certificate of Financial Responsibility (COFR)** carried on board all vessels. If the responsible party owns or operates more than one vessel, evidence of financial responsibility need be established only to meet the amount of the maximum liability applicable to the vessel having the greatest maximum liability.[2106]

The COFR regulations promulgated by the Coast Guard specifies the types of evidence vessel owners and operators must submit to the Coast Guard to demonstrate their ability to pay removal costs and damages in

2106 33 USC 2716(a).

the event of an oil or hazardous substance spill. The COFR regulation implements both OPA 90 and Comprehensive Environmental Response, Compensation, and Liability Act (CERCLA).

On July 1, 1994, four years after OPA 90 was enacted, the Coast Guard published its interim final rule on vessel COFRs. Being "interim," comments submitted to the Coast Guard before September 29, 1994 was considered before the ultimate final rule was issued and came into effect on December 28, 1994.[2107] No modifications whatsoever was made to the final rules.

## I. History of the COFR Rule.

The July 1, 1994 version of the COFR rule is virtually identical to that published by the Coast Guard in September 1991. After the September 1991 version was published, over 300 letters commenting on the proposals were submitted to the Coast Guard. The comment period closed at the end of January 1992. Although the request of several commentators for a public hearing was not granted, a subcommittee of the House of Representatives held a hearing in November 1991. Most of the substantive modifications and alternatives suggested by the shipping industry and other interested parties were rejected. For example, despite vehement objection, the direct action provision against guarantors was not changed, the net worth/ working capital requirements for self-insurance by vessel owners were not changed and the provision that COFRs encompass financial responsibility requirements for CERCLA in addition to OPA was not changed.

The July 1, 1994 rule includes a revised implementation schedule and some technical clarifications. For example, it is now clear that a COFR is not required for persons who have no operational responsibility for a vessel such as time or voyage charterers. Also, the rule now specifies that a total of up to four insurers and up to four surety bond issuers may subscribe to a single COFR. If participation is on a quota share percentage on a vertical basis of the total amount, there is no joint and several liability. In contrast, joint and several liability is imposed if the participation is on a horizontal level.

---

2107 C.F.R. § 135.401.

*Previous Law on COFRs*: Since 1970, CERCLA and the Federal Water Pollution Control Act have required vessels carrying hazardous substances to present evidence to the Coast Guard that they are capable of paying the costs of a spill, in the form of an insurance guaranty, or surety bond guaranty, or some kind of self-insurance. When a spill occurs, and the responsible party for that vessel fails to pay in full, then the provider of the insurance guaranty, surety bond guaranty, or self-insurance is required to pay, up to the limits set forth in the COFR.

The mechanics for obtaining a new COFR, one that satisfies OPA 90 as well as CERCLA, are similar to the old mechanics under CERCLA. The new COFR will differ from the old COFR in its increased monetary limits, its application to a broader range of vessels, and a broader range of removal costs and damages. The new COFR regulations is a unified document, evidencing compliance with the financial responsibility requirements of both CERCLA and OPA 90.

*The Rule's Relationship to State Law*: OPA 90 states explicitly that it does not preempt state laws regulating oil spills. In fact, a COFR which complies with OPA 90 and CERCLA may not be sufficient under applicable state environmental law. The new COFR form states explicitly that the guaranty is under federal law not state law, unless noted thereon. Further, in the past, in defense to an action for violation of state oil spill law, vessels have been able to limit their liability by resort to the Limitation of Liability Act,[2108] a federal statute which allows a vessel owner to limit its liability to the value of the vessel plus any earned freight. Under OPA 90, that defense is no longer available in oil spill actions under both federal and state law.[2109]

## II. Analysis of the criteria for obtaining the Certificate of financial responsibility (COFR).

The interim final rule identifies as acceptable various types of forms of evidence of financial responsibility: commercial insurance,

2108 U.S.C. §§ 181-189 (1988 & Supp. V 1993)

2109 *See* 33 USC §2718.

surety bonds, financial guaranties and self-insurance. The rule does not provide any means for using evidence of membership in a protection and indemnity (P & I) club as evidence of financial responsibility. All of the clubs have a stated policy that they will not provide evidence of insurance on behalf of members in the form required by OPA 90 and the new regulation, because such would require the clubs to become guarantors. The legislative history of OPA shows that the House bill included requirements for demonstration of financial responsibility, where appropriate, by the owner of oil transported as cargo on a vessel. The Conference substitute dropped the requirements for demonstration of financial responsibility by a cargo owner.[2110] Section 1016 (33 USC §2716) of the Conference substitute which was adopted is intended to ensure that there will be adequate funds immediately available to compensate injured parties.[2111] Since the primary responsibility to compensate victims of oil pollution rests with the person responsible for the source of the pollution, that person is required to establish the capability to meet at least the amount of liability specified in section 2704 of OPA (Limitation amount).[2112]

Section 106(c) of the Senate amendment and section 1019 of the House bill were similar provisions providing that a State may enforce, on the navigable waters of the State, the requirements for financial responsibility imposed under section 2716 of OPA.[2113] This authority includes the right to inspect vessels and facilities, to require the display of evidence of financial responsibility and to impose sanctions for failure to comply with the requirements.[2114]

The COFR regulations are codified in Title 33 CFR part 138.10 - 138.150. The required forms are codified at Title 33 CFR Part 138, Appendix A-F. The COFR regulations defines a guarantor as any person who provides

---

2110 H.R. CONF. REP. 101-653, 1990 U.S.C.C.A.N. 779, 796-797 (101st Cong., 2d. Sess.1990).

2111 1990 U.S.C.C.A.N. 797.

2112 Id. at 797.

2113 Id. at 800.

2114 Id. See also, 33 USC §2719.

evidence of financial responsibility, under the Acts (i.e. CERCLA and OPA), on behalf of a vessel owner, operator, and demise charterer.[2115] A vessel operator who can qualify as a self-insurer may act as both a self-insurer of vessels it operates and as a financial guarantor of other vessels, under section 138.80(b)(4).[2116]

Certificate means a "Vessel Certificate of Financial Responsibility (Water Pollution)" issued under this part, unless otherwise indicated.[2117] "Financial responsibility" means statutorily required financial ability to meet liability under the Acts.[2118] In other words COFRs are issued for the purpose of demonstrating that shipowners and operators have the financial ability to pay for removal costs and damages resulting from oil spills or hazardous substance releases.

The regulations in this part set forth the procedures whereby an operator of a vessel can demonstrate that it and the owner and demise charterer of the vessel are financially able to meet potential liability for costs and damages in the amounts established by this part.[2119] The owner, operator, and demise charterer are strictly, jointly, and severally liable for the costs and damages resulting from an incident or a release or threatened release, but together they need only establish and maintain an amount of financial responsibility equal to the single limit of liability per incident, release, or threatened release.[2120] Where a vessel is operated by its owner, or the owner is responsible for its operation, the owner is considered to be the operator and shall submit the application for a Certificate.[2121] In all other cases, the vessel operator shall submit the application. A time or voyage charterer that does not assume responsibility for the operation of the vessel is not considered an operator for the purposes of the COFR regulations.[2122]

---

2115 *See* 33 CFR §138.20(b)

2116 *See* id.

2117 Id.

2118 *See* id.

2119 *See* id. at §138.30 (a).

2120 *See* id.

2121 *See* id. at §138.30(b).

2122 *See* id.

A Certificant is an operator who has been issued a Certificate under the COFR regulations.[2123] Any mention of the word "Acts" means OPA and CERCLA.

## II. A. How to Establish Financial Responsibility - Methods

OPA provides that financial responsibility may be established by any one, or by any combination, of the following methods explained in greater detail below: evidence of insurance, surety bond, guarantee, letter of credit, qualification as a self-insurer, or other evidence of financial responsibility.[2124] Any bond filed shall be issued by a bonding company authorized to do business in the United States.[2125] OPA also requires that in promulgating requirements under this section, the Secretary or the President, as appropriate, may specify policy or other contractual terms, conditions, or defenses which are necessary, or which are unacceptable, in establishing evidence of financial responsibility to effectuate the purposes of OPA.[2126] The US Coast Guard decided not to take advantage of this flexibility. It came to the conclusion that adding policy defenses, contractual terms and conditions would not give effect to the intention of Congress in passing OPA. It was seen as something that could conflict with the intention of Congress to restrict the defenses that providers of the Evidence of Financial Responsibility can rely on.

A discussion of the various methods of establishing evidence of financial responsibility is discussed below.

An applicant shall establish evidence of financial responsibility by one or more of the following methods:

2123 *See* 33 CFR §138.20(b).

2124 *See* 33 USC §2716(e)

2125 Id.

2126 Id. at §2716(e).

*Financial Guaranty.*

This method can be established by filing with the Director, National Pollution Funds Center (NPFC), a Financial Guaranty Form CG-5586-3 executed by not more than four financial guarantors, such as a parent or affiliate acceptable to the Coast Guard.[2127] To avoid joint and several liability among the guarantors, any vertical percentage participation must be stated on the form. This means that each financial guarantor's liability is limited to its percentage of participation. A financial guarantor is required to comply with all of the self-insurance provisions of paragraph (b)(3) of this section.[2128] In addition, a person that is a financial guarantor for more than one applicant or certificant shall have working capital and net worth no less than the aggregate total applicable amounts of financial responsibility provided as a guarantor for each applicant or certificant, plus the amount required to be demonstrated by a self-insurer under this part, if also acting as a self-insurer.[2129]

*Commercial Insurance Guaranty*

This method can be established by filing with the Director, NPFC, an insurance guaranty form CG-5586, executed by not more than four insurers that have been found acceptable by and remain acceptable to the Director, NPFC, for purposes of the COFR regulations.[2130]

*Surety Bond Guaranty*

This method can be established by filing with the Director, NPFC, a surety bond guaranty form CG-5586-2, executed by not more than 10

2127 *See* 33 CFR 138.80(b)(4).

2128 Id.

2129 Id.

2130 *See* 33 CFR 138.80(b)(1).

acceptable surety companies certified by the United States Department of the Treasury with respect to the issuance of Federal bonds in the maximum penal sum of each bond to be issued under the COFR regulations.[2131] The P & I Clubs spent a lot of time trying to investigate the viability of a collective surety bond in 1994 when the deadline set by the coast guard for compliance with the COFR requirement was drawing near.[2132] Even though they were resolute in their resolve not to become financial guarantors, they were afraid of the financial implications of losing their members. However, despite their investigations they eventually failed to change their position on the issue of COFR guaranty.

### *Self-Insurance*

It was anticipated that most vessel owners, as well as most P & I club members, will not be able to satisfy the requirements for self- insurance. The requirements include demonstrating on a regular basis to the Coast Guard that the company's working capital and net worth exceed the amount of financial responsibility required under the regulations. Working capital here means the amount of current assets located in the United States, less all current liabilities anywhere in the world. Net worth means the amount of all assets located in the United States, less all liabilities anywhere in the world. The US Coast Guard rejected modifying the self-insurance criteria to delete the working capital requirement.[2133] The Director, NPFC may however permit a waiver of working capital requirement for any applicant or certificant that–

"(A) Is a regulated public utility, a municipal or higher-level governmental entity, or an entity operating solely as a charitable, non-profit making

2131 Id. at §138.80(b)(2).

2132 Shipping Editor, P & I Club says surety bond may answer OPA finance ruling, Lloyd's List Int'l, Sept. 19, 1994 at 1.

2133 James Masson and Valerie Fogleman, Gunfight at the OPA Corral, List Int'l, Aug. 27, 1993, at 8.

organization qualifying under section 501(c) Internal Revenue Code. The applicant or certificant must demonstrate in writing that the grant of a waiver would benefit a local public interest; or

(B) Demonstrates in writing that working capital is not a significant factor in the applicant's or certificant's financial condition. An applicant's or certificant's net worth in relation to the amount of its required amount of financial responsibility and a history of stable operations are the major elements considered."[2134]

Membership in a club cannot be considered evidence of self- insurance because no accounting rule allows the face value of the membership to be counted in a net worth determination because a club does not set aside assets to meet potential liabilities. P & I membership provides that an owner must pay claims out of its own pocket first before requiring reimbursement from the club, thus, the club provides no assurance of payment.

*Newly approved method - Second Line Program*

On January 26, 1996, the U.S. Coast Guard's National Pollution Funds Center announced its approval of a new method of establishing vessel financial responsibility for potential water pollution liabilities.[2135] This approved method has been dubbed the **Second Line program**. It is basically a **joint guaranty** whereby a financial guarantor and an insurance guarantor agree to back 100 percent of the other's obligation to pay for cleanup and damages resulting from a spill.[2136] Each participant in this new joint guaranty must still meet the Coast Guard's criteria as an independent guarantor.[2137] This voluntary, industry approach provides double assurance

2134 33 CFR §138.80(b)(3)(vi)(A)-(B).

2135 *See* "Coast Guard Approves Second Line As COFR Guarantor" National Pollution Funds Center – Press Release (Fri. Jan 26, 1996) (last modified Feb. 27, 2002) <http://www.uscg.mil/hq/npfc/press.htm>

2136 Id.

2137 Id.

that the costs resulting from a spill will be paid by the owner or operator, or their guarantor, rather than by the Coast Guard's Oil Spill Liability Trust Fund (the Fund or OSLTF).[2138] The Second Line program was conceived and developed for Stockton Reinsurance Limited by Mr. Graham Barnes of London, Chairman of Nicholson Leslie BankAssure.[2139] The developers of this innovative insurance product believe that it may provide the means for the COFR insurance premiums to be included in the Worldscale freight formula; thereby allowing tanker owners to pass these costs directly to vessel charterers.[2140]

### *Other Evidence (Including Specialized Letters of Credit)*

Any alternative form of evidence of financial responsibility that has been approved by the Coast Guard through its National Pollution Fund Center may be used. An earlier version of the rule specifically referred to letters of credit, but the new regulation does not. The Coast Guard explained the modification by saying that vessel owners commenting on the earlier rule failed to show an interest in using letters of credit. Importantly, no matter what the nature of the device, the person providing the guaranty is considered a guarantor under OPA 90. One could argue that the Coast Guard ought to have taken advantage of the flexibility Congress had granted it by this provision which allows other evidence of financial responsibility and letters of credit, by coming up with acceptable regulations.

The Director, NPFC, will not accept a self-insurance method other than the one described in paragraph (b)(3) of section 138.80. An applicant may in writing request the Director, NPFC, to accept a method different from one described in paragraph (b) (1), (2), or (4)(financial guaranty, insurance guaranty, and surety bond guaranty) of section 138.80 to demonstrate

2138 Id.

2139 Id.

2140 Id.

evidence of financial responsibility.[2141] An applicant submitting a request under this paragraph is required to submit the request to the Director, NPFC, at least 45 days prior to the date the Certificate is required.

The applicant is also required to describe in detail the method proposed, the reasons why the applicant does not wish to use or is unable to use one of the methods described in paragraph (b) (1), (2), or (4)(financial guaranty, insurance guaranty, and surety bond guaranty) of section 138.80 and how the proposed method assures that the applicant is able to fulfill its obligation to pay costs and damages in the event of an incident or a release or threatened release.[2142] The Director, NPFC, will not accept a method under this paragraph that merely deletes or alters a provision of one of the methods described in paragraph (b) (1), (2), or (4) of section 138.80 (for example, one that alters the termination clause of the insurance guaranty form illustrated in Appendix B of this regulation).[2143] An applicant that makes a request under this paragraph shall provide the Director, NPFC, a proposed guaranty form that includes all the elements described in paragraphs (c)(forms of guarantee – this is discussed below) and (d)(direct action) of this section.[2144] The decision of the Director, NPFC, not to accept a method requested by an applicant under this paragraph is regarded as final agency action.[2145]

As of December 31, 2001, over 80% of ship owners had used the Commercial Insurance Guaranty method. The least attractive method of guaranty has been the Surety Bond method with only 0.4% of ship owners having used it as of December 31, 2001. See Chart below.

As of December 31, 2001, the Commercial Insurance Method of Guaranty has been utilized by 15, 265 vessels. This number includes all types of vessels. See table below.

2141 *See* 33 CFR §138.80(b)(5).

2142 Id. at §138.80(b)(5).

2143 Id.

2144 Id.

2145 Id.

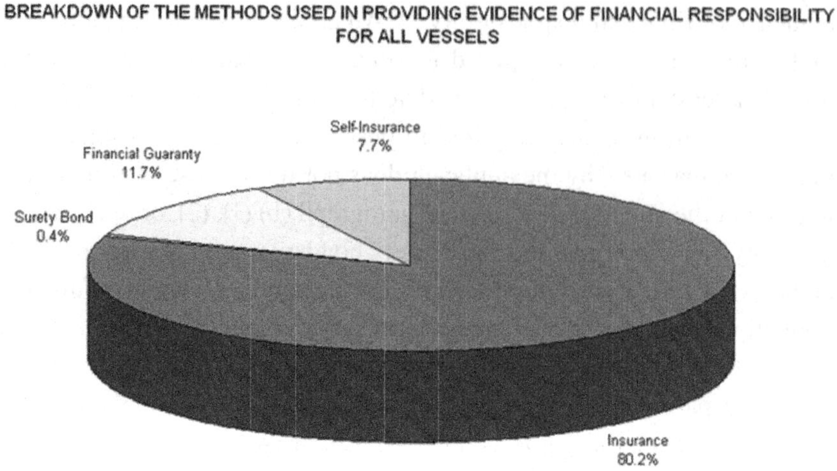


## Method of Guaranty Table.

**OPA/CERCLA VESSEL CERTIFICATES OF FINANCIAL RESPONSIBILITY AS OF 01Jan02**

| METHOD OF GUARANTY | Dry Cargo | Tanker | Tank Barge | MODU | Passenger | Fishing | Utility | TOTALS |
|---|---|---|---|---|---|---|---|---|
| Insurance | 7710 | 2081 | 1766 | 145 | 483 | 1138 | 1942 | **15265** |
| Financial Guaranty | 312 | 405 | 1149 | 87 | 2 | 57 | 213 | **2225** |
| Self-Insurance | 48 | 12 | 1041 | 65 | 49 | 0 | 250 | **1465** |
| Surety Bond | 0 | 21 | 51 | 0 | 0 | 0 | 7 | **79** |
| **TOTALS** | **8070** | **2519** | **4007** | **297** | **534** | **1195** | **2412** | **19034** |

Dry cargo includes bulk carriers, containerships, reefers, ro-ro's, etc.

Tanker includes crude carriers, product carriers, chemical tankers, OBOs, LPG and LNG carriers

Fishing includes fishing and factory vessels

Utility includes deck barges, tug/tow boats, OSVs, research vessels, and oil spill response vessels

Insurers include Shoreline Mutual, SIGCo, Arvak, WQIS, Great American Insurance, Heddington Insurance, AXA, Gyosen Chuokai, HIH, Travelers, ILU and Lloyds Syndicates

The 2519 tank vessels total 119,346,531 gross tons and approximately 238,693,062 deadweight tons.

COFR Statistics for quarter ending 31st December, 2001. The Source of the above Table is the US Coast Guard's National Pollution Funds Center.

## The U.S. Coast Guard Unveils the E-COFR System

The U.S. Coast Guard's National Pollution Funds Center (NPFC) announced in April of 2002, the introduction of an electronic Certificate of Financial Responsibility system, or E-COFR.[2146] With the E-COFR, applicants may now enroll at the National Pollution Fund Center's website, and perform the following actions, *on-line*:

- Apply as a new COFR applicant
- Apply for a supplemental COFR
- Apply for a renewal COFR
- Request a duplicate COFR
- Perform a vessel and/or applicant name change, and
- Pay COFR application fees.[2147]

Following successful enrollment, applicants may use a credit card (MasterCard, VISA, American Express, or Discover) to securely pay the appropriate COFR fees on-line.[2148]

## II.B Forms of Guaranty

As explained earlier under each method of guaranty, the COFR regulations allow multiple guarantors.[2149] Four or fewer insurers (a lead underwriter is considered to be one insurer) may jointly execute an insurance guaranty form.[2150] Ten or fewer sureties (including lead sureties) may jointly execute a surety bond guaranty form. Four or fewer financial guarantors may jointly execute a financial guaranty form. If more than one insurer, surety, or financial guarantor executes the relevant form--

---

2146 *See* "Vessel Certification Unveils E-COFR System." National Pollution Funds Center – Press Release (Wed. April 24, 2002) (last modified Oct. 23, 2002) <http://www.uscg.mil/hq/npfc/pdf/E-COFR%20Press%20Release.Pdf>

2147 Id.

2148 Id.

2149 *See* 33 CFR §138.80(c).

2150 Id. at §138.80(c).

"(i) Each is bound for the payment of sums only in accordance with the percentage of vertical participation specified on the relevant form for that insurer, surety, or financial guarantor. Participation in the form of layering (tiers, one in excess of another) is not acceptable; only vertical participation on a percentage basis is acceptable unless none of the participants specifies a percent of participation.[2151] **If no percentage of participation is specified** for an insurer, surety, or financial guarantor, the liability of that insurer, surety, or financial guarantor **is joint and several for the total of the unspecified portions**; and

(ii) The guarantors must designate a lead guarantor having authority to bind all guarantors for actions required of guarantors under the Acts, including but not limited to receipt of designation of source, advertisement of a designation, and receipt and settlement of claims."[2152]

## II.C. Direct Action Against COFR Guarantors

The COFR regulations require that any evidence of financial responsibility submitted under this regulations must contain an acknowledgment by the insurer or other guarantor that an action in court by a claimant (including a claimant by right of subrogation) for costs and damage claims arising under the provisions of the Acts, may be brought directly against the insurer or other guarantor.[2153] The evidence of financial responsibility must also provide that, in the event an action is brought under the Acts directly against the insurer or other guarantor, the insurer or other guarantor may invoke only the following rights and defenses:

"(i) The incident, release, or threatened release was caused by the willful misconduct of the person for whom the guaranty is provided.

---

2151 Id. at §138.80(c)(1)(i).

2152 Id. at §138.80(c)(1)(ii).

2153 *See* id. at §138.80(d).

(ii) Any defense that the person for whom the guaranty is provided may raise under the Acts.

(iii) A defense relating to the amount of a claim or claims, filed in any action in any court or other proceeding, that exceeds the amount of the guaranty with respect to an incident or with respect to a release or threatened release.

(iv) A defense relating to the amount of a claim or claims that exceeds the amount of the guaranty, which amount is based on the gross tonnage of the vessel as entered on the vessel's International Tonnage Certificate or other official, applicable certificate of measurement, except when the guarantor knew or should have known that the applicable tonnage certificate was incorrect.

(v) The claim is not one made under either of the Acts."[2154]

Section 2716(f) of OPA provides that the guarantor **may not invoke against a third party** claimant, any other defense that might be available in proceedings brought by the responsible party against the guarantor.

The COFR regulations provide that a guarantor that participates in any evidence of financial responsibility shall be liable because of that participation, with respect to an incident or a release or threatened release, in any proceeding **only for the amount and type of costs and damages specified in the evidence of financial responsibility**.[2155] A guarantor **shall not be considered to have consented to direct action** under any law other than the Acts, or to unlimited liability under any law or in any venue, solely because of the guarantor's participation in providing any evidence of financial responsibility under this regulation.[2156] In the event of any finding that liability of a guarantor exceeds the amount of the guaranty provided under this regulation, **that guaranty is considered null and void with respect to that excess**.[2157]

2154 Id.

2155 Id. at §138.80 (d)(2).

2156 Id.

2157 Id.

*Total applicable amount*

The required amounts of prearranged financial responsibility depend upon the vessel's type and size. The applicable amount of financial responsibility under OPA 90 is determined as follows:

"(i) For a tank vessel (except a tank vessel on which no liquid hazardous material in bulk is being carried as cargo or cargo residue, and on which the only oil carried as cargo or cargo residue is an animal fat or vegetable oil, as those terms are used in section 2 of the Edible Oil Regulatory Reform Act (Pub. L. 104-55)).

(A) Over 300 gross tons (and a vessel of 300 gross tons or less using the waters of the United States Exclusive Economic Zone to transship or lighter oil destined for a place subject to the jurisdiction of the United States, as specified in Sec. 138.12(a)(1)) but not exceeding 3,000 gross tons, the greater of $2,000,000 or $1,200 per gross ton; and (B) Over 3,000 gross tons, the greater of $10,000,000 or $1,200 per gross ton."[2158]

Tank vessel is defined by the COFR regulations as a vessel (other than an offshore supply vessel, a fishing or fish tender vessel of 750 gross tons or less that transfers fuel without charge to a fishing vessel owned by the same person, or a towing or pushing vessel (tug) simply because it has in its custody a tank barge) that is constructed or adapted to carry, or that carries, oil or liquid hazardous material in bulk as cargo or cargo residue, and that--

"(1) Is a vessel of the United States;

(2) Operates on the navigable waters; or

(3) Transfers oil or hazardous material in a place subject to the jurisdiction of the United States.[2159]

---

2158 Id. at §138.80(f).

2159 *See* 33 CFR §138.20(b).

(ii) For a vessel **other than a tank vessel** under paragraph (f)(1)(i) of this section that is over 300 gross tons or that is 300 gross tons or less using the waters of the Exclusive Economic Zone of the United States to transship or lighter oil destined for a place subject to the jurisdiction of the United States, the greater of $500,000 or $600 per gross ton.[2160]

(2) The total applicable amount is the maximum applicable amount calculated under paragraph (f)(1) of this section plus maximum applicable amount calculated under paragraph (f)(2) of this section."[2161]

Paragraph f(2) deals with CERCLA and is not germane for the purposes of this discussion.

## II.D. Provisions of the Rule Criticized by Vessel Interests: Direct Actions against Guarantors.

After the initial version of the COFR rule was issued in September 1991, the international vessel owning and operating community, acting through their P & I clubs, and Lloyd's of London (an insurer and reinsurer of the clubs) submitted numerous objections to the requirements of OPA 90, especially to the requirement that unlimited liability be imposed on vessel owners under certain circumstances. Further, vessel interests objected to liability on the levels required to satisfy the financial responsibility requirements of OPA 90 and, most strenuously, they objected to the provision for direct actions against persons providing evidence of such financial responsibility. Vessel owners also criticized the absence of an explicit provision that where the responsible party vessel owner pays the full limit of its OPA liability following a spill, that responsible party's guarantors are relieved of liability for that spill. The clubs' criticism of direct actions stems from the fact that they provide indemnity insurance, not liability insurance. There is no way for a vessel owner to use its membership or entry in a club as evidence of financial responsibility, without

2160 Id. at §138.80(f).

2161 Id.

thereby making the club subject to direct actions in connection therewith. The clubs indicated that they would not act as guarantors under OPA 90. From the perspective of the Coast Guard, this is inconsistent with the fact that clubs issue similar guaranties to other governments pursuant to the 1969 Civil Liability Convention (CLC) and to the United States government under various pre-OPA 90 statutes like the FWPCA.

The Final Regulatory Impact Analysis was issued on July 1, 1994, after issuing the Preliminary Regulatory Impact Analysis in late July 1993 and considering submitted comments. The Coast Guard concluded that in fact, vessel interests would be able to satisfy the financial responsibility requirements of OPA 90, notwithstanding the position of the Clubs, by resorting to commercial alternatives.

### *Identity of Beneficiary of Evidence of Financial Responsibility*

In order to ensure that the identity of the beneficiary is not confused with that of a successor in title to the covered vessel, the COFR regulations provide that except as provided in Sec. 138.90(f) of the regulations, at the moment a certificant ceases to be the operator of a vessel for any reason, including a vessel that is scrapped or transferred to a new operator, the individual Certificate naming the vessel, and any copies of the Certificate, are void and their further use is prohibited.[2162] In that case, the certificant shall, within 10 days of the Certificate becoming void, complete the reverse side of the original individual Certificate naming the involved vessel and return the Certificate to the Director, NPFC.[2163] If the Certificate cannot be returned because it has been lost or destroyed, the certificant is required to submit the following information in writing to the Director, NPFC, within three business days:

(1) The number of the individual Certificate and the name of the vessel. (2) The date and reason why the certificant ceased to be the operator of the vessel.

---

2162 33 CFR §138.90(e).

2163 Id.

(3) The location of the vessel on the date the certificant ceased to be the operator. (4) The name and mailing address of the person to whom the vessel was sold or transferred.[2164]

An operator shall file a written application for the renewal of a Certificate at least 21 days, but not earlier than 90 days, before the expiration date of the Certificate.[2165]

*What happened to FWPCA Evidence of Financial Responsibility between August 18, 1990 & December 28, 1994:*

The OPA provides that any regulation relating to financial responsibility, which has been issued pursuant to any provision of law repealed or superseded by OPA, and which is in effect on the date immediately preceding the effective date OPA, is deemed and shall be construed to be a regulation issued pursuant to OPA's section 2716(h).[2166] OPA provides further that such a regulation shall remain in full force and effect unless and until superseded by a new regulation issued under this section.[2167] The superseding regulation referred to was promulgated in July of 1994, and vessels were required to obtain the Evidence of Financial Responsibility by December 28, 1994. Between the time OPA was passed on August 18, 1990 and December 28, 1994, when the COFR regulations took effect, P & I Clubs continued to issue the usual required COFRs under the FWPCA to their members and sent them circulars reiterating that those COFRs were still valid by virtue of the above provision in the COFR regulations. As will be explained later in chapter nine, Clubs warned their ship owner members not to enter into any agreement with time charterers to the effect that their Clubs would provide COFR guarantees under OPA.

2164 Id. at §138.90(e)(1)-(4).

2165 Id. at 138.70(a).

2166 33 USC §2716(h).

2167 Id.

### *Financial Responsibility Civil Penalties*

Section 2716a of OPA provides that any person who, after notice and an opportunity for a hearing, is found to have failed to comply with the requirements of section 2716 of this title or the regulations issued under that section, or with a denial or detention order issued under subsection (c)(2) of that section, shall be liable to the United States for a civil penalty, not to exceed $25,000 per day of violation. This section provides further that the amount of the civil penalty shall be assessed by the President by written notice. In determining the amount of the penalty, the President shall take into account the nature, circumstances, extent, and gravity of the violation, the degree of culpability, any history of prior violation, ability to pay, and such other matters as justice may require.[2168] The President may compromise, modify, or remit, with or without conditions, any civil penalty which is subject to imposition or which had been imposed under this paragraph.[2169] If any person fails to pay an assessed civil penalty after it has become final, the President may refer the matter to the Attorney General for collection.[2170]

In addition to, or in lieu of, assessing a penalty under section 2716a(a) of OPA, the President may request the Attorney General to secure such relief as necessary to compel compliance with section 2716 of this title, including **a judicial order terminating operations**. The district courts of the United States shall have jurisdiction to grant any relief as the public interest and the equities of the case may require.[2171]

### *Rejection of the Proposed Mandatory Excess Insurance Facility*

After the September 1991 version of the COFR rule was issued, several ship owners' organizations proposed the creation of a Mandatory Excess

2168 33 USC §2716 (a).

2169 Id.

2170 Id. at § 2716(a).

2171 33 USC §2716a(b).

Insurance Facility (MEIF) to provide high levels of liability coverage as well as to act as a guarantor for the purpose of providing COFR coverage. The Coast Guard rejected the proposal, stating that establishing such a facility would require substantial legislation. The proposal goes beyond OPA 90's COFR requirements, insofar as the levels of insurance it seeks to make available far exceed any COFR-related financial responsibility requirement. The Coast Guard has noted "that the MEIF promoters agreed, that the MEIF is principally designed to alleviate the ship owners' concerns about unlimited liability, not COFRs, which have no relation to one another."[2172]

## III. The face-off between the P & I Clubs and the United States Coast Guard and its impact on the Maritime Industry.

All the International Group Clubs held board meetings prior to the release of the final regulations and agreed that there were no grounds for modifying their position. As pointed out earlier the clubs were being asked to depart from their normal and well understood role as indemnity underwriters for named ship owners and expose themselves as guarantors without policy defenses and possibly without financial limit to a multitude of unknown potential claimants and in respect of strict liability for damages of unprecedented size and scope. The clubs were also inhibited as assuming guarantor status would jeopardize their reinsurance cover. Lloyds of London provided a substantial proportion of the International Group's reinsurance cover, with US underwriters taking a less than seven- percent share. Initially, there was a search for alternative markets around the world but there was none at any price.[2173] The clubs were ready to stick to their guns even if meant the near cessation of ocean shipping traffic to and from the United States, considering the fact that they provided the marine pollution insurance for ninety percent of the world's ocean-going vessels.

2172 59 Fed. Reg. 34223.

2173 Jim Mulrenan, P & I row threatens to upset US ocean trade, Lloyd's List Int'l, July 22, 1994, at 1.

In 1991, Representatives from international insurance groups and the shipping industry warned the House Merchant Marine and Fisheries Subcommittee on Coast Guard and Navigation that U.S. Coast Guard regulations proposed under the act would prevent them from obtaining certification necessary to operate in U.S. waters.[2174] Terrence Coghlin, then chairman designate of the International Group of P&I Clubs, said:

"The U.S.A. has chosen not to ratify the international conventions in this area and has in their place created its own uniquely onerous liability regime for oil spills. Those who insure risks worldwide on behalf of an international community must take this unique risk into account." [2175]

The insurers also expressed concern about facing unlimited liability under state laws.[2176] J. Richard Yoell, a marine insurance underwriter at Lloyds of London, told the subcommittee that:

"OPA's failure to pre-empt state liability and certification laws leaves open the possibility that third-party claimants will be able to assert state law claims outside of OPA against an insurer/guarantor, creating the possibility of horizontal exposure to multiple limits against an insurer for which no premium was collected and no insurance capacity remains."[2177]

The Britannia Steam Ship Insurance Association was very critical of the Coast Guard. They alleged that clean-up in the US is about contractors making money and politicians or bureaucrats making reputations, and large and arbitrary penalties being imposed.[2178] They also described the situation in the US as a cause for grave concern, particularly if other countries try to follow a similar path.[2179]

---

2174 *See* Oil Spills: Insurers Warn They Will Not Certify Financial Responsibility Of Ship Owners, 22 Env. Rep. 1776 (Nov. 15, 1991).

2175 Id. at 1776.

2176 Id.

2177 *See* 22 ER 1776.

2178 Janet Porter, P & I Club criticizes US over oil spill handling, Lloyd's List Int'l, Jun. 25, 1998, at 2.

2179 Id.

### *Impact on Maritime Industry*

Tankers trading into the U.S. were faced with another large increase in their insurance costs from February 1994, as concern about the huge liabilities of the OPA 90 spread unabated. The additional premium payable for tankers entering U.S. waters rose by 26% from the February 20, 1994, renewal of P & I Clubs entries. The increase was driven by the reinsurers at Lloyd's and else where, who were seeking higher premiums for covering the major International Group clubs against a U.S. oil spill. The additional premium payable by tankers trading into U.S. Mainland ports rose from 23 cents per gross ton to 29 cents per gross ton, largely reflecting a revised assessment of exposure to OPA 90 by reinsurance underwriters.[2180] The additional premium payable for larger tankers trading into the Louisiana offshore Oil Port (LOOP) or lightering in U.S. Coast Guard approved locations also rose proportionately but remained half the mainland rate. Since the U.S. accounts for about 25% of the world's oil trade, the ultimate impact of the higher additional premiums on charterers and the oil industry could be large. The overall cost of what is the world's largest reinsurance increased by something over 6% on the $360m cost of 1993. The excess oil insurance cover of $200m that used to supplement the $500m of cover available through the clubs was made available in the 1994 fiscal year.[2181]

Shell Petroleum immediately withdrew its fleet of vessels from US trade waters, opting instead to use chartered vessels for the transport of its oil to the U.S. Mainland.[2182] As of 1991, Shell also started to decrease the size of its tanker fleet from ninety to fifty vessels and to phase out its third-party transportation business. [2183] Following Shell's lead, a number of international shipping companies barred their tankers from calling

2180 Jim Mulrenan - Shipping Editor, US-bound tankers face more P&I rises: Additional premium to jump from February rate renewals, Lloyd's List Int'l, Jan. 25, 1994, at 1.

2181 Id. at 2.

2182 Derek Bamber, Oil Tanker Market Never Up Long, PETROLEUM ECONOMIST, Aug. 1991, at 15.

2183 Robin Buckner Price, U.S. Oil Spill Law to Cause Growing Tanker Problem, OIL & GAS J., Sept. 30, 1991, at 21.

at U.S. ports, including Teekay Shipping, Elf Aquitaine, A.P. Moller, Petrofina, and Mearsk.[2184] Amoco trimmed its chartering business that carries oil owned by third parties, but continued to ship its own oil to its four U.S. refineries.[2185] Chevron significantly reduced its deliveries in U.S. waters.[2186] Furthermore, a number of tanker owners, including Shell, refused to carry heavy crude and other "dirty oils" to the United States. Such crudes and other heavy fuels are considered "dirty" because they are difficult and costly to clean up in the event of a spill.[2187]

The face-off between the U.S. Coast Guard and the P & I Clubs has also led to "*corporate restructuring and changes in vessel ownership*". As industry experts had further predicted, many tanker operators have reorganized their corporate structures in an effort to protect their parent companies from the reaches of OPA 90 and its potential for unlimited liability.[2188] For instance in a more subtle move, Exxon Corporation reorganized its shipping subsidiary, Exxon Shipping Company. The subsidiary received a new name, as did each of its U.S.-flagged tankers. Additionally, the subsidiary's board of directors was reshuffled and, for the first time, includes directors from outside the parent corporation. While Exxon Corporation conceded that the move was due, in part, to the impact of OPA 90, it expressly denied that it was a legal maneuver designed to shield itself from the future liabilities of its subsidiary.[2189] However it cannot be denied that the reorganization places further distance between the two companies and their respective assets. One could argue that if the present trend continues, it may pave the way for undercapitalized and substandard

2184 These companies, like Shell, do permit their vessels to call at the Louisiana Offshore Oil Port (LOOP). LOOP is the United States's only deepwater port that is located a sufficient distance from oil sensitive coastlines to ease shipper's concerns. Amy Feldman, Aloha, Forbes, May 11, 1992, at 20. See also id. at 21.

2185 Amoco Trims Charters, PLATT'S OILGRAM NEWS, Feb. 3, 1993, at 3.

2186 Robin Buckner Price, U.S. Oil Spill Law to Cause Growing Tanker Problem, OIL & GAS J., Sept. 30, 1991, at 21.

2187 Aviva Freudmann, Oil Tanker Owners Adjust to risks Under Pollution Law, J. of Com., Feb. 21, 1991, at A9.

2188 Jeffery D. Morgan, The Oil Pollution Act of 1990: A Look at its Impact on the oil industry, 6 Fordham Envtl. L. J. 1, 9 (Fall 1994)

2189 Joel Glass, Exxon Plans U.S. Shipping shake-up, Lloyd's List Int'l, Mar. 3, 1993, at 1.

operators who will simply walk away from spills, to enter into the market place. But, this is only if the OPA limit of liability is broken. If limitation is not broken, then the COFR guarantor will be directly liable for the spill up to the maximum amount of its COFR guaranty.

Considering the aforementioned examples, one must acknowledge that the Oil industry's early warnings were not totally without merit. When major oil companies cut back on transporting their own oil in favor of third-party charter vessels, the abundant assets of those companies become unavailable under OPA 90 should a spill occur. Likewise, unless litigants are able to "pierce the corporate veil," the strategic restructuring of corporate entities will place assets out of reach from potential plaintiffs.[2190] In such situations, the end result is an increased likelihood that cleanup costs and damages will be borne by the oil tax funded Oil Spill Liability Trust Fund.[2191]

## IV. Mobil Shipping and Transportation Company led the way for several other COFR applicants to follow.

*MOBIL*: The U.S. Coast Guard in the Fall of 1994 reached its eagerly sought milestone with the issuing of the first vessel Certificate of Financial Responsibility (COFR) under the controversial U.S. Oil Pollution Act (OPA 90) regime to two Mobil subsidiaries.[2192] The first new COFRs were issued for the one U.S.-flag tanker and 16 large barges operated by Mobil Shipping & Transportation Company. Mobil is a Britannia P & I Club member. The National Pollution Control Funds Center the U.S. Coast Guard Department charged with the responsibility of issuing COFRs issued the COFRs to Mobil after approving the new Mobil subsidiary Marine Guaranty corporation, which was created specifically to act

2190 Jeffery D. Morgan, The Oil Pollution Act of 1990: A Look at its Impact on the oil industry, 6 Fordham Envtl. L. J. at 11.

2191 Id. at 11.

2192 Joel Glass, Mobil sets COFRs milestone: Oil major offshoots receive certificate after company sets up guaranty corporation, Lloyd's List Int'l, Sept. 14, 1994, at 14.

as guarantor for the 49-vessel fleet.[2193] Mobil Shipping president Gerhard Kurz said that Marine Guaranty's exposure for the two subsidiaries' fleets was $285m, all of it backed by internally-generated funds. The Coast Guard hailed the Mobil vessels' certification as a very positive indication that the maritime industry would like to get about its business. They also praised Mobil's approach to solving the COFR standoff, claiming that: This is a responsible company that is looking out for its interests in light of some legitimate legislation in the U.S.[2194]

*A.P. Moeller*: In November, 1994, the US Coast Guard's National Pollution Funds Center announced the issuance of 35 Certificates of Financial Responsibility for the fleet operated by A.P. Moeller.[2195] The fleet which received their certificates consisted of 32 self propelled tankers and three non tankers. Mr. D.F. Sheehan, then Director of the National Pollution Funds Center, indicated then, that this brought the total number of COFRs issued to tank vessels to 215, a little over one month to the December 28, 1994, deadline for compliance with the COFR requirement. He indicated at the time that the number was steadily increasing on a daily basis and that the issuance of certificates to major foreign owned independent tank vessel owners and operators was a significant step in the process and commended them for their responsible actions.[2196]

In November, 1994, the Coast Guard's National Pollution Funds Center announced that it had approved the issuance of an additional 195 Certificates of Financial Responsibility under OPA 90 and the Comprehensive Environmental Response, Compensation and Liability Act (CERCLA).[2197] The following companies received approval:

---

2193 Id. at 14.

2194 Id.

2195 *See* "COFRs Issued To Major Foreign Owned Independent Fleet," National Pollution Funds Center – Press Release (Wed. Nov 16 1994) (last modified Feb. 27, 2002) <http://www.uscg.mil/hq/npfc/press.htm>

2196 Id.

2197 *See* "COFRs Issued To Additional 195 Vessels" National Pollution Funds Center – Press Release (Tue. Nov 22 1994) (last modified Feb. 27, 2002) <http://www.uscg.mil/

*Bergesen*, for 40 tank vessels and 2 non tank vessels (financial guaranty); *Shell International Shipping Limited*, for 44 tank vessels (financial guaranty); *Union Carbide Corporation*, for 1 tank vessel and 106 barges (self-insurance); and *Neptune Orient Lines, Ltd.*, for 2 non-tank vessels (surety bond guaranty).[2198] As of November 22, 1994, a little over a month to the COFR deadline, the total number of COFRs issued for tank vessels was 296, and the total of all OPA COFRs issued were 96, while the total of CERCLA COFRs issued were 1043.[2199]

There is no doubt that exponential progress has been made on the controversial issue of COFRs. Judging by the high number of COFR holders in the December 2001, NPFC chart and Table analyzed earlier in this part, there is no doubt that vessel owners have gotten used to the COFR requirements, and they have adjusted to the increased costs that it brings with it. The number of COFR holders has risen to the level that optimists would have expected considering the number of vessels that sail into US waters on a daily basis. But this increase was not within the contemplation of the P & I Clubs who promised a train wreck scenario for ocean vessel transportation to US waters.

## V. Insurance Industry's solution to the standoff and its impact on P & I Clubs:

### V.A. Who are the Leading COFR Guarantors and how do they impact the long-standing P & I Club insurance Structure?

(a) *Shoreline Mutual:* On Thursday, December 1, 1994, the Coast Guard's National Pollution Funds Center announced that it had approved the Shoreline Mutual (Bermuda) Limited, of Financial Responsibility

hq/npfc/press.htm>

2198 Id.

2199 Id.

(COFR) guaranty program.[2200] Shoreline applied for and was granted full approval as a provider of financial responsibility under the vessel financial responsibility regulations published July 1, 1994.[2201] The company was at that time authorized to issue COFR guaranties up to $300 million but expected to be able to arrange cover for tankers requiring higher amounts later on, subject to Coast Guard approval.[2202] NPFC Director Daniel Sheehan noted that with this approval there were three commercial entities that had publicly announced a willingness to act as COFR guarantors for shipowners and operators as of that date.[2203] The newly approved guaranty providers as of December 1, 1994, 27 days to the deadline for the required COFR guaranties, were Shoreline, First Line, and OPA Club.[2204] As of that date, there were 1203 vessels which had been issued COFRs under the new rule.[2205] This figure included 395 self-propelled tankers, 749 barges, and 59 other vessels.[2206]

Shoreline is not affiliated to any broker or P & I Club. This new special purpose insurance mutual started underwriting oil pollution risks shortly before the expiration of the U.S. Coast Guard deadline for obtaining the COFRs. It was set up in order to resolve the impasse between the major P & I Clubs and the U.S. Coast Guard, over the OPA 90. This company was incorporated in Bermuda and provides up to $300m of oil pollution cover to shipowners as well as providing the guaranties to the Coast Guard to back the certificates of financial responsibility that have proved a sticking point between the P & I Clubs and the Coast Guard.[2207] Shoreline is a traditional, industry-standard P& I Club, mutual and non-profit making, controlled by a shipowner's committee just

2200 *See* "Coast Guard Approves "Shoreline" As COFR Guarantor" National Pollution Funds Center – Press Release (Thurs. Dec 1, 1994) (last modified Feb. 27, 2002) < http://www.uscg.mil/hq/npfc/pdf/9.pdf>

2201 Id.

2202 Id.

2203 Id.

2204 Id.

2205 Id.

2206 Id.

2207 Jim Mulrenan, Mutual move in OPA impasse, Lloyd's List Int'l, Mar. 9, 1994, at 1.

like the International Group Clubs. Its architects were a former P & I Club manager, a retired shipowner and two marine insurance brokers: all industry insiders.[2208]

The new mutual offers cover to both U.S. and foreign owners of tankers and all other ships on a tariff basis although the managers reserve the right individually to underwrite risks where claims are recorded or other factors warrant it.[2209]

The new mutual made a $300m bond offering in the U.S. to provide initial financing and the Swiss Bank Corporation declared that it expects to underwrite the whole issue. The bond had a five-year maturity by which time it was hoped the mutual would have sufficient reserves to be self-financing.[2210] A number of prominent shipowners expressed interest in joining shoreline, but would still have to remain members of a general purpose P & I Club in respect of other risks.

The mutual is being managed through the agency of Mutual Risk Management, a leading New York Stock Exchange quoted, but Bermuda based captive manager, with claims handling organized out of Seattle.[2211] Shoreline retains a first $10m of risk and reinsure the remaining $290m exposure under a program placed by Lloyd's broker Blackwall Green, John P Tilden of New York and Peter H. Mess of Hamburg.[2212]

In the Spring of 1995 Shoreline Mutual arranged reinsurance to protect shipowners against a big supplementary call in the event that a member faces damages for an oil spill in U.S. waters and turns out to be insolvent.[2213] The Mutual's managers said that the combination of those circumstances is extremely remote, but acted in response to requests from members. The members raised fears that they might face undue exposure in the 30-days it would take to sort out the immediate problems caused

2208 Shuker, Specialist insurers offer real OPA solution for shipowners, Lloyd's List Int'l, June 21, 1996, at 8.

2209 Jim Mulrenan, Mutual move in OPA impasse, Lloyd's List Int'l, Mar. 9, 1994, at 1.

2210 Id. at 1.

2211 Id. at 2.

2212 Id. at 1.

2213 James Brewer, Shoreline arranges oil spill insurance, Lloyd's List Int'l, Mar.8, 1995, at 14.

by the insolvency of an owner with a stricken vessel. Shoreline is growing steadily, as of the Spring of 1995 it had issued more than 320 guaranties for vessels totaling more than 11m gt and had further applications.[2214] The new policy adds to cover for the range of instances where a P & I Club would exclude payment.[2215] The P & I Clubs have discretionary rules on paying where there is insolvency. This mutual policy has attracted and will continue to attract traditional P & I Club members because it is a very good offer. This invariably makes them a threat to the monopoly and dominance of P & I Clubs in vessel insurance. Shoreline said its quota share reinsurer, Center Re (Bermuda) Ltd, arranged the policy, which will cover most of the potential supplementary call which would have hit members. The policy was placed by Willis Faber & Dumas and Sedgwick Marine & Cargo, and is underwritten 100% at Lloyd's.[2216] The cost has been absorbed by shorelines's existing reinsurers, allowing published tariffs to remain unchanged. Shoreline also said that the cover further reduced the area of a substantial mutuality claim on members.[2217]

(b) *Firstline*: On November 23, 1994, the US Coast Guard's National Pollution Funds Center announced that it had approved the Certificate of Financial Responsibility (COFR) guaranty program commonly referred to as "First Line."[2218] Stockton Reinsurance Limited (Stockton Re), a Bermuda insurance company, applied for, and was granted, approval as an "other evidence" provider of financial responsibility under the vessel financial responsibility regulations published July 1, 1994. Stockton Re is reinsured through reinsurers based in Bermuda and London.[2219] The Firstline program was wound up after a few years of operation and substituted with the SIGCo program which will be discussed later in this chap-

2214 Id. at 14.

2215 Id.

2216 Id.

2217 Id.

2218 *See* "Coast Guard Approves Stockton Re As COFR Guarantor" Press Release National Pollution Funds Center - Press Release (Wed. Nov. 23, 1994) (last modified Feb. 27, 2002)< http://www.uscg.mil/hq/npfc/pdf/10.pdf>

2219 Id.

ter. Stockton Re was at that time authorized to issue COFR guaranties up to $150 million, but fully expected to later obtain additional reinsurance enabling it to write larger risks.[2220] This arrangement was spearheaded by international insurance broker Johnson & Higgins.[2221] NPFC Director Daniel Sheehan noted that this approval marked another milestone in that as of that date, November 23, 1994, there were three entities capable of providing COFR guaranties to independent shipowners and operators.[2222] These included the newly approved Stockton Re, OPA Club, and Federal Insurance Company, the latter of which intended to guaranty principally chemical tankers.[2223] Mr. Sheehan reaffirmed on that day that the then looming December 28, 1994, compliance date for self-propelled tank vessels to obtain COFR was not going to change.[2224]

This insurance program called Firstline was the second major insurance industry solution to the stand-off between P & I Clubs and the U.S. Coast Guard. Finance and reinsurance support for this specialist insurance company set up to cover oil spill liabilities in the U.S. was secured by Lloyd's broker Nicholson Chamberlain BankAssure, and Johnson & Higgins two leading insurance broking houses.[2225] This company was incorporated in Bermuda, but with managing agents in London and New York and it provided comprehensive insurance to meet shipowners' liabilities under OPA 90. This included provision of the guaranties necessary to obtain the Certificates of Financial Responsibility required by OPA 90. The company also envisaged it would separately offer sue and labor cover for the legal expenses that could fall on shipowners.[2226]

The potential reinsurers were a mixture of catastrophe and financial underwriters, largely in Bermuda. A key feature of the reinsurance

2220 Id.

2221 Id.

2222 Id.

2223 Id.

2224 Id.

2225 Jim Mulrenan, New insurance company set to cover US oil spill liabilities: Hope of end to impasse between Coast Guard and protection and indemnity clubs over OPA regulations, Lloyd's List Int'l, Sept. 28, 1993, at 3.

2226 Id. at 3.

program was that risks were individually declared to reinsurers who therefore retained control of rating.[2227] The Stockton Re initiative somewhat replaced the P & I Clubs just like Shoreline, as a primary source of U.S. oil pollution Liability cover and did not rely on reinsurance support from them. The risk was confined to pollution only while an insured vessel is in the U.S. Exclusive economic zone.[2228] Limits insured was to statutory levels only- an average of less than $20m for a dry cargo and $60m for a tanker trading into U.S. mainland ports or $240m for the large tankers that visit the Louisiana offshore oil Port and conduct offshore transshipment.[2229] Claims were supposed to be made within three years as provided under section 2717(f) of the OPA 90. Insurance was for federal OPA 90 requirements and not for liabilities imposed at state level. [2230]

(c) *Comparing Shoreline and First line and how they impact P & I Clubs*: The P & I clubs had threatened that a train wreck scenario could take place in maritime trade in the U.S. if their demand for a repeal of the harsh provisions of the OPA 90 were not met. However the threatened train wreck did not occur, and there has been no fall-off in trade with the U.S. despite the implementation of the requirement of the new Certificates of Financial Responsibility (COFR).

The two specialist insurers, Shoreline Mutual and First Line program of Stockton Re, offer guaranties acceptable to the U. S. Coast Guard for the issue of certificates for those shipowners unable to obtain COFRs through self-insurance.[2231] It was borne out of necessity, and it became a vehicle for people to look outside the P & I Clubs for a vehicle to provide COFR guaranties.

---

2227 Id.

2228 Id.

2229 Id.

2230 Id.

2231 *See* Hugh Bryant, Specialist insurers offer real OPA solution for shipowners: The realisation that **OPA** 90 is here to stay has prompted calls from **shipowners** for an 'industry **solution'** to the problem of Certificates of Financial Responsibility. Lloyd's List Int'l, June 21, 1996, at 5.

Nowadays, the COFR providers, Shoreline and First line, are sometimes criticized for being expensive, and for charging high prices simply for a ticket to trade. Is there in fact a real risk which they cover? [2232]

Real risks are indeed covered by the COFR providers, although the cover provided by Shoreline and First line differ somewhat.

Shoreline simply covers any liability for oil or other pollution under the terms of its guaranty to the U.S. government which is not met by the shipowner's P & I Club.[2233] First line provided, by contrast, what was essentially a credit risk insurance, covering any liability arising under a COFR guaranty which could not be recovered from the shipowner concerned. Both programs offer COFR guaranties up to $395m for any one ship.[2234] According to the U.S. Coast Guard, there has already been an instance where a P & I Club in the International Group has refused to provide coverage in respect of U.S. oil pollution and this fell on First line.[2235] As a matter of principle, it should be noted that the P & I Clubs have expressly insisted on their right to invoke their indemnification rule, otherwise called pay-to-be-paid principle, which in effect is reserving the right to withhold cover in certain instances. It is therefore clearly the case that the COFR providers are accepting substantial risks.

Even under the First line scheme, where any liability was recoverable from the assured, underwriters were accepting a substantial risk. How likely is it that a $200m liability could be recovered from a one-ship company?

The creation of COFR providers was done against the background of a vigorous campaign by P & I Clubs to have OPA 90 changed, in order to remove the need for the certificates altogether. This was a highly unlikely prospect. There are few votes in environment-conscious United States for changing the law in favor of potential polluters. Nevertheless shipowners supported the campaign on the ground that however unlikely, they will benefit if it did succeed. It became apparent at a very late stage that the

2232 Id. at 5.

2233 Id.

2234 Id.

2235 Id.

U.S. government was not going to back down. This made many of the tanker-shipowners to abandon their initial support for the P & I Clubs and most of them took refuge under Shoreline and First line. This may be the beginning of the end of the strangle hold or monopoly that P & I Clubs had hitherto enjoyed for the last 140 years and might also lead to environmental laws similar to the OPA 90 being passed by other countries. This is because other coastal nations would be convinced that if the train wreck scenario did not occur in the US despite the tough OPA 90 provisions, it would also not occur in their respective jurisdictions.

The International Group of P& I Clubs has maintained its refusal to provide COFR guaranties, and periodically mention in their circulars and reports to members, the need for an industry solution to the COFR requirement.[2236] Some critics say that this looks like nonsense in view of the successful operation of Shoreline and First line (and its successor SIGCo). They criticize the demand of the P & I Clubs for an industry solution, which they believe Shoreline and First line have already brought, since both companies come from the heart of the marine insurance industry. They also believe that the P & I Clubs are making that call now because some of their managers would have liked to have the fee-income which the managers of Shoreline and First line truly earn.[2237]

These days, if they ever did, shipowners do not set up mutuals or other insurance vehicles by themselves. The insurance industry, in persons of brokers, professional managers, specialist lawyers and seasoned accountants, do it for them. This is the real meaning of an industry solution.[2238] Given the fact that all ships which need COFRs can obtain them through Shoreline and Firstline (and its successor SIGCo), which provide distinctively different, competing products, if the P & I Clubs suddenly abandoned their principle and promoted a so-called industry solution, it

---

2236 *See* Hugh Bryant, Specialist insurers offer real OPA solution for shipowners: The realization that **OPA** 90 is here to stay has prompted calls from **shipowners** for an 'industry **solution'** to the problem of Certificates of Financial Responsibility, Lloyd's List Int'l, June 21, 1996, at 5.

2237 Id. at 5.

2238 Id.

might be thought that its real purpose was not to serve shipowners but simply to put Shoreline and First line (and its successor SIGCo) out of business.[2239] These criticisms were made before the first line program was succeeded by the SIGCo program. It is important to recognize that two genuine industry solutions already exist in the form of Shoreline and First line (as succeeded by SIGCo). They are doing a good job at a fair price. They deserve less grudging acceptance by the P & I Clubs, whose assets they inadvertently protect from the challenge of direct action in the U.S.[2240]

## V. B. SIGCO

On November 20, 1996 Stockton Reinsurance announced the formation of a new vehicle to provide COFR guaranties under OPA 90.[2241] The Shipowners Insurance and Guaranty Company Ltd. (SIGCo) replaced the First Line program after December 28, 1996.[2242] This is the same Stockton Re that established the now defunct Firstline program. SIGCo was incorporated as a limited liability company on the 9th October, 1996 to respond to the requirements mandated by the United States Oil Pollution Act, 1990 (OPA90). The company's formation was facilitated by the consultation between Stockton Re (the insurer behind the First Line Program that preceded SIGCO) and the managements of three leading P&I Clubs.[2243]

---

2239 Id.

2240 *See* Hugh Bryant, Specialist insurers offer real OPA solution for shipowners: The realisation that **OPA** 90 is here to stay has prompted calls from **shipowners** for an 'industry **solution'** to the problem of Certificates of Financial Responsibility, Lloyd's List Int'l, June 21, 1996, at 5.

2241 See The American Club, Ship Owners guaranty Company Limited, Circular No. 9/96 (Nov. 22. 1996).

2242 Id.

2243 http://cofr.com/about.htm

*Objective*

SIGCo's principal objective is to assist shipowners in fulfilling Financial Guaranty requirements of OPA 90 and the Comprehensive Environmental Response Compensation and Liability Act (CERCLA). SIGCo was founded with the express intention to be the long term, fixed premium Certificate of Financial Responsibility (COFR) Guaranty facility.[2244] It was established to provide low-cost guaranties while increasing control and ownership of the facility on behalf of shipowners, without unnecessary exposure to their balance sheets.[2245]

*Summary Of Services*

Just like its predecessor, the FirstLine program, SIGCo's primary function is the provision of Financial Guaranties needed to support COFRs issued by the United States Coast Guard (USCG) for the world's blue-water tonnage trading to the USA.[2246] SIGCo is approved by the USCG as a result of capitalization in excess of $25 million and a comprehensive reinsurance program supported by some of the world's largest reinsurance companies.[2247] SIGCo is liable as Guarantor for claims arising under OPA90/CERCLA that result from oil or hazardous material pollution incidents occurring within the US Exclusive Economic Zone.[2248] As a logical extension of its primary responsibility, SIGCo will also apply to the USCG for a COFR on behalf of the shipowner.[2249] In addition to removing the onerous administrative burden of such an application, SIGCo also absorbs the associated fees payable to the USCG

---

2244 *See* The Shipowners Insurance and Guaranty Company Ltd. (SIGCo): About SIGCo. (last modified Jan, 2002) <http://cofr.com/about.htm>

2245 Id.

2246 Id.

2247 Id.

2248 Id.

2249 Id.

and the US processing agent.[2250] There is no charge to the shipowner for this service.[2251]

### *COFR Guaranty Application*

COFR guaranties are provided at a fixed premium cost with vessels rated according to type.[2252] Tankers carrying either persistent or non-persistent cargoes as defined in the legislation are rated on a per voyage basis over the period of the guaranty.[2253] Dry cargo vessels are given a fixed premium cost for the period irrespective of voyages undertaken.[2254] SIGCo will also provide a guaranty for vessels on a "service fee" basis where it is not anticipated that the vessel will enter US waters, but the shipowner does not wish the COFR to lapse.[2255] This administrative procedure is undertaken by SIGCo at a nominal cost, with an increase to a full premium cost if the vessel does in fact enter US waters during the period of the cover.[2256]

### *COFR Application:*

SIGCo will also process the CG5585 application to the USCG on behalf of its clients, at no charge.[2257] Under OPA90, each operator is required to obtain a COFR from the USCG, using this CG5585 application. The resulting COFR accompanies the COFR guaranty, issued by SIGCo.[2258] Both documents are required for each vessel trading to the

2250 Id.
2251 Id.
2252 Id.
2253 Id.
2254 Id.
2255 Id.
2256 Id.
2257 Id.
2258 Id.

USA.[2259] SIGCo personnel maintain close relations with the USCG and are able to liaise with them swiftly and efficiently to resolve problems which may arise in meeting all COFR obligations of shipowners under OPA 90 and CERCLA.[2260]

The entry of SIGCo into the COFR guarantor market pushed shoreline the erstwhile number one COFR guarantor into second place as the statistics below show. In a circular sent out to its members in 1997, shoreline indicated that the COFR market had changed considerably with the advent of two new COFR facilities becoming operational that year.[2261]

**SIGCO's COFR statistics for quarter ending March 2001.**
**SIGCo Market Share as of March 2001**

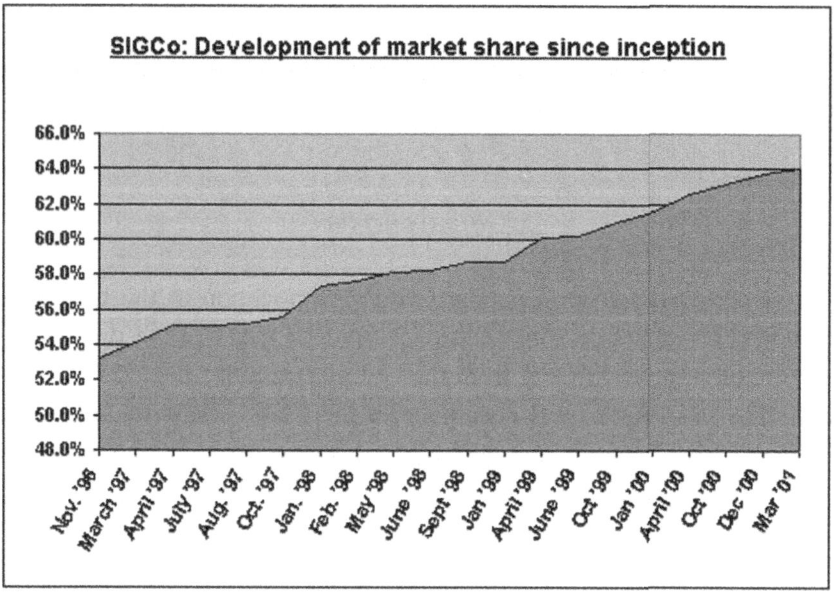


2259 Id.

2260 Id.

2261 Shoreline Leads The Way In COFR Guarantees, Circular to Members and Brokers (Wednesday February 5th 1997).

## NPFC COFR statistics for quarter ending 31 Dec. 2001

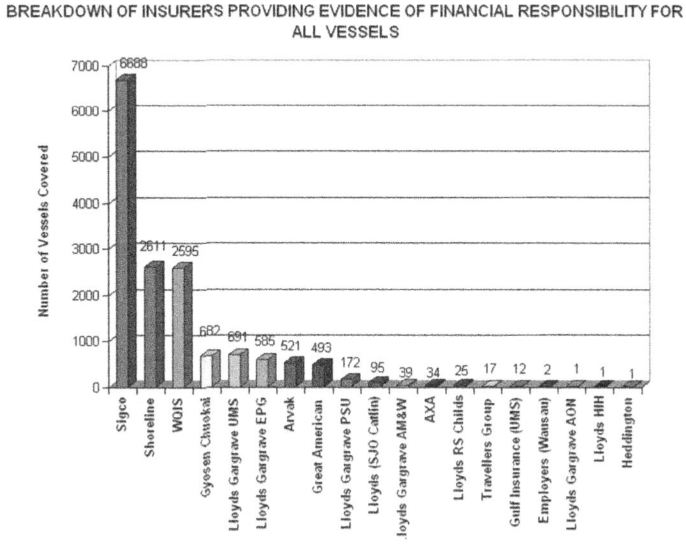


## Insurance Breakdown Table

BREAKDOWN OF INSURERS PROVIDING EVIDENCE OF FINANCIAL RESPONSIBILITY

| INSURER | Dry Cargo | Tanker | Tank Barge | MODU | Passenger | Fishing | Utility | TOTALS |
|---|---|---|---|---|---|---|---|---|
| Sigco | 4987 | 1284 | 40 | 0 | 81 | 88 | 208 | **6688** |
| Shoreline | 1804 | 677 | 4 | 2 | 96 | 7 | 21 | **2611** |
| WQIS | 424 | 15 | 871 | 46 | 212 | 103 | 924 | **2595** |
| Gyosen Chuokai | 0 | 0 | 0 | 0 | 0 | 682 | 0 | **682** |
| Lloyds Gargrave UMS | 4 | 4 | 527 | 0 | 0 | 0 | 156 | **691** |
| Lloyds Gargrave EPG | 78 | 1 | 127 | 0 | 23 | 102 | 254 | **585** |
| Arvak | 301 | 95 | 28 | 0 | 4 | 52 | 41 | **521** |
| Great American | 77 | 1 | 157 | 3 | 30 | 4 | 221 | **493** |
| Lloyds Gargrave PSU | 3 | 0 | 8 | 0 | 10 | 87 | 64 | **172** |
| Lloyds Gargrave AM&W | 1 | 0 | 1 | 0 | 2 | 13 | 22 | **39** |
| AXA | 30 | 3 | 0 | 0 | 1 | 0 | 0 | **34** |
| Lloyds RS Childs | 0 | 0 | 0 | 0 | 24 | 0 | 1 | **25** |
| Travellers Group | 0 | 0 | 0 | 0 | 0 | 0 | 17 | **17** |
| Lloyds (SJO Catlin) | 0 | 0 | 1 | 93 | 0 | 0 | 1 | **95** |
| Gulf Insurance (UMS) | 0 | 0 | 0 | 0 | 0 | 0 | 12 | **12** |
| Lloyds Gargrave AON | 0 | 0 | 0 | 1 | 0 | 0 | 0 | **1** |
| Lloyds HIH | 1 | 0 | 0 | 0 | 0 | 0 | 0 | **1** |
| Employers (Wausau) | 0 | 0 | 2 | 0 | 0 | 0 | 0 | **2** |
| Heddington | 0 | 1 | 0 | 0 | 0 | 0 | 0 | **1** |
| TOTALS | **7710** | **2081** | **1766** | **145** | **483** | **1138** | **1942** | **15265** |

Dry cargo includes bulk carriers, containerships, reefers, ro-ro's, etc.
Tanker includes crude carriers, product carriers, chemical tankers, OBOs, LPG and LNG carriers
Fishing includes fishing and factory vessels
Utility includes deck barges, tug/tow boats, OSVs, research vessels, and oil spill response vessels

## V.C. SIGCO's (COFR Guarantor's) Terms and Conditions.

The OPA allows private parties and government parties to proceed directly against guarantors like SIGCo, and it also bars them from invoking exclusion clauses and insurance policy defenses against third party claimants, **but it does not bar** the guarantors from invoking exclusion clauses and policy defenses against the insured or the beneficiary of the evidence of financial responsibility in actions by it against its COFR guarantor. For instance, SIGCo's policy provides that additional defenses not enumerated in the COFR regulations **that may be available to the Guarantor against the Covered Party arising from a contract**, if any, pursuant to which this Guaranty is provided, **may not be invoked by Guarantor against a Claimant in any direct action by a Claimant.**[2262]

The SIGCo guarantee is based on difference in conditions insurance and is provided to the Coast Guard on the basis of a difference in conditions insurance contract with the Covered Party.[2263] The guarantor (SIGCo) also certifies by its signature to the United States Coast Guard that the Covered Liabilities **are guaranteed by the Guarantor up to, but not exceeding the limit guarantied.**[2264]

SIGCo also certifies that the amount and scope of the Guaranty provided by the Guarantor is not conditioned or dependent in any way upon the existence of any contract, agreement, or understanding between it (the guarantor) and the Covered Party or between the Covered Party and a marine insurer, if any.[2265] The guarantor (SIGCo) also **consents to be sued directly with respect to any claim**, including any claim by right of subrogation, against the Covered Party.[2266] In any direct action, Guarantor's (SIGCo's) **maximum liability per covered vessel**

2262 *See* The Shipowners Insurance And Guaranty Company Ltd. (SIGCo) Standard Terms And Conditions, Appendix 1.III Form of guaranty - Defenses (28th December, 1997).

2263 Id at Appendix 1.II Form of Guaranty.

2264 Id.

2265 Id.

2266 Id.

**per incident shall not exceed the limit guarantied in respect of such incident.**[2267]

By virtue of the fact that the guarantor can still invoke policy defenses and exclusions against the COFR guaranty beneficiary in lawsuits filed by it against the guarantor for denial of insurance cover, SIGCo has included in its guaranty policy, certain warranties, representations and undertakings, which is a condition precedent to its indemnification of the insured. The undertakings include the following:

"(a) to enter and keep each of the Vessels entered in the Club for full protection and indemnity risks under law including, but not limited to, OPA 1990 and CERCLA, in the Standard Amount;

(b) to keep each of the Vessels fully insured for the full value of the Vessel for collision liabilities, either under the terms of the Club entry or under hull and machinery policies with reputable insurers or under a combination of both;

(c) for each of the Vessels that is a tank vessel, to ensure that SIGCo receives copies of the quarterly U.S. Voyage Declarations, if any, at the time such Declarations are submitted to the Club, and, with respect to tank vessels that are not subject to quarterly U.S. Voyage Declarations, to ensure that SIGCo receives notice of each voyage made by such tank vessels in U.S. waters;

(d) to keep each of the Vessels in such condition as will entitle it to maintain the highest classification for vessels of its type and service with the Classification Society and to comply with all recommendations and qualifications of such Classification Society affecting class within any period specified by the Classification Society and so as to comply with the provisions of all laws, regulations and requirements (statutory or otherwise) from time to time applicable to vessels registered under the same flag as the Vessel and engaged in the service in which the Vessel is engaged;

(e) to submit each of the Vessels to such periodic surveys as may be required for classification purposes and to supply to SIGCo copies of all survey reports and confirmations of class concerning the Vessels, as may be requested by SIGCo from time to time;

2267 Id.

(f) to comply with all statutory, regulatory and other requirements, including but not limited to such requirements established by or issued pursuant to OPA 1990 and CERCLA, as are applicable to vessels operating in the trade in which the Vessels are engaged concerning the ownership of the Vessels and their operation, management and trade;

(g) immediately to notify SIGCo if any of the Vessels is the source of a discharge or threatened discharge under OPA 1990 or CERCLA or the source of a release or threatened release under OPA 1990 or CERCLA;

(h) in the event of notification of a claim or threatened claim to take all such steps as are required by the Club and under OPA 1990 and any other applicable laws, regulations and requirements;

(i) without prejudice to any rights of SIGCo to terminate or take any other actions under the Agreement, to notify SIGCo immediately of any change in the written information, statements, representations, warranties and undertakings provided to SIGCo during the period of the Agreement that would make such previous information, statement, representation or warranty untrue or misleading, and to immediately notify SIGCo of any breach of the Agreement;

(j) to supply SIGCo with any receipts or other evidences of payment for damages or removal costs paid by the Applicants;

(k) to comply with all of the rules, regulations and requirements of the Club from time to time in force;

(l) at any time and from time to time on the written request of SIGCo promptly and duly to execute and deliver to SIGCo any and all such further instruments, documents and things as SIGCo may consider desirable in obtaining the full benefit of the Agreement and of the rights and powers therein granted;

(m) to furnish, whenever requested by SIGCo, Confirmation of Entry or of renewal of entry in the Club substantially in the form contained in Appendix 2 attached hereto, maintenance of insurances required by the Vessels mortgagee, and maintenance of such other insurances as are customarily maintained by vessel owners and/or operators entering U.S. waters;

(n) to procure execution by the Club of the Letter of Undertaking and the Letter to Member substantially in the form contained in Appendix 2 attached hereto prior to the issuance of the Guaranty and to provide to SIGCo the original

Letter of Undertaking, and the Applicants shall maintain such Letter of Undertaking and Letter to Member in full force and effect for the period of the Agreement;

(o) to pay to SIGCo at the time and in the manner agreed such Premiums in United States dollars as have been agreed with SIGCo; and

(p) to agree that all Premiums shall be deemed fully earned by SIGCo upon the issue of the Guaranty."

The guaranty agreement between SIGCo and the COFR guaranty beneficiary may be terminated by SIGCo, with respect to any or all of the Vessels by SIGCo giving notice of the termination of the Guaranty to the United States Coast Guard to be effective thirty (30) days thereafter, in the event of a breach of any of the representations, warranties or undertakings explained above.[2268] A breach of any of the COFR guaranty beneficiary's other obligations contained in the Terms and Condition; or its failure to pay Premiums when due; and failure to cure such failure within forty-eight (48) hours, would also entitle the SIGCo to terminate the guaranty agreement.[2269] The guarantee agreement could also be terminated at any other time and for any other reason.[2270]

Shoreline, the second leading COFR guarantor, also requires that their members make similar undertakings as those included in the SIGCo terms and conditions. For those insured by either shoreline or SIGCo, theoretically, it is possible that a violation of the COFR beneficiary's undertaking to comply with all of the rules, regulations and requirements of the P & I Club from time to time in force could jeopardize its guaranty with these companies and other Guaranty companies with similar requirements. This means that a violation of Club Rules would be regarded as a violation of the Guarantor's Rules. In such a case, the third party claimant could be paid its due, but then the COFR guarantors will then sue the COFR guaranty beneficiary for indemnification of what they paid to that third party that brought the claim. That third party could be government claimants

2268 Id. at Clause 4.1, Termination.

2269 Id. at Clause 4.1 (b)-(c).

2270 Id. at Clause 4.1(d).

or private claimants under OPA. This may sound contradictory because from the point of view of the ship owner, one of the practical uses of the COFR guaranty itself is for the Club member to have substitute insurance to fall back on when it is sued by a third party and its P & I Club denies Cover because of one Club Rule violation or the other. But it is likely that in most cases only egregious violations of Club Rules combined with violations of rules peculiar to the Guarantors may cause the COFR guarantor to interpret a violation of the Club Rules as a concomitant violation of the Guarantor's Rules.

SIGCo terms and conditions provide further that the moment any COFR guaranty beneficiary ceases to be the owner or operator of any Vessel for any reason, including scrapping or transferring the Vessel to a new operator; the guaranty agreement shall terminate automatically with respect to such vessel.[2271] The guaranty agreement shall also terminate automatically if any Vessel shall be covered by a COFR accepted by the United States Coast Guard on the basis of evidence of financial responsibility other than that submitted by SIGCo and notice of termination of the Guaranty for such Vessel shall be given by SIGCo to the United States Coast Guard.[2272]

These COFR guaranty beneficiary's undertakings show that the P & I Club membership is a sine qua non to the application of the insurance guaranty to claims filed by the COFR guaranty beneficiary or insured against SIGCo or any other COFR guarantor that adopts a similar policy. Shoreline also has a similar policy. This Club membership must be confirmed by a letter of confirmation of entry by the P & I Club.[2273] The letter of confirmation of entry also contains a disclaimer that the confirmation of entry is not an indemnity or evidence of any undertaking on the part of the Club, whether financial or otherwise, to any party and shall not be construed as such.[2274]

2271 Id. at Clause 4.2(a).

2272 Id. at Clause 4.2(b).

2273 Id. at Appendix 2, Confirmation of Entry From The P&I Club (Letter 1 of 3).

2274 Id.

The P & I Club letter of undertaking must be obtained from the P & I Club in order for the COFR guarantor to issue the guaranty. The P & I Club letter of undertaking contains an undertaking by the P & I Club to inform SIGCo if the Directors of the Club give the Member notice under its "expiry of cover" rule, that its insurance in the Club in respect of any of the Named Vessels is to cease at the end of the then current policy year.[2275] It also contains an undertaking by the P & I Club to give SIGCo adequate notice (the number of days must be specified in the letter of undertaking) of the Club's intention to cancel the insurance of the Member in respect of any of the named vessels pursuant to the Rules of the Club by reason of the Member's failure to pay, when due and demanded, any sum due from it to the Club.[2276]

The COFR beneficiary is also supposed to obtain letters from its P & I Club that makes certain additional undertakings. The undertakings are as follows:

(a) If the Guarantor provides a guaranty to enable the Member to obtain a Certificate of Financial Responsibility from the US Coast Guard using Coast Guard Form "Other Evidence Approval No. 004" (the "Guaranty"), the P & I Club undertakes that neither the provision of the Guaranty by the Guarantor, nor the entering into such agreement with the Guarantor by the Member constitutes double insurance for the purpose of the Club's "double insurance" rule.[2277]

(b) An acknowledgement by the P & I Club that the COFR guaranty beneficiary's instruction that payments made under the Guaranty by the Guarantor are made on the COFR guaranty beneficiary's behalf. The Club thus confirms that, under this circumstance, payment by the Guarantor shall be considered to be payment by the Member for the purposes of the "pay-to-be-paid" rule.[2278]

---

2275 *See* The Shipowners Insurance And Guaranty Company Ltd. (SIGCo) Standard Terms And Conditions, Appendix 2. Letter Of Undertaking From The P&I Club (Letter 2 of 3) (28th December, 1997).

2276 Id.

2277 Id. at Appendix 2, Letter To Member From The P&I Club (Letter 3 of 3).

2278 Id.

(c) A confirmation by the P & I Club that insofar as the Member may be required to give an indemnity to the Guarantor in relation to the provision of the Guaranty, the Managers do not approve the terms of such indemnity for the purpose of the "contracts, indemnities and guarantees" rule.[2279] Generally, based on a Club's power to exclude coverage and invoke traditional P & I Club policy defenses, the failure of the Member to get the approval of the Managers of the club before entering into indemnities, contracts or guaranties with third parties could result in the P & I Club denying both a claim by the Member or any third party.[2280] This clause was included in the Club's letter to Member to neutralize this rule for the purposes of SIGCo's guaranties, indemnities, and policies with a P & I Club Member. The undertaking further states that the Club Member shall nevertheless remain entitled to recover from the Club in accordance with the Rules of the Club and the terms of entry, such liabilities, costs and expenses as would have been recoverable by the Member from the Club if it had been sued directly as the responsible party.[2281] The undertaking further states that other than as provided above, in relation to indemnities, guaranties, and contracts, the Member's cover remains in all respects governed by the Rules of the Club and the terms of entry of the ships concerned.[2282]

The undertakings also include disclaimer clauses stating that the provision or issuance of the undertakings cannot be used in support of any application for the purposes of demonstrating evidence of insurance or evidence of financial responsibility under any applicable law relating to environmental pollution or financial responsibility.[2283] The disclaimer further states that the issuance of these letters does not

---

2279 Id. at Appendix 2, Letter To Member From The P&I Club (Letter 3 of 3).

2280 *See* North of England Protection & Indemnity Association Rules, Rule 19(16)(A)-(B) (2002 -2003). Most Clubs have similar or identical provisions in their rules and policies.

2281 *See* The Shipowners Insurance And Guaranty Company Ltd. (SIGCo) Standard Terms And Conditions, Appendix 2, Letter To Member From The P&I Club (Letter 3 of 3). (28th December, 1997).

2282 Id.

2283 Id.

amount to an agreement by the Club to be sued directly by third party claimants.[2284]

Just like most of the International Group of P & I Clubs, SIGCo terms and conditions chose English law as the applicable law, and English courts as the applicable forum for settlement of disputes that arise under the terms and conditions.

The terms and conditions also include a provision that outlines the circumstances in which the COFR guaranty beneficiary would have to indemnify SIGCo for what it pays to a third party claimant in a third party lawsuit brought directly against SIGCo because of the activities of the COFR guaranty beneficiary.

Clause 3.1 of the SIGCo terms provide that the COFR guaranty beneficiary shall on demand, jointly and severally indemnify SIGCo and hold it harmless in respect of each of the items set forth in Clauses 3.1.2 (a) through (e) below if at any time during the period of the Agreement any of the COFR guaranty beneficiaries shall be in breach of the obligations set forth in the representations, warranties and undertakings provisions discussed earlier. The items specified in Clauses 3.1.2 (a) - (e) include the following:

"(a) Payments under the Guaranty - the amount, or the aggregate of all amounts, paid by SIGCO under the terms of the Guaranty;

(b) Interest on Guaranty Payments - interest in respect of amounts paid under the Guaranty by SIGCo, as in 3.1.2(a) above, calculated at an annual interest rate of LIBOR plus 200 basis points on such amounts from the date of payment by SIGCo to the date of reimbursement by the Applicants or the Club;

(c) Costs & Expenses - all claims, demands, proceedings, liabilities, taxes, losses, costs, interest and expenses of every kind (including, but not limited to, taking or defending legal action, whether or not liability under the Guaranty was actually established on the part of SIGCo, and reasonable lawyer's fees

2284 Id. *See also* Id. at Appendix 2, Confirmation of Entry From The P&I Club (Letter 1 of 3).

and expenses) (hereinafter together referred to as 'Liability Items") which may be made or brought against, or incurred by SIGCo in any country, in relation to:

*(i) the issue and performance of the Guaranty; or*

*(ii) any action taken by any person against SIGCo under or in connection with the Guaranty; or*

*(iii) any other event, matter or question which occurs or arises at any time and which has any connection with, or any bearing on, the Guaranty or any transaction relating to the Guaranty, or any Vessel covered by the Guaranty, other than Liability Items which are shown to have been caused mainly and directly by the gross negligence or the dishonesty of SIGCo or its officers or employees;*

(d) Other Liabilities - any other liabilities arising out of or in connection with the occurrence or continuance of any breach of any provision or other default of any Applicant under or in connection with the Agreement, including the due payment of Premiums;

(e) Interest for Late Payment - upon any failure (for whatever reason) by the Applicants to pay any amount due under the Agreement within 10 days of the date of demand, interest shall be payable calculated at an annual interest rate of LIBOR plus 400 basis points on such amounts outstanding from the demand date until receipt by SIGCo of the amount outstanding."[2285]

Clause 3.1.1 of the conditions further provide that in the event there is no breach of the obligations set forth in the representations, warranties and undertakings, the COFR guaranty beneficiary shall on demand jointly and severally indemnify SIGCo and hold it harmless in respect of the items set forth in Clause 3.1.2 (a) through (e) above. It however includes

2285 *See* The Shipowners Insurance And Guaranty Company Ltd. (SIGCo) Standard Terms And Conditions, Clause 3.12, Indemnification (28th December, 1997).

a proviso that the indemnity required by this Clause (3.1.1) shall not apply to, and SIGCo undertakes to be responsible for any payments under Clause 3.1.2(a) above for which any COFR guaranty beneficiary is not entitled to be indemnified pursuant to any insurance which it is required to obtain under Clause 1.2 (provision requiring entry of the COFR guaranty beneficiary in a P & I Club) other than by reason of the application of any deductible or excess to be borne by the Applicant under the terms and conditions of such insurance.

So, this recognizes that when the Club denies insurance cover by virtue of its normal policy defenses and exclusions, then SIGCo is obligated to step in to make the needed payment, provided that there is no breach of the obligations set forth in the representations, warranties and undertakings provision discussed earlier. In all cases, when the Club denies a claim, it communicates its decision not to indemnify its member to the COFR guarantor, with the expectation that the COFR guarantor will step in to pay the claim of an aggrieved third party. In almost all cases where the Club denies a claim because of its application of one of its laundry list of exclusion clauses, the COFR guarantor will defer to the Club's decision to deny the claim, and make the needed payments under the OPA.

Clause 3.5 provides that SIGCo shall be subrogated to all of the COFR guarantee beneficiary's rights or claims against any other person or entity (including but not limited to the Club) relating to any payment made under the Guaranty to the extent of such payment. The Applicants shall provide SIGCo with all documentation and other evidence necessary for assertion of such claims and shall execute all documents necessary to secure such rights.[2286] Despite the deference that the COFR guarantors show to the Club, in the Club's decision to invoke an insurance policy exclusion clause, this provision theoretically gives them the power to sue the Club if they believe that the Club's exclusion was not applicable to the case in dispute.

Some of the provisions in SIGCo's terms and conditions are also in Shoreline's Rules. For both Shoreline and SIGCo, they only pay a third party claimant if the Club denies a claim.

---

2286 Id. at Clause 3.5, Subrogation.

In most cases the Club Rules and the Guarantor's Rules bear some striking similarities, with the exception of the pay to be paid principle and direct action principle. It appears that both of them have similar rules in terms of what is covered and what is excluded. The Guarantors are disadvantaged because they cannot wield policy defenses or exclusions as a shield in disputes with third parties, although they can use it against the COFR guaranty beneficiary itself. That was why the insurance industry came up with the COFR guarantors in the first place. Were it not for the refusal of the Clubs to subject themselves to direct action and waiver of their shopping list of policy exclusions, there would be no COFR guarantors in existence today. But necessity as they say is the mother of invention, and the insurance industry did a great job of inventing the COFR guaranty solution. Were it not for that timely invention, the train wreck scenario which was predicted for oil shipments to the US would have been a self-fulfilling prophecy.

## V. D. Additional Insurance Industry Responses to COFR Regulations

*Commercial Insurance Guaranty*

*AXA Global Risks*: In 1999, the U.S. Coast Guard National Pollution Funds Center announced its approval of AXA Global Risks as a new provider of insurance guaranties furnished as evidence of financial responsibility for vessel owners and operators who face potential water pollution liabilities.[2287] AXA Global Risks will be providing these insurance guaranties as part of their fixed premium protection and indemnity insurance package.[2288] They are represented in the United States by Lamorte Burns & Company. AXA Global Risks, licensed and regulated

2287 *See* "Coast Guard approves AXA Global Risks as OPA Guarantor" Press Release National Pollution Funds Center - Press Release (Thursday, Dec. 16, 1999) (last modified Feb. 27, 2002) <http://www.uscg.mil/hq/npfc/press.htm>

2288 Id.

as an insurer under the laws of France, is a member of the AXA Group. It is reinsured through an extensive program with reinsurers located throughout the world.[2289]

*COFRSURE program*: On June 12, 1997, the U.S. Coast Guard National Pollution Funds Center announced its approval of the COFRSURE program as a new provider of insurance guaranties furnished as evidence of financial responsibility for vessel owners and operators who face potential water pollution liabilities.[2290] The COFRSURE program is an insurance vehicle of Terra Nova Underwriting Agency Ltd., as agent for Scandinavian Reinsurance Company Limited of Bermuda.[2291] The COFRSURE program was approved to provide insurance guaranties in amounts up to four hundred million dollars.[2292] The Scandinavian Reinsurance Company Limited, the actual insurance guarantor, is licensed as an insurer under the laws of Bermuda. It is reinsured through an extensive program with reinsurers located in Bermuda and London.[2293]

In January 1999, SIGCo joined forces with Terra Nova (Bermuda) Ltd. ("Terra Nova") in providing COFR related services.[2294] As explained earlier both SIGCo and Terra Nova (the latter through the COFRSURE program) are involved in the provision of guaranties supporting Certificates of Financial Responsibility which are required under OPA 1990 for vessels entering US waters, and both also offer other COFR related services.[2295] Under the terms of the Agreement, the COFRSURE facility and rights to its renewal business was transferred to SIGCo and Terra Nova acquired a

2289 Id.

2290 *See* "Coast Guard Approves 'COFRSURE' Program As COFR Guarantor" Press Release National Pollution Funds Center - Press Release (Thursday, June. 12, 1997) (last modified Feb. 27, 2002) <http://www.uscg.mil/hq/npfc/press.htm>

2291 Id.

2292 Id.

2293 Id.

2294 *See* Press Release – SIGCo and TERRA NOVA Join Forces (January, 1999). <http://www.cofr.com/doc/PR6.doc>

2295 Id.

shareholding in SIGCo.[2296] Terra Nova and its related syndicates at Lloyds will provide SIGCo with significant reinsurance protection and will offer support to SIGCo's future sales, marketing and development efforts.[2297] The Agreement also included terms under which SIGCo will issue COFR guaranties for a P & I facility to be operated by Terra Nova and its related Lloyds syndicate J.L. Jones & Others. Neil Clemens, SIGCo's President observed; "Recent developments in the market have led both companies to recognize the long-term benefits to their respective clients of working together to provide COFR guaranties in a cost effective manner and in a stable environment."[2298] He observed further that this transaction recognizes economies of scale **associated with SIGCo's large client base and Terra Nova's substantial reinsurance capacity** which should assist the companies in meeting their long-term objectives.[2299] The capital investors are a combination of shipping interests and reinsurers whose interests are to be repaid over time, concomitant with a transition to a shipowner owned and managed facility.[2300]

*Other Evidence of Financial Responsibility:*

In 1996, the U.S. Coast Guard National Pollution Funds Center announced its approval of Arvak Limited (ARVAK) as a new provider of "other evidence" of financial responsibility for vessel owners and operators who face potential water pollution liabilities. [2301] Arvak was approved to provide "other evidence" of financial responsibility under 33 CFR 138.80 (b)(5) in amounts up to three hundred ninety-five million dollars.

---

2296 Id.

2297 Id.

2298 Id.

2299 Id.

2300 Id.

2301 *See* "Coast Guard Approves Arvak As Cofr Guarantor" National Pollution Funds Center – Press Release (Thursday Dec. 19 1996) (last modified Feb. 27, 2002) <http://www.uscg.mil/hq/npfc/press.htm>

Arvak is licensed as an insurer under the laws of Bermuda. It is reinsured through an extensive program with reinsurers located in London.[2302]

*Surety Bond Guaranty*

In 1994, the US Coast Guard's National Pollution Funds Center (NPFC) accepted the first surety bond guaranty as the basis for the issuance of Certificates of Financial Responsibility (COFRs) under the Oil Pollution Act of 1990 (OPA 90) and the Comprehensive Environmental Response, Compensation and Liability Act (CERCLA).[2303] This surety bond guaranty, one of several methods allowed by the Acts and Coast Guard regulations, was arranged by C.A. Shea 6 Co. on behalf of operators affiliated with Neptune Orient Lines, based in Singapore.[2304] Nineteen foreign flag tank vessels ranging to 55,962 gross tons in size were issued COFRs.[2305] The surety bond guaranty was underwritten by American Home Assurance Company, American Motorists Insurance Company, National Union Fire Insurance Company of Pittsburgh, PA, and Insurance Company of the State of Pennsylvania.[2306] The NPFC Director at the time, Daniel Sheehan remarked that this milestone clearly demonstrates the viability of surety bond guaranties as a method for demonstrating financial responsibility to obtain COFRs.[2307] At the time of the approval, there was a mad rush by vessel owners and operators to obtain OPA 90/CERCLA COFRs to meet the then looming December 28, 1994, compliance deadline for self-propelled tank vessels.

---

2302 Id.

2303 *See* "First Surety Bond Guaranty Accepted For COFRS." National Pollution Funds Center - Press Release (Wed. Nov. 16 1996) (last modified Feb. 27, 2002) <http://www.uscg.mil/hq/npfc/press.htm>

2304 Id.

2305 Id.

2306 Id.

2307 Id.

## VI. The United Kingdom adopts the polluter pays principle

The "polluter pays" philosophy behind the OPA 90 is tacitly spreading to other countries, especially the United Kingdom (UK). This shows that OPA 90 has set a precedent, which other countries have started to follow.

In January 1993 a Liberian tanker The Braer, broke up off the Shetland Islands. Just like the Exxon Valdez oil Spill resulted in a sudden metamorphosis of legislative attitude to oil spills, the Braer spill has achieved a similar result. A new strict liability regime for bunker oil spills off the U.K. coast was introduced on October 1 1994 as a result of the Braer Oil Spill.[2308] Shipowners and their P & I Clubs will have to pay potentially unlimited compensation for pollution damage regardless of fault for spills within the UK's 12-mile wide territorial waters.[2309]

Lord Goschen, the UK shipping minister at the time signed an order bringing into force the polluter pays principle, under section 6 of the Merchant Shipping (Salvage and Pollution) Act 1994.[2310] The question of who pays for pollution from the often highly persistent oil carried in ship's bunkers has sometimes taken lengthy litigation to resolve. The new legislation sets no upper limit for the compensation payable by shipowners and their insurers.[2311]

This new legislation shows that more countries have begun to adopt stricter oil pollution laws. This means that the P & I Clubs will have to grapple with the fact that the global attitude towards oil pollution is changing rapidly and they may also have to change their long standing traditions if they do not want to be left behind.

---

2308 Jim Mulrenan, Polluter pays regime for offshore bunker spills, Lloyd's List Int'l, Aug. 10, 1994, at 3.

2309 Id. at 3.

2310 Id.

2311 Id.

## VII. Oil Spill Financial Responsibility (OSFR) For Offshore Facilities & Deepwater Ports

### Offshore Facilities

Oil Spill Financial Responsibility (OSFR) means the capability and means by which a responsible party for a covered offshore facility will meet removal costs and damages for which it is liable under OPA, with respect to both oil-spill discharges and substantial threats of the discharge of oil.[2312] "Oil" means oil or gas condensate produced from wells or platforms with a surface location in, on, or under Federal, State, or Territorial coastal waters of the United States as described in 30 CFR 253; stored in, on, or under these waters; or transported through pipelines in or under these waters.[2313]

Section 2716(c)(1)(A) of OPA provides that subject to subparagraph (C) of this section, a responsible party is required to obtain evidence of financial responsibility (in the amount required under subparagraph (B) or (C), as applicable) with respect to an offshore facility that:

(i) (I) is located seaward of the line of ordinary low water along that portion of the coast that is in direct contact with the open sea and the line marking the seaward limit of inland waters; or (II) is located in coastal inland waters, such as bays or estuaries, seaward of the line of ordinary low water along that portion of the coast that is not in direct contact with the open sea;

(ii) is used for exploring for, drilling for, producing, or transporting oil from facilities engaged in oil exploration, drilling, or production; and

---

2312 30 CFR § 253.3

2313 *See* United States Department of Interior – Minerals Management Service (MMS), Notice To Lessees And Operators Of Federal Oil And Gas Leases In The Outer Continental Shelf And Located In Certain Areas Of Coastal States, NTL 99 N01 (Effective Date: January 6, 1999).

(iii) has a worst-case oil spill discharge potential of more than 1,000 barrels of oil (or a lesser amount if the President[2314] determines that the risks posed by such facility justify it).

The requirements for obtaining evidence of financial responsibility for offshore facilities is codified in Title 30 CFR Part 253, subpart A-F. This regulation replaces the former OSFR regulation at 33 CFR Part 135, which was written to implement the Outer Continental Shelf Lands Act (OCSLA). This regulation became effective on October 13, 1998. Title 30 CFR §253.1 provides that this OSFR regulations establishes the requirements for demonstrating OSFR for covered offshore facilities (COFs) under Title I of the Oil Pollution Act of 1990 (OPA). Whenever there is a reference to "Secretary" in the OSFR regulations, it is the Secretary of the Interior that the OSFR regulation refers to. The Executive Order (E.O.) implementing OPA (E.O. 12777; October 18, 1991) assigned the OSFR certification function to the Department of the Interior (DOI). The Secretary of the Interior, in turn, delegated this function to Mineral Management Service (MMS).[2315] Whenever there is a reference to Director in the OSFR regulations, it means the Director of the MMS.[2316]

"Bay" is defined by the OSFR regulations as a body of water included in the Geographic Names Information System (GNIS) bay feature class. "Geographic Names Information System" (GNIS) means the database developed by the United States Geological Survey (USGS) in cooperation with the U.S. Board of Geographic Names which contains the federally-recognized geographic names for all known places, features, and areas in the United States that are identified by a proper name. Each feature is located by state, county, and geographic coordinates and is referenced to the appropriate 1:24,000-scale or 1:63,360-scale USGS topographic map

2314 This power was delegated by the President to the Secretary of the Interior, who in turn delegated it to the Minerals Management Services (MMS).

2315 See 56 FR 54757.

2316 See 30 CFR 253.3.

on which it is shown.[2317] A GNIS bay includes an arm, bay, bight, cove, estuary, gulf, inlet, or sound.[2318]

To be bound by OPA and the OSFR regulations for offshore facilities, the facility involved has to be a "covered offshore facility" (COF). The OSFR regulations applies to any COF on any lease or permit issued or on any right-of-use and easement (RUE) granted under the Outer Continental Shelf Lands Act (OCSLA) or applicable state law.[2319] For a pipeline COF that extends onto land, the OSFR regulation applies to that portion of the pipeline lying seaward of the first accessible flow shut-off device on land.[2320] This provision relating the flow shut-off devise was included because the MMS recognized the possibility that a transportation pipeline could begin offshore and move production onshore.[2321]

A Covered offshore facility (COF) means a facility:

> "(1) That includes any structure and all its components (including wells completed at the structure and the associated pipelines), equipment, pipeline, or device (other than a vessel or other than a pipeline or deepwater port licensed under the Deepwater Port Act of 1974 (33 U.S.C. 1501 et seq.)) used for exploring for, drilling for, or producing oil or for transporting oil from such facilities. This includes a well drilled from a mobile offshore drilling unit (MODU) and the associated riser and well control equipment from the moment a drill shaft or other device first touches the seabed for purposes of exploring for, drilling for, or producing oil, ***but it does not include the MODU***."[2322] (Emphasis mine).

MODUs are facilities designed or modified to engage in drilling and exploration activities, but not production, separation, or storage of oil in or on Federal, State, or Territorial coastal waters of the United States

2317 30 CFR § 253.3.
2318 *See* 30 CFR § 253.3.
2319 30 CFR § 253.10.
2320 Id. at §253.10.
2321 62 FR 14052, 14053.
2322 30 CFR § 253.3.

of America.[2323] This term includes drilling vessels, semi-submersibles, submersibles, jack-ups, and similar facilities that can be moved without substantial effort.[2324] These facilities may or may not have self-propulsion equipment on board and may require dynamic positioning equipment or mooring systems to maintain their position.[2325]

Mr. Alan Spackman, International Association of Drilling Contractors' (IADC) Director of Offshore Technical and Regulatory Affairs has since the Exxon Valdez oil spill in 1989, worked assiduously on the problem of OPA 90 implementation and in 1997, reached the end of the line for the main issue of concern for drilling contractors - clarity on guarantees of financial responsibility for drilling contractors engaged in offshore activities in the event of an oil spill.[2326] IADC had objected to the definition of a COF proposed in an earlier rulemaking.[2327] Under that definition, MODUs could be considered COFs. However, the twist in the regulatory road is that MODUs are already classified as vessels under OPA's section 2704(b)(1). Therefore, they are subject to oil-spill regulations under the US Department of Transportation, specifically, the US Coast Guard, as MMS notes in its final rule.[2328] A mobile offshore drilling unit (MODU) is classified as a vessel. However, a well drilled from a MODU is classified as an offshore facility under this rule.[2329]

Mr. Alan Spackman said that drilling contractors engaged in offshore activities got the clarification they wanted with this definition of

---

2323 *See* United States Department of Interior – Minerals Management Service (MMS), Notice To Lessees And Operators Of Federal Oil And Gas Leases In The Outer Continental Shelf And Located In Certain Areas Of Coastal States, NTL 99 N01 (Effective Date: January 6, 1999).

2324 Id.

2325 Id.

2326 *See* OPA 90 Financial Responsibility: A Long and Winding Road to Closure, at 22, Drilling Contractor (September/October 1998).

2327 Id. at 22.

2328 Id.

2329 Id.

COF **that excludes MODUs.**[2330] This makes it clear that it is the operator's responsibility to obtain the evidence of financial responsibility, and to have the certificate of financial responsibility in place before drilling begins.[2331] This seemingly obvious distinction took years to emerge from the smoke and haze of the law itself. Mr. Spackman explained that it appeared from the outset that there would be confusion between MMS and the Coast Guard as to the division of responsibility for regulating financial responsibilities for drilling activities carried out by mobile offshore drilling units.[2332]

The Coast Guard issued its final rules in 1994. Those regulations left the petroleum industry little to cheer about, except when it came to mobile offshore drilling units: Owners/operators of these workhorses of the marine Exploration & Production (E&P) business are responsible only for the oil required for MODU operations not produced petroleum.[2333] Over the years IADC had commented extensively on these and related issues as well as meeting with US Coast Guard and MMS officials. The upshot is that an appropriate distinction has been made for demonstration of financial responsibility for offshore E&P operations under OPA 90, with the responsibility for the well falling squarely on the shoulders of the operator, not the drilling contractor.[2334] This is a great relief to drilling contractors, because if they were considered COFs in addition to being considered Tank vessels, it would have amounted to an over-regulation of the drilling contractors' industry with the concomitant effect of over-insurance and excessive payment of premiums by drilling contractors that may have engendered a recession in the oil drilling contractor industry.

Only "responsible parties (RP)" are covered under the OPA and its implementing OSFR regulations. Responsible party has the following meanings under the OSFR regulations:

---

2330 Id.

2331 Id. at 22.

2332 Id.

2333 Id.

2334 Id. at 22.

"(1) For a COF that is a pipeline, responsible party means any person owning or operating the pipeline;

(2) For a COF that is not a pipeline, responsible party means either the lessee or permittee of the area in which the COF is located, or the holder of a right-of-use and easement (RUE)[2335] granted under applicable state law or the Outer Continental Shelf Lands Act (OCSLA)[2336] for the area in which the COF is located (if the holder is a different person than the lessee or permittee).[2337] A Federal agency, State, municipality, commission, or political subdivision of a state, or any interstate body that as owner transfers possession and right to use the property to another person by lease, assignment, or permit is not a responsible party;[2338] and

(3) For an abandoned COF, responsible party means any person who would have been a responsible party for the COF immediately before abandonment."[2339]

---

2335 Right-of-use and easement (RUE) means any authorization to use the OCS or submerged land for purposes other than those authorized by a lease or permit, as defined herein. It includes pipeline rights-of-way. 30 CFR §253.3.

How can one identify OSFR evidence for facilities located on rights-of-use and easement?

"The following two types of rights-of-use and easement are issued by the MMS as defined in 30 CFR 253.3

1 A pipeline right-of-way is a type of right-of-use and easement issued under 30 CFR 250.1010(d) for pipelines, and any appurtenant structures, that are installed on blocks that are either unleased or leased and operated by another company(s). When required, you should identify the OSFR evidence for pipeline rights-of-way by the pipeline right-of-way number (e.g. G-2314) that MMS issues.

2 A right-of-use and easement is also issued under 30 CFR 250.107 for wells and platforms needed to explore or produce a lease from a surface location on an adjacent block that is either unleased or leased and operated by another company(s). When required, you should identify the OSFR evidence for these rights-of-use and easement by the associated well bottom-hole location lease number. However, you must note the surface facility in the application." *See* United States Department of Interior – Minerals Management Service (MMS), Notice To Lessees And Operators Of Federal Oil And Gas Leases In The Outer Continental Shelf And Located In Certain Areas Of Coastal States, NTL 99 N01 (Effective Date: January 6, 1999).

2336 43 U.S.C. 1301-1356.

2337 30 CFR §253.3.

2338 *See* 30 CFR §253.3.

2339 Id. at §253.3.

Once a facility is found to be the "source of the incident," it would be held responsible for the oil spill as provided under OPA. Source of the incident means the facility from which oil was discharged or which poses a substantial threat of discharging oil, as designated by the Director, National Pollution Funds Center, according to 33 CFR part 136, subpart D.[2340] An oil spill incident is an oil or gas condensate spill or blowout from a single well, platform, or pipeline resulting from any equipment failure, human action, or weather condition.[2341]

Any person in doubt may submit to MMS a request for a determination of OSFR applicability. Such inquirer must include in her request any information that will assist MMS in making the determination. MMS may require her to submit other information before making a determination of OSFR applicability.[2342]

In order to be a COF, the offshore facility must be either a fixed offshore or a floating offshore facility (except an offshore facility that is used to store oil).

*Fixed offshore facility* – This is a bottom anchored offshore facility permanently attached to the seabed of Federal, State, or Territorial coastal waters of the United States of America.[2343] This term includes platforms, guyed towers, articulated gravity platforms, single- and multi-well caissons, gravel and ice islands, caisson retained islands, sub-sea wells and manifolds, and similar facilities designed for drilling, production, storage, or transportation of oil.[2344] This does not include marina structure and piers, and marine loading docks not connected to offshore facilities in, on, or under Federal, State, or Territorial coastal waters of the United States

---

2340 30 CFR § 253.3.

2341 *See* United States Department of Interior – Minerals Management Service (MMS), Notice To Lessees And Operators Of Federal Oil And Gas Leases In The Outer Continental Shelf And Located In Certain Areas Of Coastal States, NTL 99 N01 (Effective Date: January 6, 1999).

2342 Id. at § 253.12.

2343 *See* United States Department of Interior – Minerals Management Service (MMS), Notice To Lessees And Operators Of Federal Oil And Gas Leases In The Outer Continental Shelf And Located In Certain Areas Of Coastal States, NTL 99 N01 (Effective Date: January 6, 1999).

2344 Id.

of America as described in 30 CFR 253.[2345] This definition also does not include facilities licensed under the Deepwater Port Act of 1994.[2346]

*Floating offshore facility* – This is a buoyant offshore facility, securely and substantially moored or otherwise connected to the seabed of Federal, State, or Territorial coastal waters of the United States of America, that cannot be moved without substantial effort. This term includes tension leg platforms, spars, and similar facilities designed or modified for drilling, production, separation, or storage of oil. These facilities may have semi-submersible or ship-shape hulls.[2347]

Section 2716(c)(1)(B) (amount required) provides that subject to subparagraph (C) of this section, the amount of financial responsibility for offshore facilities that meet the criteria of subparagraph (A) above is:

"(i) $35,000,000 for an offshore facility located seaward of the seaward boundary of a State; or
(ii) $10,000,000 for an offshore facility located landward of the seaward boundary of a State."

The OSFR regulations provides more details as to the amount of OSFR that must be demonstrated. Section 253.13 (b) of the OSFR regulations provide that the following general parameters apply to the amount of OSFR that an RP must demonstrate:

"(b) You must demonstrate OSFR in the amounts specified in this section:
(1) For a COF located wholly or partially in the OCS, you must demonstrate OSFR in accordance with the following table:

2345 Id.
2346 Id.
2347 Id.

| *COF Worst Case Oil-Spill Discharge Volume* | *Applicable Amount Of OSFR* |
|---|---|
| Over 1,000 bbls but not more than 35,000 bbls | $35,000,000 |
| Over 35,000 but not more than 70,000 bbls | $70,000,000 |
| Over 70,000 but not more than 105,000 bbls | $105,000,000 |
| Over 105,000 bbls | $150,000,000 |

(2) For a COF not located in the OCS you must demonstrate OSFR in accordance with the following table:

| *COCOF Worst Case Oil-Spill Discharge Volume* | *Applicable Amount Of OSFR* |
|---|---|
| Over 1,000 bbls but not more than 10,000 bbls | $10,000,000 |
| Over 10,000 but not more than 35,000 bbls | $35,000,000 |
| Over 35,000 but not more than 70,000 bbls | $70,000,000 |
| Over 70,000 but not more than 105,000 bbls | $105,000,000 |
| Over 105,000 bbls | $150,000,000 |

(3) The Director may determine that you must demonstrate an amount of OSFR greater than the amount in paragraphs (b)(1) and (2) of this section based on the relative operational, environmental, human health, and other risks that your COF poses.[2348] The Director may require an amount that is one or more levels higher than the amount indicated in paragraph (b)(1) or (2) of

2348 *See* 30 CFR §253.13(b)(3).

this section for your COF. The Director will however not require an OSFR demonstration that exceeds $150 million.[2349]

(4) You must demonstrate OSFR in the lowest amount specified in the applicable table in paragraph (b)(1) or (b)(2) for a facility with a potential worst case oil-spill discharge of 1,000 bbls or less if the Director (MMS) notifies you in writing that the demonstration is justified by the risks of the potential oil-spill discharge."[2350]

Congress amended Section 2716(f) of OPA in 1996,[2351] by adding provisions relating to further requirements for claims with respect to offshore facilities and authority to promulgate regulations and made minor changes in style.[2352] The new subsection f (2) provides that a claim may be asserted pursuant to paragraph (1)(direct claims against a guarantor & allowable defenses provisions) directly against a guarantor providing evidence of financial responsibility under subsection (c)(1) of this section with respect to an offshore facility only if--

"(A)the responsible party for whom evidence of financial responsibility has been provided has denied or failed to pay a claim under OPA on the basis of being insolvent, as defined under section 101(32) of Title 11,[2353] and applying generally accepted accounting principles;

(B) the responsible party for whom evidence of financial responsibility has been provided has filed a petition for bankruptcy under Title 11; or

(C) the claim is asserted by the United States for removal costs and damages or for compensation paid by the Fund under this chapter, including costs incurred by the Fund for processing compensation claims."[2354]

2349 Id. at §253.13(b)(3).

2350 Id. at §253.13(b)(4).

2351 Pub.L. 104-324, § 1125(a)(2).

2352 33 USCA §2716 (2), as amended.

2353 Insolvent has the meaning set forth in 11 U.S.C. 101, and generally refers to a financial condition in which the sum of a person's debts is greater than the value of the person's assets. 30 CFR § 253.3

2354 33 USC 2716(f)(2).

This means that claims filed against a guarantor by a private claimant that does not conform to the requirements of subsection f (2) (A) & (B) will be dismissed. This amendment gives the US government preferential treatment when it comes to filing of claims directly against guarantors, because the US government's direct action claim is not affected by the failure of the responsible party to pay because of the insolvency of the responsible party, or the responsible party's denial of a claim.

The OSFR regulations provide that if any person participates in an insurance guaranty for a COF incident (i.e., oil-spill discharge or substantial threat of the discharge of oil) that is subject to claims under this regulation, then its maximum, aggregate liability for those claims is equal to its quota share of the insurance guaranty.[2355]

The 1996 amendment added a subsection f (3) requiring that not later than 1 year after October 19, 1996, the President shall promulgate regulations to establish a process for implementing paragraph (2) in a manner that will allow for the orderly and expeditious presentation and resolution of claims and effectuate the purposes of OPA.

Section 2716(c) was amended in 1996 to reduce the evidence of financial responsibility amount to the amounts listed above due to criticism from legal commentators and industry representatives.[2356] It used to provide before the amendment that:

"[E]ach responsible party with respect to an offshore facility shall establish **and maintain** evidence of financial responsibility of $150,000,000 to meet the amount of liability to which the responsible party could be subjected under section 2704(a) of OPA in a case in which the responsible party would be entitled to limit liability under OPA."

---

2355 30 CFR § 253.61.

2356 1996 Amendments. Subsec. (c)(1). Pub.L. 104-324, § 1125(a)(1), added provisions relating to financial responsibility requirements for offshore facilities meeting specified criteria and determination of the seaward boundary of a State, struck out provisions relating to financial responsibility requirements of $150,000 in a case in which a responsible party would be entitled to limit liability under section 2704(a) of this title, and made changes in style and phraseology. 33 USCA § 2716(c).

Many critics of OPA had been quick to point out that, by adopting the $150 million Evidence of Financial Responsibility Requirement (EOFR) for offshore facilities, Congress appears to have chosen an arbitrary number that does not correspond to actual environmental risk and cleanup costs historically associated with traditional offshore facilities.[2357] These critics cite Minerals Management Service (MMS) data which indicates that since 1970 the most expensive oil spill from a facility operating on a federal OCS lease in the Gulf of Mexico resulted in cleanup costs of $10 million.[2358] Also cited were statistics that show that the level of environmental risk posed by oil tankers is historically much higher than the risk posed by offshore oil facilities.[2359] For example, since 1974 there have been ten times as many significant oil spills from oil tankers operating in U.S. waters than from oil facilities operating on federal OCS leases, resulting in a volume of spillage from tankers equivalent to approximately twenty-five times that spilled from oil facilities.[2360] These statistics also indicate that while spills associated with oil tanker operations and municipal wastes account for more than twenty percent of average daily worldwide oil pollution, spills from offshore oil production and drilling operations only account for 1.6% of the worldwide figure.[2361]

Section 2716(c)(1)(C) (Subparagraph (C)) provides that if the President (power now delegated to MMS) determines that an amount of financial responsibility for a responsible party greater than the amount required by subparagraph (B) is justified based on the relative operational, environmental, human health, and other risks posed by the quantity or quality of oil that is explored for, drilled for, produced, or transported by the responsible party, the evidence of financial responsibility required shall be for an amount determined by the President not exceeding $150,000,000.

---

2357 *See* William W. Enders, The Oil Pollution Act Of 1990: The Financial Responsibility Requirement -- Questioning Congressional Intent And The Minerals Management Service Interpretation Of "Offshore Facility" 14 Va. Envtl. L.J. 455, 463 (Spring, 1995).

2358 Id. at 463.

2359 Id.

2360 Id. at 463-464.

2361 Id. at 464.

This subsection (c)(1)(C) was added in 1996 by an amendment to section 2716.[2362]

In a case in which a person is a responsible party for more than one facility or multiple facilities subject to this subsection, evidence of **financial responsibility need be established only to meet the amount applicable to the facility having the greatest financial responsibility requirement** under this subsection.[2363] For the purpose of this paragraph (section 2716(c), the seaward boundary of a State shall be determined in accordance with section 1301(b) of Title 43.

As the designated applicant, you may satisfy your OSFR requirements by using one or a combination of the following methods to demonstrate OSFR:

Just like the COFR regulations for vessels, the OSFR regulations provide for the following methods of demonstrating financial responsibility: (a) Self-insurance; (b) Insurance; (c) An indemnity; (d) A surety bond; and (e) An alternative method the Director approves under § 253.32.[2364]

OSFR regulations provide that if you use self-insurance to satisfy all or part of your obligation to demonstrate OSFR, you must annually pass either a net worth test under § 253.25[2365] or an unencumbered net asset test under § 253.28.[2366] To establish the amount of self-insurance allowed,

---

2362 See 33 USC 2716(c)(1)(C), see also Pub.L. 104-324, § 1125(a)(1).

2363 33 USC 2716(c)(D).

2364 30 CFR § 253.20.

2365 "(a) Divide the total amount of the stockholders'/owners' equity listed on the balance sheet by ten.

(b) Divide the net amount of the identifiable U.S. assets by the net amount of the identifiable total assets.

(c) Multiply the net amount of plant, property, and equipment shown on the balance sheet by the number calculated under paragraph (b) of this section and divide the resultant product by ten.

(d) The smaller of the numbers calculated under paragraphs (a) or (c) of this section is the maximum allowable amount you may use to demonstrate OSFR under this method." 30 CFR § 253.25, see also 30 CFR 253.21.

2366 "(a) Divide the total amount of the stockholders'/owners' equity listed on the balance sheet by 4.

(b) Divide the value of the unencumbered U.S. assets by 2.

you must submit evidence of your net worth under § 253.23[2367] or evidence of your unencumbered assets under § 253.26.[2368] If you use insurance to satisfy all or part of your obligation to demonstrate OSFR, you may use only insurance certificates issued by insurers that have achieved a "Secure" rating for claims paying ability in their latest review by A.M. Best's Insurance Reports, Standard & Poor's Insurance Rating Services,

---

(c) The smaller number calculated under paragraphs (a) or (b) of this section is the maximum allowable amount you may use to demonstrate OSFR under this method." 30 CFR § 253.28.

2367 You must support your net worth evaluation with information contained in your previous fiscal year's audited annual financial statement.

(a) Audited annual financial statements must be in the form of:

(1) An annual report, prepared in accordance with the generally accepted accounting practices (GAAP) of the United States or other international accounting practices determined to be equivalent by MMS; or

(2) A Form 10-K or Form 20-F, prepared in accordance with Securities and Exchange Commission regulations.

(b) Audited annual financial statements must be submitted together with a letter signed by your treasurer highlighting:

(1) The State or the country of incorporation;

(2) The total amount of the stockholders' equity as shown on the balance sheet;

(3) The net amount of the plant, property, and equipment shown on the balance sheet; and

(4) The net amount of the identifiable U.S. assets and the identifiable total assets in the auditor's notes to the financial statement (i.e., a geographic segmented business note). 30 CFR § 253.23.

2368 You must support your unencumbered assets evaluation with the information required by § 253.23(a) and a list of reserved, unencumbered, and unimpaired U.S. assets whose value will not be affected by an oil discharge from a COF. The assets must be plant, property, or equipment held for use. You must submit a letter signed by your treasurer:

(a) Identifying which assets are reserved;

(b) Certifying that the assets are unencumbered, including contingent encumbrances;

(c) Promising that the identified assets will not be sold, subjected to a security interest, or otherwise encumbered throughout the specified fiscal year; and

(d) Specifying:

(1) The State or the country of incorporation;

(2) The total amount of the stockholders'/owners' equity listed on the balance sheet;

(3) The identification and location of the reserved U.S. assets; and

(4) The value of the reserved U.S. assets less accumulated depreciation and amortization, using the same valuation method used in your audited annual financial statement and expressed in U.S. dollars. The net value of the reserved assets must be at least two times the self-insurance amount requested for demonstration. 30 CFR § 253.26.

or other equivalent rating made by a rating service acceptable to MMS.[2369] You must submit information about your insurers to MMS on a completed and unaltered Form MMS-1019.[2370] You may use only one indemnity issued by only one indemnitor to satisfy all or part of your obligation to demonstrate OSFR and your indemnitor must be your corporate parent or affiliate.[2371]

The OSFR regulations also provide that for each bonding company that issues a surety bond that you submit to MMS as OSFR evidence must: (1) Be licensed to do business in the State in which the surety bond is executed; (2) Be certified by the U.S. Treasury Department as an acceptable surety for Federal obligations and listed in the current Treasury Circular No. 570; (3) Provide the surety bond on Form MMS-1020; and (4) Be in compliance with applicable statutes regulating surety company participation in insurance-type risks.[2372]

The OSFR regulations provide also that the Director may accept other methods to demonstrate OSFR that provide equivalent assurance of timely satisfaction of claims.[2373] This may include pooling, letters of credit, pledges of treasury notes, or other comparable methods.[2374] Proposals for these other methods should be submitted together with all the supporting documents, to the Director. The Director's decision whether to approve the proposed alternative method to evidence OSFR is committed to the Director's sole discretion and is not subject to administrative appeal under 30 CFR part 290 or 43 CFR part 4.[2375]

The OSFR regulations also provide that if you fail to comply with the financial responsibility requirements of OPA or with the requirements of this OSFR regulations, then you may be liable for a civil penalty of up to $25,000 per COF per day of violation (that is, each day a COF is

2369 30 CFR § 253.29.
2370 Id.
2371 30 CFR § 253.30.
2372 30 CFR § 253.31.
2373 30 CFR s 253.32.
2374 Id. at §253.32.
2375 Id.

operated without acceptable evidence of OSFR).[2376] MMS will determine the date of a noncompliance. MMS will assess penalties in accordance with an OSFR penalty schedule using the procedures found at 30 CFR part 250, subpart N.[2377] A copy of the penalty schedule may be obtained from MMS at its address.[2378] MMS may assess a civil penalty against you that is greater or less than the amount in the penalty schedule after taking into account the factors in section 2716a of OPA. The OSFR regulations also provide that if you fail to correct a deficiency in the OSFR evidence for a COF, then the Director may suspend operation of a COF in the OCS under 30 CFR 250.170 or seek judicial relief, including an order suspending the operation of any COF.[2379]

## VIII. A. Deepwater Ports

Section 2716(c)(2) of OPA provides each responsible party with respect to a deepwater port shall establish and maintain evidence of financial responsibility sufficient to meet the maximum amount of liability to which the responsible party could be subjected under section 2704(a) of OPA in a case where the responsible party would be entitled to limit liability under OPA. If the Secretary exercises the authority under section 2704(d)(2) of this title to lower the limit of liability for deepwater ports,[2380]

2376 Id. at §253.51.

2377 Id.

2378 Id.

2379 Id. at §253.51.

2380 "(C) Rulemaking proceeding --

If the Secretary determines, based on the results of the study conducted under this subparagraph (A), that the use of deepwater ports in connection with the transportation of oil by vessel results in a lower operational or environmental risk than the use of other ports, the Secretary shall initiate, not later than the 180th day following the date of submission of the report to the Congress under subparagraph (B), a rulemaking proceeding to lower the limits of liability under this section for deepwater ports as the Secretary determines appropriate. The Secretary may establish a limit of liability of less than $350,000,000, but not less than $50,000,000, in accordance with paragraph (1). 33 USCA §2704(d)(2)(C).

the responsible party shall establish and maintain evidence of financial responsibility sufficient to meet the maximum amount of liability so established. In a case in which a person is the responsible party for more than one deepwater port, evidence of financial responsibility need be established only to meet the maximum liability applicable to the deepwater port having the greatest maximum liability.[2381]

The industry's dooms day predictions have not proven accurate. The United States flow of imported oil has not been reduced, nor have U.S oil spills increased. A study conducted by the U.S. Department of energy ("DOE") concluded that most tanker owners have continued to trade to the U.S. at the same rate as they were prior to the enactment of OPA 90.[2382] Moreover, many companies have established closer links with independent shipowners and have fashioned thorough inspection programs for chartered vessels. These programs seem to have effected a small but noticeable improvement in the safety of chartered tankers.[2383] According to the DOE-commissioned study, the most perceptible effect of the Act, thus far, has been the change in operational procedures, safety provisions, and inspection routines implemented in the oil trades.[2384] The study noted that "the early signs of a flight to quality provides a stark contrast to the fears of many OPA critics who forecast that U.S oil imports would be carried in inferior ships by uncaring owners for unscrupulous charterers. The exact opposite is occurring."[2385]

---

2381 33 USC 2716(c)(2).

2382 Office of Domestic & Int'l Energy Policy, United States Dept of Energy, Transporting U.S. Oil Imports: The Impact of Oil Spill Legislation on the Tanker Market, prepared by the Petroleum Industry Research Foundation, June 1992. (Hereinafter PIRF Study).

2383 The Tanker Advisory Center, which annually rates the condition of the world's tankers on a scale from 1 to 5, noted that tankers in U.S. waters averaged 3.6 by March 1992. Immediately prior to the Alaskan spill, that average had been 3.4. Michael Parrish, Drop in U.S. Oil Spills Tied to Tough Laws, L.A. Times, Aug. 22, 1992, at A1.

2384 Office of Domestic & Int'l Energy Policy, United States Dept of Energy, Transporting U.S. Oil Imports: The Impact of Oil Spill Legislation on the Tanker Market, prepared by the Petroleum Industry Research Foundation, June 1992. (Hereinafter PIRF Study).

2385 Id.

# Chapter Nine

# WHAT IS COVERED BY THE P & I CLUB POLLUTION INSURANCE

This chapter, which is related to Chapter Eight, will discuss briefly the provisions of international oil pollution conventions and international voluntary agreements that ship owners used to subject themselves to (the voluntary agreements are relevant because of their historical significance). **Analysis of the interaction between OPA and these international conventions is outside the scope of this chapter.** It is being discussed primarily for the purpose of addressing the issue of the modern scope of insurance cover for oil pollution liability risks.

## I. An overview of the International Oil Pollution Regime and its interaction with P & I Club insurance

OPA does not fulfill the yearnings of the comity of nations for a uniform global approach to oil pollution issues. Some of the provisions of the OPA have rendered nugatory the concerted efforts of the global ommunity at injecting some measure of uniformity in the area of marine pollution control. The need for this uniform approach cannot be over-emphasized because all nations of the world face the threat of oil pollution either from vessels or oil facilities. Irrespective of where it occurs, oil pollution normally has a devastating effect on human (recreational activities like surfing, swimming, pleasure boating is seriously affected) and marine life (irreparable injury and death to sea creatures or marine life in general), subsistence & commercial fishing, marine research & development, as well as on landed property and drinking water.

The International Maritime Organization (IMO), a specialized agency of the United Nations Organization is charged exclusively with the task of promulgating and implementing the international legal regime for marine pollution and safety. All the marine pollution conventions that will be discussed below were midwifed by the IMO. The IMO used to be called "The Intergovernmental Maritime Consultative Organization (IMCO)" but changed its name to IMO on May 22, 1982.[2386]

In 1969 two conventions were adopted. One was the "International Convention relating to Intervention on the High Seas in Cases of Oil Pollution Casualties" (Intervention Convention), which established the right of coastal States to intervene in incidents on the high seas that are likely to result in oil pollution. It entered into force in 1975.[2387] Certain events led to the promulgation of the Intervention Convention and other conventions that were passed around that same time. In 1967, a vessel called, the Torrey Canyon spilled 119,000 tons of crude oil into the English Channel, causing extensive damage to both the English and French coastlines.[2388] The difficulties encountered in attempting to resolve various compensation claims and liability issues revealed the inadequacy of existing law covering marine oil casualties.[2389] On November 29, 1969, in reaction to the spill, an international conference sponsored by the IMCO convened in Brussels, Belgium. The conference adopted the Intervention Convention.[2390]

Article II (3) of the Intervention Convention defines "oil" as crude oil, fuel oil, diesel oil and lubricating oil. The Intervention Convention, which has no limitation provision, allows a coastal nation to take defensive action

2386 *See* Frederick J. Carr, Comment: Statutory Liability For Oil Pollution From Vessels In Marine Environments, 3 U.S.F. Mar. L.J. 267, 303 (Summer 1991) (stating that IMCO came into existence in 1958 and that as of 1990, IMO had about 110 member states).

2387 *See* International Convention Relating To Intervention On The High Seas In Cases Of Oil Pollution Casualties 26 U.S.T. 765, T.I.A.S. No. 8068 (Brussels, 29 November 1969).

2388 Daniel Kopec And Philip Peterson, Note: Crude Legislation: Liability And Compensation Under The Oil Pollution Act of 1990, 23 Rutgers L. J 597, 608 (Spring 1992).

2389 Daniel Kopec And Philip Peterson, Note: Crude Legislation: Liability And Compensation Under The Oil Pollution Act of 1990, 23 Rutgers L. J at 608.

2390 Id. at 608-09.

against a vessel on the high seas where pollution by oil is threatened.[2391] Article I (1) of The Intervention Convention provides in pertinent part:

"Parties to the present Convention may take such measures on the high seas as may be necessary to prevent, mitigate or eliminate grave and imminent danger to their coastline or related interests from pollution or threat of pollution of the sea by oil, following upon a maritime casualty or acts related to such casualty, which may reasonably be expected to result in major harmful consequences."

The United States has codified the Intervention Convention by statute in the Intervention on the High Seas Act.[2392] The US enactment tracks the Convention language as to action which may be taken in the case of imminent danger to the coastline or related interests of the United States from pollution or threat of pollution.[2393] The measures taken to abate the pollution shall be proportionate to the damage, actual or threatened, and, if they are not, the United States shall be liable for damages.[2394] It is noted that the revolving fund established under the FWPCA, which is now the Oil Spill Liability Trust Fund under OPA, is available for intervention activities.[2395] The authority of the Intervention on the High Seas Act was invoked in the 1976 Argo Merchant spill, when the United States intervened to direct cleanup operations after the tanker went aground off Nantucket spilling her cargo of approximately 178,571 barrels (7.5 million gallons) of oil.[2396] Costs incurred in responding to an intervening government's orders would normally be covered by P & I Club Pollution insurance.

The second IMO convention was the "International Convention on Civil Liability for Oil Pollution Damage," **(CLC)** which dealt with the civil liability of the owner of a ship for damage suffered as a result of an oil

---

2391 Carter T. Gunn, Limitation Of Liability: United States And Convention Jurisdictions, 8 Mar. Lawyer 29, 60 (Spring 1983).

2392 33 U.S.C. §§ 1471-1487 (Supp. IV 1980)).

2393 Carter T. Gunn, Limitation Of Liability: United States And Convention Jurisdictions, 8 Mar. Lawyer at 61.

2394 Id. at 61.

2395 Id.

2396 Id. at 61.

pollution incident.[2397] The Convention is intended to ensure that adequate compensation will be readily available to victims of pollution, and places the obligation for paying such compensation on the ship-owner.[2398] This Convention entered into force in 1975.[2399] It was the primary convention relating to liability for accidental or intentional damage caused by oil pollution.[2400] The CLC was a reaffirmation and elaboration of the general maritime law that imposes liability for damages from oil pollution caused by a ship on the persons responsible for the ship.

Although the CLC is a serious attempt to provide a remedy for damages caused by oil pollution, it applies only to damage caused in the territory of a signatory state.[2401] Article 1(5) of the CLC defines "oil" as any persistent oil such as crude oil, fuel oil, heavy diesel oil, lubricating oil and whale oil, whether carried on board a ship as cargo or in the bunkers of such a ship.

Just like its companion convention, the Intervention Convention, the adoption of the CLC in such a short space of time, was clearly due to the political pressures felt by governments to respond to the clamour of public opinion arising from the TORREY CANYON incident.[2402]

The CLC is based on the principle that the registered owners should be primarily liable for oil pollution damage caused by discharges from their vessels carrying oil in bulk as cargo.[2403] CLC provides that no claim for compensation for pollution damage shall be made against the owner otherwise than in accordance with the Convention.[2404] Whether this is a true pre-emption clause in respect to national law is not clear.[2405] It appears

---

2397 International Convention On Civil Liability For Oil Pollution Damage (Brussels, 29 November 1969).

2398 Id.

2399 Id.

2400 *See* Frederick J. Carr, Comment: Statutory Liability For Oil Pollution From Vessels In Marine Environments, 3 U.S.F. Mar. L.J. at 304-05.

2401 Id. at 305.

2402 Id. at 305.

2403 Id.

2404 Id.

2405 Id.

that this provision makes the Convention the sole remedy for oil pollution damage in the territory of a party to CLC caused by a tanker registered by another party.[2406] Thus, when a contracting state suffers an oil spill, conflicting national laws are superseded.

In 1984, a series of convention protocols were passed which applied exclusively to preventive measures, to prevent or minimize oil pollution damage, and to pollution damage caused in the territory, the territorial sea or the exclusive economic zone (EEZ) of a state, established in accordance with international law.[2407] If a contracting state has not established such a zone, a line is to be drawn to include the area beyond and adjacent to the territorial sea of that state extending not more than 200 nautical miles from the baseline from which the breadth of its territorial sea is measured.[2408] While the compensation system established by the 1969 CLC and 1971 Fund Convention (1971 Fund Convention is discussed below) had proved very useful, by the mid-1980s it was generally agreed that the limits of liability were too low to provide adequate compensation in the event of a major pollution incident.[2409] Although the 1984 Protocol set increased limits of liability, it gradually became clear that the Protocol would never secure the acceptance required for entry into force and it was superseded by the 1992 version.[2410] **A major factor in the 1984 Protocol not entering into force was the reluctance of the United States, a major oil importer, to accept the Protocol.**[2411] The United States preferred a system that guaranteed the possibility of unlimited liability, introduced in its Oil Pollution Act of 1990.[2412] As a result, the 1992 Protocol was drawn up in such a way that the ratification of the United States was not needed in order to secure entry into force conditions.[2413]

---

2406 Id.

2407 Id. at 305-06.

2408 Id. at 306.

2409 The International Maritime Organization (IMO), Liability and Compensation Conventions (last modified in January 2002) <http://www.imo.org/Home.html>

2410 Id.

2411 Id.

2412 Id.

2413 Id.

The 1992 CLC governs the liability of Ship owners for oil pollution damage. The CLC lays down the principle of strict liability for ship owners and creates a system of compulsory liability insurance, [2414] which in most cases is provided by the P & I Clubs. The Shipowner is normally entitled to limit its liability to an amount which is linked to the tonnage of its ship.[2415]The 1992 CLC applies to oil pollution damage resulting from spills of persistent oil from tankers. The 1992 CLC covers pollution damage suffered in the territory, territorial sea or the exclusive economic zone (EEZ) or equivalent area of a state party to the convention.[2416] The flag state of the tanker and the nationality of the ship owner are irrelevant for determining the scope of application.[2417]

Pollution damage is defined as "loss or damage caused outside the ship by contamination resulting from the escape or discharge of oil from the ship, wherever such escape or discharge may occur."[2418] For environmental damage (other than loss of profit from impairment of the environment) compensation is limited, however, to costs actually incurred or to be incurred for reasonable measures to reinstate the contaminated environment.[2419] Expenses incurred for preventive measures are recoverable even when no spill of oil occurs, provided there was a grave and imminent threat of pollution damage.[2420] The 1992 CLC covers spills of cargo or bunker oil from sea-going vessels constructed or adapted to carry oil in bulk as cargo, and applies thus to laden tankers and in certain circumstances also to unladen tankers (but not to dry cargo ships).[2421] Damage

2414 International Oil Pollution Compensation Fund 1992, Explanatory Note prepared by International Oil Pollution Fund Secretariat, at 1 (March 2002).

2415 Id. at 1.

2416 Id.

2417 Id.

2418 *See* IMO Protocol of 1992 to Amend The International Convention on Civil Liability for Oil Pollution Damage 1969, Art II, Para 6 IMO 1992.

2419 International Oil Pollution Compensation Fund 1992, Explanatory Note prepared by International Oil Pollution Fund Secretariat, at 2 (March 2002).

2420 Id. at 2.

2421 Id.

caused by non-persistent oil is not covered by the 1992 CLC.[2422] Spills of gasoline, light diesel oil, and kerosene, therefore do not fall within the scope of the convention.[2423] The 1992 CLC exonerates ship owners from liability if they prove that the damage resulted from an act of war, hostilities, civil war, insurrection, or a natural phenomenon of an exceptional, inevitable and irresistible character.[2424] Exoneration is also available if the damage was wholly caused by an act or omission done with intent to cause damage by a third party, or was wholly caused by the negligence or other wrongful act of any Government or other authority responsible for the maintenance of lights or other navigational aids in the exercise of that function.[2425] In addition, if the owner proves that the pollution damage resulted wholly or partially from the negligence or intentional act of the person suffering the damage, the owner may be exonerated wholly or partially from his liability to that person.[2426]

Under 1992 CLC, the owner of a ship is entitled to limit its liability in respect of any one incident to an aggregate amount calculated as follows: (a) 3 million SDRs (as of March 14, 2002, about $3.75 million) for a ship not exceeding 5,000 units of tonnage; (b) for a ship with a tonnage in excess of 5, 000 units of tonnage, for each additional unit of tonnage, 420 SDRs (as of March 14, 2002, about $525) in addition to the amount mentioned in subparagraph (a), [2427]provided, however, that the aggregate amount shall not in any event exceed 59.7 million SDRs ($74.625 million).[2428]

For purposes of availing themselves of the benefit of limitation, ship owners must establish a fund for the total sum representing the limit of their liability.[2429] They are not entitled to limit their liability if it is proved that the pollution damage resulted from their personal act or omission

---

2422 Id.

2423 Id.

2424 *See* 1992 International Convention On Civil Liability For Oil Pollution Damage, Art Iii (2)(A).

2425 Id. at Art. III(2)(c).

2426 Id. at Art. III(3).

2427 Id. at Art VI(1).

2428 Id.

2429 Id. at Art VI (3).

committed with the intent to cause such damage, or recklessly and with knowledge that such damage would probably result.[2430]

No claim for compensation for pollution damage may be made against the owner otherwise than in accordance with the provisions of the 1992 CLC. Claims under the 1992 CLC can only be made against the registered owner of the tank vessel concerned. The 1992 CLC does not allow claim for compensation for pollution damage to be made against:

> "(a) the servants or agents of the owner or the members of the crew; (b) the pilot or any other person who, without being a member of the crew, performs services for the ship; (c) any charterer (howsoever described, including a bareboat charterer), manager or operator of the ship; (d) any person performing salvage operations with the consent of the owner or on the instructions of a competent public authority; (e) any person taking preventive measures; (f) all servants or agents of persons mentioned in subparagraphs (c), (d) and (e); unless the damage resulted from their personal act or omission, committed with the intent to cause such damage, or recklessly and with knowledge that such damage would probably result."[2431]

This provision does not however prevent victims from claiming compensation outside the CLC from persons other than the owner.[2432]

Owners of vessels registered in a contracting state and carrying more than 2,000 tons of persistent oil in bulk as cargo are required to maintain insurance or other financial security in sums equal to their potential limited liability, such as the guaranty of a bank or a certificate delivered by an international compensation fund in the sums fixed by applying the limits of liability described earlier to cover its liability for pollution damage under this Convention.[2433] Such coverage would permit claims

---

2430 Id. at Art VI(2).

2431 Id. at Art IV(4).

2432 International Oil Pollution Compensation Fund 1992, Annual Report on the Activities of the IOPC Fund (March 2000).

2433 *See* 1992 International Convention On Civil Liability For Oil Pollution Damage, Art VII(1).

for pollution damage to be brought directly against the insurer or other person providing financial security for the owner's liability for pollution damage.[2434] Actions for compensation under the 1992 CLC against the shipowner or its insurer may only be brought before the courts of the state party to the CLC in the territory, territorial sea or EEZ in which damage was caused.[2435]

The 1969 CLC discussed earlier operated within carefully defined limits, such as a monetary ceiling. It covered neither oil pollution caused by the escape of bunker oils from dry cargo ships nor tankers in ballast or loss or damage caused by fire or explosion.[2436] Nor did it cover preventive measures taken before oil actually escapes form the ship, or oil pollution damage caused outside the territory or territorial sea of a contracting state.[2437] Damage caused by non- persistent oil is not covered by the 1969 CLC. Therefore, spills of gasoline, light diesel oil, kerosene, etc., do not fall within the scope of the Convention.[2438]

It was felt by some Governments that the liability limits established by the 1969 CLC were too low, and that the compensation made available could, in some cases, prove to be inadequate. As a result, another conference was convened by IMO in 1971 which adopted the "Convention on the Establishment of an International Fund for Compensation for Oil Pollution Damage." **(IOPC).**[2439] This Convention came into force in 1978.[2440] Unlike the Civil Liability Convention, which puts the onus on the shipowner, the Fund Convention is designed to provide additional compensation to victims

---

2434 International Oil Pollution Compensation Fund 1992, Explanatory Note prepared by International Oil Pollution Fund Secretariat, at 3.

2435 Id. at 3.

2436 *See* Frederick J. Carr, Comment: Statutory Liability For Oil Pollution From Vessels In Marine Environments, 3 U.S.F. Mar. L.J. at 307-08.

2437 Id. at 308.

2438 Id. at 308.

2439 *See* Preamble to the International Convention On The Establishment of an International Fund For Compensation For Oil Pollution Damage (Brussels, 18 December 1971).

2440 The International Maritime Organization (IMO), Liability and Compensation Conventions (last modified in January 2002) <http://www.imo.org/Home.html>

where an accident results in pollution damage, which exceeds the compensation available under the Civil Liability Convention.[2441] Thus the burden of compensation is spread evenly between ship owners and cargo interests. The International Oil Pollution Compensation (IOPC) Fund is operated by the IOPC Fund Organization, which has its headquarters in London. Under the regime the owner of a tanker is liable to pay compensation up to a certain limit (explained earlier) for oil pollution damage following an escape of persistent oil from its ship.[2442] If that amount does not cover all the admissible claims, further compensation is available from the IOPC Funds if the damage occurs in a State that is a Member of one of the IOPC Funds.[2443] In other words, the Fund's obligation to pay compensation is confined to pollution damage that impacts the territories including the territorial sea of Contracting States.[2444] The Fund is also obliged to pay compensation in respect of measures taken by a Contracting State outside its territory.[2445]

The limits of liability in the CLC and the IOPC Fund Conventions were increased in 1992 by means of protocols to amend them, which were adopted by a conference convened by IMO. The 1992 CLC amendments was discussed earlier. The protocols entered into force in May 30, 1996 and increased the total amount of compensation payable to victims.[2446] The Fund can also provide assistance to Contracting States that are threatened or affected by pollution and wish to take measures against it, as allowed by the Intervention Convention.[2447] This may take the form of personnel, material, credit facilities or other aid.[2448]

---

2441 Id.

2442 Id.

2443 IOPC Funds, <http://www.iopcfund.org/intro.htm>

2444 The International Maritime Organization (IMO), Liability and Compensation Conventions (last modified in January 2002) <http://www.imo.org/Home.html>

2445 Id.

2446 The International Maritime Organization (IMO), Liability and Compensation Conventions (last modified in January 2002) <http://www.imo.org/Home.html>

2447 Id. *See also*, International Convention Relating To Intervention On The High Seas In Cases of Oil Pollution Casualties 26 U.S.T. 765, T.I.A.S. No. 8068 (Brussels, 29 November 1969).

2448 The International Maritime Organization (IMO), Liability and Compensation Conventions (last modified in January 2002) <http://www.imo.org/Home.html>

Article 4 of the IOPC provides in pertinent part:

"1. For the purpose of fulfilling its function under Article 2, paragraph 1 (a), the Fund shall pay compensation to any person suffering pollution damage if such person has been unable to obtain full and adequate compensation for the damage under the terms of the Liability Convention,

(a) because no liability for the damage arises under the Liability Convention;

(b) because the owner liable for the damage under the Liability Convention is financially incapable of meeting his obligations in full and any financial security that may be provided under Article VII of that Convention does not cover or is insufficient to satisfy the claims for compensation for the damage; an owner being treated as financially incapable of meeting his obligations and a financial security being treated as insufficient if the person suffering the damage has been unable to obtain full satisfaction of the amount of compensation due under the Liability Convention after having taken all reasonable steps to pursue the legal remedies available to him;

(c) because the damage exceeds the owner's liability under the Liability Convention as limited pursuant to Article V, paragraph 1, of that Convention or under the terms of any other international Convention in force or open for signature, ratification or accession at the date of this Convention. Expenses reasonably incurred or sacrifices reasonably made by the owner voluntarily to prevent or minimize pollution damage shall be treated as pollution damage for the purposes of this Article."

As explained earlier, under the IOPC Fund Convention, victims of oil pollution damage may be compensated beyond the level of the ship owner's liability. However, the Fund's obligations are limited, so that the total payable to victims by the shipowner and the Fund shall not exceed 30 million SDR (as of March 14, 2002 it was about US$37.5 million) for any one incident.[2449] In effect, therefore, the Fund's maximum liability for

2449 The International Maritime Organization (IMO), Liability and Compensation Conventions (last modified in January 2002) <http://www.imo.org/Home.html>, See also International Monetary Fund: IMF Finances - SDR Valuation (last modified, March 14, 2002) <http://www.imf.org/external/np/tre/sdr/basket.htm>

each incident is limited to 16 million SDR (as of March 14, 2002 about $20 million) per incident (under the 1971 convention - limits were raised under the 1992 Protocol).[2450] Where, however, there is no shipowner liable (because he has a valid defense to liability or it's a mystery oil spill) or the shipowner liable is unable to meet his liability, the Fund will be required to pay the whole amount of compensation due.[2451] Under certain circumstances, the Fund's maximum liability may increase to not more than 60 million SDR (as of March 14, 2002 it was about US$75 million) for each incident.[2452]

In connection with its second main function, the Fund is obliged to indemnify the shipowner or its insurer for a portion of the ship owner's liability under the Liability Convention.[2453] This portion is equivalent to 100 SDR (as of March 14, 2002 was about US$125) per ton or 8.3 million SDR (as of March 14, 2002 it was about US$10.375 million), whichever is the lesser.[2454] The Fund is not obliged to indemnify the owner if damage is caused by its willful misconduct or if the accident was caused, even partially, because the ship did not comply with certain international conventions.[2455] The Convention contains provisions on the procedure for claims, rights and obligations, and jurisdiction.[2456] Contributions are paid into the Fund by entities that receive oil after sea transport in Contracting States, and normally not by States.[2457] The Fund's Organization consists

---

2450 Id.

2451 Id.

2452 Id.

2453 The International Maritime Organization (IMO), Liability and Compensation Conventions (last modified in January 2002) <http://www.imo.org/Home.html>

2454 The International Maritime Organization (IMO), Liability and Compensation Conventions (last modified in January 2002) <http://www.imo.org/Home.html>, See also International Monetary Fund: IMF Finances - SDR Valuation (last modified, March 14, 2002) <http://www.imf.org/external/np/tre/sdr/basket.htm>

2455 The International Maritime Organization (IMO), Liability and Compensation Conventions (last modified in January 2002) <http://www.imo.org/Home.html>

2456 Id.

2457 The International Maritime Organization (IMO), Liability and Compensation Conventions (last modified in January 2002) http://www.imo.org/Home.html. See also IOPC Funds, <http://www.iopcfund.org/intro.htm>

of an Assembly of States, a Secretariat headed by a director appointed by the Assembly; and an Executive Committee.[2458]

There are therefore two IOPC Funds: the **1971 Fund** and the **1992 Fund**. These two intergovernmental organizations were established at different times (1971 and 1992), have different maximum amounts of compensation and have different Member States.[2459] They are intergovernmental organizations, because unlike IMO, the IOPC Funds are not United Nations (UN) agencies and are not part of the UN system.[2460] They are outside the UN, but follow procedures that are similar to those of the UN.[2461]

The membership of the 1992 Fund is increasing.[2462] The 1971 Fund is losing importance as States leave to join the 1992 Fund.[2463] Contracting Parties to the 1971 IOPC Fund on 27 September 2000 signed a Protocol allowing for the early winding-up of the 1971 Fund.[2464] The 2000 Protocol was signed following a Diplomatic Conference held from 25 to 27 September 2000. From 16 May 1998, Members of the 1992 Fund ceased to be Members of the 1971 Fund Convention due to a mechanism in the Protocol that established the 1992 Fund allowing for compulsory denunciation of the "old" regime.[2465] However, with the departure of these States, the total quantity of contributing oil on the basis of which contributions to the Fund are assessed has been dramatically reduced.[2466] The effect of this reduction in the contributions base is two-fold. In the first place, a considerably increased financial burden will fall on the contributors in those States which remain Members of

2458 The International Maritime Organization (IMO), Liability and Compensation Conventions (last modified in January 2002) <http://www.imo.org/Home.html>

2459 IOPC Funds, <http://www.iopcfund.org/intro.htm>

2460 The International Maritime Organization (IMO), Liability and Compensation Conventions (last modified in January 2002) <http://www.imo.org/Home.html>

2461 The International Maritime Organization (IMO), Liability and Compensation Conventions (last modified in January 2002) <http://www.imo.org/Home.html>

2462 IOPC Funds, <http://www.iopcfund.org/intro.htm>

2463 Id.

2464 The International Maritime Organization (IMO), Liability and Compensation Conventions (last modified in January 2002) <http://www.imo.org/Home.html>

2465 Id.

2466 Id.

the 1971 Fund if a major oil spill occurs in any of those States, since the contributors will be legally responsible for the funding of the total amount of compensation due from the 1971 Fund.[2467] In addition, as long as the 1971 Fund remains in existence, the concern remains that it will face a situation in which an incident occurs where the 1971 Fund has an obligation to pay compensation to victims, but where there are no contributors in any of the remaining Member States.[2468] In such a situation, if a tanker spill should occur, the remaining 1971 Fund Member States would not have the financial protection that they would expect under the provisions of the 1971 Fund Convention.[2469] Due to a number of recent denunciations of the 1971 Fund Convention, this Convention ceased to be in force on Friday, May 24, 2002.[2470] The 1971 and 1992 Funds have a joint Secretariat, based in London.

Under the **1992 Protocol**, the maximum amount of compensation payable from the Fund for a single incident, including the limit established under the 1992 CLC Protocol, is 135 million SDR (as of March 14, 2000, about US$168.75 million).[2471] However, if three States contributing to the Fund receive more than 600 million tons of oil per annum, the maximum amount is raised to 200 million SDR (as of March 14, 2000, about US$250 million).[2472]

Another Protocol to the **1971 and 1992 Fund** was adopted on the October 18, 2000. [2473] It is expected to enter into force on Saturday, November 1, 2003.[2474] For a single incident, including the limit established

2467 Id.

2468 Id.

2469 Id.

2470 IOPC Funds, <http://www.iopcfund.org/intro.htm>

2471 The International Maritime Organization (IMO), Liability and Compensation Conventions (last modified in January 2002) <http://www.imo.org/Home.html>, See also International Monetary Fund: IMF Finances - SDR Valuation (last modified, March 14, 2002) <http://www.imf.org/external/np/tre/sdr/basket.htm>

2472 Id.

2473 The International Maritime Organization (IMO), Liability and Compensation Conventions (last modified in January 2002) <http://www.imo.org/Home.html>

2474 Id.

under the 1992 CLC amendments (discussed earlier), the 2000 amendment increased it to 203 million SDR (US$253.75 million), up from 135 million SDR (US$168.75 million).[2475] However, if three States contributing to the Fund receive more than 600 million tons of oil per annum, the maximum amount is raised to 300,740,000 SDR (US$375. 92 million), up from 200 million SDR (US$250 million).[2476]

In conclusion, what is important to bear in mind is that there is a primary and supplementary layers of compensation for the international oil pollution regime. The primary layer of compensation recognized by the P & I Clubs is the Tanker Owner and its P & I Club that provide its pollution insurance. The 1969 and 1992 CLC governs this first layer of compensation. The supplementary layer of compensation is the 1992 IOPC Fund and the Oil Cargo Receivers. The supplementary layer of compensation only kicks in if the primary layer is inadequate to meet the claims that arise out of an oil spill. The supplementary layer of compensation is governed by the 1971 and 1992 IOPC Fund.

P&I Clubs and the 1992 Fund co-operate closely in the assessment and settlement of claims, usually using joint experts. In the event of a major incident a local claims office is usually established to assist potential claimants and to facilitate the submission of claims.[2477]

Every effort is made to settle valid claims promptly, either in whole or in part, in order to minimize any financial hardship suffered by victims.[2478] On rare occasions delays might be incurred if it appears that the total sum of valid claims could exceed the maximum amount of compensation available.[2479]

---

2475 The International Maritime Organization (IMO), Liability and Compensation Conventions (last modified in January 2002) <http://www.imo.org/Home.html>, See also International Monetary Fund: IMF Finances - SDR Valuation (last modified, March 14, 2002) <http://www.imf.org/external/np/tre/sdr/basket.htm>

2476 Id.

2477 International Tanker Owners Pollution Federation Ltd.: Oil Spill Compensation – A Brief Guide to the Civil Liability and Fund Conventions, at 3 (2000).

2478 Id. at 3.

2479 Id.

## II. A. Voluntary International Oil Pollution Compensation Schemes

The damage and publicity following the grounding of the Torrey Canyon off the South West coast of the UK in 1967, with the loss of its entire cargo of 119,000 tons of crude oil, prompted the world's tanker owners to take constructive action to mitigate the effects of oil spills and to assure adequate and timely compensation for those affected.[2480] Just as the Torrey Canyon oil spill incident had led to the creation of the 1969 CLC and 1971 IOPC Fund Conventions, it had earlier galvanized the tanker and oil industries into putting together two voluntary agreements, the Tanker Owners' Voluntary Agreement concerning Liability for Oil Pollution (TOVALOP) and the Contract Regarding a Supplement to Tanker Liability for Oil Pollution (CRISTAL). TOVALOP and CRISTAL were intended to be temporary arrangements pending global ratification of the 1969 CLC and 1971 IOPC Fund Conventions. Thus, the two voluntary arrangements preceded the 1969 CLC and 1971 IOPC Fund Conventions.

Before February 21 1997, compensation in non-convention countries was addressed by these two voluntary arrangements.[2481] The Voluntary agreements were seldom called upon in Convention countries, but were of considerable importance in non-convention countries.[2482] The members of the International Tanker Owners Pollution Federation Limited (ITOPF) (organization responsible for administering TOVALOP) voted at their Annual General Meeting on November 6, 1996, in favor of a Special Resolution to terminate the TOVALOP Standing Agreement with effect from 20 February 1997.[2483] The Board of Directors of both ITOPF and CRISTAL Limited had previously agreed not to extend the TOVALOP Supplement and CRISTAL Contract when their three-year terms end on

2480 International Tanker Owners Pollution Federation Ltd. (ITOPF): History (last Modified, Jan. 2002) <http://www.itopf.com/history.html>

2481 *See* Ben Browne, Port Authorities and Marine Oil Pollution Compensation, Port Technology International, at 194, Clyde & Co, Surrey, UK.

2482 Id. at 194.

2483 *See* North of England Protection & Indemnity Association, Circular 27 (December 1996).

20 February 1997.[2484] Therefore, with effect from February 21, 1997, both TOVALOP and CRISTAL lapsed, and pollution claimants in non-convention countries must now rely on legal regimes prevailing in their own countries, if any, to obtain compensation.[2485] The voluntary agreements actually lasted far longer than any one anticipated, although their relevance was progressively eroded as countries around the world ratified the CLC and IOPC.[2486]

*Effect of TOVALOP's Demise on TOVALOP Certificates:*

Prior to the demise of TOVALOP, the P & I Clubs sent circulars to their members informing them that ITOPF will no longer be issuing TOVALOP Certificates after the 1996 policy year since TOVALOP will, of course, no longer exist after that year.[2487] Some port authorities, and others have in the past required sight of such Certificates before allowing tankers to load or discharge.[2488] Such authorities will need to amend their procedures and look instead to the CLC Certificates issued by the flag state.[2489] There may be authorities which will require sight of TOVALOP Certificates after 20 February 1997 and the P & I Clubs recommended that their members place a copy of their P & I Circular on their tankers so that it can be shown to anyone who makes such a request as an explanation as to why TOVALOP Certificates no longer exist.[2490]

---

2484 Id.

2485 *See* Ben Browne, Port Authorities and Marine Oil Pollution Compensation, Port Technology International, at 194, Clyde & Co, Surrey, UK.

2486 Dr. Ian C. White, Oil Spill Compensation, A Brief Guide on the International Conventions on Liability and Compensation for Oil Pollution Damage. International Tanker Owners Pollution Federation Ltd. (ITOPF) (October 1999).

2487 *See* North of England Protection & Indemnity Association, Circular 27 (December 1996). Almost all the P & I Clubs sent a similarly worded circular to all their members.

2488 Id.

2489 Id.

2490 Id.

*Effect of TOVALOP's Demise on TOVALOP Charterparty Clause:*

Under the standard P&I Club recommended TOVALOP Charterparty Clause, owners normally warrant that their vessels are participating tankers in TOVALOP and give charterers the right in certain circumstances to take measures at the owner's expense in response to spill or threat of a spill from the tanker.[2491] The P & I Clubs have warned their members that such a Clause is no longer appropriate and will not be recommended by the Clubs from February 20, 1997.[2492] The Clubs had heard that some charterers were considering replacing the normal TOVALOP Charterparty Clause with a requirement that the owner remains a member of ITOPF, and the Clubs were in agreement with such a requirement in the charter party.[2493] The Clubs however observed that others were proposing to amend the present Clause merely by deleting the requirement that the tanker should be a participating tanker in TOVALOP, but retaining the right of charterers in certain circumstances to conduct cleanup operations or threat removal measures at the tanker owner's expense.[2494] The P & I Clubs did not believe that such an express right is appropriate any more since, whilst the granting of such a right was consistent with the whole voluntary compensation system set up by the TOVALOP and CRISTAL Agreements, it is incompatible with a number of the provisions of the legal regimes of the 1969 Civil Liability Convention, 1971 Fund Convention and 1992 Protocols.[2495]

The P & I Clubs warned that in the event that such Clauses are agreed, their member may be committing himself to pay clean up expenses or removal expenses which are not recoverable from the P & I Clubs based on its Rules and policies.[2496]

---

2491 Id.

2492 Id.

2493 Id.

2494 Id.

2495 Id.

2496 *See* North of England Protection & Indemnity Association, Circular 27 (December 1996). Almost all the P & I Clubs sent a similarly worded circular to all their members.

## II.B. TOVALOP

One objective of TOVALOP was to relieve innocent victims of the burden of having to find some regime of liability that would give them a basis for claiming, and a sympathetic court which would give ear to their complaint.[2497] International Tanker Owners Pollution Federation Ltd. (ITOPF) was established by P & I clubs and tanker owners in 1968 as a non-profit making service organization for the principal purpose of administering the Tanker Owners Voluntary Agreement concerning Liability for Oil Pollution (TOVALOP).[2498] The administration of TOVALOP was originally ITOPF's prime function and remained an integral part of its activities for more than a quarter of a century.[2499] However, the high incidence of major tanker spills in the early 1970s underlined the need for a specialized group to provide technical advice on response techniques and effects.[2500] It was also recognized that there would be a requirement to assess objectively the reasonableness of clean-up measures and the merits of claims for compensation under both the voluntary agreements and international Conventions. So was born ITOPF's technical service function.[2501]

Membership and Funding of ITOPF continues to be arranged through the P&I Clubs and other oil pollution insurers. The organization currently has some 4,000 tanker owner Members who between them own or operate some 98% of the world's tank-vessel tonnage.[2502] With effect from 20th February 1999 the owners and bareboat charterers of other types of ship became eligible to become Associates of ITOPF and thereby have access to the organization's technical services on a similar basis to its tanker owner Members.[2503] Before the demise of TOVALOP, membership

---

2497 *See* Christopher Hill, Practical Guides, Introduction to P & I Clubs, Lloyd's Shipping Law Library (2d ed. 1996).

2498 International Tanker Owners Pollution Federation Ltd. (ITOPF): History (last Modified, Jan. 2002) <http://www.itopf.com/history.html>

2499 Id.

2500 Id.

2501 Id.

2502 Id.

2503 Id.

of ITOPF was normally arranged by the P&I Clubs and other oil pollution insurers. These bodies also paid the annual ITOPF dues on their members' behalf (for 2001//2002 these dues were calculated at the rate of 0.7 of a UK penny per gross ton).[2504] Despite the demise of TOVALOP, as before, the administrative procedures and payment of membership dues will be handled by the P&I insurers.[2505]

Although the impetus for TOVALOP's creation has been described in both negative and positive terms, the ultimate effect was to provide mitigation and compensation for damage by oil pollution from tankers.[2506] Seven tanker owners, its original sponsors, signed the "Standing Agreement" into existence in 1969.[2507] As of 1987, over ninety-eight percent of the free world's tanker owners, including many government-owned fleets, had become signatories to TOVALOP.[2508] Membership in the ITOPF required participating tanker owners to establish and maintain the financial capability to withstand limited liability claims.[2509] Typically, this would be reflected by the vessel's acquiring insurance with a P&I Club.[2510] Under TOVALOP, the tanker owner was expected to "take such [p]reventive [m]easures and/or [t]hreat [r]emoval [m]easures as are practicable and appropriate under the circumstances."[2511] TOVALOP basically defines "Preventive Measures" as any reasonable measures taken after an incident had occurred to prevent or minimize pollution damage, while it defines "Threat Removal Measures" as any reasonable measures taken

2504 International Tanker Owners Pollution Federation Ltd. (ITOPF): Membership and Funding of ITOPF (last Modified, Jan. 2002) < http://www.itopf.com/membersh.html>

2505 Id.

2506 *See* Susan Bloodworth, Comment: Death on the High Seas: The Demise of TOVALOP and CRISTAL, 13 J. Land. Use & Envtl. L. 443, 445 (Spring 1998).

2507 Id. at 445.

2508 Id.

2509 Id. (citing, Tanker Owners Voluntary Agreement Concerning Liability for Oil Pollution (TOVALOP), Jan. 7, 1969, as amended Oct. 13, 1993, II(B)(3), reprinted in 6 MICHAEL F. STURLEY, BENEDICT ON ADMIRALTY 6-136 (7th ed. 1993) [[[hereinafter TOVALOP Agreement].

2510 *See* Susan Bloodworth, Comment: Death on the High Seas: The Demise of TOVALOP and CRISTAL, 13 J. Land. Use & Envtl. L. at 445

2511 Id. at 445.

after an incident had occurred for the purposes of removing the threat of an escape or discharge of oil.[2512] Tanker owners also were expected to voluntarily, and as promptly as possible, dispose of all valid claims arising against the owner under the Standing Agreement.[2513] In the event of a dispute regarding claims, the Standing Agreement provided for the commencement of arbitration proceedings under the rules of the International Chamber of Commerce.[2514] TOVALOP's compensation scheme was keyed to the tonnage of the vessel: $160.00 per ton, with a maximum amount of compensation available of $16.8 million for a vessel of 105,000 gross tons.[2515] TOVALOP was a no-fault compensation scheme, with only limited coverage exceptions to the tanker owner's liability: (1) where the damage occurs in a geographic area covered by the CLC; (2) the damage is the result of an act of war, hostilities, civil war, insurrection or a natural phenomenon of an exceptional, inevitable and irresistible character; (3) wholly caused by an act or omission of a third party done with intent to cause damage; and (4) wholly caused by the negligence or other wrongful act of any Government or other authority responsible for the maintenance of lights or other navigational aids in the exercise of that function.[2516]

The deliberate winding up of TOVALOP has been criticized. There are several options available for countries operating in the international oil shipping realm.[2517] For example, a country may elect not to become a signatory to the 1969 & 1992 CLC as well as the 1971 & 1992 IOPC Fund Convention. They may forego these international conventions for any number of reasons.[2518] For example, they may possess the same concerns as the U.S. Senate regarding these international conventions ability to fully compensate oil spill damages; they may be in the process of designing their own legal regime (similar to OPA 90); or they may have

---

2512 Id. at 445-46

2513 Id. at 446.

2514 Id.

2515 Id.

2516 Id. at 446.

2517 Id. at 456.

2518 Id.

relied successfully on the private industry agreements in the past and simply not had time to garner whatever support their governments require to ratify the 1969/71 conventions or the 1992 protocols.[2519] Of approximately 160 maritime countries, only 75 were a party to the 1969/71 conventions. A country may be a signatory to the 1969/71 conventions but not the 1992 protocols. A country also may be a signatory to the 1969 CLC, yet not be a member of the 1971 Fund Convention.[2520] Countries who fall into such categories may not have sufficient Funds for clean up and other oil spill response expenses. Had TOVALOP and CRISTAL not lapsed, the impact of the 1969/1971 convention's shortfall would have been negligible, because of the availability of a back up voluntary fund.[2521] Even where countries are parties to both the 1969 CLC and 1971 Fund Convention, liability limits may be inadequate.[2522] And to make matters worse, as explained earlier, the 1971 Fund expired in May of 2002. As of mid-1996, there were four separate pollution incidents in which countries that were parties to the 1969/71 conventions were faced with claims that exceeded the amounts available.[2523] Without TOVALOP and CRISTAL to fall back on, countries who may not be proponents of the 1992 protocols are left with very little choice other than to ratify them or in the alternative come up with their own domestic legislation that creates a separate Fund from the IOPC 1992 Fund. By so doing, it will be following the US OPA example, when the US Congress passed its own domestic legislation that created the Oil Spill Liability Trust Fund.

## II.C. CRISTAL

CRISTAL (also referred to as the "Supplemental Agreement") was also a voluntary industry agreement designed to address oil pollution

2519 Id.

2520 Id.

2521 Id.

2522 Id.

2523 Id.

damage by supplementing TOVALOP.[2524] Unlike TOVALOP, the parties to CRISTAL were not the tanker owners, but the various oil companies "engaged in the production, refining, marketing, storing, trading or terminaling of [o]il, or any one or more of whose affiliates are so engaged or... receives [o]il in bulk for its own consumption or use."[2525] CRISTAL first took effect in 1971.[2526] Similar to TOVALOP, a separate entity, Cristal Limited (the Institute), administered CRISTAL. CRISTAL required the establishment of a fund, contributed to by all signatories to the Supplemental Agreement.[2527] The total amount of oil received, based on crude/fuel oil receipts, directly affected each signatory's contribution amount.[2528] The Institute made the determination of how much money was necessary to assure the fund's ability to make the payments under CRISTAL.[2529] The amount was prorated, by dividing the total amount needed by the total of crude/fuel oil receipts for all signatories, and then multiplying that figure by each individual signatory oil company's receipts.[2530] Once a determination was made that compensation from the tanker owner under TOVALOP proved insufficient to meet all claims, CRISTAL came into play.[2531] Earlier versions of CRISTAL required that three basic conditions exist before paying compensation: the oil carried by the vessel must have been owned by a party to CRISTAL; the tanker from which the oil was spilled must have been a party to TOVALOP; and the spill must have occurred under circumstances which would have resulted in liability had the CLC been in force at the time of the incident.[2532] However, the 1993

---

2524 Id.

2525 Id. (citing, A Supplemental to Tanker Liability for Oil Pollution (CRISTAL), as amended Oct. 11, 1993, I(H) reprinted in 6 MICHAEL F. STURLEY, BENEDICT ON ADMIRALTY 6-148.7 (7th ed. 1993) [hereinafter CRISTAL Agreement].

2526 *See* Susan Bloodworth, Comment: Death on the High Seas: The Demise of TOVALOP and CRISTAL, 13 J. Land. Use & Envtl. L. at 446.

2527 Id. at 446-47.

2528 Id. at 447.

2529 Id.

2530 Id.

2531 Id.

2532 Id. at 447.

version of CRISTAL removed both the TOVALOP signatory requirement, as well as the exclusion for CLC covered liability.[2533]

The same defenses to liability stated in TOVALOP applied to the 1993 version of CRISTAL.[2534] However, CRISTAL still would reimburse the oil company signatories for their clean-up efforts, even if the damage were the result of "negligence or other wrongful act of any Government or other authority responsible for the maintenance of lights or other navigational aids in the exercise of that function."[2535] Special Drawing Rights (SDR's), as defined by the International Monetary Fund, expressed CRISTAL's compensation scheme just like in the case of TOVALOP and the International Conventions.[2536] Like TOVALOP, payments were linked to the size of the tanker. Funds were not paid, however, until the Institute determined the oil company's costs had exceeded specific amounts.[2537] For example, for a tanker weighing 5,000 tons or less, the oil company must have paid out costs of three million SDR's (or $3.75 million); for a tanker weighing in excess of 5,000 tons, the calculation was based on 420 SDR's (or $525) for each ton over 5,000, up to a maximum of 59,700,000 SDR's (or $74.625 million).[2538] The aggregate compensation available under CRISTAL, after the minimum payouts were met, was 32 million SDR's (or $40 million) for a tanker of 5,000 tons or less, and for a tanker in excess of 5,000 tons, 652 SDR's (or $815) for each ton in excess of 5,000, up to a maximum of 120 million SDR's (or $150 million).[2539] Designed as a last resort after all other avenues of compensation were exhausted, the minimum payouts, as well as amounts due under any other available remedy, were deducted from the above amounts prior to a CRISTAL payout.[2540]

---

2533 Id.

2534 Id.

2535 Id. (citing, CRISTAL Agreement IV(D)(2)).

2536 *See* Susan Bloodworth, Comment: Death on the High Seas: The Demise of TOVALOP and CRISTAL, 13 J. Land. Use & Envtl. L. at 448.

2537 Id.

2538 Id. (citing, CRISTAL Agreement IV(D)(4).

2539 Id. at 448.

2540 Id.

In conclusion, what is important to bear in mind is that there was a primary and supplementary layer of compensation for the voluntary oil pollution regime. The primary layer of compensation recognized by the P & I Clubs was the Tanker Owner and its P & I Club that provide its pollution insurance. The TOVALOP used to govern this first layer of compensation, until its demise in 1997. The supplementary layer of compensation was the CRISTAL and the various oil companies "engaged in the production, refining, marketing, storing, trading or terminaling of [o]il, or any one or more of whose affiliates are so engaged or... receives [o]il in bulk for its own consumption or use."[2541] The supplementary layer of compensation will in most cases kick in only if the primary layer is inadequate to meet the claims that arise out of an oil spill. The supplementary layer of compensation is governed by the CRISTAL Supplemental Agreement. So, by and large the structure of the voluntary/international and international conventions pollution regimes were similar. They both emphasized the need for back up funding to supplement the financial capability of Tanker owners to respond to an oil spill.

## III. Scope of P & I Pollution Insurance Cover

Generally, P & I Club rules covers the liabilities, losses, damages, costs and expenses set out below, when and to the extent that they are caused by or incurred in consequence of the discharge or escape from an entered ship (a ship that is a member of a P & I Club) of oil or any other substance, or the threat of such discharge or escape:

(A) Liability for loss, damage or contamination; (b) Any loss, damage or expense which the Owner incurs, or for which he is liable, as a party to any agreement approved by the Directors of the Club, including the costs and expenses incurred by the Owner in performing its obligations under such agreements; (C) The costs of any measures reasonably taken for the purpose of avoiding or minimizing pollution or any resulting loss or damage together with any liability for loss of or damage to property caused

2541 Id. at 446.

by measures so taken; (D) The costs of any measures reasonably taken to prevent an imminent danger of the discharge or escape from the entered ship of oil or any substance which may cause pollution; (E) The costs or liabilities incurred as a result of compliance with any order or direction given by any government or authority, for the purpose of preventing or reducing pollution or the risk of pollution, provided always that:

(a) such compliance is not a requirement for the normal operation or salvage or repair of the entered ship; and (b) such costs or liabilities are not recoverable under the Hull Policies of the entered ship.[2542]

The P & I Club rules also include a proviso that:

> "(a) There shall be no recovery in respect of any liability, loss, damage, cost or expense arising as a consequence of the presence in, or the escape or discharge or threat of escape or discharge from, any land-based dump, storage or disposal facility, of any substance previously carried on the entered ship, whether or not as cargo, fuel, stores or waste, except to the extent that the Directors of the Club in their discretion, and without having to give any reasons for their decision, otherwise determine; (b) Unless and to the extent that special cover has been agreed in writing by the Managers, the Clubs shall not reimburse any liability, loss, cost or expense which would have been recoverable in general average if the cargo of the entered ship had been carried on terms no less favorable to the Owner than those of the York-Antwerp Rules 1994."[2543]

In addition to those listed above, most P & I Clubs Oil Pollution cover also permit the recovery of: (1) Salvors' Expenses or Special Compensation liability of the Member to reimburse a salvor of an Entered Ship for:

(i) his reasonably incurred expenses (together with any increment awarded thereon) under Clause 1(a) of the Lloyd's Standard Form of Salvage Agreement (1980); (ii) special compensation in respect of work done or measures taken to prevent or minimize damage to the environment under the provisions of Article 14 of the International Convention

---

2542 *See* 2002 UK P & I Club Rules, Rule 2, §12. Almost all the P & I Clubs have similar or identical coverage provisions.

2543 Id. at Rule 2, §12.

on Salvage 1989 or the terms of a standard form of salvage agreement equivalent thereto approved by the Club; (iii) the Special Compensation P&I Clubs clause (SCOPIC) as incorporated into Lloyd's Open Form of Salvage Agreement or any other "No Cure – No Pay" salvage contract approved by the Club.

(2) Fines: Fines or other penalties, together with costs and expenses incidental thereto, imposed in respect of an Entered Ship by any court, tribunal, or authority of competent jurisdiction, upon a Member or upon any person whom the Member may be legally liable to reimburse or reasonably reimburses with the approval of the Managers in respect of pollution; but subject always to the Member having cover for his liabilities in respect of pollution.[2544]

## The Policy Defenses And Exclusions That P & I Clubs Invoke To Avoid Liability When There Is An Oil Spill From A Covered Vessel.

P & I Clubs often include certain exclusions in their P & I Policy that entitles them to deny coverage to a member when there is an oil spill. Exclusions refer to losses or events that are not covered by the insurance. The exclusions include:

(1) Breach of warranty of seaworthiness of the vessel, (2) willful misconduct of the member, (3) avoidance of cover for non-disclosure or misrepresentation, (4) liabilities arising under contract, (5) illegal, hazardous or improper adventures, (6) war risks, (7) pay to be paid principle, (8) unpaid calls, (9) insured only as ship owner, (10) liability for damage to entered vessel, loss of hire, equipment, etc. (11) liabilities, costs and expenses of salvage vessels, drilling vessels, dredgers and others, (12) Exclusion of Nuclear risks, and (13) double insurance or "other insurance." I will not discus these exclusions.

---

2544 *See* North of England Protection & Indemnity Association Rules, Rule 19(13), 19(19)(d) (2002 -2003). Most Clubs have similar or identical provisions in their rules and policies.

## IV. A US OIL POLLUTION SURCHARGE AND EXCLUSION CLAUSE SURCHARGE CLAUSE

By virtue of the colossal liability a vessel sailing to and from US waters is subject to under the OPA, almost all the P & I Clubs have included a US Oil Pollution Exclusion and Surcharge Clause in their Oil Pollution Insurance Policy. As the Clubs have done in the past since the promulgation of the OPA, in 1999, they sent out circulars to their members emphasizing the differing treatment that will be given to vessels that sail into US waters. These Clauses cover only persistent oil. For the purposes of the policy, persistent oil includes all hydro-carbon mineral oils except the following oils which are non-persistent: Liquefied Natural Gas (LNG), Liquefied Petroleum Gas (LPG), Gasolines (AVGAS/MOGAS), White Spirit Kerosenes (Domestic, tractor, aviation, No1 fuel), Distillates (Gas oil, heating oil, auto diesel, No2 fuel), and Gasoline blending components (naphthas).[2545] Non-Persistent Oils are normally Oils which consist of hydro-carbon fractions:-

"(a) [A]t least 50% of which, by volume, distils at a temperature of 340 degrees C; and
(b) at least 95% of which distils at a temperature of 370 degrees C when tested by the ASTM Method D 86/78 or any subsequent revision thereof."[2546]

Clubs whose Members are carrying persistent oil to or from the United States again had to pay an increased contribution towards the cost of the International Group Excess Loss Reinsurance Contract for the 2000/2001 policy year.[2547] The additional costs were passed on to the Members concerned.[2548] In addition to the Members' payment of the normal calls and premiums, for the 2000/2001 policy year, the surcharge for ships with-

2545 *See* North Of England Protection & Indemnity Association Ltd., United States Oil Pollution Cover 2000/2001 Policy Year, CIRCULAR 50 (December 1999).

2546 Id.

2547 Id.

2548 Id.

out segregated ballast tanks (as defined below) amounted to 8.5 US cents per gross ton, per voyage; for ships with segregated ballast tanks the surcharge was 7.5 US cents per gross ton per voyage; in each case there was a maximum charge of "cap" of twenty voyages.[2549] The surcharge applied to all tankers carrying out a "US voyage", as defined below, and carrying persistent oils, also as defined above. Tankers of 1,000 gross tons or less had the option of either making voyage declarations in the same way as tankers over 1,000 gross tons on a flat contributory tonnage of 1,000 gt, or of paying a single annual premium of US$1,700 (US$1,500 for ships with segregated ballast tanks).[2550]

The amount of the surcharge was reduced by 50% in respect of cargoes exclusively discharged at LOOP (Louisiana Offshore Oil Port) or exclusively transferred to another ship at a place approved by the US Coast Guard and in the Exclusive Economic Zone ("EEZ") as defined in OPA 1990[2551] (these are called designated lightering zones under OPA regulations). For the 2000/2001 Policy year, the P & I Clubs also declared that, it was again mandatory for members to follow a procedure whereby the Club is regularly advised of US voyages in order that the surcharge may be applied.[2552] This surcharge policy has become a permanent feature of P & I Club's Oil Pollution Insurance policy for vessels sailing into US waters.

## IV. B US OIL POLLUTION EXCLUSION CLAUSE

The clubs resolved that unless prior arrangement is reached with a Member, the Club's cover for all tankers incorporates the following Exclusion Clause with effect from 20 February 2000.[2553] "Excluding any and all claims in respect of oil pollution arising out of any incident to

2549 Id.

2550 Id.

2551 Id.

2552 Id.

2553 Id.

which the US Oil Pollution Act 1990 is applicable".[2554] The above Exclusion Clause will apply unless the Member agrees to undertake:

"1. to make quarterly declarations in arrears, at the latest within 2 months of each quarter ending 20 May, 20 August, 20 November and 20 February as to whether the tanker has made any cargo voyages to or from the USA or to US waters and, if so, the number of such voyages and the nature of cargo (persistent oil or other cargo) and the port or place of loading or discharging; and

2. to pay such additional premium in respect of such voyages as may be agreed between the Club and the Member."[2555]

Members requesting removal of the Exclusion Clause were told that for the 2000/2001 policy year, they will again have to provide declarations which will have to be returned to the Club within 2 months of the end of each quarter, failing which US Coast Guard Certificates will be withdrawn without further notice.[2556] Club rules also provide that in the event that any declaration made by the member or on his behalf is in any material respect inaccurate, the Clubs shall be entitled to refuse cover for the period covered by such declaration.[2557] In the event that the member makes no declaration, or a late or inaccurate declaration, the Clubs shall be entitled to refuse cover in respect of all periods subsequent to the period covered by such declaration.[2558] This selective and targeted US Oil Pollution exclusion policy has become a permanent feature of the P & I Club's Oil Pollution Insurance policy for vessels sailing into US waters.

Definitions: Segregated ballast tanks: A ship will be deemed to have segregated ballast tanks if it is equipped in accordance with the requirements of Regulation 13 of Annex I to MARPOL 73/78.[2559] US Voyage:

---

2554 Id.

2555 Id.

2556 Id.

2557 Assuranceforeningen Skuld Rules, Appendix 5 – clause 1.6 (2002).

2558 Id. at App. 5 – clause 1.7.

2559 *See* North Of England Protection & Indemnity Association Ltd., United States Oil Pollution Cover 2000/2001 Policy Year, CIRCULAR 50 (December 1999).

Any cargo voyage involving loading or discharging cargo at any port or place in the USA or within the EEZ as defined in the OPA 1990. USA includes District of Columbia, Puerto Rico, Guam, American Samoa, US Virgin Islands and Northern Marianas.[2560]

## IV. C. Who pays the cost of surcharge, Owner or Charterer?

One question that has generated a number of disputes between ship owners and charterers of vessels is "who pays the cost of the surcharge?" The solution to this problem in most cases can be found in the provisions of the charter party between ship owners and charterers. Since most charter party disputes are resolved by arbitration, the disputes relating to payment for surcharge have not been an exception. It has been held in an arbitration proceeding that the payment of a US voyage surcharge or additional premium by a ship owner cannot be recovered from a charterer, where a clause in the charter party before the OPA COFR regulations came into force provides as follows:

> "[I]n the event that the financial security requirements under united states law increase during the term of this fixture so as to require pollution insurance in excess of that owner has agreed to carry under the preceding paragraph, and there is coverage available to meet such requirements, owner will at the request of charterer obtain the requested and available coverage, which additional coverage shall be paid for by charterer. Owners and vessel will bear no responsibility whatsoever if insurability of the U.S. government financial security requirements are not available and the vessel is prevented from calling at any U.S. port as a result thereof."[2561]

The panel of arbitrators emphasized that payment of additional surcharge is not the same thing as increase in financial security or insur-

---

2560 Id.

2561 *See* Metropolitan World Maritime Corp. v. Conoco Shipping Company, SMA, No. 2955 (March 12, 1993) (**Panel:** Raymond A. Connell; Alexis Nichols; Manfred W. Arnold).

ance.[2562] They observed that OPA did not increase the amount of insurance needed for oil pollution. OPA only increased the amount of limitation of liability for oil pollution. That increase was far below the $500 million insurance coverage that the P & I Clubs provided at the time. They noted further that in another charter that the owner had entered into with another charterer, which predates the charters in dispute, the Owners knew how to write a clause allocating the additional cost of oil pollution insurance to charterers where that was intended to be done.[2563] That preceding charter provided:

"SHELL OIL POLLUTION CLAUSE: Owners have in effect through their P and I Club up to 2/20/91 the above additional coverage, if after 2/20/91 additional premiums are required then such additional premiums will be for Charterer's account, provided Owners can obtain same."[2564]

The instant charters did not contain any such language.[2565] The language of the Clause was silent on insurance costs or increased costs, and neither the Clause in dispute nor any other clause supported Owners' contention that insurance expenses for Owners' account were, in effect, intended to be "fixed", to assure a profit margin on agreed hire.[2566] Finally the panel concluded that giving the language of the Clause its plain meaning, increased expenses to maintain standard oil pollution cover is for the account of Owners, no matter what form of assessment the Club might adopt to fund the risk and without regard to whether in September 1990 Owners could have foreseen the Club's resorting to surcharges.[2567]

The Club Rules provide that where a member has "other insurance" for liability, loss, costs and fines arising out of oil pollution which would otherwise fall within the cover provided by these Rules, such cover shall be excluded up to the stated limit of such insurance and the sum insured

2562 Id.
2563 Id.
2564 Id.
2565 Id.
2566 Id.
2567 Id.

under such other insurance shall be deducted from the amount to which the Club is entitled to limit its liability.[2568] This provision on the surface may seem to be very important because of the COFR requirements of OPA and its resultant creation of a non-P & I Club COFR guarantor's market due to the refusal of the International Group of P & I Clubs to serve as guarantors for their members sailing into US waters. As was extrapolated earlier in this treatise, the P & I Clubs did this to avoid submitting themselves to direct action under OPA.

The COFR guarantors normally make it mandatory for the insured to maintain membership and P & I insurance in the standard amount ($500 million) from one of the International Group of P & I Clubs.[2569] Most of these COFR guarantors of oil pollution liability provide far less than the $1 billion dollars that the International Group of P & I Clubs now make available for oil pollution incidents. But what the "other insurance" clause emphasizes is that the International Group of P & I Clubs will deduct what can be paid by another insurer from what it (the International Group of P & I Club) would pay under its policy. But this provision does not apply to COFR guarantors because the Clubs do not see them as providers of "other insurance." Apart from this it is very difficult for an insured to execute both insurance policies at the same time. So, the P&I clubs will continue to pay for oil spill liabilities, and the COFR guaranty provided under the Oil Pollution Act of 1990 will probably be used mostly in catastrophic cases to pay claims in excess of the $1 billion paid by the P&I clubs. So, for claims that exceed $1 billion, the P & I Club pays first before any COFR guarantor. But it pays only up to $1 billion. Then after the $1 billion P & I limit has been reached, the P & I Club steps out of the picture completely and the COFR guarantors step in to pay up to the limit of liability stated expressly in the insurance policy of the insured with the guarantor. Under

2568 Assuranceforeningen Skuld Rules, Appendix 5 – clause 4.

2569 "The Applicants jointly and severally undertake at all times throughout the period of the Agreement at no expense to SIGCO: to enter and keep each of the Vessels entered in the Club for full protection and indemnity risks under law including, but not limited to, OPA 1990 and CERCLA, in the Standard Amount." Shipowners Insurance And Guaranty Company Ltd. (Hereinafter Referred To As "Sigco") Terms And Conditions, Condition 1.2 (Undertakings) (28th December, 1997).

both the international oil pollution regimes and OPA there is no liability limit that comes close to $1 billion. But if claimants successfully break the liability limits of OPA or the international oil pollution regimes, the insured's and P & I Club member's liability could equal or exceed the $1 billion amount.

The COFR guarantor can sue the P & I Club on behalf of the insured if it believes that the denial of oil pollution cover is unjustified under the laws of England and the Club's rules and policies. If it sues the Club successfully, it will be entitled to indemnity from the Club for what it has paid on behalf of the insured up to the limit of the guaranty that it has provided. Because most oil spill claims are below $1 billion, the COFR guarantor will in most cases be able to get back everything that it paid claimants on behalf of the insured, provided it can sue the Club successfully. But as was explained earlier in chapter eight, it is very unlikely that a COFR guarantor will sue a Club that has denied a claim by invoking an exclusion Clause in its Club Rules.

So, even though the International Group of P & I Clubs would not act as COFR guarantors, they still underwrite Oil Pollution risks for vessels that make voyages into US waters. What the OPA has inadvertently created is additional funds for the payment of removal costs and damages for oil pollution. The funds are the P & I Club Funds and the COFR guarantor's funds. For practical purposes, the P & I Club fund is the primary fund, while the COFR guarantor's fund is the secondary or back up fund. But additional funds are not guaranteed, because it is only possible in cases where the P & I Clubs either do not invoke a defense to oil pollution insurance coverage, or invoke it unsuccessfully in arbitration or in a court of law.

The COFR guarantor's insurance would also be applied to an oil spill incident if the P & I Club successfully invokes a traditional policy defense to coverage. This can happen where there is breach of the terms, warranties and conditions of the Policy and Club rules. When the P & I Clubs deny coverage to its member, that member would most likely litigate the matter against the Club.

Where a member of a Club has provided evidence of financial responsibility to any authority in respect of any liability, cost or expense, or potential liability, cost or expense, by producing to that authority evidence of insurance other than evidence of insurance under the P & I Club Rules, there shall be no contribution by the Clubs to the Member or to any other person in respect of such liability, cost or expense.[2570] The Club rules however includes a proviso that this Rule may be waived either: (i) by prior agreement with the Club in writing or, (ii) if the Committee in its discretion so decides.[2571]

Because of the direct action provision of OPA, now when the vessels of members undertake US voyages, the Clubs include a disclaimer clause in the policies and certificate of entry that is issued to such members. It normally provides that the certificate policy is evidence only of the contract of indemnity insurance between the named Member(s) and the Club and shall not be construed as evidence of any undertaking, financial or otherwise, on the part of the Club to any other party.[2572] The Clubs maintain that if a Member tenders this certificate as evidence of insurance under any applicable law relating to financial responsibility, or otherwise shows or offers it to any other party as evidence of insurance, such use of this certificate by the Member is not to be taken as any indication that the Club thereby consents to act as guarantor or to be sued directly in any jurisdiction whatsoever,[2573] because the Club does not so consent.[2574]

This disclaimer clause enables the International Group of P & I Clubs to provide the needed Oil Pollution insurance without subjecting themselves to direct action under the US Oil Pollution Act of 1990. The Clubs' existing policy is that they will only issue **disclaimer-free certificates** under the international conventions and the Federal Water Pollution Control Act (FWPCA) but not under OPA.[2575] In fact the FWPCA Certificate of

---

2570 *See* Britannia Steam Ship Insurance Association Ltd., Club Rules, Rule 26(2) (2002).

2571 Id.

2572 *See* The Swedish Club, Circular, Pollution/United States Oil Pollution Surcharge for tankers 1998/1999, Enclosure to circular P.2376/1999 (1998).

2573 Id.

2574 Id.

2575 *ee* Metropolitan World Maritime Corp. v. Conoco Shipping Company, SMA, No. 2955 (March 12, 1993) (**Panel:** Raymond A. Connell; Alexis Nichols; Manfred W. Arnold).

Financial Responsibility includes an express provision in which the P & I Clubs consent to direct action being brought against them.

# Chapter Ten

# CONTRIBUTION –33 USC § 2709, INDEMNITY – 33 USC § 2710, & THIRD PARTY LIABILITY – 33 USC § 2702(D)

Statutory provisions:

"§ 2709. Contribution

A person may bring a civil action for contribution against any other person who is liable or potentially liable under this Act or another law. The action shall be brought in accordance with section 2717 of this title.[2576]

"§ 2710. Indemnification agreements

(a) Agreements not prohibited

Nothing in this Act prohibits any agreement to insure, hold harmless, or indemnify a party to such agreement for any liability under this Act.

(b) Liability not transferred

No indemnification, hold harmless, or similar agreement or conveyance shall be effective to transfer liability imposed under this Act from a responsible party or from any person who may be liable for an incident under this Act to any other person.

(c) Relationship to other causes of action

Nothing in this Act, including the provisions of subsection (b) of this section, bars a cause of action that a responsible party subject to liability under this Act,

2576 33 USC § 2709

or a guarantor, has or would have, by reason of subrogation or otherwise, against any person."[2577]

One of the most notable provisions of the OPA is the one that allows responsible parties to seek indemnification from sole cause third-parties and contribution from jointly and severally liable third parties.[2578] Section 2709 of the OPA provides specifically that a person may bring a civil action for contribution against any other person who is liable or potentially liable under the OPA or another law. The OPA specifically provides that nothing in its provisions prohibits any agreement to insure, hold harmless, or indemnify a party to such agreement for any liability under this Act.[2579] The statute limits this indemnification agreement provision by specifically providing that no indemnification, hold harmless, or similar agreement or conveyance shall be effective to transfer liability imposed under this Act from a responsible party or from any person who may be liable for an incident under this Act to any other person.[2580] This section also defines its relationship to other causes of action by providing that nothing in this Act, including the provisions of subsection (b) (prohibiting transfer of liability) of this section, bars a cause of action that a responsible party subject to liability under this Act, or a guarantor, has or would have, by reason of subrogation or otherwise, against any person.[2581]

Although OPA allows an RP to file contribution actions for oil spills, an OPA RP would have to look to state statutes, common law, or general maritime law for its rights to contribution in an oil pollution case. This means that the substance of an OPA RPs contribution action would have to be based on one of these legal regimes. For example, if the oil spill is caused by the negligent collision of another vessel with the RP's vessel, general maritime law would apply. One of the items in the RP's collision

2577 33 USC § 2710

2578 33 USC §§2709-2710

2579 33 USC §2710(a)

2580 33 USC §2710(b)

2581 33 USC §2710(c)

damage statement is going to be clean up costs or other damages that are paid out under section 2702(b)(2) of OPA.

In all OPA cases, where a contributorily negligent third party is in a contractual relationship with the RP, the RP can always sue the third party for contribution or indemnity. This would apply to cases involving third parties who could have been designated as jointly and severally liable RPs but were omitted for one reason or the other. Most contribution actions will involve third parties in one type of contractual relationship or the other with the RP. For instance, the third party could be the owner and operator of a tug, while the RP could be the owner and operator of a barge being pushed or pulled by the tug. If the barge owner believes the tug was partially responsible for the oil spill by a breach of any of its duties to the barge, it could sue the tug for contribution. If the tug is designated the RP and believes the barge breached its duty to it, it could also sue the barge for contribution. If the tug and barge are held liable as RPs and as a flotilla for the oil spill, the tug could sue the barge and vice versa for contribution or indemnity if there is a breach of legally imposed duty recognized under the law of tug and tow.

Alex L. Parks in his book, The Law Of Tug, Tow, & Pilotage,[2582] provides a virtual compendium of case law setting forth various duties of the tug, the breach of which may lead to a finding that the tug and its owner were negligent. A finding of negligence in an OPA contribution or indemnity action will mean that the tug will pay contribution or totally indemnify the RP for OPA removal costs and damages.

The tower must furnish a tug of sufficient power, properly equipped for the voyage, manned by a competent master and crew.[2583] The tug has a duty to properly make up to her tow, furnishing lines of sufficient length and strength, reasonably inspected for good condition.[2584] The tug is responsible for properly lighting its tow in accordance with applicable rules of the road.[2585] Perhaps most importantly, the tug is responsible for the

2582 Alex L. Parks & Edward V. Cattell, The Law Of Tug, Tow, & Pilotage 42 (3d ed. 1994).

2583 See Alex L. Parks & Edward V. Cattell, The Law of Tug, Tow, & Pilotage, at 127.

2584 Id. at 136-37.

2585 Id. at 143.

safe and proper navigation of the tow, not only with respect to rules of the road, but also with respect to weather and sea conditions.[2586] The tug must also maintain a lookout for the condition of the tow during the course of the voyage.[2587] Finally, the tug has a duty to properly anchor or moor her tow, notifying the barge owner or the pier or the fleeting area operator in appropriate circumstances.[2588]

Many of the cases in which tug negligence is alleged involve a change in condition of the barge, a manifestation of barge unseaworthiness, or a deterioration in weather during the course of the voyage in tow. In elaborating upon the standard of care of a prudent tug master, the appellate courts have held that the tug master faced with a problem once underway "need not act with the highest degree of skill and care, for that was not required of him,... but with reasonable skill and care."[2589] In *THE ALICE MORAN*, the court stated:

> "a court cannot charge a master because it seems to us, who were not there, that another choice would have been better. Only in case his conduct is outside the range of possible discretion, may we hold him for lack of seamanship; error to become fault must be gross and flagrant. It seems to us that, if error there was, it was one which lay within the discretion of capable seamen."[2590]

Furthermore, the tug has a duty, when circumstances permit, to pump out a sinking barge or to beach her.[2591] While the burden of proof is generally on the tow to show negligence, there is a narrow exception within

2586 Id. at 160-68.

2587 Id. at 145.

2588 Id. at 168-73.

2589 Eastern Tar Prods. v. Chesapeake Oil Transp. Co., 101 F.2d 30, 33, 1939 AMC 59, 63 (4th Cir. 1939); see Transp. Co. v. Steamtug Alice Moran (The Imoan), 67 F.2d 603, 605, 1933 AMC 1626, 1630 (2d Cir. 1933).

2590 *THE IMOAN*, 1933 AMC 1626, 1630 (2d Cir. 1933). In *DeMillo v. Scheepscot Pilots, Inc.*, the court distinguished and found negligent, the action of a tugmaster who proceeded to sea in the face of predicted conditions which he admitted to be unsatisfactory for towing the particular barge. 870 F.2d 746, 749, 1993 AMC 2699 (1st Cir. 1989).

2591 Curtis Bay Towing Co. v. Southern Lighterage Corp., 200 F.2d 33, 34, 1952 AMC 2034, 2036 (4th Cir. 1952).

which the courts have applied the doctrine of res ipsa loquitur, in effect, presuming the tug to have been negligent unless she can explain the incident. In *THE ANACONDA*, for example, the barge was found to have bottom damage sometime after the completion of the tow.[2592] A review of the tug's log, including some erased entries, revealed that the Anaconda was drawing less than twenty-four feet when entering the Savannah harbor channel, which was 500 feet wide with a minimum depth of thirty feet. Any grounding of the barge must have been outside the channel. While noting the dictate of *Stevens v. THE WHITE CITY*, the Fourth Circuit held:

> "But when an accident occurs under circumstances in which it would not ordinarily have occurred had the proper care been exercised, there is imposed upon the tug the duty of proving that the proper care was exercised. This is merely the application in admiralty of the well-known rule of res ipsa loquitur. And the cases amply support the application of this rule when in a reasonably wide and well-marked channel the tow leaves the channel and is grounded."[2593]

In grounding cases where the channel is ample, well charted, and well marked, the burden of proof does not shift, but the courts charge the tug with producing evidence that her fault did not cause the grounding.[2594]

Finally, tug and tow are considered as one, and collision rules are applied to the flotilla as if it were a single vessel.[2595] Only the tug, however, is responsible to third persons for navigational negligence of the flotilla.[2596] The vessel in control of the flotilla is the "dominant mind" responsible for actions of the flotilla, including damages that result from negligence.[2597]

2592 164 F.2d 224, 227 (4th Cir. 1947).

2593 Id. at 228; *see also* America Transp. Co. v. National Marine Serv., Inc., 497 F.2d 776, 1974 AMC 1943 (8th Cir. 1974).

2594 See *Mid-America Transp. Co.*, 497 F.2d at 780, 1974 AMC at 1949.

2595 *The Civilta & The Restless,* 103 U.S. 699, 700-01 (1880).

2596 Liverpool, Brazil & River Plate Steam Navigation Co. v. Brooklyn E. Dist. Terminal, 251 U.S. 48, 51-53 (1919) (holding that where a tug is at fault, only the tug and its freight need to be surrendered in limitation proceedings).

2597 See Sturgis v. Boyer, 65 U.S. (24 How.) 110, 122-23 (1861).

All these duties must be diligently performed by the tug in order to avoid being held liable as an OPA third party in a contribution action.

As explained earlier, the tow or the barge could also be held liable to the tug in its OPA contribution or indemnity suit. Generally, in the United States, the owner of a tow owes the duty to furnish a seaworthy vessel suitable to the conditions to be anticipated.[2598] If the tow has a crew aboard it, the crew must be competent and sufficient. In addition, the tow must be properly equipped with all necessary equipment, such as anchors and lights. The tow also has the duty to supply a properly equipped vessel. This means that tow must supply a vessel which has: (1) adequate anchors,[2599] (2) lights conforming to governmental regulations insofar as to placement and numbers,[2600] (3) adequate and proper lines,[2601] (4) a sound structure,[2602] and (5) proper steering equipment aboard it.[2603] Generally, whenever a tow sinks in calm weather, the tow is presumed to be unseaworthy.[2604]

Also, the tow must be properly manned if it has a crew aboard it. This means that the tow must: (1) not be undermanned,[2605] and (2) not have incompetent or negligent crew.[2606] The tow also has an absolute duty to follow the tug's instruction.[2607] The tow also has a duty to see to it that she

---

2598 See *Ruthie M.*, 1933 AMC 740 (E.D.N.Y).

2599 See *Nanticoke-Sea King*, 1929 AMC 201, 29 F.2d 5 (2d Cir. 1929).

2600 See *Asfalto*, 1931 AMC 1753 (2d Cir. 1931).

2601 See Barge Line v. Patience, 1944 AMC 871, 56 F.Supp. 200 (E.D.NY).

2602 See *Harrison*, 1927 AMC 163 (S.D.N.Y ).

2603 See *Hagood*, 1925 AMC 1646 (S.D.N.Y ).

2604 "When a vessel sinks at a sheltered berth in calm weather without any obvious explanation, a presumption arises that incursion of sea water which caused the sinking, and hence the loss, was due to unseaworthiness of vessel in some particular, but an insured can rebut such presumption by establishing that vessel was in fact seaworthy before sinking, and was neither overloaded nor improperly loaded, and if presumption is so rebutted, a counter-presumption arises that unexplained sinking and consequent loss was caused by some extraordinary, although unknown and unascertainable, peril of the sea." Boston Insurance Co. v. Dehydrating Process Co., 204 F.2d. 441 (1st Cir. 1953).

2605 See *Director*, 1927 AMC 1295 (4th Cir. 1927).

2606 See *Goodwin-Wang*, 1929 AMC 158 (E.D.N.Y) (Scow captain became unnecessarily alarmed at weather and cut his scow adrift).

2607 See *Mohawk-Harford*, 1953 AMC 1541, 207 F.2d 626 (3rd Cir. 1953).

is properly loaded and that its cargo of oil is properly stowed.[2608] Generally a tow will be held negligent if it is loaded below its Plimsoll line.[2609] By virtue of section 2709 of OPA, if a court finds that a tow has breached any of these duties and this breach contributed to the oil spill, it could be held liable in a contribution or indemnity suit by the tug against it.

An RP-owner of a discharging vessel or barge moored at a dock could also bring a contribution action against a fleeter or wharfinger. A wharfinger or fleeter is as an owner or a manager of a wharf, or one in charge of a waterfront warehouse storing landed cargo or cargo awaiting shipment.[2610] A "wharf" or "fleet" is a structure where vessels may be berthed in connection with the transfer of cargo or passengers, and wharfage is a fee charged against cargo or against the vessel.[2611] Thus, a fleet or fleeting facility is like a parking lot for barges and tugs. A fleeter has a duty to exercise due care under the circumstances, which includes the duty to adequately moor vessels in a fleet and to inspect the moorings periodically.[2612] The circumstances of each situation dictate how the fleeter should discharge its duties.[2613] As in other situations, industry custom will not excuse negligent practices.[2614] A fleeter who fails to adequately moor vessels loaded with oil in a fleet and neglects to inspect the moorings periodically could be liable for contribution in the event that an oil spill arises from the situation.

For instance, in the case of *Cargill v. Columbia Marine Services, Inc.*,[2615] a fleeter sought to avoid liability for the breakaway of barges from its fleeting facility by blaming a towboat which had picked up barges from

---

2608 See v. Elsie M., 1951 AMC 1311, 19 F. Supp. 455 (S.D. Tex. 1951).

2609 See v. Inland Waterways Corp., 1956 AMC 1760, 235 F.2d 741 (5th Cir. 1956), *rev'd on other grounds,* 349 U.S. 85 (1955).

2610 W.A. MCEWEN & A.H. LEWIS, ENCYCLOPEDIA OF NAUTICAL KNOWLEDGE 601 (1953); *see also* BLACK'S LAW DICTIONARY 1595 (6th ed. 1990).

2611 W.A. MCEWEN & A.H. LEWIS, ENCYCLOPEDIA OF NAUTICAL KNOWLEDGE, at 601.

2612 Cargill v. Columbia Marine Servs., Inc., 1986 AMC 1894, 1896 (S.D. Ohio 1986).

2613 Id. at 1896.

2614 Id. at 1896-97.

2615 Id. at 1896.

the fleeting facility and departed the fleeting facility shortly before the breakaway. The court held that the breakaway resulted solely from the fleeter's own negligent failure to order a standby tug at a time of high water and to ensure that the barges in its fleet were properly moored.[2616] The court held that the evidence did not support the fleeter's contention that the towboat had caused unreasonable or excessive swells or had traveled in an unreasonable manner.[2617] The court held that the fleeter must "anticipate the movement of vessels in the fleeting area, as that is the purpose for which the fleet exists."[2618] Thus, the fleeter should have expected and considered the tug's wake.

Likewise, in *John I. Hay Co. v. THE ALLEN B. WOOD*,[2619] a towboat had drilled or removed several barges out of a fleet and left the barges remaining in the fleet improperly moored. The watchman at the fleet had observed this unsatisfactory mooring and informed the fleeter's tug dispatcher, but neither took action to correct the unsafe condition. The court held that the towboat breached its duty to properly re-secure the remaining barges.[2620] It also found the fleeter had violated its obligations as a wharfinger and bailee for hire with respect to the remaining barges by not taking the necessary action to correct the improper mooring of the barges.[2621] These cases illustrate the fact that the fleeter could be liable in an OPA contribution action for its breach of this duty.

A fleeter must also exercise reasonable care and anticipate and consider adverse weather or river conditions which increase the potential danger to barge fleets.[2622] The fleeter is responsible for adjusting the lines

2616 Id. at 1894.

2617 Id. at 1896.

2618 Id. at 1898.

2619 121 F. Supp. 704, 706 (E.D. La. 1954), *aff'd sub nom.* Martin Oil Serv., Inc. v. John I. Hay Co., 219 F.2d 237 (5th Cir. 1955).

2620 Id. at 708.

2621 "Bisso was a wharfinger and bailee for hire of Hay's barges moored at its landing, and was responsible for caring for those vessels after they were committed to its custody." Id. at 708.

2622 See, e.g., United Barge Co. v. Notre Dame Fleeting & Towing Serv., Inc., 568 F.2d 599, 602-03, 1978 AMC 1163, 1166-67 (8th Cir. 1978); Union Mechling Corp. v. Tri-State Marine, Inc., 1981 AMC 2601, 2606 (N.D. Ill. 1981).

and moorings of barges in the fleet as conditions change and for monitoring those conditions to determine when such action is necessary.[2623] Furthermore, a fleeter may be required to provide lighting in the fleet to warn approaching vessels of dangers in the fleet.[2624] Various regulations may define light requirements.[2625] Like any wharfinger, a fleeter has the duty to mark underwater obstructions that pose a danger to vessels approaching its fleet.[2626] The failure of a fleeter or wharfinger to perform these duties could make it liable to the RP in an OPA third party contribution action. If an oil spill is caused by the failure of the wharfinger to anticipate adverse weather conditions, or by its failure to provide lighting, or by its failure to mark underwater obstructions that pose a danger to vessels approaching its fleet, it can be sued in a contribution action for the clean up costs and damages paid to claimants by the RP.

The owner or operator of a vessel from which oil has been discharged and who has been held liable as a third party may also bring a maritime product liability action based on maritime negligence or strict liability against the manufacturer, distributor or seller of a defective product or equipment that contributed to the oil spill incident. This product could be a faulty valve, storage tank, Global Positioning System, radars, plotters, engine, fire fighting equipment, cable, switches, ropes & hawsers, hoses & couplings, and tools.

The United States Supreme Court has held that tort claims for damages resulting from design and manufacturing defects in turbines which caused supertankers to malfunction while on the high seas fell within the admiralty jurisdiction.[2627] A suit for maritime product liability, confers admiralty jurisdiction on Federal District Courts, so Federal District courts can hear such suits without regard to diversity jurisdiction or Federal

---

2623 Monsanto Co. v. Port of St. Louis Invs., Inc., 350 F. Supp. 502, 517 (E.D. Mo. 1972).

2624 Radcliff Materials, Inc. v. M/V RAYCO, 1979 AMC 1362, 1370-71 (E.D. La. 1979).

2625 Id. at 1370-72.

2626 American Commercial Barge Line Co. v. Eagle Marine Indus., Inc., 1977 AMC 475, 483-84 (E.D. Mo. 1976).

2627 East River SteamShip Corp. v. TransAmerica Delaval Inc. 106 S.Ct. 2295 (1986).

question jurisdiction. Therefore, any challenge to a District Court's jurisdiction on those grounds would fail.

The court in the case of Kirkaldy v. Alamo Chemical Transport Co.,[2628] articulated the principle of product liability when it stated:

> "Thus, a manufacturer who fails to exercise reasonable care in the manufacture of a product which, unless carefully made, the manufacturer should recognize will involve an unreasonable risk of causing substantial physical injury to those who use the product for its intended purpose and to those whom the manufacturer should expect to be in the area of probable use, now may be sued in admiralty for physical injuries caused such persons during the product's use in a manner and purpose for which it was manufactured."[2629]

In the OPA context, the injury would be that which was suffered by the environment, like natural resources damages for which the RP is held liable. It would also include the damage to real or personal property as well as removal costs incurred by the RP.

In the case of *William Marshall v. Wellcraft Marine Inc.*,[2630] the court held that a products liability claim, brought by owners of a recreational yacht against yacht manufacturer, met the "connection with maritime activity" test for determining whether the tort action was governed by maritime law. The court based this finding on the fact the incident, during which yacht's electrical navigation and communication systems were disabled when vessel took on water in a storm, could have easily prompted commercial vessels in the vicinity to lend assistance, thereby diverting such vessels from their charted courses and disrupting their commercial operations.[2631] The incident could also have posed threat of collision to commercial vessels.[2632] The court pointed out that if the storage and maintenance of a pleasure boat docked at a marina is substantially related to a

---

2628 320 F.Supp. 631 (S.D. Tex. 1970).

2629 Id. at 634.

2630 103 F.Supp 2d 1099 (S.D. Ind. 1999).

2631 Id. at 1099.

2632 Id. at 1099.

traditional maritime activity, it is at least as likely that the navigation of a pleasure boat during actual maritime voyages between those dockings also involves traditional maritime activity.[2633] The maritime principle of comparative fault is applicable in maritime strict products liability cases.[2634] This means that the recovery of the RP against a third party found liable in a product liability case could be reduced by the percentage of the RP's fault.

The third party being sued for contribution could also be the negligent non-owner of a wreck or the negligent owner of a wreck that contributes to or causes an oil spill incident. The Wreck Act provides:

"It shall not be lawful to tie up or anchor vessels or other craft in navigable channels in such a manner as to prevent or obstruct the passage of other vessels or craft; or to sink, or permit or cause to be sunk, vessels or other craft in navigable channels; or to float loose timber and logs, or to float what is known as sack rafts of timber and logs in streams or channels actually navigated by steamboats in such manner as to obstruct, impede, or endanger navigation. And whenever a vessel, raft, or other craft is wrecked and sunk in a navigable channel, it shall be the duty of the owner, lessee, or operator of such sunken craft to immediately mark it with a buoy or beacon during the day and a lighted lantern at night, and to maintain such marks until the sunken craft is removed or abandoned, and the neglect or failure of the said owner, lessee, or operator so to do shall be unlawful; and it shall be the duty of the owner, lessee, or operator of such sunken craft to commence the immediate removal of the same, and prosecute such removal diligently, and failure to do so shall be considered as an abandonment of such craft, and subject the same to removal by the United States as provided for in sections 411 to 416, 418, and 502 of this title."[2635]

2633 Id. at 1107 (citing, Sisson, 497 U.S. at 367, 110 S.Ct. 2892 (1990); LEWINTER v. GENMAR INDUS., INC., 26 CAL.APP.4TH 1214, 1218-19, 32 CAL.RPTR.2D 305 (CAL. CT.APP.1994) (finding that maritime law governed tort claim arising out of a pleasure yacht's hull failure while at sea; merging its analysis on the two prongs of the connection test but concluding that the navigation of the pleasure boat bore a substantial relationship to traditional maritime activity).

2634 Alfred Lewis v. Timco Inc., 716 F.2d 1425 (5th Cir. 1983).

2635 See 33 USCA §409.

This section imposes upon the owner of a vessel sunk in a navigable channel the obligation to commence immediate removal of the vessel; the duty of an owner whose actions are responsible for the sinking is nondelegable and inescapable; if he fails to act to remove the obstruction, the government may undertake the task in the interest of navigational safety and the owner will be held liable not only for that cost but for any damages caused by the wreck in the meantime.[2636] Although responsibility for expenses incurred in removing a wreck from navigable waters of the United States may ultimately be laid at the door of a negligent party or parties, the immediate obligation to remove the obstruction has been imposed, both by statute and by regulation, upon the shipowner, regardless of whether the sinking was caused by his negligence.[2637]

Failure of an owner, and, in some circumstances, the United States to mark or remove sunken vessel does not render either liable to injured parties absent breach of their respective duties.[2638] An injured party may look solely to the owner, or alternatively, the government, in the first instance, but if both the government and the owner have satisfied their duties, a non-owning party who negligently caused the wreck is liable to an injured party.[2639] It has been held that a barge owner's search for his barge which had broken away was sufficient to satisfy its Wreck Act obligation, where: (1) the barge owner searched the surface of the river for its barge and could not find it and (2) followed up a reported sinking of a barge of its type with a fathometer and magnetometer search which led to an object under at least 67 feet of water with sufficient similarities to the missing barge to lead the magnetometer operator to identify it, mistakenly, as the missing barge, and (3) where conditions prevented a diver from identifying either that object or another object found upstream.[2640]

---

2636 Tennessee Valley Sand & Gravel Co. v. M/V Delta, 598 F.2d 930, *opinion corrected on denial of rehearing* 604 F.2d 13 (5th Cir. 1979).

2637 *In re Chinese Maritime Trust, Ltd.*, (2d. Cir), 478 F.2d 1357, *certiorari denied* 94 S.Ct. 894, 414 U.S. 1143, 39 L.Ed.2d 98 (1973).

2638 Nunley v. M/V Dauntless Colocotronis, 727 F.2d. 455 (5th Cir. 1984).

2639 Nunley v. M/V Dauntless Colocotronis, 727 F.2d. at 455.

2640 Nunley v. M/V Dauntless Colocotronis, 661 F.Supp. 1096 (E.D.La.1987), *affirmed in part, reversed in part on other grounds*, 863 F.2d 1190, *rehearing denied*, 869

Therefore, an RP whose discharge of oil was caused by its striking an unmarked sunken wreck can sue the owner of the vessel whose sinking was not caused by owner's negligence, for failing to mark the wreck as required by the Wreck Act. But if the owner was diligent as explained above and tried to do everything within its power to find it and mark it but was unable to, it will be free from liability to the RP. The RP will be able to sue a non-owning negligent tortfeasor who contributed to the sinking of the vessel that has become a navigation obstructing wreck. The court in Nunley v. M/V Dauntless Colocotronis,[2641] noted specifically:

> "We do not find either in the statutory language or in the legislative history or purposes of the Wreck Act--which in terms only places criminal liability upon those who negligently cause a wreck in the navigable waters, as well as upon a vessel's owner who fails to mark it--any legislative purpose to relieve the tortfeasor who caused the wreck of his civil liability for the damages consequent to his negligence."[2642]

This means that RPs may be able to have two bites at the apple, by being able to sue both the non-negligent owner of the wreck (did not cause its own sinking by negligence) and the negligent non-owner of the wreck who caused the sinking of the vessel constituting the wreck; provided the wreck owner failed to search diligently for the wreck and to mark it as required by law. So, if there was a previous litigation of the issue of the liability of the non-owning tortfeasor for the sinking and a judgment had been rendered holding the tortfeasor liable, it may be collaterally estopped from re-litigating the same issue in the RP's OPA contribution action.

One very important case that has addressed the OPA third party liability provision, is the case of National Shipping Company of Saudi Arabia, v. Moran Trade Corporation Of Delaware.[2643] This case involved an accident between a tugboat and a cargo vessel. The cargo vessel SAUDI DIRIYAH,

F.2d 1487 (5th Cir.1987).

2641 M/V Dauntless, 727 F.2d. at 465.

2642 Id. at 465.

2643 122 F.3d 1062, 1997 WL 560047 (4th Cir. 1997)

owned by National Shipping Company of Saudi Arabia (NSCSA), was docked at Norfolk International Terminals on the Elizabeth River. One night, the vessel was to undock and move upstream to different docks. NSCSA contracted with Moran to provide two tugboats to assist in the move; it also contracted with docking pilot John Morey to oversee the move.

After breasting away from the pier, the SAUDI DIRIYAH made a series of turns to maneuver up the river. To make these turns, the vessel used bow and stern thrusters that were mounted on the side. At some point during the turn, William Lusk, the captain of the tugboat HARRIET MORAN, brought the tug in on the SAUDI DIRIYAH's port quarter to assist with the turn into the channel. However, when the boats made contact, one of the tug's quarter bitts struck the SAUDI DIRIYAH's hull and opened a gash in the vessel's fuel oil tank. Oil began spilling into the river and continued to flow for the next two hours as the vessel moved upstream and docked.

Approximately 214.28 barrels (9,000 gallons) of oil leaked into the river from the spill. The cleanup was directed by the United States Coast Guard, which designated NSCSA as the "responsible party" under the OPA. NSCSA thus arranged and paid for all of the cleanup. NSCSA paid roughly $870,000 to those engaged to remove the oil, and it also paid $106,806.12 to settle claims of those whose property was damaged by the spill. In addition, the Coast Guard and the United States Navy incurred about $300,000 in costs, which they sought to recover from NSCSA. As of April 2001, the National Pollution Funds Center had billed NSCSA a total of $430, 335.78.[2644]

NSCSA brought an action in the United States District Court for the Eastern District of Virginia, claiming that Moran's negligence was the cause of the spill. NSCSA brought claims under OPA, the Virginia Water Control Law, and state common law. The Water Control Law claim was dismissed before trial.

---

2644 See National Pollution Funds Center Oil Spill data, p 8, M/V Saudi Diriyah, Federal Project Number 054509 (2001) (This information was provided by the National Pollution Funds Center (NPFC) in April of 2001 and the data is on file with the NPFC and is available upon request from the NPFC).

After a bench trial the district court found that Moran was negligent and that this negligence was the sole cause of the accident. The court therefore granted relief under the OPA, but it determined that OPA § 2704(a)(2) capped Moran's damages at $500,000. The court also concluded that none of the exceptions to this cap applied and that NSCSA could not circumvent the cap through its state law claims. However, under general maritime law the court awarded NSCSA $3,250 for the lost fuel and $16,050 for the damage to the hull. The court also awarded prejudgment interest.[2645]

NSCSA appealed from the district court's denial of its claims for relief under state law and from the finding that none of the exceptions to OPA's damages cap applies. Moran appealed from the district court's conclusion that Moran's negligence caused the spill.[2646] The court examined NSCSA's contentions that the district court erred in limiting Moran's liability under OPA's damage cap. Section 2702(d)(2)(A) of OPA states that:

> "if the act or omission of a third party that causes an incident occurs in connection with a vessel or facility owned or operated by the third party, the liability of the third party shall be subject to the limits provided in section 2704 of the title as applied with respect to the vessel or facility."

Section 2704(a)(2) puts the damages cap for any vessel other than a tank vessel at "$600 per gross ton or $500,000, whichever is greater." The Circuit court noted that since the tugboat weighed only 252 gross tons, the district court was right in limiting Moran's liability under OPA to $500,000.[2647] NSCSA attempted to get around this cap in two ways: it argued (a) that OPA's exceptions to the cap apply and (b) that it can recover the excess amount through state law claims under the Virginia Water Control Law and state common law.[2648] For the purposes of the current

2645 See. National Shipping Co. of Saudi Arabia (NSCSA) v. Moran Mid-Atlantic Corp., 924 F.Supp. 1436 (E.D.Va.1996).

2646 122 F.3d 1062, 1997 WL 560047, 2 (4th Cir.1997).

2647 If not for the "whichever is greater" language in the Act Moran's liability would have been limited to $151,200 instead of the greater $500,000, *see also,* NSCSA, 924 F.Supp. at 1447

2648 122 F.3d 1062, 1997 WL 560047, 2 (4th Cir.(Va.)).

legal analysis I would only focus on NSCSA's second way of trying to get around this limitation cap.

NSCSA argued that it could circumvent OPA's damages cap by bringing claims under the Virginia Water Control Act and state common law. The Water Control Act provides that "any person discharging or causing or permitting a discharge of oil into or upon state water shall be liable to any person for injury or damage to person or property, real or personal, loss of income, loss of the means of producing income, or loss of the use of the damaged property for recreational, commercial, industrial, agricultural or other reasonable uses, caused by such discharge."[2649] NSCSA argued that this section enables it to recover its response costs under OPA as well as property damage or economic losses. NSCSA also sought to bring Virginia common law indemnity and subrogation claims in order to collect its OPA expenses.[2650] In essence, NSCSA wanted to use state law to collect the costs that it incurred as the OPA "responsible party" in excess of the $500,000 liability cap.

The court concluded, however, that OPA prevents NSCSA from using state law to collect damages under OPA that exceed OPA's liability cap. Based on § 2704(a) of OPA, which specifically provides that "except as otherwise provided in this section, the total of the liability of a responsible party under section 2702 of this title and any removal costs incurred by, or on behalf of, the responsible party, with respect to each incident shall not exceed the limitations set forth herein," the court held that NSCSA was liable for the costs of the spill solely under OPA § 2702, and Moran was liable for those costs solely under § 2702.[2651] After having held that the exceptions that allow the breaking of limitation of OPA liability do not apply in the facts of this case, the court noted that the total of Moran's exposure under OPA cannot exceed $500,000.

(The court noted that under § 2702(d)(2) Moran is treated as a "responsible party" for purpose of the liability cap.)

2649 Va.Code. Ann. § 62.1-44.34:18(C)(4).

2650 1997 WL 560047, *3.

2651 1997 WL 560047, *4.

NSCSA claimed that OPA does not limit NSCSA's ability to collect its excess liability under OPA through state law claims. It cited OPA § 2718(a)(2), which states that "nothing in this chapter... shall... affect, or be construed or interpreted to affect or modify in any way the obligations or liabilities of any person under... State law, including common law." NSCSA argued that this section allows it to bring state law claims to recoup its expenses. The court in its rejection of NSCSA's argument, pointed out that NSCSA's reading of § 2718(a)(2) was far too broad, and that moreover that section only protects the rights of parties to bring additional claims based on liability that accrues under state law. The court in its reasoning also found that if NSCSA had itself been damaged by the oil, or if it had been successfully sued by others under state law for damages relating to the spill, then the OPA liability restrictions would not apply. In footnote three of its decision, the court borrowed the lower court's illustration of circumstances in which the OPA liability restrictions would not apply. The illustration goes thus:

> "a case where an oil spill causes one million dollars of damage, but the responsible party's liability under OPA is limited to $500,000. If the spill occurred in Virginia, the responsible party may have to pay for the full cost of the spill despite the liability limitation contained in OPA because a person's liability under Virginia's State Water Control Law may be higher than its liability under OPA.... If the spill was caused by the negligence of a third party, as it was in this case, it is reasonable to assume that the responsible party may: (1) sue the third party for contribution under section 2709 of OPA; and (2) be subrogated to the rights of the state and of other claimants under the State Water Control Law. In this way, the responsible party, whose ultimate liability was not restrained by OPA, could recover the full cost of the spill from the third party despite any liability limitation the third party might enjoy under OPA."[2652]

Juxtaposing this example to the case before it, the court noted that even though NSCSA was not prevented by OPA from bringing a general maritime claim for the loss of fuel and the damage to the SAUDI

2652 Id. citing, NSCSA, 924 F.Supp. at 1449.

DIRIYAH's hull, state law was never imposed to force NSCSA to cleanup the spill or to compensate its victims."[2653] But instead, "NSCSA's liability derived exclusively from OPA."[2654]

The court extrapolated further by pointing out that if a responsible party could recoup its OPA liability costs through state law claims as well as through OPA, the cap imposed by OPA § 2704(a) would be rendered meaningless. The court also found that Congress clearly intended for the cap to apply in situations like this one, since it established that "the liability of the third party shall be subject to the limits provided in section 2704 of the title."[2655] The court noted that even if anyone disagreed with this congressional policy judgment, the court is constrained by the text of the statute.

In conclusion the *NSCSA* court held that because NSCSA was seeking to recover costs imposed solely because of its liability under OPA, "the total of the liability [imposed on Moran] under section 2702 of the Act and any removal costs incurred by, or on behalf of, the responsible party, with respect to each incident shall not exceed" OPA limits-- for Moran, $500,000.[2656] Based on the foregoing the lower court decision was affirmed by the Circuit court.[2657] So, for the purposes of indemnification and contribution, this decision makes it clear that it is the tonnage capacity of a sole-cause third party vessel that will be used to compute the limitation amount, not the tonnage capacity of the responsible party's vessel. The case also makes it clear that the sole-cause third party can be made to indemnify the responsible party only to the full extent of what it expended in cleanup and other related liability, but this would always be subject to the tonnage capacity limitation of the third party's vessel except if an exception that allows the breaking of limitation applies. If NSCSA was able to prove that that one of these exceptions was applicable, Moran would not have been able to limit its liability. This decision, if it was correctly decided, only makes it clear to OPA responsible parties claiming indem-

2653 *NSCSA*, 924 F.Supp. at 1449.

2654 Id.

2655 See 33 U.S.C. § 2702(d)(2)(A).

2656 1997 WL 560047, *4.

2657 Id.

nity and contribution from a sole-cause third party that the courts would not treat a sole cause third party being sued for indemnity and contribution differently from any ordinary responsible party being sued directly by any claimant for oil spill removal costs and damages.

The decision of the *NSCSA* court appears to have some inherent flaws in it. This is so because of its erroneous application of OPA's section 2702(d)(2)(A) to the case. Section 2702(d) specifically addresses the issue of third part liability under the OPA. This section specifically provides as follows:

> "If the act or omission of a third party that causes an incident occurs in connection with a vessel or facility owned or operated by the third party, the liability of the third party shall be subject to the limits provided in section 2704 of this title as applied with respect to the vessel or facility."

The *NSCSA* court applied this subsection to Moran and limited its liability to the tonnage capacity of the tug, which had 252 gross registered tons. The *NSCSA* court's application of this limit of liability is wrong. This is due to the fact that this subsection is supposed to apply to sole cause third parties as recognized and defined by sections 2703(a)(3) and 2702(d)(1)(A). Section 2702(d)(1)(A) specifically provides that a sole cause third party can only be treated as a responsible party for purposes of determining liability if there was no contractual relationship between that sole cause third party and the responsible party. Because NSCSA had a towage contract with Moran, section 2702(d)(1)(A) should not have been applied to Moran. The court ought to have applied 2702(d)(2)(B). This section provides as follows:

> "In any other case, the liability of a third party or parties shall not exceed the limitation which would have been applicable to the responsible party of the vessel or facility from which the discharge actually occurred if the responsible party were liable."

Section 2702(d)(2)(B) ought to have been invoked by the appellant, NSCSA. So, one should not blame the court entirely for not applying it. Both the court and the appellant, NSCSA should share the blame. Section

2702(d)(2)(B) is applicable because it does not refer to sole cause third parties who were not in a contractual relationship with the responsible party but it refers specifically to "other cases" that do not fall into that category. In other words section 2702(d)(2)(B) does not apply to sole cause third parties who are supposed to be treated as responsible parties. But instead it applies to all other third parties which would include sole cause third parties in a contractual relationship with the responsible party, contributory cause third parties, as well as third parties who do not own or operate the vessel from which the oil was discharged. If section 2702(d)(2)(B) had been applied by the *NSCSA* court, Moran's liability would have been limited to the limitation which would have been applicable to the responsible party of the vessel or facility from which the discharge actually occurred. Because the appellant, NSCSA could not claim the third party defense in section 2703(a)(3) due to the towage contract between NSCSA and Moran, that means that NSCSA was absolutely liable under the OPA, because the oil was actually discharged from NSCSA's vessel. Because the gross tonnage capacity of NSCSA's vessel was 25,036 gross registered tons, the limitation provision applicable to the vessel is $1,200 per gross ton.[2658] Based on this limitation figure, NSCSA would have been able to limit its liability to a colossal amount of $15,021,600. Because of the provision of section 2702(d)(2)(B), this higher limitation figure should have been applied to Moran by the *NSCSA* court. It is my hope that a future claimant with a case with similar facts and a similar questions of law as NSCSA's would invoke section 2702(d)(2)(B), and the court involved would seize the opportunity to expose the flaws in this decision.

**Liability of Sole Cause and Non-Sole Cause Third Parties – 33 USC § 2702(d).**

Statutory provisions:

"§ 2702 -

2658 See 33 USCA §2704(a)(1)(A)-(B).

(d) Liability of third parties

(1) In general

**(A) Third party treated as responsible party**

Except as provided in subparagraph (B), in any case in which a responsible party establishes that a discharge or threat of a discharge and the resulting removal costs and damages **were caused solely by an act or omission of one or more third parties** described in section 2703(a)(3) of this title (or solely by such an act or omission in combination with an act of God or an act of war), the third party or parties shall be treated as the responsible party or parties for purposes of determining liability under this subchapter.

**(B) Subrogation of responsible party**

If the responsible party alleges that the discharge or threat of a discharge was caused solely by an act or omission of a third party, the responsible party--

**(i)** in accordance with section 2713 of this title, shall pay removal costs and damages to any claimant; and

**(ii)** shall be entitled by subrogation to all rights of the United States Government and the claimant to recover removal costs or damages from the third party or the Fund paid under this subsection."[2659]

This part of chapter ten will briefly discuss the full ramifications of the above section. Because of the provisions of this subsection, the government does not need to go after a sole-cause third party. It is very hard to find a case where the government sues a sole cause third party directly, unless the sole cause third party is a deep pocket, while the actual initial-RP-source of the oil discharge is a shallow pocket. The government will go after whoever can pay its cost of cleanup and related oil spill damages.

2659 33 USC § 2702.

Section 2702(d)(1)(A) provides that except as provided in subparagraph (B), in any case in which a responsible party establishes that a discharge or threat of a discharge and the resulting removal costs and damages were caused solely by an act or omission of one or more third parties described in section 2703(a)(3) of this title (or solely by such an act or omission in combination with an act of God or an act of war), the third party or parties shall be treated as the responsible party or parties for purposes of determining liability under this section. This section refers to the **sole cause third party**. It does not apply to a non-sole cause third party. In other words **non-sole cause third parties** cannot be treated as RPs under OPA. Non-sole cause third parties are third parties whose action or omissions were not the sole cause of the oil spill. In other words, the acts and omissions of the RP combined with their acts and omissions to cause the oil spill. An RP has a number of options against a non-sole cause third party. They include suing the non-sole cause third party for contribution as provided for under § 2709 of OPA, which specifically provides that an RP may bring a civil action for contribution against any other person who is liable or potentially liable **under OPA or another law**. It is perhaps a good idea for the owner and operator of a vessel or facility that could be potentially liable under OPA to enter into indemnity agreements with third parties with which it has privity of contract to make it easy for the RP to get 100% reimbursement from those third parties for oil spills caused solely by them. And where they merely contributed to the oil spill, the agreements will make it easy for the RP to get contribution from the third party. This is a cheap way to allocate responsibility ahead of time. If a **non-sole cause third party** is sued for contribution by the RP based on the provisions of OPA it might be able to limit its liability to OPA limits, however if it is sued under state law, common law or any other federal law, its liability limits would probably be dictated by those laws not OPA.

Unlike in oil spills involving sole-cause third parties, the RP has no subrogation rights in claims involving non-sole cause third parties.[2660] Subparagraph (B) provides that if the responsible party alleges that the

---

2660 33 USC 2702(d)(1)(B)(ii).

discharge or threat of a discharge **was caused solely** by an act or omission of a third party, the responsible party- (i) in accordance with section 2713 (claims procedure) of the OPA, shall pay removal costs and damages to any claimant; and (ii) shall be entitled by subrogation to all rights of the United States Government and the claimant to recover removal costs or damages from the third party or the Fund paid under this subsection. This section specifically addresses the question of the liability and rights of a person entitled to the third party defense in section 2703(a) of the OPA. Section 2702(d)(1)(B) clearly and unambiguously ensures that a responsible party who successfully invokes the third party defense cannot walk away from the oil spill. The responsible party must pay removal costs and damages to any claimant. After making such payments, the responsible party can sue the sole cause third party for indemnity by virtue of being subrogated to the rights of the US government or a private claimant. The initial RP can also claim indemnity from the Fund, because it is entitled to the third-party defense.[2661]

At first blush it might appear that there is a conflict between section 2702(d)(1)(A) and section 2702(d)(1)(B). Because the former says that the sole cause third party shall be treated as the RP for liability purposes, while the latter says that the initial RP must pay removal costs and damages in sole-cause third party situations and then seek indemnity from the sole-cause third party by virtue of its subrogation rights. But a closer perusal of these two subsections would reveal that there is really no conflict between both sections because the former makes its provisions subject to the provisions of the latter. Apart from this, the initial RP invoking a sole-cause third party defense in a typical oil spill may need some time to prove its entitlement to the third party defense. It is not reasonable to wait for the RP to prove the defense before determining who pays removal costs and OPA damage claims. There might be a lot of buck-passing after an oil spill involving two or more parties claiming innocence, that it would not be fair to make government or private claimants wait for the conclusion of investigations before their claims for removal costs or damages can be

2661 33 USC §2702(d)(1)(B)(ii).

paid. The rights of subrogation provided to the initial RP in subsection (B)(ii) removes any aura of unfairness in subsection (B)(i).

### Contribution Actions against the Government

Just like CERCLA, OPA allows for contribution against any other person who is liable or potentially liable under the OPA or any other law, as long as the action is brought pursuant to section 2717 of OPA (Litigation, jurisdiction, and venue provision).[2662] The US government could be held liable as a jointly and severally liable RP under OPA subject to the doctrine of sovereign immunity. For instance, if the oil spill is caused by a government owned vessel engaged in commercial activities, the government could be held liable as owner or operator of the vessel. This means that if another person has been held primarily liable as the RP, it can sue the government for contribution. The RP can sue the government based on the provisions of OPA, or common law or admiralty law. This claim would probably be made against the government **directly in personam**. But, since it is a claim for contribution against the government, the RP would have paid removal costs and damages caused by the oil spill already. All it will be asking the Federal government for is reimbursement for what it has paid.

In many cases, the government may assert that it is immune from liability for its negligence under the discretionary function exception to the government's waiver of sovereign immunity under the Suits in Admiralty Act.[2663] This discretionary function exception excludes from the waiver of sovereign immunity:

> "any claim based upon an act or omission of an employee of the Government, exercising due care, in the execution of a statute or regulation, whether or not such statute or regulation be valid, or based upon the exercise or performance or the failure to exercise or perform a discretionary function or duty on the part of a

2662 See 33 USCA §2709.

2663 See 28 USCA §2680(a).

federal agency or an employee of the Government, whether or not the discretion involved be abused."[2664]

Apart from this, the Suits in Admiralty Act provides that

"no vessel owned by the United States or by any corporation in which the United States or its representatives shall own the entire outstanding capital stock (or in the possession of the United States or of such corporation or operated by or for the United States or such corporation), and no cargo owned or possessed by the United States or by such corporation, shall after March 9, 1920,........................ be subject to arrest or seizure by judicial process in the United States or its possessions."[2665]

This provision of the suits in Admiralty Act serves various purposes. First, this section was to restore immunity from seizure that had been taken away from merchant vessels owned by United States by the Shipping Act of 1916, as interpreted by Supreme Court.[2666] Second, it was passed to forbid seizure of vessel or cargo owned, operated, or possessed by government when such vessel or cargo is being owned and operated in the merchant service, and to give a claimant against either the vessel or the cargo a right to sue the government in personam to recover upon such claim.[2667] **So, this provision was adopted to provide suit in personam in lieu of previous unlimited right to bring suit in rem against United States vessels** in United States ports.[2668] It appears that in the contribution action brought against the United States, the RP may not be able to seize the vessel and the contribution action may be subject to the discretionary function exception to the government's waiver of sovereign immunity under the Suits in Admiralty Act. But the instant analysis applies mostly to a vessel engaged in commercial activities at the time it contributed to

2664 Id. at §2680(a).

2665 See 46 App. USCA §741.

2666 Eastern Transp. Co. v. United States, 98 F.Supp. 36 (E.D.N.Y.1951).

2667 Olavarria & Co. v. United States., 56 F.Supp. 758 (S.D.Ala.1944).

2668 Szyka v. U. S. Secretary of Defense, 525 F.2d 62. (2d Cir. 1975).

an oil spill. As was explained earlier in the treatise, these types of vessels are not Public Vessels and are therefore not covered by the OPA provision, excluding oil spills from Public Vessels from OPA liability.[2669]

As for onshore and offshore facilities, although a Federal agency, State, municipality, commission, or political subdivision or any other interstate body may not be held liable as an OPA RP by virtue of merely being a lessor, assignor or permittor of a facility, it could be held liable if it is being sued as a third party who contributed directly to the oil spill. This is because of the language of section 2709 of OPA that allows an RP to sue for contribution under any other law. So, in contribution cases, the RP need not confine itself to the four walls of OPA, an RP can scale the four walls of OPA and utilize non-OPA remedies that will enable it to get appropriate contribution from the government for the government's role in the oil spill. The provision exempting government from liability when it acts as lessor, assignor, or permittor merely recognizes that the government may not be in control of the circumstances leading to an oil spill because the lessee, assignee, or permitee is the one in occupation, possession and control of the government owned facility. Where the government has not leased the facility to anyone and it is in sole occupation, possession and control of the facilities at the time of the oil spill and contributed directly to the chain of events causing the oil spill, the government could be sued for contribution but the outcome of the suit will be subject to the sovereign immunity doctrine.

2669 See 33 USCA §2702(c).

# Chapter Eleven

# THE NPFC'S OIL SPILL LIABILITY TRUST FUND – 33 USC § 2712

Statutory provisions:
"§ 2712. Uses of Fund

(a) Uses generally

The Fund shall be available to the President for--

**(1)** the payment of removal costs, including the costs of monitoring removal actions, determined by the President to be consistent with the National Contingency Plan--

**(A)** by Federal authorities; or

**(B)** by a Governor or designated State official under subsection (d) of this section;

**(2)** the payment of costs incurred by Federal, State, or Indian tribe trustees in carrying out their functions under section 2706 of this title for assessing natural resource damages and for developing and implementing plans for the restoration, rehabilitation, replacement, or acquisition of the equivalent of damaged resources determined by the President to be consistent with the National Contingency Plan;

**(3)** the payment of removal costs determined by the President to be consistent with the National Contingency Plan as a result of, and damages resulting from, a discharge, or a substantial threat of a discharge, of oil from a foreign offshore unit;

**(4)** the payment of claims in accordance with section 2713 of this title for uncompensated removal costs determined by the President to be consistent with the National Contingency Plan or uncompensated damages;

**(5)** the payment of Federal administrative, operational, and personnel costs and expenses reasonably necessary for and incidental to the implementation, administration, and enforcement of this Act (including, but not limited to, sections 1004(d)(2), 1006(e), 4107, 4110, 4111, 4112, 4117, 5006, 8103, and Title IV) and subsections (b), (c), (d), (j), and (l) of section 1321 of this title, with respect to prevention, removal, and enforcement related to oil discharges, provided that--

**(A)** not more than $25,000,000 in each fiscal year shall be available to the Secretary for operating expenses incurred by the Coast Guard;

**(B)** not more than $30,000,000 each year through the end of fiscal year 1992 shall be available to establish the National Response System under section 1321(j) of this title including the purchase and prepositioning of oil spill removal equipment; and

**(C)** not more than $27,250,000 in each fiscal year shall be available to carry out subchapter IV of this chapter.

(b) Defense to liability for Fund

The Fund shall not be available to pay any claim for removal costs or damages to a particular claimant, to the extent that the incident, removal costs, or damages are caused by the gross negligence or willful misconduct of that claimant.

(c) Obligation of Fund by Federal officials

The President may promulgate regulations designating one or more Federal officials who may obligate money in accordance with subsection (a) of this section.

(d) Access to Fund by State officials

(1) Immediate removal

In accordance with regulations promulgated under this section, the President, upon the request of the Governor of a State or pursuant to an agreement with a State under paragraph (2), may obligate the Fund for payment in an amount not to exceed $250,000 for removal costs consistent with the National Contingency Plan required for the immediate removal of a discharge, or the mitigation or prevention of a substantial threat of a discharge, of oil.

(2) Agreements

(A) In general

The President shall enter into an agreement with the Governor of any interested State to establish procedures under which the Governor or a designated State official may receive payments from the Fund for removal costs pursuant to paragraph (1).

(B) Terms

Agreements under this paragraph--

**(i)** may include such terms and conditions as may be agreed upon by the President and the Governor of a State;

**(ii)** shall provide for political subdivisions of the State to receive payments for reasonable removal costs; and

**(iii)** may authorize advance payments from the Fund to facilitate removal efforts.

(e) Regulations

The President shall--

**(1)** not later than 6 months after August 18, 1990, publish proposed regulations detailing the manner in which the authority to obligate the Fund and to enter into agreements under this subsection shall be exercised; and

**(2)** not later than 3 months after the close of the comment period for such proposed regulations, promulgate final regulations for that purpose.

(f) Rights of subrogation

Payment of any claim or obligation by the Fund under this Act shall be subject to the United States Government acquiring by subrogation all rights of the claimant or State to recover from the responsible party.

(g) Audits

The Comptroller General shall audit all payments, obligations, reimbursements, and other uses of the Fund, to assure that the Fund is being properly administered and that claims are being appropriately and expeditiously considered. The Comptroller General shall submit to the Congress an interim report one year after August 18, 1990. The Comptroller General shall thereafter audit the Fund as is appropriate. Each Federal agency shall cooperate with the Comptroller General in carrying out this subsection."[2670]

The National Pollution Fund Center (NPFC) is the fiduciary agent for the Oil Spill Liability Trust Fund and the portion of Superfund accessible to the U.S. Coast Guard.[2671] CERCLA established a national "Superfund" for response/remediation of hazardous waste incidents. Both are federally-managed funds that distinctly support liability and

2670 33 USC § 2712.

2671 United States Coast Guard-Roles and Mission of the National Pollution Funds Center < http://www.uscg.mil/hq/npfc/brochure.htm > (Last modified March 3, 2001)

compensation regimes pertaining to pollution from oil or hazardous substances, respectively.[2672]

The Oil Spill Liability Trust Fund (the Fund) was originally established under Section 9509 of the Internal Revenue Code of 1986. It was one of several similar Federal trust funds funded by various levies set up to provide for the costs of water pollution. The Oil Pollution Act of 1990 (OPA) generally consolidated the liability and compensation schemes of some prior Federal oil pollution laws and authorized the use of the Fund, which consolidated the funds supporting those regimes. [2673] Those prior legal regimes included the Federal Water Pollution Control Act; Trans-Alaska Pipeline Authorization Act; Deepwater Port Act; and Outer Continental Shelf Lands Act. The Fund is available to pay for, inter alia, removal costs and certain other expenses, claims and damages, as well as obligations under the Federal Water Pollution Control Act.[2674] The Fund is also used for costs not directly paid by a responsible party (RP) or guarantor, including costs to respond to "mystery spills" for which there is no identified RP.[2675] Mystery spills are an unfortunate reality in the US today. For instance, on 10 August, 1994, the US Coast Guard received reports of a mystery oil spill on the lower Columbia River near Wauna, Oregon, USA.[2676] Oil washed up on the shoreline approximately 5 km from Wauna. The impacted area included a nearly 2-km x 5 -m band of tar balls on the beach, 1 km of oiled rocks, and 250 pilings with a 30-cm band of oil.[2677] The USCG contracted with Foss Environmental to clean up the spill. Foss provided 11 workers and one fast response vessel. The USCG took oil

2672 Id.

2673 The Oil Pollution Act § 9001 (amending 26 U.S.C. § 9509 (1988)). The Oil Spill Liability Trust Fund was established by section 9509 of the Internal Revenue Code.

2674 Oil Pollution Act § 1012, (33 USCA §2712), 9001 (amending 26 U.S.C. § 9509).

2675 See United States Coast Guard, National Pollution Funds Center: Oil Spill Liability Trust Fund- Guidance And Information For Use During An Oil Spill, < http://www.uscg.mil/hq/npfc/media.htm > (Last updated November 29, 2000). Mystery Spills are oil spills in which there are no identifiable RPs.

2676 See Mystery Oil Spill Occurs in Columbia River, Oil Spill Intelligence Report Cutter Information,Vol.17, No. 31 ISSN: 0195-3524, 1994 WL 2521917, August 18, 1994.

2677 Id.

samples from several vessels in the vicinity at the time of the spill, but was not able to immediately match the oil on the beaches with a particular vessel.[2678] This example underlines the need to make the Fund available for costs related to "mystery spills."

Once payments are made, the Fund becomes subrogated to the rights of the claimants or of a state who received them to recover from the responsible party. The fund is on deposit with the U.S. Treasury, which has to pay interest that may further build the capital. Generally, a claim must be presented to the responsible party or guarantor before being presented to the Fund. The OPA requires these parties to follow the procedures by which claims may be presented.[2679] The OPA also allows a responsible party and indirectly the guarantor to seek indemnity from the fund for clean-up costs that exceed the statutory limit. The Fund can provide up to $1 billion per incident for uncompensated cleanup costs and can compensate oil-spill victims when liability limits have been reached or if the spiller and an injured party cannot reach an agreement on a settlement.

The Fund receives funds from four primary sources: (1) an oil tax (five cents a barrel on domestically produced or imported oil collected from the oil industry; this is suspended when the fund reaches $1 billion but may be reinstated if the fund falls below this amount), the levy was in force from 1990-1993 and it generated $20m a month in revenue, and it was turned off in 1993 when the key target of building a $1bn oil spill Liability Trust Fund was achieved.[2680] However the levy will be reinstated if the fund falls below $1bn; (2) interest on fund principal; (3) cost recovery from responsible parties (The parties responsible for oil spills are liable for costs and damages. All monies recovered go either back to replenish the Fund or to the U.S. Treasury); and (4) penalties (including civil penalties assessed to the responsible parties).

The OPA allows for claims for uncompensated removal costs consistent with the National Contingency Plan and damages resulting from an

---

2678 Id.

2679 Oil Pollution Act § 2713(a)

2680 Jim Mulrenan, Pollution fund hits $1bn target, US oil spill clean up tax suspended Lloyd's List Int'l, Aug. 2, 1993, at 1.

oil pollution incident to include the following: uncompensated removal costs; natural resource damages; real or personal property damages; loss of subsistence use of natural resources; net loss of government revenues; loss of profits or impairment of earning capacity; and net costs of providing increased or additional public services.[2681]

To better address funding needs, the Fund has been subdivided into an Emergency Fund and a Main Fund. **The Emergency Fund** ensures rapid and effective response to oil spills without requiring further Congressional appropriations. Through this portion of the Fund, up to $50,000,000 is provided each year to fund removal activities and to initiate natural resource damage assessments.[2682] Money available in the Emergency Fund also includes a carryover from prior years. This portion of the Fund (the Emergency Fund) may be used for the following removal actions and costs/services:

*Removal Actions*- containing and removing oil from water and shorelines; preventing or minimizing oil pollution where there is a substantial threat of discharge; and taking other actions related to minimizing the damage to public health and welfare.[2683]

*Removal Costs/Services*- contract services (e.g., cleanup contractors and administrative support to document removal actions); salaries for government personnel not normally available for oil-spill responses and for temporary government employees hired for the duration of the spill response; equipment used in removals; chemical testing required to identify the type and source of oil; and proper disposal of recovered oil and oily debris.[2684]

The legislative history of the OPA reveals that a dispute had arisen among several Federal agencies with respect to reimbursements from the Fund established by section 311(k) of the FWPCA for costs incurred by

---

2681 Oil Pollution Act § 2702(a)-(b)

2682 US Department of Interior, Minerals Management Services- Gulf of Mexico Region Offshore Information, The Oil Spill Liability Trust Fund (Last updated January 19, 2001) < http://www.gomr.mms.gov/homepg/regulate/regs/laws/osltf.html >

2683 Id.

2684 Id.

those agencies while responding to the Exxon Valdez oil spill.[2685] At issue during the drafting stages of the OPA bill was whether Federal agencies should be reimbursed only for the incremental costs incurred as the result of a spill (primarily travel and overtime), or whether the base salaries of individuals diverted from other duties to work on oil spill response should be included. The Congress was of the view that both incremental and base costs should be included when calculating the cost of Federal efforts to respond to a spill except for persons normally available for oil spill response. Congress however emphasized that reimbursement for these costs should be sought from the responsible party.[2686] Congress also intended that agencies that assist in oil spill response actions should be fully compensated by the Fund or by the responsible party for that assistance.[2687]

**The Main Fund** (exclusive of the Emergency Fund) can be used to pay claims without further appropriation and may be used for other actions when Congress appropriates the funds. Such additional actions may include Federal administrative, operational, and personnel costs;[2688] natural resource damage assessments and restoration;[2689] and research and development.[2690]

On February 20, 1991, the National Pollution Funds Center (NPFC) was commissioned to serve as fiduciary agent for the Fund.[2691] Since Federal On-Scene Coordinators need funds immediately to respond directly to a spill or to monitor responsible parties' actions, the NPFC established a system to provide funds 24-hours a day.[2692] In addition to dispersing funds for removal actions, the NPFC also administers the Fund by monitoring

---

2685 1990 U.S.C.C.A.N. 792, H.R. Conf. Rep. No. 653, 101ST Cong., 2nd Sess. 1990, 1990 WL 132747 (Leg.Hist).

2686 1990 U.S.C.C.A.N. 792.

2687 Id.

2688 33 USC §2712(a)(5).

2689 33 USC §2712(a)(2).

2690 33 USC §2712(a)(5), see also, §2704(d)(2).

2691 US Department of Interior, Minerals Management Services- Gulf of Mexico Region Offshore Information, The Oil Spill Liability Trust Fund (Last updated January 19, 2001) < http://www.gomr.mms.gov/homepg/regulate/regs/laws/osltf.html > .

2692 Id.

the use of funds, by processing third-party claims submitted to the Fund, and by pursuing cost recovery from responsible parties for removal costs and damages paid by the Fund. Generally the owner or operator of the vessel or facility that is the source of a discharge or substantial threat of a discharge will be liable for removal costs and damages resulting from an oil-spill incident. Therefore, claimants must first seek reimbursement from the responsible party or guarantor. If a claimant is dissatisfied with the actions of the responsible party/guarantor with respect to the claim, the claimant may elect to litigate against the responsible party or submit the claim to the Fund.[2693] The controlling legal authority for Fund claims can be found in OPA (33 U.S.C. 2701 et seq.) and that statute's implementing regulations at 33 CFR 136.

The legislative history of the OPA reveals that the US Congress had three purposes in mind for setting up the Fund. The first purpose of the Fund was to provide a source of money for immediate cleanup activities or damage compensation in the event a spiller does not act promptly.[2694] In such a case, the Fund would be used for removal costs and would be available for prompt damage compensation. The Fund would then be subrogated to all rights against the spiller for all expenditures up to the extent the spiller is liable, given any limits or defenses to liability.[2695]

The second purpose of the Fund was to provide a source of compensation for claims which are not settled by the spiller by virtue of a limit or a defense.[2696] This was to ensure compensation of victims regardless of the liability of the spiller.[2697] Congress was convinced that increased liability limits and coverage of third party damages would help fix responsibility for cleanup and damages where it belongs--on the discharger.[2698] Congress wanted to guarantee through the instrumentality of the Fund that the costs

---

2693 Id.

2694 1990 U.S.C.C.A.N. 727, S. Rep. No. 94, 101ST Cong., (1st Sess. 1989), 1989 WL 225005 (Leg.Hist).

2695 1990 U.S.C.C.A.N. 727.

2696 Id.

2697 Id.

2698 Id.

associated with a spill are compensated, not just those within the spiller's limit of liability, through a mechanism which spreads these excess costs to all users of oil.[2699]

The third purpose was to provide funds for compensation in the event the spiller cannot be identified or located, or is judgment proof.[2700] Congress believed that even though the 1851 Federal Limitation of Liability Act would be explicitly made inoperative by the OPA bill for claims arising under OPA or State law, there may be cases where the assets of the owner or operator are not sufficient to meet the liability.[2701] The Fund assures compensation in such cases, with the cost borne by all owners and users of oil.[2702]

## A. RECOVERY OF ATTORNEY'S FEES BY THE NPFC AND PRIVATE CLAIMANT'S, & NPFC'S RECOVERY OF ADMINISTRATIVE AND ADJUDICATIVE COSTS

The OPA specifically provides that at the request of the Secretary, the Attorney General shall commence an action on behalf of the Fund to recover any compensation paid by the Fund to any claimant pursuant to this chapter, and all costs incurred by the Fund by reason of the claim, including interest (including prejudgment interest), administrative and adjudicative costs, and attorney's fees.[2703] This section provides further that such an action may be commenced against any responsible party or (subject to section 2716 of this title) guarantor, or against any other person who is liable, pursuant to any law, to the compensated claimant or to the Fund, for the cost or damages for which the compensation was paid.

Even though the OPA allows the government to recover attorney's fees from a responsible party, it is not yet entirely clear whether a claimant can recover attorney's fees against the Fund. But the judicial interpretation of a similar provision in the Trans-Alaska Pipeline Authorization Act could provide some guidance.

---

2699 Id.

2700 Id.

2701 Id.

2702 Id. at 727.

2703 See 33 U.S.C.A. § 2715(c).

In *Alyeska Pipeline Service Co. v. Wilderness Society,*[2704] the Supreme Court had affirmed the American Rule that, absent express statutory authority, bad faith, or willful disobedience of a court order, each party should bear the cost of its own attorney's fees.[2705] Exceptions to the American Rule are narrowly circumscribed.[2706]

In *Re the GLACIER BAY,*[2707] plaintiffs brought an action under the Trans-Alaska Pipeline Authorization Act (TAPAA) and the Alaska Environmental Conservation Act, to recover economic and business loss damages they sustained as result of oil spill off Alaska shoreline. The court held that they were entitled to award of reasonable attorney fees from government fund as matter of fairness, inasmuch as government fund could recover attorney fees from the vessel owner and operator in a subrogation action under the Trans-Alaska Pipeline Authorization Act.[2708]

TAPAA did not contain express statutory authority for awarding attorney's fees prior to the amendments contained in the Oil Pollution Act of 1990, which was enacted subsequent to the briefing on the motions in the *GLACIER BAY* case but prior to oral argument. The Oil Pollution Act of 1990 amended TAPAA in several ways, including elimination of the $14 million vessel owner's and operator's threshold liability. The applicable amendment read as follows:

"(d) Payment Of Claims By Fund--Section 204(c)(3) of the Trans-Alaska Pipeline Authorization Act (43 U.S.C. 1653(c)(3)) is amended by adding at the end the following: "The Fund shall expeditiously pay claims under this subsection, including such $14,000,000, if the owner or operator of a vessel has not paid any such claim within 90 days after such claim has been submitted to such owner or operator. Upon payment of any such claim, the Fund shall be subrogated under

2704 421 U.S. 240, 95 S.Ct. 1612, 44 L.Ed.2d 141 (1975).

2705 Zambrano v. City of Tustin, 885 F.2d 1473, 1481 (9th Cir.1989).

2706 Miller-Wohl Co., Inc. v. Commissioner of Labor & Industry, 694 F.2d 203, 204 (9th Cir.1982).

2707 In re the GLACIER BAY, 746 F.Supp 1379 (D. Alaska 1990).

2708 746 F.Supp. 1379, Trans-Alaska Pipeline Authorization Act, §§ 202-206, as amended, 43 U.S.C.A. §§ 1651-1655.

applicable State and Federal laws to all rights of any person entitled to recover under this subsection. In any action brought by the Fund against an owner or operator or an affiliate thereof to recover amounts under this paragraph, the Fund shall be entitled to recover prejudgment interest, costs, reasonable attorney's fees, and, in the discretion of the court, penalties."[2709]

The *GLACIER BAY* court noted that all of the litigation which had occurred in this case had been over the $14 million threshold liability of the vessel owner and operator. Plaintiffs had been doing, in effect, what has now become the Fund's job, only now the Fund is authorized to collect its attorney's fees.[2710] The defendant argued that because TAPAA does not specifically provide for award of attorney's fees to plaintiffs bringing claims against the government Fund, all attorneys' fees claims against the fund should be denied. In its rejection of the defendant's argument, the court held that attorney's fees do not necessarily have to be denied simply because TAPAA does not specifically award them to plaintiffs. Although a congressional intent to include attorney's fees must be clear, it may be expressed in terms other than the use of those specific words. The court found that congress clearly intended for TAPAA to provide adequate compensation to those who suffered damages from a TAPS oil spill. Congress also intended for victims of a TAPS oil spill to recover without necessarily resorting to lengthy and expensive litigation. In contrast, the environmental statutes cited by the defendants (to defeat recovery) which specifically provide for attorney's fees all involve private attorney general suits where citizens are authorized to enforce compliance with certain environmental standards through litigation.[2711] The court found that as amended, TAPAA provides for the burden of litigation to shift to the Fund, through the mechanism of subrogation, if the vessel owner and operator fail to pay TAPAA claims within ninety days.

---

2709 The Oil Pollution Act, 33 USCA § 8102(d), The Trans Alaska Pipelines Authorization Act, 43 U.S.C. 1653(c)(3).

2710 746 F.Supp. 1379, 1393.

2711 See Outer Continental Shelf Lands Act, 43 U.S.C. § 1349(a)(5); Clean Air Act, 42 U.S.C. § 7604(d); Clean Water Act, 33 U.S.C. § 1365(d).

Since the Fund can now recover attorney's fees from the vessel owner and operator in any subrogation action that the Fund brings, it is only fair that the plaintiffs, who have already done much of the Fund's work for it, should also recover reasonable attorney's fees.[2712] Since the OPA has similar subrogation provisions as TAPAA, the GLACIER BAY case should be applicable to OPA claims against the Fund for the recovery of attorney's fees. It should apply to OPA cases also because Congress intended for victims of an OPA oil spill to recover without necessarily resorting to lengthy and expensive litigation. The OPA just like the TAPAA provides for the burden of litigation to shift to the Fund, through the mechanism of subrogation, if the responsible party fails to pay OPA claims within ninety days.[2713]

The arguments I made in the preceding paragraphs in favor of recovery of attorneys fees by claimants from the responsible party were made bearing in mind that there is a dearth of case law on this issue and one would need to wait for a few more months or years before the law on this issue becomes settled. The Ninth Circuit Court of Appeals in a 2000 case discussed the issue of recovery of attorneys fees under OPA. In the Ninth Circuit Court of Appeals case of *Unocal Corp. v. United States,*[2714] the plaintiff argued that the lower district court should have awarded attorney's fees to him pursuant to the OPA. This appellate court reviewed the district court's interpretations of federal and state statutes de novo. The circuit court based its decision upon a plain reading of section 2715(c) of the OPA. This section provides:

> "At the request of the Secretary, the Attorney General shall commence an action on behalf of the Fund to recover any compensation paid by the Fund to any claimant pursuant to this chapter, and all costs incurred by the Fund by reason of the claim, including... attorney's fees."[2715]

---

2712 746 F.Supp. at 1393.

2713 33 CFR §136.103

2714 *Unocal Corp*, 222 F.3d 528 (9th Cir. 2000).

2715 33 USCA §2715(c).

The court also relied on its own 1999 decision in *United States v. Hyundai Merchant Marine Co.*[2716] In *Hyundai*, the United States government sued a responsible party for costs incurred by the Coast Guard in monitoring the cleanup of an oil spill.[2717] The Ninth Circuit approved an award of fees to the government at the close of the case, reasoning that section 2715's attorney's fees provision applies equally to suits on behalf of the Fund and suits on behalf of other branches of the federal government.[2718] The *Hyundai* court concluded that, because the government's recovery would be paid into the Fund, a denial of attorney's fees to the Coast Guard would defeat the purpose of the OPA.[2719]

*Unocal* attempted to extend this reasoning one step further, arguing that, as a vindicated owner/operator, it, too, is subrogated to the rights which the Fund might have asserted had it filed the claim.[2720] Unocal pointed to 33 U.S.C. § 2702(d)(1)(B), which states that a responsible party who pays for removal costs after a spill and later alleges that the spill was caused by an unrelated third party "shall be entitled by subrogation to all rights of the United States Government and the claimant to recover removal costs or damages from the third party or the Fund."[2721] Unocal argued that this provision grants to the "responsible party" all the rights of the federal government in a suit under the OPA, including the right to fees discussed in *Hyundai*. Rejecting the plaintiff's argument, the court held that the argument contradicts the plain language of section 2702(d), which provides for subrogation only to the government's right to recover removal costs or damages from a third party. In other words, section 2702(d) permits owners/operators such as Unocal to sue for damages in the stead of the United States government, but does not necessarily give to the responsible party the benefit of all the rights held by the federal government.[2722]

2716 *Hyundai*, 172 F.3d 1187 (9th Cir.1999).

2717 172 F.3d at 1189.

2718 Id. at 1192-99.

2719 Id.

2720 *Unocal Corp*, 222 F.3d at 542.

2721 Id at 542.

2722 Id. at 543

Based on this reasoning, the court held that Unocal could not recover fees in the stead of the federal government.

The court concluded by holding that the OPA specifically permits attorney's fee awards for the government, not for private parties, therefore Unocal's interpretation of the statute skews that provision, to require an award of fees in every suit by a responsible party against a third party. The court further concluded that in the absence of congressional or contractual authority, the court cannot award fees to a prevailing non-government party in an OPA suit.[2723]

In the case of the *United States v. Hyundai Merchant Marine Co., Ltd,*[2724] the Ninth Circuit Court of Appeals noted the provision of the OPA that states that funds recovered for removal costs are paid to the Oil Spill Liability Trust Fund, which is available to the President for the payment of removal costs.[2725] Although Hyundai (the responsible party in this case) did not dispute that the recovery in this case will be paid into the Fund, it contended that the government could not recover attorney's fees because it was not clear that the Fund itself was suing as a subrogee. Hyundai latched onto the phrase "compensation paid by the Fund," used in 33 U.S.C.A. § 2715(c) and argued that no attorneys' fees were due to the United States unless the Coast Guard first was compensated by the fund for its removal costs.[2726] Rejecting this argument, the circuit court noted that the Coast Guard and the Fund are both part of the federal government, and that this action was necessarily brought on behalf of the Fund because the recovery will go to the Fund. The court also reiterated that it was clearly Congress's purpose that the United States be reimbursed its attorneys' fees when it must sue for such a recovery.[2727] The court concluded that the Congressional purpose would be frustrated

2723 Id., *quoting*, Stanton Road Associates, v.Lohrey Enterprises, 984 F.2d 1015,1018 (9th Cir. 1993).

2724 48 ERC 1385, 1999 A.M.C. 1521, 172 F.3d 1187 (9th Cir. 1999)

2725 172 F.3d 1187, 1192, see also, 33 U.S.C. §§ 2706(f), 2712(a)(1).

2726 Id.

2727 Id.

if recovery of fees was defeated by the happenstance that, as a matter of accounting, the Fund paid for the removal costs after, rather than before, the claim against the responsible party was litigated. The court thereby affirmed the lower court's decision to award the United States attorneys' fees.[2728] Based on this decision, any agency of the federal government (like the Environmental Protection Agency (EPA) and the United States Coast Guard (USCG), that sues to recover attorney's fees can recover such fees even if the Fund reimburses such government agency for the removal costs after the attorneys fees claim against the responsible party is litigated.

## B. JUDICIAL REVIEW OF CLAIMS AGAINST THE FUND

In the case of *International Marine Carriers v The Oil Spill Liability Trust Fund (IMC)*,[2729] it was has held that section 2717(b) of the OPA, providing that United States district court shall have exclusive original jurisdiction over controversies, though a grant of original jurisdiction, does not provide for judicial review of claims against the Oil Spill Liability Trust Fund. The same court also held that a vessel operator's suit for reimbursement from Oil Spill Liability Trust Fund was suit against United States, barred by sovereign immunity absent consent to suit or waiver, which does not appear in the OPA.[2730] Waiver of sovereign immunity must be express and any waiver is to be construed narrowly, with ambiguities resolved in favor of government.[2731]

The *IMC* court also decided that despite the fact that Fund claims cannot be reviewed under the provisions of the OPA, the Administrative Procedure Act's (APA) [2732] waiver of sovereignty immunity **applied to**

2728 172 F.3d 1187, 1193

2729 International Marine Carriers v The Oil Spill Liability Trust Fund, 903 F.Supp. 1097 (S.D. Tex. 1994), *see also*, 33 U.S.C.A. § 2717(b).

2730 International Marine Carriers, 903 F.Supp. 1097, *see also*, 33 U.S.C.A. §§ 2712, 2713, 2715.

2731 Id. at 1097

2732 5 U.S.C. § 704.

**a vessel operator's suit for judicial review of denial of its claim for reimbursement of removal cost from the Oil Spill Liability Trust Fund.**[2733] Subject to certain exceptions, section 704 of the APA provides for judicial review of "final agency action for which there is no other adequate remedy in a court.[2734]

The *IMC* court held that the Administrative Procedure Act's (APA) waiver of sovereignty immunity applies to a vessel or facility operator's suit for judicial review of its unsuccessful removal costs Fund claim despite the fact that sovereign immunity bars review of money damages claims.[2735] The court held that reimbursement of removal costs by the Fund required under the OPA, constitutes restitution, not damages (damages deals specifically with compensation for harm caused).[2736] The court observed that a money award may be equitable relief where it results from an action enforcing a statutory mandate to pay money.[2737] Implicit in the *IMC* decision is the fact that if the court claim against the NPFC involves reimbursement of money damages recognized under the damages section of the OPA,[2738] it would not be recoverable through a suit in a court of law, because the damages involved deals specifically with compensation for harm caused. This implicit holding of the *IMC* decision on money damages is consistent with the provision of section 702 of the APA.

The *IMC* court found a close analogy in cost recovery actions under section 9607 CERCLA,[2739] and section 7003(a) of the Resource Conservation and Recovery Act ("RCRA").[2740] The *IMC* court noted that

---

2733 *Marine Carriers*, 903 F.Supp. 1097

2734 Id.at 1102

2735 Id. at 1102.

2736 Id.

2737 International Marine Carriers v. Oil Spill Liability Trust Fund, 903 F.Supp., 1102, (*quoting*, Bowen v. Massachusetts, 487 U.S. 879, 899-901, 108 S.Ct. 2722, 2735, 101 L.Ed.2d 749 (1988); Beverly Hosp. v. Bowen, 872 F.2d 483, 487 (D.C.Cir.1989).

2738 33 USC §2702(b)(2)

2739 42 U.S.C.A. § 9607

2740 42 U.S.C.A. § 6973(a), CERCLA section 107 and RCRA section 7003(a), like OPA section 2712, provide for reimbursement of costs incurred from remediation of a discharge or response to a threat of discharge

courts recognize CERCLA's cost recovery actions as restitution claims.[2741] The IMC court noted that when the government seeks recovery of its response costs under CERCLA or its abatement costs under RCRA, it is in effect seeking equitable relief in the form of restitution or reimbursement of the costs it expended in order to respond to the health and environmental danger presented by hazardous substances.[2742] It therefore concluded that OPA removal costs claims should not be categorized as damages for sovereign immunity purposes, but rather as restitution which is not barred by sovereign immunity.[2743] Therefore, OPA damage claims may be barred because of sovereign immunity. APA Section 702 provides in pertinent part:

> "An action in a court of the United States seeking relief "other than money damages" (emphasis mine) and stating a claim that an agency or an officer or employee thereof acted or failed to act in an official capacity or under color of legal authority shall not be dismissed or relief therein be denied on the ground that it is against the United States or that the United States is an indispensable party."[2744]

This section could bar judicial review of Administrative decisions relating to OPA damage claims because in substance they are money damages.

The decision of the *IMC* court appears to be incorrect because of its classification of the action of IMC to recover removal costs refund from the NPFC as restitution and equitable. Based on my analysis in the latter part of this treatise on jury trial availability under OPA, one can conclude

---

2741 See International Marine Carriers v. Oil Spill Liability Trust Fund, 903 F.Supp. 1102, (*quoting*, States v. Northeastern Pharmaceutical Chemical Co. Inc., 810 F.2d 726, 749 (8th Cir.1986)), *cert. denied*, 484 U.S. 848, 108 S.Ct. 146, 98 L.Ed.2d 102 (1987)).

2742 See International Marine Carriers v. Oil Spill Liability Trust Fund, 903 F.Supp. 1102, (*quoting*, United States v. Northernaire Plating Co., 685 F.Supp. 1410, 1413 (W.D.Mich.1988), *aff'd sub nom.* United States v. R.W. Meyer, Inc., 889 F.2d 1497 (6th Cir.1989), *cert. denied*, 494 U.S. 1057, 110 S.Ct. 1527, 108 L.Ed.2d 767 (1990); G.L. Indus. of Michigan, Inc. v. Forstmann-Little, 800 F.Supp. 695, 698 (S.D.Ind.1991) (CERCLA cost recovery actions are equitable in nature when brought by private parties).

2743 See IMC, 903 F.Supp. at 1102.

2744 5 U.S.C. § 702 (1988).

that the courts classification of removal costs as restitution and equitable, based on the flawed decisions of the CERCLA case laws, is an error of law, and ought to be reviewed de novo on appeal. Based on my analysis in that part of the treatise, one can argue that removal costs actions are actions at law to recover a sum certain and is analogous to the type of remedies that the 18th century common law courts adjudicated. By virtue of this, they are not reliefs "other than money damages." In fact they resemble money damages more than restitution. This makes section 702 of the APA inapplicable to actions to recover removal costs from the NPFC. This means that judicial review should not be available for claims that are administratively closed by the US Coast Guard's National Pollution Funds Center.

Assuming arguendo that cost recovery actions amount to restitution, historical analysis reveals that it is not an action at equity, but, rather an action at law. This issue is developed further in my discussion of the jury trial issue in the latter part of this treatise.

NPFC final decisions denying claims have been subject to limited judicial review of the NPFC administrative record under the Administrative Procedures Act "arbitrary and capricious" standard.[2745] As earlier explained, OPA does not waive the sovereign immunity of the United States and the NPFC and OSLTF are not subject to suits for money damages. This means that after a final decision has been made denying a claim, the claimant would have to either accept the decision as final or try to challenge it in a court of law since it is final agency action, but such a challenge will only be successful if the claimant satisfies the "arbitrary and capricious" standard. But such a challenge would also be subject to all administrative law doctrines such as the sovereign immunity doctrine as earlier explained.

If other courts follow the *IMC* court's reasoning, claimants asking for judicial review of NPFC's denial of refund of removal costs will succeed under section 702 of the APA. If other courts reject the *IMC* reasoning as I

2745 NPFC Fund, User Reference Guide, Supplement to The US Coast Guard Marine Safety Manual, Volume IX, Chapter 6, 621 (May 2000).

have done here, then the possibility of obtaining judicial review of NPFC's decision to deny refund of removal costs is very slim.

## C. PROCEDURAL MECHANISM FOR PRESENTMENT OF CLAIMS TO THE NATIONAL POLLUTION FUND CENTER – 33 USC § 2713.

The Coast Guard National Pollution Funds Center is the body charged with the responsibility of disbursing the Fund. The OPA 90 lays down a clear and unambiguous procedure for the presentment of claims to a responsible party and the National Pollution Fund Center (hereinafter NPFC). Failure to follow the procedure stipulated in the statute and regulations to the letter might be a bar to recovery of claims against a responsible party and/or the NPFC.

*General Order Of Presentment Of Claims:* 33 C.F.R. § 136.103, which mirrors Section 2713 of the OPA (a) provides that except as provided in paragraph (b) of this section, all claims for removal costs or damages must be presented first to the responsible party. Subsection (b) allows claims for removal costs or damages to be presented first to the fund only, if the Director, NPFC, has advertised, or otherwise notified claimants in writing. In all cases where the source of the pollution cannot be ascertained, a claim may be made against the Fund. Subsection (c)(1) provides that if the responsible party to whom a claim was presented denies all liability for the claim or the claim is not settled by any person by payment within 90 days after the date upon which (A) the claim was presented, or (B) advertising was begun, whichever is later, the claimant may elect to commence an action in court against the responsible party or to present the claim to the fund. This doctrine of election must be strictly adhered to.

The most important subsection is (d), which states categorically:

> "No claim of a person against the Fund will be approved or certified for payment during the pendency of an action by the person in court to recover costs which are the subject of the claim."

Thus, if any claimant has a suit currently pending against a responsible party who has denied a claim, it is required that such suit be discontinued by that claimant in order to satisfy this requirement of the implementing regulations.[2746] This requirement creates a time bar problem for a claimant who has filed a suit against the RP but subsequently decides to withdraw the suit in order to pursue a claim against the Fund directly. If the time limitation has expired, the claimant may be barred from filing a claim against the Fund. However, submitting a claim to the NPFC during the pendency of a lawsuit may be to the claimant's advantage in order to comply with the Statute of Limitations for claims to the NPFC. In the event that the action in court is no longer pending, the claimant may then wish to proceed with the claim to the NPFC.[2747] In other words the claim may be on file with the NPFC, pending the time that the claimant is ready to actively pursue it. The NPFC during this time will not adjudicate the claim because it will be inactive pending the discontinuance of the court claim against the RP. This also means that the claim cannot be approved or certified for payment until the court action is discontinued.

OPA's claims presentation provision is inconsistent with CERCLA's provision, which limits the presentation requirement to claims asserted against CERCLA's Fund.[2748] Unlike OPA's claims provision, which states that "all claims... shall be presented...," CERCLA's claims provision states that all claims which may be asserted against the Fund... shall be presented.[2749] § 9612, CERCLA's claims procedure provision states as follows:

"(a) Claims against the Fund for response costs ***No claim may be asserted against the Fund*** ........**unless** such claim is presented in the first instance to the owner, operator, or guarantor of the vessel or facility from which a hazardous

2746 33 C.F.R. § 136.103(d)

2747 NPFC Fund User Reference Guide, Supplement to The US Coast Guard Marine Safety Manual, Volume IX, Chapter 6, at 618 (May 2000).

2748 See 42 U.S.C.A. § 9612(a). *See, e.g.*, United States v. Carolina Transformer Co., 978 F.2d 832, 841 (4th Cir.1992) (holding that CERCLA's claims presentation provision only applies to claims asserted against the Fund).

2749 *Compare* 33 U.S.C.A. § 2713(a) *with* 42 U.S.C.A. § 9612.

substance has been released, if known to the claimant, and to any other person known to the claimant who may be liable under section 9607 of this title."

While §2713, OPA's claims procedure provision states:

"(a) Presentation [*A]ll claims* **for removal costs or damages** shall be presented first to the responsible party or guarantor of the source designated under section 2714(a) of this title.

**(b) Presentation to Fund**

(1) In general Claims for removal costs or damages may be presented first to the Fund."

This significant textual change does suggest that courts should interpret OPA's claims provision as having a different scope from CERCLA's. The change in the text, combined with evidence that Congress was aware of CERCLA when it enacted OPA, suggests that Congress intended the change in OPA's language to have substantive consequences and purposely rejected the CERCLA approach limiting the presentation requirement to those claims asserted against the Fund. There is evidence in OPA's text, and legislative history,[2750] that Congress was aware of, and occasionally borrowed from, CERCLA when enacting OPA. However, when that fact is coupled with a comparison of the respective claims procedures' text, the most logical conclusion is that Congress rejected the CERCLA limitation when adopting OPA's claims presentation provision.[2751] The implication of this is that while CERCLA does not require adherence to its claims presentation procedure in claims by a private party against a Responsible Party (RP) for clean up and remediation costs,[2752] OPA requires a strict observance of

2750 See S.Rep. No. 94, 101st Cong., 1st Sess. 2 (1989).

2751 See Boca Ciega Hotel Inc. v. Bouchard Transportation Company Inc, 51 F.3d 235, 240 (11th Cir. 1995).

2752 "A private party must prove four elements before they can prevail in a cost recovery action: (1) the site where the "hazardous substance" is found is a "facility," as per CERCLA's definition of that term, 42 U.S.C. § 9601(9); (2) there has been a "release" or "threatened release" of a "hazardous substance" from the facility, 42 U.S.C. § 9607(a)(4);

its claims presentation procedure in removal costs and damages suits by a private party against the RP as well as in suits by the private party against the Oil Spill Liability Trust Fund (the Fund). This means that OPA's claim presentation procedure is broader in scope than that of CERCLA.

The NPFC's Claims Division adjudicates all claims presented to the NPFC, except for Natural Resources Damage (NRD) Claims, which is adjudicated by the NPFC's Natural Resources Damage Claims Division. The Officials of the NPFC who adjudicate the claims are called the NPFC Claims Managers.

*The claims presentation procedure: (Section 2713 of the OPA & 33 C.F.R. § 136.103) jurisdictional or a mere condition precedent to filing an OPA claim?*

There is a split among the courts on this question. In the United States District Court of the Eastern District of Louisiana, there has been two inconsistent decisions on this question. In the first case of *Marathon Pipeline Co. v. LaRoche Industries Inc*,[2753] the owner of a ruptured gasoline pipeline, a responsible party under Oil Pollution Act (OPA), and gasoline owner brought action against the owner of brine pipeline, whose excavation activities were allegedly sole cause of rupture of gas pipeline, alleging federal question jurisdiction based on OPA and Declaratory Judgment Act. The defendant/responsible party based its motion to dismiss for lack of subject matter jurisdiction on the OPA's presentation requirement outlined above.[2754] LaRoche, the responsible party argued that the presentation requirement of § 2713 is jurisdictional and that the failure

(3) the "release" or "threatened release" has caused the private party to incur "response costs" that were "necessary" and "consistent with the national contingency plan," 42 U.S.C. § 9607(a)(4)(A) and (B); and (4) the Defendants fall within one the four classes of parties subject to the liability under the Act. 3550 Stevens Creek Assoc. v. Barclays Bank, 915 F.2d 1355, 1358 (9th Cir.1990); Ascon Properties, Inc. v. Mobil Oil Co., 866 F.2d 1149, 1152 (9th Cir.1989). Richard E. BUNGER and REB of Florida, Inc., v. Jack M. HARTMAN and Texaco, Inc., 797 F.Supp. 968, 971 (S.D. Fla. 1992).

2753 See *LaRoche Industries Inc.*, 944 F.Supp. 476 (E.D. La. 1996)

2754 33 U.S.C. § 2713, 33 C.F.R. § 136.103.

to comply with that section results in a lack of subject matter jurisdiction. The Court agreed that § 2713's presentation requirement is jurisdictional and mandates dismissal when that provision is applicable and not complied with by the claimant.[2755]

Also in the case of *Johnson v. Colonial Pipeline Company*,[2756] property owners sued a pipeline company seeking damages for oil spill. On the oil company's (defendant's) motion to dismiss or for summary judgment, the District Court held that the plaintiffs had failed to make presentment required for suit under the Oil Pollution Act. The court noted that OPA provides that all claims for damages shall be presented first to the party responsible for the spill, and if such a claim is presented and the responsible party denies all liability or the claim is not settled within 90 days, the claimant may elect to commence an action in court against the responsible party.[2757] The court therefore held that the plaintiffs failure to comply with the clear-cut prerequisites for bringing such a claim, must lead to the dismissal of the OPA claim.[2758]

The court pointed out that the purpose of the claim presentation procedure is to promote settlement and avoid litigation and Congress believed that lawsuits against parties are appropriate only "where attempts to reach a settlement with the responsible party... were unsuccessful."[2759] The court observed that, that was why Congress mandated a 90-day period in which the parties would attempt to resolve monetary disputes arising from oil spills prior to commencing litigation in the hope that costly and cumbersome litigation can be avoided.[2760]

---

2755 944 F.Supp. 476, 477.

2756 37 ERC 1852, 1994 A.M.C. 2702, 24 Envtl. L. Rep. 20,162, 830 F.Supp. 309 (E.D. Va. 1993).

2757 See 33 U.S.C. § 2713(c).

2758 830 F.Supp. 309, 310 (citing with approval, Cf. Hallstrom v. Tillamook County, 493 U.S. 20, 31, 110 S.Ct. 304, 311, 107 L.Ed.2d 237 (1989) (plaintiff's failure to comply with Resource Conservation and Recovery Act's 60-day notice and presentation requirement mandates dismissal of case).

2759 See H.R.Rep. No. 242, 101st Cong., 1st Sess., pt. 2, at 66 (1989).

2760 See 135 Cong.Rec. at H 7962, 7965 (statements of Rep. Hammerschmidt and Rep. Lent).

The court found that the plaintiffs had not complied with the presentation requirement of OPA.[2761] The plaintiffs filed this suit on April 2, 1993 without having first presented a claim to Colonial (the responsible party). Thereafter, apparently realizing their failure to comply, the plaintiffs sent a letter to Colonial on April 7, 1993, which purported to present an OPA claim. However, the court held that the April 7 letter failed to cure the jurisdictional defect for two reasons, first, Colonial had not denied all liability under OPA and 90 days have not passed since the claim was presented. The court pointed out that at least one of these events must occur before an OPA action may proceed. Second, the plaintiffs' April 7 letter failed to "present" a claim within the meaning of 33 U.S.C. § 2713(a), because the purpose of OPA's claim presentation requirement is to enable the parties to negotiate, if possible, a settlement of potential claims resulting from an oil spill without having to resort to litigation. The settlement is to be in the form of "payment within 90 days after the date upon which the claim was presented." 33 U.S.C. § 2713(c)(2). The court also found that in order to accomplish this purpose, the claim presented must inform the responsible party with some precision of the nature and extent of the damages alleged and of the amount of monetary damages claimed. Otherwise, the responsible party will be unable to make an informed offer of its own, unable to engage in meaningful substantive negotiations, and thus unable to settle the matter by agreeing to a final amount. Instead, the responsible party will have to ask for a more definite statement of the claim, as Colonial had done, and the 90-day period will be spent trying to obtain basic information rather than actually negotiating a settlement.

The court observed that the need for specificity in OPA claims is underscored by the regulations issued by the United States Coast Guard pursuant to OPA, setting forth the specific requirements for filing such claims against the OPA Fund.[2762] These regulations have been discussed in the earlier part of this treatise.

Turning to the April 7th letter of claim written by the claimant, the court held that measured against the purposes of the OPA claims presentation

2761 See *Colonial Pipeline Company,* 830 F.Supp. 309, 311(E.D. Va. 1993).

2762 33 C.F.R. § 136.103.

procedure, as well as the Coast Guard regulations, the plaintiffs' April 7 letter was plainly inadequate. The controversial claims letter conclusorily recited that the claim was for "damages for injury to or economic losses resulting from the destruction of rent property owned by the claimants," as well as for loss of income, elimination of property value, mental distress, loss of use and enjoyment of property, loss of quality of life, and disruption. Plaintiffs made no effort to describe the nature or extent of these alleged damages, much less to explain the basis for claiming that these damages had been sustained. They also failed to state a sum certain for any of the types of damages alleged. Indeed, they did not give any suggestions as to the amount of damages they were claiming.

The court held further that the plaintiffs' letter did not provide Colonial with enough information to accept the claim and make a payment that will settle the matter, or even to formulate an offer of its own that might lead to settlement. The court pointed out that Colonial was unable to negotiate meaningfully with plaintiffs, as it had done with other claimants, many of whose claims have been resolved, and that the Plaintiffs' letter was simply an afterthought, sent to Colonial after the plaintiffs had already sued in the hope of curing a profound jurisdictional defect.

In conclusion the court held that the plaintiffs had thus never "presented" their claims as required by OPA, and that even if they had, they could not maintain this lawsuit because Colonial Pipeline had not denied all liability and the 90-day negotiating period had not expired.[2763] This case underscores the need for claimants to comply with the claim presentation procedure spelt out in the OPA and the Code of Federal regulations. Despite this decision, the National Pollution Funds Center on its part was able to collect oil spill removal costs it incurred from Colonial Pipeline. It billed Colonial Pipeline a total of $580, 416.59.[2764]

---

2763 Johnson v. Colonial Pipeline Company 830 F.Supp. at 311.

2764 See National Pollution Funds Center Oil Spill data, p 8, Colonial Pipeline Company, Federal Project Number 053520 (2001) (This information was provided by the National Pollution Funds Center (NPFC) in April of 2001 and the data is on file with the NPFC and is available upon request from the NPFC).

Another important case on point is the case of *Boca Ciega Hotel Inc. v. Bouchard Transp. Co., Inc.*,[2765] a case in which, four vessels collided in Tampa Bay, spilling thousands of gallons of oil and other oil pollutants in the process on August 10, 1993. Pursuant to OPA, the Coast Guard designated Appellees Bouchard Transportation (Bouchard), as owner and operator of the vessel "Tug Captain Fred Bouchard" and barge "B. 155," and Maritrans Operating Partners (Maritrans), as owner and operator of the vessel "Seafarer" and barge "Ocean 255," (collectively, Appellees) as the "responsible parties" for the spill. The Appellants brought this action individually and on behalf of several plaintiff classes to recover business, property, and tourist damages sustained as a result of the spill. The complaint alleged liability under OPA's citizen suit provisions and various Florida statutory and common-law theories.[2766]

Appellees Bouchard and Maritrans moved to dismiss the complaint for lack of subject matter jurisdiction. According to the appellees, federal subject matter jurisdiction did not exist because Appellants had failed to comply with OPA's claims presentation procedure. Conforming to OPA, Bouchard and Maritrans had organized a claims clearing-house to identify, process, and settle claims arising from the spill. Appellees took the position that resort to this claims presentation process is a mandatory condition precedent to any OPA lawsuit, and that Appellants' failure to present their claims rendered them unripe for judicial resolution.[2767]

In responding to Appellees' motions, the appellants never claimed that they satisfied OPA's claims presentation requirement. Instead, they maintained that the claims presentation requirement only applies to actions seeking to recover from the OPA-created cleanup fund (Fund), not to actions brought directly against the responsible parties.

In rejecting the appellants argument, the court noted that the appellants did not claim that the language of § 2713 is ambiguous, nor could they. The *Boca Ciega* court noted that the appellants' complaint constituted a "claim" as OPA defines that term, and section 2713 makes it very

2765 844 F.Supp. 512 (M.D. Fla. 1994), *aff'd*, 51 F.3d 235 (11th Cir. 1995).

2766 51 F.3d 235, 236.

2767 Id. at 237, see also 33 U.S.C.A. §§ 2713-2714.

clear that "all claims... shall be presented first to the responsible party...." The court found that the Congressional use of the word "shall" in § 2713(a) is naturally read to place a mandatory condition on all claims.[2768] The court reasoned that no reading of § 2713(a)'s language suggests that Congress intended to limit its applicability to claims against the Fund. The court pointed out that the language of § 2713(c)'s election of remedies provision, discussed earlier in this chapter, bolsters its interpretation of § 2713(a). As pointed out in the earlier part of this chapter, section 2713(c) allows a claimant whose "claim is presented in accordance with subsection (a)" to "elect to commence an action in court against the responsible party... or to present the claim to the Fund."[2769] The court in supporting its conclusion that § 2713(a) applies to all claims, held that the natural reading of § 2713(c) is that claimants like the appellants, filing "in court against the responsible parties," as well as claimants seeking recovery from the Fund, must present their claims in accordance with § 2713(a). The court noted that if it accepts the appellants' interpretation of § 2713(a), it would render parts of §2713(c) superfluous or nonsensical, a result to be avoided when interpreting statutes.[2770]

The appellants argued that limiting the claims presentation requirement to claims against the Fund is more consistent with the overall structure and purpose of the Act. The court noted that while discovery of the plain meaning of an unambiguous statute will almost always end an inquiry, in rare and exceptional circumstances, a court of law may decline to follow the plain meaning of a statute because overwhelming extrinsic evidence demonstrates a legislative intent contrary to the text's plain meaning.[2771] The appellants' contention that the structure and purpose of OPA so clearly contradicts the plain meaning of the claims presentation provision

---

2768 *Id.* (*citing with approval*, v. United States Dist. Court for the Southern Dist. of Iowa, 490 U.S. 296, 300-02, 109 S.Ct. 1814, 1818, 104 L.Ed.2d 318 (1989)).

2769 33 U.S.C § 2713(c).

2770 *Boca Ciega Hotel Inc* 51 F.3d 235, 238, (*citing*, *Ratzlaf* v. *United States*, 510 U.S. 135, 114 S.Ct. 655, 659, 126 L.Ed.2d 615 (1994)).

2771 Id. at 238, (*citing*, v. Tillamook County, 493 U.S. 20, 28-30, 110 S.Ct. 304, 310, 107 L.Ed.2d 237 (1989); Garcia v. United States, 469 U.S. 70, 73-75, 105 S.Ct. 479, 482, 83 L.Ed.2d 472 (1984); Kirkland, 12 F.3d at 202.

that the court should limit that provision to claims against the Fund, the court held that the appellants' reliance on the "overall purpose" of OPA--which they claim is "to expand the liability of responsible parties"--is misplaced, because courts have long recognized that statutes, especially large, complex statutes like OPA, are the result of innumerable compromises between competing interests reflecting many competing purposes and goals.

The court in its reasoning found that "vague notions" about a statute's overall purpose cannot be allowed "to overcome the words of its text regarding the specific issue under consideration."[2772] In its refusal to attempt to adjust the balance between competing goals that the text adopted by Congress had struck, the court pointed out that the appellants presented nothing from OPA's text and little from its legislative history to convince the court that expanded liability was the only, or even primary, goal of the Act. Relying heavily on some passages from the legislative history of OPA, the court agreed with the appellees' claim that one goal of the claims presentation provision was to temper the Act's increased liability with a congressional desire to encourage settlement and avoid litigation.[2773] The court took note of the fact that even if the appellants could produce textual evidence of an overall congressional purpose, the pursuit of broad policy goals in some portions of a statute generally does not demonstrate an intent to alter the plain statutory command of another provision. The court reasoned that the appellants' claim that OPA's preservation of state oil spill remedies (saving to suitors clause in section 2718(a) of OPA), contradicts § 2713's plain meaning fails for the same reason. The court also reasoned that while the side-by-side co-existence of state remedies requiring no presentation and OPA remedies requiring presentation might be relevant if we were interpreting a facially ambiguous statute, the clarity of § 2713(a) forecloses that possibility. A general statutory provision like OPA's savings clause does not trump the more specific command of

---

2772 Id. at 238, (*citing*, v. Hewitt Associates, 508 U.S. 248, 113 S.Ct. 2063, 2071, 124 L.Ed.2d 161 (1993)) (emphasis in original).

2773 *Id.* at 239, (*citing*, H.R.Rep. No. 242, 101st Cong., 1st Sess., pt. 2, at 66 (1989); 135 Cong.Rec., 101st Cong., 1st Sess. H7962 (Nov. 2, 1989) (remarks of Rep. Lent); *see also*v. Colonial Pipeline Co.,830 F.Supp. 309, 310 (E.D.Va.1993).

§ 2713(a).[2774] The court also rejected the appellants' policy objections to the claims presentation requirement because only Congress, not the court of law can create an exception to the current OPA procedure. The court also alluded to the Supreme Court's reasoning in a case that noted that when construing the notice provision of the Resource Conservation and Recovery Act of 1976 (RCRA)[2775], a provision similar to the one before the instant court--the court is not at liberty to create an exception where Congress has declined to do so."[2776] The court reasoned that in the long run, experience teaches that strict adherence to the procedural requirements specified by the legislature is the best guarantee of evenhanded administration of the law. The court pointed out that any perception of a policy shortcoming caused by OPA's claims presentation requirement, arises as a result of the balance struck by Congress, and is properly remedied by congressional action.[2777]

In concluding, the court found nothing in the text or legislative history of OPA remotely approaching the type of extraordinarily clear evidence needed to justify departing from the plain meaning of a statute's text.[2778]

In 1998, another United States District judge in Louisiana reached a slightly contrary opinion from that reached in the earlier *Marathon* case discussed above. In *Leboeuf v. Texaco*,[2779] plaintiffs filed a class action against an oil company and environmental cleanup companies in state court, alleging damages suffered from oil spill on a lake. After removal to federal court on diversity grounds and remand to state court, the oil company removed the action again based on federal question jurisdiction. The defendants' position was that not until the state court determined that the plaintiffs complied with the presentment requirements of 33 U.S.C. § 2713, did the defendants learn that plaintiffs' claims were viable and

2774 Id. at 239, (*citing*, v. TWA, Inc.,504 U.S. 374, 384-85, 112 S.Ct. 2031, 2037, 119 L.Ed.2d 157 (1992); v. Bock Laundry Machine Co., 490 U.S. 504, 523, 109 S.Ct. 1981, 1992, 104 L.Ed.2d 557 (1989)).

2775 42 U.S.C.A. § 6972 (West 1989 & Supp.1994).

2776 Id at 239, (*citing*, v. Tillamook County, 110 S.Ct. 304, 309 (1989)).

2777 Id.

2778 Id. at 239.

2779 9 F.Supp.2d 661, 663

that this case was removable. In other words, the defendants argued that 33 U.S.C. § 2713(c) deprives any court of subject matter jurisdiction over OPA claims where the plaintiff has not first complied with OPA's presentment and claims procedure. Thus, defendants concluded that removal of this case when they were contesting the justiciability of the OPA claims would have been improper. Generally removal must be effected within 30 days after receipt by the removing defendant, "through service or otherwise," of a copy of the initial pleading setting forth the claim for relief upon which the action is based, or within 30 days after the service of summons if the initial pleading has been filed in court and is not required to be served upon the defendant, whichever period is shorter.[2780] So, in this case the defendant claimed that his second removal was timely because he had not validly been informed about the claim and thus the time does not begin to run until the state court finally determines the issue of whether the plaintiffs' claim is barred because of non-compliance with § 2713's presentment requirements. The court found that the defendants were placed on notice of a federal question arising under the OPA when plaintiffs responded to an interrogatory request on March 2nd, 1998, the time for removal expired on April 2nd, 1998, (Thirty days). Thus the defendants' removal on May 20th, 1998 was untimely.[2781]

*Marathon* is distinguishable from *Leboeuf* in two respects. The issue of § 2713's presentment requirements was before the *Marathon* court on a motion to dismiss pursuant to Rule 12(b)(1) of the Federal Rules of Civil Procedure and the plaintiffs originally filed their action in federal court and not in state court.

Relying on the decision of the Eleventh Circuit Court of Appeals in *Boca Ciega Hotel v. Bouchard Transp. Co.*,[2782] the *Leboeuf* court held that the clear text of the § 2713 creates only a mandatory condition precedent barring all OPA claims unless and until a claimant has presented its claims in compliance with § 2713(a) and either: (1) all responsible parties deny all liability; or (2) the claim is not settled within 90 days after (A) the claim

2780 28 U.S.C. § 1446(b).

2781 9 F.Supp.2d 661, 666

2782 51 F.3d 235 (11th Cir.1995)

was presented, or (B) advertising was begun under section 2714(b) of the Act, whichever is later. 33 U.S.C.A. § 2713(c)."[2783] It rejected the reasoning of the *Marathon* court and held that § 2713 is not jurisdictional. Rather, it concluded that the Eleventh Circuit merely found the presentment requirements a mandatory condition precedent. The *Leboeuf* court held that the reasoning of the Eleventh Circuit is more in accord with an exhaustion of administrative process rather than jurisdictional requirements.

The court expressed its frustration at being unable to locate a case addressing removal and the presentment requirements of 33 U.S.C. § 2713. However, it reasoned that it is not uncommon for defendants to remove cases and then contest the failure to exhaust administrative remedies/procedures.[2784] The court pointed out the fact that OPA gives the United States district courts exclusive original jurisdiction over all controversies arising under OPA, without regard to the citizenship of the parties or the amount in controversy. It also pointed out that OPA also grants to state trial courts of competent jurisdiction, jurisdiction over claims for removal costs or damages under OPA. Such state courts may consider claims under OPA or State law and any final judgment of such state court (when no longer subject to ordinary forms of review) shall be recognized, valid, and enforceable for all purposes of OPA."[2785] Thus, a plaintiff may file an OPA claim for removal costs or damages in either state or federal court. The court concluded that if the court were to accept defendants' argument, then no court would ever have jurisdiction to hear whether a plaintiff has complied with § 2713. So, a federal court or state court of competent jurisdiction must consider whether the condition precedent to the filing of an OPA claim has been satisfied. It would take a couple of years or months before the law on this issue becomes settled, but it is an interesting issue that should be monitored closely.

---

2783 Id. at 240

2784 See Boudreaux v. Hoffman, et al, 1997 WL 610874 (E.D.La. 1997.), (The defendant removed and then moved the court for partial summary judgment of plaintiff's Title VII claim because the plaintiff failed to file and EEOC charge of discrimination prior to instituting suit in court).

2785 33 USC § 2717.

*Availability of an Appeals process for claims that are denied by the NPFC.*

When a claim is presented and it is denied, the claimant can file for a reconsideration of its claim and it would have the opportunity of presenting additional legal arguments and evidence that could lead to a change of outcome. But this request must be made in writing.[2786] Sometimes a claimant may succeed in a reconsideration claim, sometimes the claim may be denied again. The claims regulations provide that NPFC denial of a claim after reconsideration is final.[2787]

Until 1999 NPFC did not pay NRD claims. NPFC relied on a Comptroller General opinion, issued in late 1995, that OPA provides for payment of NRD from the Oil Spill Liability Trust Fund (OSLTF) only by appropriation.[2788] NPFC pays other damage and removal cost claims direct from the OSLTF without appropriation. In late 1997 the Department of Justice, Office of Legal Counsel, adopted a different interpretation of OPA, opining that natural resource damages are payable from the OSLTF without further appropriation, like other damages and removal costs.[2789] In accordance with the opinion of the Department of Justice, the NPFC began to adjudicate and pay NRD claims just as it pays other damage and removal cost claims.[2790]

*Claims by a responsible party against the Fund*: Section 2708 of OPA 90 allows the responsible party for a vessel or facility from which **oil** is discharged, or which poses the substantial threat of a discharge of **oil**, to assert a claim for removal costs and damages only if the responsible party demonstrates that --

2786 NPFC Fund User Reference Guide, Supplement to The US Coast Guard Marine Safety Manual, Volume IX, Chapter 6, at 621.

2787 Id. at 621.

2788 Id. at 616.

2789 Id.

2790 Id. at 617.

"(1) the responsible party is entitled to a defense to liability under section 2703; or

(2) the responsible party is entitled to a limitation of liability under section 2704."[2791] This means that once the responsible party can prove that it is entitled to limitation of liability, it can recover whatever it has paid in excess of its liability limits. If it is entitled to a defense to liability, then the responsible party can claim complete indemnity from the Fund for all the money and resources the responsible party has expended on the spill. This would include the entire amount spent on removal and damages. Even if it is entitled to limit its liability, what is refunded to it depends on its liability limits.

*The extent of recovery by a responsible party*: the responsible party who is entitled to a limitation of liability may assert a claim under section 2713 only to the extent that the sum of the removal costs and damages incurred by the responsible party or by the guarantor on behalf of the responsible party, exceeds the amount to which the total of the liability of the responsible party is limited under section 2704. So, the responsible party would be entitled to seek a refund of any amount it spends on removal and damages that exceeds the OPA limit.

## D. OTHER LIMITATIONS TO ACCESSING THE OIL SPILL LIABILITY TRUST FUND

- Maximum of $1 billion per case or balance in the FUND, whichever is less.
- Removal (including response to substantial threat) and Initiation of Natural Resources Damage Assessment (NRDA) funding are limited to funds available in Emergency Fund subset of the OSLTF. Since OPA, the Emergency Fund has had as much as $125 million and as little as $6 million. $50 million is added to the Emergency Fund balance on October 1st of each year.

2791 See 33 U.S.C §2708.

- Maximum of $500,000,000 per case to satisfy Natural Resource Damage claims and assessments.
- The discharge must impact waters of the U.S., including the 200-mile Exclusive Economic Zone (EEZ).[2792]
- Not all the response phase activities qualify for funding from the OSLTF as removal costs, e.g., Phase I, Discovery or Notification does not qualify for Funding.[2793] Phase I Activities are activities conducted to discover oil spills or to notify appropriate authorities of oil spills, for example, patrols, notifications to the National Response Center, notifications to the predesignated FOSC. With the exception of the costs incurred by the FOSC to notify appropriate Federal, State, and local officials of an OPA incident, these costs are not directly chargeable to the OSLTF as removal costs but are funded through normal operating appropriations (e.g., Coast Guard OE).[2794]
- Groundwater Contamination: Removal costs may be incurred to handle oil discharges in groundwater which are tributary to surface waters of the United States. However, the FOSC must have a reasonable basis to conclude that there is a clear hydrological nexus to surface waters before taking removal action to clean up groundwater. The Fund is not available for removal actions to clean up groundwater where there is no discharge or substantial threat of a discharge into surface waters. Even when the OSLTF may be used, its use is limited to cleaning up the surface waters or eliminating the substantial threat thereto, not remediation of the groundwater contamination. The 1986 amendments to the Resource Conservation and Recovery Act (RCRA) established a Federal Trust Fund to finance the cleanup of petroleum releases from underground storage tanks (USTs). This is an EPA program

---

2792 Oil Spill Liability Trust Fund, Guidance and Information for use During An Oil Spill, < http://www.uscg.mil/hq/npfc/media.htm#access> (Last Updated, March 3, 2001).

2793 US Coast Guard National Pollution Funds Center, Technical Operating Procedures For Determining Removal Costs Under The Oil Pollution Act of 1990, 110 (January 16, 1996).

2794 Id. at 112.

largely administered through grants and cooperative agreements with the states. The OSLTF may be used when the discharge affects navigable waters or to mitigate a substantial threat of a discharge into navigable waters, but remediation of the groundwater contamination from an UST should be financed by the RP or the Federal Trust Fund provided for that purpose.[2795]

2795 The US Coast Guard National Pollution Fund Center, Technical Operating Procedures for Determining Removal Costs Under The Oil Pollution Act of 1990, 118 (January 16, 1996).

# Chapter Twelve

# RECOVERY BY FOREIGN CLAIMANTS UNDER OPA – 33 USC § 2707

Under section 2707 of OPA, foreign claimants are entitled to recover from responsible parties for discharges of oil in or on the territorial sea, internal waters or adjacent shoreline of a foreign country if the discharge is from an Outer Continental Shelf facility or a deep water port; a vessel in the navigable waters of the US; a vessel carrying oil as cargo between two United States ports or a tanker that received oil at a terminal of the Trans-Alaska Pipeline for transportation to a port in the United States. In addition, the foreign claimant must show that it has not otherwise been compensated and that recovery is authorized by a treaty or executive agreement between the United States and the claimant's country or that the Secretary of State has certified that the claimant's country provides a comparable remedy for United States claimants. The prerequisites do not apply to a Canadian resident in the case of a discharge from a vessel under the Trans-Alaska Pipeline Authorization Act. It is important to point out that foreign claimants cannot bring a claim for discharge of oil from a Trans Alaska Pipeline. It must be from a tanker that received oil from the terminal of a Trans Alaska Pipeline.

During the drafting stages of the OPA, the foreign claimants section of the US House of Representatives OPA bill was similar to the Senate's bill except that it did not specify recovery for a discharge, or threat of a discharge, from a vessel carrying oil as cargo between two ports subject to the jurisdiction of the United States.[2796] But this provision was added to the bill at the advanced stage of the legislative process. The House bill also required foreign claimants to seek compensation under two international

2796 H.R. Conf. Rep. No. 653, 101ST Cong., 2ND Sess. 1990, 1990 U.S.C.C.A.N. 779, 1990 WL 132747 (Leg.Hist.)

oil pollution conventions before presenting a claim to the Fund.[2797] This part of the House bill died prematurely because it failed to survive strict congressional scrutiny.

Another provision of the House OPA bill which was added in the drafting stages in Congress was the section that required that only Canadian residents may present claims for Trans Alaska Pipelines related spills, notwithstanding the requirement for an authorizing treaty or certification of comparable treatment for U.S. citizens.[2798] The only part of this proposed section that survived is the provision that did away with the requirement for an authorizing treaty or certification of comparable treatment for US citizens, in Canadian claims for removal costs and damages resulting from a discharge, or substantial threat of a discharge of oil in or on the territorial sea, internal waters, or adjacent shoreline of Canada;[2799] if such discharge emanates from a tanker that received the oil at the terminal of a pipeline constructed under the Trans-Alaska Pipeline Authorization Act (43 U.S.C. 1651 et seq.), for transportation to a place in the United States.[2800] This evinces the fact that the US Congress wanted OPA liability to be extensive. Now claimants residing in other countries can bring OPA claims for Trans Alaska Pipelines related oil spills.

One question that readily comes to mind is whether the OPA allows for foreign claimants or foreign trustees to proceed with OPA natural resources damage assessment claims when there are US based trustees also seeking the same damages from the same responsible party. The answer to this should be in the affirmative. The only thing that the foreign trustees need to do is work together with other trustees seeking the same damages. This is particularly important because the OPA does not allow double recovery for the same damaged resource. This means that whatever damage is awarded eventually would have to be shared by the trustees. The OPA Fund is limited to $1 billion dollars per incident and natural resources damage assessment cannot exceed $500 million per incident. In a very

2797 1990 U.S.C.C.A.N. 779.

2798 Id.

2799 See 33 USCA §2707(a)(2).

2800 See 33 USCA §2707(a)(2).

cataclysmic oil spill, the trustees would not have enough money to satisfy their respective claims especially if (1) the responsible party invokes an OPA defense successfully, (2) it is a mystery oil spill, or (3) the responsible party is entitled to limit its liability. In these type of cases the foreign trustees and the US based trustees would have to share the $500 million dollars even though it may not be sufficient for natural resources damage assessment and restoration.

A "foreign claimant" is defined in 2707 (c) as: (1) a person residing in a foreign country; (2) the government of a foreign country; and (3) an agency or political subdivision of a foreign country. The clear-cut provision of section 2707 (c)(1) may mean that a citizen of a foreign country residing outside that country may lack standing to sue under this section. It may also mean that a non-citizen of a foreign country residing in that country has standing to sue. The provision of section 2707 (c)(3) means that state, municipal or provincial governments have standing to sue under this section.

The provisions of the OPA do not directly indicate that foreign trustees can recover removal costs and damages from the Fund, so it may be assumed that this was not intended. For instance section 2712 of the OPA provides that "the Fund shall be available to the President for: (1) the payment of removal costs, including the costs of monitoring removal actions, determined by the President to be consistent with the National Contingency Plan-- (A) by Federal authorities; or (B) by a Governor or designated State official under subsection (d) of this section; (2) the payment of costs incurred by Federal, State, or Indian tribe trustees in carrying out their functions under section 2706 of this title for assessing natural resource damages and for developing and implementing plans for the restoration, rehabilitation, replacement, or acquisition of the equivalent of damaged resources determined by the President to be consistent with the National Contingency Plan; (3) the payment of removal costs determined by the President to be consistent with the National Contingency Plan as a result of, and damages resulting from, a discharge, or a substantial threat of a discharge, of oil from a foreign offshore unit; (4) the payment of claims in accordance with section 2713 of this title for uncompensated removal costs determined by the President to be consistent with the National

Contingency Plan or uncompensated damages; (5) the payment of Federal administrative, operational, and personnel costs and expenses reasonably necessary for and incidental to the implementation, administration, and enforcement of this chapter."

Section 2713 of the OPA referred to in section 2712(a)(4) specifically provides that claims for removal costs or damages may be presented first to the Fund-- (A) if the President has advertised or otherwise notified claimants in accordance with section 2714(c) of this title; (B) by a responsible party who may assert a claim under section 2708 of this title; (C) by the Governor of a State for removal costs incurred by that State; or (D) by a United States claimant in a case where a foreign offshore unit has discharged oil causing damage for which the Fund is liable under section 2712(a) of this title. Nowhere in all these provisions is a foreign claimant or trustee mentioned. So, it can be argued that as far as removal costs are concerned, the intent of Congress was not to allow foreign claimants to recover removal costs directly from the Fund, but rather from the responsible party directly or from an international pollution Fund or a Fund set up by the government of the foreign country in which the foreign claimant resides. Because the OPA specifically emphasizes the need for state Funds to co-exist with the Oil Spill Liability Trust Fund, the US government would not expect anything less from foreign governments. Apart from this, the OPA specifically limits recovery of removal costs for state governments in emergency response cases to a meager sum of $250,000 per incident. Apart from the meager sum provided to states for emergency clean up, the implementing regulations governing state governments' access to the Fund also imposes other additional requirements that state governments must satisfy to recover this amount. This is proof of Congressional desire for every state government or foreign government to have its own separate Fund for payment of removal costs. The US Coast Guard formulated regulations to govern state government access to the Fund but did not provide similar regulations to govern foreign government access to the Fund. This evinces the fact that Congress did not want the Fund to pay for a foreign government's removal costs.

But one can counter the above assertion by arguing that the intent of Congress may have been to allow foreign claimants to recover removal costs from the Fund, because the OPA provides in section 2706(f) that sums recovered under the OPA by a Federal, State, Indian, or foreign trustee for natural resource damages under section 2702(b)(2)(A) of the OPA shall be retained by the trustee in a revolving trust account, without further appropriation, for use only to reimburse or pay costs incurred by the trustee under subsection (c) of this section with respect to the damaged natural resources. It further provides that any amounts in excess of those required for these reimbursements and costs shall be deposited in the Fund. The fact that this section compels foreign trustees to deposit excess amounts in the Fund is an indication that Congress may have intended that the Fund should pay foreign trustees their removal costs.

One other thing that is worth noting is the fact that damages and removal costs for spills from foreign offshore units are not recoverable by foreign claimants suing under the OPA. If the US Congress had wanted foreign claimants to recover damages and removal costs for these type of spills it would have provided for it specifically in the statute.[2801] To buttress the fact that Congress may not have intended recovery for foreign offshore units oil spills, section 2712(a)(3) (provision on uses of the Fund) provides that the Fund shall be available to the President for the payment of removal costs determined by the President to be consistent with the National Contingency Plan as a result of, and damages resulting from, a discharge, or a substantial threat of a discharge, of oil from a foreign offshore unit. Section 2713(b)(D) (claims presentation procedure) of the statute further provides that a claim may be presented to the Fund by a "United States claimant" (emphasis mine) in a case where a foreign offshore unit has discharged oil causing damage for which the Fund is liable under section 2712(a) of the OPA. This provision limits possible claimants for foreign offshore unit oil spills to United States Claimants. This means that foreign claimants cannot claim removal costs and damages from the Fund where a foreign offshore unit has discharged oil thereby causing damage to that foreign claimant. It has no locus standing to sue because the OPA has failed to confer standing on it. It is difficult to rationalize the failure of the US Congress to include foreign offshore unit oil spills in

2801 See 33 USCA §2707(b).

section 2707(b). This means that no matter how devastating such oil spills are, the foreign claimants would have no recourse under OPA.

Another thing that is worth pointing out is the fact that the provision in section 2704(c)(3) relating to oil discharges from Outer Continental shelf facilities may not be applicable to foreign claimants. It is not inconceivable that an oil spill from an Outer Continental shelf facility could be carried by the waves of the sea from the Outer Continental Shelf area to the "Exclusive Economic Zone" (EEZ) of an adjoining nation. As explained earlier the "Exclusive Economic Zone" is a zone beyond and adjacent to the territorial sea, in which a coastal state possesses sovereign rights to explore, exploit, conserve, and manage its natural resources, whether living or non-living, of the seabed, subsoil, and superadjacent waters.[2802]

Section 2704(c)(3) provides in pertinent part:

> "Notwithstanding the limitations established under subsection (a) of this section and the defenses of section 2703 of this title, all removal costs incurred by the United States Government or any State or local official or agency in connection with a discharge or substantial threat of a discharge of oil from any Outer Continental Shelf facility (OCS) or a vessel carrying oil as cargo from such a facility shall be borne by the owner or operator of such facility or vessel."

This section specifically mentions (a)United States Government, (b)any State, (c) local official, and (d) agency, but it does not mention foreign claimants. This could mean that the responsible party for Outer Continental Shelf facilities may not have to pay for the entire removal costs without regard to limitation where an oil spill from the Outer Continental Shelf area impacts an adjoining nation's EEZ. It also means that a responsible party will be able to raise the defenses to liability provided in section 2703(a) of the OPA. The question then is, what limits of liability are

---

2802 See United Nations Convention on the Law of the Sea, Dec. 10, 1982, arts. 56, U.N.Doc. A/CONF. 62/122 (1982), reprinted in 21 I.L.M. 1261, 1280 (1982) [hereinafter UNCLOS III]. The territorial sea is the ocean area extending from the shore of a coastal nation to a maximum of 12 nautical miles under international law. Id. art. 3, 21 I.L.M. at 1280. The coastal nation has complete sovereignty over this area including the air space over the sea as well as its bed and subsoil. Id. art. 2, 21 I.L.M. at 1280.

applicable to OCS oil spills that impact foreign countries? My suggestion is that foreign OCS facility oil spills should be given the MODU treatment. This was discussed earlier under the chapter on "Limits of Clean-Up Liability." Under this treatment, the facility or vessel responsible for the spill should be treated as tank vessels. If however the removal costs plus damages exceed the tank vessels limitation amount, such a vessel or facility should be treated as offshore facilities. Getting the excess liability treatment would mean that the responsible party will still be liable for the entire clean-up costs, but with a right to invoke the defenses provided for in section 2703(a). He would then have to pay up to $75m for OPA damages. An alternative suggestion is that if the spill emanates from a tank vessel or "other vessels," the limitation provisions relating to these vessels as provided in section 2704(a)(1)-(2) should be applied to the responsible party.[2803] However, if the source of the oil spill is an OCS facility the responsible party should be treated as an offshore facility for limitation purposes.[2804]

This analysis appears to have limited application because of the restrictive provision of section 2707 of the OPA. It does not seem as if Congress intended for OPA to apply to foreign Outer Continental Shelf facilities. Rather it was meant to apply to the US Outer Continental Shelf. If it was meant to apply only to US Outer Continental shelf facilities, the only foreign countries that the analysis would apply to are coastal foreign countries whose territorial border or waters are contiguous or adjacent to that of the United States. It would in most cases apply to those countries because the breadth of the exclusive economic zone could extend beyond 200 nautical miles from the baselines from which the breadth of the territorial sea is measured.[2805] This means that the waves of the sea could carry an oil spill to the EEZ of an adjoining nation. This means countries like Canada, Mexico, Venezuela, Panama, and Cuba will be able to benefit

2803 See 33 USCA §2704(a)(1)-(2).

2804 33 USCA §2704(a)(3).

2805 See United Nations Convention on the Law of the Sea, Dec. 10, 1982, arts. 57, U.N.Doc. A/CONF. 62/122 (1982), reprinted in 21 I.L.M. 1261, 1280 (1982) [hereinafter UNCLOS III].

from section 2707 of OPA, while other nations may not be able to, because it is very difficult to imagine a situation where an oil spill that occurs within US territory would impact foreign nations that are very far away from US waters.

Even if the foreign nation is a contiguous territory to the US, if it does not have a subsisting treaty or executive agreement with the United States government, the only other way it can benefit from the OPA is for its legislature to pass a statute similar to the OPA that provides a comparable remedy for US claimants. If it does not have the political will to pass a statute that mirrors OPA, it should without further delay negotiate a treaty or executive agreement with the US so that it can benefit from this very comprehensive statute. The beauty of the OPA section conferring OPA rights on foreign claimants is that those foreign claimants who are qualified can not only sue US flag vessels or US owned facilities, but they can sue any vessel and facility properly identified as a responsible party under the OPA. Even though foreign claimants generally might not be able to recover removal costs from the Fund, foreign trustees can recover natural resources damages from the Fund. Private claimants residing in foreign countries can recover damages for loss of subsistence use of natural resources, loss of profits and earning capacity, as well as economic losses resulting from loss of real or personal property, directly from the responsible party.[2806] Foreign governments cannot recover damages for loss of revenue and the cost of providing increased public services from anyone. For the former, only the Government of the US, a state, or a political subdivision of a state can recover damages. For the latter, only a state or political subdivision of a state can recover damages.[2807]

2806 33 USCA §2702 (B)(C) & (E).

2807 See 33 USCA §2702(b)(2)(D) & (F).

# Chapter Thirteen

# JURISDICTIONAL & PROCEDURAL ISSUES – 33 USC § 2717

Statutory provisions:
"§ 2717. Litigation, jurisdiction, and venue

(a) Review of regulations

Review of any regulation promulgated under this Act may be had upon application by any interested person only in the Circuit Court of Appeals of the United States for the District of Columbia. Any such application shall be made within 90 days from the date of promulgation of such regulations. Any matter with respect to which review could have been obtained under this subsection shall not be subject to judicial review in any civil or criminal proceeding for enforcement or to obtain damages or recovery of response costs.

(b) Jurisdiction

Except as provided in subsections (a) and (c) of this section, the United States district courts shall have exclusive original jurisdiction over all controversies arising under this Act, without regard to the citizenship of the parties or the amount in controversy. Venue shall lie in any district in which the discharge or injury or damages occurred, or in which the defendant resides, may be found, has its principal office, or has appointed an agent for service of process. For the purposes of this section, the Fund shall reside in the District of Columbia.

(c) State court jurisdiction

A State trial court of competent jurisdiction over claims for removal costs or damages, as defined under this Act, may consider claims under this Act or State law and any final judgment of such court (when no longer subject to ordinary forms of review) shall be recognized, valid, and enforceable for all purposes of this Act."[2808]

## A. Jurisdiction & Venue

A most regrettable feature of the OPA 90, which will undoubtedly result in vessel interests incurring unnecessarily significant legal expenses in defending oil spill cases is contained in the provisions relating to jurisdiction and venue.[2809] The Act grants United States district courts federal question jurisdiction with regard to all controversies arising under the Act.[2810] Venue is proper in any district in which the discharge, injury, or damages occurred.[2811] It is easy to conceive of a situation in which the spill might affect several shorelines, thus causing OPA damages in different districts, and OPA removal costs in yet another district.

Additionally, OPA allows a claimant to sue in any district in which the RP resides, may be found, has its principal office, or has appointed an agent for service of process.[2812] Under this provision, a defendant might face suits all over the country for a single spill.[2813]

A more significant problem is that the OPA also grants state courts jurisdiction to consider claims under the Act.[2814] While state court actions under the Act may be removable to federal courts, there is a very real prospect of a defendant facing suits in several different state courts, as well as in different federal courts.[2815] Furthermore, the devise of the

---

2808 33 USC § 2717.

2809 33 USC § 2717.

2810 33 USC § 2717(b)

2811 Id.

2812 Id.

2813 Antonio J. Rodriguez & Paul A. C. Jaffe, The Oil Pollution Act of 1990, 15 Tul. Mar. L.J. 1, 21 (1990).

2814 33 USC § 2717(c).

2815 Antonio J. Rodriguez & Paul A. C. Jaffe, The Oil Pollution Act of 1990, 15 Tul. Mar. L.J. at 21.

concursus available under the Limitation Act is not a part of the defendant vessel owner's arsenal for consolidating oil pollution cases.[2816] These provisions are not conducive to a global and efficient resolution of disputes arising from an oil spill. Rather, the Act encourages piecemeal litigation of oil spill matters in various courts at added legal expense.[2817] Prior to the passing of the OPA the vessel could consolidate all actions against it into a single court and liability could be fixed, now under the OPA regime the possibility of consolidating such legal actions and restricting liability to the OPA limit has been foreclosed. The concursus mechanism is more important in the OPA context than in the context of previous statutes like the FWPCA and CERCLA because, OPA unlike these statutes has created direct private right of action to recover damages and cleanup costs, thus encouraging the filing of OPA suits by private parties in many US jurisdictions. The combined effect of the provisions allowing states to impose unlimited liability and allowing claimants to proceed to both state courts and federal courts, is that the responsible party may have to pay billions of dollars in claims for a single oil spill. If this happens, it might become insolvent if it is not a "deep pocket" defendant.

Professor Force, a renowned legal commentator considered the effect of Section 2717(c) of OPA which provides:

> "A State trial court of competent jurisdiction over claims for removal costs or damages, as defined under this Act, may consider claims under this Chapter or State law and any final judgment of such court (when no longer subject to ordinary forms of review) shall be recognized, valid, and enforceable for all purposes of this chapter..."

He reiterated the view that this means that in most instances, a claimant will have the option of bringing an OPA claim either in federal or state court.[2818] But he believes that section 2717(c), should be read in pari

2816 33 USC § 2718(a)(2).

2817 33 USC § 2717(b)-(c).

2818 See Robert Force Jonathan M. Gutoff, Limitation Of Liability In Oil Pollution Cases: In Search Of Concursus or Procedural Alternatives To Concursus, 22 Tul. Mar.

materia with section 2704(a) of OPA which provides that "the total of the liability of a responsible party under section [2702 (recovery of removal costs and damages under OPA) of this title],... with respect to each incident shall not exceed... [an amount calculated under the formula for limiting liability provided in the remainder of section 2704."[2819]

He also emphasized that this combined reading of the provisions of OPA makes it fairly clear that "OPA's limitation of liability provision applies to OPA claims regardless of whether such claims are filed in a federal court or a state court."[2820] He also observed that if OPA claims filed in state courts were not subject to section 2704's limitation provisions, then section 2704 would be superfluous because it could be so easily circumvented by the filing of OPA claims in state court.[2821]

## B. In Rem Action and Maritime Liens Under OPA:

The admiralty doctrine of personification treats the ship as the true defendant in an in rem action, with rights and responsibilities separate (at least in concept) from those of its owner. [2822] In rem actions are quite unique to American Admiralty practice.[2823] Specific rules on arrest in rem in the United States are established by Supplemental Rule C of the Supplemental Rules for Certain Admiralty and Maritime Claims, Federal Rules of Civil Procedure. The action in rem in the United States, under Supplemental Rule C, permits the arrest of any ship or other maritime

---

L.J. 331, 379 (Summer 1998).

2819 See Robert Force Jonathan M. Gutoff, Limitation Of Liability In Oil Pollution Cases: In Search of Concursus or Procedural Alternatives To Concursus, 22 Tul. Mar. L.J. at 379-380.

2820 Id at 380.

2821 Id.

2822 Martin Davies, In Defense of Unpopular Virtues: Personification and Ratification, 75 Tul. L. Rev. 337 (December 2000).

2823 See. T.J. Schoenbaum, Admiralty & Maritime Law, §18-3, at 894, West Group Hornbook Series (2d ed. 1994).

property to enforce a maritime lien,[2824] provided that the res (maritime property or vessel) is within the territorial jurisdiction of the federal district court concerned at the time the suit is filed or during the pendency of the action.[2825] Arrest perfects the lien, obtains jurisdiction, and procures pre-judgment security for the claim.[2826] Under Rule C, arrest is obtained by the filing of a complaint, verified on oath or solemn affirmation, accompanied by an affidavit.[2827] Judicial review is required before a warrant of arrest may issue (Rule C(3)), unless "exigent circumstances" make the review "impracticable."[2828] The warrant of arrest, accompanied by a summons to the defendant, are issued by the clerk, on the order of the court, and the Marshal arrests the vessel by posting the notice of arrest aboard the ship and serving a copy of the complaint and warrant upon the master or person in charge.[2829] Any person claiming an interest in the property arrested is entitled to a prompt post-arrest hearing, also compulsory under Supplemental Rule E(4)(f) of the Supplemental Rules for Certain Admiralty and Maritime Claims, Federal Rules of Civil Procedure. The vessel may be sold to satisfy the lien claim, but if the sale proceeds are insufficient to cover the claim, the owner is not liable for the balance, because the action in rem is directed exclusively against the ship or other res that has been arrested.[2830]

The relevant question for OPA purposes is whether a maritime lien exists under OPA to provide an in rem remedy against a polluting vessel.

---

2824 See William Tetley, Arrest Attachment and Related Maritime Law Procedures, 73 Tul. L. Rev. 1895, 1933 (June 1999) (hereinafter Tetley), (*citing*, Navieros Inter-Americanos v. M/V Vasilia Express, 120 F.3d 304, 313, 1997 AMC 2845, 2856 (1st Cir. 1997); Sembawang Shipyard, Ltd. v. Charger, Inc. & M/V Charger, 955 F.2d 983, 987, 1993 AMC 1341, 1345 (5th Cir. 1992); Rainbow Line, Inc. v. M/V Tequila, 480 F.2d 1024, 1028, 1973 AMC 1431, 1436 (2d Cir. 1973); Garcia v. M/V Kubbar, 4 F. Supp. 2d 99, 103, 1998 AMC 893, 896 (N.D.N.Y. 1998)).

2825 Tetley id. at 1933.

2826 Id.

2827 Id.

2828 Id.

2829 Id.

2830 Id. (citing Bay Casino, LLC. v. M/V Royal Empress, No. 98 CV 2333 (SJ), 1998 WL 566772, *2, 1998 AMC 2226, 2233 (E.D.N.Y. 1998).

First of all it is important to point out that unlike in maritime law where the owner may not be liable for the balance of a claim, OPA makes owners and operators of vessels jointly and severally liable. So, if a maritime lien exists under OPA to provide an in rem remedy against a polluting vessel, the owner of that vessel will always be liable for the balance of the claim. This also means that if a maritime lien exists under OPA to provide an in rem remedy against a polluting vessel, the claimant always gets a better deal because the operator and owner of the vessel, and the vessel itself will be jointly and severally liable. The OPA claimant can sue all of them at the same time for the entire claim or pick and choose the one that has the deepest pockets to pay the entire claim. It will now be up to the jointly and severally liable responsible parties to sue each other for contribution and indemnity pursuant to tort or contract principles. The OPA allows responsible parties to sue third parties who contribute to an oil spill for indemnity or contribution.[2831] An in rem action differs from maritime attachment in that an in rem action is brought against the vessel itself as defendant.[2832] By contrast, a vessel is attached only as an auxiliary to an in personam claim because the vessel is property belonging to the defendant.[2833]

The OPA does not specifically address whether a maritime lien exists under OPA to provide an in rem remedy against a responsible party's vessel. This issue was addressed by the district court in the case of *M/V EMILY S.*[2834] This court addressed whether a maritime lien exists under OPA to provide an in rem remedy against the tug EMILY S., who only towed the barge that actually discharged the oil.

First of all the court emphasized that it is well established that oil pollution claims are among the claims for which a maritime lien traditionally exists under the general maritime law.[2835] A maritime tort lien is an

---

2831 33 USCA §§2709-2710.

2832 See T.J. Schoenbaum, Admiralty & Maritime Law, §18-3, at 894, West Group Hornbook Series (2d ed. 1994).

2833 Id. at 894-95.

2834 See Puerto Rico v. M/V EMILY S., 1998 WL 938585, No. CIV. 94-1019CCC, at *1, 1998 AMC 2726 (D.P.R. 1998).

2835 M/V EMILY S., 1998 WL 938585, at *1, (*quoting*, T.J. Schoenbaum Admiralty and Maritime Law (2d Ed.1994) at 485)).

established right under the admiralty and maritime law, and oil pollution has consistently been held to be a maritime tort.[2836] The court acknowledged the fact that by its express terms, OPA does not specifically create a maritime lien, but instead preserves admiralty and maritime law remedies.[2837] OPA's predecessor statute, the FWPCA, was amended in 1970 to expressly reference the existence of an in rem remedy against a non-discharging vessel.[2838] The legislative history supporting this amendment confirmed that the FWPCA did not create such a remedy, but only acknowledged the existence of that remedy.[2839] In view of earlier judicial treatment of the in rem remedy under the FWPCA, the district court held that an in rem remedy is available under OPA against a non-discharging vessel for the maritime tort of oil pollution.[2840] Apart from this, the district court noted that the savings provisions of OPA[2841] preserve admiralty and maritime law remedies. The court relied on section 2751(e) of OPA,[2842] which provides in pertinent part:

"(e) Admiraity and maritime law

Except as otherwise provided in this chapter, this chapter does not affect-- )

(1) admiralty and maritime law; or

---

2836 Id. at *1, (*citing*, United States v. M/V BIG SAM, 681 F.2d 432, 440 (5th Cir.1982), *cert. denied* 462 U.S. 1132 (1983) (Oil spill resulting from collision between tug and tank barge on navigable waters is a maritime tort); United States v. City of Redwood City, 640 F.2d 963, 969-70 (9th Cir.1981) ("Oil pollution in navigable waters has been deemed a tort for which the United States is entitled damages."); In Re Exxon Valdez, 767 F.Supp. 1509, 1512 (D.Alaska 1991) (Courts have consistently held that oil spills from vessels into the navigable waters to be maritime torts); Burgess v. M/V TAMANO, 370 F.Supp. 247, 249 (D.Me.1973) (An oil spill constitutes a maritime tort), *aff'd. without opinion*, 559 F.2d 1200 (1st Cir.1977).

2837 See M/V EMILY S., 1998 WL 938585 at *1; see also, 33 U.S.C. §§ 2702, 2718, and 2751(e).

2838 Id. at 2.

2839 Id.

2840 Id.

2841 33 U.S.C. §§ 2718 and 2751(e).

2842 33 U.S.C. § 2751(e).

(2) the jurisdiction of the district courts of the United States with respect to civil actions under admiralty and maritime jurisdiction, saving to suitors in all cases all other remedies to which they are otherwise entitled."[2843]

The court observed that similarly, section 2718 of OPA,[2844] provides for preservation of additional requirements and liabilities under the state and federal laws for oil spill discharges and the threat of oil spill discharges.[2845] Based on the above reasoning, the court concluded that the provisions of OPA which preserve admiralty and maritime law, guarantees the existence of an in rem remedy under OPA. The court further concluded that a maritime lien had attached to the M/V EMILY S because of the maritime tort of pollution.[2846]

This decision is consistent with the provisions of sections 2751(e) and 2718 of the OPA. If the court had reached a different decision, it would have surprised well informed maritime scholars considering the fact that the OPA was supposed to expand on FWPCA's liability provisions. The US Congress tried to amend the OPA in 1992 by adding a subsection (e) to section 2702. The then proposed subsection (e) would have provided in pertinent part:

"(e) The costs and damages described in subsection (b) (OPA damages section) shall constitute a maritime lien on the vessel that may be recovered in an action in rem in the district court of the United States for any district within which a vessel may be found."[2847]

The US Congress was only trying to do the same thing it did to the FWPCA in 1970, when it added a similar provision to the statute. The at-

---

2843 See M/V EMILY S., 1998 WL 938585 at *2.

2844 33 U.S.C. § 2718.

2845 M/V EMILY S., 1998 WL 938585 at *2.

2846 Id. at *2.

2847 1992 U.S.C.C.A.N. 2422,2433, H.R. Rep. No. 102-474(IX), 102ND Cong., 2ND Sess. 1992, 1992 WL 136097 (Leg.Hist). If the proposed amendment of the House of Representatives' Committee on Merchant Marine & Fisheries had passed, it would have been codified as section 2102 of Energy Policy Act of 1992, Pub.L. 102-486, Oct. 24, 1992, 106 Stat. 2776.

tempt to amend the OPA in order to add this provision died prematurely in Congress. But with the clarification and construction of the *M/V Emily S.* court no one should be in doubt as to what the law is on this issue. What Congress could not accomplish due to lack of Congressional consensus, has been partly accomplished by the decision in *M/V Emily S.*, provided other courts adopt its reasoning.

The Congress noted with frustration in its unsuccessful amendment deliberations, that with regard to foreign vessels, in personam enforcement is commonly unavailable against foreign owners or operators.[2848] Therefore, the authority to detain a vessel would be a particularly effective collection technique against commercial vessels.[2849] Observing that operating costs can run to hundreds of thousands of dollars per hour of delay, Congress was convinced that the mere threat of such a collection action is a powerful, and often the only motivating, factor for owners of foreign vessels to pay their penalties.[2850] The Congress therefore wanted to use the amendment to restore the authority to impose liability in rem on a vessel whose owner, operator, or person in charge is liable for removal costs or damages resulting from an oil spill.[2851] The main focus of Congress in the failed amendment is foreign vessels that are not owned by foreign governments, not vessels that are foreign government owned.

The Foreign Sovereign Immunities Act of 1976 (FSIA)[2852] governs the issue of the liability of foreign-government owned vessels for oil pollution. The FSIA codifies the restrictive theory of sovereign immunity in the United States.[2853] In broad terms, it functions "to facilitate and depoliticize litigation against foreign states and to minimize irritations in foreign

2848 1992 U.S.C.C.A.N. 2434.

2849 Id. at 2434.

2850 Id.

2851 Id.

2852 28 U.S.C. §§1330, 1602-1611 (1976), amended by 28 U.S.C. §§1605(a)(6), (b)(1), (c)-(d), 1610 (a)(6), (e) (1988 & Supp. V 1993).

2853 Russell J. Pope, Maritime Arrest Under The Foreign Sovereign Immunities Act: An Anachronism, 62 Tex. L. Rev. 511, 521 (1993).

relations arising out of such litigation,"[2854] by entrusting the resolution of questions of sovereign immunity to the judicial branch of Government.[2855]

"Section 1605(b) of the FSIA is tailored to suits in admiralty where a private claimant seeks to enforce a maritime lien against a vessel of a foreign state engaged in commercial activity."[2856] The purpose of this subsection is to permit a plaintiff to bring suit in a U.S. district court arising out of a maritime lien involving a vessel or cargo of a foreign sovereign without arresting the vessel, by instituting an in personam action against the foreign state.[2857] In other words Section 1605(b) is designed to avoid arrests of such vessels.[2858]

Thus, "the FSIA replaces the in rem action against the ship of a foreign state with a pseudo in personam action."[2859] The claimant serves the master of the ship, forwards a copy of the summons and complaint to the foreign state itself,[2860] and thereby acquires jurisdiction in a United States court.[2861] The codification of this procedure for obtaining in personam jurisdiction over the foreign state thus renders unnecessary the practice of attaching a vessel to obtain in rem jurisdiction.[2862]

---

2854 Id. at 521 (quoting, Letter from Deputy Secretary of State Robert S. Ingersoll and Deputy Attorney General Harold R. Tyler, Jr., to Speaker of the House Carl O. Albert (Oct. 31, 1975), H.R. REP. NO. 94-1487, 94th Cong., 2d Sess., 1, 45, reprinted in 1976 U.S.C.C.A.N. 6604, 6634).

2855 Letter from Deputy Secretary of State Robert S. Ingersoll and Deputy Attorney General Harold R. Tyler, Jr., to Speaker of the House Carl O. Albert (Oct. 31, 1975), H.R. REP. NO. 94-1487, 94th Cong., 2d Sess., at 45, reprinted in 1976 U.S.C.C.A.N. at 6634.

2856 Russell J. Pope, Maritime Arrest Under The Foreign Sovereign Immunities Act: An Anachronism, 62 Tex. L. Rev. at 521-522.

2857 Id at 522.

2858 Id.

2859 Id.

2860 Id. at 522, *see also* 28 U.S.C. § 1608 (1976).

2861 Id, see also 28 U.S.C. § 1330(b) (1976), which states: '[p]ersonal jurisdiction over a foreign state shall exist as to every claim for relief over which the district courts have jurisdiction... where service has been made under section 1608 of this title.'

2862 Russell J. Pope, Maritime Arrest Under The Foreign Sovereign Immunities Act: An Anachronism, 62 Tex. L. Rev. at 522, (citing Congressional historical statement that "[T]his bill would for the first time in U.S. law, provide a statutory procedure for making service upon, and obtaining in personam jurisdiction over, a foreign state. This would render unnecessary the practice of seizing and attaching the property of a foreign

The definition of "commercial activity" for the purposes of the FSIA is codified in Section 1603 of the Act which provides:

"(d) A "commercial activity" means either a regular course of commercial conduct or a particular commercial transaction or act. The commercial character of an activity shall be determined by reference to the nature of the course of conduct or particular transaction or act, rather than by reference to its purpose.
(e) A "commercial activity carried on in the United States by a foreign state" means commercial activity carried on by such state and having substantial contact with the United States."[2863]

Section 1603 of the FSIA's defines a foreign state:

(a) A "foreign state"... includes a political subdivision of a foreign state or any agency or instrumentality of a foreign state as defined in subsection (b).
(b) An "agency or instrumentality of a foreign state" means any entity -
(1) which is a separate legal person, corporate or otherwise, and
(2) which is an organ of a foreign state or political subdivision thereof, or a majority of whose shares or other ownership interest is owned by a foreign state or political subdivision thereof, and
(3) which is neither a citizen of a State of the United States as defined in section 1332(c) and (d) of this title, nor created under the laws of any third country."

Section 1603(b)(3) of the FSIA is very important because it would prevent a foreign country from relying on this in rem action immunity if the country's agency or instrumentality that owns the discharging vessel is a corporation created **under the laws of a third country**.

If a vessel is demise chartered to a foreign country or its agency or instrumentality, it will be entitled to the immunity in the FSIA because

---

government for the purpose of obtaining jurisdiction.' H.R. REP. NO. 1487, 94th Cong., 2d Sess. at 8, reprinted in 1976 U.S. CODE CONG. & AD. NEWS 6606).

2863 28 U.S.C. § 1603(d)-(e).

a demise charterer is owner pro hac vice.[2864] In *Coastal Cargo Company, Inc. v. M/V Gustav Sule*,[2865] it was held that a corporation wholly owned by the Estonian government constituted a "foreign state" for purposes of section of the Foreign Sovereign Immunities Act providing that property of foreign state in the United States is immune from attachment, arrest and execution. The court also held that a vessel was immune from seizure under section of the FSIA protecting property of foreign state in the United States from attachment, arrest or execution, where demise or bareboat charterer, as owner pro hac vice of vessel, was corporation wholly owned by foreign state.[2866] The court also held that the fact that the vessel was time chartered to another corporation did not preclude the invocation of the FSIA.[2867]

## C. REMOVAL OF OPA CASES FROM STATE COURT TO FEDERAL COURT

One question that agitates the mind of lawyers is whether an OPA case already filed in state court can be removed by an OPA defendant to a US Federal District Court.

In *Alicia Tanguis v. M/V Westchester*,[2868] the District Court, for the Eastern District of Louisiana held inter alia that claims under Oil Pollution Act were removable to federal court. In this case, plaintiffs with fishing and oyster interests in area affected by oil spill filed putative class action lawsuit in state court against defendants allegedly responsible for the spill.

---

2864 The demise or bareboat charter is, typically, a long-term agreement 'vesting in one person most of the incidents of ownership in a capital asset of that business--the ship--while another retains the general ownership and the right of reversion.' Grant Gilmore & Charles Black, Jr., The Law of Admiralty 239 (2d ed. 1975). In contrast to the time and voyage charters, in a demise charter the owner of the vessel relinquishes control and possession of the vessel to another. As a result of the unique nature of the demise, the charterer is considered to be the owner pro hac vice. Gilmore & Black, id. at 242.

2865 Coastal Cargo Co., Inc. V. M/V Gustav Sule, 942 F.Supp. 1082 (Ed. La. 1996).

2866 Id. at 1082.

2867 Id. at 1082.

2868 153 F.Supp.2d 859 (E.D. La 2001).

After removal to federal court, plaintiffs moved to remand the case to state court. In the alternative, the plaintiffs asserted the novel theory that OPA, by its own terms, prevents removal. The removal statute states that:

"[e]xcept as otherwise expressly provided by Act of Congress, any civil action brought in a State court of which the district courts of the United States have original jurisdiction, may be removed" to an appropriate federal court."[2869]

Although OPA does not expressly preclude removal, the plaintiffs argued that a Congressional intent to prevent removal nevertheless could be divined from OPA's jurisdictional provision, in section 2717, and its savings provision, section 2751. This was apparently a question of first impression anywhere, as none of the parties cited any authority on point, and the Court had found none.[2870]

With respect to federal courts, OPA's jurisdictional provision states that

"[e]xcept as provided in subsections (a) and (c) of this section, the United States district courts shall have **exclusive original jurisdiction** over all controversies arising under this chapter, without regard to the citizenship of the parties or the amount in controversy."[2871]

The court found that this provision clearly establishes original federal district court jurisdiction over OPA claims.[2872] The plaintiffs seemed to imply that the inclusion of the word "original" in subsection (b) means that federal courts have jurisdiction over OPA claims only if they are originally filed in federal court.[2873] Hence, a federal court would have no jurisdiction over OPA claims originally brought in state court, and such actions could not be removed. In its rejection of this argument, the court found that it

2869 28 U.S.C. § 1441(a).

2870 Alicia Tanguis v. M/V Westchester, 153 F.Supp.2d 859, 862.

2871 33 U.S.C. § 2717(b).

2872 M/V Westchester, 153 F.Supp.2d at 862-63.

2873 Id. at 863.

painfully distorts the ordinary understanding of the concept of "original jurisdiction," which is generally understood to be a "court's power to hear and decide a matter before any other court can review the matter."[2874] The court explained further that a court invested with original jurisdiction is a court "of first instance," as opposed to an appellate court.[2875]

With respect to state courts, OPA's jurisdictional provision states that a "State trial court of competent jurisdiction over claims for removal costs or damages, as defined under this chapter, may consider claims under this chapter or State law and any final judgment of such court (when no longer subject to ordinary forms of review) shall be recognized, valid, and enforceable for all purposes of this chapter."[2876] This section is an express exception to exclusive original federal jurisdiction over certain OPA claims and establishes concurrent state court jurisdiction in those cases.

The court observed that as a general matter, "the existence of concurrent state and federal jurisdiction does not preclude removal of an action to a federal court."[2877] The court reasoned that the mere fact that OPA creates concurrent state court jurisdiction for some types of OPA claims does not demonstrate a Congressional intent to prohibit removal.[2878]

In its dismissal of the plaintiff's argument, the court held that section 2717(c) of OPA (jurisdictional & venue provisions) by itself does not indicate an intent to prohibit removal, as plaintiffs had argued, but merely provides that state and federal claims for removal costs or damages can be brought together in a state forum, rather than requiring plaintiffs to bring their OPA claims exclusively in federal court.[2879]

---

2874 I. (quoting, BLACK'S LAW DICTIONARY 856 (7th ed.1999)).

2875 Id. (quoting, MARY KAY KANE, CIVIL PROCEDURE IN A NUT SHELL 8 (4th ed.1996)).

2876 33 U.S.C. § 2717(c).

2877 M/V Westchester, 153 F.Supp.2d at 863, (citing, B CHARLES ALAN WRIGHT, ARTHUR R. MILLER & Edward H. Cooper, Federal Practice and Procedure § 3721, at 303 (3d ed.1998) (footnote omitted); Baldwin v. Sears, Roebuck & Co., 667 F.2d 458, 460 (5th Cir.1982). ("Unless... there is an express declaration by Congress to the contrary, all types of civil actions, in which there is concurrent original jurisdiction in both federal and state courts, are removable.")).

2878 Id. at 863.

2879 Id. at 864.

The court reasoned further that even if these two jurisdictional provisions could be considered ambiguous, the corresponding legislative history did not support plaintiffs' theory.[2880] First, the legislative history concerning jurisdiction does not mention any intent to prevent removal, as would be expected in the face of 28 U.S.C. § 1441(a)'s requirement that an exception to removal be "express." Second, the Senate description of these two sections is remarkably straightforward:

> "Appropriate United States district courts are given jurisdiction arising under the Act. Appropriate State courts are given jurisdiction over claims under section 102, and final judgments of such courts are valid and enforceable for all purposes of sections 102 and 103."[2881]

In other words, state courts have concurrent jurisdiction over certain OPA claims, while federal district courts have jurisdiction over all OPA claims (except for challenges to regulations promulgated under OPA, which subsection (a) of the jurisdictional provision assigns to the D.C. Circuit). The Court rejected the plaintiffs' reading of this legislative history.

The plaintiffs' also argued that OPA's "saving-to-suitors" clause[2882] is an express declaration of Congressional intent to prohibit removal of OPA claims. This argument has its foundation in 28 U.S.C. § 1333 and its interpretive jurisprudence.[2883]

28 U.S.C. § 1333 provides that federal district courts shall have "original jurisdiction, exclusive of the courts of the States, of... [a]ny civil case of admiralty or maritime jurisdiction, saving to suitors in all cases all

---

2880 Id.

2881 Id. (citing,. REP. NO. 101-94, U.S.Code Cong. & Admin.News (USCCAAN) 1990, pp. 722, 738).

2882 (e) Admiralty and maritime law

Except as otherwise provided in this chapter, this chapter does not affect--

(1) admiralty and maritime law; or

(2) the jurisdiction of the district courts of the United States with respect to civil actions under admiralty and maritime jurisdiction, saving to suitors in all cases all other remedies to which they are otherwise entitled. 33 USCA § 2751.

2883 M/V Westchester, 153 F.Supp.2d at 864-65.

other remedies to which they are otherwise entitled...." "The effect of the saving- to-suitors clause essentially is to provide a plaintiff who has an in personam claim the choice of proceeding in an ordinary civil action in a state or federal court, rather than bringing a libel in admiralty in federal court."[2884] The court pointed out that general maritime claims do not provide the basis for federal question jurisdiction and generally cannot be removed, on their own, under the terms of the removal statute.[2885] The court reasoned further that admiralty saving-clause cases properly filed in state court cannot be removed unless admiralty jurisdiction is exclusive.[2886] Removal in admiralty is therefore limited to (1) claims meeting the test of diversity jurisdiction where none of the defendants properly served is a citizen of the state in which the suit is filed; and (2) claims with an independent jurisdictional basis outside the Romero rule."[2887]

Here, plaintiffs originally filed suit in state court, expressly alleging state court jurisdiction "pursuant to the Savings to Suitors clause of 28 U.S.C. § 1333" (even though they also brought suit against the vessel, which they successfully attached under Louisiana law). Defendants did not allege diversity of jurisdiction in their Notice of Removal, and the First Amending Petition, indicated an absence of complete diversity. Thus, the question was whether plaintiffs' OPA claims provided the Court with an independent jurisdictional basis outside the Romero rule. Plaintiffs argued that OPA claims do not provide a basis for federal question jurisdiction because Congress included a "saving-to-suitors" clause in OPA to achieve the same result for OPA claims as would be attained for general maritime claims under the Romero rule. The provision in question comes within OPA's "Savings provisions," 33 U.S.C. § 2751. Subsection (e) states:

---

2884 Id. at 865. (citing, A CHARLES ALAN WRIGHT, ARTHUR R. MILLER & Edward H. Cooper, Federal Practice and Procedure § 3672, at 301 (3d ed.1998)).

2885 Id., salso 28 U.S.C. § 1441(b) (providing for removal based on federal question jurisdiction).

2886 Id. at 865.

2887 In Romero v. International Terminal Operating Co., 358 U.S. 354, 79 S.Ct. 468, 3 L.Ed.2d 368 (1959), the Supreme Court held that general maritime claims do not "arise under the Constitution, treaties, or laws of the United States" within the meaning of 28 U.S.C. § 1331. Id. at 865.

"Admiralty and maritime law Except as otherwise provided in this chapter, this chapter does not affect--

(1) admiralty and maritime law; or
(2) the jurisdiction of the district courts of the United States with respect to civil actions under admiralty and maritime jurisdiction, saving to suitors in all cases all other remedies to which they are otherwise entitled."

Plaintiffs argued that, because "saving-to-suitors" clauses are "extremely rare in the United States Code,... the clear intent of OPA's savings provision... is that removal is prohibited."[2888] While the court agreed with plaintiffs that OPA's "saving-to-suitors" language is conspicuous, it however concluded that the inclusion of this language instead of an express removal prohibition is a rather elliptical way to achieve a simple result.[2889] For example, the Jones Act contains an express removal prohibition: it incorporates the express non-removal provision of 28 U.S.C. § 1445(a), which provides that "A civil action in any State court against a carrier or its receivers or trustees... may not be removed to any district court of the United States."[2890] The court pointed out that this provision, unlike the OPA provision, clearly satisfies 28 U.S.C. § 1441(a)'s requirement that exceptions to the general removal rule be "express" and does not require courts to engage in any further statutory interpretation.[2891] Moreover, using a saving-to-suitors clause to prohibit removal would be rather anomalous, since 28 U.S.C. § 1333's saving- to-suitor clause, in and of itself, does not guarantee a non-federal forum. It only saves to suitors in all cases, all other remedies to which they are otherwise entitled. As the Fifth Circuit stated in *Poirrier v. Nicklos Drilling Co.*, 648 F.2d 1063, 1066 (1981):

"The "saving to suitors" clause does no more than preserve the right of maritime suitors to pursue non-maritime remedies. It does not guarantee them

---

2888 M/V Westchester, 153 F.Supp.2d at 866.

2889 Id. at 866.

2890 Id.

2891 Id.

a nonfederal forum, or limit the right of defendants to remove such actions to federal court where there exists some basis for federal jurisdiction other than admiralty."[2892]

The court also held that OPA is an independent basis for federal jurisdiction. To the extent that any ambiguities in the statutory language remain, the legislative history also supports the view that OPA establishes an entirely new federal cause of action.[2893] Referring to the Congressional Record, the court in *Rice v. Harken Exploration Co.*,[2894] recognized that OPA "represents Congress's attempt to provide a comprehensive framework in the area of marine oil pollution." Indeed, the Senate Report states that OPA "create[s] a single Federal law providing cleanup authority, penalties, and liability for oil pollution."[2895] The Senate found that "the Nation need[ed]... a package of complementary international, national, and State laws that will adequately compensate victims of oil spills, provide quick, efficient cleanup, minimize damage to fisheries, wildlife and other natural resources and internalize those costs within the oil industry and its transportation sector" to replace the inadequate and "fragmented collection of Federal and State laws" in existence prior to OPA.[2896] Thus, the legislative history makes clear Congress's desire to create "an entirely new [OPA] cause of action," previously unknown to maritime law.

The legislative history also militated against plaintiffs' position that OPA's admiralty and maritime law savings clause was intended to bar removal. The Conference report indicates that, at the time the proposed legislation reached the Conference, it contained some non-preemption provisions but lacked others. Accordingly, the Conference added the admiralty and maritime law savings clause, "as well as certain other boilerplate savings provisions, including those regarding repealed laws and legislative construction" to make clear that "there is no change in current

2892 Id.

2893 Id. at 867.

2894 89 F.Supp.2d 820, 822 (N.D.Tex.1999).

2895 S. REP. NO. 101-94, U.S.Code Cong. & Admin.News 1990, pp. 722, 730.

2896 Id.

law unless there is a specific provision to the contrary."[2897] Consistent with this principle, OPA does not "change the jurisdiction in incidents that are within the admiralty and maritime laws of the United States."[2898] The court held that this language indicates that, insofar as OPA does not preempt maritime law, the *Romero* rule is unchanged. Conversely, where OPA does remove an incident from traditional maritime law, jurisdiction is changed.[2899]

Even more important, the same legislative history says nothing about prohibiting removal. If Congress did intend, as plaintiffs argued, to take the long way to removal preclusion, one would expect that this intention would at least be expressed in the legislative history.

Based on all of these reasons, the Court concluded that OPA claims arise under the "Constitution, treaties or laws of the United States" and are removable to federal court pursuant to 28 U.S.C. § 1441(b). The defendants' removal was therefore proper.[2900]

## D. RIGHT TO JURY TRIAL

This part of chapter thirteen will examine the question of whether a right to a jury trial is available under the OPA. It will examine the possibility of having a jury trial in: (1) actions to recover damages against a responsible party, (2) actions to recover removal costs against a responsible party, & actions for contribution by a responsible party against a third party.

Over two centuries ago, William Blackstone described the civil jury trial as 'the glory of the English law.'[2901] While the precise origin of the civil jury trial remains somewhat of a mystery, legal scholars estimate that

---

2897 H.R. Conf. Rep. 101-653 (1990), reprinted in 1990 U.S.C.C.A.N. 779.

2898 Id.

2899 M/V Westchester, 153 F.Supp.2d at 867.

2900 Id. at 869.

2901 See Richard S. Altman, United States v. Tull: A Polluters Right To A Jury Trial, 4 Pace Env. L. Rev. 473, 474 (Spring 1987) (*citing*, 3 W. Blackstone, Commentaries on the Laws of England 379 (Bell ed. 1972).)

the modern version of this judicial entity took form by the year 1408.[2902] Realizing the importance of the civil jury trial in the English system, that right was written into the United States Constitution by the framers. This right to civil jury trial was enshrined in the Seventh Amendment to the Constitution of the United States. The Seventh Amendment of the Constitution provides that "in Suits at common law, where the value in controversy shall exceed twenty dollars, the right of trial by jury shall be preserved."[2903] The framers recognized three basic types of courts, existing at the time the Constitution and, later, the Seventh Amendment were ratified; common law courts, equity courts and admiralty courts. Jury trials were available then only in the common law courts, and that is what the Seventh Amendment preserves; a jury trial in cases that would have been common law cases in 1791.[2904] The Amendment applies to the trial by jury right in federal court, governed by federal law, irrespective of whether the claim at issue arises under state or federal law.[2905]

If the claim originates under state law, the determination of rights and remedies is governed by state law, even though the right to trial by jury is controlled by federal law.[2906] Further, in federal court, the Seventh Amendment guarantees and preserves the same rights for claims arising under both federal and state law, unless the state law claim "disrupts the judge-jury relationship in the federal courts."[2907] The Seventh Amendment right has been strictly upheld throughout U.S. judicial history. As Justice Sutherland so accurately explained in *Dimick v. Schiedt*;[2908] "maintenance of the jury as a fact-finding body is of such importance and occupies so firm a place in our history and jurisprudence that any seeming curtailment of the right to a jury trial should be scrutinized with the utmost

---

2902 Id. at 474 (*citing*, D. Nasmith, The Institutes of English Public Law 141 (1980)).

2903 U.S.Const. amend. VII.

2904 See South Port Marine v. Gulf Oil Limited Partnership, 56 F. Supp. 2d 104, 107, 1999 AMC 2113 (D. Me. 1999).

2905 Simler v. Conner, 372 U.S. 221, 222 (1963) (per curiam).

2906 Id. at 222.

2907 See Byrd v. Blue Ridge Rural Elec. Coop. Inc., 356 U.S. 525, 538 (1958) (*citing* Herron v. Southern Pacific Co., 283 U.S. 91 (1931)).

2908 293 U.S. 474 (1934).

care."[2909] In *Jacob v. City of New York*,[2910] the Supreme Court noted that ' a right so fundamental and sacred to the citizen, whether guaranteed by the Constitution or provided by statute, should be jealously guarded by the courts.'[2911] The Seventh Amendment only requires a jury trial for 'suits at common law.'[2912] Thus, while such actions have historically been granted a jury trial,[2913] suits in equity[2914] have been tried to the court or judge.

When do plaintiffs have the right to a jury trial in civil cases in federal courts?[2915] There are two basic answers to this question. One is that plaintiffs have this right whenever a federal statute supplies it.[2916] Defendants generally cannot assail such a statutory right because they have no offsetting constitutional right to a nonjury trial in federal courts upon which they can argue that the terms of the statute should not be

---

2909 Id. at 486; see also United States v. Regan, 232 U.S. 37 (1914) (holding that in civil actions, juries are to decide factual issues by a reasonable preponderance of the evidence).

2910 315 U.S. 752 (1942).

2911 Id. at 752-53.

2912 Under Fed. R. Civ. P. 38(d) this right may be waived. Furthermore, the right is not automatic, but must be affirmatively demanded by one of the parties to the action. Fed. R. Civ. P. 38(b).

2913 James, Right To A Jury Trial In Civil Actions, 72 Yale L.J. 655 (1963).

2914 See Richard S. Altman, United States v. Tull: A Polluters Right To A Jury Trial, 4 Pace Env. L. Rev. 473, 475, n17 (Spring 1987) (Stating that at common law, a citizen of England could, in some instances, take his case into the Court of Chancery to seek equitable remedies. The equity courts evolved into a parallel system of justice, existing side by side with the courts of law. The chancery system developed its own system of principles and rules. In the United States, the federal government, as well as most of the states, has merged law and equity into one system. As in England, though, equity remains an 'extraordinary' remedy. One may seek equity only if there is not an adequate remedy at law. Although the same courts now administer both legal and equitable relief, equity jurisdiction requires that its own principles be applied. 30 C.J.S. Equity §§ 1-10, 18-21 (1965). *Also citing*, Infusaid Corp. v. Intermedics Infusaid, Inc., 739 F.2d 661, 668 (1st Cir. 1984) ('[T]he general rule is that if there is an adequate remedy at law, equitable relief is unavailable.'); Suchan v. Rutherford, 90 Ida. 288, 295, 410 P.2d 434, 438 (1966) ('[E]quity will not intervene where the aggrieved party has a plain, speedy, adequate, and complete remedy at law.'); Smith v. Hauser 262 N.C. 697, 701, 138 S.E.2d 501, 504 (1964) ('[E]quity is intended to supplement, and not usurp the functions of the courts of law').

2915 Jason Weeden, Note: Historically Immune Defendants and The Seventh Amendment, 74 Tex. L. Rev. 655 (February 1996).

2916 Id. at 655.

followed.[2917] The central problem this scenario causes for courts is deciding with which statutes Congress intended to create a cause of action triable to a jury.[2918]

The second answer is that plaintiffs have the right to a jury trial in civil cases in federal courts when the Seventh Amendment guarantees it as earlier explained above.[2919] The central problem for courts here is deciding to which cases the Amendment applies. The language of the Seventh Amendment, it seems, declares the scope of the guarantee: The "right of trial by jury" is "preserved" for "Suits at common law."[2920] This language, however, only serves to create a further question: What is a suit at common law?[2921] Although this question is facially simple, it has spawned a highly unstable jurisprudence that has been described as "a cumbersome system replete with anomalous and inconsistent rules."[2922]

This jurisprudence, and the academic literature surrounding it, have produced one central theme for determining a plaintiff's right to a jury under the Seventh Amendment, as well as a number of tangents.[2923] The central tenet of Seventh Amendment jurisprudence is that the Amendment's reference to "common law" implicates English practice in 1791, the year the Amendment was ratified.[2924] Following this tenet, conventional wisdom provides that the current rule in Seventh Amendment cases involves a two-part test for determining when a given action is to be considered a suit at common law: Parties in federal district courts may receive a jury trial for claims (1) that more resemble those claims tried in law courts

---

2917 Id.

2918 Id.

2919 Id.

2920 Id at 655 (quoting, U.S. Const. amend. VII).

2921 Id. (citing, Mary K. Kane, Civil Jury Trial: The Case for Reasoned Iconoclasm, 28 Hastings L.J. 1, 1-4 (1976) (discussing the "deceptively precise language" of the Seventh Amendment).

2922 Id.

2923 Id. at 656.

2924 Id. (*citing*, United States v. Wonson, 28 F. Cas. 745, 750 (C.C.D. Mass. 1812) (No. 16,750) ("Beyond all question, the common law here alluded to... is the common law of England....")).

than those in courts of equity or admiralty in eighteenth-century England, and (2) for which the remedies sought more resemble those historically provided in law courts rather than equity courts.[2925]

In *Curtis v. Loether*,[2926] the Supreme Court noted that it was primarily the intention behind the Seventh Amendment to preserve the right to trial by jury as it existed in 1791 when the Amendment was originally enacted. However, the Court held that the right to trial by jury extends beyond those common law forms of action accepted and practiced during that time.[2927] For example, in *Pernell v. Southall Realty*,[2928] the Supreme Court held that the Seventh Amendment requires trial by jury in even those actions that were not known at common law as long as the action involves those rights and remedies that are traditionally involved in an action at law rather than an action at equity or admiralty.[2929] This example of the *Parnell* Supreme court case is particularly important because a lot of jurisdictions in the US have modified several common law principles. So, even if the modified rule is not analogous to the common law rule of old, it still remains firmly rooted in its common law foundations without which its superstructures could not have evolved. Even modified common law rules have been re-modified over the years and many will still undergo dynamic metamorphosis. For instance, the old trend in most jurisdictions in the United States was the contributory negligence theory whereby a plaintiff that had contributed to its own damages or injury could not recover in tort even if its damages was 1% or less, now the new trend in

---

2925 Id. Stating that one of the Supreme Court's more recent articulations of the conventional test appeared in Chauffeurs, Teamsters & Helpers Local No. 391 v. Terry, 494 U.S. 558, 565 (1990) ("First, we compare the statutory action to 18th-century actions brought in the courts of England prior to the merger of the courts of law and equity. Second, we examine the remedy sought and determine whether it is legal or equitable in nature." (quoting Tull v. United States, 481 U.S. 412, 417-18 (1987))), *citing also*, Matthew F. Davis, Comment, Beyond the Dicta: The Seventh Amendment Right to Trial by Jury Under Title VII, 38 U. Kan. L. Rev. 1003, 1012-15 (1990) (discussing the Court's two- part test as developed in *Tull*, Granfinanciera, and Terry)).

2926 415 US 189 (1974).

2927 *Curtis*, 415 US at 189 (1974).

2928 416 US 363 (1974).

2929 *Pernell*, 416 US at 375.

majority of US jurisdictions is the comparative fault principle whereby a plaintiff's contribution to its own damages will not bar its recovery of damages, rather the damages will be reduced by the plaintiff's percentage of fault. Some of these types of modernization or modification of common law principles is done by statutory enactments.

The phrase "common law" in the Seventh Amendment, as interpreted by the Supreme Court, is used in "contradistinction" to equity and admiralty and includes not only suits recognized by common law in its earlier and historical proceedings, but also those suits in which legal rights were to be ascertained and determined. Thus, those cases that recognized equitable rights and where equitable remedies were administered were not entitled to trial by jury.[2930] The *Curtis* case is recognized for holding that the Seventh Amendment applies to those new causes of action that are created by Congress as long as the statute creates legal rights and remedies that are enforceable in an action for damages in courts of law.[2931] In *Shields v. Thomas*,[2932] the Supreme Court declared that the Seventh Amendment does not include the exclusive jurisdiction of an equity court, but rather is restricted to rights and remedies that are legal by nature.[2933]

An interesting aspect of this issue comes to light when there is a joinder of legal and equitable or admiralty issues.[2934] In *Dairy Queen, Inc. v. Wood*[2935] and *Beacon Theatres, Inc. v. Westover*,[2936] it was held that when both legal and equitable claims are presented in a single case, only in the rarest of circumstances can the right to a jury trial of legal issues be lost through prior determination of equitable claims. In sum, if a legal claim is joined with an equitable claim there is a Seventh Amendment right to a jury trial on the legal claim as well as on all the issues common to both the legal and equitable claim. The right to a jury trial cannot be abridged by

---

2930 Parsons v. Bedford, 28 US 433, 446-47 (1830).

2931 *Curtis*, 415 US at 194.

2932 59 US 253 (1856).

2933 *Shields*, 59 US at 262.

2934 See FRCP 18(a), allowing for the joinder of legal and equitable claims.

2935 369 US 469 (1962).

2936 359 US 500 (1959).

merely characterizing the legal claim as incidental to the equitable relief that is sought.[2937]

**(1) Actions to Recover Damages against a Responsible Party:**

It appears that there is a right to a jury trial under section 2702(b)(2) (providing for damages) of the OPA. Unlike its predecessor statutes like the FWPCA and CERCLA, OPA specifically creates a damages right of action for private parties in section 2702(b)(2)(B), (C) & (E). It also creates a damages right of action for government parties in section 2702(b)(2)(A), (D) & (F). If the two part test earlier discussed is applied to this section a right to jury trial can be established.

*Applying the test:*. Parties in federal district courts may receive a jury trial for claims (1) that more resemble those claims tried in law courts than those in courts of equity or admiralty in eighteenth-century England, and (2) for which the remedies sought more resemble those historically provided in law courts rather than equity courts.[2938] Based on this test for a party to enjoy a jury trial in damage claims under the OPA, we have to look to see if the damages/remedy allowed in the OPA: (1) more resemble those claims tried in law courts than those in courts of equity or admiralty in eighteenth-century England, and (2) more resemble the remedies historically provided in law courts rather than courts of equity. OPA liability is strict, joint and several. Joint and several liability is a rule in common law of torts.[2939] Joint and several liability arises under the common law in several situations. A group of individuals acting in concert to commit a tort or failing to perform a common duty are jointly liable.[2940] A relationship

2937 Ross v. Bernhard, 396 US 531, 539 (1970).

2938 Chauffeurs, Teamsters & Helpers Local No. 391 v. Terry, 494 U.S. 558, 565 (1990) ("First, we compare the statutory action to 18th-century actions brought in the courts of England prior to the merger of the courts of law and equity. Second, we examine the remedy sought and determine whether it is legal or equitable in nature." (*quoting* Tull v. United States, 481 U.S. 412, 417-18 (1987))).

2939 USA Group Loan Services, Inc. v. Riley, 82 F.3d 708 (7th Cir. 1996).

2940 *The Atlas*, 3 Otto 302, 93 U.S. 302, 23 L.Ed. 863 (1876).

between two individuals strong enough to create vicarious liability (e.g. master-servant) also can produce joint and several liability.[2941] Courts have extended the doctrine to cases where individuals acting independently produce an indivisible injury, essentially for the public policy reason that it is unfair to give the victimized plaintiff the difficult burden of proving each defendant's share of the injury. [2942] When a third party has sustained an injury to his property, from the combination of two causes, though the persons producing them may not be in intentional concert to occasion such a result, the injured person is entitled to compensation for his loss from either one or both of them according to the circumstances of the incident.[2943] Acts wrongfully done by the combination and joint agency of several persons constitute all thc parties wrong-doers and they may be sued jointly or severally, and anyone of them is liable for the injury done by all, if it appears either that they acted in concert or that the act of the individual sought to be charged ordinarily and naturally produced the acts of the others. [2944] Multiple tort-feasors who concurrently cause indivisible injury are jointly and severally liable; it is not essential that all who concurrently caused the harm be joined as defendants.[2945] Under the OPA, divisible injury would still warrant the imposition of joint and several liability. So, the OPA's joint and several liability provision is stricter than that of the common law.

Statutory strict, joint and several liability creates a basis for recovery where none previously existed and violation by itself renders the violator liable without any showing of fault. In suits filed by claimants who have sustained damages and incurred cleanup costs, there need not be any analysis about the possible negligence of the tortfeasors or role actor, even though fault may ultimately determine liability among tortfeasors inter se. Under the OPA, the responsible party is liable without fault. When the

---

2941 *The Atlas*, 3 Otto 302, 93 U.S. 302, 23 L.Ed. 863 (1876).

2942 *The Atlas*, 3 Otto 302, 93 U.S. 302, 23 L.Ed. 863 (1876).

2943 *The Atlas*, 3 Otto 302, 93 U.S. 302, 23 L.Ed. 863 (1876).

2944 Id. at 302.

2945 Restatement (Second) of Torts §§ 433A, 433B, 879-882, see also, Northington v. Marin, 102 F.3d 1564 (10th Cir. 1996).

principle of strict, joint and several liability is applicable in a case, the principle of comparative negligence cannot be applied because negligence is not a factor in determining strict liability. This means that the claimant does not have to sue all jointly and severally liable responsible parties and recover from each of them their percentage of liability. As explained earlier they are each liable to the claimant for the entire claim. It is then up to the claimant who has paid more than its actual percentage of the liability to go after it co-responsible party to obtain contribution or indemnity.

Strict liability and joint and several liability are common law doctrines or concepts and their adoption by the US Congress as a remedy for oil pollution; (1) more resemble those claims tried in law courts than those in courts of equity or admiralty in eighteenth-century England, and (2) more resemble the remedies historically provided in law courts rather than courts of equity. Although maritime law has also embraced the strict liability doctrine in certain contexts, it was borrowed from the common law. Application of the two tests shows that damage claims under the OPA entitles a claimant to a jury trial. The nature of the damage remedies provided in the OPA are historically common law remedies that historically sound in law rather than in equity or admiralty.

Apart from the foregoing, OPA allows for monetary compensation for oil pollution in the form of damages. The damages are in the form of liquidated damages because OPA limits the liability of responsible parties to specific amounts. Money damages actions are typically common law actions. The Seventh Amendment right to jury trial applies to actions enforcing statutory rights and requires jury on demand if the statute creates legal rights and remedies enforceable in action for damages in ordinary courts of law.[2946] Where Congress provides for enforcement of statutory rights in ordinary civil action in district courts and there is obviously no functional justification for denying jury trial right, a jury trial must be available if the action involves rights and remedies of sort typically enforced in an action at law.[2947]

---

2946 See, Curtis v. Loether, 415 US 189, 94 Sct 1005 (1974).

2947 Id. at 189.

Section 2717(b) of the OPA provides that:

"Except as provided in subsections (a) and (c) of this section, the United States district courts shall have exclusive original jurisdiction over all controversies arising under this Act, without regard to the citizenship of the parties or the amount in controversy. Venue shall lie in any district in which the discharge or injury or damages occurred, or in which the defendant resides, may be found, has its principal office, or has appointed an agent for service of process."

Because the OPA has conferred original jurisdiction on Districts Courts and concurrent jurisdiction on state courts[2948] and the damages remedy involves rights and remedies of sort typically enforced in an action at law, a jury trial must be available in OPA damage claims filed in state and federal court. There is obviously no functional justification for denying jury trial right in OPA damage claims.

## Jury Trial for Claims Cognizable in Admiralty and Common Law

The general rule is that no right to jury trial exists under general maritime and admiralty law.[2949] If a plaintiff chooses to designate its claim as an admiralty case, federal admiralty jurisdiction, with no jury right, and not general federal jurisdiction, which grants the right to make a jury demand to all parties, is invoked.[2950] Unlike the Jones Act that specifically

---

2948 "(c) State court jurisdiction---

A State trial court of competent jurisdiction over claims for removal costs or damages, as defined under this chapter, may consider claims under this chapter or State law and any final judgment of such court (when no longer subject to ordinary forms of review) shall be recognized, valid, and enforceable for all purposes of this chapter." 33 USC §2717(c).

2949 Vassalos v. Hellenic Lines, Ltd., 482 F.Supp. 906 (E.D. Pa. 1979). See also Fed. Rules Civ.Proc. Rule 38(e).

2950 Vassalos v. Hellenic Lines, Ltd., 482 F.Supp. at 906. See also, Fed.Rules Civ.Proc. Rules 9(h), 38(e), 28 U.S.C.A.

provides for the right to jury trial,[2951] OPA is silent on the issue. However, because OPA preserves admiralty remedies,[2952] a claimant may elect to bring an OPA claim in Admiralty. This implies that otherwise, it is brought in law and jury trial would be available.

The approach of the courts explained above under the sub-topic "applying the test," also applies to OPA damage claims where the nature of the legal remedy involved is also recognized in admiralty. In *South Port Marine v. Gulf Oil Limited Partnership*,[2953] the court applied the two part test explained above to a ship to shore OPA damage case. The court analyzed whether the Seventh Amendment authorized a jury trial for property and economic loss claims arising out of physical damage to a marina's docks caused by the discharge of 476.19 – 714.28 barrels (20,000 to 30,000 gallons) of gasoline.[2954] Relying heavily on the jury trial cases referred to above, the court noted that although none of those cases involves admiralty (all are conflicts between common law and equity jurisdiction); those cases clearly give precedence to the common law and to jury trial in any competition. Based on this assertion the court saw no principled basis to treat admiralty any differently than equity for such purposes.[2955] The court observed that the US Supreme Court has regularly referred to them in equivalent terms.[2956]

The court recognized that prior to 1948, a plaintiff could not have proceeded in admiralty to recover for pollution related damages to a marina and its business; such an action would only have been cognizable under the common law.[2957] The court also noted that in 1948, Congress enacted

---

2951 Under the Jones Act, a seaman is entitled to a jury trial unless he waives it. Ballard v. Moore-McCormack Lines, Inc., 285 F.Supp. 290 (S.D.N.Y. 1968). (citing, Jones Act, 46 U.S.C.A. § 688).

2952 See 33 USC §2751.

2953 56 F. Supp. 2d 104, 107, 1999 AMC 2113 (D. Me. 1999), *aff'd in part, rev'd on other grounds*, 234 F.3d. 58, 2001 A.M.C. 609 (1st Cir. 2000).

2954 See South Port Marine, 56 F. Supp. 2d at 106.

2955 56 F. Supp. 2d at 111.

2956 Id. at 111-12.

2957 Id. at 109.

the Admiralty Extension Act,[2958] which legislatively expanded the scope of admiralty jurisdiction to "ship-to- shore" torts, but does not provide a right to a jury trial. The district court concluded that the Supreme Court had consistently found that "ship-to-shore" cases were recognized historically only at common law, not in admiralty.[2959] Thus, although the Admiralty Extension Act extended the reach of admiralty jurisdiction to a "ship-to-shore" case, the Seventh Amendment preserved the right to a jury trial for an OPA cause of action to "shoreline structures." The court held that if the Seventh Amendment preserves the right to jury trial at common law and if this action for damages caused by a ship's pollution traveling to shore structures would have been cognizable only at common law when the Seventh Amendment was ratified, then the jury trial right prevails.[2960] The *South Port Marine* court also held that Congress simply cannot extend either equity or admiralty jurisdiction into areas where the common law traditionally provided the remedy, without preserving the right to jury trial.[2961] This court however noted in dicta that the broad class of damages available under the § 2702(b)(2) of the OPA certainly constitutes legal relief rather than equitable relief, but, it does not follow that a suit to recover such damages would be a suit "at common law" in every case.[2962]

In *Max & Lilli Clausen v. M/V NEW CARISSA,*[2963] the court held that the owners of oyster beds were entitled to a jury trial on their claim under OPA against the vessel owner, the vessel, its captain, and others to recover for damages resulting from death of several million oysters following an oil spill from the vessel. The court held that the oyster operation was more analogous to common law claim of farming, to which Seventh Amendment right to jury trial attached, than to traditional maritime activity of fishing.[2964]

---

2958 46 U.S.C. § 740 (1994).

2959 South Port Marine, 56 F. Supp. 2d at 112.

2960 Id. at 112.

2961 Id.

2962 Id. at 113, n 12.

2963 171 F.Supp.2d 1127 (D. Oregon 2001).

2964 171 F.Supp.2d 1127, see also 33 U.S.C.A. § 2701.

## Jury Trial for Natural Resources Damage Assessment Claims

Both CERCLA and OPA allow the government to recover damages for injury to and destruction of natural resources. The OPA allows a United States trustee, a State trustee, an Indian tribe trustee, or a foreign trustee to recover damages for injury to, destruction of, loss of use of, natural resources, including the reasonable costs of assessing the damage.[2965] Earlier in this treatise, I undertook an analysis of the Natural Resources Damage Assessment (NRDA) provisions of OPA. The Department of Interior (DOI) promulgated the implementing regulations for the CERCLA NRDA, while the National Oceanic and Atmospheric Administration (NOAA) promulgated the implementing regulations for OPA's NRDA. Although there are some minor differences between the DOI NRDA and the NOAA NRDA, for the purposes of this analysis, both of them will be treated similarly.

Nature of the Cause of Action: A legal commentator by the name of Frederick Anderson has noted that a paradox existed in environmental law before CERCLA was enacted; while private homeowners could bring legal actions for compensation when their property was damaged, the public had no similar common law mechanism to protect its common resources.[2966] In enacting CERCLA, Congress built upon basic common law doctrines, extending liability beyond the traditional rules to include damage to natural resources.[2967] CERCLA actions for natural resource damages

---

2965 33 USCA 2702(b)(2)(A).

2966 See Frederick R. Anderson, Natural Resource Damages, Superfund, and the Courts, 16 B.C. Envtl. Aff. L. Rev. 405, 406 (1989) (discussing differences between common law and CERCLA strict liability rules).

2967 See In re Acushnet River & New Bedford Harbor: Proceedings re Alleged PCB Pollution, 712 F. Supp. 994, 1000 (D. Mass. 1989) (noting that "the common law has long recognized a duty not to injure the property of another" and therefore "the legal duty found in CERCLA is only 'new' as a matter of federal law"); Dan B. Dobbs, Dobbs Law of Remedies, §5.2(5), at 503 (2d ed. 1993) (noting that natural resource trustee is in similar position to landowner claiming common law property damages); Frederick R. Anderson, Natural Resource Damages, Superfund, and the Courts, 16 B.C. Envtl. Aff. L. Rev. at 426-27, 449-50 (noting that common law is most important source for interpreting natural resource damage provisions); Duane Woodard & Michael R. Hope, Natural Resource Damage Litigation Under the Comprehensive Environmental Response, Compensation and Liability Act, 14 Harv. Envtl. L. Rev. 189, 189-90 (1990) (arguing that

thus developed from the common law tort action for property damages.[2968] Because property damage claims have always been triable as of right to a jury,[2969] the first prong of the two part test analysis dictates that natural resource damage claims receive similar treatment.

Nature of the Remedy: Natural resource damage actions seek monetary relief for injury, destruction, or loss of publicly owned or managed natural resources. Money damages are a traditional form of compensatory relief granted by courts of law for which jury trials are available.[2970] The Supreme Court, however, has recognized two exceptions to this general rule: (1) where the relief is restitutionary, and (2) where the relief is "incidental to or intertwined with injunctive relief."[2971] In these cases, the relief will be considered equitable and a jury trial will be unavailable. I argue in this subpart that natural resource damage actions seek compensatory damages, thus satisfying the second prong of the Seventh Amendment inquiry.

The goal of all forms of tort relief, whether restitutionary or compensatory in nature, is to restore the status quo that existed prior to the invasion of the protected interest.[2972] The distinction between the two forms

---

CERCLA "builds upon the traditional approaches to natural resource damages in the common law").

2968 Lashins Arcade I, 881 F. Supp. 101, 104 (S.D.N.Y. 1995) (finding "recovery for loss of natural resources is similar to an action in tort or trespass"); Acushnet, 712 F. Supp. at 1000 (finding suits for damages caused by releases of hazardous substances were maintainable at law under theories of both nuisance and trespass).

2969 See, e.g., Pernell v. Southall Realty Co., 416 U.S. 363, 370 (1974).

2970 See, e.g., Wooddell v. International Bhd. of Elec. Workers Local 71, 502 U.S. 93, 97 (1991); Chauffeurs, Teamsters & Helpers Local 391 v. Terry, 494 U.S. 558, 570 (1990); see also Crocker v. Piedmont Aviation, Inc., 49 F.3d 735, 746 (D.C. Cir. 1995) ("The Supreme Court has held that as a general rule awards of pecuniary relief... are legal."), *cert denied*, 133 L.Ed.2d 118, 516 US 865, 116 S.Ct 180 (1995).

2971 *Terry*, 494 U.S. at 570-71 (1990) (quoting Tull, 481 U.S. at 424).

2972 See, e.g., Board of County Comm'rs v. Slovek, 723 P.2d 1309, 1314 (Colo. 1986) (" 'The law of torts attempts primarily to put an injured person in a position as nearly as possible equivalent to his position prior to the tort.' " (quoting Restatement (Second) of Torts s 901 cmt. a (1979))); *see also* In re Acushnet River & New Bedford Harbor: Proceedings re Alleged PCB Pollution, 712 F. Supp. 994, 1002 (D. Mass. 1989) ("Were the Court to accept the argument that a monetary reward is restitutionary simply because it returns a party to pre-injury status, little would be left in the realm of compensatory damages.").

of relief lies in the means by which the award is meant to accomplish this goal. Legal damages are substitutionary relief providing the plaintiff money to compensate for a loss that was not originally monetary in form.[2973] As compensatory relief, damages are measured by the loss sustained by the plaintiff.[2974] In contrast, equitable restitution is relief awarded to prevent unjust enrichment of the defendant.[2975] Therefore, restitutionary awards are measured by the gain to the defendant that equitable principles mandate should be transferred to the plaintiff.[2976] In the natural resources damage context, a defendant who has discharged oil has not been enriched unjustly or otherwise.

Natural resource damage claims seek a monetary award in substitution for the injured natural resources. The measurement of the claim is based on the loss suffered by the plaintiff -- the public as represented by the government, tribal and foreign trustee. As was discussed earlier in greater detail in another part of this treatise, the general damage elements claimable are restoration costs, lost use and nonuse values, and assessment costs. All of these figures are calculated solely from the vantage point of the plaintiff. In addition, unlike restitutionary awards of response costs that cover only those costs already incurred,[2977] there is no requirement

2973 See, e.g., Motor Vehicle Mfrs. Ass'n v. New York, 550 N.E.2d 919, 922 (N.Y. 1990); Potter v. Oster, 426 N.W.2d 148, 151 (Iowa 1988); Dan B. Dobbs, Dobbs Law of Remedies, § 3.1, at 209 (2d ed. 1993).

2974 See, e.g., Motor Vehicle Mfrs. Ass'n v. New York, 550 N.E.2d 919, 922 (N.Y. 1990); Potter v. Oster, 426 N.W.2d 148, 151 (Iowa 1988); Dan B. Dobbs, Dobbs Law of Remedies, § 3.1, at 209.

2975 See, e.g., Dursteler v. Dursteler, 697 P.2d 1244, 1249 (Idaho Ct. App. 1985); Dan B. Dobbs, Dobbs Law of Remedies, § 3.1, at 210; see also Crocker v. Piedmont Aviation, Inc., 49 F.3d 735, 747 (D.C. Cir. 1995) (" 'Restitution is defined as that body of law in which (1) substantive liability is based on unjust enrichment, (2) the measure of recovery is based on defendant's gain instead of plaintiff's loss, or (3) the court restores to plaintiff, in kind, his lost property or its proceeds.' " (*quoting,* Douglas Laycock, The Scope and Significance of Restitution, 67 Tex. L. Rev. 1277, 1293 (1989)), *cert denied*, 133 L.Ed.2d 118, 516 US 865, 116 S.Ct 180 (1995)).

2976 See Dan B. Dobbs, Dobbs Law of Remedies, § 3.1, at 210.

2977 See Stanton Road Assoc. v. Lohrey Enters., 984 F.2d 1015, 1021 (9th Cir. 1993), *cert. granted sub nom.* Key Tronic Corp. v. United States, 114 S. Ct. 633, and cert.

that trustees spend money before they can recover damages.[2978] Just like traditional tort plaintiffs, trustees may recover money for future use.[2979] Damages claims therefore seek legal, compensatory relief.

The DOI regulations expressly state that natural resource damages seek to compensate the public through a monetary award that is meant to substitute for the natural resources lost. Damages are defined as "the amount of money sought by the natural resource trustee as compensation for injury, destruction, or loss of natural resources."[2980] According to DOI, the "regulations are designed to calculate a monetary damage figure for injuries to natural resources."[2981] Therefore, "the purpose of the Damage Determination phase is to establish the amount of money to be sought in compensation for injuries to natural resources."[2982] After determining and quantifying injury, the trustees must develop a plan to restore the injured natural resource. Before selecting their preferred restoration plan, the trustees must develop and consider a range of possible alternatives, including natural (no action) restoration.[2983] Each alternative must provide for two different restoration requirements: (1) a primary restoration action, which consists of a plan to return the damaged area to its baseline physical, chemical, and biological condition; and (2) compensatory restoration, which is a monetary damage assessment that represents the interim resource loss between the time of damage to the time of full recovery.[2984]

---

dismissed, 114 S. Ct. 652 (1993); North Carolina ex rel. Howes v. W.R. Peele, Sr. Trust, 876 F. Supp. 733, 740-41 (E.D.N.C. 1995).

2978 See New York v. General Elec. Co., 592 F. Supp. 291, 298 (N.D.N.Y. 1984).

2979 CERCLA restricts trustee use of recovered sums to restoration, replacement, or acquisition of the equivalent of the injured resources. 42 U.S.C. s 9607(f)(1). OPA restricts the trustee use of recovered sums to – (A) cost of restoration, rehabilitation, replacement, or acquisition of the equivalent of, the damaged natural resources; (B) the diminution in value of those natural resources pending restoration; plus (C) the reasonable cost of assessing those damages. 33 USCA 2706(d).

2980 Natural Resource Damage Assessments, 43 C.F.R. s 11.14 (l) (1994).

2981 See Dep't of Interior, Natural Resource Damage Assessments, 59 Fed. Reg. 14,262, 14,262 (1994) [hereinafter DOI, Final Rule].

2982 43 C.F.R. s 11.80(b) (1994).

2983 15 CFR § 990.53

2984 Id. § 990.53 (c)

The NOAA's NRDA regulations specifically provide that in selecting between alternatives methods of restoration in the planning phase of restoration, the trustees must employ a process referred to in the regulations as scaling, which ensures that the restoration action appropriately addresses the injury resulting from the discharge. Scaling appears to be a way for determining the appropriate extent of a restoration action. The scaling process, which is employed both for primary and compensatory restoration, is an analysis of the injury on the basis of resources and/or services lost.[2985] If the trustees determine that neither the resource or service approaches to scaling are appropriate, they may use a valuation approach. In this proceeding natural resources must be explicitly valued in monetary terms. Both use and nonuse values can be considered. For the latter, a wide variety of speculative techniques are allowable, including contingent valuation, hedonic price models and models of market supply and demand. The use of scaling, valuation and other methods in order to arrive at a precise and definite monetary amount evinces the fact that the award of precise money damages is a major objective of the NOAA regulations.

Finally, the type of relief claimed in natural resource damage actions is the same type of relief that was granted by common law courts for property damage. Two widely applied measurement rules for property damages were the diminution in market value,[2986] or, alternatively, the lesser of restoration costs or diminution in market value.[2987] However restoration costs that exceed diminution in market value were awarded as an exception to these general rules when the property had a special value to the plaintiff; when no competitive market existed for the property; or when

2985 15 CFR § 990.53(d)(2)

2986 See, e.g., Board of County Comm'rs v. Slovek, 723 P.2d 1309, 1313-15 (Colo. 1986); Clark v. J.W. Conner & Sons, Inc., 441 So. 2d 674, 676 (Fla. Dist. Ct. App. 1983), rev. denied, 449 So. 2d 264 (Fla. 1984); Trinity Church v. John Hancock Mutual Life Ins. Co., 502 N.E.2d 532, 535 (Mass. 1987).

2987 See, e.g., Mikol v. Vlahopoulos, 340 P.2d 1000, 1001 (Ariz. 1959); Heninger v. Dunn, 162 Cal. Rptr. 104, 106-07 (Ct. App. 1980); Jenkins v. Etlinger, 432 N.E.2d 589, 591 (N.Y. 1982); see also, Dan B. Dobbs, Dobbs Law of Remedies, §5.2(1), at 498-99 (noting that award of restoration costs greater than diminution in value can be seen as windfall to plaintiff or economic waste).

diminution in market value would otherwise be insufficient compensation.[2988] Indeed, as originally issued, the DOI regulations mandated that trustees follow the common law "lesser of" rule and seek only the lesser of restoration costs or lost use values of the injured resources.[2989]

Although this rule was rejected by the D.C. Circuit as inconsistent with congressional intent,[2990] the court found only that Congress intended to modify the common law rule.[2991] By "placing a thumb on the scales in favor of restoration" costs,[2992] Congress in effect mandated that the common law exception become the general rule under CERCLA. Natural resource damages are therefore still a form of substitutionary compensation of the same type as that sought in general property damage cases. Simply changing the rule of measurement in this manner does not constitute an affirmative transformation by Congress of a legal form of relief into an equitable remedy. Apart from this, as explained earlier, the remedy promulgated by regulations or statute need not mirror the one available at common law in 1791. It will still resemble a common law remedy even where it is a statutorily modified form of the old common law remedy. Thus natural resource damage actions seek a legal damage remedy.

The argument that natural resource damage awards are restitutionary focuses on the statutory requirement that trustees may only use their damage recoveries for restorative purposes.[2993] According to this argument, the relief, therefore, is not truly substitutionary like traditional tort compensation;[2994] the use limitation in effect transforms the monetary recovery into an in-kind, restitutionary remedy.

---

2988 See, e.g., Heninger, 162 Cal. Rptr. at 107-09; Slovek, 723 P.2d at 1315-16; Clark, 441 So. 2d at 676; Trinity Church, 502 N.E.2d at 536; Denoyer v. Lamb, 490 N.E.2d 615, 619 (Ohio App. 1984).

2989 See 43 C.F.R. s 11.35(b)(2) (1993).

2990 See Ohio v. United States Dep't of the Interior, 880 F.2d 432, 459 (D.C. Cir. 1989).

2991 See id. at 455 ("The legislative history illustrates, however, that a motivating force behind the CERCLA natural resource damage provisions was Congress' dissatisfaction with the common law.").

2992 Id. at 456.

2993 See CERCLA, 42 U.S.C. §9607(f)(1), OPA 33 USCA §2706(d).

2994 See. Frederick R. Anderson, Natural Resource Damages, Superfund, and the Courts, 16 B.C. Envtl. Aff. L. Rev. at 437-38.

There are several flaws in this argument, however. First, the damage measurement rules remain based on the plaintiff's loss rather than the defendant's gain, and the defendant is still not returning to the plaintiff any property taken. Thus, the damage awards remain substitutionary. Second, an analysis of the legislative history of this provision demonstrates that the requirement was imposed as part of the underlying public trust doctrine and as a mechanism to maintain congressional control over the recovered sums.[2995] Therefore, it does not affect the characterization of natural resource damage awards as legal or equitable.

The second type of monetary relief that will be considered equitable is relief "incidental to or intertwined with injunctive relief."[2996] An analysis of this exception demonstrates the clear division in the statutory scheme between the equitable response costs and the legal natural resource damage remedy.

In *Crocker v. Piedmont Aviation, Inc.*,[2997] the D.C. Circuit held that "the status of a claim as 'intertwined' or 'incidental' with injunctive relief depends on the remedial structure of the statutory scheme."[2998] An award of damages will be considered sufficiently removed from injunctive relief where the court's authority to grant relief is based on a "sepa-

---

2995 In declaring that "[t]he President, or the authorized representative of any State, shall act on behalf of the public as trustee of such natural resources to recover for such [natural resource] damages," 42 U.S.C. § 9607(f)(1), Congress adopted the common law public trust doctrine into the CERCLA statutory scheme. According to this doctrine, the government holds certain natural resources in trust for the public. This trustee relationship places restrictions on the government's ability to alienate its interests in the resources. See Illinois Cent. R.R. v. Illinois, 146 U.S. 387, 435 (1892) (stating that government's control over land under tidal waters is constrained by fact that it must not "substantial[ly] impair[ ]" public's interest in resource); Anthony R. Chase, Remedying CERCLA's Natural Resource Damages Provision: Incorporation of the Public Trust Doctrine into Natural Resource Damage Actions, 11 Va. Envtl. L.J. 353, 363-71 (1992) (examining NOAA's attempt to use role of public trustee to recover natural resource damages under CERCLA). See generally Joseph L. Sax, The Public Trust Doctrine in Natural Resource Law: Effective Judicial Intervention, 68 Mich. L. Rev. 471 (1970) (tracing evolution of public trust doctrine).

2996 Chauffeurs, Teamsters & Helpers Local 391 v. Terry, 494 U.S. 558, 571 (1990) (quoting Tull v. United States, 481 U.S. 412, 424 (1987)).

2997 49 F.3d 735, 748 (D.C. Cir. 1995).

2998 Id. at 748.

rate and distinct statutory provision."[2999] Natural resource trustees have no statutory authority to seek injunctive relief.[3000] Such relief may only be obtained under CERCLA by federal authorities responding to an imminent and substantial threat to the public health or the environment.[3001] Furthermore, the entire statutory scheme in OPA and CERCLA maintain a division between response costs and natural resource damages. Not only are natural resource damage actions authorized in a separate subsection from response cost actions,[3002] but they also have a different statute of limitations.[3003] As the discussion above demonstrates, natural resource damage actions satisfy both prongs of the Supreme Court's Seventh Amendment two part test. Natural resource damage actions are analogous to common law tort claims for property damages and seek a legal remedy. Therefore, the constitutional jury trial right should attach to these suits, making a jury available if it is properly demanded.

*Who should do the Assessment of Damages in OPA Jury trials; Judge or Jury?*

Once we have concluded that jury trials are allowed for OPA damage claims the other question that needs to be answered is whether it is the judge or the jury that has the authority to assess the quantum of the OPA damages. Generally, once liability has been found by the jury, the next phase of the trial entails a determination of the quantum of damages.

While the Supreme Court has not yet ruled on this precise issue, the Circuit Courts have settled the point that when the issue of liability is submitted to a jury, the task of determining damages is also submitted. In *Hawkes v. Ayers*,[3004] the Fifth Circuit stated that ' a fundamental principle

---

2999 Id. at 749 (*quoting*, Tull, 481 U.S. at 425).

3000 See Carol E. Dinkins, Natural Resource Damages: Another Opportunity for Litigation, C855 ALI-ABA 623, 626 (1993) (noting that natural resource damage trustee cannot issue unilateral administrative orders as EPA can for response actions).

3001 42 U.S.C. s 9606(a); see New York v. Shore Realty Corp., 759 F.2d 1032, 1041 (2d Cir. 1985).

3002 See CERCLA 42 U.S.C. § 9607(a)(4)(A)-(C), OPA 33 USCA §2702(b)(2)(A)-(F).

3003 See CERCLA 42 USCA 9613(g)(1), OPA 33 USCA §2717(f)(1)-(5).

3004 537 F.2d 836 (5th Cir. 1976).

of American jurisprudence is that the fact-finder determines the quantum of damages in civil cases.'[3005] In *Borough v. Duluth, Missabe & Iron Range Ry. Co.,*[3006] the Eighth Circuit clearly articulated the principle that the 'calculation of damages' is a question 'of fact and peculiarly within the province of the jury.'[3007] Other circuits have also accepted this position.[3008] In these cases, the Supreme Court has consistently denied certiorari and let the Circuit Court decisions stand.

Therefore, when a jury has been chosen to decide a civil case, it should also determine the amount of damages to be awarded, since it is clearly a question of fact. The trier of the facts, who has the first-hand opportunity to hear the testimony and to observe the demeanor of the witnesses, is clothed with a wide latitude and discretion in fixing damages, pursuant to the court's instructions, deemed proper to fairly compensate the injured party.[3009] The courts have held that the amount of damages awarded by a jury can be supported by any competent evidence tending to sustain it.[3010] The courts will not disturb a jury's finding on damages unless it is so unreasonable "as to shock the judicial conscience and to raise an irresistible inference that passion, prejudice, corruption, or other improper cause invaded the trial..."[3011] It is very difficult to find a jury trial record that discloses evidence to support a finding of passion or prejudice on the part of a jury, or a record that does not fully support the amount of damages awarded by a jury. Therefore the decision of juries on OPA damages in most OPA cases would be unassailable.

---

3005 Id at 837.

3006 762 F.2d 66 (8th Cir. 1985).

3007 Id. at 69. See also Herold v. Burlington Northern, Inc., 761 F.2d 1241, 1248 (8th Cir.), cert. denied, 106 S. Ct. 208 (1985) ('The assessment of damages lies within the sound discretion of the jury.').

3008 See Rosen v. LTV Recreational Development, Inc., 569 F.2d 1117 (10th Cir. 1978) (holding that the fixing of damages is the peculiar function of the jury, or of the trial judge if there is no jury).

3009 See Rosen v. LTV Recreational Development, Inc., 569 F.2d 1117, 1123 (10th Cir.1978).

3010 Hitchcock v. Weddle, 304 F.2d 735, 737 (10th Cir.1962).

3011 Barnes v. Smith, 305 F.2d 226, 228 (10th Cir.1962).

**(2) Actions to recover removal costs against a responsible party & actions for contribution and indemnity by a responsible party against a third party:**

The OPA allows claimants to recover removal costs from a responsible party up to the limits of limitation provided in the statute. As explained earlier in this treatise, there are situations in which removal costs cannot be limited under the OPA. Section 2709 of the OPA also allows a responsible party to recover what it has paid as removal costs from a jointly and severally liable responsible party through a common law contribution or indemnity claim. The question that arises in this situation is whether the actions by claimants to recover removal costs from the responsible party and the actions by the responsible party to recover the same through a contribution action are equity or common law actions. In other to arrive at the right conclusion, a brief analysis of the courts treatment of this same issue under the CERCLA will be useful. This analysis will not lead to the endorsement of most of the CERCLA case law, because it appears that the courts in these CERCLA cases incorrectly applied the two part test for determining whether a jury trial is warranted.

The bulk of cases addressing the right to trial by jury in CERCLA cost- recovery actions have arisen under subsections (A), (B), and (C) of §9607(a)(4).[3012] Because the nature of the issues and the remedy sought varies with each subsection, each presents different issues for consideration under Seventh Amendment jurisprudence.

**Removal Costs – CERCLA Section 9607(a)(4)(A) & OPA Section 2702(a)**

Section 9607(a)(4)(A) permits the government to recover from a liable person "all costs of removal or remedial action incurred by the United States Government or a State not inconsistent with the national contingency plan." The bulk of cases addressing the issue of the Seventh Amendment right to trial by jury in a CERCLA cost-recovery action have

3012 42 U.S.C. §9607(a)(4)(A)-(C), ELR Stat. CERCLA §107(a)(4)(A)-(C).

arisen in the context of a section 9607(a)(4)(A) government enforcement proceeding. All federal courts considering a demand for a jury in a subsection (A) proceeding have held that there is no right to trial by jury.[3013] The OPA on its part in section 2702 makes a responsible party liable for the entire costs of removal up to its maximum limit of liability in section 2704. This shows that there is a striking similarity between OPA & CERCLA cost recovery provisions.

Under CERCLA, *United States v. Northeastern Pharmaceutical & Chemical Co.,*[3014] and *United States v. Reilly Tar & Chemical Corp.,*[3015] were the first cases to address the issue. Neither case conducted the historical inquiry that the Supreme Court precedents require. Although both cases properly examine whether the remedy sought is legal or "purely equitable,"[3016] their analyses and conclusions are flawed.

The *Northeastern Pharmaceutical* and *Reilly Tar* decisions follow the same basic pattern of analysis. First, the courts characterize the remedy the government seeks as "restitution."[3017] Second, the courts conclude that no right to a jury trial exists because restitution is a traditional equitable remedy. *Reilly Tar* states that "(restitution involves) restoring the status quo and ordering the return of what rightfully belongs to a party.

3013 See for example, United States v. Northeastern Pharmaceutical & Chem. Co., 810 F.2d 726, 749, 17 ELR 20603, 20614 (8th Cir. 1986), cert. denied, 484 U.S. 848 (1987); Town of Jaffrey v. Town of Fitzwilliam, 846 F. Supp. 3, 7, 24 ELR 21021, 21023 (D.N.H. 1994); Hatco Corp. v. W.R. Grace & Co., 859 F. Supp. 769, 773 (D.N.J. 1994); United States v. Witco Corp., No. 94-0662, slip op. at 1 (E.D. Pa. July 12, 1994); American Cyanamid Co. v. King Indus., Inc., 814 F. Supp. 209, 214 (D.R.I. 1993); Thaler v. PRB Metals Prods., Inc., 810 F. Supp. 49, 50 (E.D.N.Y. 1993); United States v. Giles Armature & Elec. Works, No. S91-0042-C, slip op. at 1 (E.D. Mo. Jan. 27, 1992); United States v. Peppers Steel & Alloys, Inc., Nos. 85-0571, -1531, slip op. at 6 (S.D. Fla. Jan. 17, 1992).

3014 United States v. Northeastern Pharmaceutical & Chem. Co., 19 Env't Rep. Cas. (BNA) 2186 (D. Mo. 1983).

3015 United States v. Reilly Tar & Chem. Corp., 13 ELR 20897 (D. Minn. June 23, 1983).

3016 Northeastern Pharmaceutical, 19 Env't Rep. Cas. (BNA) at 2187; Reilly Tar, 13 ELR at 20898.

3017 Northeastern Pharmaceutical, 19 Env't Rep. Cas. (BNA) at 2188 ("Restitution is equitable relief with the ultimate goal to return the plaintiff to his status quo."); Reilly Tar, 13 ELR at 20898.

Restitution is within the recognized power and within the highest tradition of a court of equity."[3018]

Most courts subsequently addressing the right to a jury trial cite either *Northeastern Pharmaceutical* or *Reilly Tar*, or cite cases relying on that pair of decisions. Most of these later cases make short work of the Seventh Amendment issue.[3019] The few cases that meaningfully discuss the issue employ the two-step approach taken by *Northeastern Pharmaceutical* and *Reilly Tar*: First, the cases classify the relief sought by the government as restitution, and second, they state that restitution is an equitable remedy.[3020] The *Northeastern Pharmaceutical* or *Reilly Tar* analysis is relevant for OPA purposes because of the similarity of OPA and CERCLA provisions on recovery of removal costs. But it is an analysis that OPA courts will do well to reject, because as will be explained below, this analysis is incorrect.

*The District Courts Have Wrongly Assumed That the Government Is Seeking Restitution in CERCLA Cost-Recovery Actions*

The district courts have analogized the claim the government pursues in a §9607(a)(4)(A) action to the restitution action articulated in §115 of the Restatement of Restitution.[3021] Section 115 states:

"A person who has performed the duty of another by supplying things or services, although acting without the other's knowledge or consent, is entitled to restitution from the other if: (a) he acted unofficiously and with intent to charge

3018 Reilly Tar, 13 ELR at 20898; see Northeastern Pharmaceutical, 19 Env't Rep. Cas. (BNA) at 2189.

3019 See, e.g., United States v. Tyson, 22 Env't Rep. Cas. (BNA) 1471, 1472 (E.D. Pa. 1984) (two paragraphs); United States v. Union Gas Co., 22 Env't Rep. Cas. (BNA) 1603 (E.D. Pa. 1984).

3020 See, e.g., United States v. Mottolo, 605 F. Supp. 898, 913 (D.N.H. 1985) and United States v. Wade, 653 F. Supp. 11, 13 (E.D. Pa. 1984). Both *Mottolo* and *Wade* adopt the analysis of *Northeastern Pharmaceutical* and *Reilly Tar.*

3021 See, e.g., Northeastern Pharmaceutical, 19 Env't Rep. Cas. (BNA) at 2188 (citing Restatement provision); Reilly Tar, 13 ELR at 20898 (citing Restatement provision); United States v. Georgeoff, 22 Env't Rep. Cas. (BNA) 1601, 1602 (N.D. Ohio 1984) (citing Restatement provision). See also, Restatement of Restitution §115 (1937).

therefore, and (b) the things or services supplied were immediately necessary to satisfy the requirements of public decency, health, or safety."

Careful analysis of what the government seeks in a CERCLA & OPA cost-recovery action reveals that the remedy sought is not restitution.

The OPA specifically provides that the RP is responsible for removal costs.[3022] The president of the United States through the US Coast Guard is required to take charge of the response and containment activities after an oil spill or substantial threat of an oil spill.[3023] So, the OPA merely imposes a legal duty on the RP to pay a sum certain for cleanup expenses to the government or a private claimant. The President and not the RP is required to undertake removal activities. This means that the government is not performing any duty for the RP when it undertakes the removal of spilt oil. It is performing a duty that has been imposed on it by the OPA. The fact that the President, through the US Coast Guard may permit the RP to do the removal itself, does not transform the duty imposed on the President to one imposed on the RP. Section 2702 of OPA only confers on the government, a right to indemnification from the RP for the specific sums of money it expended on removal.

Also, this legislative provision imposing clean up duty on the president, clearly removes OPA oil spill removal from the realm of equity or

3022 See 33 USC §2702(a).

3023 "SEC. 4201. FEDERAL REMOVAL AUTHORITY.

33 USCA § 1321

(a) IN GENERAL.--Subsection (c) of section 311 of the Federal Water Pollution Control Act (33 U.S.C. 1321(c)) is amended to read as follows:

"(c) FEDERAL REMOVAL AUTHORITY.--

"(1) GENERAL REMOVAL REQUIREMENT.--(A) The President shall, in accordance with the National Contingency Plan and any appropriate Area Contingency Plan, ensure effective and immediate removal of a discharge, and mitigation or prevention of a substantial threat of a discharge, of oil or a hazardous substance--

"(i) into or on the navigable waters;

"(ii) on the adjoining shorelines to the navigable waters;

"(iii) into or on the waters of the exclusive economic zone; or

"(iv) that may affect natural resources belonging to, appertaining to, or under the exclusive management authority of the United States." Oil Pollution Act 33 USCA 4201, 33 USCA 1321, PL 101-380, 1990 HR 1465.

restitution, because the statute provides for a money remedy. The fact that the statute includes removal costs in a separate sub-section from damages makes no difference. Section 2702(a) is not an injunction to clean up or an injunction to move a vessel, that could arguably be equitable, but rather, it is a requirement to pay a sum certain. By including both removal costs and damages in the same section,[3024] the US Congress must have intended that all claims should be resolved by a single trier of fact instead of bifurcation of claims in which some issues are tried to the judge, while other are tried to the jury. That could not have been the intention of Congress.

There are 18th century common law analogies to an RPs payment of removal costs. For example, 'A' owns a piece of land called Black acre, and 'B' owns an adjacent piece of land called White acre. 'B' discharges noxious substances to the 'A's land from his land. 'A' can bring a private nuisance action against 'B.' 'A' can recover a sum certain for what it cost it to clean up its property from 'B.' 'A' can also recover for loss of use of the land and for physical damage to the land. In this example, a jury trial is definitely available.

Assuming for instance that the oil spill causes damage to state natural resources, and the state did the cleanup of the oil spill by hiring state and local government police officers to work overtime on the oil spill removal activities. Is it reasonable under this situation to bifurcate a case and say the judge should determine one issue and the jury should determine the others? OPA could not have contemplated that, because there is no basis for that in the statute. By providing a wide range of recovery, clearly Congress must have intended the same decision maker to adjudicate the whole dispute.

Another argument is that in a multiple OPA RP situation the government has the discretion to pursue one of the RPs with the deepest pocket. It only needs to designate that RP as the RP. When the government is seeking "all costs of removal or remedial action incurred" from a single PRP or RP, the nature of the remedy sought is quite unlike restitution. To analogize a CERCLA §9607(a)(4)(A) or OPA §2702(a) claim to restitution, the government must be seeking compensation for performing

3024 33 USC §2702.

"the duty of another" and demonstrate that it "is entitled to restitution from the other."[3025] Restitution imposes on the defendant a duty to restore the plaintiff insofar as the defendant has been unjustly enriched.[3026] The doctrine of joint and several liability makes each defendant liable for the entire government cleanup costs (subject to limitation figure in the statute) nevertheless, when there are multiple RPs involved, and the government is seeking "all costs" from a single RP, the government is seeking more from the RP than what the duty of restitution requires. This is a compelling argument in the CERCLA and OPA context because both statutes impose strict joint and several liability. OPA's strict joint and several liability is even more potent than that of CERCLA, because in the OPA even when the oil spill incident that injures a claimant is caused by multiple responsible parties, and liability is divisible, one party can nevertheless be held liable for the entire liability that flows from the spill. So, the government in the OPA context will be suing to collect from the responsible party more than its fair share of the removal costs.

The competing argument could be made that the PRP's or RP's duty under CERCLA and OPA is to reimburse the government for all its response costs. Thus, the government's remedy is restitution because it is seeking reimbursement only for its performance of the PRP's or RPs duty. This argument, however, is not convincing. First, CERCLA and OPA liability for all response costs is premised on joint and several liability, even though both statutes on their face do not require imposing such liability. Joint and several liability is a legal doctrine the law courts invented.[3027] Thus, if the duty to reimburse the government for all its response costs is premised on a court imposing joint and several liability, the government actually is seeking legal relief and the right to trial by

---

3025 Restatement of Restitution, §115.

3026 Id., §1 ("(A) person who has been unjustly enriched at the expense of another is required to make restitution to the other.").

3027 See W. Page Keeton et al., Prosser and Keeton on the Law of Torts s47, at 328 (5th ed. 1984) ("Quite apart from any question of vicarious liability or joinder of defendants, the common law developed a separate principle, that a defendant might be liable for the entire loss sustained by the plaintiff, even though the defendant's act concurred or combined with that of another wrongdoer to produce the result.").

jury should be available. Second, principles of CERCLA liability provide that a PRP does not owe the government all response costs when "there is a reasonable basis for determining the contribution of each cause to a single harm."[3028] The government cannot claim to be seeking restitution, much less equitable relief, when it seeks all its response costs but is only entitled to some. Similarly in the OPA context section 2702(d)(1)(B) provides that if the responsible party alleges that the discharge or threat of a discharge was caused solely by an act or omission of a third party, the responsible party- (i) in accordance with section 2713 (claims procedure) of the OPA, shall pay removal costs and damages to any claimant; and (ii) shall be entitled by subrogation to all rights of the United States Government and the claimant to recover removal costs or damages from the third party or the Fund paid under this subsection. This section specifically addresses the question of the liability and rights of a person entitled to the third party defense in section 2703(a) of the OPA. Section 2702(d)(1)(B) clearly and unambiguously ensures that a responsible party who successfully invokes the third party defense cannot walk away from the oil spill. The responsible party must pay removal costs and damages to any claimant. After making such payments, the responsible party inherits the rights and claims of all the claimants it has paid and can go ahead to sue the sole cause third party for removal costs and damages. Government and private OPA claimants cannot claim to be seeking restitution, much less equitable relief, when they seek all their response costs but are entitled to none. Since the Restatement only allows restitution when a person has performed the duty of another by supplying things or services, there is no restitution in this OPA provision because the responsible party is entitled to a defense of sole cause third party (not in a contract relationship with the RP), and therefore had no duty that he ought to perform, but for the statutory mandate that he should pay any claimant's damages and removal costs.

3028 See. United States v. Alcan Aluminum Corp., 964 F.2d 252, 268, 22 ELR 21124, 21126 (3d Cir. 1992); In re Bell Petroleum Servs., Inc., 3 F.3d 889, 895, 23 ELR 21474, 21475 (5th Cir. 1993).

*The District Courts Have Wrongly Assumed in CERCLA Cost-Recovery Actions That Restitution Is a Historically Equitable Remedy*

Assuming arguendo that cost recovery actions amount to restitution, historical analysis would reveal that it is not an action at equity, but, rather an action at law. Historical scholarship on restitution demonstrates the divided jurisdiction over claims that fell under the rubric of "restitution" during the late 18th century. Both law courts and equity courts entertained "restitution" actions.[3029] The Restatement specifically notes that a person entitled to restitution "is entitled, in an appropriate case, to... (f) a judgment at law or a decree in equity for the payment of money."[3030] The interrelation of tort and contract was further complicated when the common law courts, late in the seventeenth century, began to take over into the law some of the principles and remedies of equity. The judges, becoming conscious of their shortcomings and jealous of the expanding powers of the chancery courts, sought to broaden their own jurisdiction into equity fields, and found a means ready to their hand in the action of assumpsit.... The common law courts recognized that they were invading the province of equity, and the relief which they granted by way of restitution has continued to be subject to equitable rules.[3031] The Restatement also sets forth the forms of action at law for restitution.[3032]

CERCLA §9607(a)(4)(A) cases do not consider the divided jurisdiction between the law courts and the equity courts over claims of restitution. Rather, the district courts have simply assumed that restitution is an equitable remedy.[3033] This approach turns a blind eye to the fact that the

3029 Dan B. Dobbs, Dobbs Law of Remedies §§2.6(3), 4.2 (2d ed. 1993); see In re Acushnet River & New Bedford Harbor, 712 F. Supp. 994, 1003, 19 ELR 21198, 21202 (D. Mass. Feb. 27, 1989) ("(M)uch of the relief thought of as restitutionary was available in the English common law courts in an action of assumpsit.").

3030 Restatement of Restitution §4.

3031 W. Page Keeton et al., Prosser and Keeton on the Law of Torts §94, at 672 (5th ed. 1984)

3032 Restatement of Restitution §5.

3033 See, e.g., United States v. Mottolo, 605 F. Supp. 898, 913, 15 ELR 20444, 20450 (D.N.H. 1985) ("The Court finds these decisions persuasive and concludes that no Seventh Amendment right to jury trial attaches (when) plaintiffs seek merely equitable relief, the return of monies expended for the cleanup of hazardous waste. Plaintiffs seek restitution,

jurisdictions of law courts and equity courts have always overlapped with respect to restitution.[3034] The quintessential types of restitution claims equity courts historically entertained hardly seem analogous to CERCLA or OPA removal cost claims. One commentator clarified the issue succinctly when he said:

> "The most notable equitable procedures to enforce restitution are the constructive trust, the equitable lien, and subrogation. These procedures give the plaintiff restitution by giving the plaintiff title to, or a security interest in a particular property; or in the case of subrogation, by giving the plaintiff the rights formerly held by another person."[3035]

In fact, CERCLA cost-recovery claims resemble more closely restitution actions heard at law. In particular, CERCLA cost-recovery actions seem more analogous to a particular form of restitution action entertained in the law courts: The assumpsit action of quantum meruit. The district courts postulate that CERCLA cost-recovery actions effect a return to the status quo ante by reimbursing the government.[3036] Similarly, the quantum meruit action at law effected a return to the status quo ante by restoring a defendant's unjust enrichment to the plaintiff:

> "Quantum meruit is a count used where the plaintiff has performed services for the defendant. As in many common count cases, the services may be performed at the defendant's request, so that an implied in fact contract might be found. However, services might be performed without the request of the defendant, but which nevertheless benefited him in some way. If recovery is allowed for such unrequested services, it is clear that the recovery is the quasi-contract sort, that is, based upon the principle against unjust enrichment and not on contract."[3037]

---

that is, to restore the status quo by receiving their rightful reimbursement. This restitution remedy is under the jurisdiction of a court of equity, and there is no jury trial right (when) purely equitable relief is sought.").

3034 In re Acushnet River, 712 F. Supp. at 1003, 19 ELR at 21202.

3035 Dan B. Dobbs, Dobbs Law of Remedies, §4.1(3), at 565.

3036 *Mottolo*, 605 F. Supp. at 913, 15 ELR at 20450.

3037 Dan B. Dobbs, Dobbs Law of Remedies, s4.2(3), at 583.

The district courts have invoked restitution as a magical charm to conclude that the remedy must be equitable.[3038] A look behind the tag, however, demonstrates that courts entertained restitution claims both at law and equity. Indeed, CERCLA removal cost claims more closely resemble the type of restitution claims over which law courts historically had jurisdiction than the kind of restitution claims over which equity courts historically had jurisdiction. OPA removal cost claims in as much as they are similar to CERCLA removal costs claims would warrant the same conclusion. The removal cost claims in OPA are more in the form of quantum meruit action at law effecting a return to the status quo ante by restoring an OPA defendant's unjust enrichment to the OPA claimant.

**The District Courts Have Wrongly Concluded That the Remedy the Government Seeks in a CERCLA Cost-Recovery Action Is Equitable**

The nature of the remedy sought is dispositive of the Seventh Amendment issue. Regardless of whether restitution is at issue, if the remedy sought in a CERCLA or OPA cost-recovery action is legal, the right to trial by jury exists. This subpart demonstrates that the nature of the relief the government seeks in a cost-recovery action is legal, not equitable. This sub-part's analysis of this misclassification of legal remedies as equitable remedies by the courts, will be interspersed with discussion of the historical grounds for seeking or claiming equitable remedies. Such historical analysis is needed because without it, it will be difficult to demonstrate that OPA or CERCLA cost-recovery action is a legal remedy, rather than an equitable remedy.

To determine the nature of the remedy requires careful scrutiny of the relief the government actually seeks. Careful scrutiny of the relief sought is precisely the approach the Supreme Court cases require.[3039] Many district courts have failed to examine the relief the government seeks. As

3038 In re Acushnet River, 712 F. Supp. at 1002, 19 ELR at 21202.

3039 See Tull v. United States, 481 U.S. 412, 422-27, 17 ELR 20667, 20670- 71 (1987).

previously discussed, the cases simply assert that the government seeks return of the status quo ante.[3040]

The government typically seeks recovery of all its response costs through its attempt to impose joint and several liability. But the government's reliance on joint and several liability defeats any pretense that what it seeks is equitable. As noted above, PRPs or RPs may be liable to the government for only a divisible portion of the response costs the government incurred.[3041] In *re Bell Petroleum Services, Inc.*,[3042] incisively illustrates this point. The case holds that a PRP is liable only for a portion of the costs when the damages are "reasonably capable of apportionment."[3043] Thus, the government seeks more than it is equitably entitled to when it seeks all its response costs from a single PRP. Government claimants and private claimants under OPA also seek all the removal costs from the responsible party even if he is only liable for a portion of the oil spill because there are multiple responsible parties. Indeed, it is a prerequisite to equity jurisdiction that "he who seeks equity must do equity."[3044] As Pomeroy's Equity Jurisprudence states this principle, it would also deprive an equity court of jurisdiction over the government's attempt to recover all response costs from a single PRP:

> "The meaning is, that whatever be the nature of the controversy between two definite parties, and whatever be the nature of the remedy demanded, the court will not confer its equitable relief upon the party seeking its interposition and aid, unless he has acknowledged and conceded, or will admit and provide for, all the

---

3040 United States v. Mottolo, 605 F. Supp. 898, 913, 15 ELR 20444, 20450 (D.N.H. 1985).

3041 United States v. Alcan Aluminum Corp., 990 F.2d 711, 23 ELR 20706 (2d Cir. 1993); United States v. Alcan Aluminum Corp., 964 F.2d 252, 22 ELR 21124 (3d Cir. 1992); In re Bell Petroleum Servs., Inc., 3 F.3d 889, 23 ELR 21474 (5th Cir. 1993).

3042 *In re Bell Petroleum*, 3 F.3d at 903 (5th Cir. 1993).

3043 *In re Bell Petroleum*, 3 F.3d at 903

3044 See John N. Pomeroy's Equity Jurisprudence §385, at 51 (5th ed. 1941) ("He who seeks equity must do equity."). Where the government is entitled to all response costs from a single PRP, this may constitute restitution. Even in this situation, however, the relief sought by the government is not equitable. Money is the relief at issue and that is the classic form of legal relief.

equitable rights, claims, and demands justly belonging to the adversary party, and growing out of or necessarily involved in the subject-matter of the controversy."[3045]

When the government seeks all costs from a PRP or RP, it is not seeking to do equity. Doing equity means seeking a PRP's fair share of the response costs. So also under OPA when a government or private claimant seeks all removal cost from a jointly and severally liable RP even when the RP is entitled to the third party defense, such OPA claimants are not seeking to do equity, because they are not seeking an RP's fair share of the response costs. This objection is still more acute when the government is seeking to recover from a PRP all the government's costs associated with a site and the government itself is also a PRP. Certainly, the government is not seeking an equitable remedy when it attempts to recover all its costs but may be liable for at least some of those response costs.[3046] In OPA oil spills, a government public vessel responsible for a discharge of oil can escape liability, but if a court finds that the vessel was engaged in commercial activities like the transportation of cargo for hire for private shippers it would not be regarded as a public vessel and it will be subject to OPA liability. Where an oil spill is caused due to the combined fault of both a government vessel that has been found not to qualify as a public vessel and a private vessel, a Federal government agency like the US Coast Guard or the EPA can sue the owner and operator of the private vessel and recover the entire removal costs from that RP. So, under the OPA the government of the United States can be a responsible party (RP). Black's Law Dictionary defines equity as "justice administered according to fairness as contrasted with the strictly formulated rules of common law."[3047] It is unfair, and certainly not equitable, for a PRP or RP to seek recovery

---

3045 Id. at 52.

3046 For example, in United States v. Witco Corp., the United States sought to recover all its unreimbursed response costs associated with a Superfund site, despite the fact that it has been adjudicated liable under CERCLA s107(a)(2) as an owner of facilities at the site. United States v. Witco Corp., No. 94-0662, slip op. at 6 (E.D. Pa. July 12, 1994); see also Elf Atochem, Inc. v. United States, No. 92-7458, slip op. at 13 (E.D. Pa. Sept. 26, 1994).

3047 Black's Law Dictionary 540 (6th ed. 1990).

for the harm it caused. The prerequisite to equity jurisdiction that "he who comes into equity must come with clean hands" bolsters this objection.[3048] As Pomeroy states, this principle also would deprive an equity court of jurisdiction over a claim by the government when it is a PRP:

> "He who comes into equity must come with clean hands, is much more efficient and restrictive in its operation. It assumes that the suitor asking the aid of a court of equity has himself been guilty of conduct in violation of the fundamental conceptions of equity jurisprudence, and therefore refuses him all recognition and relief with reference to the subject-matter or transaction in question. It says that whenever a party, who, as actor, seeks to set the judicial machinery in motion and obtain some remedy, has violated conscience, or good faith, or other equitable principle, in his prior conduct, then the doors of the court will be shut against him in limine; the court will refuse to interfere on his behalf, to acknowledge his right, or to award him any remedy."[3049]

These arguments do not obtain, however, when the government is an innocent party and the site involves a single PRP or RP. In that case, arguably, the government is seeking only what is fair and just--that the polluter pay. Under these limited circumstances, the government's argument that it is seeking an equitable remedy is at its strongest. In OPA cases the government's argument that it is seeking an equitable remedy is at its strongest when one of the vessels involved, though a government vessel, is found to be a public vessel under the law. In this kind of situation, the government vessel can be tagged an innocent vessel by virtue of the OPA provision that excludes public vessels from OPA liability.

But even in this situation, the relief sought is not equitable. Yet another prerequisite to equity jurisdiction--the prerequisite that no adequate remedy exists at law--demonstrates that jurisdiction over CERCLA cost-recovery claims lies at law.[3050]

---

3048 See John N. Pomeroy's Equity Jurisprudence §397 at 90 (5th ed. 1941).

3049 Id. at 91.

3050 Beacon Theatres, Inc. v. Westover, 359 U.S. 500, at 509 (1959); John N. Pomeroy's Equity Jurisprudence, §176 at 239.

In a CERCLA §9607(a)(4)(A) and OPA §2702(a) claim, all the government seeks is money. The Supreme Court has stated many times that money is the classic form of "relief offered in the courts of law."[3051] The Court never has held, however, that an award of monetary relief is by definition legal.[3052] It would be a poor argument to assert that the relief sought is legal strictly because money is sought, as it is well within a court's equity powers to order monetary relief.[3053] But the Supreme Court has stated that the "general rule" is that monetary relief is legal.[3054] Similarly, the Court has stated that to characterize monetary relief as other than legal would require demonstrating "attributes" to justify an "exception to the general rule."[3055] The party seeking to strike the jury demand should bear the burden of demonstrating this exception.

Hence, the nature of the relief the government seeks in a cost-recovery action is not equitable but legal. The government's recovery of all costs from a single PRP or RP at a site in the multiple PRP or RP context is not fair. And even when the government claims entitlement to full recovery from the single PRP or RP, a court of law can give the government all the relief it seeks.[3056] Since there is adequate relief at law, equity need not

3051 Curtis v. Loether, 415 U.S. 189, 196 (1974); see Dairy Queen v. Wood, 369 U.S. 469, 476 (1962) ("(I)nsofar as the complaint requests a money judgment it presents a claim which is unquestionably legal."); Granfinanciera, S.A. v. Nordberg, 492 U.S. 33, 47-49 (1989).

3052 Chauffeurs, Teamsters & Helpers, Local No. 391 v. Terry, 494 U.S. 558, 570 (1990).

3053 See John N. Pomeroy's Equity Jurisprudence, §§112 & 186; Restatement of Restitution, §4(f).

3054 *Chauffeurs*, 494 U.S. at 570.

3055 Id. at 570.

3056 In CERCLA and OPA cases, the government usually brings cost-recovery claims while response activities at a site are ongoing. Thus, the government's future response costs are unknown. But this is no bar to an adequate legal remedy, because the court can award known response costs against the PRP or RP and issue a declaratory judgment on future costs. See 42 U.S.C. §9613(g)(2), 28 U.S.C. §2201, 33 U.S.C. §2717(f)(2). Thus, the court can give complete relief at law to the government. While an equity court has the power to award monetary relief, that power is delimited by a court of law's inability to award such relief. John N. Pomeroy's Equity Jurisprudence, §173. §2717(f)(2) provides: "[a]n action for recovery of removal costs referred to in section 2702(b)(1) of this title must be commenced within 3 years after completion of the removal action. In any such action described in this subsection, the court shall enter a declaratory judgment

step in. The legislative history of OPA does not show any indication that Congress wanted to classify removal costs as equitable relief and thus preclude claimants from invoking their Seventh Amendment right to trial by jury.

One thing that is clear from the above analysis on the availability of the right to jury trial in OPA cases is the jurisprudential embracement of the two part test established by the United States Supreme Court. This two part test should continue to guide the courts to the right decision, however for the courts that have misapplied this test, it is time for them to reconsider their decisions and apply the test the correct way in line with the above analysis. Especially in regard to removal cost cases as well as contribution cases under the CERCLA there needs to be a reexamination of the continuing trend of a lot of the Districts Courts in the US towards denial of the right to jury trial. The right to jury trial is a constitutional right that should not be denied by the courts unless the courts have undertaken a painstaking application of the two-part test of the United States Supreme Court.

---

on liability for removal costs or damages that will be binding on any subsequent action or actions to recover further removal costs or damages." See also, O'Neil v. Picillo, 883 F.2d 176 (Ist Cir. 1989) (holding that hazardous waste generators could be held jointly and severally liable for future removal costs at hazardous waste site even if it were not shown that such work would ever be needed. See also 42 U.S.C.A. § 9607.

# Chapter Fourteen

# THE NON-PREEMPTION CLAUSE - 33 U.S.C. § 2718(A)-(C)

Statutory provisions:
"§ 2718. Relationship to other law

(a) Preservation of State authorities; Solid Waste Disposal Act

Nothing in this Act or the Act of March 3, 1851 shall--

**(1)** affect, or be construed or interpreted as preempting, the authority of any State or political subdivision thereof from imposing any additional liability or requirements with respect to--

**(A)** the discharge of oil or other pollution by oil within such State; or

**(B)** any removal activities in connection with such a discharge; or

**(2)** affect, or be construed or interpreted to affect or modify in any way the obligations or liabilities of any person under the Solid Waste Disposal Act (42 U.S.C. 6901 et seq.) or State law, including common law.

(b) Preservation of State funds

Nothing in this Act or in section 9509 of Title 26 shall in any way affect, or be construed to affect, the authority of any State--

**(1)** to establish, or to continue in effect, a fund any purpose of which is to pay for costs or damages arising out of, or directly resulting from, oil pollution or the substantial threat of oil pollution; or

**(2)** to require any person to contribute to such a fund.

(c) Additional requirements and liabilities; penalties

Nothing in this Act, the Act of March 3, 1851 (46 U.S.C. 183 et seq.), or section 9509 of Title 26, shall in any way affect, or be construed to affect, the authority of the United States or any State or political subdivision thereof--

**(1)** to impose additional liability or additional requirements; or

**(2)** to impose, or to determine the amount of, any fine or penalty (whether criminal or civil in nature) for any violation of law; relating to the discharge, or substantial threat of a discharge, of oil."[3057]

Earlier in this treatise, I briefly discussed the non-preemption issue in the context of the liability of dissolved corporations. In this chapter I will be discussing the general application of the non-preemption provision of OPA. Some of the recommendations made in the earlier discussion may be generally applicable as well.

The OPA specifically includes a non-preemption or savings clause, which states that state laws are not preempted by the provisions of the Act or any other law. It also allows states to impose additional liabilities, penalties, and other requirements on vessel and facility owners and operators for oil pollution.[3058] This non-preemption or savings clause of the Oil Pollution Act was added to allow states to enact legislation protecting their citizens and their resources to a greater extent than protection offered by OPA; it was meant to allow states to go beyond basic protection of federal law, and beneficiaries of the savings clause are the victims of oil spills; the clause was clearly not intended to affect liability between two vessels involved in an oil spill.[3059]

---

3057 33 USC § 2718.

3058 33 U.S.C. § 2718(a)-(c).

3059 National Shipping Co. of Saudi Arabia (NSCSA) v. Moran Mid-Atlantic Corp, 924 F.Supp. 1436 (E.D. Va. 1996), see also, Oil Pollution Act of 1990, 33 U.S.C.A. § 2718(a).

Of particular note is the fact that the additional state liabilities are not subject to limitation either under the Act itself, or pursuant to the Limitation of Liability Act.[3060] This provision represents a significant departure from the interaction of the Limitation Act and state statutes under the FWPCA. As most states now have the incentive and green light to enact unlimited liability statutes, the limits of the new Act are largely theoretical with respect to the actual exposure to which a vessel owner may be subject. The implication of this is that OPA's liability limits provide no protection for responsible parties and their guarantors or insurers sued under state law. The insurers argue that if they insure and become guarantors of vessels that sail to states that impose or will impose unlimited liability under their laws, actions for claims could be brought directly against them and they might become subject to unlimited liability, which could trigger their insolvency. This is because one oil spill can lead to liability running into billions of dollars. It is worthy of note that a number of States now have oil pollution statutes that do not limit liability.[3061] One can make a counter argument that in practice, it is very rare for an insurer to be held liable above the limit of its insurance policy.

In drafting OPA, Congress deliberately chose not to preempt state laws governing oil pollution liability and compensation.[3062] OPA's "non-preemption" clause was designed to give states the right to impose greater liability requirements than those in the federal scheme.[3063] The theory is that the federal statute is designed to provide basic protection for the

---

3060 Id. § 2718 (c).

3061 1990 U.S.C.C.A.N. 728, S. Rep. No. 94, 101ST Cong., 1ST Sess. 1989, 1989 WL 225005 (Leg.Hist.). The vast majority of coastal states have enacted unlimited liability statutes. See Survey, The 1993 Maritime Survey of State Pollution Statutes, 5 USFMLJ 452-512 (Spring 1993), *see also* N.Y. Times, Nov. 9, 1989, at A32, col. 1. At least 14 coastal states had no limit on liability in the event of an oil spill, according to a 1983 survey of state oil spill laws. Both Alaska and Maine, for example, have an unlimited, strict joint and several liability standard. U.S. Coast Guard, Oil Spill Liability And Compensation Legislative Pre-Emption Considerations, APP.A. (Mar. 1, 1985), *see also*, Ala. Code §§ 22-22-1 to –14(1990).

3062 Matthew P. Harrington, Necessary and proper, but still unconstitutional: The Oil Pollution Act's Delegation of Admiralty Power to the states, 48 Case W. Res. 1, 14.

3063 Id.

environment and victims damaged by spills of oil. Any state wishing to impose a greater degree of protection for its own resources or citizens is entitled to do so. On the other hand a state may feel adequately protected by the federal statute and therefore choose not to enact additional state law. In any event, the Congress chose not to impose, arbitrarily, the constraints of the federal regime on the states while at the same time preempting their rights to their own laws.[3064] Permitting states to legislate in this area was a source of great concern, and OPA was roundly criticized by many both within and outside the shipping industry because of this decision.[3065]

In *Anthony Williams v. Potomac Electric Power Company(PEPCO)*,[3066] the court held that OPA did not preempt property owners' state common law claims for negligence, trespass, strict liability, and nuisance against a power company for damages resulting from oil discharge from the company's pipeline.[3067]

Plaintiffs in this case clearly pleaded purely state law causes of action. Based on the defendant, PEPCO's argument, the question was whether OPA is sufficiently pre-emptive to displace those causes of action and validate the removal of the action from state court to Federal court pursuant to the removal provisions as encapsulated in 28 USCA §1441(a)-(b).

PEPCO's argued that OPA preempts state common law causes of action to recover removable costs and damages in oil spill cases because the state actions would conflict with OPA's "full purposes and objectives."[3068] The court relied on the Supreme Court case of *United States v. Locke*,[3069] in which the matter was effectively put to rest on March 6, 2000. This case is discussed later on below. *Locke* involved state regulations governing tanker operations and their interrelation with federal statutes and international instruments applicable to such operations. Finding preemption as

3064 S. Rep. No. 101-94, at 6 (1989), reprinted in 1990 U.S.C.C.A.N. 722, 728.

3065 Philip Peterson & Daniel Kopec, Crude Legislation: Liability and Compensation Under The Oil Pollution Act of 1990, 23 RUTGERS L.J. at 624-25.

3066 115 F.Supp.2d. 561 (D. Maryland 2000).

3067 115 F.Supp.2d. at 561. See also 33 USCA 2718.

3068 115 F.Supp.2d. at 564.

3069 INTERTANKO, 529 U.S. 89, 120 S.Ct. 1135, 146 L.Ed.2d 69 (2000).

to a number of the state regulations, the Court had occasion to comment upon the savings clauses of Title I of OPA:

"Title I of OPA contains two saving clauses, stating:
(a) Preservation of State authorities...
Nothing in this Act or the Act of March 3, 1851 shall--
(1) affect, or be construed or interpreted as pre-empting, the authority of any State or political subdivision thereof from imposing any additional liability or requirements with respect to--
(A) the discharge of oil or other pollution by oil within such State

(c) Additional requirements and liabilities; penalties
Nothing in this Act, the Act of March 3, 1851 (46 U.S.C. § 183 et seq.), or section 9509 of [the Internal Revenue Code of 1986 (26 U.S.C. § 9509] ), shall in any way affect, or be construed to affect, the authority of the United States or any State or political subdivision thereof--
(1) to impose additional liability or additional requirements "relating to the discharge, or substantial threat of a discharge, of oil."[3070]

The *Potomac* court noted the savings clauses are found in Title I of OPA, captioned "Oil Pollution Liability and Compensation" and creating a liability scheme for oil pollution.[3071] The court explained that the placement of the saving clauses in Title I of OPA suggests that Congress intended to preserve state laws of a scope similar to the matters contained in Title I of OPA, not all state laws similar to the matters covered by the whole of OPA or to the whole subject of maritime oil transport.[3072] Relying heavily on *Locke,* the court pointed out that the evident purpose of the saving clauses is to preserve state laws which, rather than imposing substantive regulation of a vessel's primary conduct, establish liability rules and financial requirements relating to oil spills.[3073]

---

3070 33 U.S.C. § 2718.

3071 115 F.Supp.2d. at 564.

3072 Id. at 564-565.

3073 Id. at 565.

The court explained that Title I of OPA permits recovery of damages involving vessels "from which oil is discharged or substantial threat of a discharge, or which pos[e] the substantial threat of a discharge of oil.[3074] The saving clauses, in parallel manner, permit States to impose liability or requirements "relating to the discharge, of oil."[3075]

The court followed the reasoning in *Locke*, where the Supreme Court said:

"In its titles following Title I, OPA addresses matters including licensing and certificates of registry, 104 Stat. 509; duties of senior licensed officers to relieve the master, id., at 511; manning standards for foreign vessels, id., at 513; reporting of marine casualties, ibid.; minimum standards for plating thickness, id., at 515; tank vessel manning requirements, id., at 517; and tank vessel construction standards, id., at 517-518, among other extensive regulations. If Congress had intended to disrupt national uniformity in all of these matters, it would not have done so by placement of the saving clauses in Title I.[3076] Limiting the saving clauses as we have determined respects the established federal-state balance in matters of maritime commerce between the subjects as to which the States retain concurrent powers and those over which the federal authority displaces state control. We have upheld state laws imposing liability for pollution caused by oil spills. See Askew v. American Waterways Operators, Inc., 411 U.S. at 325, 93 S.Ct. 1590, 36 L.Ed.2d 280. Our view of OPA's savings clauses preserves this important role for the States, which is unchallenged here."[3077]

Based on the foregoing reasoning of the Supreme Court, the *Potomac* court concluded that the Supreme Court has thus effectively foreclosed any argument as to pre-emption in this case.[3078] The court also held that OPA does not preempt "state laws of a scope similar to the matters contained in Title I of OPA," such as the state common law actions pleaded in this

3074 Id. at 565, see also 33 U.S.C. § 2702(a).

3075 Id. see also 33 USCA § 2718(c).

3076 Id. at 565.

3077 Locke, 120 S.Ct. at 1145-47.

3078 115 F.Supp.2d. at 565.

case.[3079] Therefore the court held that there is no basis for removal jurisdiction predicated on OPA, since the action in state court is based on state common law remedies.[3080] And there is, in consequence, no requirement for the presentment of claims under OPA prior to commencing suit, since their action is predicated on state common law remedies.[3081]

Congress further provided that states might create their own compensation funds similar to the Federal Oil Spill Liability Trust Fund, to be funded and maintained with state taxes on the oil and shipping industry.[3082] This provision goes beyond merely "grand-fathering" already-existing state funds.[3083] Rather, it is clear that Congress envisioned that states would establish new oil spill compensation funds and that these funds would be supported by taxing "oil landings."[3084] States would be free to set their own rates, and the federal tax rate would neither be a ceiling nor a floor for state rates.[3085] The intent behind this provision is to leave the states flexibility in funding their responses to oil pollution incidents. This is particularly important because the Fund is authorized to pay to a state government an amount not to exceed $250,000 for emergency removal costs consistent with the National Contingency Plan, provided it is required for the immediate removal of a discharge, or the mitigation or prevention of a substantial threat of a discharge of oil.[3086] This clean up amount is very small and would not make any difference in medium or major oil spills. Apart from this, the state government has to satisfy the Fund that the money being sought is to be used for immediate removal of a discharge, or the mitigation or prevention of a substantial threat of a discharge of oil. If the Fund is not convinced that the removal is consistent with the National Contingency Plan, the state government's request may be denied even though the amount statutorily

3079 Id at 565.

3080 Id.

3081 Id.

3082 See 33 U.S.C. § 2718(b).

3083 Matthew P. Harrington, Necessary and proper, but still unconstitutional: The Oil Pollution Act's Delegation of Admiralty Power to the states, 48 Case W. Res. at 15

3084 See S. Rep. No. 101-94, at 6 (1989), reprinted in 1990 U.S.C.C.A.N. 722, 728.

3085 Id.

3086 33 USC §2712(d)

available is very small. That is why it is imperative for the states to have their own Oil Pollution Trust Fund.

Preemption of state funds would compromise the ability of states to prevent or limit oil spill damage to the natural resources and property of its own citizens.[3087] Unfortunately, situations have arisen in the past where federal clean-up efforts have been inadequate. Preemption of state funds would make the states wholly dependent on the Federal funds and response system. The result might be a decrease in the degree of protection from oil spill damage, rather than an increase.[3088]

However, Congress's decision not to preempt state action has had some unintended effects. Following the passage of OPA, the states of Washington sought to impose added design and safety requirements on vessels operating in state waters.[3089] This is in spite of the fact that in crafting OPA's preemption clause, Congress appears to have intended that states be permitted to supplement the liability provisions of federal law. The clause does not seem to address on its face, the question of whether states may supplement federal vessel safety and construction standards with legislation imposing greater requirements or restrictions on vessel operation and manning.[3090] The Supreme court has ruled on this issue and this is discussed immediately below.[3091]

**Analysis of The Supreme Court's Decision in International Association of Independent Tanker Owners (Intertanko) v. Gary Locke.[3092]**

As of the date of this research, the only Supreme Court case on the effect of the non-preemption clause of OPA on state oil pollution laws and

3087 Matthew P. Harrington, Necessary and proper, but still unconstitutional: The Oil Pollution Act's Delegation of Admiralty Power to the states, 48 Case W. Res. at 16.

3088 See S. Rep. No. 101-94, at 7 (1989), reprinted in 1990 U.S.C.C.A.N. 722, 728.

3089 See Intertanko v. Gary Locke, 148 F3d 1053 (9th Cir. 1998).

3090 See H.R. Conf. Rep. No. 101-653, at 122 (1990), reprinted in 1990 U.S.C.C.A.N. 722, 800-01.

3091 See Intertanko v. Gary Locke, 120 S.Ct 1135 (2000).

3092 Intertanko, 146 L.Ed.2d 69, 2000 A.M.C. 913, 120 SC.t 1135 (2000)

on the doctrine of preemption is *Intertanko*, which was decided on March 6, 2000.

## A. Background

Intertanko is a trade association representing approximately eighty percent of the world's oil tanker fleet.[3093] Its members call at oil facilities at Puget Sound and travel to Oregon Ports by way of the Columbia River.[3094] In doing so, Intertanko oil tankers must navigate the waters of Puget Sound through fog and vessel traffic. Additionally the rocky coastlines along Puget Sound and the Strait of Juan de Fuca create confined and shallow waters. These waters produce diverse ecosystems which are especially vulnerable to oil pollution. Because of this potential threat to the environment, three environmental groups intervened in the Intertanko law suit to defend state interests.[3095] Intertanko sought a declaratory judgment that certain Washington state statutes and regulations concerning vessel operations in Washington state waters were unconstitutional.[3096] Specifically, Intertanko challenged sixteen regulations promulgated by the State office of marine safety ("OMS")[3097] and two sections of the Washington Revised Codes[3098] on the theory that these provisions were preempted, or otherwise invalidated, by the federal statutes, regulations, and treaty obligations.[3099]

Therefore, the district court confronted the issue of whether federal law prohibits states from enacting oil spill prevention laws.[3100] Arguably,

---

3093 *Intertanko*, 947 F.Supp.1484 (W.D. Wash. 1996), Intertanko is comprised of 253 members and 152 associate members.

3094 See id.

3095 See id.

3096 See id.

3097 See id. at 1488-89. A list of the challenged regulations appears in the Intertanko decision.

3098 See Wash. Rev. Code. §§ 88.46.010,88.46.040(3) (1996).

3099 See Intertanko, 947 F. Supp. at 1490.

3100 See id.

oil spill prevention could step into the province of ship design, an area exclusively regulated by federal maritime law.[3101] The district court upheld the constitutionality of all applicable Washington State statutes and regulations, thereby granting defendants' and intervenors' motions for summary judgement.[3102] The court decided that the oil spill prevention laws legitimately protect Washington State's delicate and valuable marine resources through the exercise of the state's police powers.[3103] Accordingly, the challenged statutes were deemed valid notwithstanding federal preemption laws, the Commerce Clause, or the Foreign Commerce Clause.[3104] However on appeal, the Ninth Circuit affirmed in part, reversed in part, and remanded. The court reversed the district court's holding that the Wash. Admin. Code section 317-21-265 is not preempted by federal law, but affirmed the district court's judgment as to all other challenged Washington regulations.[3105] The Ninth Circuit was confronted with similar issues on appeal. The Ninth Circuit Court of Appeals upheld most of the state regulations, **save one requiring vessels to install certain navigation and towing equipment.** After granting certiorari, the Supreme Court, Reversed and remanded, holding that: (1) the preemptive effect of the Ports and Waterways Safety Act (PWSA) and its regulations is not affected by the Oil Pollution Act; (2) Title I of the PWSA allows a state to regulate its ports and waterways, so long as the regulation is based on the peculiarities of local waters that call for special precautionary measures; (3) under Title II of the PWSA only the federal government may regulate the design, construction, alteration, repair, maintenance, operation, equipping, personnel qualification, and manning of tanker vessels; and (4) Washington's tanker regulations regarding general navigation watch procedures, English language skills, training, and casualty reporting are therefore preempted.[3106]

---

3101 See id. at 1491.

3102 See id. at 1500.

3103 Id.

3104 See. id., U.S. Const. art. I, § 8, cl. 3.

3105 148 F.3d 1053,1069 (9th Cir. 1998).

3106 *Intertanko*, 120 S.Ct. 1135.

The Supreme Court criticized the Ninth Circuit for placing too much weight on OPA's saving clauses than they can bear.[3107] The Supreme Court held that like Title I of OPA, in which the saving clauses are found, the saving clauses are limited to regulations governing liability and compensation for oil pollution, and do not extend to rules regulating vessel operation, design, or manning. Thus, the pre-emptive effect of the PWSA and its regulations is not affected by OPA, and the Supreme Court's previous holding in which the preemptive effect of the PWSA was upheld, survives OPA's enactment undiminished.

The Supreme Court relied heavily on its earlier decision in *Ray v. Atlantic Richfield Co.*[3108] The *Ray* Court had held, among other things, that Congress, in PWSA Title I, preserved state authority to regulate the peculiarities of local waters, such as depth and narrowness, if there is no conflict with federal regulatory determinations, but PWSA Title II, mandated uniform federal rules on the subjects or matters there specified.[3109] Thus, under *Ray's* interpretation of the Title II provision now found at 46 U.S.C. § 3703(a), only the Federal Government may regulate the design, construction, alteration, repair, maintenance, operation, equipping, personnel qualification, and manning of tankers. The Supreme Court in *Intertanko* thus reaffirmed *Ray's* holding on this point. The Supreme Court held that Congress has left no room for state regulation of these matters.[3110]

The Supreme Court further held that the field pre-emption rule surrounding PWSA Title II and 46 U.S.C. § 3703(a) and the superseding effect of additional federal statutes are illustrated by the pre-emption of four of Washington's tanker regulations, the attempted reach of which was well demonstrated by the briefs and record.[3111]

The Supreme court pointed out that, the imposition of a series of training requirements on a tanker's crew do not address matters unique to Washington waters, but imposes requirements that control the staffing,

3107 Id. at 1138-39

3108 Ray, 435 U.S., 151, 171-172, 178, 98 S.Ct. 988 (1978)

3109 Id. at 168, 98 S.Ct. 988

3110 *Intertanko*, 120 S.Ct. 1135, 1139

3111 Id. at 1139

operation, and manning of a tanker outside of those waters.[3112] The court thus found that the training and drill requirements pertain to "operation" and "personnel qualifications" and so are pre-empted by § 3703(a).[3113] The Supreme Court further held that training is a field reserved to the Federal Government and this is further confirmed by the circumstance that the STCW Convention addresses crew "training" and "qualification" requirements, and that the United States has enacted crew training regulations.

The court rejected the imposition of English language proficiency requirements on a tanker's crew and held that it is not limited to governing local traffic or local peculiarities.[3114] In addition to this it is pre-empted by § 3703(a) as a "personnel qualification" and by 33 U.S.C. § 1228(a)(7), which requires that any vessel operating in United States waters have at least one licensed deck officer on the navigation bridge who is capable of clearly understanding English.[3115]

The *Intertanko* Court also invalidated Washington's general requirement that the navigation watch consist of at least two licensed deck officers, a helmsman, and a lookout because it is pre-empted as an attempt to regulate a tanker's "operation" and "manning" under § 3703(a).[3116]

The Supreme Court also struck down the requirement that vessels in Washington waters report certain marine casualties regardless of where in the world they occurred because the Coast Guard regulates the same subject that Congress intended be the sole source of a vessel's reporting obligations.[3117]

One of the most important parts the Supreme Court decision is the part that invalidated the navigational equipment requirements of the Washington State regulations. Considering the fact that most of the tanker-vessels involved in the transportation of oil had been built several years ago, thus lacking modern design and construction requirements,

---

3112 Id.

3113 Id.

3114 Id.

3115 Id.

3116 Id. at 1139-40

3117 See 46 U.S.C. §§ 6101, 3717(a)(4).

this would have put a lot of vessel owners out of business. Because of this specific requirement under the Washington laws, most of these vessel owners will find it difficult to obtain financing from banks. This is because upholding the Washington State's attempt to regulate design will be an encouragement to other states to enact similar statutes. Most banks will not want to get involved in the financing of this category of tanker-vessels since they may not be able to ascertain what the potential liabilities of the vessel would be, because of the network of conflicting state regulations on tanker design and construction that a contrary Supreme Court decision would have engendered. This in turn would have translated into distress in the shipping industry.

*Reactions to the Intertanko Decision*: As Svein Ringbakken, Intertanko's Washington-based general counsel, put it: "The last major decision on this issue - Ray v Atlantic Richfield - was in 1978. I believe this decision will continue to be the standard for at least another 20-30 years.' He added: 'It restores predictability as regards who is regulating maritime affairs."[3118] Matthew Vafidis, a partner at Haight Gardner Holland & Knight who submitted an earlier amicus brief in the case on behalf of the International Chamber of Shipping, added that states such as California, Rhode Island and Maine 'will have to take a long, hard look at each of their tanker regulations to see if they fall foul of this decision'.[3119]

The Intertanko decision was no doubt a blow to the ability of the states to regulate the operation of tanker vessels that trade in their waters. But one approach some states are considering now is the option of increasing the liability limits under their state statutes or in the alternative making liability unlimited. In fact Washington State is considering one of such options. But apart from this, some state governments have taken the battle to Capitol Hill. In fact just two months after dealing what seemed a fatal blow in the US Supreme Court to Washington state's onerous tanker safety

3118 See John Mclaughlin, Insight: Supreme win but battle not over: Intertanko's US Supreme Court victory is a welcome boost for battered tanker owners with the case likely to be a legal benchmark for years to come, Lloyd's List Int'l, March 13, 2000, at 7.

3119 Id at 7.

rules, Intertanko found itself girding for another fight on the same issues, with the battleground this time on Capitol Hill.[3120] In early May 2000, one of Washington State's Senators at the time, Slade Gorton introduced the 'States Prevention of Oil Tanker Spills Act' into the Senate. It is a simple bill, and a brief one, amending the Oil Pollution Act of 1990 to allow states free reign to introduce their own regulations on tanker safety.[3121] Senator Gorton warned last year that if the Supreme Court ruled against his state's tanker regulations, he would go the legislative route. Intertanko is not underestimating the challenge it faces.[3122] 'Absolutely we are taking it seriously,' said Intertanko's senior vice-president and general counsel, Svein Ringbakken, of the bill. 'It has the potential to undermine what we gained in the Supreme Court case.' However, 'better to have this discussion going on at federal level' he states, 'than at the more closed local level where the international maritime community has a very limited opportunity to participate.'[3123] For Representative Jack Metcalf, also of Washington, who introduced a companion bill in the House of Representatives - the bill 'will allow all states to implement the best achievable protection from the damage caused by oil spills.'[3124] Introducing the bill, the senator added that it 'won't eliminate all oil spills. I believe, however, that it will help to prevent some. Laws protecting our shores from dangerous oil spills should not be brought to the lowest common denominator. Rather, allowing states to enhance federal laws will ensure an even greater level of protection.' [3125]

Intertanko sees it differently. It contends that a proliferation of discrete local regulations would weaken the existing international maritime safety regime, thus endangering the environment these laws were designed to protect.[3126] Senator Gorton's bill attacks federal pre-emption head-on, in its single amendment to OPA '90 stating that: 'Nothing in this chapter, or any

3120 See John Mclaughlin, International: Capitol Hill: Intertanko gears up again to combat Washington tanker safety legislation, Lloyd's List Int'l May 18, 2000, * 5

3121 Id at 5.

3122 Id.

3123 Id.

3124 Id.

3125 Id.

3126 Id.

other provision of law, pre-empts the authority of a state to adopt additional standards regarding maintenance, operation, equipping, personnel qualification or manning of vessels to which the regulations apply.[3127]' As of December of 2002, there was no indication that there is a Congressional move towards adding this amendment to the OPA. But another catastrophic oil spill on the scale of Exxon Valdez may be all that it takes for the momentum for the enactment of this OPA amendment to pick up.

The inclusion of the non-preemption clause in OPA means that an RP cannot recover from the Fund what it paid as removal costs in clean up efforts directed by a state government environmental official.[3128] In the case of *United States v. Gatlin Oil,*[3129] the RP, Gatlin Oil sought reimbursement for the costs of complying with the directives of the North Carolina environmental officials. These state directives required Gatlin Oil to clean up soil and groundwater contamination. Gatlin Oil argued that the federal coordinator by virtue of his position assumed responsibility for the entire cleanup.[3130] Gatlin Oil also asserted that the entire oil spill posed a substantial threat of oil reaching navigable waters.[3131] In contrast, the Coast Guard maintained that the Fund was not liable for the work performed pursuant to North Carolina directives. The court agreed with the Coast Guard's superior argument because of the provisions of OPA's section 2718(a)(1)(A)-(B) (Non-preemption clause) and the OPA implementing regulations.[3132] The court also noted that the OPA authorizes proceedings by which the Fund may be obligated to assist states. The court noted particularly the provisions of Section 2712(d)(1) which provides that "upon request of the Governor of a State" or pursuant to an agreement between the President and a Governor, the President may obligate the Fund for removal costs incurred by a state. The court pointed out that Gatlin Oil had not shown any request by the

3127 Id.

3128 See. United States v. Gatlin Oil, 169 F.3d 207, 212 (4th Cir. 1999).

3129 169 F.3d 207, 212 (4th Cir. 1999).

3130 Id. at 212.

3131 Id. at 212.

3132 Id. at 212-213, see also, 33 CFR 133.1-133.25.

Governor of North Carolina or an agreement between the Governor and the President.[3133] Noting that procedures for state access to the Fund are set forth in 33 CFR Part 133, the court observed Gatlin's non-introduction of any evidence showing compliance with either OPA or the regulations concerning cleanup costs that the North Carolina authorities directed.[3134]

For instance, *Gatlin Oil* failed to prove that the removal of the contamination of the soil and groundwater, which was required by North Carolina, posed a substantial threat of a discharge of oil into navigable waters.[3135] In other words they met the threshold requirement for the state of North Carolina but failed to meet the "navigable waters" threshold requirement of the OPA. In addition to this the court found that Gatlin's theory that the federal coordinator is deemed to have directed all state and federal removal costs is contrary to 33 CFR § 136.205.[3136] 33 CFR § 136.205 specifically provides that the amount of compensation allowable for removal costs in general is the total of uncompensated reasonable removal costs of actions taken that were determined by the FOSC to be consistent with the National Contingency Plan or were directed by the FOSC. It further provides that except in exceptional circumstances, removal activities for which costs are being claimed must have been coordinated with the FOSC. The *Gatlin* Court noted that the federal coordinator did not determine that the cleanup ordered by North Carolina authorities was consistent with the National Contingency Plan, and he did not direct Gatlin Oil to comply with North Carolina's directives.[3137] Based on the foregoing, the *Gatlin* court concluded that the Fund was not liable for Gatlin's expenditures that were directed by North Carolina authorities.[3138]

The *Gatlin* court's reading of section 2718 is correct. A contrary decision would defeat the purpose of that section, and would cause states to

---

3133 Id. at 213.

3134 Id.

3135 Id.

3136 Id.

3137 Id.

3138 Id.

disinvest in State Oil Spill Funds. Why is a state Fund needed if an RP or a third party claimant can go cap in hand to the Oil Spill Liability Trust Fund to recover cleanup costs even when the FOSC did not determine that the cleanup was in any shape or form consistent with the National Contingency Plan or where he did not direct the cleanup? A contrary decision would have been a license for all claimants to raid and dissipate the limited Oil Spill Liability Trust Fund.

*The interaction of the OPA's non-preemption clause with the Limitation of Liability Act:*

The Shipowner's Limitation of Liability Act[3139] was enacted in 1851, to encourage shipbuilding and the investment of money in the shipping industry.[3140] The Act provides that "the liability of the owner of any vessel, whether American or foreign,... for any act, matter, or thing, loss or damage, or forfeiture, done, occasioned or incurred, without the privity or knowledge of such owner or owners, shall not... exceed the amount or value of the interest of such owner in such vessel, and her freight then pending."[3141] It creates a procedure whereby the vessel owner may petition the federal district court for limitation and deposit a sum equal to the value of the vessel and pending freight with the court for the satisfaction of all claims. All proceedings against the owners are stayed pending disposition of the limitation petition.[3142] A single forum is then used to determine (1) whether the vessel and its owner are liable at all, (2) whether the owner may in fact limit its liability to the value of the vessel, (3) the amount of the claims, and (4) how the fund should be distributed.

Until the passage of the FWPCA, CERCLA, and TAPAA, the Limitation of Liability Act was routinely applied to claims for pollution damages. These statutes set specific liability limits (higher than the post

3139 Act of March 3, 1851, ch. 43, 9 Stat. 635 (1851) (codified at 46 U.S.C. §§ 18189).

3140 See Flink v. Paladini, 279 U.S. 59, 62 (1929).

3141 46 U.S.C. app. § 183(a) (1994).

3142 See 46 U.S.C. app. § 185 (1994).

casualty value of a vessel) that is in conflict with and renders inapplicable the limitation policy of the Limitation of Liability Act. OPA, just like these statutes, sets specific liability limits that conflict with the policy of the Limitation Act. Also, OPA specifically provides that the Limitation Act does not apply to oil spill cases pursued under it or under state statutes and common law. However, after OPA, the Limitation Act might still be a viable defense to admiralty claims, but unavailable for the defense of common law claims for pollution damage. It appears that OPA's non-preemption clause is evidently intended only to exempt statutory and common law actions for pollution damages. OPA's savings clause, provides that OPA does not affect the general maritime law, other than as is set forth in the preemption clause:

"2751. Savings provision
(e) Admiralty and maritime law.
Except as otherwise provided in this Act, this Act does not affect--
(1) admiralty and maritime law; or
(2) the jurisdiction of the district courts of the United States with respect to civil actions under admiralty and maritime jurisdiction, saving to suitors in all cases all other remedies to which they are otherwise entitled."[3143]

The Limitation of Liability Act survives to the same extent that admiralty and common law claims (incidental to oil pollution) survive OPA, because limitation is a right and a defense granted by the maritime law. The savings clause, when read in conjunction with the preemption clause, reveals that OPA was not intended to abrogate the Limitation of Liability Act, except with respect to the liability of a responsible party for claims asserted under OPA or a state statute or common law. Nothing else in OPA indicates a congressional intent to effect a total repeal of the right to limitation.[3144]

---

3143 33 U.S.C. § 2751(e) (1994).

3144 See William M. Duncan, The Oil Pollution Act of 1990's Effect on the Shipowners' Limitation of Liability Act, 5 U.S.F. Mar. L.J. 303, 314 (1993).

It is true that OPA contains a number of prohibitions on the use of the Limitation of Liability Act. It prevents limitation as to claims by the United States, and it also prohibits a responsible party from relying on the Limitation of Liability Act as a defense to actions under OPA itself, regardless of the person or entity bringing the claim. OPA also abrogates the Limitation of Liability Act's provisions in cases wherein states have imposed additional or unlimited liability.[3145] OPA's repeal of the Limitation of Liability Act is not complete, however. OPA does not affect the right of a responsible party to limit liability where the claim is brought under the general maritime law.[3146] Thus, where a claim is brought under a maritime tort theory, a vessel owner should be able to raise the Limitation of Liability Act as a defense. Such cases are most likely to arise in situations where a state has not enacted an unlimited liability statute.[3147]

The provisions of OPA's section 2718(a)(2) (non-preemption) seems to indicate that the Limitation Act is no longer applicable to common law claims for oil pollution. This section provides in pertinent part:

"(a) Preservation of State authorities; Solid Waste Disposal Act
Nothing in this chapter or the Act of March 3, 1851 shall--
(2) affect, or be construed or interpreted to affect or modify in any way the obligations or liabilities of any person under the Solid Waste Disposal Act (42 U.S.C. 6901 et seq.) or State law, including common law."

The specific inclusion of "common law" in this section is an indication that Congress wanted all those suing under common law for oil pollution removal cost and damages, to recover from an RP without being subject to the Limitation Act. The use of the words "Nothing in this chapter or the Act of March 3, 1851 shall modify in any way the obligations or liabilities of any person under.......common law" indicates that Congress wanted those suing under common law theories to have their day in court, without

3145 33 U.S.C. § 2718(c) (1994).

3146 See id. § 2751(e) (OPA's admiralty and maritime law savings provision).

3147 See Ballard Shipping Co. v. Beach Shellfish, 32 F.3d. 623 (1st Cir. 1994) (holding that exoneration was available to defeat shellfish dealers' claim for purely economic loss).

OPA or the Limitation Act standing in the way of their full recovery. In such oil pollution common law claims, the limitation provisions of OPA and the limitation provisions of the Limitation Act will be inapplicable. Amount of damages or cost will be determined by the jury.

*Recent jurisprudence on the OPA & the Limitation of Liability Act:* Majority of courts have overwhelmingly held that the provisions of the Limitation of Liability Act do not apply to OPA claims.[3148]They have also found that Rule F of the Supplemental Rules for Certain Admiralty and Maritime Claims of the Federal Rules of Civil Procedure ("Rule F") (concursus procedural mechanism) usually utilized to enjoin and consolidate all multiple and multi-jurisdictional suits against pre-OPA responsible parties or oil polluters have no application whatsoever to post-OPA suits.[3149]Some notable legal commentators have however criticized these decisions.[3150]

The main focus of this part of chapter fourteen is the effect that OPA has on Rule F and the Limitation Act with respect to post-OPA oil spills. One very notable decision is that of *Bouchard Transport Co. Inc., v. Updegraff,*[3151] a case where vessel owners filed complaint for exoneration from or limitation of liability in connection with collision of freighter and two tugs pushing petroleum- carrying barges. Among other claimants, Florida Department of Environmental Protection (DEP) filed oil pollution claims, and the United States District Court for the Middle District of Florida ordered mediation. The Court of Appeals, vacated and remanded for ruling on Florida's claim of Eleventh Amendment immunity. On remand, the United States District Court for the Middle District of Florida, ruled that Florida was entitled to sovereign immunity from limitations

3148 See e.g., Transport Co. Inc., v. Updegraff, 1998 A.M.C. 2409, 147 F.3d 1344 (11th Cir. 1998).

3149 147 F.3d at 1344.

3150 See Robert Force & Jonathan M. Gutoff, Limitation Of Liability In Oil Pollution Cases: In Search Of Concursus Or Procedural Alternatives To Concursus, 22 Tul. Mar. L.J. 331 (1998) (Hereinafter Force).

3151 47 ERC 1353, 29 Envtl. L. Rep. 20,139, 23 Fla. L. Weekly Fed. C 1690, 1998 A.M.C. 2409, 147 F.3d 1344 (11th Cir. 1998).

proceeding, and it dismissed claims under the Oil Pollution Act (OPA) and Florida's Pollution Discharge Prevention and Control Act. The vessel owners appealed.

The Court of Appeals held that: (1) as matter of first impression, Florida was not entitled to Eleventh Amendment immunity from limitations proceeding, but (2) claims brought pursuant to OPA and Florida Pollution Discharge Prevention Act were not subject to Rule F of the Supplemental Rules for Certain Admiralty and Maritime Claims, and were not constrained to Rule F limitation of liability proceedings. So, the lower court's decision was affirmed in part, reversed in part, and remanded.[3152]

In response to the owners contention that Rule F generally applies to all limitation statutes, the court in its reasoning found that Rule F does not specify the limitation statutes to which it applies. The Owners argued that the OPA is a limitation statute insofar as it limits the Owners' liability to $1,200 per gross ton for cleanup costs and natural damages, and that the OPA claims against them therefore must be resolved in a Rule F limitation proceeding.[3153] More specifically, the Owners asserted that there are two sets of limited funds that must be distributed among valid claims arising from the collision: (1) a set of funds, each equal to the value of the respective vessel, to be distributed pro rata among all valid maritime and common law claims subject to the Limitation Act; and (2) a set of funds, each equal to $1,200 per gross ton for the respective vessel, to be distributed pro rata among all valid OPA claims. Therefore, the Owners contend, Rule F should apply to the OPA claims to the same extent it applies to claims subject to the Limitation Act.

In rejecting this argument, the court in its reasoning said that the OPA is not subject to Rule F for two reasons: (1) OPA claimants do not face a limited fund necessitating a pro rata distribution; and (2) Congress has specifically set forth procedures to implement the strictures of the OPA. The court observed that the Owners' theory was based on a false premise, because OPA claimants do not face a limited fund in that OPA uses the Oil Spill Liability Trust Fund (Fund) to ensure that every claim made

3152 Updegraff, 147 F.3d 1344.

3153 Id. at 1350.

pursuant to the OPA will be paid in full.[3154] The court pointed out that even though the OPA limits the liability of the Owners for certain costs and damages arising from the oil spill in this case to $1,200 per gross ton, the Fund backstops the Owners' limited liability and ensures that every valid claim will be paid in full.

The court also pointed out that while the OPA is a limitation statute in some sense (i.e., it limits the ship owner's liability), it is not a limitation statute in the relevant sense--it does not limit the total amount of money that can be recovered by the claimants in this case, thus there is no need to bring all of the claimants into a single proceeding to make a pro rata distribution because every claim will be paid in full. In footnote eight of the decision the court rejected the owners argument that the OPA does create a limited fund because the maximum amount that may be paid by the Fund with respect to any single incident is $1 billion.[3155] The court pointed to the fact that there had been no allegation that the claims in this case posed any danger of exceeding the $1 billion cap and that even if the OPA were judicially analogous to the Limitation Act and therefore subject to Rule F, traditionally, this Circuit does not require claimants to proceed in a Rule F limitation proceeding absent the real possibility that some claims will not be paid.

It appears that this statement by the court opens a small window of opportunity for a responsible party in a big oil spill where claims actually could exceed $1 billion, to invoke Rule F in that the first rationale behind the *Updegraff* court's refusal to allow Rule F would be absent. That rationale, as explained before is that the claims did not exceed the amount in the Oil Spill Fund. In those situations, the vessel owner will be exposed to liability in excess of the amount in the oil spill fund, and thus the vessel owner's should be able to use Rule F.[3156]

The *Updegraff* court also observed that the OPA is not subject to Rule F because, unlike the Limitation Act, which was enacted without procedural

3154 See 26 U.S.C. § 9509; 33 U.S.C. §§ 2712, 2713.

3155 See 26 U.S.C. § 9509(c)(2)(A)(i).

3156 *Updegraff*, 147 F.3d 1344,1350, (*quoting*, *Beiswenger*, 86 F.3d 1032, 1037 (11th Cir. 1996)).

mechanisms, Congress expressly set forth procedures for implementing the OPA. In reaching this conclusion, the First Circuit summarized the claims procedures set forth in the OPA. Comparing the OPA statutory procedures with the Rule F procedures, the court found that it reveals two largely conflicting frameworks for resolving OPA claims. For example, the OPA gives claimants three years to bring claims against a responsible party.[3157] The OPA also requires that claimants first present their claims to the responsible party, and then, if a claim is not settled within the requisite period of time, the claimant may proceed in court.[3158] In some instances, claimants may proceed directly to the OPA Fund and then subrogate to the United States the claims against the responsible party.[3159] The court in its reasoning pointed out that if OPA claims were subject to Rule F, every claim (including claims subrogated to the United States) would have to be brought within the period announced by the district court in the notice sent to potential claimants, which was 60 days in this case.[3160] The court expressed the fear that subjecting OPA claims to Rule F would effectively allow ship owners to opt out of the Congressionally mandated procedures for resolving OPA claims. To buttress this point the court noted that, the venue provisions of the OPA permits claimants to proceed "in any district in which the discharge or injury or damages occurred, or in which the defendant resides, may be found, has its principal office, or has appointed an agent for service of process."[3161]

The court noted that the injunction issued by the district court in a Rule F proceeding would require OPA claimants to proceed only in the district court chosen by the vessel owners, and the process envisioned by the OPA's jurisdiction and venue provisions would be rendered meaningless. Noting that the OPA's section 2717(c) grants jurisdiction to state courts to hear claims arising thereunder, the court was afraid that this grant of concurrent jurisdiction would be rendered meaningless if OPA

3157 33 U.S.C. § 2717(f).

3158 33 U.S.C. § 2713(a) & (c).

3159 33 U.S.C. § 2715.

3160 147 F.3d at 1351.

3161 33 U.S.C. § 2717(b).

claims were subject to Rule F, in that Rule F complaints must be filed in federal court.

The Owners asserted that this conflict of procedures is no different than the conflict that occurs when Jones Act claims are required to be brought in a Rule F limitation proceeding (e.g., the 3-year statute of limitations normally enjoyed by Jones Act claimants is replaced with the shorter period announced pursuant to Rule F). While it acknowledged that Rule F procedures govern in the small percentage of Jones Act cases that implicate the liability limits of the Limitation Act, the court rejected this argument because it was convinced that it would subject every OPA claim to Rule F, giving ship owners the option to replace OPA's 3-year statutory period in every case.

The court invoked what it called the fundamental principles of statutory construction or interpretation to resolve the conflict between the Rule F procedures and the OPA procedures. The court held that, a fundamental principle of statutory construction requires that a specific statute take precedence over a more general one.[3162] Furthermore, the court said it was avoiding statutory constructions that render provisions meaningless.[3163] The court held that consistent with these principles of statutory construction, OPA claims must be resolved pursuant to the procedures contained in that statute, rather than replacing those procedures with Rule F. The court noted that although the Supplemental Rules for Certain Admiralty and Maritime Claims are not part of a Congressionally-enacted statute, the decision whether to apply those rules or the more specific procedures contained in the OPA is informed by general principles of statutory construction.

The Owners argued that Rule F must be applied to preserve judicial resources and avoid the burden of defending a multiplicity of suits in various fora. Rejecting this argument, the court ruled that the owners'

---

3162 147 F.3d at 1351, (*quoting*, Pedro v. United States, 79 F.3d 1065, 1069 (11th Cir.), *cert. denied*, 519 U.S. 980, 117 S.Ct. 431, 136 L.Ed.2d 330 (1996)).

3163 Id. (*citing*, v. Marine Cooks & Stewards Union, 642 F.2d 966, 970-71 (5th Cir. Apr.1981) ("A basic principle of statutory construction is that a statute should not be construed in such a way as to render certain provisions superfluous or insignificant." (internal quotations and citations omitted)).

understandable interest in consolidating this potentially unwieldy litigation does not overcome the congressionally mandated procedures for adjudicating OPA claims. The court pointed out that it does not view the convenience of the shipowner as a legitimate goal of a Rule F limitation proceeding:

"Absent an insufficient fund (1) the statutory privilege of limiting liability is not in the nature of a forum non conveniens doctrine, and (2) the statute gives a ship-owner, sued in several suits no advantage over other kinds of defendants in the same position. Concourse is to be granted only when necessary in order to distribute an inadequate fund. The purpose of limitation proceedings is not to prevent a multiplicity of suits but, in an equitable fashion, to provide a marshalling of assets--the distribution pro rata of an inadequate fund among claimants, none of whom can be paid in full.[3164] Furthermore, neither Rule F nor the Limitation Act grants the owners a right to a concursus. Rule F merely provides a procedure for distributing a limited fund among competing claimants where the real possibility exists that some claims will not be paid in full:
Where the value of the vessel and the pending freight, the fund paid into the proceeding by the offending owner, exceeds the claims made against it, there is no necessity for the maintenance of the concourse...."[3165]

The court also stated that to expand the jurisdictional provisions of the Act to prevent the respondent from now proceeding in her state case would transform the Act from a protective instrument to an offensive weapon by which the shipowner could deprive suitors of their common-law rights, even where the limitation fund is known to be more than adequate to satisfy all demands upon it. The court also pointed out that the shipowner's right to limit liability is not so boundless and that the Act is not one of immunity from liability but of limitation of it.[3166] In order to debunk the

---

3164 Id. at 1351 (citing, Pershing Auto Rentals, Inc. v. Gaffney, 279 F.2d 546, 550-51 (5th Cir.1960) (internal citations and quotations omitted)).

3165 Id. at 1351-1352.

3166 Id. at 1352, (*citing*, Tankers Corp. v. Henn, 354 U.S. 147, 152-53, 77 S.Ct. 1269, 1272, 1 L.Ed.2d 1246 (1957)).

owners argument that the affirmative defense of limited liability will not work if multiple actions proceed in different courts, the court held that because the OPA establishes a limit of liability for the owners, after paying out that amount, no cause of action will lie against the owners pursuant to the OPA. The remaining claims (or the remaining portions of claims) will be paid from the Fund. The court is in other words saying that the possibility of the multiplicity of claims in various courts should not and would not break the OPA limitation (except for the situations where OPA provides for unlimited liability).[3167]

The court noted that Rule F was designed to distribute a limited fund to multiple claimants where Congress has provided no statutory procedure for that distribution and where all claims cannot be paid in full. The court found that the instant case satisfies neither of these requirements--Congress has provided a procedure for implementing the OPA and the Fund will guarantee full payment of all valid OPA claims arising from this [particular] oil discharge.[3168]

In another very interesting case, *In the Matter of The Complaint of Metlife Capital Corp., v. M/V EMILY S*,[3169] the Commonwealth of Puerto Rico brought action seeking damages under OPA, general federal maritime law, and Puerto Rico law after parted towing wire between a tug and a barge caused the grounding of the barge which resulted in an oil spill. Demise charterers, operator, and owner of the tug filed complaints under the Limitation of Liability Act and Admiralty Rule F, seeking exoneration from or limitation of liability. After initially enjoining actions other than those filed in limitation proceeding, the United States District Court for the District of Puerto Rico, permitted claims for oil spill removal costs or damages to be asserted independently of limitation of liability proceedings. Charterers, operator, and owner appealed. The Court of Appeals held that: (1) OPA repealed both substantive limitations and procedures of Limitation Act with respect to removal costs and damages claims against responsible parties, and (2) admiralty Rule F which

3167 See 33 U.S.C §2704(c)(1)-(3).

3168 Updegraff, 147 F.3d 1344, 1352.

3169 M/V EMILY S, 132 F.3d 818 (1st Cir. 1997).

governed filing and adjudication of limitation actions did not apply to actions under OPA.

The decision of the court in this case is mutatis mutandis with the decision of the court in *Updegraff.*

One concern the *Metlife* court had with the shortened claims period under Rule F is that it would interfere with the United States' subrogation rights under the OPA. The court in its reasoning said that if oil spill claims are subject to Rule F concursus, claimants who are barred by the court imposed deadline from recovering against the responsible party, are likely to present their claims to the Fund,[3170] and once the Fund pays a claim, the United States acquires all rights of subrogation.[3171] The court expressed the fear that at that point, the United States may then be denied access to the proceedings against the responsible party, consequently the Fund will bear the financial burden of these late claims. The appellants responded that, under Rule F, the government's subrogation rights do not necessarily lapse because "for cause shown, the court may enlarge the time within which claims may be filed."[3172] In rejecting this argument, the court observed that subjecting the government's subrogation rights to the whims and caprices of the trial court in every oil spill action fails to adequately secure those rights.[3173] The court also noted that Congress specifically examined this issue in creating the OPA's statute of limitation and giving the courts discretion over this matter is contrary to legislative intent. The court concluded that, even if the courts consistently enlarge the monition period for subrogation claims, in many instances, the limited fund established by the concursus procedure would already have been exhausted.[3174]

*Criticisms of the Anti-Rule F OPA decisions:* Some renowned commentators have criticized some of the anti-Supplemental Rule F OPA decisions. Notable among the critics of these decisions are Professors Robert

3170 Id. at 823.

3171 See 33 U.S.C. §§ 2712(f), 2713, 2715(a).

3172 Rule F(4).

3173 M/V EMILY S, 132 F.3d at 824.

3174 Id.

Force and Jonathan Gutoff ("Hereinafter Professor Force").[3175] After a scholarly extrapolation of the workings of Supplemental Rule F, Professor Force noted that Rule F provides a complete procedure for achieving a concursus of claims by anyone seeking "limitation pursuant to statute," and that the plain language of the Rule is broad enough to include limitation under OPA.[3176] He, however, agreed with the courts on the fact that OPA itself removes OPA claims from the substantive provisions of the Limitation Act. He pointed out that a combination of factors, including the specific and greatly increased limits on liability set out in OPA, the relative ease with which liability can be broken under OPA, and the fact that states are not precluded from imposing additional liability on parties without regard to the Limitation Act, clearly seem to undercut the applicability of the substantive provisions of the Limitation Act to OPA claims.[3177] But he frowned at the fact that some courts have carried this approach over to the procedural provisions of the Limitation Act and Rule F. He particularly criticized *Metlife's* suggestion that OPA provides a procedure for effecting limitation of liability under the Act. He believes that the court confused the term "claims procedure" (Emphasis mine) with the term "limitation procedure" (Emphasis mine).[3178] He noted that contrary to the court's suggestion, Rule F requires that the person filing a limitation petition must do so within six months of having received notice of a claim,[3179] the Rule then leaves it to the discretion of the limitation court to set the time in which claims may be made against the limitation fund.[3180] Professor Force believed that there is absolutely no reason why a court would not take into account the time needed to complete removal activities or to formulate and implement a plan for restoration of natural resources.[3181] He also noted that,

---

3175 See Robert Force & Jonathan M. Gutoff, Limitation Of Liability In Oil Pollution Cases: In Search Of Concursus Or Procedural Alternatives To Concursus, 22 Tul. Mar. L.J. at 331 (Summer 1998).

3176 Id. at 360.

3177 Id. at 361.

3178 Id. at 365.

3179 Id. at 363.

3180 Id. at 364.

3181 Id.

the Oil Spill Liability Trust Fund could likewise file a contingent claim in any situation where it appears that it may have a right to do so. Professor Force pointed out that the importance of the only time limit specified in Rule F is that it would require a responsible party to act promptly to invoke the right of limitation, but it would in no way impinge on the discretion of the trial judge to allow claimants a fair and realistic opportunity to present and prove their claims.[3182] But it is important to point out that the even though the court could tinker with the time frame, it does not appear that that was the intent of Congress when OPA was drafted.

Professor Force also indicated that the limitation period analysis would, if carried to its logical conclusion, completely eviscerate both Supplemental Rule F and the Limitation Act in non-OPA cases. Pointing out that the court's reasoning was not logical in any way, he noted that if the position of the court were valid, the Act of 1851 itself would conflict with later legislation. He pointed to the fact that Congress by statute has provided for a three-year statute of limitations for personal injury claims, but personal injury claims are subject to limitation.[3183] He noted that, there very well may be situations where a personal injury plaintiff may have to file a claim in a limitation proceeding prior to the expiration of the three years in order to assure a share in the distribution of the limitation fund. The same may be said as to Carriage of Goods by Sea Act (COGSA) claims where there is a one year limitation period. In the event of a collision that results in cargo damage and personal injury there is nothing to prevent a vessel owner from filing for limitation of liability two weeks after the incident as long as claims have been made against it. Professor Force also noted that virtually every claim for damages that may be brought as an admiralty claim in federal court may also be brought in a state court under the "saving to suitors" provision of 28 U.S.C.A. § 1333. These claims are no different than OPA claims where a party who has incurred removal costs or sustained damages may sue in federal or state court. He pointed out further that, just as ordinary "admiralty" claims brought in state court are subject to the exclusive jurisdiction of a federal limitation court, so

3182 Id.

3183 See *In re Texaco, Inc.*, 1991 AMC 2624 (E.D. La. 1991) (The M/V Anatole B).

could OPA claims brought in state court be made subject to the exclusive jurisdiction of a federal limitation court. This is a very strong argument.

But it appears that the main concern of the courts in the companion cases, *Metlife* and the *Updergraff* is that if Congress had intended the status quo to prevail, it would not have indicated expressly in the statute that the Limitation of Liability Act is inapplicable to OPA cases. Apart from this, the court would not want claimants' ability to recover within the three year time limit set by Congress to be subject to the whims and caprices or unwieldy discretion of any judge.

What probably informed the court's rigid approach to Rule F in the OPA context as opposed to the COGSA context is the goal of Congress to ensure that those that have been damaged by oil pollution, be fully compensated under OPA. The courts over the years have devised ways of broadening the scope of environmental statutes to maximize their reach. The analysis on piercing the corporate veil in environmental pollution cases discussed earlier in this treatise underlines this modern judicial approach to environmental statutes.

Professor Force also believes that the court never came to grips with the limitation provision of OPA.[3184] He asked the following questions:

"Did Congress provide responsible parties with a right to limit their liability? If so, how is this right to be implemented in the light of OPA's total silence on the subject of limitation procedures? What are the responsibilities of courts in regard to limitation of liability?"[3185]

Professor Force noted that the upshot of *Metlife* and other similar decisions is that they have construed "limitation" out of the Act.[3186] For instance Professor Force noted as follows:

"The matter is brought home when one considers suits brought not against the discharger, who may or may not be able to limit according to the facts, but suits brought directly against a guarantor who is clearly li-

---

3184 See Robert Force & Jonathan M. Gutoff, Limitation Of Liability In Oil Pollution Cases: In Search Of Concursus Or Procedural Alternatives To Concursus, 22 Tul. Mar. L.J. at 364.

3185 Id. at 365.

3186 Id.

able only up to the amount of the guarantee. Under the holding of the court of appeals, what procedure may a guarantor invoke to limit its liability to the amount of its guarantee?"[3187]

It appears that the *Updegraff* court has answered these questions to some extent. The *Updegraff* court made it very clear that owners' understandable interest in consolidating potentially unwieldy litigation does not overcome the Congressionally mandated procedures for adjudicating OPA claims. The court also stated clearly that because the OPA establishes a limit of liability for responsible parties, after paying out that amount, no cause of action will lie against the owners pursuant to the OPA. The remaining claims (or the remaining portions of claims) will be paid from the Fund, which means that the possibility of multiple claims in various courts should not and would not break the OPA limitation.

Professor Force also argued that Congress's intention to supersede the substantive provisions of the Limitation Act does not mean that it necessarily intended also to supercede the procedures specified in Rule F. He noted that there is nothing in OPA or its legislative history that makes any reference to the procedures established by the Supreme Court for limitation of liability in admiralty claims which are now contained in Rule F of the Supplemental Rules, and OPA does not specify in any respect the procedures to be followed in effecting limitation under its own limitation provision.[3188] Professor Force argued that since the Supplemental Rules specifically provide that they apply "to maritime claims within the meaning of [Federal] Rule [of Civil Procedure] 9(h) with respect to... (4) Actions for exoneration and limitation of liability," a claim pursuant to OPA's limitation provisions is an admiralty claim, and it should be subject to the Supplemental Rules.[3189]

Professor Force contended that concursus under Rule F of the Supplemental Rules is available regardless of whether OPA was enacted by Congress pursuant to its power to prescribe rules in admiralty and maritime cases inferred from article III of the Constitution or its power to

3187 Id.

3188 Id.

3189 Id.

regulate commerce as provided in article I.[3190] Professor Force pointed out that the provision of OPA that states that it is not intended to affect admiralty jurisdiction along with OPA's legislative history provide strong indication that Congress contemplated actions under OPA as coming within the admiralty jurisdiction.[3191] He also pointed out that an incident arising out of the discharge of oil from a vessel on navigable waters would ordinarily come within the admiralty jurisdiction of the federal courts because the incident would have the required locus (navigable waters) and maritime nexus (the discharge would affect maritime commerce and would result from the most traditional maritime activity imaginable, the operation of a vessel). He concluded that the fact that a party seeking relief from a vessel owner may not be seeking that relief under the admiralty jurisdiction does not prevent a vessel owner from taking advantage of the limitation provisions of Supplemental Rule F, so long as the incident for which the owner is seeking to limit its liability would come within the admiralty jurisdiction.[3192]

He noted further that claims under the Jones Act come within the jurisdiction of the federal courts as arising under federal law and not under the admiralty jurisdiction, and yet, Jones Act claims are regularly subject to the provisions of the Limitation Act.[3193] He also noted that similarly, under the "savings to suitors" provision contained in 28 U.S.C.A. § 1333, claims that could otherwise be brought in federal court under the admiralty jurisdiction may be brought in a state court as actions at law. Such claims, even if brought in state court, are subject to limitation of liability under the Limitation Act. He concluded by saying "Accordingly, OPA actions come within the admiralty jurisdiction; because OPA provides for "limitation of liability pursuant to statute," parties seeking limitation under OPA should be able to take advantage of the concursus provisions of Rule F."[3194]

3190 Id. at 365.

3191 Id. at 366.

3192 Id. at 367.

3193 Id.

3194 Id. at 367.

# Chapter Fifteen

## A BRIEF COMPARISON OF SOME PREVIOUS FEDERAL MARINE/OIL POLLUTION STATUTES WITH OPA, AND HOW OPA AFFECTS THEM

Having discussed OPA itself in great detail over several chapters of this treatise, the main purpose of this part is to provide a very brief summary of the effects of OPA's enactment on pre-OPA marine pollution legislation. This sub-part will not go into a detailed analysis of these Pre-OPA statues. The discussion will refresh the reader's memory on some of the topics discussed throughout the treatise.

The United States Coast Guard is one of the primary government bodies responsible for safeguarding the navigable waters of the United States from oil and hazardous substance pollution. The Coast Guard's authority flows from domestic legislation, some broadly worded and others aimed at specific issues. The broader legislation includes:

14 U.S.C. § 2 is the specific statutory basis for the Coast Guard law enforcement mission. The environmental protection program is considered an enforcement area within this mission.

14 U.S.C. § 89 is the principle source of Coast Guard enforcement authority. It provides authority for Coast Guard active duty commissioned, warrant, and petty officers to enforce applicable U.S. law. It authorizes such personnel to enforce all applicable federal law on waters subject to U.S. jurisdiction, and in international waters, as well as on all vessels subject to U.S. jurisdiction.

14 U.S.C. § 141 provides for other federal, as well as state and local, agencies to request Coast Guard assistance when Coast Guard facilities and persons are especially qualified to perform a particular activity. Under this statute, the Coast Guard may provide assistance to foreign governments.

The above statutes establish the authority of the Coast Guard to enforce and assist in the enforcement of all Federal laws on the high seas and waters over which the U.S. has jurisdiction as well as the authority of the Coast Guard to make inquiries, examinations, inspections, searches, seizures and arrests to prevent, detect and suppress violations of U.S. laws.

### *The Federal Water Pollution Control Act.*[3195]

The Federal Water Pollution Control Act (FWPCA) was enacted by the ninety-second US Congress in 1972. It was substantially amended by the Clean Water Act (CWA) in 1977 and both names are now in general use for the statute. The FWPCA was further amended by the passage of OPA. Before OPA amended the FWPCA, it had been amended on eight different occasions. It is codified at 33 USC § 1251-1330. The most relevant section of the statute for the purposes of this analysis is section 311 which is codified at 33 USC §1321. In the course of this discuss, section 1321 may be used interchangeably with section 311.

The FWPCA was enacted in 1972 as the government's primary statutory weapon in recovering the United States' costs of responding to marine pollution resulting from the discharge of oil and other hazardous substances. The FWPCA was in part a modification and reenactment of the Water Quality Improvement Act of 1970 ("WQIA"),[3196] which was a response to the massive spill of 833, 333 barrels (35 million gallons) of oil by the TORREY CANYON off the southwest coast of England in 1967.[3197] Of the subsequent amendments of the FWPCA in 1977, 1978, and 1987,

3195 The FWPCA is codified at 33 U.S.C. §§ 1251-1330 (1988 & Supp.1991). The portion of the FWPCA which addresses liability arising out of the discharge of oil into the waters of the United States is usually referred to as section 311 of the FWPCA, or § 311 of the Clean Water Act.

3196 Pub.L. 91-224, Title I, Apr. 3, 1970, 84 Stat. 91 (1970).

3197 The United States had no effective remedy specifically targeted at oil spills until 1966, when Congress amended the Oil Pollution Act of 1924 to provide for limited recovery based upon a showing of grossly negligent or willful misconduct. See United States v. Dixie Carriers, 627 F.2d 736, 738 (5th Cir. 1980).

the additions of the Clean Water Act of 1977[3198] were perhaps the most significant by providing for recovery of environmental restoration or replacement costs of damaged natural resources, and not merely the government's costs of removing oil and hazardous substances from the environment.[3199]

*Structure of Section 311 of the FWPCA*

This sub-part will undertake a very brief overview of the Pre-OPA 90 provisions of section 311 of the FWPCA.

*Policy*: In section 311(b) (1) of the FWPCA, the US Congress declared that its goal is that "there should be no discharges of oil or hazardous substances into or upon the navigable waters of the United States, adjoining shorelines, or into or upon the waters of the contiguous zone, or in connection with activities under the Outer Continental Shelf Lands Act, or the Deepwater Port Act of 1974, or which may affect natural resources belonging to, appertaining to, or under the exclusive management authority of the United States." Although this goal is laudable, the provisions of the FWPCA lacked the bite that was required to discourage oil pollution. The OPA left this policy unaffected but added provisions that made OPA more potent than the FWPCA.

*Liability & Defenses provisions*: Section 311(f) of the FWPCA exculpates an owner or operator of a vessel or facility from liability if it can prove that a discharge of oil or hazardous substance was caused solely by "(A) an act of God, (B) an act of war, (C) negligence on the part of the United States Government, or (D) an act or omission of a third party without regard to whether any such act or omission was or was not negligent, or any combination of the foregoing clauses."[3200] The OPA does not directly amend subsection (f), although it did reduce the number of defenses available to a responsible party.

---

3198 91 Stat. 156 (1977).

3199 See Pub.L. 95-217, The Clean Water Act of 1977, 95th US Congress, S.Rep. 95-370, *92, 1977 U.S.C.C.A.N. 4467.

3200 See 33 USC §1321(f)(1).

Section 311(b)(3) is the most important section of the FWPCA. It prohibits owners and operators of vessels or facilities from discharging oil or hazardous substances "in such quantities as may be harmful as determined by the President, (i) into or upon the navigable waters of the United States, adjoining shorelines, or into or upon the waters of the contiguous zone, or (ii) in connection with activities under the Outer Continental Shelf Lands Act, the Deepwater Port Act of 1974 or which may affect natural resources belonging to, appertaining to, or under the exclusive management authority of the United States, including resources under the Magnuson-Stevens Fishery Conservation and Management Act."[3201] The OPA left subsection (b)(3) intact.

Reference was made to the Magnuson-Stevens Fishery Conservation and Management Act in order to extend the jurisdiction of section 311 out to the 200-mile limit of the fisheries management zone.[3202] The Magnuson Fishery Conservation and Management Act established a 200-mile fishery conservation zone, effective March 1, 1977, and established Regional Fishery Management Councils comprised of Federal and State officials, including the Fish and Wildlife Service. The concept of a fishery conservation zone was subsequently jettisoned by amendment and the geographical area of coverage was changed to the Exclusive Economic Zone (EEZ), with the inner boundary being the seaward boundary of the coastal States.

In its justification of the extension of the coverage of the FWPCA to the EEZ, the US Congress observed that many incidents of tanker spills, especially the disaster caused by the Argo Merchant off the coast of New England, underscored the immediate need for improved protection from and jurisdiction over marine pollution.[3203] Congress noted that the absence of clear legal authority to deal with oil spills beyond the territorial seas was indefensible. Congress also declared:

---

3201 Id. at §1321(b)(3).

3202 Public Law 94-265, approved April 13, 1976; 16 U.S.C. 1801-1882; 90 Stat. 331; as amended by several subsequent public laws.

3203 See 1977 USCAAN 4326, 4390, Pub. L. 95-217, S. Rep. 95-370, *65.

"Our capacity to act to clean up oilspills and recover costs, regardless of their location, so long as they potentially adversely affect the interests of the United States, must be assured and this legislation attempts to do that."[3204]

The 200-mile extension was made in the 1977 amendment to the FWPCA. The US Congress retained the 200-mile extension in OPA.

The original 1972 FWPCA only prohibited discharge of oil in harmful quantities, however the 1978 amendments to the statute substituted "such quantities as may be harmful" for "harmful quantities," thereby liberalizing the threshold requirements for holding a polluter liable under the Act.[3205]

Section 311(f)(4) stipulates that the costs of removal of oil or a hazardous substance for which the owner or operator of a vessel or onshore or offshore facility is liable under subsection (f) of this section must include any costs or expenses incurred by the Federal Government or any State government in the restoration or replacement of natural resources damaged or destroyed as a result of a discharge of oil or a hazardous substance in violation of the liability provisions of section 311. One small draw back in subsection (f)(4) is its lumping together of natural resources damages with removal costs. It is bad legislative drafting. Subsection (f)(4) was not amended by OPA, but OPA avoided mixing apples with oranges, by separating damages from removal costs. Subsection (f)(4) was part of the sweeping amendments made to the FWPCA in 1977.

Section 311(o) emphasizes that "nothing in this section shall affect or modify in any way the obligations of any owner or operator of any vessel, or of any owner or operator of any onshore facility or offshore facility to any person or agency under any provision of law for damages to any publicly owned or privately owned property resulting from a discharge of any oil or hazardous substance or from the removal of any such oil or hazardous substance." In other words, those whose properties are affected by the spill may look to statutory provisions that allow recovery for property damage caused by a spill.

---

3204 S. REP. 95-370, *65, 1977 U.S.C.C.A.N. at 4390.

3205 See Pub. L. 92-500, 86 Stat. 816, § 311(b)(3) (1972).

Section 311(o)(2) provides that "nothing in this section shall be construed as preempting any State or political subdivision thereof from imposing any requirement or liability with respect to the discharge of oil or hazardous substance into any waters within such State." Subsection (o)(2) is a savings provision, and it has been held that none of the savings clauses of Federal Water Pollution Control Act preserved non-statutory remedies grounded in negligence and nuisance which the government may assert in claims for costs incurred in cleaning up oil spills in territorial waters.[3206] It has also been decided that claims based on traditional maritime law, on federal common law of nuisance and on Refuse Act for costs incurred by United States were preempted by Federal Water Pollution Control Act.[3207] Subsection (o)(2) of the FWPCA is somewhat dissimilar to section 2718(a)(1) (preservation of state authorities provision) of OPA, which specifically preserves or saves State law, **including common law** (Emphasis mine).[3208]

Section 311(i) provides that "where an owner or operator of a vessel or an onshore facility or an offshore facility from which oil or a hazardous substance is discharged in violation of the liability provisions of this section acts to remove such oil or substance in accordance with regulations promulgated pursuant to this section, such owner or operator shall be entitled to recover the reasonable costs incurred in such removal upon establishing" its entitlement to any one or a combination of any of the four defenses provided for in section 311(f). Section 311(i) is similar to section 2708(a) of the OPA.

Section 311(n) confers jurisdiction on all the district courts of the United States for any law-suits brought under section 311. OPA does not directly amend section 311(n), it however modifies subsection 311(n) for oil pollution cases.

*Limit of Liability*: The owner or operator of any vessel from which oil or a hazardous substance is discharged is "liable to the United States Government for the actual costs incurred for the removal of such oil or

3206 See Unites States v. Oswego Barge Corporation, 664 F.2d 327 (2d Cir. 1981).

3207 *Oswego*, 664 F.2d at 327.

3208 33 USC 2718(a)(2).

substance by the United States Government in an amount not to exceed, in the case of an inland oil barge $125 per gross ton of such barge, or $125,000, whichever is greater, and in the case of any other vessel, $150 per gross ton of such vessel (or, for a vessel carrying oil or hazardous substances as cargo, $250,000), whichever is greater."[3209] Section 311(f)(1) includes a proviso that "where the United States can show that such discharge was the result of willful negligence or willful misconduct within the privity and knowledge of the owner, such owner or operator shall be liable to the United States Government for the full amount of such costs." Such costs shall constitute a maritime lien on such vessel which may be recovered in an action in rem in the district court of the United States for any district within which any vessel may be found.[3210] The United States may also bring an action against the owner or operator of such vessel in any court of competent jurisdiction to recover such costs.[3211]

The above limitation amount was included in the 1977 amendment to the statute. The 1972 FWPCA imposed a limitation figure of "$100 per gross ton of such vessel or $14,000,000, whichever is lesser."[3212]

The owner or operator of an on-shore or offshore facility from which oil or a hazardous substance is discharged in violation of the statute is liable to the United States Government for the actual costs incurred for the removal of such oil or substance by the United States Government in an amount not to exceed $50,000,000.[3213] The statute also includes a proviso that "such owner or operator shall be liable to the United States Government for the full amount of such costs where the United States can show that such discharge was the result of willful negligence or willful misconduct within the privity and knowledge of the owner."[3214] Owners and operators of on-shore and offshore facilities are also allowed to invoke the four defenses outlined earlier. The $50,000,000 limitation amount was

3209 33 USC §1321(f)(1).

3210 Id.

3211 Id. at §1321(f)(1).

3212 See Pub. L. 92-500, 86 Stat. 816, § 311(f)(1) (1972).

3213 33 USC §1321(f)(2)-(3).

3214 Id.

included in the 1977 amendment to the statute. Under the original 1972 FWPCA, the limitation figure was $8,000,000.[3215] OPA does not directly change the limitation figures in the FWPCA, but it imposes drastic changes to the limitation figures in the FWPCA for oil spills.[3216]

*The President*: Section 311(c) (1) of the FWPCA authorized the President to act to remove or arrange for removal when there is discharge or substantial threat of a discharge of oil or hazardous substance at any time unless he determines that such removal will be done properly by the owner or operator of the vessel, onshore facility, or offshore facility from which the discharge occurs. The phrase "substantial threat" of such discharge was added in the 1977 amendment to the Act. By including "substantial threat of a discharge," the 1977 amendment widened the removal powers of the President of the United States.[3217]

The President was also empowered to prepare and publish a National Contingency Plan (NCP) for removal of oil and hazardous substances.[3218] The NCP should provide for efficient, coordinated, and effective action to minimize damage from oil and hazardous substance discharges, including containment, dispersal, and removal of oil and hazardous substances.[3219]

Section 311(d) provided that:

"whenever a marine disaster in or upon the navigable waters of the United States has created a substantial threat of a pollution hazard to the public health or welfare of the United States, including, but not limited to, fish, shellfish, and wildlife and the public and private shorelines and beaches of the United States, because of a discharge, or an imminent discharge, of large quantities of oil, or of a hazardous substance from a vessel the United States may (A) coordinate and direct all public and private efforts directed at the removal or elimination of

3215 See Pub. L. 92-500, The Federal Water Pollution Control Act, 86 Stat. 816, § 311(f)(2)-(3), (1972).

3216 See 33 USC §2704.

3217 See Pub. L. 92-500, The Federal Water Pollution Control Act, 86 Stat. 816, § 311(c)(1) (1972), see also, Pub.L. 95-217, § 58(b), (c)(1).

3218 33 USC §1321(c)(2).

3219 Id.

such threat; and (B) summarily remove, and, if necessary, destroy such vessel by whatever means are available without regard to any provisions of law governing the employment of personnel or the expenditure of appropriated funds."

This section further provided that any expense incurred under this subsection or under the Intervention on the High Seas Act would be regarded as a cost incurred by the United States Government for the purposes of subsection (f) (liability and defenses provisions) in the removal of oil or hazardous substance. Subsection (d) did not specifically saddle the President with the responsibility of coordinating or destroying the erring vessel. It merely referred to the United States, thereby making it difficult to know who to hold responsible in the Federal government if these statutory mandates are not properly implemented.

Section 311(f)(5) authorizes the President, or the authorized representative of any State, to act on behalf of the public as trustee of the natural resources to recover for the costs of replacing or restoring such resources. Sums recovered is supposed to be used to restore, rehabilitate, or acquire the equivalent of such natural resources by the appropriate agencies of the Federal Government, or the State government.[3220] Subsection (f)(5) was part of the sweeping amendments made to the FWPCA in 1977. The OPA made sweeping changes that widens the oil spill removal powers of the President, which the President in turn delegated to such government agencies as the US Coast Guard or the Environmental Protection Agency (EPA).

*Judicial relief*: Section 311 (e) made it clear that when the President determines there is an imminent and substantial threat of a spill into US waters, he may require the United States attorney of the district in which the threat occurs to secure such relief as may be necessary to abate such threat. Subsection (e) also conferred jurisdiction on the district courts of the United States "to grant such relief as the public interest and the equities of the case may require." This provision was repealed by the OPA and

---

3220 See 33 USC §1321(f)(5).

the functions that were conferred on the US attorneys were shifted to a cabinet rank Federal government official.

### *Civil Penalties*

*Lower Administrative Penalty*: Section 311(b)(6)(A) imposed a maximum fine of $5,000 on the owner, operator, or person in charge of any onshore facility or offshore facility from which oil or a hazardous substance is discharged in violation of the liability provisions of the Act.[3221] This is an administrative fine or penalty. The same amount of penalty was imposed on the owner, operator, or person in charge of any vessel from which oil or a hazardous substance is discharged in violation of the liability provisions of the Act. Each violation of the statute was a separate offense.

*Higher Judicial Penalties*: Section 311(b)(6)(B) allowed the Administrator of the EPA, to take into account the gravity of the offense, and the standard of care manifested by the owner, operator, or person in charge, and to commence a civil action against any such person who could be subject to the $5,000 penalty. The EPA may impose a penalty based on consideration of the size of the business of the owner or operator, the effect on the ability of the owner or operator to continue in business, the gravity of the violation, and the nature, extent, and degree of success of any efforts made by the owner, operator, or person in charge to minimize or mitigate the effects of such discharge.[3222] The Act emphasizes that the amount of such penalty should not exceed $ 50,000, but included a proviso that where the United States can show that such discharge was the result of willful negligence or willful misconduct within the privity and knowledge of the owner, operator, or person in charge, such penalty shall not exceed $ 250,000.[3223] Each violation of the statute was a separate offense. This section also provided that any law suit under this provision may be brought "in the district court of the United States for the district

3221 See 33 USC §1321(b)(3).

3222 33 USC §1321(b)(6)(B).

3223 Id.

in which the defendant is located or resides or is doing business, and such court shall have jurisdiction to assess such penalty."[3224] This subsection included a caveat that "[n]o action may be commenced under this clause where a penalty has been assessed under clause (A) of this paragraph." In other words, a person cannot be made to pay both the lower administrative fine of $5,000 and the higher judicial fine of $50, 000, even though similar factual scenarios could make a polluter liable under either penalty provisions. So, the government cannot get two bites at the same apple. The civil penalty provisions are strict liability provisions.

OPA repealed paragraph (6) of subsection (b) and replaced it with a new paragraph that materially altered the amount and nature of civil penalties imposed on oil polluters.

*Criminal Penalty:* Section 311(b)(5) imposes upon any person in charge of a vessel or of an onshore facility or an offshore facility from which oil or hazardous substances is discharged in violation of the liability provisions of section 311(b)(3) to immediately notify the appropriate agency of the United States Government of such discharge as soon as he becomes aware of the discharge. Section 311(b)(5) of the FWPCA imposed a fine of not more than $ 10,000, or imprisonment for not more than one year, or both on any responsible party who fails to notify the government. Subsection(b)(5) was amended by OPA, and a harsher term of imprisonment was imposed.

Section 309(c) (1) & (2) of the FWPCA imposed harsh criminal penalties on the owner or operator of a vessel, or on-shore, or offshore facility from which hazardous substance is discharged into US waters, negligently or knowingly. Negligent violations was punished by a fine of not less than $ 2,500 nor more than $ 25,000 per day of violation, or by imprisonment for not more than 1 year, or by both. Also, if a conviction of a person is for a violation committed after a first conviction of such person under this provision, punishment shall be by a fine of not more than $ 50,000 per day of violation, or by imprisonment of not more than 2 years, or by both.[3225] For a person who knowingly violates the statute by discharging hazardous

---

3224 Id.

3225 See. 33 USC §1319(c)(1)(B).

substance into US waters, a punishment of not less than $ 5,000 nor more than $ 50,000 per day of violation, or by imprisonment for not more than 3 years, or by both is imposed.[3226] If a conviction of a person is for a violation committed after a first conviction of that person under this provision, punishment shall be by a fine of not more than $ 100,000 per day of violation, or by imprisonment of not more than 6 years, or by both.

Section 309(c) (3) of the FWPCA also imposes a harsh criminal penalty on owners and operators of vessels and onshore, or offshore facilities who discharge hazardous substance into US waters, and know at that time that he or she thereby places another person in imminent danger of death or serious bodily injury. Such a violator shall, upon conviction, be subject to a fine of not more than $ 250,000 or imprisonment of not more than 15 years, or both.[3227] A person which is an organization shall, upon conviction of violating this provision, be subject to a fine of not more than $ 1,000,000.[3228] If a conviction of a person is for a violation committed after a first conviction of such person under this provision, the maximum punishment shall be doubled with respect to both fine and imprisonment.[3229]

OPA made a small but noticeable change to section 309(c)(1)-(3) by applying the penalty provisions of these sections to violation of section 311(b)(3) (liability provision of FWPCA for **Oil Spills discharges**). With a stroke of its legislative pen, the US Congress was able to bring oil pollution cases within the purview of the criminal penalty provisions of section 309 of the FWPCA. Before OPA's enactment, the criminal provisions of the FWPCA did not apply to oil spill discharges. By virtue of this change, corporate and individual violators could pay millions of dollars in criminal fines. Individuals could also be sentenced to between 1 and 15 years imprisonment for oil pollution, depending on whether they are "negligent," "knowing," or "knowing endangerment" violators. The civil penalty provisions are therefore markedly different from the criminal penalty provisions because the civil penalty provisions are strict liability provisions.

3226 See id. at §1321(c)(2)(B).

3227 See 33 USC §1319(c)(3).

3228 Id.

3229 Id.

This also invariably means that a person could acquire a criminal record for negligently causing an oil spill.

The US Congress added violation of section 311(b)(3) to section 309(c)(1)-(3) as a criminal violation because some court decisions had confirmed that **oil is a "pollution"** within the definition of the FWPCA and discharges of oil to the navigable waters are **subject to the general penalty provisions of section 309** of the FWPCA.[3230]

*Third Party Liability*: Section 311 (g) governs third party liability under the FWPCA. Under subsection (g), if the owner or operator of a vessel or an onshore or offshore facility from which oil or a hazardous substance is discharged in violation of the liability provisions of this section alleges that such discharge was caused solely by an act or omission of a third party, such owner or operator must pay to the United States Government the actual costs incurred for removal of such oil or substance and shall be entitled by subrogation to all rights of the United States Government to recover such costs from such third party.

If the third party was the owner or operator of a vessel which caused the discharge of oil or a hazardous substance in violation of the liability provisions of section 311, the liability of such third party is the same as that which would have applied to the vessel of a responsible party.

If the sole cause third party that caused the discharge is not the owner or operator of the vessel, "the liability of such third party shall not exceed the limitation which would have been applicable to the owner or operator of the vessel or the onshore or offshore facility from which the discharge actually occurred if such owner or operator were liable."[3231] If the United States can prove that "the discharge was the result of willful negligence or willful misconduct within the privity and knowledge of such third party, such third party shall be liable to the United States Government for the full amount of such removal costs."[3232] This subsection allows the United

3230 S. REP. 101-94, at 9, 1990 U.S.C.C.A.N. 722, 730. See also United States v. Hamel 551 F.2d. 107 (6th Cir. 1977).

3231 33 USC §1321(g).

3232 Id. at §1321(g).

States to bring an action against the third party in any court of competent jurisdiction to recover such removal costs.[3233]

Section 311(h) stipulates that "the liabilities established by this section shall in no way affect any rights which (1) the owner or operator of a vessel or of an onshore facility or an offshore facility may have against any third party whose acts may in any way have caused or contributed to such discharge, or (2) The United States Government may have against any third party whose actions may in any way have caused or contributed to the discharge of oil or hazardous substance." Subsection 311(h) is similar to section 2702(d) of OPA.

*The Revolving Fund:* Section 311(k) authorized "to be appropriated to a revolving fund to be established in the Treasury such sums as may be necessary to maintain such fund at a level of $ 35,000,000" to carry out the provisions of this section relating to removal of spilt oil or substances. Subsection (k) further mandated that any other funds received by the United States under this section shall also be deposited in the revolving fund. The OPA repealed subsection (k) and created a more robust Oil Spill Fund.[3234]

Financial Responsibility: Section 311(p) provided that:

> "any vessel over three hundred gross tons, including any barge of equivalent size, but not including any barge that is not self-propelled and that does not carry oil or hazardous substances as cargo or fuel, using any port or place in the United States or the navigable waters of the United States for any purpose shall establish and maintain under regulations to be prescribed from time to time by the President, evidence of financial responsibility of, in the case of an inland oil barge $ 125 per gross ton of such barge, or $ 125,000, whichever is greater, and in the case of any other vessel, $ 150 per gross ton of such vessel (or, for a vessel carrying oil or hazardous substances as cargo, $ 250,000), whichever is greater, to meet the liability to the United States which such vessel could be subjected under this section."

---

3233 Id.

3234 See Pub.L. 101-380, Title I, § 2002(b)(2), Aug. 18, 1990, 104 Stat. 507.

Subsection (p) stipulated that in cases where an owner or operator owns, operates, or charters more than one such vessel, financial responsibility need only be established to meet the maximum liability to which the largest of such vessels could be subjected. "Financial responsibility may be established by any one of, or a combination of, the following methods acceptable to the President: (A) evidence of insurance, (B) surety bonds, (C) qualification as a self-insurer, or (D) other evidence of financial responsibility. This subsection further requires that any bond filed shall be issued by a bonding company authorized to do business in the United States.

Section 311(p)(3) provided that "any claim for costs incurred by such vessel may be brought directly against the insurer or any other person providing evidence of financial responsibility." Subsection(p)(4) imposed a $10, 000 penalty on any owner or operator of a vessel subject to this subsection, who failed to comply with the provisions of this subsection or any regulation issued under it.

Subsection (p)(6) empowered the US Coast Guard to "deny entry to any port or place in the United States or the navigable waters of the United States, and detain at the port or place in the United States from which it is about to depart for any other port or place in the United States, any vessel subject to this subsection, which upon request, does not produce evidence furnished by the President that the financial responsibility provisions of this subsection have been complied with."

The OPA repealed subsection (p) and replaced it with 33 USC §§2716 & 2716(a). These OPA provisions increased the amount of the financial responsibility to reflect the OPA liability limits in section 2704 of OPA. The amount of the penalty for violating the financial responsibility requirement was also increased by OPA.

Under the FWPCA, the Coast Guard has two closely-related principal responsibilities. One is as vice-chair of the National Response Team (NRT), with leadership in administering the National Response System for events occurring in the coastal zone. (EPA has primary responsibilities for the inland zone.) The second principal responsibility under the FWPCA involves developing and implementing pollution prevention, preparedness and response regulations for certain vessels and facilities under Coast Guard jurisdiction. (EPA, Research Special Programs Administration [RSPA], and Minerals Management Service [MMS] assume this role for facilities in other jurisdictions.)

Authority and Responsibilities Within the National Response System: The National Response System is established under the National Contingency Plan (NCP) and it is the Federal government's blueprint for responding to releases of oil and hazardous substances. The NCP, codified at 40 CFR Part 300, was developed originally more than 20 years ago to implement section 311 of the FWPCA. Initially, the NCP addressed oil and FWPCA hazardous substances only. However, after Congress passed the Comprehensive Environmental Response, Compensation, and Liability Act of 1980 (CERCLA or Superfund), the NCP was revised to address prevention, preparedness and response planning for an expanded list of hazardous substances. The most recently revised NCP reflects changes required by OPA 90, and was published on September 15, 1994.[3235]

## OPA Amendments to the FWPCA

In summary, the OPA amends section 311 of the FWPCA to clarify federal response authority, pump up penalties for oil spills, establish U.S. Coast Guard response organizations, mandate tank vessel and facility response plans, and provide for contingency planning in designated areas. OPA also abrogates several statutory provisions and consolidates the funds established under several laws in order to create a national pollution trust fund.

OPA revised the FWPCA to strengthen and expand the nation's oil and hazardous substances spill prevention, preparedness, and response activities. It further required the President to promulgate an amended National Oil and Hazardous Substances Pollution Contingency Plan (NCP) that expands the Federal government's removal authority,

3235 See United States Coast Guard Marine Safety Manual, Marine Environmental Protection Volume IX, at 25 (COMDTINST MI 6000.14).

increases the responsibility of Federal On Scene Coordinators (FOSC) during responses, and broadens coordination and preparedness planning requirements.[3236] OPA requires that the NCP describe the duties and responsibilities assigned to new OPA -created entities like the National Strike Force Coordination Center (NSFCC), for better coordination and execution of Federal response efforts. Under OPA 90, vessel and facility owners and operators must develop oil and hazardous substances response plans.[3237]

(1) OPA 90 amended the FWPCA to require owners and operators to develop oil spill response plans for certain tank vessels, certain onshore marine transportation-related facilities, and deepwater ports. In 1993 the Coast Guard published interim final oil response plan rules for vessels and transportation-related onshore facilities.[3238] The response plan regulations for tank vessels are codified at 33 CFR Part 155; the regulations for marine transportation-related facilities—including deepwater ports—are codified in 33 CFR Parts 150 and 154.

(2) A major feature of the OPA 90 spill response plans is the requirement for covered vessel and facility owners and operators to identify and ensure the availability of — by "contract or other approved means" — private personnel and equipment necessary to remove the "worst case discharge" to the "maximum extent practicable." The Coast Guard created an oil spill removal organization (OSRO) classification process administered by the NSFCC to assist vessel and facility owners and operators in meeting this requirement.[3239]

(3) The OPA 90 amendments to the FWPCA also require that the President conduct periodic drills of removal capability for the areas covered by Area Contingency Plans (ACPs), and for tank vessel and facility response plans. The Coast Guard has been delegated this responsibility for the coastal zone, and it fulfills this responsibility through the National Preparedness for Response Exercise Program (PREP). PREP is

---

3236 Id. at 24.

3237 Id.

3238 Id.

3239 Id.

the framework for conducting Area drills and exercises, and provides a means for covered vessel and facility owners and operators to satisfy their internal drill requirements.[3240]

(4) Congress increased substantially the penalties for strict liability offenses that the Coast Guard and EPA could levy under their administrative penalty authority. Before OPA, the maximum civil penalty that could be imposed in a **judicial civil penalty action** under the FWPCA was $50,000 per incident. OPA amended the FWPCA to allow judicially imposed strict liability penalties as great as $25,000 per day or violation, or $1000 per barrel of oil for a discharge of oil or hazardous substance in violation of section 311(b)(3) of the FWPCA.[3241] The volumetric calculation of the penalty affords the courts the option of imposing enormous civil penalties.[3242] For example, a discharge of 1000 barrels would translate into a maximum civil penalty of $1 million.

The OPA amendments to the FWPCA imposes a duty on the owner or operator of a vessel or facility to carry out removal of spilt oil or substance, and to obey administrative or Presidential orders relating to removal activities.[3243] The OPA amends section 311(b)(6) of the FWPCA, by imposing a penalty of $25,000 per day of violation of this duty or an amount up to 3 times the costs incurred by the Oil Spill Liability Trust Fund as a result of such failure. Under the OPA amendments to the penalty provisions of the FWPCA, any person who fails or refuses to comply with any regulation issued under section 311 (j) (Response plan, equipment, area drills requirements) is made to pay a civil penalty in an amount up to $25,000 per day of violation.[3244]

Another OPA amendment to the FWPCA penalty provisions, stipulates that in any case in which a violation of the liability provisions of the FWPCA was the result of gross negligence or willful misconduct of the

3240 Id. at 25.

3241 See 33 USC §1321(b)(7)(A).

3242 See Breaux Has Lost Will to Push OECD, Cong. Info. Bureau Inc., Oct. 21, 1999, at 2.

3243 See 33 USC §1321(b)(7)(B).

3244 Id. at §1321(b)(7)(C).

responsible party, the responsible party shall be subject to a civil penalty of not less than $100,000, and not more than $3,000 per barrel of oil or unit of reportable quantity of hazardous substance discharged.[3245] Another OPA amendment added paragraph (9) to subsection (b) of the FWPCA. This paragraph makes it clear that in addition to establishing a penalty for the discharge of oil or a hazardous substance, the Secretary of the department in which the Coast Guard is operating may act to mitigate the damage to the public health or welfare caused by such discharge, and the cost of such mitigation shall be deemed a cost incurred under subsection (c) (Federal removal authority) of this section for the removal of such substance by the United States Government.

The OPA repealed section 311(p) of the FWPCA. The amount of the penalty for violating the financial responsibility requirements was also drastically increased by OPA from a fine of not more than $10, 000 under the defunct subsection (p) to $25,000 per day of violation under the new provision.[3246] Section 2716a(b) of OPA adds more teeth to its financial responsibility provisions by providing that "[i]n addition to, or in lieu of, assessing a penalty under subsection (a) of this section, the President may request the **Attorney General** to secure such relief as necessary to compel compliance with this section, including a judicial order terminating operations."

(5) Although the FWPCA did **preserve** or save the rights of private claimants for property damage by oil or hazardous substance **under state statutory provisions**, OPA's treatment of Responsible Parties (RPs) is a sharp departure from the FWPCA, as the FWPCA did not directly make an RP liable to anyone other than the United States, and then only for removal costs and natural resources damages.

(6) OPA limits a RP's liability for removal costs and damages.[3247] The limitation amount is based upon the type of vessel and its tonnage. Generally, OPA's limitation scheme follows that of the FWPCA except

---

3245 Id. at §1321(b)(7)(D).

3246 Pub.L. 101-380, Title II, § 2002(b)(4), Aug. 18, 1990, 104 Stat. 507. See also 33 USC §2716a(a).

3247 33 USCA §2704.

that OPA's limits are much higher.[3248] Just like the FWPCA, OPA allows a sole cause third party to limit its liability for removal costs and damages.[3249] Also, like in the FWPCA, OPA does not directly impose any liability upon a non-sole-fault third party, therefore it may not be able to look to OPA for limitation of liability.[3250] The FWPCA's limitation does not affect the government's right to seek a greater amount from a non-sole cause third party under some other basis such as a common law tort cause of action.[3251]

One of the most important differences between limitation under OPA and the FWPCA is the scope of application. The FWPCA's limitation applies only to the federal government's right to seek reimbursement for removal costs and natural resources damages.[3252] The scope of OPA's limitation is broader as it applies to any person's right to recover damages and removal costs under OPA. The limitation therefore applies to a private or public party's right to recover damages and removal costs.

(7) There is a slight amendment in the defenses provisions of OPA to the four defenses that were available under the FWPCA. OPA just like its contemporary statute FWPCA, allows the three defenses of, act of God, act war, and act of a third party not in any contractual relationship with the RP.[3253] But it excludes the defense of negligence by the United States Government, which is a fourth defense under the FWPCA.[3254]

(8) The OPA has amended and broadened the scope of damages and who may be a plaintiff. One of the most important distinctions between the OPA and the FWPCA is the identity of parties allowed to sue as plaintiffs.

---

3248 See id.

3249 Section 2702(d)(2)(A)-(B).

3250 The OPA provision which imposes liability states "each responsible party... is liable for the removal costs and damages specified in subsection (b) that result from such an incident." 33 U.S.C. § 2702. A non-sole- fault third party is not a responsible party and has no direct liability under OPA. See 33 USC §2702(d)(1)(A).

3251 M/V BIG SAM, 681 F.2d 432, 444 (5th Cir. 1982).

3252 For example, in Steuart Transp. Co. v. Allied Towing Co., 596 F.2d 609, 620-21 (4th Cir.1979), the court held that the FWPCA does not limit the amount of removal costs the Commonwealth of Virginia may recover from the RP.

3253 See 33 USCA §2703(a)(1)-(3).

3254 See 33 USCA § 1321(f)(1).

Under the FWPCA, private parties had no standing whatsoever to sue for monetary damages or cleanup costs. The FWPCA only allowed private parties to bring citizen suits:

"(1) against any person (including (i) the United States, and (ii) any other governmental instrumentality or agency to the extent permitted by the eleventh amendment to the Constitution) who is alleged to be in violation of (A) an effluent standard or limitation under the Act or (B) an order issued by the Administrator or a State with respect to such a standard or limitation, or (2) against the Administrator where there is alleged a failure of the Administrator to perform any act or duty under the Act which is not discretionary with the Administrator."[3255]

Under the OPA, the private party has become highly favored, and can now sue for costs of clean up as well as damages.[3256]

(9) Section 2717(b)-(c) of OPA is a tacit amendment of the jurisdictional provisions of section 311(n) of the Federal Water Pollution Control Act. This is because these OPA provisions confer concurrent jurisdiction on Federal District Courts and state courts for oil pollution cases.

(10) OPA substituted the provisions of section 311(c) by authorizing federal removal authority, by the President, over discharges of oil or hazardous substances into or on navigable waters of the U.S., waters of the exclusive economic zone and waters that may affect the natural resources of the U.S., in accordance with the specifics of the National Contingency Plan.[3257] This means that unlike the defunct subsection (c)(1), the President no longer needs to wait and hope that the removal will be done properly by the owner or operator of the vessel, onshore facility, or offshore facility from which the oil has been discharged. He can take a more pro-active role in response activities and ensure that the Federal government employs adequate resources. The President is authorized to coordinate public and

3255 See 33 USCA §1365(a).

3256 See 33 USCA §2702(b)(1)(2).

3257 See 33 USCA § 1321(c). Pub.L. 101-380, § 4201(a).

private clean up efforts when a substantial threat of a pollution hazard to public health exists from an oil or hazardous substance spill.

The Legislative history of OPA provides some insight into the reason Congress decided to jettison section 311 (c)(1) of the FWPCA. Congress said:

"Section 311(c)(1) of the Clean Water Act allows the vessel or facility owner or operator responsible party to clean up spills and does not require federal removal. The Act allows, but does not require, federal removal unless the President determines that the spill will be cleaned up properly by the responsible party. Thus, the Act currently does not require federal removal even if the spill is not being cleaned up properly. The reported bill would require the President to cleanup or arrange for cleanup of oil or hazardous substances unless the President determines that the cleanup is being done properly and promptly by the responsible party, and that the responsible party has the financial resources and technical capability to clean up. In addition, the President is authorized under the reported bill to order the owner or operator to remove, or arrange to remove, oil or hazardous substances and to continue the cleanup until the President determines that it has been removed, as defined under section 311(a)."[3258]

(11) OPA repealed section 311(e) which provided that the "President, upon determination of threat to the public health, may require the U.S. attorney of the district in which threat occurs to secure such relief as may be necessary to abate such threat." OPA replaced it with a new subsection (e) that empowers the President to require the Attorney General to secure relief to abate the threat of oil or hazardous substance pollution, upon determination of threat to public health. Under this provision, the President can require the Attorney General to take any other necessary action, including issuance of administrative orders.[3259] The direct inclusion of the Attorney General in place of the US Attorneys shows the importance that the US Congress attaches to the issue of strict and adequate enforcement of the provisions of the OPA and the FWPCA.

---

3258 S. REP. 101-94, at 7-8, 1990 U.S.C.C.A.N. 722, 729.

3259 See 33 USC § 1321(e),.L. 101-380, § 4306.

Finally, FWPCA case law would no doubt continue to provide invaluable guidance in the interpretation of some OPA provisions that mirror FWPCA provisions, as it has done throughout this treatise.

## *THE TRANS-ALASKA PIPELINE AUTHORIZATION ACT*

The Trans-Alaska Pipeline Authorization Act of 1973[3260] *(TAPAA),* was enacted to facilitate the speedy construction of a trans-Alaska pipeline and to make use of available low-sulfur oil reserves.[3261] TAPAA applied inter alia to vessels loaded with oil transported through the Trans-Alaska Pipeline destined for ports or terminal facilities under United States jurisdiction.[3262] Section 1653(c) of TAPAA, established a scheme of strict liability and a liability fund applicable to all vessels and onshore facilities transporting or handling pipeline oil.

In general, the TAPAA imposed strict liability of up to $100 million for all cleanup costs and other damages sustained by any public or private entity as a result of the discharge of TAPS oil from a vessel.[3263] Generally, the vessel owner, operator, and guarantor are liable for the first $14 million in damages; the Trans-Alaska Pipeline Liability Fund is liable for the remaining shortfall of $86m.[3264] Claims in excess of $100 million could be "adjudicated under other applicable Federal or state law."[3265] In order to avoid strict liability, the owner or operator of the vessel, or the Fund, had to prove that the damages were "caused solely" by (1) act of war or (2) negligence of the United States or other governmental agency. OPA repealed TAPAA.

Section 1656 of OPA codified in 43 USC § 1656 also empowers the Secretary of the Interior to assess and collect a civil penalty of no less

3260 43 U.S.C, §§ 1651-1655 (1988 & Supp. II 1992).

3261 See 43 U.S.C. §1652 (1994).

3262 See 43 U.S.C. § 1653(c)(7).

3263 See 43 U.S.C. § 1653(c)(3).

3264 Id.

3265 43 U.S.C. § 1653(c)(3) (1988).

than $1,000 per barrel of oil discharged: (1) during transit from fields or reservoirs supplying oil to the trans-Alaska pipeline; or (2) **during transportation through the trans-Alaska pipeline** or handling at the terminal facilities, that causes damage to, or threatens to damage, natural resources or public or private property.[3266] The persons liable for the civil penalty imposed by this OPA provision include: (1) the person causing or permitting the discharge, (2) the owner or owners of the oil at the time the discharge occurs; who shall be jointly, severally, and strictly liable for the full amount of penalties assessed pursuant to this section. However, the United States and the several States, and political subdivisions thereof, shall not be liable under this section.[3267]

In determining the amount of civil penalty under this section, the Secretary shall consider: (1) the seriousness of the damages from the discharge, (2) the cause of the discharge, (3) any history of prior violations of applicable rules and laws, and (4) the degree of success of any efforts by the violator to minimize or mitigate the effects of such discharge.[3268] The Secretary may reduce or waive the penalty imposed under this section if the discharge was solely caused by an act of war, act of God, or third party action beyond the control of the persons liable under this section. No civil penalty assessed by the Secretary pursuant to this section shall be in addition to a penalty assessed pursuant to section 1321(b) of the Federal Water Pollution Control Act.[3269]

Until passage of the OPA, the vessel liability provisions of the TAPAA applied to vessels carrying North Slope crude transported through the Trans-Alaska Pipeline.[3270] As part of OPA, Congress passed the Trans-Alaska Pipeline System Reform Act of 1990.[3271] In effect, the 1990

3266 See 43 USCA §1656 (a) & (c).

3267 See 43 USCA §1656(b).

3268 See 43 USCA §1656(c)(2).

3269 Id. at §1656(c)(3)-(4).

3270 See 43 USCA § 1653(c)(1), *see also*, §1651(a) which provides: "The early development and delivery of oil and gas from Alaska's North Slope to domestic markets is in the national interest because of growing domestic shortages and increasing dependence upon insecure foreign sources."

3271 See Pub. L. No. 101-380, §§ 8101-8103 [codified at 33 U.S.C. §§ 1651-1653].

provision stipulates that the OPA shall apply to all post-OPA-enactment spills of TAPS oil; conversely, the TAPAA, **though repealed for post-OPA TAPS oil spills**, covers pre-OPA spills.[3272] TAPAA has therefore been replaced by OPA, although it is still applicable as passed with respect to pre-OPA claims.

## *THE DEEPWATER PORT ACT OF 1975*

The Deepwater Port Act of 1974[3273] (DWPA), codified at 33 U.S.C. § 1501 *et seq.*, creates a structure and authority to regulate any port or terminal for loading and unloading oil in waters off the coast and beyond the territorial sea of the U.S. when the oil is transported to any state in the U.S. Section 1502(9) of the Act defines "deepwater port" to mean:

> "any fixed or floating manmade structures other than a vessel, or any group of such structures, located beyond the territorial sea and off the coast of the United States and which are used or intended for use as a port or terminal for the loading or unloading and further handling of oil for transportation to any State, except as otherwise provided in section 1522 of this title. The term includes all associated components and equipment, including pipelines, pumping stations, service platforms, mooring buoys, and similar appurtenances to the extent they are located seaward of the high water mark." [3274]

---

3272 See Pub.L. 101-380, Title VIII, § 8102(a)(1), (5)(A), Aug. 18, 1990, 104 Stat. 565, 566, which provides: subsection (c)(covering: Discharges of oil from vessels loaded at terminal facilities of pipeline; strict liability; limitation on liability; apportionment of liability; establishment and operation of Trans-Alaska Pipeline Liability Fund) of this section is repealed effective 60 days after the date on which the Comptroller General certifies to Congress that: (i) all claims arising under subsection (c) of this section have been resolved, (ii) all actions for the recovery of amounts subject to subsection (c) of this section have been resolved and (iii) all administrative expenses reasonably necessary for and incidental to the implementation of subsection (c) of this section have been paid.

3273 33 U.S.C. §§ 1501-1524 (1988 & Supp. II 1992).

3274 33 U.S.C. § 1502(9), (1988 & Supp. II 1992). There is only one such deepwater port, in Louisiana. See Frederick J. Carr, Statutory Liability for Oil Pollution from vessels in Marine Environments, 3 U.S.F.MAR.L.J. 266, 290 (1991).

The regime Congress established under this statute provides for protecting the marine and coastal environment from the effects of deepwater port operations and for regulating deepwater port location, ownership, construction, and operation.[3275] The Department of Transportation (DOT) may promulgate and enforce operational and training procedures to be used at deepwater ports. Civil penalties, unaffected by OPA, are set at $25,000 per violation with each day of a continuing violation considered a separate violation.[3276]

The statute provided for clean up costs and damages against the owner or operator of a vessel or the licensee of a deepwater port from which oil is discharged in violation of the statute. The statute defined "cleanup costs" as "all actual costs, including but not limited to costs of the federal government, of any state or local government, of other nations or of their contractors or subcontractors incurred in the (a) removing or attempting to remove, or (b) taking other measures to reduce or mitigate damages from, any oil discharged into the marine environment….."[3277] While it defined damages as "all damages (except cleanup costs) suffered by any person, or involving real or personal property, the natural resources of the marine environment, or the coastal environment of any nation, including damages claimed without regard to ownership of any affected lands, structures, fish, wildlife, or biotic or natural resources."[3278]

However, the civil liability provisions of the DWPA were repealed and replaced by OPA.[3279] Before the repeal of the civil liability provisions of the DWPA, owners and operators of a vessel were "jointly and severally liable, without regard to fault, for cleanup costs and for damages that result from a discharge of oil from such vessel within any safety zone, or from a vessel which has received oil from another vessel at a deepwater port, except when such vessel is moored at a deepwater port."[3280] The statute

---

3275 See 33 USCA §1501.

3276 33 U.S.C. §1514(b) (1988).

3277 See 33 USC §1517(M)(1). Superceded by 33 USC §§2702 & 2704.

3278 33 USC §1517(M)(2). Superceded by 33 USC §§2702 & 2704.

3279 See 33 U.S.C. §§ 2702, 2704 (Supp. II 1992) for OPA's liability scheme.

3280 33 USC §1517(D). Superceded by 33 USC §§2702 & 2704.

limited such liability to $150 per gross ton or $20,000,000, whichever was lesser, except that if it was shown that such discharge was the result of gross negligence or willful misconduct within the privity and knowledge of the owner or operator, such owner and operator was jointly and severally liable for the full amount of all cleanup costs and damages.[3281]

The statute also held the licensees of a deepwater port liable, without regard to fault, for cleanup costs and damages that result from a discharge of oil from such deepwater port or from a vessel moored at such deepwater port.[3282] The statute further provided that such liability could not exceed $50,000,000, except that if it was shown that such damage was the result of gross negligence or willful misconduct within the privity and knowledge of the licensee, such licensee shall be liable for the full amount of all cleanup costs and damages.[3283]

OPA also amended the criminal liability provision of the DWPA to make violation a class A misdemeanor for each day of a continuing violation.[3284]

## *THE OUTER CONTINENTAL SHELF LANDS ACT*

The Outer Continental Shelf Lands Act[3285] (OCSLA), governs the activities of facilities on the outer continental shelf and vessels operating off-shore which transport oil from such facilities. OCSLA imposes strict liability on vessels and operators for cleanup expenses and damages incurred by the United States.[3286] While liability is generally limited, if

3281 33 USC §1517(D). Superceded by 33 USC §§2702 & 2704.

3282 33 USC §1517(E). Superceded by 33 USC §§2702 & 2704.

3283 Id. at §1517(E). Superceded by 33 USC §§2702 & 2704.

3284 Act of Aug. 18, 1990, Pub.L. 101-380, Title IV, Subtitle C § 4302(m), 104 Stat. 539. This 1990 Amendment substituted "commits a class A misdemeanor for each day of violation," for "shall on conviction be fined not more than $25,000 for each day of violation or imprisoned for not more than 1 year, or both."

3285 Act of Aug. 7, 1953, ch. 345, 67 Stat. 462, codified as 33 U.S.C. §§ 1331-1356 (1988 & Supp. II 1992)

3286 43 U.S.C. § 1350 (1988 & Supp.1991).

willful misconduct, gross negligence, or violations of certain safety regulations can be proven, there is no limitation.[3287] OCSLA's liability provisions have been amended by the OPA.[3288] OCSLA's civil penalties have similarly been increased to $20,000 per day continuing violation fine, adjustable every three years.[3289] Citizen suits are restricted to compelling compliance with OCSLA, and the suitor must have a "valid legal interest" that is adversely affected to assert standing.[3290]

OPA section 2004 amends the OCSLA Amendments of 1978 by repealing Title III of that Act.[3291] Title III encapsulated the compensation and liability provisions of the OCSLA. OPA includes provisions superseding those contained in the repealed Title. In addition, the OPA eliminates the Offshore Oil Spill Pollution Fund established by that Title,[3292] transfers monies remaining in that fund to the Oil Spill Liability Trust Fund (OSLTF or the Fund), and provides that the OSLTF assumes all liabilities incurred by the OCSLA Fund.[3293] Through these amendments, OPA creates a single fund to handle the costs and damages previously covered by three separate funds.

## *THE COMPREHENSIVE ENVIRONMENTAL RESPONSE, COMPENSATION AND LIABILITY ACT OF 1980.*

The Comprehensive Environmental Response, Compensation and Liability Act of 1980[3294] (CERCLA), is a statute of general application

---

3287 Id. at §1350.

3288 33 U.S.C. §§ 2702-2704 (Supp. II 1992).

3289 Act of Aug. 18, 1990, Pub.L. 101-380 Title VIII, Subtitle B § 8201, 104 Stat. 570, codified at 33 U.S.C. § 1350(b) (1988 & Supp. II 1992).

3290 33 U.S.C. § 1349(a) (1988 & Supp. 1992).

3291 OPA § 2004, 104 Stat. 484, 507 (1990) (to be codified at 43 U.S.C. §§ 1811-1824 (1989)).

3292 See 43 U.S.C. § 1812 (1989).

3293 OPA § 2004, 104 Stat. 484, 507 (1990).

3294 94 Stat. 2767, codified at 42 U.S.C §§ 9601-9675(1988).

dedicated primarily to landside matters.[3295] One of the purposes of the statute is to ensure that parties responsible for the release of **hazardous substances**, and not the taxpayers, bear the cost of the cleanup. Congress passed the CERCLA to make responsible parties liable for cleanup costs of hazardous waste disposal facilities and for natural resource damages.[3296]

CERCLA's statutory framework imposes liability on any (1) current owner or operator of a facility, (2) owner or operator of a facility at the time hazardous substances were disposed there, (3) person who arranged for disposal or arranged for the transport of hazardous substances for disposal, or (4) person who accepts any hazardous substances for transport or disposal.[3297] Those falling within the scope of this section can be held liable for "all costs of removal or remedial action" and "any other necessary costs of response incurred... consistent with the national contingency plan [NCP],"[3298] but only if (1) they are also found to have disposed of the hazardous substances at a "facility,"[3299] (2) there is a **"release"**[3300] or threatened release of the hazardous substances from the facility, and (3) the release causes the incurrence of "response" costs.[3301] "Release" means "any spilling, leaking, pumping, pouring, emitting, emptying, discharging, injecting, escaping, leaching, dumping, or disposing into the environment

3295 See 42 U.S.C. § 9601(14) (1988) for a definition of "hazardous substance" to which CERCLA applies. However, CERCLA's regulatory reach includes all marine pollution by substances other than oil.

3296 "Potentially responsible parties"' (PRPs) under CERCLA include past and present owners and operators of hazardous waste disposal facilities, transporters of hazardous waste, and persons who have "arranged for disposal or treatment... of hazardous substances." 42 U.S.C 9607(a)(3).

3297 42 USC §9607(a).

3298 Id.

3299 A facility is defined under CERCLA as:

"(A) any building, structure, installation, equipment, pipe or pipeline (including any pipe into a sewer or publicly owned treatment works), well, pit, pond, lagoon, impoundment, ditch, landfill, storage container, motor vehicle, rolling stock, or aircraft, or (B) any site or area where a hazardous substance has been deposited, stored, disposed of, or placed, or otherwise come to be located; but does not include any consume product in consumer use or any vessel." 42 USC §9601(9).

3300 See id. §9601(22).

3301 Id. at §9601(25).

(including the abandonment or discarding of barrels, containers, and other closed receptacles **containing any hazardous substance** or pollutant or contaminant)."[3302]

Once a CERCLA plaintiff has made *a prima facie* showing of liability, a defendant can only avoid responsibility by establishing that the release or threatened release of hazardous materials was caused by an act of God, an act of war, certain acts or omissions of third parties other than those with whom the defendant has a contractual relationship, or any combination of these factors.[3303]

Although CERCLA does not state explicitly a scheme of liability, courts consistently have interpreted CERCLA as creating strict, joint, and several liability.[3304] Thus, without regard for notions of intent or fault, full liability for all cleanup costs extends to any person falling in one of the four categories of responsible parties outlined above. RPs under CERCLA are called Potentially Responsible Parties (PRPs).

OPA liability provisions relating to removal costs and natural resources damages are similar in many ways to the CERCLA liability section at 42 U.S.C. § 9607, and CERCLA case law on recovery of removal costs and natural resources damages definitely plays a role in judicial interpretation of OPA.[3305] For example, both acts deny a discharger the defense that the discharge was caused solely by a third party when that third party has a direct or indirect contractual relationship with the discharger.[3306] Both statutes also provide the two defenses of "act of God" and "act of war."

One major difference between OPA and CERCLA is that OPA civil liability provisions does not hold the owner of spilled cargo liable for oil spills, except for the imposition of civil penalties on the owner or owners of oil discharged: (1) during transit from fields or reservoirs supplying

3302 42 U.S.C. § 9601(22).

3303 See 33 USC §9607(b).

3304 See. United States v. Northeastern Pharmaceutical & Chem. Co., 579 F. Supp. 823, 843-845 (W.D. Mo. 1984).

3305 Gregg L. McCurdy, An Overview of OPA 1990 And Its Relationship To Other Laws, 5 U.S.F. Mar. L.J. 423, 437 (1993).

3306 *See* 42 U.S.C. § 9607(b)(3) (1988) (CERCLA) and 33 U.S.C. § 2703(a)(3) (Supp. II 1992) (OPA).

oil to the trans-Alaska pipeline; or (2) during transportation through the trans-Alaska pipeline or handling at the terminal facilities, that causes damage to, or threatens to damage, natural resources or public or private property.[3307] So, OPA does not impose removal cost and damage liability on owners of oil. Unlike CERCLA that holds a person who arranged for disposal or arranged for the transport of hazardous substances for disposal **liable** for spill of hazardous substances. Persons who have "arranged for disposal or treatment... of hazardous substances"‘ are commonly referred to as "generators."‘ Generators often have produced the waste and have shipped it to a disposal site from which there is a subsequent release of hazardous substances. However, to be liable under CERCLA, the generator need not have actually produced the waste; rather, liability is linked to an act of "arranging for the disposal"‘ of hazardous substances.[3308] This means that CERCLA liability is broader in its reach than OPA liability.

One other difference between OPA and CERCLA is that CERCLA applies retroactively to spills of hazardous substances that precede the enactment of the statute, while OPA does not apply to oil spills that occurred prior to August 18, 1990, the date it was enacted.[3309] Because of the retroactive application of CERCLA, spills of hazardous substances that occurred during World War II are covered by the statute. One judge has stated that CERCLA "is by its very nature backward looking."[3310] It is clear from the legislative history that Congress, in enacting CERCLA, intended it as a tool to effectuate cleanup of the 30,000-50,000 improperly managed toxic waste sites already in existence at the time of CERCLA's enactment.[3311]

3307 See 43 USCA §1656 (a) & (c).

3308 See 42 U.S.C. § 9607(a)(3). *See also* Note, Developments in the Law--Toxic Waste Litigation, 99 HARV. L. REV. 1458, 1516 (1988).

3309 See 33 USCA §2717(e).

3310 United States v. Shell Oil Co., 605 F.Supp. 1064, 1072 (D.Colo.1985). *Accord* United States v. South Carolina Recycling and Disposal, Inc., 20 Env't Rep.Cas. (BNA) 1753 (D.S.C.1984); Ohio ex rel. Brown v. Georgeoff, 562 F.Supp. 1300 (N.D.Ohio 1983); Jones v. Inmont Corp., 584 F.Supp. 1425 (S.D.Ohio 1984).

3311 5 U.S.Code Cong. & Ad.News 6119, 6119-20 (1980).

OPA unlike CERCLA broadens the scope of private claimants rights, by creating direct private causes of action for damages like loss of profits and earning capacity, loss of subsistence use of natural resources, as well as economic losses resulting from destruction of real or personal property.[3312] The only private cause of action allowed under CERCLA against an RP or PRP is an action to recover remedial or clean up costs.[3313]

OPA also broadens the scope of damages recoverable by public claimants such as the federal government, state governments and municipalities, by creating a damages cause of action for loss of taxes, royalties, rents, and net profit shares caused by injury, destruction, or loss of real or personal property, or natural resources.[3314] It also creates a damages cause of action for state governments and political subdivisions of states for net costs of providing increased or additional public services during or after removal activities.[3315]

### *THE ACT TO PREVENT POLLUTION FROM SHIPS*

The Act To Prevent Pollution From Ships (APPS)[3316] implements part of the International convention for the prevention of pollution from ships[3317], called MARPOL 73/78.

APPS applies to all United States flag ships anywhere in the world, and to all foreign flag vessels operating in the navigable waters of the United States or while at a port or terminal under the jurisdiction of the United States.[3318] The oil and noxious liquid substances provisions apply

---

3312 See 33 USCA §2702(b)(2)(B),(C) & (E).

3313 See 42 USCA §9607(a)(4)(B).

3314 See 33 USCA §2702(b)(2)(D).

3315 Id. at §2702(b)(2)(F).

3316 Act of Oct. 21, 1980, Pub.L.96-478, 94 Stat. 2297, *codified at* 33 U.S.C. §§ 1901-1911 (1988).

3317 Protocol of 1978 Relating to the International Convention for the Prevention of Pollution from Ships, Feb. 16, 1978, reprinted in 17 I.L.M. 546 (1978).

3318 33 U.S.C.A. § 1902(a) (West Supp. 1996).

only to seagoing ships.[3319] The regulations implementing Annex I and Annex II of MARPOL (1) limit discharges of oil and noxious substances, (2) establish reporting requirements for discharges, and (3) establish specific requirements for monitoring equipment and record keeping aboard vessels.[3320] In particular, the regulations require that vessels covered by APPS and MARPOL keep Oil Record Books in which all discharges, disposal and transfers of oil are kept.[3321]

APPS was amended by the Marine Plastic Pollution Research and Control Act of 1987, which implemented the provisions of Annex V of MARPOL relating to garbage and plastics.[3322] Annex V of MARPOL and the regulations implementing it apply to all vessels, whether seagoing or not, regardless of flag, on the navigable waters of the United States and in the EEZ of the United States.[3323] It applies to U.S. flag vessels wherever they are located.[3324]

Under the regulations implementing APPS, the discharge of plastics, including synthetic ropes, fishing nets, plastic bags and biodegradable plastics, into the water is prohibited.[3325] Discharge of floating dunnage, lining and packing materials is prohibited in the navigable waters and in areas offshore less than 25 nautical miles from the nearest land.[3326] Food waste or paper, rags, glass, metal, bottles, crockery and similar refuse cannot be discharged in the navigable waters or in waters offshore inside 12 nautical miles from the nearest land.[3327] Food waste, paper, rags, glass and other similar garbage that is comminuted or ground may not be

3319 Id. at § 1903(a). The Coast Guard uses the term "oceangoing" ships and defines it at 33 C.F.R. § 151.05.

3320 33 C.F.R. §151 (1996).

3321 Id. at § 151.25.

3322 Pub. L. No. 100-220, Title II, 1987 U.S.C.C.A.N. (101 Stat.) 1460.

3323 33 U.S.C.A. § 1902(a)(3) (West Supp. 1996). Navigable waters of the United States for purposes of APPS are those waters defined under the traditional Commerce Clause test.

3324 33 U.S.C.A. § 1902(a)(1) (West Supp. 1996).

3325 33 C.F.R. § 151.67 (1996).

3326 Id. at § 151.69(a)(1).

3327 Id. at § 151.69(a)(2).

discharged in the navigable waters or in waters offshore inside three nautical miles from the nearest land.[3328]

The violation of MARPOL's prohibition against the discharge of harmful substances, including oil, was changed by OPA to a class D felony, if the violation is done with knowledge.[3329] The Coast Guard may refer violations to a vessel's flag country for prosecution.

### *THE OCEAN DUMPING ACT OF 1972*

The Ocean Dumping Act of 1972,[3330] also known as the Marine Protection, Research and Sanctuaries Act (MPRSA), prohibits the transport and dumping of any material for which a permit is not granted. The MPRSA implements the 1972 International Convention on the Prevention of Marine Pollution by Dumping of Wastes and Other Matter (the London Dumping Convention).[3331] The London Convention commits party states to promoting effective control of pollution into the marine environment from all sources. This Convention specifically targets dumping waste and other matter likely to create a human health hazard, to harm living resources and marine life, or to interfere with legitimate uses of the sea. Just like the Convention, the MPRSA recognizes that the unregulated dumping of **material** into ocean waters endangers human health, welfare, and amenities, and the marine environment, ecological systems, and economic potentialities.[3332]

---

3328 Id.

3329 33 U.S.C. § 1908(a) (Supp. II 1992). Amended by the Act of Aug. 18, 1990, Pub.L. 101-380 § 2027. The criminal penalty has been up to 5 years in prison and $50,000.

3330 Act of Oct. 23, 1972, Pub.L. 92-532, 86 Stat. 1052, codified at 33 U.S.C. §§ 1401-1445 (1988 & Supp. II 1992)

3331 Convention on the Prevention of Marine Pollution by Dumping of Wastes and Other Matter, done Dec. 29, 1972, 26 U.S.T. 2403, T.I.A.S. No. 8165. While this Convention is commonly termed the 'London Convention,' the 'London Dumping Convention,' or the 'London Ocean Dumping Convention,' it is more appropriately referred to as the 'Ocean Dumping Convention.'

3332 33 USC §1401(a).

MPRSA defines dumping as "the disposition of material."[3333] "Material" is defined as "matter of any kind or description, including, but not limited to, dredged material, solid waste, incinerator residue, garbage, sewage, sewage sludge, munitions, radiological, chemical, and biological warfare agents, radioactive materials, chemicals, biological and laboratory waste, wreck or discarded equipment, rock, sand, excavation debris, and industrial, municipal, agricultural, and other waste."[3334] However, it includes a qualification that the term "material" does not mean sewage from vessels within the meaning of section 1322 of the FWPCA.[3335] Oil within the meaning of section 1321 of the FWPCA **shall be included only to the extent that such oil is taken on board a vessel or aircraft for the purpose of dumping.**[3336]

The MPRSA was amended in 1988 by Public Law 100-688, Title I of which is the Ocean Dumping Ban Act of 1988, and Title IV of which is the Shore Protection Act. The purpose of MPRSA is to regulate the transportation of material from the U.S. or by U.S. vessels, aircraft, or agencies for the purpose of dumping the material into ocean waters, and the dumping of material transported by any person from a location outside the U.S. if the dumping occurs in the territorial sea or the contiguous zone of the U.S.[3337] The law applies to U.S. flag vessels regardless of the origin of the dumped material, and to foreign flags if the voyage originates in the U.S.[3338] Under the MPRSA, no dumping is allowed in U.S. waters except some sewage, sludge, dredge materials, and fish wastes.[3339] Except for radiological, chemical, and biological warfare agents, high-

3333 33 USC §1402(c).

3334 Id.

3335 ""[S]ewage" means human body wastes and the wastes from toilets and other receptacles intended to receive or retain body wastes except that, with respect to commercial vessels on the Great Lakes, such term shall include graywater." 33 USC §1322(a)(6). ""[G]raywater" means galley, bath, and shower water." Id. at §1322(11).

3336 "[O]il" means oil of any kind or in any form, including, but not limited to, petroleum, fuel oil, sludge, oil refuse, and oil mixed with wastes other than dredged spoil. 33 USC §1321(a)(1).

3337 33 USC §1401(c).

3338 33 U.S.C. § 1411(a) (1988).

3339 33 USC §1412(a) & (d).

level radioactive waste, and medical waste, for which no permit may be issued, the Environmental Protection Agency (EPA) may issue a permit for dumping of other materials under extraordinary circumstances.[3340]

The Act contains a non-preemption clause but states are barred from applying more stringent laws to federal projects.[3341] Unlike OPA that provides a shopping list of private right of action against polluters,[3342] MPRSA provides no right of private action, not even for injunctive relief or equitable relief to compel performance of a statutory duty.[3343]

OPA specifically excludes oil discharges permitted by a permit issued under a federal, state and local law.[3344] This means that if the dumping of oil is allowed by specific EPA permits issued under section 1412(a) of the MPRSA, the discharging or dumping party would be excluded from OPA liability, because it would amount to excluded discharge under OPA provisions.

---

3340 Id. §1412(a).

3341 33 U.S.C. § 1416(d) (1988).

3342 33 USCA §2702(a) & (b)

3343 33 U.S.C.A. § 1415(d). This section exclusively vests the right to seek injunctive relief in the Attorney General of the United States. See also Middlesex County Sewarage Authority et al v. National Sea Clammers Association et al, U.S. 1, 101 S.Ct. 2615 (1981) (holding that Citizen suit provisions of FWPCA and MPRSA apply only to persons who can claim some sort of injury and there is no basis for inferring existence of separate cause of action for "injured" as opposed to "noninjured" plaintiffs, also holding that Structure of FWPCA and MPRSA and their legislative history lead to conclusion that Congress intended that private remedies in addition to those expressly provided by the Acts should not be implied).

3344 33 USCA §2702(c).

# Chapter Sixteen

# TIME LIMITATIONS UNDER OPA

## A. TIME LIMITATIONS FOR ALL CLAIMS AGAINST THE RESPONSIBLE PARTY – 33 USC § 2717(f).

*Time Limitation for Recovery of Damages*: Except as provided in paragraphs (3)(Contribution claim time limitation) and (4) (minor & incompetent person time limitation) of section 2717(f) of the OPA, **an action for damages** under OPA shall be barred unless the action is brought within 3 years after the date on which the loss and the connection of the loss with the discharge in question are reasonably discoverable with the exercise of due care, or in the case of natural resources damages under section 2702(b)(2)(A) of OPA, within 3 years after the date of completion of the natural resources damage assessment under section 2706(c) of OPA.[3345]

*Time Limitation for Recovery of Removal Cost*: The OPA provides for a shorter time limit for removal costs claims against a responsible party compared with the longer period (6years) of limitation for removal cost claims against the Fund.[3346] The OPA provides that an action for recovery of removal costs referred to in section 2702(b)(1) of the OPA must be commenced within 3 years after completion of the removal action, and in any such action described, "the court shall enter a declaratory judgment on liability for removal costs or damages that will be binding on any subsequent action or actions to recover further removal costs or damages."[3347] (Emphasis mine). This subsection also provides that except as otherwise provided in this paragraph, an action may be commenced under this subchapter for recovery of removal costs at any time after such costs have

3345 33 USCA §2717.

3346 *Compare* 33 USCA §2712(h) *with* 33 USCA §2717(f)(2).

3347 33 U.S.C.A § 2717(f)(2).

been incurred. This section covers exclusively removal cost claims by all claimants against the RP. The provision allowing courts of law to make declaratory judgments on liability for removal costs or damages that will be binding on any subsequent action or actions to recover further removal costs or damages is a very useful tool to prevent re-litigation of removal and damages claims over and over again at great costs to the court and all the parties involved. It appears that its main aim is to ensure closure. By virtue of the declaratory judgment, the court fixes the liability limits (removal costs+ damages) based on the facts of the case before it. Once this is accomplished, its judgment binds any subsequent trial court where the same question of liability for damages and removal costs is considered. The courts would base its declaratory judgment on a thorough analysis of the defenses to liability provisions[3348] as well as the limits on liability[3349] provisions of OPA.

If a court of law finds that the person designated the responsible party was not liable for the oil spill because he has a sole cause third party defense to liability,[3350] that fact alone does not warrant a declaration that the third party is the responsible party for the purposes of future litigation.[3351] Such declaration as regards future litigation is inappropriate because the statute required only declaration of liability for removal costs or damages, not declaration that would act as prophylactic measure preventing any future suits against the original responsible party for any act relating to the spill.[3352] This point cannot be overemphasized because of the fact that the original responsible party who is later found to be blameless for the oil spill in question could be liable for negligent actions taken during the removal of the discharged oil. Such negligent actions could include use of inappropriate clean-up methods that causes further harm to the environment and to other claimants, as well as maritime casualties that

3348 33 U.S.C.A § 2703.

3349 33 U.S.C.A § 2704.

3350 33 USCA §2703(a)(3).

3351 Unocal Corp. v. United States, 222 F.3d 528 (9th Cir. 2000), *see also*, 33 U.S.C.A. § 2717(f)(2).

3352 Unocal Corp., 222 F.3d at 528.

could occur during cleanup and removal. These types of claims need not be brought under the OPA. They could be brought under general maritime law or common law principles. This declaratory judgment mechanism is not available for claims against the Fund, rather it is only available for claims against the RP.

The application of the three year limitation required in section 2717(f)(2) of the OPA was discussed in the case of *United States Of America v. George MIZHIR.*[3353] The United States brought this action for reimbursement of funds expended by the Oil Spill Liability Trust Fund for the cleanup of an oil spill allegedly caused by the defendant, George Mizhir d/b/a Mizhir Oil Co.("Mizhir"). Pending before the Court were the motion for summary judgment filed by the United States (Docket No. 11) and the cross motion for summary judgment filed by Mizhir (Docket No. 14). (D.Mass.) Mizhir lived and operated an oil delivery business in Winchendon, Massachusetts. On December 20, 1994, he took his oil truck to be serviced at Bergevin's Enterprises, Inc. of Keene, New Hampshire ("Bergevin's"). Bergevin's service records indicated that a mechanic inspected the truck and told Mizhir the brakes were "unsafe" and "not to drive truck."

The following day, Mizhir crashed his oil delivery truck into a house in Marlborough, New Hampshire causing a spill of 71.42 barrels (3,000 gallons) of No. 2 fuel oil into the house and surrounding area. That area included the Minnewawa Brook, which flows into the Ashuelot River. Mizhir made no attempt to remove the oil himself. On the day after the accident, the homeowner's insurance company retained Clean Harbors Environmental Services, Inc. ("Clean Harbors") to provide emergency oil removal from the house. The same day, the New Hampshire Department of Environmental Services notified the Environmental Protection Agency ("EPA") of the spill. An EPA coordinator, who arrived at the scene the following day, observed oil seeping into the Minnewawa Brook. Because Mizhir made no effort to remove the oil, EPA notified the U.S. Coast Guard to secure immediate funding for the cleanup and contracted with Clean Harbors to remove the oil from the brook.

---

3353 No. Civ.A. 98-40093-NMG., 2000 WL 914108 (D. Mass).

All phases of the cleanup were completed on August 4, 1995. The total cost of the cleanup was $242,587, including the EPA contract costs of $209,861 charged by Clean Harbors, $6,067 for EPA's supervisory costs, $20,759 for the cleanup of the house and interest. The homeowner's insurance company arranged for the cleanup of the house but later disclaimed liability. The government sent invoices to the defendant, but he failed to pay any portion of the cleanup costs. The government filed the instant lawsuit and thereafter the pending motion for summary judgment to be reimbursed for removal costs.[3354] The court noted that OPA provides that an action for recovery of removal costs "must be commenced within 3 years after completion of the removal action."[3355] The court pointed out that the complaint in this case was filed on May 22, 1998. Mizhir asserted that the removal action was completed on May 20, 1995. Rejecting the assertion of Mizhir, the court noted that invoices from the cleanup clearly showed that work was performed as late as August 4, 1995, which means that the three year time limit had not yet expired. Mizhir argued that 90% of the oil removal was completed before May 20 and that any action taken after that time was not part of the removal action. The court found that Clean Harbors, the company retained to perform the work, conducted cleanup work on seven occasions after May 22, 1995 (three years prior to filing) and all work was completed on August 4, 1995, well within the three-year statute of limitations period. The court regarded Mizhir's argument that work was complete by May 20, 1995 as groundless. In granting the government's motion for summary judgment, the court noted that even though the date upon which removal work was completed is a question of fact, no reasonable jury could find that the government filed this action more than three years after the completion of the oil removal.[3356]

3354 2000 WL 914108, *1 (D.Mass.).

3355 33 U.S.C. § 2717(f)(2).

3356 2000 WL 914108, *4 (D.Mass.).

## B. TIME LIMITATIONS FOR ALL CLAIMS AGAINST THE FUND

The implementing regulations also provide that except as provided under section 2712(h)(3) (minors and incompetents) of OPA, the Fund will consider a claim only if presented in writing to the Director, NPFC, within the following time limits:

"(1) For damages, within three years after--

(i) The date on which the injury and its connection with the incident in question were reasonably discoverable with the exercise of due care.
(ii) In the case of natural resources damages under section 1002(b)(2)(A) of the Act (33 U.S.C. 2702(b)(2)(A)), within three years after the date on which the injury and its connection with the incident in question were reasonably discoverable with the exercise of due care, or within three years from the date of completion of the natural resources damage assessment under section 1006(e) of the Act (33 U.S.C. 2706(e)), whichever is later.[3357]

(2) For removal costs, within six years after the date of completion of all removal actions for the incident. [3358] As used in this paragraph, "date of completion of all removal actions" is defined as the actual date of completion of all removal actions for the incident or the date the FOSC determines that the removal actions which form the basis for the costs being claimed are completed, whichever is earlier.[3359] Unless the Director, NPFC, directs in writing that the claim be submitted elsewhere, a claim is deemed presented on the date the claim is actually received at the National Pollution Funds Center, suite 1000, 4200 Wilson Boulevard, Arlington, Virginia 22203-1804. If the Director, NPFC, directs that the claim be presented elsewhere, the claim is deemed presented on the date the claim is actually received at the address in the directive."[3360]

---

3357 33 CFR s 136.101(a).

3358 33 C.F.R. § 136.101 (a) (2).

3359 Id.

3360 33 C.F.R. § 136.101 (a)(2)(b).

# Chapter Seventeen

# CRITICISMS OF THE LIABILITY & COMPENSATION PROVISIONS OF OPA

1. OPA's Attack on Uniformity

The wisdom of the non-delegation principle is made manifest by the confusion created by OPA's failure to preempt state oil spill legislation. Indeed, the chaos created by the dizzying array of remedies and defenses applicable to post-OPA oil pollution incidents demonstrates that the decision not to preempt state action was a poor policy choice.[3361] Failing to preempt state action has given rise to a situation wherein the uniformity of maritime law is made but an illusion. The law applicable to an oil spill is now almost wholly dependent on the law of the state in which the spill occurs.

After OPA, there are now at least four types of remedies available to parties injured by an oil spill, each with a different statutory or legal basis, namely, OPA, Admiralty, Common Law, and State oil spill statutes. Each of these remedies is subject to different limitations on liability. In addition, several defenses remain available to the shipowner, each of which impacts the remedies differently. A shipowner faced with plaintiffs seeking these various remedies might rely on OPA's statutory limit on damages for the OPA claims, have varying defenses available under a state statute, and assert the Limitation of Liability Act against the oil spill claims brought in admiralty.[3362]

Moreover, the decision not to preempt has also created an entirely new procedural problem, namely the end of the concursus, or joinder of claims into a single proceeding. The courts have held in a number of cases that

3361 Matthew P. Harrington, Necessary and proper, but still unconstitutional: The Oil Pollution Act's Delegation of Admiralty Power to the states, 48 Case W. Res. at 52.

3362 Id.

the concursus mechanism is no longer available to consolidate claims in one forum so as to achieve an orderly and swift adjudication. Renowned legal commentators, such as Professor Force have criticized the refusal of the courts to allow concursus in OPA cases.

Perhaps, the OPA has inadvertently unnecessarily complicated the substantive and procedural aspects of oil pollution litigation.

A. The Substantive Problem: Conflicting Remedies and Defenses

1. Sorting Out the Claims

After passage of OPA, a party injured by an oil spill will be entitled to assert claims (1) under the OPA, (2) under any applicable state statute (3) in admiralty, and (4) under the common law.

A. OPA Claims

OPA claims include actions for recovery of removal costs and damages. These must be brought within three years of the date of the spill.[3363] Because the scope of covered damages is quite broad, OPA is seen by many as the primary avenue for the recovery for most oil pollution claims. As noted earlier, it permits injured parties to recover removal costs, property damage, economic loss, and natural resource damages. At the same time, OPA's potential to provide full recovery is limited, at least when the spill is found to be not the result of recklessness, gross negligence, or the violation of a federal operating or safety standard. In such a case, the OPA claims will be subject to the statutory limits. This means in some cases the responsible party's liability, although strict, could be limited to an amount far less than the actual removal costs and damages.[3364] If a 1,000 GRT tank barge spills oil over a large area, its liability may be capped at $2 million, even though amounts far in excess of that were spent in cleanup. The amount available to satisfy public and private claims might actually be even lower, since the responsible party is permitted to offset any costs

3363 See 33 U.S.C. § 2702(b) (1994).

3364 33 U.S.C. § 2704(a) (1) (1994).

it incurs in cleaning up the spill against its statutory limit.[3365] Hope of full compensation from the responsible party under OPA may, therefore, prove to be illusory in many cases. When claims are in excess of the statutory limitation, many plaintiffs may be left to seek compensation either from the Oil Spill Liability Trust-Fund (Fund) or in a legal proceeding grounded in some other remedy.

B. Claims Based on State Statute

Almost all the coastal states have enacted some sort of oil pollution legislation. These statutes take a variety of forms, provide for various forms of liability and permit recovery for a variety of different claims. The non-uniformity in state pollution legislation is staggering. Many states have enacted oil pollution compensation statutes providing for strict and unlimited liability for discharges. Some of these statutes are far broader than OPA, in that they provide for a broader range of recoverable costs and damages.[3366] Some states provide for unlimited liability, but with types of recoverable damage more limited than under OPA.[3367] Others provide for liability limits and recoverable damages that are almost identical to those in OPA.[3368] Finally, a few states have statutes that provide for neither strict nor unlimited liability, essentially leaving injured parties to use common law or admiralty remedies.[3369]

This variety in state legislation not only subjects a vessel owner to differing liabilities depending on the location of the spill--a proposition that would seem to be at odds with the purposes of the admiralty grant--it

3365 See 33 U.S.C. § 2704 (a) (1995).

3366 See, e.g., The Rhode Island Environmental Injury Compensation Act, R.I. Gen. Laws § 46-12.5-6 (1996) (providing for strict and unlimited liability for discharges of oil into state waters).

3367 See Massachusetts Oil and Hazardous Materials Prevention Act, Mass. Gen. Laws ch. 21E, § 5 (West 1983) (providing for strict and unlimited liability but permitting recovery only for removal costs and damages to natural resources and real or personal property).

3368 See La. Rev. Stat. Ann. § 30:2025 (E) (West 1996).

3369 See, e.g., 35 Pa. Cons. Stat. § 691.401 (1996) (a water pollution law, permitting the Commonwealth to maintain a nuisance action against a discharger, but providing no specific remedies to private parties).

permits different opportunities for recovery to claimants. Injured parties in states with more generous compensation statutes, such as Rhode Island, which provides for strict and unlimited liability for a wide range of damages, may fare better than those in states such as Pennsylvania,[3370] where a vessel owner's liability is more limited. Where damages exceed OPA's statutory limits, a vessel owner's liability and a plaintiff's ultimate right to recovery are wholly dependent on the fortuity of an accident occurring in a state with a generous compensation regime.

The interaction between OPA and claims based on state legislation is complicated by this patchwork regime. One need only imagine an incident involving a vessel with an OPA limit of $10 million and cleanup costs and damages in excess of that limit to see the effect. Assuming that neither the vessel nor the Fund have paid the claim, recovery of amounts in excess of the OPA limit will be entirely dependent on the state legislation in force. If the state imposes strict and unlimited liability for all costs and damages, a plaintiff might conceivably recover. However, a spill in a state with a less generous recovery regime might not result in recovery in excess of the OPA limits. The situation is even more complicated when one factors in the types of damages that might be at issue. Economic losses in excess of the OPA limit might be recoverable in some states with an unlimited liability regime, but not in others. Still other states might permit recovery for economic losses, but only up to a specified state limit.

It is clear, therefore, that OPA's promised recovery may not only be illusory in some cases, but it may open the claims resolution process to a great deal of confusion and uncertainty. After OPA, vessel owner's liability and claimant's recovery remains a function of an inconsistent statutory regime.

C. Admiralty Claims

OPA did not abrogate the right to recover in admiralty for oil pollution damages.[3371] States and private individuals may, therefore, maintain

---

3370 See id.

3371 33 U.S.C. § 2751(e) (1994) (savings provision).

an action in admiralty, in rem[3372] and in personam[3373] to recover when oil pollution damages or interferes with a property interest.

Damages recoverable in admiralty for oil pollution are similar to those available in other maritime tort actions. Property damage and cleanup costs are recoverable items of damage, but recovery for economic loss is severely limited by the Robins Dry Dock rule. Although this rule is frequently criticized, it nevertheless operates as a limit on proximate causation, barring claims that might be considered too remote to have been foreseeable.

It is clear, therefore, that admiralty recognizes a maritime cause of action in tort for damages caused by oil pollution,[3374] and this is true whether the claim involves damage to property, either real or personal, or where the claimant seeks the costs of cleaning up a spill.[3375] Nonetheless, it is also important to note that oil spills will frequently give rise to admiralty claims that do not involve damages from pollution. A grounding or collision undoubtedly will give rise to all manner of admiralty claims, which may sound in tort or contract. None of these ancillary claims are cognizable under OPA or any state oil pollution statute. Maritime casualties will create claims from cargo owners for lost cargo.[3376] Vessels involved in a collision may have claims for damage. Seamen, passengers, or other maritime workers will have personal injury claims.[3377] Charterers might

3372 See The Barnstable, 181 U.S. 464. 467 (1901).

3373 See Salaky v. Atlas Tank Processing Corp., 120 F. Supp. 225 (E.D.N.Y. 1953) (allowing a cause of action for damage to small boats fouled by oil sludge), rev'd on other grounds sub nom. Salaky v. The Atlas Barge No. 3, 208 F.2d 174 (2nd Cir. 1953).

3374 See Ballard Shipping, 32 F.3d at 626 (1st Cir. 1994) (holding that claims arising from pollution may sound in maritime tort or at common law).

3375 See Puerto Rico v. S.S. Zoe Colocotroni, 628 F.2d 652 (1st Cir. 1980) (allowing the Commonwealth of Puerto Rico to pursue a claim for loss of value of land).

3376 See In re Lloyd's Leasing, Ltd., 764 F. Supp. 1114 (S.D. Tex. 1990).

3377 See Petition of Odin Marine Corp., No. 96-CV-5438 (S.D.N.Y. 1996).

claim for breach of charter party.[3378] Terminal operators will claim for damage from allision or grounding.[3379]

Recovery for these injuries or breaches is not provided for either in OPA or state pollution statutes, and thus, claimants are required to maintain actions in admiralty. Claims in admiralty, however, are subject to admiralty defenses and procedures. OPA's preemption of the Limitation of Liability Act was not absolute. It specifically left in place traditional admiralty rights and defenses, where damages unconnected with the pollution itself are concerned. Thus the Limitation of Liability Act survives as a defense to admiralty claims, even though it does not apply to claims brought under OPA's damage provisions.[3380] Moreover, it appears that the Robins Dry Dock rule may remain in force for the same reason.

D. Common Law Claims

Maritime plaintiffs have long enjoyed the right to bring a claim pursuant to common law in addition to any right of action they might have had in admiralty. This right was enshrined in the first Judiciary Act and has remained a fundamental principle of federal civil procedure ever since. OPA makes specific provision for common law actions by "saving to suitors in all cases all other remedies to which they are otherwise entitled."[3381] While courts were somewhat slow to recognize common law remedies for water pollution, at least three (and possibly four) theories would seem to be available: These include actions for trespass, nuisance, negligence, and strict liability.

While trespass has been recognized by the English courts as a cause of action to recover damages for oil pollution, few, if any, American courts have been faced with similar claims. The primary obstacle to a successful trespass action is the requirement that the injured party show intent on the

---

3378 See In re Lloyd's Leasing, Ltd., 764 F. Supp. at 1114.

3379 See In re Nautilus Motor Tanker Co., 900 F. Supp. 697 (D.N.J. 1995) (allowing a berth operator a claim for pure economic damages from a grounding and resulting oil spill).

3380 See 33 U.S.C. § 2751(e) (1994).

3381 Id. § 2751(e) (2).

part of the wrongdoer.[3382] Unless the pollution is intentional, as in the case of a discharge of oily ballast, the chances of showing intent are small.[3383]

A nuisance action might be maintained either by the state to abate a public nuisance or by a private citizen to recover damages for a particularized injury.

An action in negligence is perhaps the most viable cause of action at common law for damages resulting from oil spills. In order to be successful, the plaintiff will be required to show the vessel owner has some duty with respect to the plaintiff and some act amounting to a breach of that duty resulted in damage to the plaintiff's interests. All the difficulties attendant with proof in claims for land-based torts are magnified in oil spill cases. This is primarily because of the rule that a vessel owner's duty of care is determined by resort to the principles of maritime law.[3384]

Finally, one other theory that might support a common law claim for oil pollution is strict liability for ultra-hazardous activities. Admittedly this theory is as yet undeveloped, but at least one court has held that a motor carrier's transportation of large quantities of gasoline is an ultra-hazardous activity.[3385] The rationale for the decision was that "in many respects hauling gasoline as freight is no more unusual, but more dangerous, than collecting water. When gasoline is carried as cargo--as distinguished from fuel for the carrier vehicle--it takes on uniquely hazardous characteristics, as does water impounded in large quantities."[3386]

2. Applying the Defenses

After OPA, a vessel which discharges oil into navigable waters within a state is subject to a variety of differing obligations. As noted in the previous section, claimants might make out claims under OPA for removal costs

3382 See W. PAGE KEETON ET AL., PROSSER & KEETON ON THE LAW OF TORTS § 13, at 73-75 (5th ed. 1984).

3383 See Joseph C. Sweeny, Oil Pollution of the Oceans, 37 Fordham L. Rev. 155, 170-71 (1968) (discussing the requirements for intent or negligence under the various formulations of the doctrine of tresspass).

3384 In Ballard Shipping Co. v. Beach Shellfish, 32 F.3d 623, 626 (1st Cir. 1994).

3385 See Siegler v. Kuhlman, 502 P.2d 1181, 1187 (Wash. 1972).

3386 Id. at 1184.

and damages up to the statutory limit. Amounts in excess of those recoverable under the federal statute might be recoverable under a state statute. But, because such statutes provide for differing levels of recovery, a vessel owner's liability will differ depending on the statute in force in a particular state. Where both federal and state statutory regimes are inadequate, or where the claim is not cognizable under an oil pollution statute, a party might also make out a claim in admiralty or at common law for damages.

While this scheme appears to provide a broad right of recovery, it also results in some confusion. OPA creates a complex array of liabilities that are met by an equally complex array of defenses. Moreover, even where the vessel lacks a complete defense, it may still limit its liability for damage in various ways, again depending on the cause of action being asserted. Keeping the claims, defenses, and limitations all straight requires the dexterity of a juggler or inventive lawyering.

A. Defenses to the Statutory Claims

OPA provides several defenses to liability. Under the statute, a responsible party may be relieved of liability where it can show that the spill was the result of an act of God, act of war, or the act or omission of a third party.[3387] The limited nature of the third party defense, along with the improbability that a party will be able to show that a spill was the result of an act of God or act of war means that there is very little possibility of escaping liability under OPA. Nonetheless, while liability may be strict, liability under OPA is not unlimited. A responsible party will still be able to take advantage of the limit on damages provided in the statute.

State statutes also provide defenses to liability, and these are as variable as the statutes themselves. Some provide almost no defenses, to the point of requiring a responsible party even to show that the spill was the result of an act of God, which could not have been guarded against.[3388] Others provide defenses for acts of God, acts of war, negligent or criminal acts of third parties, sabotage, and negligent acts on the part of governments.[3389]

---

3387 See 33 U.S.C. § 2703 (1994).

3388 See Alaska Stat. §§ 46.03.758,.760 (Michie 1996).

3389 See Or. Rev. Stat. § 468B.305 (1995).

Some states contain monetary caps on liability, while others impose unlimited liability.

With respect to statutory claims, therefore, different defenses to liability may be asserted, and different limits on liability are imposed. Statutory rights of action are wholly dependent on the location of the spill.

B. Defenses to Admiralty and Common Law Claims

In drafting OPA, Congress was intent on preventing the Limitation of Liability Act from being used to limit recovery, at least where OPA, state statutory and common law claims are at issue. OPA thus repeals the Limitation of Liability Act with respect to "any additional liability or requirement" imposed by the states or by common law.[3390] Congress did not, however, undertake a repeal of the Limitation of Liability Act with respect to oil spill or non-oil spill claims brought in admiralty. Thus, a vessel owner may assert a right to exoneration or limitation under the Limitation of Liability Act for oil spill claims not based on OPA, state statute or common law. At the same time, Congress made no provision for the repeal of the Robins Drydock rule, except to provide a federal statutory remedy for recovery of economic loss in OPA. As a result, both the Limitation of Liability Act and the Robins Drydock rule may be applicable to bar oil spill and non-oil spill claims brought in admiralty.

3. The US Congress should probably have adopted additional measures to combat the problem of oil pollution in US waters. These measures are discussed below.

A. The Problem of Unseaworthiness and Classification Societies

The US Congress missed the opportunity to include a reform of the vessel classification system in the OPA statute. Classification societies are independent legal entities, usually assuming the corporate form, that establish basic minimum standards for the design, construction, and maintenance of the principal hull and machinery components of ves-

3390 33 U.S.C. § 2718(a) (1994).

sels.[3391] They are hired and paid for by the owner(s) of the vessels that are classified. The certificates of class, which are issued by classification societies, are relied upon by all sectors of the marine industry, including the P & I Clubs, as assurance that the classed vessel is reasonably fit for its intended use.[3392]

The more prominent classification societies are the American Bureau of Shipping (ABS) in the United States, Lloyd's Register of Shipping in the United Kingdom, Germanischer Lloyd in Germany, Det Norske Veritas in Norway, Nippon Kaiji Kyokai (NKK) in Japan, Bureau Veritas in France, Registro Italiano Navale (RINA) in Italy, and Polski Rejestr Stratkow (PRS) in Poland.[3393]

In order to enhance public confidence in classification societies the International Association of Classification Societies (IACS) was formed. IACS prescribes certain minimum requirements for classification, the purpose of which is to ensure, to the extent practicable, that a shipowner gains no economic advantage in terms of seaworthiness requirements by enrolling in one classification society as opposed to another.[3394] *In other words, the IACS standards are designed to prevent classification society shopping.*

Classification societies perform a vital role within the maritime community.[3395] As said earlier, they strive to set the standards for the design, construction, and maintenance of vessels,[3396] and through scientific research and by gathering empirical data over decades, they have developed rules and standards that, if followed, will produce a vessel that is seaworthy and fit for its intended service over its useful life of twenty years or more.[3397] Classification societies serve as the unofficial policemen of the

---

3391 Machale A. Miller, Liability Of Classification Societies From The Perspective Of United States Law, Tul. Mar. L.J. 75, 77 (Winter 1997).

3392 Id. at 77.

3393 Id. at 77.

3394 Id.

3395 Machale A. Miller, Liability Of Classification Societies From The Perspective Of United States Law, Tul. Mar. L.J. 75 (Winter 1997).

3396 Id. at 75.

3397 Id.

maritime world, using independent verification processes to ensure that seaworthy vessels are in service.[3398] Over the years the maritime industry has grown to depend heavily on classification societies. Indeed, the smooth and efficient working of maritime commerce depends heavily upon the efforts of classification societies.[3399] As vessels become more complex, the demands for prompt and efficient service grow, and the pressures to operate vessels more economically mount, the role of classification societies becomes increasingly more critical.[3400] When classification societies do their job, classed vessels usually are seaworthy and catastrophic losses rarely occur. However, when a classification society fails to perform its mission, disaster looms over the horizon.[3401]

In order to ensure that members keep their vessels in a seaworthy condition, the P & I Clubs include classification requirements in their policies and rules to ensure that their members enroll in one of the known and reputable classification societies.

The P & I Club rules and policies normally make the following provisions in relation to Classification Society requirements:

"Unless otherwise agreed in writing between the Member and the Managers, the following are conditions of the insurance of an Entered Ship.

(a) (i) The Ship must be and remain throughout the period of entry classed with a classification society approved by the Managers, and

(ii) the Member must promptly report to that classification society any incident or condition in respect of which it might make recommendations as to repairs or other action to be taken by the Member.

(iii) The Member authorizes the Managers to inspect any information, relating to the maintenance of class of the Entered Ship, in the possession of any classification society with which that Ship is or at any time has been classed, and will where necessary authorize such classification society or societies to disclose and make available that information to the

3398 Id.

3399 Id. at 75-76.

3400 Id. at 76.

3401 Id.

Managers upon request by the Managers and for whatsoever purposes the Managers may consider necessary.

(iv) The Member must immediately inform the Managers if, at any time during the period of entry, the classification society with which the Entered Ship is classed is changed and advise the Managers of all outstanding recommendations, requirements or restrictions specified by any classification society relating to that Ship as at the date of such change.

(v) A Member shall cease to be insured by the Association in respect of an Entered Ship from the happening of any failure to comply with this Rule in relation to such Ship."[3402]

As stated earlier, mere enrolment with a classification society is not a guarantee that an otherwise unseaworthy vessel will not be dubiously classified as a seaworthy vessel by the classification society involved. Many of the tanker vessels that have been responsible for oil spills in international waters like the Erika were found to have been unseaworthy and their unseaworthiness caused the discharge of their oil cargo into international waters. Representatives of the United States Coast Guard occasionally board vessels to check their classification certificates to ensure that they are current. In addition, United States Customs regulations require a shipowner to supply the loadline certificate that is issued by the classification society before a vessel may leave port.[3403] While the inspection of the certificates by the US Coast guard and the enrolment of the vessel in a classification society are commendable measures they are clearly not adequate. The US Congress ought to have included a provision in the liability section of OPA that makes Classification Societies jointly and severally liable without fault if they wrongly certify an unseaworthy vessel as seaworthy. Such a provision should have allowed government and private parties to recover damages arising from the failure of a

3402 See North of England Protection & Indemnity Association, P & I Rules 2002-2003, Rule (a). All other P & I Clubs have similar or identical provisions in their Rules and Policies.

3403 Machale A. Miller, Liability of Classification Societies From The Perspective of United States Law, Tul. Mar. L.J. at 105.

classification society to detect defects and deficiencies that compromise the seaworthiness of the classified vessel to such an extent that it does not comply with the classification society's rules and standards. In addition, the classification society should have been held liable under OPA, if they are found not to have formulated sound rules that, if adhered to, will produce a seaworthy vessel. Should a classification society devise an inadequate rule or standard, liability just as readily should be imposed as when the classification society fails to survey a vessel in accordance with its rules.[3404] The classification society should be held accountable if it discovers a serious defect posing an imminent danger and nevertheless fails to take measures that will remove the vessel from service.[3405] Most classification societies have a provision in their rules that allows the classification society to suspend or revoke class whenever the ship owner has failed to comply with the rules and standards.[3406] Revocation will ensure that the vessel, as a consequence, will no longer remain in service.[3407] There is nothing wrong with holding the classification societies directly liable under OPA since they all benefit financially indirectly from the oil transportation business. Because they benefit from the transportation of Oil into US waters it is reasonable to hold them liable for the consequences of their actions. They should internalize the cost of oil pollution as part of the cost of doing business.

In addition to the above, maybe a provision ought to have been included in the OPA shifting the primary responsibility of certifying the seaworthiness of vessels sailing into US waters to the US Coast Guard. This would probably have ensured a process devoid of compromises and financial pressure which the classification societies are subject to. The financial pressure to grant certification of a rust-bucket vessel is real because if one classification society is not ready to play along with the desire of a vessel owner to get its vessel certified as quickly as possible, the vessel owner could easily take its vessel to a competing classification society. The

3404 Id. at 90-91.

3405 Id. at 91.

3406 Id.

3407 Id.

current structure of the classification system does not inspire a flight to quality or a race to the top as far as certification standards are concerned. Perhaps, if a direct government assumption of the role played by classification societies is seen as too drastic or disruptive of the free flow of commerce, then OPA should have included a compromise provision that would have allowed the US Coast Guard to play a very visible and effective supervisory role in the classification system to ensure that unseaworthy vessels do not make it into US waters. The US should also lead the charge for this same approach to be adopted internationally through the IMO.

B. The problem of not holding cargo owners liable under OPA

Most of the oil cargo that is transported on vessels in the US is owned by small-independent or big multinational oil companies or crude oil refiners. The brief discussion that follows uses the term cargo owners and oil companies interchangeably. An argument could be made against the non-inclusion of oil cargo owners or oil companies in the liability scheme of OPA, because it reduces the amount of assets that could be available in OPA cases. This becomes a very serious issue when an RP vessel is unable to limit its liability but nevertheless has insufficient assets to meet all the OPA claims against it. Since the P & I insurer or COFR guarantor cannot be held liable above the amount of its insurance coverage or guaranty, and the Fund is limited to $1b, all OPA claimants must look exclusively to the assets of the RP as the only means of satisfying their claims in unlimited liability situations. The non-inclusion of oil companies or cargo owners could provide an incentive for cargo owners to use rust-bucket vessels that charge very low freight rates, unfortunately, this practice could engender a race to the bottom. The response to this criticism will be that it is the job of classification societies to certify seaworthiness, and the job of the US Coast Guard to enforce seaworthiness, and cargo owners should not have to do their job for them by undertaking safety and seaworthiness inspections of vessels.

Most of the offshore facilities are owned or leased by oil companies, thus owners and operators of off shore facilities are usually oil companies. Under OPA, oil companies involved in the production and exploration of oil in the offshore or outer-continental shelf area are strictly liable for oil spills that occur in those areas and as explained earlier cannot limit their liability for removal costs, in addition oil companies cannot invoke any of the OPA defenses to liability in outer-continental shelf oil spills. It is mostly in oil spills from vessels that oil companies are not included as RPs. The cargo owners or oil companies are in a position to control standards and quality of facilities in offshore oil spills where they take a primary role in the production and exploration process, whereas in the vessel transportation process they take a back seat in the determination, measurement and management of quality and standards. It is the vessel owner, the classification societies, as well as the US Coast guard that should lead the charge on the issue of vessel quality and seaworthiness. One the other hand, one could argue that it makes social and political sense to hold the cargo owners liable because of the effect that oil spills have on the marine environment. By not holding oil companies liable, the risk undertaken by the oil companies is reduced; therefore, their expected profit margin will be higher, because they do not have to purchase oil pollution insurance. It also means that gasoline will be cheaper for the consumer because of reduced distribution cost. So, not holding the cargo owner liable is good for the oil companies and their continued viability and it is also good for consumers.

A deeper but brief economic analysis is necessary to determine whether it makes economic sense to make the cargo owner or oil companies share in OPA oil spill liability. Generally one could opine that holding cargo owners jointly liable under OPA will make them proactive when it comes to the selection of vessels for the transportation of their oil on US waters because of the dramatic effect it could have on their profit margin. Thus they will select vessels of the highest quality, which will in turn engender a race to the top or a quick flight to quality. This means that the current situation where the cost of oil spills from vessels is externalized by oil companies will give way to a system of cost internalization. The immediate effect of holding cargo owners liable and the flight to quality that it engenders is that the freight rate demanded by high quality or seaworthy vessels will increase because the demand for such vessels will be higher due to the fact that they are less prone to oil spills than low quality ships. This is however contingent on a market where there is symmetric information. Symmetric information is information that is equally available to all parties. So, if cargo owners generally are in a position to know whether vessels are seaworthy, then this theory applies. However currently, the information in the vessel transportation market is asymmetric in nature. Asymmetric information is information concerning a transaction which is unequally shared between the two parties to the transaction.[3408] The most famous application of the problems that asymmetric information can create has been Akerlof's discussion of the second-hand car market. Other important applications relate to the principal-agent problem and moral hazard.[3409] Much of economics in the 1970s and 1980s has been devoted to the discussion of mechanisms for coping with these types of problem.[3410]

George Akerlof illustrated the most famous example of asymmetric information in his 1970 paper on "The Market for Lemons." The paper examined the market for used cars to illustrate the importance of informational asymmetries.[3411] The scenario is quite simple – the seller of a used car usually knows more about it than does the buyer.[3412] They know, for example, how well it runs on the highway, in the snow, when it is hot outside, etc.[3413] The buyer knows relatively little, So if a seller offers to sell the car for, say, $5,000, the buyer should be suspicious, since, if the car were worth more than $5,000, the owner would not be selling it at that price. Just like in the used car sales situation, the owner of a vessel may intentionally misrepresent the quality or seaworthiness of its vessel. In this case, Akerlof showed, the market may break down completely.[3414] The consequences of asymmetric information can be profound. In the extreme, markets with asymmetric information may simply cease to exist. In other cases, asymmetric information will cause the market to "behave badly" and thus create an opportunity for a government or some exter-

---

3408 The penguin Dictionary of Economics (1998).

3409 Id.

3410 Id.

3411 See. ArgMax – Economics News Data and Analysis, Nobel Prize for "Asymmetric Information," John Irons (last updated March 31, 2003) <http://www.argmax.com/mt_blog/archive/000289.php>

3412 Id.

3413 Id.

3414 Id.

nal organization to come in and intervene to improve the private market outcome.

If there is symmetric information in the vessel charter transaction between vessel owners and cargo owners, equilibrium will be socially optimal, in other words the freight rate will be just about right. Based on Akerlof's theory, the only way in which we can have symmetric information is legislative reform of OPA that makes the cargo owner jointly liable for oil spills if it fails to undertake an inspection of the vessel that it charters to make sure that it is seaworthy. In other words, cargo owners would have to perform the inspection duty of the classification societies and internalize the cost of seaworthiness of the vessel or in the alternative cargo owners would have to start transporting their oil cargo in seaworthy vessels owned by them, instead of third party rust-bucket vessels. The current practice of some multinational oil companies of selling off their own oil tank vessels and using vessels owned by unrelated third parties will stop immediately if cargo owners are jointly liable for oil spills under OPA.

In the absence of legislative intervention, if the market has asymmetric information, it will be wrong to hold cargo owners liable because due to the unavailability of equal information in the market place they cannot distinguish between good or bad vessels, and in this case, the freight rate for the vessels will not be the proper price. This will keep unseaworthy or low quality vessels in business and good ships will go out of business because the demand for unseaworthy ships will increase steadily and the freight rate that they charge cargo owners will be much lower than that charged by good or seaworthy vessels. Seaworthy vessels will go out of business because they will not be able to offer the lower freight rates that are offered by unseaworthy vessels because it will not make economic sense for them to do so. Based on Akerlof's theory, the market is likely to behave badly in this situation because in the long run, the unseaworthy vessel will be charging higher than it is supposed to charge, while oil spills are likely to increase. The market may eventually break down or cease to exist, which is unthinkable considering the importance of oil to the US and world economy. On the flip side however, OPA could have intervened by including a provision which requires cargo owners to inspect the vessels that they charter to ensure that they are in fact seaworthy, in order to make information equally available to both parties concerned as suggested by Akerlof. But, the problem with this approach is that it could have an unintended punitive effect on cargo owners because the cost of inspecting every single vessel that they use will be too high and this will significantly diminish their profit margin. If they decide to pass the cost of inspection to consumers, it might change consumer behavior and cause a drastic reduction in demand for oil or gasoline. Many people may resort to public transportation if they cannot afford to pay for the product. This will have the concomitant effect of driving oil companies out of business. Unfortunately, this means that the inspection requirement which was originally meant to create symmetric information in a market with asymmetric information would have created cargo owner and oil consumer unhappiness. If consumers do not change their rate of consumption despite the higher prices and continue to consume at the same rate, then the cargo owners and owners of seaworthy vessels will stay in business while oil spills continue to decrease steadily.".

However if the ship owner is the only liable party, then in time charter party situations it will prefer to charter its vessel to the cargo-owner that uses the vessel in the most environmentally friendly manner, for example, by ordering the vessel's master to terrains that are not too dangerous or by transporting light crude oil as opposed to very thick or dirty crude oil that is very costly to clean up when it is spilt. If there is symmetric information, the ship owner will charge the good user a lower freight rate and the bad user a higher freight rate. So, a good cargo owner user may be charged $100,000, while a bad user may be charged $125,000. If we have a market that has asymmetric information, then a bad user cargo owner will misrepresent itself as a good user and by doing so gets an equal freight rate with a good user, which means that the freight rate of the good user will increase while that of the bad user will decrease. This means that the good user is paying too much, while the bad user is paying a freight rate that is too low. This means that it inadvertently punishes good users and this could push good users of vessels out of the market. But, if consumers are still happy to consume crude oil at the same rate despite the increasing price of gasoline caused by increased freight rate paid by good users, then good-user cargo owners may be able to remain in business.

This economic analysis shows that good arguments could be made against or in favor of holding cargo owners/oil companies jointly and severally liable with vessel owners for oil spills from vessels, but in the light of the prohibitive and crippling transactional cost of inspecting every single vessel that oil cargo owners charter, it will be very difficult to create a symmetric information market by legislative fiat. This type of exorbitant cost could drive many oil companies out of business and reduce the supply of crude oil in the market thereby making the price of crude oil artificially high by virtue of the law of demand and supply. The heavy dependence of the US economy on oil will make it difficult to include a provision that holds oil cargo owners liable for oil spills because of the negative vertical and horizontal impact that it could have on all sectors of the economy; the legislative creation of symmetric information by requiring oil cargo owner inspection of vessels would also be difficult to do for the same reason.

C. The Problem of Unlimited Liability

In a situation in which the liability of the RP is unlimited under OPA, an RP is normally supposed to pay the entire cost of clean up and damages by private and governmental claimants. This means that claimants first of all look to the COFR guarantors who are held liable up to the maximum amount of their COFR guaranty and the P & I Club of the RP (even though the P & I club cannot be held directly liable under OPA and can raise their traditional defenses to liability). The COFR guaranty as discussed earlier, runs between $250-$400m, while the P & I Club insurance is now about $1b. An additional layer of funding for cleanup and damage claims is the Oil Spill Liability Trust Fund, which provides another $1b. If we add everything up in an ideal situation we will have $400m (COFR Guaranty) + $1b (P & I Insurance) + $1b (OPA Oil Spill Fund) = $2.4b. The total damage and clean up claims in most oil spills would be below the COFR guaranty amount, the P & I Club amount, and the Oil Spill Liability Trust Fund amount. But in the most catastrophic oil spills where the total claims for cleanup and damages exceed the maximum COFR guaranty plus the

P & I Club insurance amount, then the question then becomes how do you deal with the situation in order to ensure that all claims are paid.

When the maximum available insurance and guaranty money has been exhausted by all claimants, it means that the RP has to pay the balance of the excess claim. If the owner or operator of the vessel is a well-capitalized corporation, it might be able to pay most or all of the claim, but this depends on the pristine nature of the area of the oil spill, and the amount of oil spilt. The most capitalized corporation does not have unlimited financial resources to meet the most extreme type of claims. But the picture is even gloomier for undercapitalized vessel owners and operators who may not have enough financial resources to meet a large percentage of the excess claims. In both the undercapitalized and adequately capitalized vessel owner and operator situation there is a possibility that a huge percentage of clean up and damage claims will not be met. In fact, in the most catastrophic oil spills, the Oil Spill Liability Trust Fund may not cover the entire cost of cleanup, thereby creating an ecological disaster. This problem should perhaps have been addressed legislatively under OPA. This problem can be solved by holding the oil companies who own the oil cargo that is spilt jointly and severally liable for oil spills, so that when the COFR guaranty, P & I Club insurance, and the Fund's money runs dry, claimants can look to the oil companies to meet their claims. An alternative or additional solution may be to make sure that the 5 cents a barrel tax on the crude oil of the oil companies is not turned off when it reaches $1b, but instead to require that the taxes be paid continuously until the Fund reaches $20b. The tax on the oil could also be increased to 20 cents a barrel so that it reaches the $20b amount very quickly.

D. Problem of not joining the international liability regime

This problem was analyzed earlier in the "Introduction" section of this treatise. The arguments for and against the adoption of the international regime by the US was discussed in detail. The international regime for oil pollution and the domestic law of many European Union countries are becoming less and less hospitable to the ship owner and operator and are beginning to move closer to OPA in terms of liability limits and basis of liability. What the United States simply did at the expense of global uniformity was provide leadership on the problem of oil pollution by providing through OPA, standards of liability that set the pace for the rest of the world. The domestic legislators of many EU countries are beginning to talk about the possibility of adopting an oil spill regime that is similar to OPA. One can safely conclude that OPA is the driving force behind the steady increase in the liability limits in the international regime since the early 90s. This steady increase was discussed in chapter nine.

# Chapter Eighteen

# CONCLUSION

The US Congress should probably have categorized oil cargo owners and classification societies as jointly and liable RPs under the OPA, thereby increasing the amount of RP assets available in OPA oil spill cases. In addition, Congress ought to have provided for a $20b OPA Oil Spill Fund instead of a $1b Fund.

It is commonly thought that oil spill legislation prior to OPA had two great failings. The first was that none of the legislation provided adequate limits of liability. The second centered on the lack of adequate statutory remedy available to states or private parties. In many respects, OPA corrected these deficiencies and achieved the goals of real legislative reform. OPA expanded the remedies for oil pollution both by increasing the classes of parties entitled to seek a remedy and by broadening the types of damages that might be recoverable. OPA also attempted a delicate balance, permitting expanded recovery while at the same time avoiding the possibility that responsible vessel operators would be driven out of the market by potentially crushing liability.

Yet, in drafting OPA's non-preemption clause, Congress appears to have been working at cross-purposes with itself. Having settled upon a scheme to impose strict, but limited, liability, Congress then undercut the uniformity of the oil pollution regime by permitting the states to impose additional liabilities. It further exacerbated the problem by abrogating the-Limitation of Liability Act with respect to those liabilities. The result is an oil pollution statute that is neither comprehensive nor uniform.

Allowing states to supplement the limited liability regime created by OPA works material prejudice to the essential harmony of the federal oil pollution regime. The problem is not that Congress chose to abrogate the Limitation of Liability Act. There seems little doubt that Congress could have done so and still preserved the constitutional requirement of uniformity. Rather, the problem is that having expressed a preference for a regime that imposes strict liability but limits recoverable damages,[3415] Congress cannot be permitted to upset that balance by permitting states to enact non-uniform legislation. The result is that vessel owners are now subject to inconsistent statutory liabilities, liability in excess of that provided for in Robins Dry Dock, and the possibility of a multiplicity of suits with the threat of inconsistent and insolvency-inducing judgments.

It is important to bear in mind that the issue is not one of preemption. None of the problems discussed above result from a conflict between state and federal law. Rather, they result from the fact that Congress has chosen to delegate its exclusive power to legislate over maritime affairs. One commentator ably summed up the problem, arguing that "the Framers intended that the Courts and Congress would work together in preserving the intended uniformity of the national maritime law, leaving the states the power to develop those legal areas that did not directly impinge on the national interest."[3416] In abdicating its responsibility to provide a uniform national admiralty policy, Congress has created a confusing and contradictory statutory regime. Because it does not preempt supplemental state legislation, OPA is truly a "missed opportunity" to make some good of the "emotional reaction to the Exxon Valdez disaster."[3417] However, by and large, it is a sophisticated statute that has changed forever the way owners and operators of vessels and facilities involved in the transportation, exploration and production of oil conduct their day to day business. Any future amendments made to OPA will most likely be to make its provisions more sympathetic to environmental concerns about the impact of oil spills on the marine environment.

3415 United States v. Dixie Carriers, Inc., 627 F.2d 736, 739 (5th Cir. 1980) (discussing Congressional intent in creating a similar liability scheme under the FWPCA).

3416 Davis J. Bederman, Uniformity, Delegation and the Dormant Admiralty Clause, 28 J. Mar. L. & Com. 1, 35 (1997) (arguing for a strong "dormant Admiralty Clause").

3417 Steven R. Swanson, Federalism, the Admiralty, and Oil Spills, 27 J. Mar. L. & Com. 379, 407 (1996) (evaluating "how best to deal with the legal ramifications of oil spills" under admiralty law).

regelmäßige Rollen konnte der Index nachgebildet werden und war somit investierbar. Durch die Beschränkung auf liquide handelbare Rohstoff-Futures ist sichergestellt, dass auch große Vermögen angelegt werden können. Die Beschränkung auf Kontrakte, die in den OECD-Staaten in US-Dollar notieren, sichert ein Vermögen gegen unangenehme Entwicklungen ab.

### *Sonstige Rohstoffindizes*

Bemerkenswert ist, dass die führenden Index-Provider der Welt in den vergangenen Monaten ihre bekannten Messlatten zuletzt immer stärker in unzählige Sub-Indizes aufgeteilt haben, mit denen nicht nur die verschiedenen Rohstoffproduktgruppen (Energie, Metalle, Agrarwirtschaft und Viehwirtschaft) abgebildet werden, sondern es auch innerhalb dieser Gruppen dann noch zu Unterteilungen kommt. Weltweit dürfte es inzwischen mehr als 500 Rohstoffindizes geben. Darüber hinaus erhalten die oben genannten vier führenden Rohstoffindizes der Welt seit geraumer Zeit immer stärkere Konkurrenz durch die Kreation neuer Benchmarks, die Investmentbanken und Börsen seit kurzem publizieren (vgl. Tabelle 85):

- Deutsche Bank Liquid Commodity Index (DBLCI) – Neben den vier genannten, weltweit populären Rohstoffindizes hat in den vergangenen Jahren auch die seit 17. Februar 2003 berechnete Messlatte der Deutschen Bank in der Finanzwelt eine große Bedeutung erlangt. Der Index wies im Jahr 2005 eine Steigerung um 17,5 Prozent und im Jahr 2006 von 8,1 Prozent auf.
- CX Commodity Index – Die Deutsche Börse hat in der zweiten November-Woche 2006 sowohl einen neuen Rohstoffindex unter der Bezeichnung CX Index als auch mehrere Subindizes auf den Markt gebracht. Der aus 20 Rohstoff-Futures bestehende CX ist in der Art gewichtet, dass hier die liquidesten Rohstoffe – gemessen am Umsatzvolumen der jeweiligen Futures-Kontrakte an den entsprechenden Terminbörsen – in die Berechnung einfließen. In diesem Kontext ist anzumerken, dass die Deutsche Börse und ihre Derivate-Tochter Eurex in den vergangenen Jahren den Aufschwung der Rohstoffmärkte und das seit dem Jahr 2000 daraus

entstandene gigantische Anlegerinteresse an der Anlageklasse Rohstoffe regelrecht verschlafen haben.

- Lehman Brothers Rohstoffindex – Das US-Investmenthaus veröffentlicht seit 27. Juni 2006 einen aus 20 Rohstoffen (Energie, Metalle, Agrarwirtschaft, Viehwirtschaft) bestehenden Index.
- Merrill Lynch Rohstoffindex – Die amerikanische Investmentbank berechnet seit 23. Juni 2006 einen aus 18 Produkten bestehenden Rohstoffindex.
- UBS Commodity Strategy Index – Die Schweizer Großbank kam erstmals am 19. Juni 2006 mit einem neuen Index an den Markt.
- UBS und Diapason Commodites Biofuels Index – Die beiden Finanzhäuser kamen im März 2006 mit einem neuen Biotreibstoffindex an den Markt, der die Preisentwicklung jener Rohstoffe abdeckt, die zur Produktion von Ethanol und Biodiesel verwendet werden.

Die unterschiedliche Wertentwicklung von Rohstoffindizes ist nicht zuletzt auf die stark unterschiedliche Gewichtung einzelner Rohstoffe zurückzuführen. Wie verschieden die Gewichtung von fünf führenden Rohstoffindizes – an einem zufällig ausgewählten Tag – ausfallen kann, ist aus Tabelle 85 zu ersehen.

# Spezialitäten I

## *Investieren in Uran*

In diesen letzten beiden Abschnitten werden ausgewählte Themen und einige oftmals nach dem Zufallsprinzip ausgewählte Produkte dargestellt, mit denen sich der Anleger im Bereich Rohstoffe und Urstoffe auch längerfristig positionieren kann.

Uran ist eines der spannendsten Anlagethemen dieser Zeit. Grund: Das unter der Überschrift »Peak Oil« stehende absehbare Ende des Ölzeitalters hat die Atomenergie zurück in den Fokus der Öffentlichkeit gebracht. Und dies, obwohl Atomkraftwerke nicht erst seit dem Reaktorunfall von Tschernobyl nicht unumstritten sind. So ist kaum vorstellbar, dass es eine Energiezukunft ohne Uran geben kann.